POWERING CIVILIZATION THE COMPLETE ENERGY READER

POWERING CIVILIZATION THE COMPLETE ENERGY READER

JAMES RIDGEWAY

PANTHEON BOOKS, NEW YORK

 Published in the United States by Pantheon Books, a division of Random House, Inc., New York, and simultaneously in Canada by Random House of Canada Limited, Toronto.

Since the permissions acknowledgments cannot all be accommodated on this copyright page, they appear on the following pages.

Library of Congress Cataloging in Publication Data
Ridgeway, James, 1936–
Powering civilization.

Bibliography: p.
Includes index.
1. Power resources. I. Title.
TJ163.2.R53 1982 333.79 82–47878
ISBN 0–394–51471–8 AACR2
ISBN 0–394–71129–7 (pbk.)

Manufactured in the United States of America

First Edition

Text design: Karin Gerdes-Kincheloe

Grateful acknowledgment is made to the following for permission to reprint previously published material:

Appalachian Land Ownership Task Force: From "Land Ownership Patterns and Their Impacts on Appalachian Communities: A Survey of 80 Counties" by the Appalachian Land Ownership Task Force. Reprinted by permission.

Steve Baer: From "The Clothesline Paradox" by Steve Baer, *Sunpaper*, Summer 1975. Reprinted by permission of the author.

Ballinger Publishing Company: From *Radioactive Waste: Politics, Technology and Risk* by Ronnie D. Lipschultz. Copyright © 1980 by The Union of Concerned Scientists. Reprinted with permission from Ballinger Publishing Company.

Thomas N. Bethell: From *Coal Patrol* by Thomas N. Bethell. Copyright © 1972 by Thomas N. Bethell. Reprinted by permission of the author.

Joseph Bowring: From pre-publication draft of "Federal Subsidies to Nuclear Power: Reactor Design and Fuel Cycle" by Joseph Bowring, March 1980. Reprinted by permission of the author.

The Bulletin of the Atomic Scientists: From "Is Nuclear Energy Necessary?" March 1980. Copyright © 1980 by the Educational Foundation for Nuclear Science. Reprinted by permission of *The Bulletin of the Atomic Scientists,* A Magazine of Science and Public Affairs.

Corporate Data Exchange, Inc.: From Corporate Data Exchange press release, June 27, 1980. Reprinted by permission of Corporate Data Exchange, Inc.

Dresser Industries, Inc.: From advertisement, "I Was the Only Victim of Three Mile Island." Reprinted by permission of Dresser Industries, Inc.

E. P. Dutton, Inc.: From *The Elusive Bonanza* by Chris Welles. Copyright © 1970 by Christopher J. Welles. Reprinted by permission of the publisher, E. P. Dutton, Inc.

Foreign Affairs: From "Oil and the Decline of the West" by Walter Levy, and "Nuclear Power and Nuclear Bombs" by Amory B. Lovins, L. Hunter Lovins, and Leonard Ross, Summer 1980. Copyright © 1980 by the Council of Foreign Relations, Inc. Reprinted by permission of *Foreign Affairs.*

Fortune magazine and Robert Sheehan: From "Coal Man at Chrysler" by Robert Sheehan, September 1962. Copyright © 1962 by Time Inc. All rights reserved. Reprinted by permission of *Fortune* magazine and Robert Sheehan.

Harcourt Brace Jovanovich, Inc.: Abridged from *Technics and Civilization* by Lewis Mumford. Copyright 1934 by Harcourt Brace Jovanovich, Inc.; renewed 1962 by Lewis Mumford. Reprinted by permission of the publisher.

Harper & Row, Publishers, Inc., and Weidenfeld & Nicolson Ltd.: Abridged from *The Age of Revolution, 1789–1848* by E. J. Hobsbawm (World Publishers). Copyright © 1962 by E. J. Hobsbawm. Reprinted by permission of Harper & Row, Publishers, Inc., and Weidenfeld & Nicolson Ltd.

Macmillan Publishing Co., Inc.: From *The Crime and Punishment of I.G. Farben* by Joseph Borkin. Copyright © 1978 by The Free Press, a Division of Macmillan Publishing Co., Inc. Reprinted by permission of Macmillan Publishing Co., Inc.

Monthly Review Press: From "Oil Exploration Strategies: Alternatives for the Third World" by Michael Tanzer, *Monthly Review,* March 1978. Copyright ©

1978 by Monthly Review, Inc. Reprinted by permission of Monthly Review Press.

Mother Jones magazine: From "The Nuclear Frontier" by Amanda Spake, September/October 1979. Reprinted by permission of *Mother Jones* magazine.

The Nation: From "OPEC at 20 (1980)" by Joe Stork (reprinted in *America's Energy,* edited by Robert Engler). Table, "U.S. Nuclear Weapons Accidents (1950–1980) Acknowledged by The Pentagon," February 7, 1981. Copyright © 1980/1981 by The Nation Associates. Reprinted by permission of *The Nation.*

Nuclear Information and Resource Service: From "Nuclear Dangers," Energy Fact Sheet no. 2, Nuclear Information and Resource Service, Washington, D.C. Reprinted by permission.

Penguin Books Ltd. and Fred Halliday: From *Iran: Dictatorship and Development,* 2nd ed., by Fred Halliday. Copyright © 1979 by Fred Halliday. Reprinted by permission of Penguin Books Ltd. and the author.

The Philadelphia Inquirer: From "Energy Anarchy" by Donald L. Barlett and James B. Steele, December 7–13, 1980. Reprinted by permission of *The Philadelphia Inquirer.*

The Progressive: From "Ripping Off the Sun" by Richard Munson, September 1979. Copyright © 1979 by The Progressive, Inc. Reprinted by permission of *The Progressive.*

Ramparts magazine: From "Out of Gas" by James Ridgeway, October 1973. Copyright © 1973 by Noah's Ark, Inc. Reprinted by permission of *Ramparts* magazine.

Random House, Inc.: Cartoon, "The Nuclear Fuel Cycle," from *The Anti-Nuclear Handbook* by Stephen Croall and Kaianders. Copyright © 1978 by Beginners Books Ltd. Text Copyright © 1978 by Stephen Croall. Illustration Copyright © 1978 by Kaianders. From *The Control of Oil* by John M. Blair. Copyright © 1976 by John M. Blair. Reprinted by permission of Pantheon Books, a Division of Random House, Inc.

Vic Reinemer: From "The Dominant Dozen: Who Owns the Energy Corporations?" by Vic Reinemer, *Public Power,* November–December 1980. Reprinted by permission of the author.

Charles Scribner's Sons: From *The World Crisis* by Winston Churchill. Copyright 1923, 1927, 1929, 1931 by Charles Scribner's Sons; Copyright renewed 1951, © 1955, 1957, 1959 by Winston Churchill. Reprinted with the permission of Charles Scribner's Sons.

Southern Exposure: Map, "Nuclear Shipment Routes," from "Tower of Babel," special issue of Winter 1979 on the nuclear industry in the south. Copyright © 1979. Reprinted by permission of *Southern Exposure.*

Stanford University Press: From *The Condition of the Working Class in England* by Friederich Engels, translated and edited by W. O. Henderson and W. H. Chaloner. Copyright © 1958 by Basil Blackwell. Reprinted by permission of the publishers, Stanford University Press.

Times Books: From *John L. Lewis* by Melvyn Dubofsky and Warren Van Tine. Copyright © 1977 by Melvyn Dubofsky and Warren Van Tine. Reprinted by permission of Times Books, a division of Quadrangle/The New York Times Book Co., Inc.

The Union of Concerned Scientists: From *The Nugget File,* edited by Robert D. Pollard. Reprinted courtesy of The Union of Concerned Scientists.

United Mine Workers Journal: From "Dying the Slow Death" by Don Stillman, June 1–15; 1975. Reprinted by permission of *United Mine Workers Journal.*

Viking Penguin Inc.: From *The Seven Sisters: The Great Oil Companies and the World They Shaped* by Anthony Sampson. Copyright © 1975 by Anthony Sampson. Reprinted by permission of Viking Penguin Inc.

The Village Voice: From "The Big Switch, A Plan to Save New York" by Geoffrey Stokes and Leonard Rodberg, February 18, 1980, and "The Nuclear Power Structure, Where It Came From, What It Is" by Alexander Cockburn and James Ridgeway, May 7, 1979. Copyright © 1980/1979 by News Group Publications, Inc. Reprinted by permission of *The Village Voice.*

The Washington Monthly: From "The Pittston Mentality: Manslaughter on Buffalo Creek" by Thomas Bethell and Davitt McAteer, May 1972, and "Conspiracy in Coal" by Thomas Bethell, March 1969. Copyright © 1972/1969 by The Washington Monthly Co. Reprinted by permission of *The Washington Monthly.*

The Washington Post: From "Coal Miners: Energy War Casualties" by Curtis Seltzer, May 27, 1979. Copyright © 1979 by *The Washington Post.* Reprinted by permission of *The Washington Post.*

Harvard Business Review: From "Capital Investment to Save Energy" by G. N. Hatsopoulos, E. P. Gyftopoulos, R. W. Sant, and T. F. Widmer (March/April 1978). Copyright © 1978 by the President and Fellows of Harvard College; all rights reserved. Reprinted by permission of *Harvard Business Review.*

The JG Press: From *Energy-Efficient Community Planning* by James Ridgeway with Carolyn Projensky, 1979. Reprinted by permission of the JG Press

Alfred A. Knopf, Inc.: From *The Politics of Energy* by Barry Commoner. Copyright © 1979 by Barry Commoner. Reprinted by permission of Alfred A. Knopf, Inc.

Charles Komanoff: From "Doing Without Nuclear Power" by Charles Komanoff, *New York Review of Books,* May 17, 1979. Reprinted by permission of the author.

Worldwatch: From "The Solar Energy Timetable" by Denis Hayes, Worldwatch Paper 19. Copyright © 1978 by Worldwatch Institute. Reprinted by permission of *Worldwatch.*

CONTENTS

ACKNOWLEDGMENTS

I wish to thank Tom Engelhardt of Pantheon, without whose encouragement and good ideas this book never would have been written. He is responsible for much of the structure and interrelationship of the different sections. I also want to thank Len Rodberg, Curtis Seltzer, Alexander Cockburn, Vic Reinemer, Betsy Taylor, Peter Pringle, Mike Locker of Corporate Data Exchange, John Gaventa, and Tom Bethell for all their help. Special thanks go to Dan Cullen, who shepherded the manuscript through Pantheon.

INTRODUCTION

In reading this book you will want to keep several things in mind. The technical aspects of energy and its production can be fascinating, even mesmerizing—at least for experts in the field. Although, that's no reason for the rest of us to be presented with energy only in its narrow, technical sense, most energy writings take just such an approach. The first and most important theme in this book is that energy must instead be viewed as an integral part of the history of our modern industrial world.

Energy after all, forms the underpinnings of our entire economic existence. Our daily lives, the routine of our households, the work we do, our collective productivity, our leisure activity—all depend on the kinds and amounts of energy we consume. To cite but one obvious example, the suburb, engine of growth in the post-World War II period, could never have existed without the automobile, which, in turn, depended on large quantities of cheap oil.

This book follows the way our civilization has been fueled over the last two centuries—from the beginning of the Industrial Revolution to the current time. At the same time, it raises basic questions about how each of our key energy sources has affected the way our world has been organized and controlled. The major fuels in this process have, of course, been coal, oil, and natural gas. Nuclear power, synthetic fuels, and solar energy all have become potentially important in recent years, but it was coal and oil in particular which formed the underpinnings of the industrial world. These fuels are absolutely crucial to our economy. Their availability has depended on rapidly expanding markets which made their production profitable. Economic growth proved fundamental to use of coal and oil. As you will see, there is no more riveting story that the way in which Britain's abundant supplies of coal and numerous workers were harnessed together in the conquest of expanding markets for railroads, ships, and and a growing economic empire.

THE ORGANIZATION OF ENERGY

Surplus and concentration—these are the two key concepts that will help us understand energy in the pages that follow. Historically they have long been linked, though you would hardly think so from the news stories we read day after day which emphasize energy scarcity and economic competition. However, surplus, not shortage, has generally determined the fortunes of the petroleum industry since its founding in Pennsylvania in 1859. It was partly the fear of profit-devouring surplus which first drew the major oil companies together in an international petroleum cartel in the mid-1920s. It was also in the 1920s that the Standard Oil Company of New Jersey (predecessor of Exxon) joined with the giant German chemical firm I.G. Farben in a cartel. Both meant to control an expected and much feared surplus of synthetic gasoline which Standard thought Farben could otherwise unleash on the market with its discovery of coal synthetics. During the late 1920s the U.S. oil industry first sought federal approval for a government-sanctioned industry-wide cartel to control its domestic surplus. Herbert Hoover, who had originally supported the idea, turned against it as President. However, the New Deal ultimately provided such a federal sanction for industry-sponsored control programs through the passage of the Connally "hot oil" act. That act permitted producing states, often under the thumbs of the major oil companies, to establish levels of oil production. The federal government then banned shipment in interstate commerce of oil produced in excess of those quotas.

The prospect of glut and competition based on glut repeatedly dogged the oil industry. It was one of the reasons the oil companies began buying up coal and uranium firms in the 1960s, thereby enabling one set of giant energy companies to control the release of other types of energy into the marketplace—another way of reducing fears of an overall energy glut which might make prices for all forms of energy tumble. The more recent purchases of small solar energy companies by such energy giants seem to have a similar goal. One of the persistent questions, as we shall see, is whether and to what extent private industry can actually organize and control the energy markets so as to avoid ruinous surpluses or whether they must in the end turn to government for assistance.

THE SOCIAL COSTS OF ENERGY

The debate over energy swirls around costs: the costs of a barrel of oil from the Middle East versus the cost of a barrel of oil from Texas versus the equivalent amount of coal from Appalachia versus the equivalent derived from solar energy. But in such considerations of cost, we seldom take into account the larger human and environmental costs of energy production. It's these hidden, largely untallied social costs on which this book concentrates.

Coal could never have come to form the underpinnings of the world industrial economy from the late nineteenth through the early twentieth century were it not for the large numbers of very young children and women who worked with men in the underground mines of England and the United States, often under the worst possible conditions. Increased profitability in coal has always depended on increasing the productivity of the men and machines in the mines. That, in turn, has invariably meant reduced safety standards. In quite another energy sphere, few considering the production of synthetic fuels have seriously dealt with the human costs in terms of the potential for cancer and other diseases for those who work in or live near synthetic fuel operations; nor until recently have we had a serious debate on the effects of nuclear power plants on those who live near them.

As you read this book, you should be asking questions: What are the real, if often hidden, costs of the energy we use, especially in terms of human exploitation and environmental waste? Why do we use the kind of energy we do? Why, for example, do we continue to rely on fossil fuels, not on the "soft path" of solar alternatives? Who gains and who loses from the use of each particular type of energy? What is the role of government? Is it an impartial arbiter in the general public interest or does it represent the interests of industry?

Endings to books of this sort usually tend toward the upbeat, with rosy predictions of a world of renewable alternative energy systems. Such systems are dealt with in some detail here and I do indeed hope that someday they might come into widespread use. However, it ould hardly seem right to ignore the evidence of my own book, and so *Powering Civilization* ends on a more realistic, if grimmer, note —a possible future of immense energy concentration in a few giant companies.

The goal in publishing this collection is to make the subject of energy more accessible to the general reader. Putting energy back into history gives us a perspective from which to judge, question, and grasp the confusing energy events of the present moment which are presented to us in fragments on television or in the press and always in a mood of a historical crisis.

There are, however, limitations to a book like this which the reader should keep in mind. I have attempted to keep the narrow, technical details of energy to a minimum, but as you'll see, this isn't always possible. There are necessary stretches of this book where you will have little choice but to plow through complex materials. Space is another problem. The topic is enormous, and the debate over the last ten years has been extensive. Undoubtedly I have made omissions where material should have been included. To cite but one example, natural gas receives short shrift in the discussion. Natural gas is indeed an important fuel, accounting for nearly one-third of the U.S. energy market, but in its general outline the gas industry is extraordinarily similar to the oil industry, and the issues dealt with in the oil chapter apply to gas as well. It should also be noted that while gas has been an important fuel in the United States since before the Second World War, it is just becoming a significant factor in the energy picture of Europe and Asia. Thus, the literature dealing with gas is somewhat scant.

For those who want to pursue in more detail the subjects discussed under the different chapter headings, a bibliography at the back of the book will provide further guidance. A glossary also explains the different industrial processes

POWERING CIVILIZATION THE COMPLETE ENERGY READER

ORIGINS OF THE MODERN ENERGY INDUSTRY

THE history of industrial development in our Western world is, at base, the story of the growth and exploitation of new forms of energy, and that history begins with the development of coal mining into a mass industry in nineteenth-century England.

Traditionally the major source of England's domestic fuel needs had been wood; but by 1800 there were not enough forests in Britain to supply wood for household fuel in the nation's burgeoning cities. Coal proved to be the answer. From the turn of the century to about 1840 the coal industry, incorporating the first steam engines into prototypes of the first railway systems, changed the nature of the Industrial Revolution and, as we shall see, gave birth to other mass industries. From 1840 through the end of the century coal sparked the rapid mechanization of British industry and the development of new markets for heavy capital goods made of iron and steel—especially railroads and later ships.

The growth in the coal industry was astonishing. In 1850 Britain produced 49 million tons of coal. By 1880 the output had jumped to 147 million tons. This startling increase in production came not through technological innovation but simply by increasing the number of coal miners. It might be said that as the Industrial Revolution was propelled forward by modern fuel industries, so these industries themselves were being fueled by human power and a massive waste of human lives. In fact, one of the main problems during this period of the Industrial Revolution was the need to condition labor to long, steady hours of tedious work. This was especially true in the textile mills (as well as in the mines), where women and children proved more tractable than men. In general, strict discipline and low pay forced workers to labor through the week to make a minimum income.

After the railroads were built, the productive capacity of England's coal-powered steel mills was gainfully employed in the building of metal steamships, which the Royal Navy was persuaded to buy. Under the pressure of American competition, British shipping had declined in influence during the first part of the nineteenth century. However, with the birth of the iron steamship it recaptured supremacy. Shipbuilding then provided Britain with a major source of revenue as other aspects of its economy settled into decline.

With steamships there was not only a market for iron and steel (in the manufacture of which coal was employed) but an immense market for coal itself to fire the boilers of the vessels. As a result, the growth of steamships initially meant expanding exports for the British coal industry. However, as the colonies and other parts of the industrializing world became more self-sufficient, these exports declined.

In 1911 in a single stroke Sir Winston Churchill, first lord of the admiralty, irreversibly changed all this by formally deciding to fuel the British Navy with oil, not coal. Until this moment the Standard Oil Trust had dominated the world oil market, exporting from its empire in the United States. Churchill's decision, signaled the beginning of a new energy era, the age of adventuring for oil abroad.

Such a dramatic change had been some years in the making. In 1901 William Knox D'Arcy, an Australian financier living in London, had obtained a sixty-year concession to explore for and produce petroleum "throughout the whole extent of the Persian Empire," an area of 500,000 square miles. D'Arcy failed to strike any sizable amount of oil, and with funds exhausted, he desperately sought additional capital, at first in America and then, when that failed, on the Continent. It was at this point that the Navy entered the picture. Since 1882 naval officers had argued that the fleet could increase its fighting capacity by changing to oil. In 1904 the chairman of the Admiralty's oil committee approached the Burmah Oil Company and encouraged that firm to join D'Arcy in establishing a syndicate. The syndicate, the Anglo-Persian Oil Company (later the Anglo-Iranian Oil Company and today BP [British Petroleum]), was formed. Eventually D'Arcy hit an immense oil field.

When Churchill became first lord of the admiralty, he set out to expand an oil-fueled navy. With no other oil source at hand and fearful of becoming dependent on Standard Oil or Shell, the government turned to Anglo-Persian. In 1914 it signed a long-term supply contract and agreed to buy an interest in the company. Of the Persian concessions, Churchill said at the time, "Over the whole of these enormous regions we obtain the power to regulate developments according to naval and national interests, and to conserve and safeguard the supply of existing wells pending further development."

THE MINE

The descent into the mine begins this book, reminding us from the start that people produce energy in ways which are often painful and from a human point of view wasteful in the extreme. Indeed, from the beginning the foreboding works of the mine reflected all the human and environmental costs now associated with what we view as industrial progress: ruined land; polluted streams; weary, sick workers. With the onset of the Industrial Revolution in England, men, women, and children by the hundreds of thousands came to spend their short lives laboring in the dark galleries of the mine to unearth the coal on which the new world of capital ran.

As Lewis Mumford points out, the production of the mine has been closely linked to the development of modern warfare. As with the waste of human lives, the linking of military and energy endeavors is a phenomenon which we will meet over and over again in the history of energy production.

Taken from Technics and Civilization, *by Lewis Mumford, New York, Harcourt, Brace & Co., 1934.*

. . . DE RE METALLICA

Quarrying and mining are the prime extractive occupations: without stones and metals with sharp edges and resistant surfaces neither weapons nor tools could have passed beyond a very crude shape and a limited effectiveness—however ingeniously wood, shell and bone may have been used by primitive man before he had mastered stone. The first efficient tool seems to have been a stone held in the human hand as a hammer: the German word for fist is *die Faust,* and to this day the miner's hammer is called *ein Fäustel.* . . . In contrast to the forethought and sober plodding of the peasant, the work of the miner is the realm of random effort: irregular in routine and uncertain in result. Neither the peasant nor the herdsman can get rich quickly: the first clears a field or plants a row of trees this year from which perhaps only his grandchildren will get the full benefits. The rewards of agriculture are limited by the known qualities of soil and seed and stock: cows do not calve more quickly one year than another, nor do they have fifteen calves instead of one; and for the seven years of abundance seven lean years, on the law of averages, are pretty sure to follow. Luck for the peasant is usually a negative fact: hail, wind, blight, rot. But the rewards of mining may be sudden, and they may bear little relation, particularly in the early stages of the industry, either to the technical ability of the miner or the amount of labor he has expended. One assiduous prospector may wear out his heart for years without finding a rich seam; a newcomer in the same district may strike luck in the first morning he goes to work. While certain mines, like the salt mines of the Salzkammergut, have been in existence for centuries, the occupation in general is an unstable one.

Until the fifteenth century A.D., mining had perhaps made less technical progress than any other art: the engineering skill that Rome showed in aqueducts and roads did not extend in any degree to the mines. Not merely had the art remained for thousands of years in a primitive stage: but the occupation itself was one of the lowest in the human scale. Apart from the lure of prospecting, no one entered the mine in civilized states until relatively modern times except as a prisoner of war, a criminal, a slave. Mining was not regarded as a humane art: it was a form of punishment: it combined the terrors of the dungeon with the physical exacerbation of the galley. The actual work of mining, precisely because it was meant to be burdensome, was not improved during the whole of antiquity, from the earliest traces of it down to the fall of the Roman Empire. In general, not merely may one say that free labor did not enter the mines until the late Middle Ages; one must also remember that serfdom remained here, in the mines of Scotland for example, a considerable time after it had been abolished in agriculture. Possibly the myth of the Golden Age was an expression of mankind's sense of what it had lost when it acquired control of the harder metals.

Was the social degradation of mining an accident, or does it lie in the nature of things? Let us examine the occupation and its environment, as it existed through the greater part of history.

Except for surface mining, the art is pursued within the bowels of the earth. The darkness is broken by the timid flare of a lamp or a candle. Until the invention of the Davy safety lamp at the beginning of the nineteenth century this fire might ignite the "mine-damp" and exterminate by a single blast all who were within range: to this day, the possibility of such an explosion remains, since sparks may occur by accident even when electricity is used. Ground-water filters through the seams and often threatens to flood the passages. Until modern tools were invented, the passage itself was a cramped one: to extract ore, children and women were employed from the earliest days to crawl along the narrow tunnel, dragging a laden cart: women indeed were so used as beasts of burden in English mines right up to the middle of the nineteenth century. When primitive tools were not sufficient to break up the ore or open a new face, it was often necessary to light great fires in the difficult seams and then douse the stone with cold water in order to make it crack: the steam was suffocating, and the cracking might be dangerous: without strong shoring, whole galleries might fall upon the workers, and frequently this happened. The deeper down the seams went the greater the danger, the greater the heat, the greater the mechanical difficulties. Among the hard and brutal occupations of mankind, the only one that compares with old-fashioned mining is modern trench warfare. . . .

Mining and refining and smithing invoke, by the nature of the material dealt with, the ruthlessness of modern warfare: they place a premium on brute force. In the technique of all these arts the pounding operations are uppermost: the pick-ax, the sledge-hammer, the ore-crusher, the stamping machine, the steam-hammer: one must either melt or break the material in order to do anything with it. The routine of the mine involves an unflinching assault upon the physical environment: every stage in it is a magnification of power. When power-machines came in on a large scale in the fourteenth century, it was in the military and the metallurgical arts that they were, perhaps, most widely applied.

Let us now turn to the mining environment. The mine, to begin with, is the first completely inorganic environment to be created and lived in by man: far more inorganic than the giant city that Spengler has used as a symbol of the last stages of mechanical desiccation. Field and forest and stream and ocean are the environment of life: the mine is the environment alone of ores, minerals, metals. Within the subterranean rock, there is no life, not even bacteria or protozoa, except in so far as they may filter through with the ground water or be introduced by man. The face of nature above the ground is good to look upon, and the warmth of the sun stirs the blood of the hunter on the track of game or the peasant in the field. Except for the crystalline formations, the face of the mine is shapeless: no friendly trees and beasts and clouds greet the eye. In hacking and digging the contents of the earth, the miner has no eye for the forms of things: what he sees is sheer matter, and until he gets to his vein it is only an obstacle which he breaks through stubbornly and sends up to the surface. If the miner sees shapes on the walls of his cavern, as the candle flickers, they are only the monstrous distortions of his pick or his arm: shapes of fear. Day has been abolished and the rhythm of nature broken: continuous day-and-night production first came into existence here. The miner must work by artificial light even though the sun be shining outside; still further down in the seams, he must work by artificial ventilation, too: a triumph of the "manufactured environment."

In the underground passages and galleries of the mine there is nothing to distract the miner: no pretty wench is passing in the field with a basket on her head, whose proud breasts and flanks remind him of his manhood: no rabbit scurries across his path to arouse the hunter in him: no play of light on a distant river awakens his reverie. Here is the environment of work: dogged, unremitting, concentrated work. It is a dark, a colorless, a tasteless, a perfumeless, as well as a shapeless world: the leaden landscape of a perpetual winter. The masses and lumps of the ore itself, matter in its least organized form, complete the picture. . . .

There is a passage in Francis Bacon that makes one believe that the alchemists had perhaps a glimpse of this fact. He says: "If then it be true that Democritus said, *That the truth of nature lieth hid in certain deep mines and caves,* and if it be true likewise that the alchemists do so much inculcate, that Vulcan is a second nature, and imitateth that dexterously and compendiously, which nature worketh by ambages and length of time, it were good to divide natural philosophy into the mine and the furnace: and to make two professions or occupations of natural philosophers, some to be pioneers and some smiths; some to dig, and some to refine and hammer." Did the mine acclimate us to the views of science? Did science in turn prepare us to accept the products and the environment of the mine? The matter is not susceptible to proof: but the logical relations, if not the historical facts, are plain.

The practices of the mine do not remain below the ground: they affect the miner himself, and they alter the surface of the earth. Whatever could be said in defense of the art was said with great pith and good sense by Dr. Georg Bauer (Agricola), the German physician and scientist who wrote various compendious treatises on geology and mining at the beginning of the sixteenth century. He had the honesty to sum up his opponents' arguments in detail, even if he could not successfully refute them: so that his book De Re Metallica remains to this day a classic text, like Vitruvius on Architecture.

First as to the miner himself: "The critics," says Dr. Bauer, "say further that mining is a perilous occupation to pursue because the miners are sometimes killed by the pestilential air which they breathe; sometimes their lungs rot away; sometimes the men perish by being crushed in masses of rock; sometimes falling from ladders into the shafts, they break their arms, legs, or necks. . . . But since things like this rarely happen, and only so far as workmen are careless, they do not deter miners from carrying on their trade." This last sentence has a familiar note: it recalls the defenses of potters and radium watch-dial manufacturers when the dangers of their trades were pointed out. Dr. Bauer forgot only to note that though *coal* miners are not particularly susceptible to tuberculosis, the coldness and dampness, sometimes the downright wetness, predispose the miner to rheumatism: an ill they share with rice cultivators. The physical dangers of mining remain high; some are still unavoidable.

The animus of the miner's technique is reflected in his treatment of the landscape. Let Dr. Bauer again be our witness. "Besides this the strongest argument of the detractors is that the fields are devastated by mining operations, for which reason formerly Italians were warned by law that no one should dig the earth for metals and so injure their very fertile fields, their vineyards, and their olive groves. Also they argue that the woods and groves are cut down, for there is need of endless amount of wood for timbers, machines, and the smelting of metals. And when the woods and groves are felled, there are exterminate the beasts and birds, very many of which furnish pleasant and agreeable food for man. Further, when the ores are washed, the water which has been used poisons the brooks and streams, and either destroys the fish or drives them away. Therefore the inhabitants of these regions, on account of the devastation of their fields, woods, groves, brooks, and rivers, find great difficulty in procuring the necessaries of life, and by reason of the destruction of the timber they are forced to a greater expense in erecting buildings."

There is no reason to go into Dr. Bauer's lame reply: it happens that the indictment still holds, and is an unanswerable one. One must admit the devastation of mining, even if one is prepared to justify the end. "A typical example of deforestation," says a modern writer on the subject, "is to be seen on the eastern slopes of the Sierra Nevada, overlooking the Truckee Valley, where the cutting of trees to provide timber for the deep mines of the Comstock left the hillside exposed to erosion, so that today they are bleak, barren and hideous. Most of the old mining regions tell the same tale, from Lenares to Leadville, from Potosi to Porcupine." The history of the last four hundred years has underlined the truths of this indictment; for what was only an incidental and local damage in Dr. Bauer's time became a widespread characteristic of Western Civilization just as soon as it started in the eighteenth century to rest directly upon the mine and its products, and to reflect, even in territories far from the mine itself, the practices and ideals of the miner.

One further effect of this habitual destruction and disorganization must be noted: its psychological reaction on the miner. Perhaps inevitably he has a low standard of living. Partly, this is the natural effect of capitalist monopoly, often exerted and maintained by physical compulsion: but it exists even under relatively free conditions and in "prosperous" times. The explanation is not difficult: almost any sight is brighter than the pit, almost any sound is sweeter than the clang and rap of the hammer, almost any rough cabin, so long as it keeps the water out, is a more hospitable place for an exhausted man than the dark damp gallery of a mine. The miner, like the soldier coming out of the trenches, wants a sudden relief and an immediate departure from his routine. No less notorious than the slatternly disorder of the mining town are the drinking and gambling that go on in it: a necessary compensation for the daily toil. Released from his routine, the miner takes a chance at cards or dice or whippet racing, in the hope that it will bring the swift reward denied him in the drudging efforts of the mine itself. The heroism of the miner is genuine: hence his simple animal poise: his profound personal pride and self-respect. But the brutalization is also inevitably there.

Now, the characteristic methods of mining do not stop at the pithead: they go on, more or less, in all the accessory occupations. Here is the domain, in northern mythology, of the gnomes and the brownies: the cunning little people who know how to use the bellows, the forge, the hammer and the anvil. They, too, live in the depths of the mountains, and there is something a little inhuman about them: they tend to be spiteful and tricky. Shall we set this characterization down to the fear and mistrust of neolithic peoples for those who had mastered the art of working in metals? Perhaps: at all events one notes that in Hindu and Greek mythology the same general judgment prevails as in the North. While Prometheus, who stole the fire from heaven, is a hero, Hephaestus, the blacksmith, is lame and he is the sport and butt of the other gods despite his usefulness.

Usually pocketed in the mountains, the mine, the furnace, and the forge have remained a little off the track of civilization: isolation and monotony add to the defects of the activities themselves. . . . In the main . . . the mining and metallurgical arts were outside the social scheme of both classic and gothic civilization. That fact proved a sinister one as soon as the methods and ideals of mining became the chief pattern for industrial effort throughout the Western World. Mine: blast: dump: crush: extract: exhaust—there was indeed something devilish and sinister about the whole business. Life flourishes finally only in an environment of the living.

. . . MINING AND MODERN CAPITALISM

More closely than any other industry, mining was bound up with the first development of modern capitalism. By the sixteenth century it had definitely set the pattern for capitalist exploitation.

When mining was undertaken by free men in the fourteenth century in Germany the working of the mine was a simple partnership on a share basis. The miners themselves were often ne'er-do-wells and bankrupts who had seen better days. Partly abetted no doubt by this very application of free labor, there was a rapid advancement in technique in the German mines: by the sixteenth century those in Saxony led Europe, and German miners were imported into other countries, like England, to improve their practices.

The deepening of the mines, the extension of the operations to new fields, the application of complicated machinery for pumping water, hauling ore, and ventilating the mine, and the further application of waterpower to work the bellows in the new furnaces—all these improvements called for more capital than the original workers possessed. This led to the admission of partners who contributed money instead of work: absentee ownership: and this in turn led to a gradual expropriation of the owner-workers and the reduction of their share of the profits to the status of mere wages. This capitalistic development was further stimulated by reckless speculation in mining shares which took place as early as the fifteenth century: the local landlords and the merchants in the nearer cities eagerly followed this new gamble. If the mining industry in Dr. Bauer's day showed many of the modern improvements in industrial organization—the triple shift, the eight hour day, the existence of guilds in the various metallurgical industries for social intercourse, charitable self-help and insurance—it also showed, as the result of capitalist pressure, the characteristic features of nineteenth century industry throughout the world: the division of classes, the use of the strike as a weapon of defense, the bitter class war, and finally the extinction of the guilds' power by a combination of mine-owners and the feudal nobility during the so-called Peasants' War of 1525.

The result of that conflict was to abolish the cooperative guild basis of the mining industry, which had characterized its technical resurrection in Germany, and to place it on a free basis—that is, a basis of untrammeled acquisitiveness and class domination by the shareholders and directors, no longer bound to respect any of the humane regulations that had been developed by medieval society as measures of social protection. Even the serf had the safeguard of custom and the elementary security of the land itself: the miner and the iron-worker at the furnace was a free—that is, an unprotected—worker: the forerunner of the disinherited wage-worker of the nineteenth century. The most fundamental industry of the machine technics had known only for a moment in its history the sanctions and protections and humanities of the guild system: it stepped almost directly from the inhuman exploitation of chattel slavery to the hardly less inhuman exploitation of wage slavery. And wherever it went, the degradation of the worker followed.

But in still another way mining was an important agent of capitalism. The great need of commercial enterprise in the fifteenth century was for a sound but expansible currency, and for capital to provide the necessary capital goods—boats, mills, mine-shafts, docks, cranes—for industry. The mines of Europe began to supply this need even before the mines of Mexico and Peru. Sombart calculates that in the fifteenth and sixteenth centuries German mining earned as much in ten years as trade in the old style was able to accomplish in a hundred. As two of the greatest fortunes of modern times have been founded upon monopolies of petroleum and aluminum, so the great fortune of the Fuggers in the sixteenth century was founded upon the silver and lead mines of Styria and the Tyrol and Spain. The heaping up of such fortunes was part of a cycle we have witnessed with appropriate changes in our own time.

First: improvements in the technique of warfare, especially the rapid growth of the artillery arm, increased the consumption of iron: this led to new demands upon the mine. In order to finance the ever more costly equipment and maintenance of the new paid soldiery, the rulers of Europe had recourse to the financier. As security for the loan, the lender took over the royal mines. The development of the mines themselves then became a respectable avenue of financial enterprise, with returns that compared favorably with the usurious and generally unpayable interest. Spurred by the unpaid notes, the rulers were in turn driven to new conquests or to the exploitation of remote territories: and so the cycle began over again. War, mechanization, mining, and finance played into each other's hands. Mining was the key industry that furnished the sinews of war and increased the metallic contents of the original capital hoard, the war-chest: on the other hand, it furthered the industrialization of arms, and enriched the financier by both processes. The uncertainty of both warfare and mining increased the possibilities for speculative gains: this provided a rich broth for the bacteria of finance to thrive in.

Finally, it is possible that the animus of the miner had still another effect on the development of capitalism. This was in the notion that economic value had a relation to the quantity of brute work done and to the scarcity of the product: in the calculus of cost, these emerged as the principal elements. The rarity of gold, rubies, diamonds: the gross work that must be done to get iron out of the earth and ready for the rolling mill—these tended to be the criteria of economic value all through this civilization. But real values do not derive from either rarity or crude manpower. It is not rarity that gives the air its power to sustain life, nor is it the human work done that gives milk or bananas their nourishment. In comparison with the effects of chemical action and the sun's rays the human contribution is a small one. Genuine value lies in the power to sustain or enrich life: a glass bead may be more valuable than a diamond, a deal table more valuable esthetically than the most tortuously carved one, and the juice of a lemon may be more valuable on a long ocean voyage than a hundred pounds of meat without it. The value lies directly in the life-function: not in its origin, its rarity, or in the work done by human agents. The miner's notion of value, like the financier's, tends to be a purely abstract and quantitative one. Does the defect arise out of the fact that every other type of primitive environment contains food, something that may be immediately translated into life—game, berries, mushrooms, maple-sap, nuts, sheep, corn, fish —while the miner's environment alone is—salt and saccharin aside—not only completely inorganic but completely inedible? The miner works, not for love or for nourishment, but to "make his pile." The classic curse of Midas became perhaps the dominant characteristic of the modern machine: whatever it touched was turned to gold and iron, and the machine was permitted to exist only where gold and iron could serve as foundation.

MINE RAILROAD

England's burgeoning coal-mining industry provided both the necessary energy and the crucial invention on which the Industrial Revolution was to be based. Coal originally had been hauled from mine face to pithead by hand. Slowly, in the coal fields around Durham, this changed, and miners began to haul coal out of the mines in carts placed on iron tracks. Finally, movable engines replaced human beings and prototypical railroads were in operation. The first modern railroads were elaborations of this basic process and were used to haul coal across country from pithead to port. The railroad itself then became the primary impetus for the further development of the coal industry, since ever larger amounts of iron and coal were needed simply to build more railroads, until England was crisscrossed with iron rails and a completely new system of transportation had been built.

Coal, of course, is a crucial ingredient along with iron ore in the manufacture of steel. The invention at mid-nineteenth century by Sir Henry Bessemer of a process to make steel by combining molten iron with oxygen vastly enlarged the potential for the industry.

Taken from The Age of Revolution, 1789–1848, *by E. J. Hobsbawm, London, World, 1962.*

It is evident that no industrial economy can develop beyond a certain point until it possesses adequate capital-goods capacity. This is why even today the most reliable single index of any country's industrial potential is the quantity of its iron and steel production. But it is also evident that under conditions of private enterprise the extremely costly capital investment necessary for much of this development is not likely to be undertaken for the same reasons as the industrialization of cotton or other consumer goods. For these a mass market already exists, at least potentially: even very primitive men wear shirts or use household equipment and foodstuffs. The problem is merely how to put a sufficiently vast market sufficiently quickly within the purview of businessmen. But no such market exists, e.g., for heavy iron equipment such as girders. It only comes into existence in the course of an industrial revolution (and not always then), and those who lock up their money in the very heavy investments required even by quite modest ironworks (compared to quite large cotton-mills) before it is visibly there, are more likely to be speculators, adventurers and dreamers than sound businessmen. In fact in France a sect of such speculative technological adventurers, the Saint-Simonians

. . . acted as chief propagandists of the kind of industrialization which needed heavy and long-range investment.

These disadvantages applied particularly to metallurgy, especially of iron. Its capacity increased, thanks to a few simple innovations such as that of puddling and rolling in the 1780s, but the non-military demand for it remained relatively modest, and the military, though gratifyingly large thanks to a succession of wars between 1756 and 1815, slackened off sharply after Waterloo. It was certainly not large enough to make Britain into an outstandingly large producer of iron. In 1790 she out-produced France by only forty per cent or so, and even in 1800 her output was considerably less than half of the combined Continental one, and amounted to the, by later standards, tiny figure of a quarter of a million tons. If anything, the British share of world iron output tended to sink in the next decades.

Fortunately they applied less to mining, which was chiefly the mining of *coal.* For coal had the advantage of being not merely the major source of industrial power in the nineteenth century, but also a major form of domestic fuel, thanks largely to the relative shortage of forests in Britain. The growth of cities, and especially of London, had caused coal mining to expand rapidly since the late sixteenth century. By the early eighteenth it was substantially a primitive modern industry, even employing the earliest steam-engines (devised for similar purposes in non-ferrous metal mining, mainly in Cornwall), for pumping. Hence coal mining hardly needed or underwent major technological revolution in our period. Its innovations were improvements rather than transformations of production. But its capacity was already immense and, by world standards, astronomic. In 1800 Britain may have produced something like ten million tons of coal, or about 90 per cent of the world output. Its nearest competitor, France, produced less than a million.

This immense industry, though probably not expanding fast enough for really massive industrialization on the modern scale, was sufficiently large to stimulate the basic invention which was to transform the capital-goods industries: the railway. For the mines not only required steam-engines in large quantities and of great power, but also required efficient means of transporting the great quantities of coal from coal-face to shaft and especially from pithead to the point of shipment. The "tramway" or "railway" along which trucks ran was an obvious answer; to pull these trucks by stationary engines was tempting; to pull them by moving engines would not seem too impractical. Finally, the costs of overland transport of bulk goods were so high that it was likely to strike coal-owners in inland fields that the use of these short-term means of transport could be profitably extended for long-term haulage. The line from the inland coalfield of Durham to the coast (Stockton–Darlington 1825) was the first of the modern railways. Technologically the railway is the child of the mine, and especially the northern English coal mine. George Stephenson began life as a Tyneside "engineman," and for years virtually all locomotive drivers were recruited from his native coalfield.

No innovation of the Industrial Revolution has fired the imagination as much as the railway, as witness the fact that it is the only product of nineteenth-century industrialization which has been fully absorbed into the imagery of popular and literate poetry. Hardly had they been proved technically feasible and profitable in England (*c.* 1825–30), before plans to build them were made over most of the Western world, though their execution was generally delayed. The first short lines were opened in the USA in 1827, in France in 1828 and 1835, in Germany and Belgium in 1835, and even in Russia by 1837. The reason was doubtless that no other invention revealed the power and speed of the new age to the layman as dramatically; a revelation made all the more striking by the remarkable technical maturity of even the very earliest railways. (Speeds of up to sixty miles per hour, for instance, were perfectly practicable in the 1830s, and were not substantially improved by later steam-railways.) The iron road, pushing its huge smoke-plumed snakes at the speed of wind across countries and continents, whose embankments and cuttings, bridges and stations, formed a body of public building beside which the pyramids and the Roman aqueducts and even the Great Wall of China paled into provincialism, was the very symbol of man's triumph through technology.

In fact, from an economic point of view, its vast expense was its chief advantage. No doubt in the long run its capacity to open up countries hitherto cut off by high transport costs from the world market, the vast increase in the speed and bulk of overland communication it brought for men and goods, were to be of major importance. Before 1848 they were economically less important: outside Britain because railways were few, in Britain because for geographical reasons transport problems were much less intractable than in large landlocked countries.[*] But from the perspective of the student of economic development the immense appetite of the railways for iron and steel, for coal, for heavy machinery, for labour, for capital investment, was at this stage more important. For it provided just that massive demand which was needed if the capital-goods industries were to be transformed as profoundly as the cotton industry had been. In the first two decades of the railways (1830–50) the output of iron in Britain rose from 680,000 to 2,250,000 [tons]; in other words it trebled. The output of coal between 1830 and 1850 also trebled from 15 million tons to 49 million tons. That dramatic rise was due primarily to the railway, for on average each mile of line required 300 tons of iron merely for track. The industrial advances which for the first time made the mass production of steel possible followed naturally in the next decades.

The reason for this sudden, immense, and quite essential expansion lay in the apparently irrational passion with which businessmen and investors threw themselves into the construction of railways. In 1830 there were a few dozen miles of railways in all the world—chiefly consisting of the line from Liverpool to Manchester. By 1840 there were over 4,500 miles, by 1850 over 23,500. Most of them were projected in a few bursts of speculative frenzy known as the 'railway manias' of 1835–7 and especially in 1844–7; most of them were built in large part with British capital, British iron, machines, and know-how. These investment booms appear irrational, because in fact few railways were much more profitable to the investor than other forms of enterprise, most yielded quite modest profits and many none at all: in 1855 the average interest on capital sunk in the British railways was a mere 3.7 per cent. No doubt promoters, speculators, and others did exceedingly well out of them, but the ordinary investor clearly did not. And yet by 1840 £28 millions, by 1850 £240 millions, had been hopefully invested in them.

Why? The fundamental fact about Britain in the first two generations of the

[*]No point in Britain is more than 70 miles from the sea, and all the chief industrial areas of the nineteenth century, with one exception, are either on the sea or within easy reach of it.

Industrial Revolution was that the comfortable and rich classes accumulated income so fast and in such vast quantities as to exceed all available possibilities of spending and investment. (The annual investible surplus in the 1840s was reckoned at about £60 millions.) No doubt feudal and aristocratic societies would have succeeded in throwing a great deal of this away in riotous living, luxury building, and other uneconomic activities.[*] Even in Britain the sixth Duke of Devonshire, whose normal income was princely enough, succeeded in leaving his heir £1,000,000 of debts in the mid-nineteenth century (which he paid off by borrowing another £1,500,000 and going in for the development of real estate values). But the bulk of the middle classes, who formed the main investing public, were still savers rather than spenders, though by 1840 there are many signs that they felt sufficiently wealthy to spend *as well as* to invest. Their wives began to turn into "ladies," instructed by the handbooks of etiquette which multiply about this period, their chapels began to be rebuilt in ample and expensive styles, and they even began to celebrate their collective glory by constructing those shocking town halls and other civic monstrosities in Gothic and Renaissance imitations, whose exact and Napoleonic cost their municipal historians recorded with pride.

Again, a modern socialist or welfare society would no doubt have distributed some of these vast accumulations for social purposes. In our period nothing was less likely. Virtually untaxed, the middle classes therefore continued to accumulate among the hungry populace, whose hunger was the counterpart of their accumulation. And as they were not peasants, content to hoard their savings in woollen stockings or as golden bangles, they had to find profitable investment for them. But where? Existing industries, for instance, had become far too cheap to absorb more than a fraction of the available surplus for investment: even supposing the size of the cotton industry to be doubled, the capital cost would absorb only a part of it What was needed was a sponge large enough to hold all of it. . . .

Whether it [capital] could have found other forms of home investment—for instance in building—is an academic question to which the answer is still in doubt. In fact it found the railways, which could not conceivably have been built as rapidly and on as large a scale without this torrent of capital flooding into them, especially in the middle 1840s. It was a lucky conjuncture, for the railways happened to solve virtually all the problems of the economy's growth at once.

WOMEN AND CHILDREN IN THE MINES

The social costs of this burst of railroad construction and the Industrial Revolution which followed were high. Nowhere were they more apparent than in the mines, where the need to create an enormous, pliant labor force led mine owners to employ vast numbers of women and children in conditions so appalling that various parliamentary commissions were formed to investigate them.

[*]Of course such spending also stimulates the economy, but very inefficiently, and hardly at all in the direction of industrial growth.

Taken from First Report of the Commissioner for Mines, 1842. *Children's Employment Commission, Great Britain*

90. The Sub-Commissioner says, "I visited the house of the parents of a little boy whom I saw keeping a door down Flatworth Pit, on the 20th of May; it was about seven o'clock on the Sunday evening, and the boy, Thomas Roker, was in bed asleep. His mother said he was aged about six years and seven months, and that he had been down the pit about a month or six weeks. The boy was at school at three years old, and his father wished to make him a better scholar before he went down. Always puts him to bed early, because he must get up every working morning at three o'clock: and he often rubs his eyes when he is woke, and says he has only just been to sleep. He gets up at 3 A.M., and goes down the pit at 4 o'clock A.M. He gets his dinner directly he comes home, about half-past 4 P.M., or a quarter to 5 P.M., and then he washes himself and goes to bed between six and seven; so that he will never be up more than two hours from the pit for eating, washing, and playing. When his son gets a little more hardened to the pit, his father means to send him to night-school, and stop an hour off his sleep. Thomas generally goes down the pit in a corf,[*] with a good few boys in it, and sometimes he goes up on his father's knee. It is a dusty pit, but he never complains, though he tells many a queer story of the pit. The pit does not hurt him, but makes him a little whiter and perhaps thinner. He was a very fat boy when he was three years old. . . .

98. . . .[S]tatements as to the early age at which Children commence work in the pits are confirmed by the most abundant evidence derived from examinations of the Children themselves; and it must be borne in mind that many of the youngest of these Children have to carry coals on their backs, from the workings to the surface, up steep ladders. . . .

> Margaret Leveston, six years old, coal-bearer, says: "Been down at coal-carrying six weeks; makes 10 to 14 rakes a-day; carries full 56 lbs. of coal in a wooden backit. The work is na guid; it is so very sair". . . .—Robert Seton, eleven years old, coal-putter: "Father took me down when I was six years old, and I have wrought below ever since." . . .—Mary Neilson, ten years old, coal-bearer: "Sister was six years old when she first wrought, and I went down at that age." . . .—Margaret Watson, sixteen years of age, coal-bearer: "I was first taken below to carry coals when I was six years old, and have never been away from the work, except a few evenings in the summer months, when some of us go to Carlops, two miles over the moor, to learn the reading." . . .—Thomas Brown, ten years old, putter: "Wrought below four years;" so that he began work at six years of age." . . .

296. When a child has to drag a carriage loaded with coals through a passage "not more than 18 inches in height," some ingenuity is required to get his body and the carriage through this narrow space. "The boys," says Mr. Tranter, "crawl on their hands and knees." But an expedient has been adopted with a view of facilitating this labour, of which the Sub-Commissioner gives the following description: "A girdle is put round the naked waist, to which a chain from the carriage

[*]Small wooden or iron wagon used to carry coal in and out of mines.

is hooked and passed between the legs, and the boys crawl on their hands and knees, drawing the carriage after them." This is called "Drawing by the Girdle and Chain." "This practice," he adds, "is not totally unknown in South Staffordshire in working some thin seams of coal; and is still more in use in the thin beds of ironstone; but it is not nearly so common as in Shropshire. About thirty years ago it was a very general custom to employ young boys, both in the coal-pits and iron-pits, to draw carriages by this means. The custom is not yet entirely out of use, though the respectable companies have many years discontinued it, and have substituted instead small iron railways, and small carriages called dans, which the boys push before them. All persons who have spoken of the girdles, both in Staffordshire and Shropshire, have described the labour as very severe, and the girdle as frequently blistering their sides, and occasioning great pain." . . .

> James Pearce, twelve years of age: "About a year and a half ago I took to the girdle and chain; I do not like it; it hurts me; it rubs my skin off; I often feel pain. I have often had blisters on my side; but when I was more used to it it would not blister, but it smarted very badly. The chain was made of the same stuff as the rope that goes down the pit. I crawled on hands and feet. I often knocked my back against the top of the pit, and it hurt it very sore. The legs ached very badly. When I came home at night I often sat down to rest me by the way, I was so tired. The work made me look much older than I was. I worked at this drawing with girdle and chain three or four months. I thought that if I kept at this work I should be nothing at all, and I went and worked upon the bank. Many boys draw with girdle and chain now. There is not the railway and the dans. It is like drawing on the roads. I think it is a great hurt to a boy: it must be, to draw the same as a horse draws. A great many boys find that they are unable, and give over drawing with girdle and chain. It is very hard, very hard, sir. If they were to lay down rails, and push the coals on dans, it would be very convenient for the boys, though the expense might not be convenient for the masters." . . .
>
> Betty Harris, aged thirty-seven, drawer, in a coal-pit at Little Bolton: "I have a belt round my waist, and a chain passing between my legs, and I go on my hands and feet. The road is very steep, and we have to hold by a rope; and, when there is no rope, by anything we can catch hold of. There are six women and about six boys and girls in the pit I work in: it is very hard work for a woman. The pit is very wet where I work, and the water comes over our clog-tops always, and I have seen it up to my thighs: it rains in at the roof terribly; my clothes are wet through almost all day long. I never was ill in my life but when I was lying-in. My cousin looks after my children in the day-time. I am very tired when I get home at night; I fall asleep sometimes before I get washed. I am not so strong as I was, and cannot stand my work so well as I used to do. I have drawn till I have had the skin off me: the belt and chain is worse when we are in the family way. My feller [husband] has beaten me many a time for not being ready. I were not used to it at first, and he had little patience: I have known many a man beat his drawer. I have known men take liberty with the drawers, and some of the women have bastards." . . .—Rosa Lucas, nearly eighteen years old, drawer at Mr. Morris's, Lamberhead Green: "What distance did you draw? 23 score yards in length.

> That is 460 yards each way, or 920 yards? Yes.—How many times had you to draw this distance? 16 and sometimes 18 times. [Taking 16 times, she would have to draw 14,720 yards daily]." . . .—Dinah Bradbury, waggoner at Mr. Evans's, Haydock Colliery: "Draws for two men. *Girl.*—At what age do you intend to turn us out of the pit? Put me down 15 years old. I should like to be turned out.—Do you then not like your present employment?—No, I don't, and I would not go down if I could get anything else to do." . . .

359. The persons employed in coal-bearing are almost always girls and women. Boys are sometimes engaged in the same labour, but that is comparatively rare. The coal-bearers have to carry coal on their backs in unrailed roads with burdens varying from ¾ cwt. to 3 cwt. The Sub-Commissioner represents this labour as "a cruel slaving revolting to humanity;" yet he found engaged in this labour a child, a beautiful girl, only six years old, whose age he ascertained, carrying in the pit ½ cwt. of coals, and regularly making with this load fourteen long and toilsome journeys a-day.

> . . . William Burnside, ten years old, coal-bearer, same colliery: "I gang with brother and sister; have done so two months. I can fill one tub in the day: it takes me 17 journeys, as my back gets sore. A tub holds near 5 cwt. I follow sister with bits of coal strapped over my head and back. The work fatigues me muckle." . . .—Ellison Jack, a girl eleven years old, coal-bearer: "I have been working below three years on my father's account; he takes me down at two in the morning, and I come up at one and two next afternoon. I go to bed at six at night to be ready for work next morning; the part of the pit I bear in the seams are much on the edge. I have to bear my burthen up four traps, or ladders, before I get to the main road which leads to the pit bottom. My task is four to five tubs; each tub holds 4¼ cwt. I fill five tubs in 20 journeys. I have had the strap when I did not do my bidding. Am very glad when my task is wrought, as it sore fatigues." . . .

360. "A brief description of this Child's place of work will better illustrate her evidence. She has first to descend a nine-ladder pit to the first rest, even to which a shaft is sunk, to draw up the baskets or tubs of coals filled by the bearers: she then takes her creel (a basket formed to the back, not unlike a cockle-shell flattened towards the neck, so as to allow lumps of coal to rest on the back of the neck and shoulders), and pursues her journey to the wall-face, or as it is called here, the room of work. She then lays down her basket, into which the coal is rolled, and it is frequently more than one man can do to lift the burden on her back. The tugs or straps are placed over the forehead, and the body bent in a semicircular form, in order to stiffen the arch. Large lumps of coal are then placed on the neck, and she then commences her journey with her burden to the pit bottom, first hanging her lamp to the cloth crossing her head. In this girl's case she has first to travel about 14 fathoms (84 feet) from wall-face to the first ladder, which is 18 feet high: leaving the first ladder she proceeds along the main road, probably 3 feet 6 inches to 4 feet 6 inches high, to the second ladder, 18 feet high, so on to the third and fourth ladders till she reaches the pit-bottom, where she casts her load, varying from 1 cwt to 1½ cwt., into the tub. This one journey is designated a rake; the height

ascended, and the distance along the roads added together, exceed the height of St. Paul's Cathedral; and it not unfrequently happens that the tugs break, and the load falls upon those females who are following. However incredible it may be, yet I have taken the evidence of fathers who have ruptured themselves from straining to lift coal on their Children's backs." . . .

THE HEALTH OF MINERS

Among the most vigorous criticisms of the treatment of workers in England during the Industrial Revolution was that made by Friedrich Engels, son of a prosperous German cotton manufacturer who himself was trained in a Manchester cotton firm.

Taken from The Condition of the Working Class in England, *by Friedrich Engels, Palo Alto, California, Stanford University Press, 1958.*

. . . All the children and young people employed in hauling coal and ironstone complain of being very tired. Not even in a factory where the most intensive methods of securing output are employed do we find the workers driven to the same limits of physical endurance as they are in the mines. Every page of the report to which we have referred gives chapter and verse for this assertion. It is a very common occurrence for children to come home from the mine so exhausted that they throw themselves on to the stone floor in front of the fire. They cannot keep awake even to eat a morsel of food. Their parents have to wash them and put them to bed while they are still asleep. Sometimes the children actually fall asleep on the way home and are eventually discovered by their parents late at night. It appears to be the almost universal practice of these children to stay in bed most of Sunday in an attempt to recover from the exertions of the previous week's work. Only a few go to church or Sunday school. The teachers at these schools complain that their pupils are very tired and listless. The women and older girls are also habitually exhausted owing to the brutal way in which they are overworked. This utter weariness, actually painful to bear, naturally affects the physique of these women adversely. The most obvious consequence of their unnatural physical exertions is that all the strength in their bodies is concentrated into muscular development. In particular, the muscles of the arms, legs, back, shoulders and chest are overdeveloped because they take the strain of pushing and pulling [the heavy coal tubs]. The rest of their bodies, on the other hand, are crippled owing to lack of nourishment. Nearly all miners are physically stunted, except those in Warwickshire and Leicestershire who work under particularly favourable conditions. Next it may be mentioned that both among boys and girls puberty is delayed—among boys often until as late as the eighteenth year. J. C. Symons actually came across a 19-year-old youth who, except for his teeth, had the physique of a boy aged between 11 and 12. This prolongation of the period of childhood is a proof of retarded development and naturally has its consequences in later years. Miners are either bandy-legged or knock-kneed and suffer from splayed feet, spinal deformities and other physical defects. This is due to the fact that their constitutions have been weakened and they are nearly always forced to work in a cramped position. Many people, including even doctors, say that in Yorkshire, Lancashire, Northumberland and Durham it is possible to pick a miner out from among a hundred other people because of his physical defects. The women, in particular, appear to be half crippled. They seldom, if ever, have backs which are as straight as those of other women. Distortion of the pelvis leads these women to have difficult and sometimes fatal confinements. All this is to be attributed to the nature of their work. In addition to these physical deformities, which are peculiar to coal mining, there are the illnesses which they share with all types of miners. It is easy to see the connection between these illnesses and the nature of the occupation they follow. They suffer particularly from stomach troubles. They lose their appetites and are subject to internal pains, nausea and vomiting. In addition they are liable to become very thirsty and very often the only water available is the filthy, tepid water in the mine. They suffer from severe indigestion and this aggravates the other stomach troubles mentioned. Further complaints among miners are various diseases of the heart—particularly enlargement and inflammation of the heart and pericardium, contraction of the auriculoventricular communications, and contortion of the commencement of the aorta. There is much evidence to show that all these diseases are common among miners, and it can easily been seen that they are almost certainly caused by undue physical exertion. The same is true of ruptures, which are also due to excessive muscular strain.

Many miners suffer also from painful and dangerous lung diseases, particularly asthma. This is due partly . . . to the foul dusty atmosphere impregnated with carbonic acid gas and carburretted hydrogen gas. These gases could easily be dispersed. In some districts most miners suffer these diseases by the time they are 40, and then they are soon unfit for further work. Sometimes the effects of these diseases are seen as early as the age of 30. Those employed in wet workings are naturally the first to suffer from chest complaints. In some districts of Scotland young miners aged only between 20 and 30 are particularly susceptible to inflammation of the lungs and other feverish complaints. A disease which is largely confined to miners is "black spittle." It arises because the lungs become impregnated with fine coal dust and this leads to general debility, headaches, constriction of the chest and the expectoration of thick black mucus. In some coalmining districts this complaint occurs only in a mild form, but in certain areas, particularly in Scotland, it is so virulent as to appear to be quite incurable. In Scotland the symptoms of black spittle—in addition to those already mentioned—are constant shortness and quickness of breath, a rapid pulse (over 100 beats in a minute), and a hacking cough. When general emaciation and weakness set in, the patient is soon unfit for work. The illness is always fatal. Dr. Makellar of Pencaitland, East Lothian, states that this illness does not occur in those mines which are adequately ventilated. Many examples could be given of miners who moved from well-ventilated to badly-ventilated mines and caught the disease. It is solely due to the colliery owners' greed for profit that this illness exists at all. If the coalowners would pay to have ventilation shafts installed the problem would not exist. Except in Warwickshire and Leicestershire rheumatism is an occupational disease of miners. It is naturally most severe in the wetter coal mines.

Owing to these illnesses the coalminers in all districts, *without exception,* become prematurely aged and unfit for work after they are 40 years old. The average age of retirement, of course, varies from district to district. It is very rare for a miner to be still at work after he is 50 or even 45. It is generally agreed that a miner is practically an old man at the age of 40. That is true of the coalhewers. The loaders who lift heavy lumps of coal into the tubs, become old when they are 28 or 30, so that there is a saying in the coal districts: "Loaders are . . . old men before they are young ones." It goes without saying that, since miners age prematurely, they die young. It is very rare indeed to come across a miner who is 60 years of age. Even in South Staffordshire where the coal mines are relatively healthy, comparatively few workers reach the age of 51. Since the workers become old so soon it is natural that there should be much unemployment among parents in the mining as well as in the factory districts. The parents are often supported by children who are still very young.

Dr. Southwood Smith, one of the Commissioners, briefly summarises the effects of their occupation on the miners as follows. He points out that the period of childhood is unduly prolonged while the period of adult life is curtailed. Consequently, when a man should be in the prime of life and in full possession of his powers, his life is prematurely cut short by an early death. And for all this the middle class is solely responsible. . . .

THE ROMANCE OF DESIGN

When there were no more railroads to be laid in England, British industrial power turned to the building of steel steamships, mainly for the British Navy. Though by the end of the nineteenth century the Navy had begun to fuel a few of its ships with oil, the bulk of them were still coal-powered. However, in 1911, Winston Churchill, the new first lord of the admiralty, decided to seek a fleet which would be able to outgun as well as outmaneuver Germany's newest warships. With this in mind, he set out to build a "Fast Division" of battleships, armed with fifteen-inch guns and run on oil.

Churchill's fateful decision to power the British Navy with oil-burning ships led the government to seek a secure and inexpensive supply of oil in Persia. In underwriting the Anglo-Persian Oil Company, the government set off a scramble for Middle Eastern oil concessions and opened a new period in the world's energy (as well as colonial) history—the Imperial Age of Oil.

Taken from The World Crisis, *by Winston S. Churchill,* 1911–1915, *New York, Scribners, 1931*

. . . The gun dominated the ship, and was the decisive cause of all the changes we then made in design. The following was in those days the recipe in very unexpert language for making a battleship:—

You take the largest possible number of the best possible guns that can be fired in combination from one vessel as a single battery. You group them conveniently by pairs in turrets. You put the turrets so that there is the widest possible arc of fire for every gun and the least possible blast interference. This regulates the position of the turrets and the spacing between them. You draw a line around the arrangement of turrets thus arrived at, which gives you the deck of the ship. You then build a hull to carry this deck or great gun platform. It must be very big and very long. Next you see what room you have got inside this hull for engines to drive it, and from this and from the length you get the speed. Last of all you decide on the armour.

. . . On this vast process of juggling and higgling we now embarked.

From the beginning there appeared a ship carrying ten 15-inch guns, and therefore at least 600 feet long with room inside her for engines which would drive her 21 knots and capacity to carry armour which on the armoured belt, the turrets and the conning tower would reach the thickness unprecedented in the British Service of 13 inches. For less armour you could have more speed: for less speed you could have more armour, and so on within very considerable limits. But now a new idea began to dawn. Eight 15-inch guns would fire a simultaneous broadside of approximately 16,000 lb. Ten of the latest 13.5-inch would only fire 14,000 lb. Therefore, we could get for eight 15-inch guns a punch substantially greater than that of ten 13.5-inch. Nor did the superiority end there. With the increased size of the shell came a far greater increase in the capacity of the bursting charge. It was not quite a geometric progression, because other considerations intervened; but it was in that order of ideas. There was no doubt about the punch. On the other hand, look at the speed. Twenty-one knots was all very well in its way, but suppose we could get a much greater speed. Suppose we could cram into the hull a horse-power sufficient to drive these terrific vessels, already possessing guns and armour superior to that of the heaviest battleship, at speeds hitherto only obtained by the lightly armoured 12-inch gun battle-cruisers, should we not have introduced a new element into naval war?

And here we leave the region of material. I have built the process up stage by stage as it was argued out, but of course all the processes proceeded in simultaneous relation, and the result was to show a great possibility. Something like the ship described above could be made if it were wanted. Was it wanted? Was it the right thing to make? Was its tactical value sufficient to justify the increase in cost and all the changes in design? We must turn for the answer to the tactical sphere.

Here I felt able to see a little more clearly. As cannot be too often repeated, war is all one; and the same principles of thought which are true in any form are true *mutatis mutandis* in every other form. Obviously in creating an Army or an Air Force or a squadron of battleships you must first of all have regard to their highest tactical employment, namely, decisive battle. Let us therefore, first of all, visualize the battle. Let us try to imagine what its conditions will be; what we shall have to meet and what would help us most to win. The first naval idea of our supreme battle at this time was that it would be fought about something: somebody would want to be going somewhere and somebody else would try to stop him. One of the Fleets would be proceeding in a certain direction and the other Fleet would come along and try to prevent it. However they might approach, the battle would soon resolve itself into two lines of ships steaming along parallel and bringing all their broadsides to bear upon each other. Of course if one Fleet is much stronger than the other, has heavier guns and shoots better, the opposite line begins to get the worst of it. Ships begin to burn and blow up and fall out of the line, and every one that falls out increases the burden of fire upon the remainder. The Fleet which has more ships in it also has a tail which overlaps the enemy, and a good many ships in this tail can concentrate their fire upon the rear ships of the enemy, so that these unlucky vessels have not only to fight the ships opposite to them, but have to bear the fire of a number of others firing obliquely at them from behind. But smashing up the tail of an enemy's Fleet is a poor way of preventing him from achieving his objective, i.e. going where he wants to go. It is not comparable to smashing up his head. Injuries at the head of the line tend to throw the whole line into confusion, whereas injuries at the tail only result in the ships dropping astern without causing other complications. Therefore the Admiralissimo will always try to draw a little ahead if he possibly can and bring his van nearer and nearer to the enemy and gradually, if he can, force that enemy to turn off, so that he can then curl round him. . . .

If the speeds of the Fleets are equal, how can this be done? The heads of both lines will be abreast and the fire will only be given and returned ship for ship.

But suppose you have a division of ships in your Fleet which go much faster than any of your other ships or of your enemy's ships. These ships will be certainly able to draw ahead and curl round the head of the enemy's line. More than that, as they draw ahead they will repeat in a much more effective fashion the advantage of an overlapping tail, because the ships at the head of the enemy's line will have to bear the fire of the overlapping ships as well as the fire of those which are lying opposite to them, and therefore two or three ships might be firing on every one of the leading ships of the enemy, thus smashing to pieces the head of the enemy's line and throwing his whole formation into confusion.

Here then in simple outline is the famous argument for the Fast Division. A squadron of ships possessing a definite superiority of speed could be so disposed in the approaching formation of your own Fleet as to enable you, whichever way the enemy might deploy, to double the fire after a certain interval upon the head of his line, and also to envelop it and cross it and so force him into a circular movement and bring him to bay once and for all without hope of escape. . . .

Suppose . . . we could make a division of ships fast enough to seize the advantageous position and yet as strong in gun-power and armour as any battleship afloat. Should we not have scored almost with certainty an inestimable and a decisive advantage? . . .

At this stage the War College were asked to work out on the tactical board the number of knots superiority in speed required in a Fast Division in order to ensure this Division being able to manoeuvre around the German Fleet as it would be in the years 1914 and 1915.

The answer was that if the Fast Division could steam in company 25 knots or better, they could do all that was necessary. We therefore wanted 4 or 5 knots additional speed. How were we to get it? With every knot the amount of horsepower required is progressively greater. Our new ship would steam 21 knots, but to steam 25 to 26 she wanted 50,000 horse-power. Fifty thousand horse-power meant more boilers, and where could they be put? Why, obviously they could be put where the fifth turret would go, and having regard to the increased punch of the 15-inch gun we could spare the fifth turret.

But even this would not suffice. We could not get the power required to drive these ships at 25 knots except by the use of oil fuel.

The advantages conferred by liquid fuel were inestimable. First, speed. In equal ships oil gave a large excess of speed over coal. It enabled that speed to be attained with far greater rapidity. It gave forty percent greater radius of action for the same weight of coal. It enabled a fleet to re-fuel at sea with great facility. An oil-burning fleet can if need be and in calm weather, keep its station at sea, nourishing itself from tankers without having to send a quarter of its strength continually into harbour to coal, wasting fuel on the homeward and outward journey. The ordeal of coaling ship exhausted the whole ship's company. In wartime it robbed them of their brief period of rest; it subjected everyone to extreme discomfort. With oil, a few pipes were connected with the shore or with a tanker and the ship sucked in its fuel with hardly a man having to lift a finger. Less than half the number of stokers was needed to tend and clean the oil furnaces. Oil could be stowed in spare places in a ship from which it would be impossible to bring coal. As a coal ship used up her coal, increasingly large numbers of men had to be taken, if necessary from the guns, to shovel the coal from remote and inconvenient bunkers to bunkers nearer to the furnaces or to the furnaces themselves, thus weakening the fighting efficiency of the ship perhaps at the most critical moment in the battle. For instance, nearly a hundred men were continually occupied in the *Lion* shovelling coal from one steel chamber to another without ever seeing the light either of day or of the furnace fires. The use of oil made it possible in every type of vessel to have more gun-power and more speed for less size or less cost. It alone made it possible to realize the high speeds in certain types which were vital to their tactical purpose. All these advantages were obtained simply by burning oil instead of coal under the boilers. Should it at any time become possible to abolish boilers altogether and explode the oil in the cylinders of internal combustion engines, every advantage would be multiplied tenfold.

On my arrival at the Admiralty we had already built or were building 56 destroyers solely dependent on oil and 74 submarines which could only be driven by oil; and a proportion of oil was used to spray the coal furnaces of nearly all ships. We were not, however, dependent upon oil to such an extent as to make its supply a serious naval problem. To build any large additional number of oil-burning ships meant basing our naval supremacy upon oil. But oil was not found in appreciable quantities in our islands. If we required it, we must carry it by sea in peace or war from distant countries. We had, on the other hand, the finest supply of the best steam coal in the world, safe in our mines under our own hand.

To change the foundation of the Navy from British coal to foreign oil was a formidable decision in itself. If it were taken it must raise a whole series of intricate problems all requiring heavy initial expense. First there must be accumulated in Great Britain an enormous oil reserve large enough to enable us to fight for many months if necessary, without bringing in a single cargo of oil. To contain this reserve enormous installations of tanks must be erected near the various naval ports. Would they not be very vulnerable? Could they be protected? Could they be concealed or disguised? The word *"Camouflage"* was not then known. Fleets of tankers had to be built to convey the oil from the distant oilfields across the oceans to the British Isles, and others of a different pattern to take it from our naval harbours to the fleets at sea.

Owing to the systems of finance by which we had bound ourselves, we were not allowed to borrow even for capital or "once for all" expenditure. Every penny must be won from Parliament year by year, and constituted a definite addition to the inevitably rising and already fiercely challenged Naval Estimates. And beyond these difficulties loomed up the more intangible problems of markets and monopolies. The oil supplies of the world were in the hands of vast oil trusts under foreign control. To commit the Navy irrevocably to oil was indeed "to take arms against a sea of troubles." Wave after wave, dark with storm, created with foam, surged towards the harbour in which we still sheltered. Should we drive out into the teeth of the gale, or should we bide contented where we were? Yet beyond the breakers was a great hope. If we overcame the difficulties and surmounted the risks, we should be able to raise the whole power and efficiency of the Navy to a definitely higher level; better ships, better crews, higher economies, more intense forms of war-power—in a word, mastery itself was the prize of the venture. A year gained over a rival might make the difference. Forward, then!

The three programmes of 1912, 1913 and 1914 comprised the greatest additions in power and cost ever made to the Royal Navy. With the lamentable exception of the battleships of 1913—and these were afterwards corrected—they did not contain a coal-burning ship. Submarines, destroyers, light cruisers, fast battleships —all were based irrevocably on oil. The fateful plunge was taken when it was decided to create the Fast Division. Then, for the first time, the supreme ships of the Navy, on which our life depended, were fed by oil and could only be fed by oil. The decision to drive the smaller craft by oil followed naturally upon this. The camel once swallowed, the gnats went down easily enough.

A decision like this involved our national safety as much as a battle at sea. It was as anxious and as harassing as any hazard in war. It *was* war in a certain sense raging under a surface of unbroken peace. . . .

An unbroken series of consequences conducted us to the Anglo-Persian Oil Convention. The first step was to set up a Royal Commission on Oil Supply. . . .

Simultaneously with the setting up of this Commission we pursued our own Admiralty search for oil. . . . I sent Admiral Slade with an expert Committee to the Persian Gulf to examine the oil fields on the spot. These gentlemen were also the Admiralty representatives on the Royal Commission. To them the principal credit for the achievement is due. At the later financial stage the Governor of the Bank of England, afterwards Lord Cunliffe, and the directors of the Anglo-Persian and Royal Burmah Oil Companies were most serviceable. All through 1912 and 1913 our efforts were unceasing.

Thus each link forged the next. From the original desire to enlarge the gun we were led on step by step to the Fast Division, and in order to get the Fast Division we were forced to rely for vital units of the Fleet upon oil fuel. This led to the general adoption of oil fuel and to all the provisions which were needed to build up a great oil reserve. This led to enormous expense and to tremendous opposition on the Naval Estimates. Yet it was absolutely impossible to turn back. We could only fight our way forward, and finally we found our way to the Anglo-Persian Oil agreement and contract, which for an initial investment of two millions of public money (subsequently increased to five millions) has not only secured to the Navy a very substantial proportion of its oil supply, but has led to the acquisition by the Government of a controlling share in oil properties and interests which are at present valued at scores of millions sterling, and also to very considerable economies, which are still continuing, in the purchase price of Admiralty oil. . . .

COAL IN AMERICA

IN early times America was almost entirely an agricultural country with abundant wood for fuel. Wood, in fact, remained America's principal fuel until 1840 and then vied with coal and natural gas for another fifty years.

The first coal in the New World was reported at Cape Breton Island, off Canada's east coast in the sixteenth century. In 1673 Joliet's expedition to the Mississippi noted coal deposits along the Illinois River. Coal was discovered on the James River above Richmond, Virginia, around 1701, although actual mining did not begin there for another fifty years. A smattering of coal was traded in the early eighteenth century—from Nova Scotia to Boston and other New England communities as well as from England itself to the northeast American colonies. However, this tiny trade did not amount to more than 9,000 tons a year before the Revolution.

The American Revolution caused a brisk growth in the coal trade, for coal was in great demand at Pennsylvania forges for use in the manufacture of arms and ammunition (remember Lewis Mumford's linkage of the mine to military endeavor). However, the large-scale use of coal in the United States, as in Britain, traces its origins to the growth of cities and commerce. The coal industry spurted ahead in the 1820s as canals began to establish a path between resources and markets. Although a commerce in coal was not anticipated when it was built, the Schuylkill Canal linked the coal fields of eastern Pennsylvania to Philadelphia. The construction of steamships in the mid-nineteenth century increased the demand for coal, as did the development of steam-powered factories. The salt industry was a great user of coal. Yet wood remained an important fuel, and the slow development of the American coal industry compared with Britain's can be gauged from the fact that all mining was done by hand until the end of the nineteenth century. (Some mines in Virginia were actually manned by slaves until the Civil War.)

As in Britain, the Industrial Revolution changed this picture by increasing the demand for large, steady supplies of fuel. Nonetheless, up through the First World War the bituminous or soft coal industry consisted of myriad small firms, engaged in bitter boom-and-bust competition.

The enormous demand for coal during the First World War rescued the industry but also became the first of a series of factors which forced its restructuring. The continued buoyancy of coal prices as a result of increased demand from postwar Europe led the coal industry's major American customers—railroads, steel companies, and utilities—to reduce costs by reducing consumption through fuel efficiencies. This initial cutback in the domestic coal market was compounded by the challenge of new energy sources—cheap oil and natural gas. For it was just at this moment, in the 1920s, that the international oil companies organized themselves into a cartel to harness the oil surplus beginning to pour out of the Middle East (see p. 29). The resulting growing surplus of oil on world fuel markets threatened the stability of the whole coal industry.

It was in this international context that mine operators, eager to lower their own costs and increase their efficiency, began seriously to consider the mechanization of the industry and a major slash in their work force, then numbering 400,000.

As will be seen in the entries that follow, the struggle over mechanization and employment was to consume both labor and management for a quarter century. There were two major actors in this struggle: John L. Lewis, president of the United Mine Workers (UMW), and George Love, president of the Consolidation Coal Company, the nation's largest coal operator. The pact eventually hammered out by these two men not only established a long period of labor-management peace but, beyond that, created the conditions on which the modern coal industry was founded.

John L. Lewis remains an immense but clouded figure in the history of labor. After a brief stint in the mines he made a business of union organizing. First as president of the United Mine Workers' local at Panama, Illinois, then as special agent for the American Federation of Labor under Samuel Gompers, Lewis worked his way quickly up the union ladder. He became statistician for the international UMW, then a vice-president, and finally, in 1918, acting president. In 1920 he was elected president, a post he filled until 1960.

A Princeton-educated, Pennsylvania blueblood, George Love made his mark by taking lackluster coal properties from the Rockefellers, Hannas, and Mellons and stitching them together into successful enterprises. In an industry where small companies tore each other to pieces in head-to-head competition, Love carefully consolidated holdings and successfully practiced concentration, making himself the John D. Rockefeller of the coal business.

The future of the coal industry in America came to depend on the views of these two men—what they saw ahead and, just as important, what they did not see.

The period over which John L. Lewis presided was one of immense change. When Lewis took up his first official role in the UMW, coal was still dug with picks and strip mining was a peripheral aspect of the business. By the end of the Second World War the coal mine had been turned into a veritable underground assembly line, with machines gouging the coal from the face and loading it onto trucks for the trip to the surface.

Just as mechanization transformed the mine, so the markets for coal were being subjected to fierce competition from oil and natural gas. In 1920 nearly 80 percent of primary energy consumption was provided by coal. By the 1970s, with consumption more than three times what it had been in the twenties, coal's share of the market had shrunk to 18 percent, with oil and natural gas now accounting for close to 80 percent.

Under the impulse of these twin forces, the coal mine work force dramatically declined from 400,000 at the peak of the union's power following the Second World War to 100,000 today.

MACHINES AND JOBS

For Lewis, as for the coal operators, the persistent question was how to control the ruinous cycle of boom and bust that constantly gripped the hundreds of little companies that made up the coal industry. Throughout his long tenure as head of the United Mine Workers union Lewis was consistent in his answer: fair wages and mechanization. He believed the union's push for higher wages would have a beneficial effect on the coal operators by forcing them to reduce costs through the introduction of the machine. Increased productivity would result. Indeed, Lewis viewed coal industry attacks on the union as efforts by inefficient, uneconomic coal operators to stay in business. Much later, as will become clear from subsequent entries, Lewis actually made the union join with mine owners in an effort to hasten mechanization and drive the uneconomic mines out of business. In the following selection, Lewis advances an essentially technocratic argument rooted in his belief in the capitalist system and in the inherent beneficence of the machine.

It is important to remember that Lewis was not a socialist. He did not believe in government ownership of the mines. His abiding faith was in the marketplace, and it affected both the way he negotiated for the miners and the solutions he espoused for the improvement of the coal industry. In this light, it is important to note not just the matters Lewis discussed, but the larger context he often ignored.

At the very moment he was proposing his technical solution to the coal industry's problems—mechanization—the world's major oil companies were meeting in Europe to cartelize the giant surplus of oil beginning to pour out of the Middle East. Mechanization proved far too limited a context in which to challenge successfully the rapid expansion of oil and gas into markets hitherto reserved for coal, and as the uses of these two fuels were extended into industry and the home, the economic viability and even independence of both the coal miners' union and the coal industry were eroded.

For all his knowledge of the industry and his fervent belief in long-range cycles of historical behavior, Lewis never seemed able to look beyond the coal mine to grasp the larger picture. Although he greatly admired the methods of American big business, he seemed incapable of learning its lessons in the energy industry.

We must remember, after all, that the 1920s were formative years in the modern energy industry we now take for granted. Not only were the leaders of the world's great oil companies meeting to carve up the Middle East's supplies, but during the same decade representatives of the Standard Oil Company met with German industrialists to organize a cartel so as to avoid cutthroat competition between oil and coal in the new field of synthetic fuels (see p. 233). Since that time the integration of the coal industry into the rest of the energy industry has proceeded apace.

As the industry gradually coalesced in the direction of integration and concentration, Lewis did not rise to meet the challenge. Although he had been an imaginative founder and driving force in the Congress of Industrial Organizations (CIO) which organized workers in mass production industries, as head of the UMW he never sought to form a union of all the workers in different sectors of the energy industry. Either it simply never occurred to him, or he saw no advantage in taking that route.

Taken from The Miners' Fight for American Standards, *by John L. Lewis, Indianapolis, Bell, 1925.*

Engineering and economic authorities, and all of the official commissions which have passed judgment upon the coal industry, agree that it is in that critical stage, sooner or later reached by most of the major divisions of productive enterprise, the transition from human to mechanical power, the transformation of the laborer from a prime mover to a machinery control.

It is not surprising that the reactionary element of the industry has charged the United Mine Workers of America with opposing the introduction of machinery and scientific methods.

This was the conventional thing to do. Because of certain perfectly natural reactions on the part of displaced hand labor at the outset of the industrial revolution in England, one hundred and fifty years ago, it has become a fixed article of faith with the superficial that it is always labor which opposes the further mechanization of the industry.

This idea was born in the age of ox carts and that is where it belongs. The files of the patent office alone will disclose that from the ranks of ambitious and dissatisfied labor, have come many of the inventions which have transformed our life.

The economic history of the United States in the last half century is replete with instances in which great inventions have been resisted by reactionary management or suppressed by shortsighted finance, unwilling to scrap obsolete equipment. It is unnecessary here to recount instances in which the strong arm of government, called into play by organized labor, has been needed to force upon backward management in interstate commerce many labor and life-saving inventions. . . .

The policy of the United Mine Workers of America will inevitably bring about the utmost employment of machinery of which coal mining is physically capable. The policy of those who seek a disruption of the existing wage structure would only postpone mechanization of the industry and perpetuate obsolete methods.

Fair wages and American standards of living are inextricably bound up with the progressive substitution of mechanical for human power. It is no accident that fair wages and machinery will walk hand in hand.

All will agree that fair wages are only possible, because of the increased productivity per worker, secured largely by advanced methods and means of production. It is equally true that such wage rates are the principal incentive for the invention and installation of new devices.

Leaders of the electrical industry have pointed out in an interesting manner why there are so few inducements in cheap labor countries, like China, to install the immensely expensive equipment necessary for the generation and distribution of electric power. When the labor of men can be bought for a few cents a day there is little reason to invest $10,000 in devices that will enable one man to do the work of five. But when men cost from $5.00 to $10.00 per day, the capital outlay is more easily justified.

We have industries in this country, which use over $10,000 worth of machinery per worker. Such equipment is a sound investment here. In America, where machinery costs the most, it is scrapped most frequently. Fair wages are not only a result of the high productivity of machinery but relatively high wage costs are an ever-present incentive to the introduction of more and better machinery. Obviously in a Chinese province where the labor of a vigorous man for 12 hours costs less than twice the daily ration of oats consumed by an Iowa farm horse, there are few such incentives. In so far as organized labor is responsible for maintenance of fair wage standards it may justly claim a share of the credit for the mechanization of American industry. The paradox of our industrial history is that the relative scarcity of labor in this country made production so difficult and costly, that it had to be done more easily and cheaply than anywhere else, by machinery.

There have been times when rice produced on high priced American land by American farmers, employing machinery and machine pumping in irrigation, has been laid down in Oriental ports at lower prices than the native grain produced by men doing work assigned in this country to beasts, tractors, gasoline pumps, and locomotives. Cheap men do not produce the cheapest rice, and in the long run cheap men will not mine cheap coal.

Those who seek to cheapen coal by cheapening men simply seek to reverse the evolution of American industry. It cannot be done. We must take the American route to the betterment of mining. But before the technique of the coal industry can be brought to a state commensurate with what the nation has a right to expect, there must be a great change in the financial structure of the coal business.

The installation of modern machinery in coal mines is a vastly more complicated and expensive matter than alterations of the technique and equipment of manufacturing and transportation.

Mining is fundamentally distinct from manufacture in that it must be carried on where the minerals lie, and must conform to the varying physical characteristics of the coal deposits and their surroundings. This condition affects every mining problem and none more than installation of improved equipment.

One reason why mining machinery will always be relatively expensive is that it must be adapted to all sorts of mines, "roof conditions," thickness of seams, hardness of coals and many other varying phases of mining which pertain to the industry. Therefore, it can never be standardized to the same extent as textile machinery or even railway equipment.

It is obvious that only solvent corporations, sufficiently financed, can undertake the improvements that the times demand. It is equally plain that only properties enjoying the physical conditions which permit the profitable employment of machinery can be successfully operated.

The United States Coal Commission summed up the present situation relative to machinery, as follows:

"In most industries remarkable progress has been made during the last century in the development of machinery to replace slow and arduous hand labor and reduce production costs.

"The bituminous coal mining industry is just entering the last stage of reducing manual labor through the introduction of machinery.

"The first stage was the use of undercutting machines . . . The importance of the problem, both to the workman in lessening his toil and to the consumer in reducing the cost of coal, is evident when we consider that some seventy per cent of the cost of the coal at the mine is labor, and more than one-half of this labor is for cutting and loading coal into the mine cars.

"From this transition there will, of course, result a decrease in the quantity of human labor at any given point or for a given production. This is inevitable and desirable. However, unlike the introduction of automatic machines, such as spinning frames, the transition will naturally be slow because of the necessity of adapting machinery to the physical conditions of different mines . . . This change will gradually come to the industry, as will also the development of coal storage, resulting in more regular and lower cost of production.

"Development of enough low cost operations to supply the demand will automatically eliminate the high cost mines . . . which under existing conditions in periods of car shortage absorb so large a portion of the transportation service as to lower the working time of the better mines, thus unduly increasing their costs also."

The observation that labor costs constitute seventy per cent of the cost of coal recalls the fact that even in highly developed machine industries, labor is about the same per cent of costs. The studies of the National Bureau of Economic Research indicate that for manufacturing, mining and transportation as a whole, labor absorbs about seventy per cent of the income.

The Commission's observation as to the effect of the operation of high cost mines on transportation service is not germane to the issue at this time because of the passing of the evil day of car shortages. But that the development of low cost operations will automatically eliminate the uneconomic mine is certainly true, and anything which retards the development of low cost operations and forces them to divide the market with less well equipped mines will inevitably delay the mechanization of the industry.

Stripped to its essentials, the present crusade against the Union and the existing wage rates is nothing but an effort to prolong the life of uneconomic mines. And the cry for lower wages is in the ultimate a cry for higher production costs.

The stronger companies possessing properties physically adapted to modernization can only hope to attain the necessary financial strength, when they are enabled to command a market not demoralized by distress coal, and the cut-throat competition of coal companies, which can only operate under obsolete and un-American cheap labor conditions. . . .

The miners face the future of mine mechanization in the same spirit of willingness to co-operate in the introduction of loading machinery and every other mechanical aid that has characterized their past policy. The figures showing the progressive increase in production per man per day in American mines are the irrefutable testimony as to what that past policy has been. In the face of the most discouraging conditions, the cold figures of the Geological Survey show that American miners have been producing more coal year by year, when aided by machinery, and even when denied such aids.

But the mine worker insists, and will continue to insist, that the introduction of loading machinery and other devices which will revolutionize the industry on its mechanical side, make no difference in the fundamental human side of the industry as now expressed in wage scales, working conditions and Union relationship, and therefore the mechanical changes to be inaugurated cannot be taken advantage of by management to impair those standards.

In the period of development, and experimentation, when the new devices are receiving their tryout, the mine worker should not be called upon to finance indirectly by any sacrifice of his pay or working conditions, this now departure which will ultimately redound to the benefit of ownership.

Payment for such innovation and experiment, by all the economic canons, is the capitalist's role. The profits of capital are partly the rewards of the risks in such experiment. Labor cannot be called upon to finance it by money deducted from its pay envelope for which there would be no return by way of interest or dividend, if success is achieved.

For that reason mine labor demands and will enforce the right to such consultation in the period of mechanization, as will prevent the sacrifice of its standards in the process.

"YOUR NIGGARDLY AND ANTI-SOCIAL PROPENSITIES"

With the work force of coal miners growing older, Lewis attempted to turn the union's negotiations with the operators in 1946 away from a discussion of wages toward the establishment of a miners' health and welfare fund. But the operators would have none of it. They were not there, as one of their leaders said, in the capacity of "sanitary experts." In early April the miners struck. Still the operators would not budge. On April 10 Lewis scribbled the few thoughts that follow on a piece of paper, rose before the assemblage of negotiators, and read them out. The talks were terminated at once. President Harry Truman eventually ordered the mines seized, and the government and union wrote the first welfare and retirement fund agreement. It was subsequently taken over by the industry and became the bedrock of the union's political and financial power.

Here is the Lewis that coal miners like to remember.

Statement of John L. Lewis to the National Bituminous Joint Conference, Shoreham Hotel, Washington, D.C., April 10, 1946, 11:00 A.M.

For four weeks we have sat with you; we attended when you fixed the hour; we departed when weariness affected your pleasure.

Our effort to resolve mutual questions has been vain; you have been intolerant of suggestions and impatient of analysis.

When we sought surcease from blood-letting, you professed indifference. When we cried aloud for the safety of our numbers you answer—Be content—'twas always thus!

When we urged that you abate a stench you averred that your nostrils were not offended.

When we emphasized the importance of life, you pleaded the priority of profits; when we spoke of little children in unkempt surroundings you said —Look to the State!

You aver that you own the mines; we suggest that, as yet, you do not own the people.

You profess annoyance at our temerity; we condemn your imbecility.

You are smug in your complacency; we are abashed by your shamelessness; you prate your respectability; we are shocked at your lack of public morality.

You scorn the toils, the abstinence and the perils of the miner; we withhold approval of your luxurious mode of life and the nights you spend in merriment.

You invert the natural order of things and charge to the public the pleasure of your own indolence; we denounce the senseless cupidity that withholds from the miner the rewards of honorable and perilous exertion.

To cavil further is futile. We trust that time, as it shrinks your purse, may modify your niggardly and anti-social propensities.

GEORGE LOVE

Had John L. Lewis been a modern titan of energy he could not have put the arguments for efficiency and productivity more persuasively. Indeed, his most successful labor agreements were made with businessmen who saw things the same way. George Love, the president of the Consolidation Coal Company, was perhaps the most important of these.

By 1950 Love had made his mark on the coal industry by doing exactly what Lewis had counseled in the 1920s—hammering together small, inefficient mining companies into one profitable venture. Love was imaginative and, like Lewis, a great believer in progress through the machine. But unlike Lewis, Love looked far beyond the mine. He clearly saw the threat of oil and, with plans for making synthetic oil from coal, moved to do battle. He was an early advocate of the slurry pipeline,* which would have dramatically resuscitated the coal industry, reducing costs. Most important, it was Love who set the trends in the coal industry, bringing about reforms that resulted in concentrated business organizations that still sold coal. These companies were, in turn, bought by oil companies, beginning in the mid-1960s. It is safe to say that without Love, and the labor truce he arranged with Lewis in the coal fields, the modern energy industry would not exist today.

Taken from "Coal Man at Chrysler," by Robert Sheehan, Fortune, *September 1962.*

. . . [W]hat George Love did in the coal business was not only to restore a series of sick companies to sound health and profitability, but by the force of his example, lead a whole ailing and archaic industry into the light of modern ways. This is not hyperbole. In the early 1940's, when George Love (with George Humphrey at his

*To transport coal by pipeline requires that the coal be first crushed and then mixed with water to create slurry.

shoulder) set out to acquire control of and to merge Consolidation Coal Co. and Pittsburgh Coal Co., those two venerable companies between them had, over the years 1925–40, lost the fantastic sum of $100 million. In Love's first year, 1946, as head of the merged company he turned in a net profit of $5,600,000. He has never had a losing year, and in the past five years Consol's net has averaged $20 million. But the important thing about this performance is the imagination that went into it, and the odds against which it was accomplished, for coal is an industry in a chronic condition of oversupply, and its traditional markets are prey to the increasing incursion of cheap residual oil and natural gas.

Love waged his battle on all fronts. He was the first operator to spend major money on coal research and development, and one of the first to mechanize his mines completely, and to concentrate on the cleansing, preparation, and beneficiation of coal in order to fit the product more precisely to the individual needs of customers. In the field of industrial relations, he first mopped up the bad working conditions in his own mines, then took up the cudgels for the industry in its perennial struggle with John L. Lewis, with whom he eventually established remarkable accord, and laid the basis for a dozen years of uninterrupted labor peace. Later, Love and Lewis joined hands in the formation of the National Coal Policy Conference, which gives voice to the industry's interests on government regulation of oil import quotas and the like. Perhaps the most dramatic Love accomplishment has been Consol's development, after years of research, of a successful method for pipelining coal. . . .

. . . In the Hanna tradition, Love believes in thorough delegation of authority: you pick your operating man carefully; let him run his own show; and if he doesn't deliver, replace him. Though a well-educated man, Love is a far cry from such executive types as Robert McNamara, for example, who goes in for those exhaustive statistical surveys of problems. Love is not much of a hand for either writing or reading memos; he likes to judge people, and their problems, face to face. Finally, he has sheer physical energy that many a much younger man could envy, and the mental mobility to shift quickly and effectively from problem to problem, and from coal to cars.

Most photographs of Love, with the lens bearing down on his bald head and square-cut features, are apt to suggest strength (correct) or even stolidity (incorrect). The camera does not convey his informality and lightness of touch. He has a tendency, even when he is most absorbed and most alert, to let his 6-foot-2½-inch, 190-pound frame slide well down in his chair, hands clasped behind his neck. An executive who has served on boards with Love says, "To me, he's one of the most intriguing men in business today. He seems to have a capacity for doing so many things so well, and to do them in such an apparently painless fashion. He reminds me of those golf pros you see on TV who make the hard shots look so easy." . . .

George Hutchinson Love was born to a well-circumstanced family in Johnstown, Pennsylvania, on September 4, 1900. George's grandfather had been in the coal business, as were two of his sons, but George's father elected to go into the wholesale food business with a partner whose square monicker, incredibly, was Sunshine; fortune smiled, naturally, on the firm of Love & Sunshine. George prepped at Phillips Exeter Academy in New Hampshire, then enrolled in the class of 1922 at Princeton, where he majored in English and economics. His roommate for the four years was Don Lourie, All-American quarterback, who is now president of Quaker Oats Co. Love was manager of the football team in his senior year. He then went on for a two-year course at Harvard Graduate School of Business Administration, which had a rather small and select student body in those days. After Harvard, Love joined the investment firm of Lee Higginson Corp., specializing in the bond business. Following a training period, he served as a salesman and counselor in the firm's Chicago office, and later the St. Louis office.

In 1926, George's uncle, Frank Love, asked him to come back to Pennsylvania and help out with the management of the less-than-flourishing Love family coal properties. The company, called Union Collieries, owned three bituminous mines northeast of Pittsburgh that produced around two million tons of coal a year. George came in as assistant to the president, and became president upon Uncle Frank's death in 1933. In those days coal was the most primitive of industries, a relic, in most every respect, of the nineteenth century. There were some 5,000 different companies in the business, most of them marginal producers making spot sales to spot markets at cut prices. In many of the mines, the workers were still hacking away at the walls with picks, and as late as 1924 the census reported 36,000 mules and horses still in service for underground haulage in U.S. coal mines (not to mention the canaries for the detection of gas).

It was out of such depths that George Love, over the years 1933–40, led Union Collieries into the light. By borrowing heavily to build a first-rate cleaning plant he was able to reduce the high sulfur and ash content of his coal and sell it to the coking markets at 40 cents a ton more than it had been bringing as steam coal. And by mechanizing his mines 100 per cent with the latest cutting and loading equipment, he raised output per man from five to eight tons per day, and sheared his costs by as much as 25 cents a ton.

The Love-Humphrey relationship began in late 1929, when Love was twenty-nine, Humphrey thirty-nine. One of Union Collieries' properties, the Renton mine, bordered smack on a mine owned by M. A. Hanna Co. Neither mine was doing well by itself, and the Loves thought that some kind of joint operation might be a solution. Frank Love and his nephew went to Cleveland to see Mr. Hanna (Howard Hanna, nephew of founder Mark Hanna) about it, and were referred to George Humphrey, who had just become president of the company. The upshot was that Hanna turned over its mine to the Loves for an equity interest in Union Collieries, and Humphrey became a member of Union Collieries' board. He and young George Love hit it off at once—they do indeed seem to be cut of the same cloth—and thereafter went on to make coal history together.

Around 1942, the late Gordon Rentschler, of the National City Bank, came to George Humphrey with an offer to sell to Hanna a large block of Consolidation Coal Co. stock that was kicking around in the bank's trust department. Consolidation had been controlled by the Rockefellers, who had sold off their holdings at a heavy loss shortly before the company went through a 77-B bankruptcy in 1935. Consolidation, everybody said, was a "dog," but it had extensive holdings in the indubitably rich Fairmont coalfields in northern West Virginia, and Humphrey said that if George Love would consent to come in and run the company Hanna would buy it. The purchase was effected in 1943, and George Love took over as executive vice president. In a year's time, Consolidation was doing so well that George Love decided to merge his Union Collieries into it, thus completely intertwining the Love family fortunes with those of Hanna. (George Love today owns 113,900 shares of Consol, worth at present prices around $4 million, and a more substantial interest in M. A. Hanna.)

Meanwhile the Mellons, who had been as luckless in coal as the Rockefellers, came around with a proposition to merge their Pittsburgh Coal Co. with Consolidation. The Mellons were glad to sell a major interest in Pittsburgh to Hanna in order to get their coal holdings under Love's management. When the merger papers were signed in November, 1945, George Love became president of the largest coal company in the U.S. Thereafter Consol added many other coal companies, large and small, to its complex. In 1946, most of Hanna's other coal properties, including its extensive strip mines in Ohio, were put into Consol. Pocahontas Fuel Co. of Virginia, which produces high-grade metallurgical coal, was a major purchase in 1956, and just this year Consol took over Truax-Traer Coal Co. of Chicago.

There is an old Pittsburgh adage to the effect that any thing can be made out of coal except money. "But we had a dream," says Love. "The trouble with the coal industry was that it was fragmentary in its organization, and wasteful in its technology. We reasoned first that if we could get our hands on enough properties, we could close down or sell off the bad mines, exploit only the good ones. A company with the best thirty to forty million tons could capture the top 3 to 5 per cent of the market, and could make money on that market, which is exactly what Consol did." And second, Love and Humphrey reasoned that by putting profits into research and development Consol could hope to find new uses and markets for coal, through new coal-process technology, and perhaps a cheaper way of shipping it.

In 1947, Love contracted with Standard Oil Development, New Jersey, for joint research on the gasification of coal, and for some years thereafter the business world was agog at the revolutionary prospect of coal being burned close to the minehead, producing a gas that could be piped directly as a cheap domestic and industrial fuel, or converted into gasoline and chemicals. A $300,000 pilot plant was built, a successful public demonstration of the process staged, and plans were announced for the construction of a $125-million refinery to be in operation by 1951. But Consol never quite managed to get the economics of the process in line with competitive fuel prices, and when the vast new oil fields in the Middle East began opening up in 1950, Love grimly ordered the gasification project shelved. Consol keeps on top of the technology, however, and Love thinks he'll live to see the day when a Consol plant is turning Consol coal into gas for the pipelines in the winter, and into liquid gasoline in the summer. . . . [See pp. 234ff. for a present-day version of Love's scheme.]

THE LABOR PACT OF 1950

The problems of competition and inefficiency in the coal industry were largely resolved by Lewis and Love in the National Bituminous Wage

Agreement of 1950, which they wrote. This pact established a lengthy period of labor peace in the coal fields and set into motion forces which led to dramatic change in the entire energy industry. Small, marginal mines gave way to larger ones or went out of business, and as Thomas Bethell argues in the following selection, the United Mine Workers itself became a working partner in the new coal industry.

Taken from "Conspiracy in Coal," by Thomas N. Bethell, Washington Monthly, *March 1969.*

. . . For a period of 60 years after the United Mine Workers of America came into being in 1890, and particularly after John L. Lewis became president of the union in 1920, the coal business was a saga of hostility between labor and management, with almost a dozen years of uninterrupted warfare in the period immediately before 1950. But with the signing of the National Bituminous Coal Wage Agreement of 1950, all that changed—abruptly, permanently, and somewhat mysteriously. Reminiscing later about the 1950 contract negotiations, George Love—then president of Consol and later chairman of its board of directors—would observe happily that "we haven't had any major strikes or labor trouble in coal" since then. And John L. Lewis would say that "George Love is an industrial statesman. Our nation would fare well had we more of his breed."

Harry Moses, who was head of U.S. Steel's mining division during the stormiest years of union-management warfare, would say of the UMW after 1950 that "they have joined us without reservation in all our efforts to combat the influences of competitive fuels, government interference, and unreasonable safety regulations."

By 1959, moreover, Lewis and Love were getting together to form the National Coal Policy Conference, an unprecedented lobbying operation in which coal operators and union leaders, like lions and lambs lying down together, joined forces to assault the halls of Congress. A year later, when Lewis retired, labor writer Paul Jacobs noted that "he was heaped with lavish praise by the mine owners."

But this was the very same John L. Lewis who had vilified management for 30 years in some of the most splendidly rococo oratory ever heard in America; who had condemned two Democratic Presidents without mercy; who had once ironically compared George Love to Samson by saying that Love was "so successful in putting his shoulders to the columns and supports of the temple [of industry] that he pulled it down about his ears." This was the same Lewis who, just a few months before an apparently permanent peace came to the industry, described the corporations which Love represented as "a tremendous group of immense power who have apparently decided to make this struggle . . . final and significant in American economic history." The turnabout after 1950, seen with the benefit of hindsight, was startling and complete. . . .

. . . Nowhere were the labor battles bloodier than in eastern Kentucky during the Depression. In Harlan County, where U.S. Steel, International Harvester, and other industrial giants had staked out enormous claims, the coal operators' association budgeted most of its funds for warfare. "Which side are you on?" the union organizers demanded. You could choose either side and run about an equal risk of getting killed. "You'll either be a union man or a thug for J. H. Blair," the miners sang, thereby immortalizing the county sheriff who, like his deputies and friends, was also a coal operator. Pitched gun battles were fought regularly in the streets of company towns. One was even fought in a company bathhouse, where thugs ambushed naked miners in the showers and shot them down in cold blood and hot water.

Coal operators gave ground to the union with the utmost reluctance. The years during and immediately after World War II were unbelievably chaotic. Three times during the war national strikes resulted in government seizure of the mines. The end of hostilities with the Germans and the Japanese did not end hostilities between the miners and the coal operators. With the War Labor Disputes Act still in effect, President Truman seized the mines again in May, 1946, during a particularly paralyzing national strike, and the government controlled coal production for more than a year.

In March, 1947, while the mines were still under federal control, a mine explosion at Centralia, Illinois, killed 111 men in the worst disaster since Monongah. Lewis declared a week of mourning, and mines shut down all over the country. At almost the same time, Congress rammed through the Taft-Hartley Act[*] over Mr. Truman's veto while coal labor-contract negotiations were under way. Lewis, calling Taft-Hartley "the first ugly, savage thrust of fascism in America," sent 200,000 miners out on strike the day it became law. A week later he suddenly declared a national vacation period. During the summer of 1947 a new contract was finally signed; but in March, 1948, Lewis claimed that the operators were "dishonoring" it, and the miners struck again. The Justice Department used the new Taft-Hartley law to get a restraining order against the union; Lewis ignored it and found himself convicted of contempt. Not until the Supreme Court upheld the conviction several weeks later did the miners go back to work.

In June, 1949, they were out on strike again. Lewis said it wasn't really a strike this time; he called it "a stabilizing period of inaction" that was prompted by overproduction. It lasted a week. When it ended, Lewis ordered a three-day work week. The miners struck again in September, went back to work in November, struck once more in December, experimented briefly again with a three-day week, then struck—and stayed struck as 1949 ended.

Someone suggested to President Truman that the problem could be resolved by making Lewis ambassador to Moscow, but Mr. Truman saw little humor in the idea; Lewis, he said, wouldn't even make a good dog-catcher. The President was no oratorical match for Lewis, who described Truman as "totally unfitted for the position. His principles are elastic, and he is careless with the truth. He has no special knowledge of any subject, and he is a malignant, scheming individual who is dangerous not only to the United Mine Workers but also to the United States."

[*The Taft-Hartley law was used most vigorously against the coal miners in the late 1940s. Under the law, the President orders a three-member commission, which he names, to determine whether or not there is a national emergency. If so, he can invoke the law and order the strikers back to work. It should be noted that the President appoints the members of the commission, and there is no required fact finding involved.]

As for the coal operators, they were, said Lewis, simply "human leeches" making fat profits from men who worked and died in unsafe mines.

The cheerless three-way impasse between union, operators, and government—all of it precipitated by the refusal of anyone to negotiate seriously with anyone else for a generally acceptable contract—might have gone on indefinitely if Truman had not created an emergency board of inquiry which found, in mid-February, 1950, that the country was down to a two-week supply of coal. Several states promptly declared emergencies, and the railroads, which had already sliced service in half, threatened additional cutbacks. Public opinion aligned itself against the miners, and editorials belabored Lewis with remarkable fervor. On March 3, Truman went to Congress to ask for authorization to seize the mines. Congress was more than ready to accommodate him. Neither the operators nor the union wanted the industry saddled with a law that would have made Taft-Hartley look libertarian by comparison; if there was one thing they could agree on, it was their determination not to let the federal government dictate to the industry. Both union and management suddenly found it possible to sit down on a Sunday afternoon and negotiate a contract with each other. On Monday morning, March 6, 1950, the last great coal strike ever engineered by John L. Lewis came to an end.

The National Bituminous Coal Wage Agreement of 1950 was significant not only because it marked the end of large-scale labor warfare in the coal industry but also because it was the first industry-wide contract in the history of the coal business. [Was] there . . . more than a coincidental connection between these two facts[?]

Until 1950 the UMW had been in the habit of negotiating contracts separately with three different groups of coal operators: the Northern Coal Operators Association, which represented companies mining principally in Pennsylvania, northern West Virginia, Ohio, Illinois, and western Kentucky; the Southern Coal Producers Association, representing companies in southern West Virginia, Virginia, eastern Kentucky, Tennessee, and Alabama; and the so-called "captive" mines, which were owned outright by steel-producing companies and did not sell coal commercially (except at times when steel required less than their total production).

Contract negotiations were invariably long drawn-out affairs featuring heavily publicized theatrical performances by both sides. Originally the UMW spokesmen had enjoyed the public spectacle hugely; even if most of the newspapers in the country took sides with the operators, the publicity did wonders for organizing efforts among the rank and file and created a solidarity within the union that might never have been possible otherwise. Over the years, however, Lewis and his two principal UMW lieutenants, vice-president Thomas Kennedy and secretary-treasurer John Owens, found themselves arguing more and enjoying it less. Owens, who went to work in the mines when he was 10 years old and [was] still handling the union's finances at the age of 78, admits to having felt considerable awe when he faced the coal operators: "It was rather embarrassing sometimes to Lewis and Tom Kennedy and myself," he once said, "not being able to cope with the intelligence and leadership that the coal industry provided when they met us." Lewis would never have admitted that, but Owens wasn't Lewis; there was only one Lewis.

The Northern operators produced more coal than the other two groups, and their negotiations with the union were invariably the noisiest and the most heavily reported—partly because Lewis himself represented the union (Kennedy was generally assigned to bargain with the captive mines, Owens with the Southern operators) and partly because the Northern operators were represented for nearly 20 years by Charles O'Neill, a blusteringly intractable man almost as fond as Lewis of melodramatic speech-making. Whenever the two men met, the resulting furor resembled a supremacy battle between bull walruses in mating season. Negotiations between O'Neill and Lewis were generally attended by scores of reporters who reacted much like fight fans at Madison Square Garden, scribbling happily while Lewis elaborately castigated the coal operators for endless perfidies and O'Neill predicted economic disaster for the entire world if American coal companies were forced to pay their miners a penny more. O'Neill backed himself up with a portable squad of statisticians who attended the negotiations with him and supplied impressive data to support his claims. "Ringling Brothers," one reporter remembers fondly now, "had nothing on Charlie O'Neill."

But by 1950 Charlie O'Neill was dead and the Northern operators were represented by George Love of Consolidation Coal Company. Negotiating was something new for him, he claims now that he didn't enjoy it. After all, Love said, Lewis "was an old hand at negotiating and it was something new for me . . . that was sort of like matching an elephant and a mouse."

George Love's self-description is appealing, but wide of the mark. By 1950 George Love was the largest mouse in the coal business. . . .

Love remembers the negotiations as a "long, bitter struggle." The presence of so many reporters "forced both . . . the union and the operators to take a public position," and he was opposed to that. He was not accustomed to involving the public in his work. He was also profoundly opposed to government intervention in the coal industry, and when Mr. Truman finally went to Congress to ask for enabling legislation to seize the mines, Love caved in immediately and signed with Lewis. The Southern operators and the captive mines followed suit the same day.

The signing of the contract under such unfavorable circumstances left Love determined not to repeat the experience. The 1950 agreement went into effect in March; by July, after a number of private meetings with Harry Moses of U.S. Steel, Love succeeded, without any publicity at all, in engineering an alliance between the Northern operators and the captive mines. A new organization, the Bituminous Coal Operators Association, came into being for the purpose of representing both groups in future negotiations with the United Mine Workers. Love chaired the first meeting of the new BCOA and arranged the election of Moses as its president.

There was nothing innocuous about the BCOA. It's members outproduced the Southern operators more than two to one. They mined approximately half of all the coal in the United States. This gave them far more than domination of the industry, since much of the remaining production came from small mines, many of which belonged to no association and were too busy struggling for survival to participate in national contract negotiations.

Just as George Humphrey had stayed behind the scenes during George Love's campaign to make Consol the biggest company in the industry, so now did Love stay behind the scenes in the development of the BCOA. As usual, he is beguilingly modest about his role in the organization. . . . [Asked] whether he had what might be described as a special relationship with the BCOA, "None," Love said firmly. "Somebody from Consol was a director, along with 23 or 24 others, but we had no particular arrangement with anybody. We were one member out of a great number."

Humility is George Love's long suit. However, BCOA's bylaws clearly provided that voting was to be carried out in accordance with the tonnage produced by each member—one vote per million tons. Consol accounted for 15.5 million tons, but Love also served as representative of other companies with 37.5 million tons. The total tonnage of the BCOA's members was 110.5 million; at each BCOA meeting, therefore, Love controlled 52 votes out of 110. If by some exceedingly remote chance that had not been enough to give him control of the organization, he had only to join forces with his friend Harry Moses, who represented the 19.2 million tons produced by U.S. Steel and therefore had 19 votes. By no possible combination could the other members of the BCOA defeat Love's aggregate 71 votes with their 39; voting was by a simple majority, not by two-thirds. . . .

The public and the press were not aware in 1950 of the means by which a single company had come to hold a commanding position in one of the nation's largest industries. John L. Lewis must have been very much aware of it, and he may also have been impressed by the speed and sophistication with which George Love had engineered such a coup. At any rate Lewis wasted no time in dealing with the new Bituminous Coal Operators Association. Less than six months after the formation of the BCOA, Lewis approached Harry Moses about renegotiating the 1950 contract—although it still had nearly a year to run.

Moses was ready and willing to meet with Lewis. They conferred in complete secrecy—the first time since 1890 that labor negotiations in the coal industry had been closed to the press, public, and the union membership. Moses agreed wholeheartedly with George Love's views on doing things in private; the public negotiations of the past had resulted, he thought, in "too much government, too little private initiative." . . . The agreement, when they reached it, was immediately ratified by the BCOA and by the membership of the UMW. Lewis came out of the negotiations sounding like a new man. "The country," he said, "is now freed from any thought of a so-called coal crisis for an indefinite period of time."

. . . The threat of a paralyzing national strike had always been Lewis's principal weapon against the coal operators and he had always held it over them like a Damoclean sword. He removed that sword in 1950 by stating publicly that there would be no further crises in the coal industry. It was not the kind of thing anyone expected, and it was inconsistent with historical patterns.

The pattern in Lewis's case was particularly clear. Since 1920 he had been hammering away without variation on three principal themes; employment for the maximum possible number of men; pay at the highest possible levels; work in the best possible conditions. He was basically opposed to socialism, but he favored government regulation of the industry whenever it would advance his goals. The coal industry had a tendency to overproduce, resulting in unpredictable layoffs of large numbers of men and temporary closing of mines. Lewis wanted the government to help with the problem. At the union's 1936 convention, for example, he called on President Roosevelt to set up "a system of proper federal regulation which will encompass a synchronized system of price-fixing and allocation of tonnage on a basis equitably fair to mine workers and operators alike." Two years later he was demanding "a parity in competitive conditions which will as nearly as practicable allow each of the operators in the several [union] districts an opportunity to secure their fair share of the markets and, at the same time, provide as equitably as possible equal work opportunities for all the mine workers employed in various districts."

Ten years later, in 1948, he was battling the post-war overproduction that was creating new turmoil in the industry. "If the operators of this country can't give any leadership on the commercial side of this industry," he thundered, "the United Mine Workers can and will . . . if there are only three days' work in this industry, we will all have the three days' work." It was no idle threat; the three-day week that Lewis imposed in 1949 was his method of imposing a production control on the industry.

Production control, whether imposed by Lewis or by the government, was anathema to free-enterprise boosters like George Love. "We complained bitterly," he said, "about trying to operate our mines one day, three days, any number of days that we didn't decide." Love thrived in the chaos of the coal industry. In a well-regulated industry untroubled by overproduction, he might never have built the colossus of Consol. Nor could he have so shrewdly maneuvered half the industry into an association that he controlled. Conditions in the coal industry were allowing him to build an unprecedented economic empire with unprecedented speed; by his own admission, he was not about to let Lewis or anyone else take that away from him.

. . . By 1952 [Lewis] sounded like Love's alter ego. The smaller coal operators, he said, "are just a drag on the industry. The constant tendency in this country is going to be for the concentration of production into fewer and fewer units . . . more of the obsolete units will fall by the board and go out of production." He was, in essence, giving his powerful blessing to the building of the economic empire that George Love had been working on since 1926.

There may have been other reasons for Lewis's whole-hearted conversion to the basic tenets of big business. He may well have been influenced by the pathological fear of communism sweeping through the country during the McCarthy years. He had been something of a red-baiter himself as early as the 1920's, when he went after the Wobblies, and unquestionably the communist threat later became an obsession with him. In 1966, when asked whether his policies after 1950 had tended to create monopolies and restrain trade, Lewis countered: "The Communist threat that looms on the horizon and occupies the daily attention of every citizen of this land—what about it?" The free enterprise system was at stake, he said. When he was asked whether he considered competition the backbone of that system, his answer made clear how much the man had changed since the militant days of the 1930's and '40's. "You may have that viewpoint," Lewis said. "At the moment, I am a little cloudy how to fit it into the complex economy and the interdependence of our economic units upon each other." He would not discuss the subject further.

Lewis's attitudes after 1950 must also have been influenced by forces more directly threatening than communism. The spectacular labor warfare of 1948 and 1949 had been less than a triumph for the UMW. With every strike, coal markets declined. Oil and gas made major inroads—nowhere more dramatically than on the railroads, which rapidly converted from coal-fired to diesel locomotives. The Damoclean sword of the great national strike began to lose its effectiveness. Lewis could not form alliances with labor bosses in the oil and gas industries because neither industry employs large numbers of men; a major coal mine cannot be operated with supervisory personnel during a strike, but a major oil refinery can.

The strikes of 1948 and 1949 had also undercut Lewis's prestige as a labor leader—not necessarily with his own rank and file, but certainly in the eyes of the public and of other union leaders. Men who had once paid homage to Lewis as a larger-than-life champion of workers in the world's most dangerous industry now saw him as a threat to an economy deeply shaken by post-war problems. He had begun to lose allies at a time when he might reasonably have been expected to want to keep them; at 70, with three decades of a brilliant career behind him, he had earned a place as an elder statesman in American labor, and it must have been a bitter pill for him to find himself so widely condemned for his strikes and rumors of strikes.

Under these circumstances, the understated persuasiveness of George Love must have had a profound effect on Lewis: the 1950–1951 negotiations between Lewis and Harry Moses were marked by cordiality between the two men—who now, between them, held the power to determine the labor policies of an entire industry. . . .

Through this concentration of power a peace descended on the coal industry that was awesome to behold. Successive contracts were negotiated and signed, without publicity, in 1952, 1955, 1956, and 1958. . . .

THE UNION AS BUSINESS

As Tom Bethell suggests, the most intriguing side of Lewis's character was his admiration for the world of big business. The public picture of Lewis, of course, was just the opposite: the rough-hewn lad from Wales, who had worked his way up from the pits to leadership of his union; a union man who had learned the hard way. In fact, Lewis's forebears were mostly farmers, not miners, although his father did work in the mines. On his mother's side the family was related to the iron and coal industry elites of Wales, a fact that Lewis was actually fond of recalling. As a young man Lewis worked only briefly in the mines, then quit to start a feed and grain business. All along identifying with business, he dabbled in Republican party politics and was even discussed as a possible vice-presidential nominee in 1924. He was a great friend of Jacob Harriman, the banker, who bailed out the union in the early 1920s, and was later involved in business deals with Cyrus Eaton.

Although Lewis's entrepreneurial inclinations and high regard for business are not well known, they played an important part in his management of the union.

Taken from John L. Lewis, *by Melvyn Dubofsky and Warren Van Tine, New York, Quadrangle, 1977.*

. . . Lewis followed his own rules of social etiquette religiously. He kept fellow officers of the UMW at a distance, practiced regal aloofness, and acted in the union as a king to his court. Lewis reserved his friendship for business executives, high public officials, and members of the hereditary American elite. They dined with the Lewises on a reciprocal basis, and he charmed them with well-told stories and stimulating conversation. The Herbert Hoovers, the Gardner Jacksons, the Harrimans, the Cyrus Chings, corporation executives in general—they were the type of people John L. Lewis cultivated. Cyrus Ching, a United States Rubber Company executive and later a prominent federal labor mediator, described Lewis as "a brilliant conversationalist," the "soul of courtesy . . . a typical Southern gentleman." Nonflamboyant in private conversation, Lewis, according to Ching, had a dry, keen sense of humor, one that enabled him and George Love, a leading coal company executive, to swap stories for seven consecutive hours as Ching laughed ceaselessly.

During the 1920s Lewis established a particularly close business and personal relationship with the Harriman family. Not only did Jacob Harriman, president of the Harriman National Bank, extend a substantial line of credit to the UMW during the 1922 strike, he also personally phoned President Harding to plead the union's case. Lewis, for his part, deposited UMW funds in Harriman's bank and sought to obtain other union business for his banker friend. Harriman regularly extended credit simply on the basis of Lewis's personal signature without collateral. For example, W. Jett Lauck, the UMW's economic adviser and Lewis's personal tax and real estate consultant, financed his own many—and mostly unsuccessful—real estate ventures through loans obtained from the Harriman National Bank on the signatures of Lewis and Phil Murray [a faithful lieutenant]. Averell Harriman occasionally invited Lewis to polo matches in which the former played. And Lewis, the trade union leader and miners' spokesman, felt no embarrassment appearing at the matches attended largely by members of New York's "400."

Later in the 1930s, when Jacob Harriman ran afoul of the law as a result of his bank's practices before and during the Great Depression, Lewis came to his aid. His bank ruined, his health shattered, his trial for fraud scheduled to open in federal court, Harriman, in May 1934, pleaded with Lewis to appear for him as a character witness. Writing to Lewis from Doctor's Hospital in New York, Harriman lamented: "My good name is in jeopardy and I am *fighting for my life.* And as you, too, are a good fighter you will appreciate my position and I leave it all to you!" Lewis proved a loyal friend, not only testifying in court himself but also urging William Green [head of the AFL] to bear witness concerning Harriman's good character. Lewis also visited Harriman in the hospital, a visit that Harriman wrote "built me up—my months back have been filled with heart-breaking cracks —but I'm keeping my head up and am fighting back as you told me to. . . . God bless you for your kindness—and I shall never forget it." Thus did Lewis pay off his debt to the man who, in the 1920s, assisted the UMW financially, provided liberal loans to Lewis's friends, and, in 1924, promoted John L. Lewis's candidacy for the Republican vice-presidency.

Lewis's relationship to the world of banking went considerably beyond his acquaintance with Jacob Harriman. In September 1923 Lewis agreed to become president of the United Labor Bank and Trust Company of Indianapolis, Indiana (capitalized at nearly $1 million) and demanded "a salary commensurate with the character of the institution and the degree of responsibility involved." He also suggested that the bank's organizers appoint his brother-in-law Floyd C. Bell cashier and a member of the board of directors at a starting salary of $4,000 to $5,000 per annum, to rise when business increases [*sic*]. In his letter of acceptance, Lewis enclosed two separate personal checks for $1,100 in payment for ten shares of bank stock each for himself and Floyd Bell in order to qualify them for their executive positions.

The reasons for establishing a labor bank and appointing Lewis as its president seem obvious. Three of the largest labor unions in the nation—the miners, the teamsters, and the carpenters—and many smaller ones had their national headquarters in Indianapolis. Unions, moreover, maintained an enormous cash flow as dues receipts trickled in and benefits poured out. A bank fortunate enough to become a depository for union funds gained substantial economic advantages, which is what the directors of the United Labor Bank likely expected from Lewis's presidency. The bank did, to be sure, become a depository for substantial UMW funds; but, in the absence of complete financial records, one cannot know to what extent it was patronized by other Indianapolis unions. Lewis's bank presidency during the 1920s and his business relationship with Harriman served as an apprenticeship for his subsequent banking enterprises in Washington and his financial manipulations with entrepreneur Cyrus Eaton. . . . Lewis . . . had long dabbled in business. Among other things, he had engaged in grain sales in the 1900s, launched a "labor bank" in the 1920s, and formed the Lewmurken Corporation in the 1930s to support the sagging businesses of his friends. He long had invested both the union's and his own money in the stock market with great skill. Since moving the union's headquarters to the nation's capital, the UMW had quietly purchased an impressive array of downtown real estate. Beginning with the University Club Building at 15th and I streets, for which the union paid $275,000, it went on to acquire 1453 K Street for $600,000; the Insurance Building at 15th and I for $1 million; and finally, in 1949, the eleven-story Chandler Building at 1427 I Street for $550,000. All in all, then, his entrepreneurial activities of the 1950s merely expanded and elaborated his earlier business endeavors.

With the establishment of the welfare and retirement fund in the late 1940s, Lewis gained access to a multimillion-dollar treasury that he decided to invest in the banking business. This decision was perhaps inevitable, given his personal fascination with high finance, the counseling of such friends as Cleveland tycoon Cyrus Eaton, and his belief that financiers controlled the economy. In the 1960s, Secretary-Treasurer John Owens would inform convention delegates that the union purchased a bank because the establishment where the UMW kept its funds repeatedly insulted Owens by asking for identification each time he cashed a check. Although an apt tale for individuals angered by the impersonality of the times, it was not the real explanation for the union's actions. Closer to the truth was Lewis's contention that he saw no reason why the welfare and retirement fund should sit in other people's banks and not be put to work for the union. In this exploit, as well as in his other entrepreneurial activities, Lewis was not seeking personal financial profit but rather trying to strengthen the union and, consequently, his own position of power. Unfortunately, activities advantageous for the institution were not necessarily beneficial to the membership.

Apparently, in the spring of 1949, Lewis employed the investment firm of Johnston, Lemon and Company secretly to purchase for the UMW controlling interest in the National Bank of Washington. By April, the firm had completed the arrangements. Over the next thirteen months the union transferred the welfare and retirement fund into the bank's vaults, which increased the institution's total deposits from $22,610,346 to $83,676,875. By June 1950, the National Bank had become fourth largest among nineteen banks in the city. Even then, Lewis refused to acknowledge his connection to the institution, although he had personally chosen Barnum L. Colton to be the bank's president and his brother Dennie and UMW attorney Welly K. Hopkins sat on the board of directors. In 1956 they would be joined by Lewis's son, John Jr., and then later by the comptroller of the welfare and retirement fund, Thomas Ryan, in an appointment that raised seriously the issue of conflict of interest.

The scope of the UMW's banking activities, as with most of its financial adventures, increased as Lewis became further isolated from the labor movement. Shortly after the A. F. of L. and CIO made known their merger plans, Lewis directed the National Bank to outbid all competitors for controlling interest in the Hamilton National Bank. This accomplished[,] the National Bank of Washington subsequently absorbed the Liberty National Bank and the Anacostia Banks so that by 1964 it was the second largest bank in Washington, with eighteen units and total assets of $432 million. By 1964, Secretary-Treasurer John Owens proudly boasted that the union's $23 million investment in bank stocks over the previous fourteen years was worth $72 million.

The deposits in the National Bank of Washington provided Lewis with tremendous financial leverage. Full details on the actual use of the bank's resources are unavailable, but it is clear that the institution responded to Lewis's will. It made loans to coal operators wishing to modernize their properties, and it bought heavily in the electric power field, where it then used its position to convince companies to burn union coal. Like all financial institutions, moreover, it made loans to people of influence when the need arose. Perhaps because of the possibility of government scrutiny of the bank's affairs, in delicate situations Lewis generally relied directly on the UMW treasury.

The UMW hierarchy intentionally cloaked the disposition of the union's monies. With unintended irony, John Owens told the 1960 convention delegates: "We differ from other labor unions in this country. We haven't publicly bragged about the resources of our Union." More accurately, the leadership mystified its financial activities. For years, the officers had reported the union's assets at approximately

$30 million. Then the passage of the Labor-Management Reporting and Disclosure Act in 1959 compelled them to reevaluate the organization's worth at more nearly $110 million. This dramatic disclosure, combined with a series of legal cases, created enough of a stir among the membership and the press to force the officials to offer more detailed information on the UMW's financial empire.

At the 1960 convention, John Owens presented a murky report on the union's financial resources that named names and cited figures, at least, even if it did not measure up to the standards of intelligible accounting. Owens made clear that he was speaking for "Mr. Labor Leader himself, who has so ably guided and directed me in whatever I have done, in whatever we have accomplished." According to Owens, the $21,646,174.72 tied up in the National Bank of Washington was the union's largest outright investment. Next came Lewis's 1951 investment of $9,421,518.45 in securities of the coal-carrying Chesapeake and Ohio Railway, which was managed by his close friend and economic counselor Cyrus Eaton. "I am only sorry to report to you," Owens gloated to the delegates, "that we have made just a few million dollars out of that investment for which no coal miner worked in the coal mines." Finally, since 1956, when the union allied with business interests to sell coal abroad through the American Coal Shipping Corporation, Lewis invested $8,346,489 into that venture and, through it, into the Bull Steamship Line. . . .

The most opaque section of Owens's report concerned the UMW's financial ties with actual mining properties. With great warmth, he told of advancing $5,200,000 to the Coaldale Mining Company in an effort to keep at least one segment of the decaying anthracite industry alive. He also defended the union's $26 million investment in the West Kentucky and Nashville Coal Companies.[*] Yet on all other arrangements he was incredibly fleeting, asserting something about bringing stability to the Pittsburgh Midway properties and blurting out that the union had attained mines in Kansas under contract. "We brought about hundreds and thousands of other tons of production on which men are receiving the wage scale, and the 40 cents a ton is going into the Welfare and Retirement Fund," he concluded without further elaboration. Nonetheless, he had said enough to substantiate the *New York Times'* conclusion that the United Mine Workers was the "wealthiest union in the land." . . .

[*Lewis used union funds to take over West Kentucky Coal, a supplier to the Tennessee Valley Authority (TVA). The deal worked like this: Lewis got together with Cyrus Eaton, the multimillionaire Cleveland industrialist and board chairman of the Chesapeake & Ohio Railroad, a major coal hauler. The UMW lent funds to Eaton on Lewis's say-so. Eaton began buying West Kentucky stock in a strategy to take over the company. By 1952 Eaton was a West Kentucky director. The following year he was chairman of the board. His first official act as chairman was to sign a wage contract with the UMW.

With control over West Kentucky, the UMW was able to move into the huge new TVA market (one of the reasons this market was so big was that TVA was supplying electricity to the government for the enrichment of uranium, used to make nuclear bombs and then, of course, as fuel for nuclear power plants). Eaton and the UMW eventually had more than 16 percent of the TVA business for West Kentucky.

Long-term contracts with large coal companies like West Kentucky were displacing small coal operators, also employing UMW members, in Tennessee. Many of these small, marginal mines went out of business, and the men who worked in them became unemployed.]

WHO OWNS THE COAL?

The United States probably has the most bountiful supplies of coal in the world, as the first selection which follows indicates. Ownership and control of this coal are increasingly viewed as a cornerstone of the energy industry, whether for production of electricity, as a feedstock for synthetic oil or gas, or as an export to other nations.

As the previous section made clear, the arrangements achieved by Lewis and Love during the immediate post-World War II period set the stage for a newly structured coal industry, by creating the conditions for its consolidation and expansion. The organization of much larger companies meant a far greater concentration of ownership of the coal reserves themselves. Although the overall issue of concentration is discussed in the section on monopoly (see p. 315), here we look at the specific issue of concentration of ownership of the coal in the ground.

Historically most of the coal that fostered the nation's economic growth has come from Appalachia. Most of that mineral-rich land is held by corporations or by wealthy individuals from New York or Philadelphia, Cleveland or Houston—anywhere but Appalachia. Within Appalachia, West Virginia has been one of the most important coal-producing states, and here three major owners stand out. The first two are railroads: Norfolk & Western and the Chessie System (formerly the Chesapeake & Ohio, owned by Lewis's friend Cyrus Eaton). These railroads crisscross the mountains, hauling coal from mines to markets. The third owner is Continental Oil, which in the mid-1960s bought George Love's company, Consolidation Coal.

In 1980 the Appalachian Alliance, a coalition of community groups, completed a detailed analysis of ownership in eighty different Appalachian counties in the states of Alabama, Kentucky, North Carolina, Tennessee, Virginia, and West Virginia and found that almost half of about 20 million coal-rich acres are held by a few corporations, government agencies, and absentee individuals. Put another way, the alliance investigation showed that only 1 percent of the people actually living in the eighty counties owned their own land.

The Appalachian Alliance study shows how as the coal industry was reorganized into an energy industry, so, too, was the land which held the coal.

Taken from Coal Resources of the United States, January 1, 1974, *by Paul Averitt, U.S. Geological Survey Bulletin 1412, Washington, D.C.*

Coal Resources of the United States, January 1, 1974

ABSTRACT

The coal resources of the United States remaining in the ground on January 1, 1974, are estimated to total 3,968 billion tons, distributed in several major categories, as shown below:

Estimated remaining coal resources of the United States, January 1, 1974
[Figures are for resources remaining in the ground]

Category	Billions (10^9) of short tons
1. Identified resources:	
A. Reserve base	424
B. Additional identified resources	1,307
C. Total identified resources	1,731
2. Hypothetical resources:	
A. 0–3,000 ft overburden[*]	1,849
B. 3,000–6,000 ft overburden	388
C. Total hypothetical resources	2,237
3. Total remaining resources	3,968

[*The earth between the coal and the surface.]

The new United States estimate is a 23-percent increase over previous estimates . . . made possible by an increased program of geologic mapping, exploration, and study during the past few years by Federal and State agencies and by private industry. The new estimate is based on detailed published estimates of identified resources in individual States and on generalized estimates of additional hypothetical resources for unmapped and unexplored areas in these States.

The identified tonnage has been classified in all States according to rank. It has also been classified by thickness of overburden, degree of reliability of estimates, and thickness of beds in 21 States. Coal thus classified is well distributed in all coal provinces and represents about 60 percent of the total identified tonnage. This large classified tonnage is, therefore, reasonably representative of the total identified resources. The distribution of the classified tonnage in several meaningful categories, each expressed as a percentage of the total, is as follows: (1) 91 percent is 1,000 feet or less below the surface, (2) 43 percent is bituminous coal, (3) 33 percent is in thick beds, and (4) 24 percent is in the reserve base.

The United States contains about 25 percent of the world's identified coal resources and about 20 percent of the world's estimated total coal resources. In 1972 the United States accounted for about 19 percent of the total world production. Between 75 and 80 percent of United States production is obtained from 23 thick, continuous beds.

A comparison on a uniform Btu basis of resources of coal and other fossil fuels in the United States shows that coal constitutes 69 percent of the total estimated recoverable resources of fossil fuel, whereas petroleum and natural gas together constitute only 7 percent, and oil in oil shale—which is not currently used as a fuel—constitutes only 23 percent. The disparity between the large resources of coal and the small resources of petroleum and natural gas is sharply emphasized by the fact that in 1973 the combined production of petroleum and natural gas in the United States was 3 times that of coal. . . .

Taken from "Land Ownership Patterns and Their Impacts on Appalachian Communities: A Survey of 80 Counties," submitted to the Appalachian Regional Commission by the Appalachian Land Ownership Task Force, February 1981.

COAL AND COAL LANDS

When surface and mineral acres are combined, 17 coal-mining and coal-landowners own 1,520,261 acres. The surprising characteristic of these owners is that only three—Pittston, Alabama By-Products, and the Blue Diamond Coal Company—are engaged primarily in the business of mining coal. The others simply lease their land and minerals to coal operators, who do the mining.

In 1965 *Dun's Review of Modern Business* wrote of these coal land corporations that "for all their small numbers . . . these coal royalists hold what may be one of the most lucrative investments in all of America." The "coal royalists," as they are called, simply oversee their land (usually through a local manager), negotiate leases, and collect the royalties, currently as high as $2 to $3 per ton. The companies that lease the land for the mining incur most of the risks.

On the national economic scene, these coal landholding companies are small and often relatively unknown. Even their trade group, the National Coal Lessers' Association, is not highly visible. Yet locally these companies are often viewed as having enormous power. Through single decisions of their offices, the land use of huge portions of certain counties can be affected. Coal operators are dependent upon good relations with them to negotiate the leaseholds necessary to mine the coal, which often provides the jobs in an area. Tenants living in old coal camps on their property may also be dependent upon these companies' goodwill for housing. Whole communities are potentially affected by the taxes and economic base which their resources provide.

Despite their profitability and power, these coal royalists are often absentee and relatively anonymous. Only one of the owners, Plateau Properties, has its headquarters in the county where most of its holdings are located—most are headquartered outside the region altogether. Only three—Pittston, Penn-Virginia, Alabama By-Products—are public companies (in the sense that they have over $1 million in assets and over 500 shareholders and are thus required to register public information with the Securities & Exchange Commission). Others are often family-owned, relatively small operations with merely post office boxes as their addresses or small offices serving as their corporate headquarters. A lawyer in West Virginia describes his attempts to research the Cotiga Development Company, a Philadelphia-based operation which owns 25,081 surface acres and 39,648 mineral acres in Mingo County:

> Two years ago I wanted to do some research into the background of Cotiga. . . . I wanted to see the makeup of a company such as Cotiga. I went to Cotiga's office, which you have some trouble finding because it's a one-room office in a suburban home. Not only is it the office for Cotiga Development

Coal Fields of the Conterminous United States

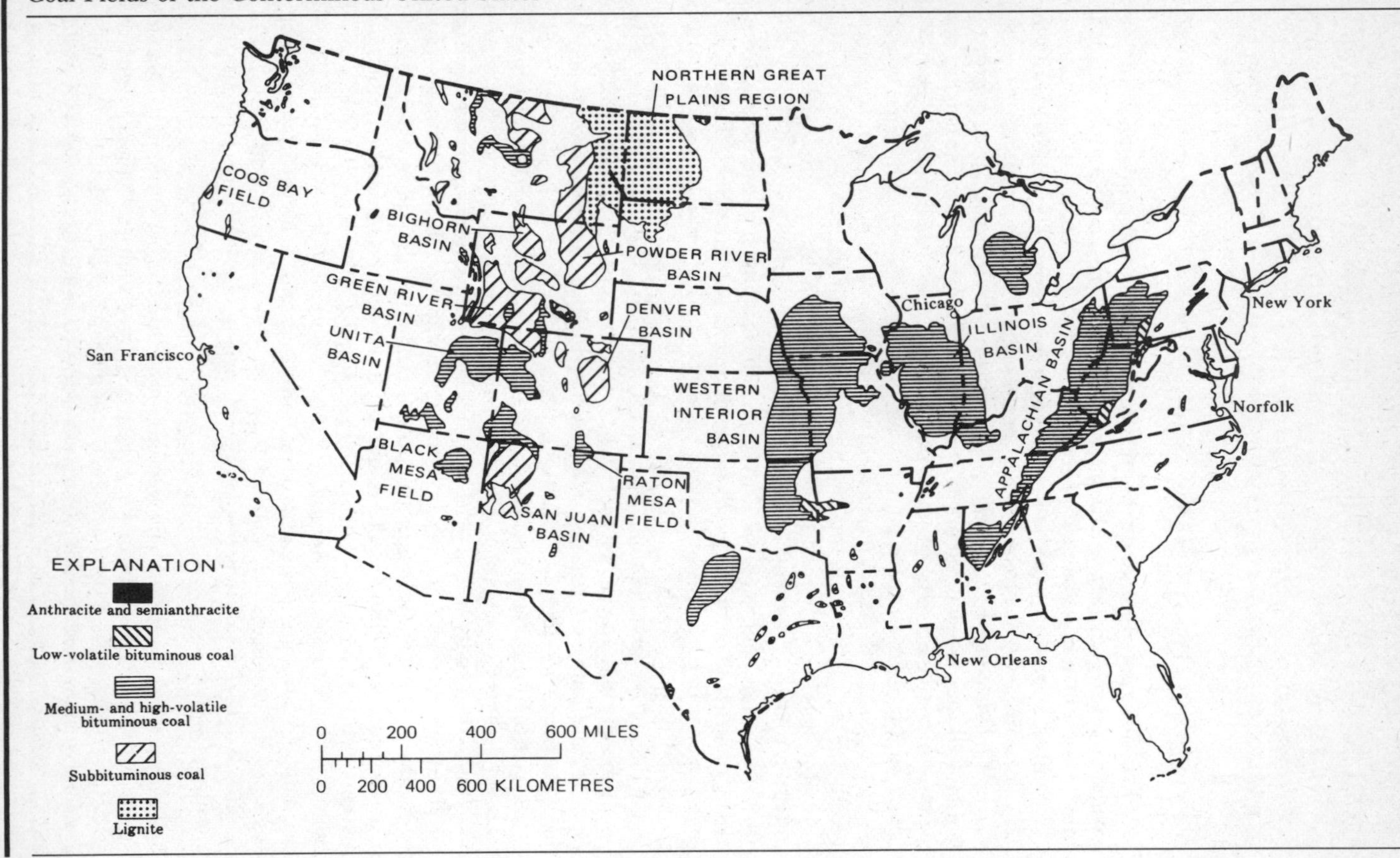

Company, one of the largest landowners in Mingo County, but it's also the office, according to the mailbox, for several other land companies in West Virginia. Thompson wasn't home, and when I talked to one of the secretaries in the office next door, she said, "Well, he comes in one or two days a week. And sometimes there's a secretary that comes in to answer letters." But what was interesting to me was how little it really took once you've acquired the land, to keep it going.

According to interviews in Mingo County, the Cotiga holdings were acquired by an enterprising sewing machine salesman who traveled the hills of the county early in the century trading sewing machines for land. Others of these companies also have interesting backgrounds:

Coal Creek Mining and Manufacturing: Along with its affiliates, Poplar Creek Coal and Winter Gap Coal Company, Coal Creek owns 64,374 acres in Anderson, Campbell, Morgan, and Scott counties in Tennessee. The company is headquartered in Knoxville and is controlled by approximately 155 shareholders throughout the United States. Most of its properties were acquired before the turn of the century and have remained virtually the same since that time.

The Brimstone Company: This company is owned primarily by John Rollins, a Delaware businessman and financier, who also controls the Orkin Pest Control Company, trucking lines, Jamaican resorts, and a group of television and radio stations—to name a few. Rollins acquired the 40,261 acres in Scott and Morgan counties in Tennessee from the family of Senator Howard Baker in 1972. Senator Baker was a principal partner in the operations until 1977, when charges of conflicts of interest were raised concerning mining and potential recreation developments on the property and legislation supported by the senator.

Kentucky River Coal and Coke Company: Located in Lexington, Kentucky, Kentucky River owns thousands of acres of land and mineral rights throughout eastern Kentucky—as many as 180,000 acres according to some published reports. This survey found 82,551 recorded on the tax rolls. Most of this property was obtained by John C. C. Mayo, a schoolteacher from Paintsville, Kentucky, who in the late nineteenth century received backing from eastern financiers, becoming one of eastern Kentucky's most successful coal buyers.

Kentenia Corporation: Owning 25,335 acres, primarily in Harlan County, this company is based in Boston, Massachusetts. The company was founded in the early 1900s by Warren Delano, a wealthy northerner and uncle of Franklin Delano Roosevelt, who invested heavily in the eastern Kentucky region.

Historically most of these coal land companies have held their land and minerals for decades, many since before the turn of the century. However, the last decade has seen in Appalachia a new wave of corporate amalgamation in the coal fields. With the energy crisis, as more, often multinational, corporations have moved into the energy field, a number of these coal land companies have been bought by larger interests. Look at some of the examples of the trend:

—In east Tennessee, the 50,940 acres of Tennessee Land and Mining, owned for decades by a family from Scarsdale, New York, has been bought by the Koppers Company, a multinational metal and chemical corporation from Pittsburgh. In 1980 Koppers also bought the 36,092 acres owned by the High Top Coal Company, giving it 169,376 acres in four eastern Tennessee counties.

—In Tennessee and Kentucky, the J. M. Huber Corporation purchased the 65,000 acres of the American Association, Ltd., a British-owned firm formerly controlled by the interests of Sir Denys Flowerdew Lowson, a former lord mayor of London. American Association had developed Middlesboro and Cumberland Gap in the 1890s. The largest owner found in the study, Huber owns 227,000 acres in the survey area.

—In Kentucky and Virginia the properties of the Virginia Iron, Coal and Coke Company have been purchased by the Bates Manufacturing Company. Shortly afterward they were acquired by the American Natural Resources Corporation, a diversified energy corporation from Detroit.

—In Tennessee a family-held coal-mining and landholding company, the Tennessee Consolidation Coal Company, has been purchased by St. Joe's Minerals. St. Joe's has also signed an agreement with Scallop Coal Corporation, a subsidiary of Royal Dutch Shell, jointly to develop its coal properties throughout the region, with much of the new production possibly to be used for export. . . .

The trend toward ownership and control of Appalachia's land and energy resources by larger, more multinational units can be seen as we turn to ownership by the second largest category of owners, the oil, gas, and energy conglomerates.

OIL, GAS, AND ENERGY COMPANIES

The last decade has seen growing national concern over the extent of control of the nation's energy resources by a small number of holders, particularly the oil companies. In 1963 Gulf Oil took over the Pittsburgh and Midway Coal Company; in the years following, other companies followed suit. According to the Office of Technology Assessment of the U.S. Congress, these "horizontally integrated" companies will mine about 385 to 465 million tons of coal by 1986, representing almost one-half of the total domestic consumption of coal used for energy purposes.

As they acquired coal companies, oil companies also gained control over vast amounts of mineral reserves. According to the President's Coal Commission, oil and gas companies now own 41.1 percent of all privately owned coal reserves in the country, concentrated primarily in the West. Six of the top ten national coal reserve owners are partially owned by larger oil and gas companies: Continental Oil, Exxon, El Paso Natural Gas, Standard Oil of California, Occidental Petroleum (Island Creek). The largest of these, Continental Oil, owns an estimated 13.7 billion tons of coal, theoretically enough to supply the nation's needs for fifteen years to come.

Of these big oil companies, Continental Oil (Consolidation Coal) and Occidental Petroleum (Island Creek Coal) are in the list of the top fifty owners in the survey area, together owning 422,320 acres of surface and mineral rights. They control thousands more acres through leasing. Altogether in the survey area, eleven oil and gas companies own approximately 1,239,698 acres of surface and mineral rights combined, an average of over 100,000 acres each.

While controlling thousands of acres of coal reserves on the one hand, the oil companies are now leasing thousands of acres of oil and gas rights on the other. According to the New York Times News Service, as much as 10 million acres have already been leased in what is called the Eastern Overthrust Belt, a geologic formation running 1,000 miles along the Appalachian mountains from Alabama to New England. Exactly who is leasing how much of this oil and gas is difficult to determine because the rights rarely appear on the tax rolls. When the leases are recorded in county deed books, they often appear in the names of individuals serving as land agents for the oil companies. However, from other evidence, it is clear that the leasing activity extends well beyond the coal fields. Speculating about the presence of oil atop "Old Smokey," *South* magazine reports a "land war going on for drilling rights in the Appalachian region. . . . Gulf, Exxon, Weaver Oil and Gas Corporations of Houston are all known to be crawling the foothills in search of landowners." Already, for instance, Standard Oil of Indiana has leased 122,000 acres in just four western North Carolina counties.

The oil and gas company presence is seen, too, in the development of new synthetic fuels plants in the region. In Wayne and Lincoln counties, West Virginia, for instance, Columbia Gas has been exploring possibilities of synthetic fuels development on its over 300,000 acres of minerals. In Catlettsburg, Kentucky, Ashland Oil has spearheaded a consortium (which includes Mobil Oil, Standard Oil of Indiana, and Conoco) that has built a pilot liquefaction plant, funded primarily by Department of Energy funds. In Monongalia County, West Virginia, Gulf Oil is building another liquefaction plant, which would use 6,000 tons of coal a day. The Koppers Company, already the largest developer of synfuels technology in the world, plans five plants on its Tennessee properties. The synthetic fuels industry is likely to have major impacts on land use, as well as air and water quality, employment, and services in the communities where it is located.

MINGO COUNTY

In this history of one county in southern West Virginia, it is possible to follow at a microlevel the effects of the recent history of the coal industry, hard hit during the era of cheap oil from the end of World War II to the early 1970s and then on the upswing as the price of oil soared in the 1970s.

Taken from Volume VIII, "West Virginia," of "Land Ownership Patterns and Their Impact on Appalachian Communities: A Survey of 80 Counties," submitted to the Appalachian Regional Commission by the Appalachian Land Ownership Task Force, February 1981.

POPULATION CHARACTERISTICS

The development of Mingo County [West Virginia] has been inextricably linked to coal ever since its creation. Following the extension of the railroad link from the coalfields to Huntington, Charleston, and the industrial Northeast at the turn of the century, Mingo County experienced phenomenal growth. Between 1890 and 1950 the population multiplied twelvefold from 4,381 to 47,409. These were boom years—industrialization and war in the national and international arenas supported the coal market, and within the county the mines supported the railroad, timber, and a host of construction, retail, and service activity. Today the composition of economic activity is much the same, though on a reduced scale.

Mechanization and a slump in the coal market in the 1950s had a disastrous effect on the county, generating severe unemployment and outmigration. By 1960 the population had fallen to 39,742 and in 1970 to 32,780. As the county lost 40 percent of its jobs, including 75 percent of its mining jobs between 1950 and 1977, it lost 31 percent of its residents. An increase in population of 8.3 percent between 1970 and 1976 is one of a number of signals that the county may be growing again. . . .

Ultimately . . . Mingo County is fraught with contradictions. The county possesses some of the highest quality natural resources in the region, yet these resources are developed according to marketing strategies designed elsewhere. As a result, the county's prosperity is predicated upon a pattern of landownership which has not necessarily been consistent with the preservation of the land and the well-being of the population. Because of the intensity of this contradiction, Mingo County can serve as an object lesson for other areas only recently targeted by corporate interests.

The history of the "opening" of Mingo County parallels the history of the region. The timber and coal boom came with the Norfolk & Western Railroad in the 1880s. In fact, the county itself was created as the result of commercial activities which followed the construction of the railroad. A group of West Virginia and Kentucky speculators came into the area early in the decade and established hotels, a bank, and a newspaper in Williamson, which became the county seat, as well as rural settlements all geared to the railroad, timber, and coal. By 1895 their enterprise had been affirmed by the establishment of Mingo County as an independent political entity. The history of farming, hunting, trapping, and trading of the 1800s was now displaced by the coal boom.

Absentee control has come a long way since the small syndicate of developers traveled the county, piecing together holdings by buying outright, maneuvering heirships, and making claims on heretofore-forfeited land grants originating in the nineteenth century. As was true throughout the region, unsuspecting and illiterate property owners were often intimidated and misled as they put their *X* on broad form deeds which resulted in the loss of their rights to minerals and surface.

Today the landownership and use patterns in many ways represents the culmination of that early effort. Of Mingo County's 270,000 acres, out-of-state corporations own 126,410 acres of surface (47 percent) and 161,649 acres of minerals (60 percent).* Out-of-county (but in-state) corporations own 40,511 acres of surface (15 percent) and 53,450 acres of minerals (20 percent). Four companies alone—Cotiga Development, Island Creek Coal, Georgia-Pacific, and U.S. Steel—own 101,851 acres of surface (38 percent) and 130,563 acres of minerals (48 percent). Out-of-county and out-of-state individuals own 17,070 acres of surface and 23,351 acres of minerals. As a result, less than 30 percent of the surface and 10 percent of the minerals are owned locally.†

The precariousness of the county's economic fate is due to the disproportionate presence of coal. In 1976, fifty-five mining establishments employed 35 percent of the working population with a payroll of almost $30,000,000 annually. . . . In rank order, retail trade establishments employed 25 percent of the labor force with an annual payroll of only $9,684,000. Manufacturing ranked fourth with only 414 employees or 7.4 percent of the work force and a payroll of $3,539,000.

The absence of substantial manufacturing leaves the county extremely vulnerable. In 1970 only 6.7 percent of those employed were involved in manufacturing, as opposed to over 20 percent in Lincoln and over 30 percent in Wayne immediately to the north. The manufacturing which does exist is small-scale and predominantly coal-related. In 1972 none of the manufacturing operations employed over 100 people, and their capital expenditure of $200,000 was the smallest in the region.

The nature of landownership has also restricted the potential for diversification and growth by inhibiting the construction of the infrastructure necessary to sustain commercial development. Because of the huge rural holdings by mineral and timber interests, there has never been any reason to extend sewage and water facilities beyond the incorporated residential areas. The ad hoc facilities which were built to handle the old company towns were inadequate then and are dilapidated now. Even the public systems in residential areas are inadequate because of insufficient maintenance, a situation which has lately generated widespread public protest. Thus any commercial site development would have to start from scratch even if suitable land were made available by corporate owners.

Given this predicament, the first concern is simply holding onto the nonmining business that is already in place.

Because of the unavailability of land, there has been nothing akin to industrial park development and little or no effort to apply the [state's] incentive program for economic development. While [new highways] will supplement, if not replace, the fledgling rail system and a road network overcrowded with coal trucks, it cannot lure new commercial activity to the area as long as there is no place to build.

EMPLOYMENT CONSEQUENCES

Over the years the coal companies have also shaped the size, skills, and thus the fate of the local labor force. Population has moved in and out of the county as a

*The figures for minerals include all types; thus there may be some duplication in acreage when gas and oil are owned independent of coal or where there are duplicate coal seams.
†For purposes of this study, 76 percent of the surface acreage and 97 percent of the mineral acreage were surveyed.

reflection of the amount of coal being mined. Between 1950 and 1970 coal production fell 3 million tons and mining jobs declined by 73 percent, and population fell by 15,000 people. As production began to pick up again in the 1970s, jobs appeared and population grew.

In Mingo County, as in any predominantly single commodity economy, layoffs and strikes can and do have a paralyzing impact. Unemployment in the county has consistently been above the state average. In 1977 the state classified Mingo County in the "high unemployment" category—i.e., over 6.6 percent as against the state average of 4.6 percent. As the coal market became more and more uncertain in the late 1970s, mines shut down and layoffs increased. As production dropped in 1978 back to the 1970 level of 3 million tons, unemployment rose to 9.3 percent. According to the mayor of Williamson, one mining job generates four nonmining jobs, and for each mining job lost, four nonmining jobs are also lost.

A number of mines have closed down. . . . The West Virginia Department of Employment Security estimates that as many as 600 miners were out of work in January 1980, and the outlook is not too good for 1980. . . .

Recently a new element has eroded the traditional relationship between production and employment. Increased emphasis on strip mining is providing the tonnage but not the jobs. One estimate is that a given production underground mining operation employs three to five times the work force of a strip-mining operation. . . .

. . . Impact on Fiscal Development

> If taxes are what we pay for a civilized society . . . then the cost of civilization is an arguable issue in Mingo County.

Almost everyone in Mingo County seems to understand that there is a connection between taxes and the quality of services, but there is less agreement on which comes first. Georgia-Pacific's lawyer argues that "the services they get for the taxes they pay are zero"—i.e., nonexistent services justify Georgia-Pacific's low taxes. Concerned citizens, on the other hand, argue that the reason for the lack of services is the gross underassessment of prime surface, timber, and minerals and the fact that those least able to pay suffer a disproportionate amount of the tax burden.

SOURCES OF COUNTY REVENUE

Mingo County's fiscal situation is representative of West Virginia coal fields in general—resource-rich, yet tax-poor. Because of years of intimidation, negligence, and/or a shortage of expertise and staff, county assessors have avoided any accurate determination of the actual value of corporate holdings for tax purposes. Until the advent of grants-in-aid and revenue sharing the county simply went without the services they now provide. The increased availability of external funds since the "New Frontier" and "Great Society" has allowed local officials to continue to ignore the reservoir of revenue within their own county. . . .

Budgeted expenditures for fiscal year 1979–1980, excluding schools, total $1,373,746. Only 56 percent of that amount, or $772,442, is expected to come from property taxes. Almost 18 percent of the needed revenue, or $257,804, will come from various fees, interest, and outstanding balance. The remaining 25 percent will come from federal grants ($340,000) and state grants ($3,500). . . .

Mingo County has been at the forefront of the property tax issue in West Virginia. The Tug Valley Recovery Center maintains that on the basis of research done in 1977, county residents living on 1 percent of the land paid 70 percent of the taxes. Our data approximate this contention. According to the 1979 books, absentee corporate landowners owned approximately 60 percent of the surface and 80 percent of the minerals, yet were responsible for only 36.6 percent of the county's total property valuation, in some cases paying less than $1 an acre in taxes. . . . Our data also indicate that in-county corporations, and in some cases individual property owners, were paying more tax per acre than were the large, absentee corporate owners. . . . In combination, the history of unassessed minerals, the continued underassessment of minerals, underassessed corporate surface, and the intermittent assessment of corporate machinery has cost the county millions of dollars in much needed tax revenue over the years.

Prior to 1979 there was, for all intents and purposes, no value put on coal, the county's most valuable resource. According to the county assessor, it was a "hit or miss proposition" at best. The state coal appraisal done in response to statewide pressure finally established an average appraisal in Mingo County of $360 per acre of coal. The assessor, in turn, has the power to assess that coal within a range of 50 to 100 percent of that appraisal. Typically, the Mingo County assessor chose to put the coal on the books at a value of $180 per acre.

Prior to the state appraisal, concerned citizens working through the Tug Valley Recovery Center challenged the low assessments before the county Board of Equalization and Review, pointing out that 39,000 acres of Cotiga coal were on the books at only $18 per acre.

. . . The figures on Cotiga's coal were only the most graphic example in a history of subsidies to corporate land and mineral owners through the negligence of the assessor and the county commission. . . .

. . . The hard-won increases have occurred as residents have gone over the heads of the County Commission to the Supreme Court, or gained the advantage of state-wide appraisals and the visibility of successful challenges by citizen groups in other counties. The obstructionism within much of the county political structure is evident in the sympathies of the president of the County Commission, a coal company personnel manager who, as chairman of the Board of Equalization and Review, defended corporate landowners during the 1980 session. "If it was not for them I would not be working today and drawing my salary." . . .

BLACK LUNG

Black lung is the common name for coal workers' pneumoconiosis, the lung disease that is estimated to have killed hundreds of thousands of miners in this century. Four thousand miners are believed to be dying prematurely each year because of black lung. The disease begins gradually and usually after a buildup of years begins to affect the lungs. There is no cure. The process cannot be reversed. Put more abstractly, black lung is part of the social cost of mining coal, a cost carried by labor, specifically by miners who are incapacitated in middle age, so that a few large corporations can profitably produce the fuel.

Taken from "Dying the Slow Death," by Don Stillman, United Mine Workers Journal, *June 1–15, 1975.*

Even in the summer, darkness still shrouds Mud Fork hollow at 4:30 A.M. Already, he is up, sitting in the old, brown chair that is his favorite in the dim light of the small table lamp next to him.

The only sounds are those of his wife sleeping in the next room and the coffee pot perking on the counter between the dining room and the kitchen. Knowing his problem, she usually puts the coffee and water in the pot the night before so that all he has to do is plug it in when he gets up.

He sits in pajama tops and trousers with one hand against his forehead and wonders what kind of day it will be. In a moment, he has the answer. There is a rattling sound in his chest, a brief gasp and then he is almost doubled over with a massive coughing fit.

His left hand flies to his mouth while the right clutches at his chest—one to catch the black-red spittle and the other to fight the spasm and the pain in his lungs. Cheeks puff out and throat muscles tighten hard as he struggles for breath.

For a moment he is clearly losing that struggle, then it is over. He slumps back hard, his eyes shut and his face color changing from red to white as he makes throat-clearing noises. It is not warm, but there are tiny beads of sweat on his forehead.

Another day has begun for Luther David—age 47; occupation, disabled coal miner.

For him, it is an ordinary day. One full of coughing fits, massive chest pain, headaches, muscle aches, spitting up blood and a shakiness and irritability David calls "the nerves."

David, a UMWA miner for 28 years and, at 47, a man theoretically in the prime of his working life, has black lung. He knows it. His wife and two young sons know it. His doctors know it. His fellow union members know it. His neighbors know it. Anyone who spends 30 minutes with him knows it.

Everybody knows it, except the people who run the federal black lung compensation program. They don't know it. They've told Luther twice now that he doesn't have it and they aren't going to pay him for it. It is, of course, a long way from the handsome new building in Washington, D.C., where Labor Department "experts" process black lung claims to the little, onetime company town called "15-Camp" where Luther passes each remaining day.

There are other men like Luther David in 15-Camp who spend their days struggling for a decent breath, just as there are in 16-Camp and 18-Camp up the hollow. In fact, there are men like Luther David in the next hollow and the one after that and the one after that. Men who gave their country the coal it needed, their companies the profits they craved and, in the process, lost their health, their livelihood, even their manhood.

Luther's wife, Myrtle, is up at 5:30 to get the kids off to school. Allen is 18, Timmy 15. Some mornings Luther is awake by 3:30 or 4 and can't get back to sleep. If he's coughing a lot, he may get up and drag himself to his chair in the adjoining room. Or he may just continue to toss and turn and do his best not to wake Myrtle.

After taking his array of pills and cough medicine, he "tries to stay out of the way" while the rest of the family has breakfast. Once Allen and Timmy have departed, Luther eats some cream-of-wheat or perhaps a couple of eggs and a biscuit with his coffee.

"After breakfast, I have to rest up, rest from using my arm and eating," he says. "You wouldn't think that would tire a man out at the beginning of the day, would you? Well, it does."

The remainder of the early morning routine is familiar, each act so simple to a healthy man is an ordeal for Luther David. Shaving to him is like running a mile to a normal person. He has to rest for a half hour or more afterwards. Then, he has the strength to brush his teeth.

Bathing is the worst of all. "We don't have a shower and bending over to get in the tub, it's like I'm tearing everything loose," Luther says. "Sometimes it takes me over half a day to get ready to go for breathing treatments at the hospital and by the time I'm ready I wouldn't even feel like going."

The rest of the day is not much better. Luther sits in his chair. Or he moves into the living room and sits there. Or, in the weeks of the year when it is not too hot or too cold, he'll sit outside on the porch. Then he goes in and lays [sic] down on the bed. He doesn't really nap, because he can't sleep. Sometimes he lays [sic] down on the bed in his son's room, just to vary his routine.

He doesn't read and seldom watches television. Occasionally, he listens to country music on a small, portable radio, but even that wears thin. Mostly, he sits. Just about any exertion tires him tremendously and brings on coughing fits. About once a week, Luther tries to go to the post office in nearby Mt. Gay. In the past, he has been able to walk out to the road that runs between the two rows of company-built houses and stand in the alley talking with neighbors. Lately, even that is too tiring for him.

Luther David looks like a fairly vigorous middle-aged man and indeed, that is what he was up until about two years ago. He used to hunt deer, rabbit, squirrels and love[d] the outdoors. He had a horse he rode and loved to go motorcycle riding on the winding roads through the mountains of southern West Virginia where he lives. He is a big man, with the look of one you would think twice before provoking.

He has purchased his hunting license the last two years with the hope that somehow things would get better. They didn't and he was unable to go out. Recently, a friend took him to [a] nearby state park to go fishing. The walk down the path to the water tired Luther so that he was unable to bait a hook. . . .

. . . Both Luther and his wife say that what he misses most of is being able to work. While disliking the unsafe conditions, he enjoyed the jobs he had, the men he worked with and, put simply, felt proud to be a coal miner. It was a job he did well and in turn it provided him and his family with a good income. Now, he misses not just the money, but also the job itself. He thinks about work a great deal. "I wish I could go back," he says. "But I can't.

"Every day I feel the effects of it. The doctor at the hospital said I'll just have to live with it. Well, I know that's true, but it's a hard thing to accept, particularly at my age. Think how you would feel if someone said to you that you'll just have to live with constant pain and not being able to work or hardly go out of the house." . . .

Luther has received "breath shots" at a nearby hospital. He stopped going for them because of the pain they cause him. "I like to have tore up the sheets after the last one and I said that's it". He still receives "mist treatments" aimed at helping him get his breath more easily.

Other than that, and an incredible assortment of drugs prescribed by various doctors, there is little that can be done by the medical experts.

Luther's wife, Myrtle, has been forced to quit her job at the local dime-store to stay home with him. Because he needs virtually constant care, she now finds it difficult to get out of the house for even the few minutes it takes to walk several hundred yards down the road to her mother's home. The strain has made her "a little nervous, too, like Luther." . . .

"Yes, I suppose I'm a little bitter," she says. "When Luther was working, I just never dreamed this could happen, at least until he was older. My dad was 63 when he died from black lung—he had it pretty bad, too. There is nothing we can do now but look to the good Lord and try not to worry.

"I don't understand why they can get the dust down in other countries where coal is mined and not here. I thought we were ahead of them in these things. If my sons go in (to the mines) I hope the companies will bring the dust down so they're not disabled like Luther so young."

Black lung disease was something that Luther David had little occasion to think about during all but the last of his mining career. . . .

During his 28 years as a miner, he worked in a variety of jobs, many of them at or close to the face. "I wanted to get all the coal I could for the company—for the royalty for the Fund and all," he says. "I'd run a buggy and I couldn't even see what coal I had in it because it was so dusty. Buddy, you just ate that dust all the time." . . .

David worked for Omar Mining Co., owned by Wheeling-Pittsburgh Steel Corp., at its No. 15 mine for the bulk of his final years as a miner. He noticed no major chest or lung problems until 1971.

"There used to be some steps up the hill from the bathhouse to where we'd go in the mine and I can remember being able to run up them without even breathing hard. I used to go up those steps when the day shift would be coming down.

"I seen this man I knew who carried on a lot and I got to notice him coming down those steps. He'd come down some and have to knock off and rest—going down, not coming up and he'd have to rest. And he'd be hanging on to the bannister.

"I wondered why that was. I didn't make light of him, but it was hard to believe that a man would have to stop going down steps—he was a big, healthy man. After he got down, he'd be a cut-up in the bathhouse—then all of a sudden he'd quiet down and couldn't do anything. I felt sorry for him.

"He was a big, jolly fellow. I got to watching him and wondering if that would ever happen to me."

About two years later, it did. Luther began to notice that he had shortness of breath after hanging curtains or shoveling or just about any rigorous activity. He noticed things seemed to "act up a little" after a hard day in the mines. Then, right before vacation in 1972, he developed bad pains in the chest and was off five days.

"The thing kept up and the doctor I went to thought maybe it was an ulcer so I heard to try a little of this sweet milk. That didn't help and neither did aspirin. Finally, the pain started in my chest and come up to the throat and nearly killed me."

Future visits to physicians finally resulted in one doctor telling Luther it was his lungs. "It never occurred to me it could be the dust," he says now. "I'd just gone into debt on a Super Beetle (Volkswagen) and had a mortgage loan and I figured I could keep on working without too much trouble, though."

Luther did just that. But the more he worked, the clearer it became that, even at his age, he was trading his health for a paycheck. "I'd always been strong, but pretty soon I found I was having to rest going up them steps. There's 196 of them steps to the top and I'd have to stop after 8 or 9 of them. Finally, I told my wife I thought I was going to have to start driving my car from the lot down below up to the top where we'd go in."

In July, 1973, it got so bad Luther was forced to spend eight days in the hospital. "I was a hurtin' and a miserin', but I wouldn't holler for a pain shot, cause one time I hurt my back in the mines and the pain shot they gave me liked to have killed me, buddy."

After missing many days of work, Luther went back to Omar No. 15. But he noticed that the problems kept getting worse. "My feet got heavy and my face felt like it had big welts on it and I would be breathing hard and finally I'd just have to stop and rest," he relates.

"Then, on June 10 of 1974, it got to me. The boss had me shovelin'. He was strictly a company man, but you could reason with him. Just because a man's going to work me, I don't feel hard toward him.

"I'd done come to the point I couldn't shovel. I'd put both hands at the top of the shovel and brace it against my knee and try to push it, but finally I just had to sit down even if it meant getting fired. I just couldn't do nothin'.

"By the time I got to the bathhouse, I felt better. There's an old saying about how you get better right before you die. But before I got home it hit me again. The next day I drove to the doctor to get a breathing shot and on the way home I just about didn't make it—it just tore me up.

"I started to stop my car and turn my flashers on and lay down and figure the state police would come by and think they had a drunk on their hands—I was feeling funny and my head was shakin' and I looked blue. I made it home somehow and yelled for a neighbor and he helped me or I wouldn't have made it."

Several days later, on the way to a doctor to get a slip so he could return to work, Luther "took another spell" and Mrs. David demanded that he quit work. "I told him to turn around and we'd go home," she says. "He wanted to keep working, but I said I didn't care if we lost the home and everything—he had to stop killing himself."

Luther never went back.

On the dining room table, Luther holds an envelope with all of his black lung claim correspondence. On the outside, the envelope has written on it in magic marker: "Black Lung Turndowns." For someone so sick, it is extremely difficult for him to understand how he has been rejected twice for black lung compensation by the federal government. . . .

"I feel the company and the government are shielding one another," Luther says. "They pass the buck back and forth but it never gets to me."

If the black lung law contained the 15-year presumption the United Mine Workers of America is demanding in legislation now pending in Congress, miners with breathing disabilities like Luther's would be assumed to have contracted their impairment as the result of working in the mines. His case, and others like it, make it clear that X-rays and breathing-exercise tests alone are insufficient to prove real occupational disability from black lung.

"I fought for my country in Korea on the front lines and the federal government knew me then," he says. "I came back and worked in the mines and paid my taxes and the federal government knew me then. Now, when I ask them for something that is my right under the law, they don't know me. Buddy, I don't like the way they done me."

BUFFALO CREEK

As has been true from its historic beginnings, coal mining remains the work of an underclass. Here a whole community is wiped out by an "act of God."

Taken from "The Pittston Mentality: Manslaughter on Buffalo Creek," by Thomas N. Bethell and Davitt McAteer, Washington Monthly, *May 1972.*

Buffalo Creek, in Logan County, is reasonably typical for the southern part of West Virginia—a long, winding hollow, snaking between steep ridges on both sides for more than 20 miles from the town of Saunders, at its headwaters, to the town of Man, where the creek empties into the Guyandotte River, which flows north to join the Ohio River at Huntington. The narrow valley is just wide enough for the creek, the railroad, and an almost unending line of company-built houses stretching along both sides of the tracks. There are occasional wide places in the valley where tributaries flow into Buffalo Creek, and in the wide places there used to be towns—small towns that nobody ever heard of, places like Kistler, Crown, Accoville, Braeholm, Fanco, Becco, Amherstdale, Robinette, Latrobe, Crites, Stowe, Lundale, Craneco, Lorado, and Pardee. Some of the names come from coal companies that no longer exist. As coal towns go, these were old, most of them built before World War I. They were in varying stages of decline. Some of them were not much more than post-office addresses. The old frame two-family houses were settling unevenly. Some had collapsed altogether. Others, considering their age and the haste with which they had been built, were in surprisingly good shape. As a general rule, if a house was freshly painted you could assume that a working miner lived there.

The population of Buffalo Creek has fluctuated with the times, declining when the industry declined, recovering when the industry recovered. In 1970, coal had its best year since 1947, and a rosy glow of optimism suffused National Coal Association predictions for the future. Big companies opened new mines along Buffalo Creek and stepped up production in their old ones.

When coal comes up out of the ground, the impurities that come with it are separated out in preparation plants—tipples, as they are more commonly called. The coal rolls away in long, black trains; the impurities stay behind, and something has to be done with them. They have a way of accumulating with staggering speed: a ton of raw coal generally contains up to 25 per cent of extraneous material, and a good-sized tipple, handling the production of several mines at once, will separate out thousands of tons of waste every day. Miners have different names for it—"gob" or "slag" or "culm"—but whatever you call it, it still has to be piled somewhere. In the crowded hollows of West Virginia, finding places to pile slag is a problem of major proportions. As a general rule, no engineer is ever called in to consult on the best and safest locations. Instead, the company superintendent simply hunts around for some vacant space convenient to his tipple, and the slag is dumped there, either by trucks climbing up a mountainside and dumping down the slope, or by an aerial tramway strung between peaks and dumping in the middle. Whatever system is used, the slag is piled up until it is higher than the dumping spot, and then a new pile is started.

Since 1946 a tipple has been in operation at the head of Buffalo Creek. The plant was built by the Lorado Coal Mining Company, a mostly local outfit that sold out to the Buffalo Mining Company in 1964. Buffalo Mining, in turn, sold out in 1970 to the Pittston Company, which is headquartered in New York and is the largest independent producer of coal in the United States. All this time the tipple continued in operation. And all this time it grew. Originally designed to process coal from a single mine, it was expanded periodically as new mines were opened nearby. By 1972 Pittston was operating a total of eight mines in the Buffalo Creek vicinity—five of them underground, three of them stripping jobs. The coal from all eight was processed in the single tipple. On average, the tipple operated six days a week, two shifts a day, handling about 5,200 tons of raw coal daily, shipping out about 4,200 tons of cleaned coal on the long Chesapeake and Ohio trains. That meant that every day a thousand tons of gob, more or less, had to be dumped.

Three tributaries run into Buffalo Creek near the Pittston tipple. From 1947 until about 1955, the refuse was dumped along the hillside a few hundred yards upstream from the tipple, but by 1955 the available space was mostly exhausted and the tipple began dumping a little farther away, across the mouth of a small hollow where the Middle Fork tributary met the creek. At first the gob pile grew slowly—it had to, because most of the hollow behind it was occupied by miners living in company houses. But when production at the tipple increased, the growing gob pile began to menace the houses, and the miners were forced out. The houses were abandoned—some of them were knocked down for the lumber—and the gob was dumped where they had stood. The families moved away, some of them out of West Virginia entirely, some of them only a few hundred yards, settling in vacant houses in the small community of Saunders, which stood facing the gob pile at the intersection of Middle Fork and Buffalo Creek.

The gob pile grew, and grew, and grew more swiftly as the tipple kept expanding production. At first this grotesque black mountain was only an eyesore. Later it became a source of air pollution and a fire hazard. Gob piles may be nothing but waste, but much of that waste is flammable, and a combination of compaction and oxidation can result in spontaneous combustion. Once a fire gets going deep within a gob pile, extinguishing it is nearly impossible. The fire smoulders, sometimes bursts into open flame, fouls the sky with acrid smoke, and occasionally produces an explosion. The federal Bureau of Mines has spent millions of dollars in research on the problem, but the end result is that hundreds of gob piles are smouldering in the Appalachian coalfields right now, and nothing is being done about them. The gob pile at Middle Fork began burning years ago and kept on smouldering.

As the dumping continued, another problem arose. Tipples require vast quantities of water in the cleaning-separating process, but water can be a scarce commodity at times in West Virginia. Partly to provide itself with a reliable year-round supply of water, partly to comply with new state regulations governing stream pollution, Buffalo Mining began to build a series of settling ponds in 1964 (previously the contaminated wash water had simply been sluiced directly into Buffalo Creek, despite the objections of people who liked to fish there). The ponds were created by building retaining dams in the most immediately convenient location —on top of the huge Middle Fork gob pile. By that time the pile had reached stupefying proportions: as high as a 10-story office building, 600 feet across, stretching back into the hollow more than a quarter of a mile. Seeping down through the pile and wandering across the top, the waters of Middle Fork ran sluggishly to join the main stream of Buffalo Creek. Damming the water was a relatively easy task, using the material closest at hand: mine waste. No civil engineer in his right mind would permit the construction of a dam from such materials—as many a civil engineer would later confirm—but no engineer, it now appears, was consulted.

In operation, the settling ponds not only contained runoff water from the hills, but refuse-filled water piped from the tipple. The solid refuse would settle out and clear water could be piped back to the tipple. The first of the ponds impounded a relatively small volume of water, however, and it silted up within a couple of years. A second dam was built in 1967, slightly farther upstream. When the tipple was operating full blast, it required 500,000 gallons of water a day, pumping back between 400 and 500 gallons of waste-filled water every minute. Some of the water would seep out through the porous dam, but the waste settling to the bottom—500 tons every day—rapidly filled the pond, and a third dam was built in 1970. Again, no engineering was involved—just truckloads of mine waste, a bulldozer to push them around, and *presto!* a dam grew across the hollow, built of nothing but junk, standing on a foundation of slime and silt and dead trees. The trees were there because nobody had bothered to cut them down. It was simpler and faster just to dump on top of them.

In West Virginia, February means snow and rain. February meant it this year, as always. In Logan County, there were heavy snows and flash floods—but they were, as the state meteorologist would later point out, "nothing uncommon." At the head of Buffalo Creek, the waters rose behind Pittston's makeshift dam. Early on the morning of February 26, Pittston's local mine boss, Steve Dasovich, sent a bulldozer operator up the access road to the dam with instructions to cut a drainage ditch to relieve the pressure from the swollen lake. The access road winds around a mountainside, with the dam out of sight much of the way. When the bulldozer operator finally came around the last bend and looked through the rain at the dam, he saw with a sudden, terrible shock that it wasn't there.

The dam was gone, and 21 million cubic feet of water and an immeasurable mass of mud and rock and coal wastes were charging through the narrow valley of Buffalo Creek. From where he sat on his suddenly useless machine, the bulldozer operator could look down toward the little town of Saunders—a town consisting of nothing more than a church and some two dozen houses. Now it consisted of nothing at all. Saunders was gone, eradicated completely. Beyond Saunders, the valley curved away out of sight, but the air was filled with the terrifying sound of the flood bearing down on the 15 communities in its path.

There are no slag heaps on Park Avenue and no floods will ever wash through the offices of Joseph P. Routh unless the island of Manhattan sinks into the sea. Thirty-five floors up in the Pan American building, the chairman of the Pittston Company has a commanding view. When he looks down to the street below, he can see Brinks armored trucks moving the wealth of America from place to place. The trucks belong to Joe Routh. A good deal of the money does, too.

Routh is 79 . . . , and he has been making money longer than most men have been alive. He was already a power to be reckoned with when the Pittston Company, which then operated a dozen anthracite mines in Pennsylvania, stumbled into bankruptcy during the Depression. A friend at Manufacturers Trust suggested to Routh that he take over the company and lead it out of the wilderness. The bank sweetened the offer with a $10-million loan—essentially unsecured, since there would be no way to recoup the loss if Pittston went under—and Routh moved in. Anthracite, he concluded, was a dying industry. The future lay in the vast bituminous fields of Virginia and West Virginia. He unloaded most of Pittston's properties in Pennsylvania and began buying up tracts of coal in central Appalachia.

At a time when coal prices fluctuated wildly, he had discovered that the best way to tear loose a chunk of coal in time to take advantage of favorable trends was to strip it from the mountainsides, rather than go through the difficult, two-year-or-more process of engineering and constructing a deep mine. By 1950, when strip-mining was still an infant industry in Appalachia and conservationists hadn't the foggiest notion of the plague to come, one of Routh's companies, Compass Coal, was profitably tearing the hills of Harrison County, West Virginia, to shreds. Since there were no state or federal reclamation requirements, no money had to be spent on binding up the wounds. It must have been the best of all possible worlds, unless you lived near one of Routh's mines. He, of course, didn't.

Routh kept himself busy with other conquests, picking up coal companies in Kentucky, West Virginia, and Virginia, buying up trucking companies and warehouses in New York, enlarging his oil-distributing operations, hatching long-range plans for a giant refinery on the Maine coast. Money flowed from Routh's various holdings into his Manhattan office in a never-ending stream, and Routh bought Brinks, Inc., to carry the cash in his own armored cars.

Despite abundant evidence that he was in no danger of going soft, Routh decided in 1969 to bring in a new president. He looked around for a man to match his own toughness and found one—a 53-year-old native of West Virginia named

Nicholas T. Camicia who had already made a mark in the industry as a notable scrambler. "The coal industry is run by men who got where they are by not being nice," says one former federal official in a position to know, "and when Camicia smiles, you can hear his jaws making a special effort." Routh liked him fine.

But Camicia already had a good job when Routh approached him about taking over Pittston. Routh reportedly told him to write his own ticket, possibly remembering his own reluctance to sign on until Manufacturers Trust gave him the $10 million to play with. Camicia did, in fact, write his own ticket, putting his signature to a contract that has never been publicized, but makes fascinating reading in the archives of the Securities and Exchange Commission. The contract runs until 1976 and not only guarantees Camicia . . . a minimum salary of $100,000 (increased now to $134,000), but stipulates that a deferred salary of $25,000 will be set aside each year, compounded, and paid out to him in 120 monthly installments whenever he quits or gets fired; if he reaches retirement age before that happens, he also qualifies for a hefty pension. The contract also appears to have included some highly attractive stock options; SEC records show, for example, that Camicia picked up 7,200 shares, worth approximately $270,000, for a price of $78,000—less than a third of their market value. That wasn't all. Camicia was living comfortably in an exclusive Chicago suburb when Routh signed him up; in return for agreeing to move to New York, Camicia got Pittston to buy his house for $90,000 and furnish him, cost-free, an equivalent home within commuting distance of Manhattan. He went to work for Joe Routh, reportedly satisfied with the terms of his employment.

If ever there was any doubt that Routh and Camicia were a pair of industry touchdown-twins, it was dispelled early in 1970, when Pittston signed a contract with the Japanese steel industry. The Japanese wanted a long-term contract and were willing to make concessions to get a reliable supply of American coking coal. By 1970 Pittston had gained control of a third of all the available commercial metallurgical coal in the U.S., and no one could offer more reliability than Routh and Camicia. They would not offer it without certain stipulations, however. The contract they signed with the Japanese calls for Pittston to deliver 140 million tons of coal over the next 10 years at a reported average of $15 per ton, which is about twice the going rate elsewhere.

Pittston's directors were so happy last year that they boosted dividends twice. . . . The company now has more than 50 mines working, with nine more under development, and there is no end to the good times in sight.

Is everybody happy? No. Federal mine inspectors in Appalachia are not pleased with Pittston's safety record; they never have been particularly pleased with it, but the past couple of years have been especially bad. Nine miners lost their lives in 1971 in Pittston mines (two of them in the newly acquired Buffalo Mining division), another 743 were seriously hurt, and the company's accident frequency rate was one of the highest in the coal industry. The record in 1970 was even worse: 18 dead. Investigators found that in a solid majority of the fatal accidents bad management practices (rather than personal carelessness) were to blame. "The company appears to be sincere in its desire for health and safety throughout its mines," one inspector wrote. "This desire," he added drily, "is not always fulfilled." Not always. All told, some 98 men have been killed in Pittston's mines in the past decade, and a 1963 explosion in which 22 men died still ranks as one of the worst of recent disasters. Three or four thousand men have been seriously injured or maimed in the company's mines since 1962, and the U.S. Public Health Service estimates that as many as 5,000 Pittston miners may have developed pneumoconiosis during that time. The profit margin of the new Japanese contract is a reported 24 per cent, almost three times the normal profit margin in the coal industry; you can't help marveling at how much of that money will be going back to the disabled derelicts living out their lives in Appalachia after destroying themselves to help make Joe Routh a millionaire for the third or fourth time.

Pittston's stockholders don't have to concern themselves with such things, because they don't hear about them. The company's handsome four-color annual reports talk about money, not about people. There are pictures of freshly painted oil storage tanks, spotless armored trucks, gleaming computer banks—and aerial pictures of the long, black coal trains winding their way through seemingly virgin Appalachian valleys. The pictures are taken with care: on the inside back cover of the 1971 report there is a color shot of lovely hills and hollows with a sturdy complex of mine buildings prominent in the foreground. "Aerial view of the Lorado Mine of newly acquired Buffalo Mining Company," the caption reads. Beyond the mine, railroad tracks stretch away, disappearing behind a hill. If you could see beyond that hill, you would see the massive, smouldering gob pile that stood at the head of Buffalo Creek, and on top of it the jerry-built dams that Pittston used with its preparation plant. But those things are not part of the picture, not part of the annual report. As far as Pittston's stockholders were concerned, they never existed—not until the morning of February 26, when suddenly the dams collapsed and the burning gob pile erupted and all hell broke loose.

Helicopters were still thrashing back and forth between Buffalo Creek and the nearest hospitals when reporters began calling Pittston's New York headquarters to find out what the company had been doing to cause such a monstrous disaster. Camicia and Routh weren't available, wouldn't answer the telephones, wouldn't return calls. Finally, Mary Walton of the Charleston *Gazette* flushed out a Pittston lawyer who insisted on remaining anonymous, but was willing to give the company's point of view. "It was an act of God," he said.

" 'Act of God' is a legal term," Robert Weedfall remarked when he heard about Pittston's explanation of the flood. "There are other legal terms—terms like 'involuntary manslaughter because of stupidity' and 'criminal negligence.' " Weedfall is the West Virginia state climatologist, the man who keeps track of basic acts of God such as rain and snow. He was in a better position than anyone else to know whether there could be any possibility that Pittston's dam had collapsed from natural causes, and he was convinced that it had not—could not have—not by any stretch of the imagination. There had been heavy rainfall in Logan County during the week of February 26, and considerable flooding. But it was nothing uncommon for February, Weedfall said, and he had the statistics to prove it. When reporters called him they were impressed with his conviction. Pittston officials had called, too, looking for ways to document their private theory of divine intervention. Weedfall wasn't much help.

Nor were the technical specialists of the Department of the Interior who arrived from Washington and, in the aftermath of the disaster, poked and probed among the ruins in search of clues. The U.S. Geological Survey sent a crew, as did the Bureau of Mines; the Bureau of Reclamation summoned a former chief of its

Earth Dams Section from retirement. The investigators examined the remains of the dam in microscopic detail, interviewed Pittston workers and company officials (who would not talk to reporters), and pieced together a convincing account of what had happened and why. None of the investigators showed any doubt that the dams had been badly engineered. Fred Walker, the retired Bureau of Reclamation expert, went further, refusing to use the word "dam" to describe the structures. "Locally these barriers are called dams, but to me this is unacceptable nomenclature," he wrote. "These structures were created by persons completely unfamiliar with dam design, construction, and materials, and by construction methods that are completely unacceptable to engineers specializing in dam design."

West Virginia law, Walker noted, "requires permits, approval of plans, and inspection during construction for impoundments more than 10 feet deep. I was unable to find that such requirements had ever been complied with." Suggesting that similar potentially disastrous situations could be found elsewhere in the coalfields, Walker commented scathingly that "fortunately most of these barriers are built in valleys that have small watersheds above them, as apparently little if any consideration is given to the flood hazard involved." . . .

. . . Apparently no one saw the actual moment when the dam finally gave way. It seems to have happened very fast, the dam settling until water was running across the top, the water cutting a cleft into the dam, more water hurrying through, and then complete and total collapse, and millions of gallons of water and hundreds of thousands of tons of sludge streaming across the top of the slag pile at the beginning of catastrophe.

The water cascaded into the burning section of the slag heap and erupted in a volcanic explosion. Men were coming off shift at the tipple and saw what was happening; they saw a mushroom cloud burst into the air from the explosion, saw mud and rock thrown 300 feet into the sky, saw the windshields of their pick-up trucks covered with steaming mud. They raced back up the road and tried to use the telephone at the tipple to send out a warning, but the line was already dead. The tipple was safe—it was upstream, up another fork of the creek, out of the path of the destruction—but the men were cut off from the mainstream of Buffalo Creek and there was no way they could help anyone. They could only watch as the water and sludge crested over the top of the exploding gob pile and burst into the valley, "boiling up like dry flour when you pour water on it."

The flood traveled at first at a speed of at least 30 miles an hour—in a solid wall 20 or 30 feet high. People who saw it coming as they headed up the Buffalo Creek road barely had time to throw their cars into reverse, turn around wherever there was room, and head back downstream, leaning on their horns, flashing their lights, trying to warn other people who had heard the explosions but still did not know what was happening. There was very little time to do anything. It takes a few seconds to collect your wits when you see a wall of water bearing down on you, especially when you live in a valley where there are only a few exits—hollows running at right angles to the main valley. For most of the people who died, it was like being in the barrel of a gun and seeing the bullet coming. There was nowhere to go.

That so many people did escape is something of a miracle. Nearly 5,000 people lived in the path of the flood. Probably a thousand were caught up in it, battered, left shaken and sometimes badly hurt, but alive. From the wreckage of 16 communities, the bodies of 118 people have been found. There are others still missing; the final toll may be close to 150.

What happens after a disaster of such magnitude? There are inquiries, of course, and inquiries are under way in West Virginia. But in Appalachian affairs, the official response tends to have a common theme. After the Farmington mine disaster killed 78 miners, it was an Interior Department assistant secretary who said brightly: "We don't know why these things happen, but they do." After the 1970 mine explosion that killed 38 men in Kentucky, it was a newly installed director of the Bureau of Mines who said: "We can almost expect one of these every year." While the search for bodies was still continuing in Logan County, West Virginia's Governor Arch Moore was already defending the Pittston Company: the sludge-built dam had served a "logical and constructive" use by filtering mine wastes that would otherwise have gone unfiltered into Buffalo Creek. It didn't seem to matter much how the thing was built. The state legislature chose not to investigate, instead, leaving to the governor the selection of an official commission which would be told to report back by the end of summer. "It's easy to say that the dam shouldn't have been there," Moore said at one point. "But it had been there for 25 years." He was technically wrong, of course, but the inference seemed to be that if a hazard simply exists long enough, it has a right to be left alone. And by the same token, the Governor made it painfully clear that he would ask the same treatment for the problems of West Virginia. The real tragedy, he said, a tragedy greater even than what had befallen the people of Buffalo Creek, was the unflattering coverage of West Virginia in the national press.

In fact there had been precious little of that. The flood had been on page one for two or three days, but it was eclipsed by the President's tour through China (from Shanghai, where he learned of the flood, Nixon sent an expression of regret, concluding from a distance of many thousands of miles that it was a terrible "natural disaster" and promising speedy federal aid), and within a week it would be forgotten, dismissed as one of those things—*Time*, for example, observed that the people of Buffalo Creek would have been well-advised to live elsewhere, but that they had stayed on in the shadow of the smouldering gob pile presumably because "that was the only life they knew."

The Interior Department, meanwhile, explained through Assistant Secretary Hollis Dole that there was, in its opinion, no federal responsibility in the matter, despite the fact that regulations within the 1969 Federal Coal Mine Health and Safety Act specifically cover the construction and use of gob piles and retaining dams. There were no indications that the government would move to take action against Pittston, unless it was prodded by an outraged Congress; on Capitol Hill there was no outraged Congress to be found.

There would be room for doubt, in any event, about the kind of action that Interior would take even if it were forced to do something. The Department is reluctant to think of itself as a regulatory agency, or as a federal cop, and among all of the subordinate agencies within Interior, the Bureau of Mines is a standout example of one that has refused to grasp the idea of representing the public interest. The problem might not be serious if a system of countervailing power were in operation—if, for example, the people of Buffalo Creek could have counted on the United Mine Workers to represent them against the overwhelming resources and indifference of the Pittston Company. There had been scattered efforts along Buffalo Creek to protest against the slag heaps and the sludge dams —petitions had been circulated, attention had been demanded. But the effort never went anywhere, and it never went anywhere partly because no powerful organization—like the union—chose to push it. . . . The result is that on one side of the equation there is a powerful industry deeply dedicated to its own interests; on the other side there is, most of the time, nothing at all. And in the middle, where there should be an even-handed government agency, there is instead the Bureau of Mines, an organization so encrusted with age and bureaucracy that it will not even support its own inspectors when they try to do their jobs.

They had, for example, been trying to do their jobs at Pittston's mines, trying to cut down the number of men killed in needless accidents. Over the past year they had slapped thousands of violation notices on the company. The idea is that the notices will cost money; get fined often enough and hard enough, the theory goes, and you will become safety-conscious in the extreme. It hasn't worked that way. Thanks to a highly complex assessment system set up in Washington by a former lobbyist who is now in charge of the Bureau's fines-collection operation, Pittston has been able to defer, seemingly indefinitely, any payment for its sins. Specifically, over the past year inspectors had fined Pittston a total of $1,303,315 for safety violations. As of April 1, the company had appealed every one of the notices it had received, and had paid a grand total of $275 to the government.

Meanwhile, on Buffalo Creek, the investigations continue, the reports are compiled, the survivors try to plan a future; the mines, only briefly disrupted by the raging flood, are back at work, and the long trains roll. One month after the disaster, Pittston set up an office to process claims—without, however, accepting liability. The company's official view is still that God did it—and if, by any chance, God should pass the buck back down, "we believe that the investigations of the tragedy have not progressed to the point where it is possible to assess responsibility." It's possible that such a point will never be reached. Who was responsible, for example, for deciding to spend $90,000 to buy Nicholas Camicia's house, but *not* to spend the $50,000 that it might have cost—according to one of the federal reports—to build a safe dam at the head of Buffalo Creek? There are sticky questions like that rising in the aftermath of the disaster, questions that will be hard to answer. "There is never peace in West Virginia because there is never justice," said Mother Jones, the fiery hell-raiser of West Virginia's early labor wars. On Buffalo Creek these days there is a strange kind of quiet, a peacefulness of sorts, but it is not the kind that comes with justice.

WESTERN COAL

Since the mid-1960s the focus of the coal industry has shifted away from Appalachia to the rich, virgin fields of the West. There vast deposits of coal lie just beneath the surface of the land, all along the eastern slope of the Rockies. Although oil companies have increasingly large holdings in coal in the West, much of the coal is still owned either by individual states or by the federal government. The Council on Economic Priorities provides a summary of the situation in the western coal fields, along with an analysis of the impact of mining.

Although this report was first published in 1974, there has been little substantive change in the basic policies portrayed here. In 1981 the Department of the Interior made its first coal leases after a ten-year moratorium during which the government studied the effect of coal leasing on public lands. In late 1980 there were 565 federal coal leases outstanding in fourteen states, covering 812,000 acres and containing 16.5 billion tons of recoverable coal.

The Council on Economic Priories is a nonprofit organization which periodically publishes information on practices of U.S. corporations in areas that vitally affect society, including environmental quality, military production, consumer practices, and so on.

Taken from "Leased and Lost, a Study of Public and Indian Coal Leasing in the West," Economic Priorities Report, *Vol. 5, No. 1, 1974.*

If the energy shortage pushes coal development in the western states as far and as fast as present predictions tell us it will, the land and the life of those states will be profoundly changed. Some 20 billion tons of coal under nearly one million acres of public and Indian land have been leased by the Department of Interior to private industry. Interior has leased this land in the absence of a national energy strategy, without considering the environmental effects of strip mining, and without taking into account the economic and social impact coal development will have on the lives of the people in the leasing areas. If this leased coal is mined and used to fuel the huge energy producing projects that are planned for the West, the economic and social patterns of the affected states will be changed from rural agrarian to mining, and perhaps to urban industrial. The environmental quality that has made the intermountain West a recreation capital for the nation will be substantially degraded.

. . . Coal development raises even graver questions for the Indians of the West. Bob Bailey, a Northern Cheyenne from Montana, says, "The question is, do we perpetuate ourselves or do we extinguish ourselves? The very land we stand on, sleep on, eat on, will be torn up. This is our last piece of land, and if we lose it, we'll be Indians without lands in the future."

Most of the large scale coal development projects planned for the West by coal developers and utilities will be located in the Northern Plains which stretch across northeastern Wyoming, southeastern Montana, and western North Dakota, or in the Indian lands of the Southwest. This land includes some of the most beautiful country in the United States.

In October, 1971, the Bureau of Reclamation and 35 power companies jointly released the *North Central Power Study* which suggested that since the nation's overall fuel reserves were running low, the time had come to tap the huge coal reserves of the Fort Union Formation. These coal beds contain close to 40% of the nation's total coal reserves, almost 85% of which belong to the public or to Indian tribes.

The study located potential sites for 42 power plants. Thirteen of them were to have a generating capacity of more than 10,000 megawatts. The study suggested that an additional 50,000 megawatts of generating capacity be built for the area by 1985, rising to 197,000 megawatts by the end of the century. This would give the Northern Plains alone more generating capacity than the current electrical production of any country in the world except the US and Russia.

Coal gasification facilities are also planned for the Northern Plains. A draft report of the combined federal and state Northern Great Plains Resource Program, released in 1974, concludes that the "most probable scenario" for the Northern Plains includes seven gasification plants operating by 1985 and 16 by the end of the century.

Coal companies have begun to lease reserves to supply these planned gasification plants. Between 1969 and 1971, the Northern Cheyenne tribe auctioned prospecting permits for 52% of their reservation, or 243,000 acres, for about $2.5 million. Six prospecting permits, all owned by Peabody Coal Company, have been converted into leases. Peabody has pledged 500 million tons of coal from its leases to supply at least two gasification plants which will be built near the reservation by Northern Natural Gas Company and Cities Service Gas Company jointly. The first plant is scheduled for completion in 1979.

Consolidation Coal Company, a subsidiary of Continental Oil, has asked the Northern Cheyenne to lease an additional 70,000 acres. The company would like to build four gasification plants on the reservation. The 30,000,000 tons of coal needed to fuel them each year would be strip mined from the lease tract.

Shell Oil, American Metal's Climax (AMAX) and Westmoreland Resources hold leases to 75,358 acres of Crow reservation land adjacent to the Northern Cheyenne. Westmoreland has already invested $34 million in strip mining operations and plans to mine four million tons each year. The company has contracted to supply nearly 80 million tons of coal over the next 20 years to four Midwestern utilities. Three hundred million more tons of Crow coal have been optioned to Colorado Interstate Gas Company to be used in a gasification plant that is now planned for Montana.

The Southwest will be another major coal development target. Most of the coal there is owned by the Navajo and Hopi tribes in northeastern Arizona and northwestern New Mexico. In 1964, 23 investor and publicly owned utilities and several government agencies formed a consortium to plan, construct, and operate an electricity generating network to feed power hungry southern California and the burgeoning southwestern cities. Called WEST (Western Energy Supply and Transmission Associates), the consortium has built two power plants and has three more under construction. The group hopes to add 36,000 megawatts of generating capacity to the Southwest by 1990. That will give it three times the capacity of the nation's largest utility, the Tennessee Valley Authority.

These power plants will be fueled primarily by coal mined on land leased from the Hopi and Navajo tribes. The two plants in operation are Arizona Public Service's Four Corners facility, a 2,085 megawatt behemoth located in Fruitland, New Mexico, and Southern California Edison's 1,580 megawatt Mohave Plant. The spewing smokestacks of the Four Corners plant earned notoriety several years back as the only manmade creation visible to the Apollo astronauts. These plants burn a total of 12 million tons of coal each year.

Seven gasification plants are under construction in the Southwest. Each will produce 250 million cubic feet of natural gas a day and consume eight million tons of coal and 20,000 acre feet of water a year. One hundred square miles of Indian land will be strip mined to provide coal for these plants over the next 35 years.

Over 1500 square miles of land, about the area of the Great Salt Lake, could be stripped to extract western coal in the next 35 years. Strip mining destroys the economic role of the surface land during mining and the existing surface ecosystem permanently. A debate is now raging over the true reclamation potential of stripped land.

The land loses its usefulness for any purpose other than mining while coal is being stripped. The surface that covers 63% of the strippable coal in the West is privately owned by farmers and ranchers who make a living from it. The surface rights to much of this land passed into private hands under the Homestead Act of 1863 while the mineral rights were retained by the government. In Montana, 97% of the publicly owned strippable coal lies under privately owned surface; in North Dakota, the figure is 100%. Strip mining will destroy a segment of the area's largest industry, agriculture, and uproot the people who now work the land.

The economic impact of this preemption will vary. Navajo reservation land atop Black Mesa is so arid that sheep ranchers need 30 acres to support each sheep. Stripping 400 acres a year in this region will displace only 13 sheep annually. This land will probably be lost to sheep ranching for centuries, however, because of the extremely low reclamation potential of desert land.

The Northern Plains are also dry, but there is enough moisture and fertile soil to support farming. Wheat yields are among the highest of any part of the country, and cattle ranchers need only two to two and a half acres a head. As food prices skyrocket, this land is becoming more valuable to farmers and to the nation.

In addition to the temporary dislocation that strip mining causes, some evidence suggests that the surface is permanently altered. Draglines remove the topsoil along with the overburden, destroying the ecosystem which has developed over slow centuries of biological succession. Deep pits disrupt the groundwater system, causing the water table to fall and creating hydrological repercussions in areas far from the mine site. Coal seams are the principal aquifers, or underground waterways, in the Northern Plains. They are often close to the surface, providing the underground irrigation that makes much of that arid area surprisingly lush, but this very closeness to the surface also makes them attractive to strip miners. Once they are removed, groundwater must find new channels. It often goes deep underground, leaving reclaimed areas too dry to support the kinds of vegetation that grew there before the land was stripped.

Stripping also contaminates surface runoff water with subsoil chemicals, that are shaken loose during the digging. Additional areas where the overburden is dumped are defaced with sterile spoils banks.

The National Academy of Sciences (NAS) report, *Rehabilitation Potential of Western Coal Lands,* was released in the fall of 1973. Probably the most comprehensive document on reclamation to date, the report bluntly states that restoration of stripped land "is not possible anywhere." What is possible, at best, is "the rehabilitation of land to a stable ecological state that does not contribute to environmental destruction and is consistent with surrounding aesthetic values." Carl Wambolt, Ph.D. and range specialist at Montana State University, says "reclamation efforts in the West have not yet provided the diversity and other characteristics required to return mined lands to their former wildlife carrying capacity."

No strip mined land in the West has been successfully reclaimed to date. The President's Council on Environmental Quality concluded in a recent report to the Senate Committee on Interior and Insular Affairs that "acceptable reclamation of these semi-arid lands has yet to be demonstrated."

Strip miners promise that land can be adequately reclaimed, although they are quick to add that much more research is needed. Utah International has said its reseeding program at the Navajo mine in New Mexico "will ultimately provide a higher grade of livestock forage than ever existed on this arid rangeland." . . .

The Northern Plains Resource Council (NPRC), a coalition of ranchers in eastern Montana, points out that even if some test plots are revegetated successfully, so much fertilizer, seed and water would be needed to maintain them, that the cost would be prohibitive and quantities of water unavailable to apply the method on a large scale.

Bill Mitchell, a biologist with the NPRC, says, "In Ohio AMAX planted crown vetch. Its forage value is not very high. From a rancher's point of view, that's not reclamation. It's a question of semantics. What does reclamation mean? That they can get something to grow, or that they've created a successful, reproducing ecosystem?

"They're mining native perennial range here in Montana. That short grass prairie is some of the best beef country in the world. The annual grasses they plant on the reclamation plots are invasive, squeezing out the perennials on good land, so you get double damage. Burlington Northern smoothed over a lot of 50 year-old spoils banks and planted rye with water and fertilizer. No rancher in his right mind wants that in his hay. They can't grow alfalfa, and they plant a lot of it.

"They don't know how whether these revegetated spots will survive an extreme season. That will take years. They'll have to use biological succession [the progression of plant communities from the simple to the complex, each stage prepares the soil for the succeeding community], and that takes time. Acceptable reclamation for a rancher would be the development of a native perennial range.

"I think revegetation is a kind of red herring because no one claims they can restore the ground water. They want to mine the lush meadows. That's sub-irrigated pastureland, the water is near the surface. They don't know how to restore a sub-surface aquifer." . . .

The NAS study determined that over and above the willingness of corporations to invest large sums of money in reclamation programs, the amount of rainfall in an area is the "limiting factor" in reclamation. The NAS concluded that areas that received over 10 inches of rain a year have a "high potential" for reclamation if large sums are expended on the effort over a number of years. About 60% of western coal land, including the Northern Plains, receives more than 10 inches of rain a year.

In the Southwest, with its less than 10 inches of annual rainfall, revegetation "may not occur for centuries," no matter how extensive a reclamation project is attempted. The NAS says that surface mining in these areas "amounts to sacrificing such values [as aesthetics] permanently for economic reward." The report suggests that these areas either be spared the burden of mining, or that they will be declared "National Sacrifice Areas" where reclamation will not even be attempted.

WATER

The most staggering changes facing the West may result not from stripping the land itself, but from the secondary effects of mining. Foremost among these will be the changes in water use patterns that large scale development will cause. The Montana Coal Task Force says, "Water controls all activity in this semi-arid region."

The plans for coal development project that have been announced to date will severely tax available water supplies. The National Academy of Sciences says that the water supply in Montana is "completely committed, perhaps overcommitted," that Wyoming's supply is nearly accounted for, and that the Colorado River Basin water options represent a "de facto overcommitment." *Science* reported the NAS findings in October, 1973, noting, "there simply is not enough water in the Western states to permit the enormous congregations of coal-fired generating, gasification, and liquefication plants envisioned in recent years by utilities and oil companies . . . any large-scale commitment of water to on-the-spot consumption of coal would lock such states as Montana, Wyoming, and the Dakotas into a coal based economy they hadn't bargained for."

Coal development is proceeding despite the scarcity of water. A single gasification plant will consume 20,000 acre feet of water a year. [An acre foot is the quantity of water necessary to cover one acre of land to a depth of one foot, or 326,000 gallons.] Water needed to supply the 14 gasification plants planned for 1985 will drain over a quarter million acre feet, with sharper rises expected after that. The gasification process hydrolizes the water into hydrogen and oxygen, so it will not be returned to the river, aqueduct or aquifer from which it was drawn, but will actually be consumed in the production system. Unlike water used for irrigation or industrial cooling, this water will be lost to the western ecosystem permanently, further drying out an already arid land.

About 28 cubic feet of water per second, or 20,270 acre feet a year, are required to cool the generating equipment for a 1,000 megawatt plant. Development of the 50,000 megawatt capacity predicted for the Northern Plains by 1985 will create a demand for 1,000,000 acre feet of cooling water. Most of this water will be returned to a waterway 10° to 15° hotter than it was before it entered the plant. The rest will be lost through evaporation.

The diversion of large quantities of water to coal development will severely strain the water resources in the West and preempt agriculture in favor of coal development even in non-mining areas. For example, an estimated 2,000,000 acre feet of water a year will be needed for coal development in the upper Missouri River Basin by 1990. The estimated total potential, as opposed to present, water supply will be only 3,100,000 acre feet. Coal development in eastern Montana could cut the flow of the Yellowstone River by one-third of its normal rate, and will reduce it to a mere trickle in times of drought. The Navajo tribe has already assigned two-thirds of its Colorado River water allotment to coal development corporations, eliminating the possible future use of that water for irrigation. . . .

Some compromises will have to be made between agriculture and coal development if an equitable distribution of the West's scarce water resources is to be made. The speed with which coal development companies have been acquiring water rights threatens to negate any chances for a balance. The Northern Plains Resource Council fears that present and future diversions of water for coal development "could result in the severe curtailment of future urban, recreational, and agricultural water use in this area."

DIRT

Mining and generating electricity are water polluting activities. Strip mining disrupts the chemical composition of the ground. Much of the soil in the Northern Plains and the Southwest is high in alkaline salts. Normally the salts are leached out of the upper soil layers. The deeper the soil, the higher the concentration of salts, so vegetation grows near the surface in the least alkaline soil. Stripping mixes surface and deep soil together, resulting in a uniform salt concentration that is too high for most vegetation to withstand.

Rain or irrigation water that soaks through the stripped surface carries the freed salts into the subsurface aquifers. This water eventually flows into rivers or its tapped by wells where the effects of alkaline pollution become significant. Fish begin to die, cattle are sickened by contaminated wells, and crops irrigated with this water are stunted or killed.

Increased sedimentation is another water pollution problem. Stripping loosens the normally compact soil. Rain or irrigation water carries some of the loose soil away to streams and rivers. Fish suffocate in the murky water, and aquatic plants are buried under the sludge banks which form along river banks.

Fly ash, an air pollutant created by coal burned in power plants, can become a water pollutant. The fly ash is collected before it passes into the atmosphere and is usually dumped in landfills. Rainwater soaks through the fly ash, picking up chemicals from it and contaminating the groundwater supplies. Finally, domestic sewage can be a water pollution problem. Local treatment facilities will be overwhelmed by the larger numbers of people who migrate into the area to build and operate the mines, the power and gasification plants, and ancillary businesses.

Air pollution is already emerging as a problem in the Southwest, and it is increasing. The sight of majestic Shiprock and other natural wonders of the Canyon de Chelly have been cheapened by the brown cloud that clings to the earth. The fly ash and soot which reduce visibility and contrast pose a serious health hazard. The particles can lodge in the lungs, aggravating or causing respiratory ailments.

Strip mining kicks some dust into the air, but the major air pollution sources are the coal-burning power plants near the mines. One to two hundred pounds of soot and fly ash can be released by every ton of coal that is burned. Air pollution control devices such as electrostatic precipitators, scrubbers, and baghouse filters can capture more than 99% of these emissions, but a single plant burning tens of thousands of tons of coal every day will still produce a staggering amount of pollution. Even after removal of 99.5% of the fly ash, the power plants planned for the Northern Plains by 1985 will pour 100,000 tons of particulates into the air every year.

Some 50,000 megawatts of additional electrical generating capacity are planned for the Northern Plains by 1985. According to Environmental Defense Fund calculations, the air pollution that will result from development on such a scale will produce more air pollution than that which now chokes the 9,219 square-mile Los Angeles basin.

Most of the coal in the West is low sulfur coal (less than 1% sulfur content), but the vast quantities which will be burned when large scale coal development takes place will still release huge amounts of sulfur dioxide. Sulfur dioxide is poisonous to human beings and other animal and plant life. It reacts with water in the atmosphere to form sulfuric acid which comes to earth during storms as "acid rainfalls." The acid can severely damage crops. By 1985, power plants in the Northern Plains alone are expected to emit over two million tons of sulfur dioxide a year.

Nitrogen oxide is another major air pollutant caused by burning coal. It combines with ozone and carbon in the air to form the brown clouds known as smog. Nearly 1,250,000 tons of nitrogen oxide will be released by power plants in the Northern Plains by 1985.

In addition to this pollution, the air in the West will be tainted with exhaust fumes from the cars and trucks of the people who follow the new jobs into the area, by the smokestacks of other industries that will move near the new power sources, and by the garbage incinerators of the new towns that are springing up in the West. . . .

PEOPLE IMPACT

It is extremely difficult to estimate the effect that coal development will have on the lives and culture of the people who live in the West. It is even harder to say whether the changes will be for better or worse. . . .

The sudden jump in population growth, the emergence of urban centers, and the possible "boom-bust" economic cycle will cause many social and cultural changes. The Bureau of Reclamation predicts that coal development in the Northern Plains could result in "the sevenfold increase in the present population." Between 200,000 and 400,000 people are expected to migrate into eastern Montana. The Northern Cheyenne will be outnumbered ten to one by whites on their own reservation if Consolidation Coal Company proceeds with its mining plans.

The Council on Environmental Quality reports, "There are few, if any, cities and villages in the [region] that could absorb these new employees and their families without extensive changes in their public and private capital facilities and, in many cases, their way of life."

. . . It is probable that in the next quarter century, several cities of one hundred thousand people will spring up in the Northern Plains in the wake of massive coal development.

This growth will provide increased income and a larger tax base for western communities, but it will overstrain public facilities and services. Hundreds of miles of highways must be built, and dozens of schools, hospitals and sewage treatment facilities must be provided. Government services, including police and fire protection and garbage collection, must expand to meet the demand. All of this must come in a hurry because, in terms of urban planning timetables, development will happen overnight.

State and local governments are struggling to do the best they can, often without knowing exactly what to prepare for. Eldon Rice, the head of Montana's brand new Rosebud County planning agency, is trying to deal with rising housing costs, the influx of trailers, additional school children, sewage problems, and increased crime and bar fights. "It's the people impact," says Rice. "I'm not sure the industrial impact would be so bad, but it's the people impact."

The West is ill-prepared to deal with rampaging growth, and very little regional planning has been done on the state or federal level. . . .

The spectre of boom-bust economics weighs heavily on the West. The region must equip itself to deal with changes that could be as temporary as they are rapid. The average coal mine produces for about 35 years. Power and gasification plants last the same length of time. When the coal is gone, the mining and related industries move on to new supplies of coal, taking much of the economic life and the tax base of the community with them. Congressman Ken Hechler (D-W. Va.) says, "Strip mining is like taking seven or eight stiff drinks. You are riding high as long as the coal lasts, but the hangover comes when the coal is gone and the jobs are gone and the bitter truth of the morning after leaves a barren landscape and a mouth full of ashes."

The West is no stranger to the boom-bust economics of mining, but the extent of strip mined coal development will be unprecedented. Westerners are afraid that their homeland will become another Appalachia. If reclamation is not successful, the region's cultural base will be permanently destroyed, and the people will not be able to pick up the remnants of their old life style. The Northern Plains Resource Council asks. "Will we have at the end [of 35 years] a series of dying and ghostly towns spread across the prairie, an Indian community submerged in a white mining culture and a marginally productive agricultural community?"

. . . The growth which coal mining in the West absorbs is growth the eastern coal regions will not get. With Appalachian coal reserves of 240 billion recoverable tons, including 80 billion tons of low sulfur coal, and with unemployment in many Appalachian regions running over 9%, western coal expansion could be at the expense of Appalachia.

It could make better economic sense for the nation to turn to Appalachian coal to meet the needs of the energy crunch. This point of view is given some support, for a different reason, by Howard Odum, professor of environmental engineering at the University of Florida, and Joel Shatz, an energy consultant for the state of Oregon. They point out that the true value of an energy producing resource is not equal to the energy of the fuel where it is found but rather to the energy which is available to do work producing goods and services for our society *after* the expenditure of the energy necessary to extract the fuel and transport it to its point of use.

Odum and Shatz say that as we move farther away from markets to find energy, the net amount of energy available to society decreases. This means that even if a dollar will buy the same amount of coal five years from now as it buys today, more of its energy content will be consumed to transported it to the place where it can do work. To get the same amount of work done and to produce the same amount of goods and services, you will have to buy more coal, so the same standard of living will be more costly.

Odum and Shatz suggest that if the nation develops energy sources far away from markets or in hard-to-mine regions, it will push the nation into an inflationary spiral, eroding the standard of living. Their theories do not preclude the use of western coal to meet short term energy needs or its use as part of a well organized national energy policy. In the absence of such a policy, however, they believe that massive western coal development could do more economic harm than good to the country. . . .

The nation has enough time and expertise to plan coal development and minimize its adverse effects. The present system of planning by default threatens to lock the West and the country as a whole into a long term commitment which has more liabilities than any of us ever bargained for.

WORK IN THE MINE

John L. Lewis believed that mechanization, wrought under the pressure of increasing labor costs, would push the coal industry into a coherent framework and lead to improvement in the working conditions of mine workers.

There is little question that there have been improvements in the mine. But the mine, as depicted by Lewis Mumford in the opening passages of this book, remains a dangerous and brutal place of work. As Curtis Seltzer argues below, the revival of coal as a primary fuel source in all likelihood will lead to more injuries and deaths, raising once more the issue of social costs in this form of energy production. Indeed, these social costs of injury, death, and disease in deep mines must be weighed against the purely environmental damage described in the preceding section.

Taken from "Coal Miners: Energy War Casualties," by Curtis Seltzer, Washington Post, *May 27, 1979.*

That nobody died at Three Mile Island is a cliché from pro-nuclear circles. But the long-run political fallout may prove something else: that the Three Mile Island nuclear scare killed a lot of coal miners.

Since Washington is a town where pressures rather than problems are resolved, the search is on for a quick fix for the nuclear jitters, and coal is likely to be the windfall fuel of the Harrisburg accident. It is abundant and readily mined; output can be tripled with current technology.

Many utilities will turn to coal-fired electricity if a moratorium or phaseout on nuclear power is imposed. And the reason is simple: Coal costs are reasonably predictable and profits fairly dependable. With fuel-supply forecasts predicting that utilities will swing away from oil and gas, less nuclear generation means even greater use of coal.

Coal, however, carries its own risks and costs to human health and safety. The administration's plan to substitute coal for oil (and perhaps nuclear power) will endanger tens of thousands of miners unless mining is done differently.

Coal mine fatalities and injuries are likely to increase 35 percent and 39 percent respectively if annual production in 1985 is two-thirds greater than in 1977 (688 million tons), a new study, "The Direct Use of Coal," by the Congressional Office of Technology Assessment predicts.

If production almost triples by 2000, so will the body count. OTA suggests 370 fatalities and 42,000 disabling injuries is the likely annual toll.

Coal comes relatively cheap in dollars and relatively dear in human lives. From a work force of 230,000, 139 miners were killed in 1977 and 15,000 injured, each injury disabling the worker for two months on the average. That's both better and worse than 10 years ago.

After a 78-victim disaster in 1968 at a Consolidation Coal mine, Congress passed radical mine safety legislation to eliminate the causes of multi-victim explosions.

The 1969 Federal Coal Mine Health and Safety Act worked. Many fewer miners are now killed in disasters. Yet little change has been recorded since 1973 in the annual number of coal mine fatalities. Without the disasters—and the finger-pointing publicity they generated—the catalyst for tighter regulation is gone.

The 1969 act did not deal specifically with preventing injuries. For every million hours worked, 50 underground miners suffered a disabling injury in 1977. That is the same rate recorded throughout the 1950s and 1960s. Further, the number of disabling injuries has been rising steadily as more miners are hired to mine more coal.

Ten years ago, Congress also addressed the scandal of work-related lung disease among coal miners.

A strict dust standard was phased in that, the legislators were told, would prevent new cases of disabling lung disease and arrest the progression of those already in evidence. Today questions are asked about the inherent safety of this standard. And other questions have been raised about how many of the nation's 6,000 mines actually comply with the standard every day. A recent study done in east Kentucky found that more than one-quarter of the workplace dust samples the operators submitted to the government were no higher than those taken in fresh air. That, the study said, is "unrealistically low."

Compliance with the current dust standard should drastically reduce the number of miners disabled by pneumoconiosis in the future. Yet it is not a zero-risk standard. Assuming diligent compliance, OTA says that more than 10,000 cases of pneumoconiosis will be found among working miners in 2000. Even more cases of bronchitis, emphysema and other lung impairments are likely.

Anyone with grade-school multiplication skills can work up such body counts. Indeed, several in the executive branch already have. Yet mine safety stands cold on the political back burner, and I think the following reasons and attitudes explain why.

Coal miners are a small, back-country, working-class group. As such, they lack clout in Washington, especially in the administration. They are viewed more often as a necessary nuisance than as a constituency.

The industry and the country have traditionally underwritten cheap coal through cheap safety. More than 110,000 miners have been killed on the job since 1900 and at least 4 million have been injured.

Casualties are to be expected on any battlefield, and the "moral equivalent of war" is no different. This attitude is akin to that expressed by an official of the 1910 census who said, "The best interests of society will be served by permitting the least valuable members of the mining communities to be the victims."

Miners are segregated from the general population, as are their hurts. Nuclear power, on the other hand, democratizes risk by spreading it across class lines and by involving millions of people across the country (instead of only thousands in Appalachia). Were miners conscripted from the general population, their safety would no longer be swept under the moldy rugs of federal bureaucracy. Montgomery County wouldn't stand for it.

Industry has argued for seven decades that most mine accidents are caused by miners themselves because they are ignorant, careless, untrained, accident-prone or foolhardy. By this logic, most mine accidents are inevitable since human nature can't be changed. This argument is dusted off every few years to weaken efforts to establish better workplace and equipment standards. It persists despite credible research to the contrary.

Miners are said to be different from the rest of us, more accustomed to—and deserving of—their troubles. During their 3½-month-long strike in 1977–1978, *Newsweek* barefacedly called them a "breed apart": "clannish and fatalistic, wary and independent, hell-raising and violent, promiscuous and enduring." Such alien folk have these attitudes—so appropriate to their work—bred into them, were *Newsweek* to be believed.

Federal officials and industry will deny that miners are expected to subsidize future electricity. But it doesn't take long to wade through the perfunctory statements about "the health and safety of American coal miners is our highest priority" to get to the bottom line: Miners themselves—and greater protection of their health and safety—are "constraints" on coal production. The natural inclination of energy problem solvers is to minimize constraints.

Without a clear national commitment to mine safety, nothing much will change. That commitment has not been made. . . .

THE GREENHOUSE EFFECT

Those who fear a large-scale switch to coal in the United States for energy needs, including proponents of nuclear power, point to the so-called greenhouse effect as the most awesome and longest-term hazard from coal that exists. The greenhouse effect involves a buildup of carbon dioxide, an essential component of the earth's atmosphere. The danger of the greenhouse effect pertains to any industry that is based on coal, synthetics included. What follows is an analysis of the CO_2 problem by the Council on Environmental Quality. (For further discussion of the implications of this problem, see both the nuclear power and alternatives sections.)

Taken from "Global Energy Futures and the Carbon Dioxide Problem," by the Council on Environmental Quality, January 1981.

Carbon dioxide (CO_2) is a small but essential component of the earth's atmosphere. In recent decades the concentration of CO_2 in the atmosphere has been increasing in a manner that corresponds closely with the increasing global use of fossil fuels. The burning of fossil fuels—oil, natural gas, and coal—releases CO_2, about one-half of which appears to be retained in the atmosphere. The permanent clearing of forests and the decay of soil humus may also be net sources of CO_2.

Atmospheric CO_2 plays a critical role in warming the earth; it absorbs heat radiation from the earth's surface, trapping it and preventing it from dissipating into space. As the concentration of CO_2 in the atmosphere increases, more of the earth's radiated heat is trapped. Many scientists now believe that, if global fossil fuel use grows rapidly in the decades ahead, the accompanying CO_2 increases will lead to profound and long-term alteration of the earth's climate. These climatic changes, in turn, could have far-reaching adverse consequences, affecting our ability to feed a hungry and increasingly crowded world, the habitability of coastal areas and cities, and the preservation of natural areas as we know them today. . . .

Carbon dioxide is a gas that is a normal component of the earth's atmosphere. Before the Industrial Revolution (about 1800), the atmospheric concentration of CO_2 was about 290 parts per million (ppm). Since then it has increased an estimated 15–25 percent, and it is known that the concentration has increased about 7 percent between 1958 and 1979. (The present [1979] concentration of CO_2 is about 335 ppm. The pre-industrial level is estimated to lie within the range of 260–300 ppm. This report assumes a pre-industrial level of 292 ppm.) (See Figure 1.) During the last two centuries, and particularly in the post-World War II period,

FIGURE 1 Mauna Loa Monthly Averages of Atmospheric CO_2 Concentrations, with Seasonal Effect Removed.

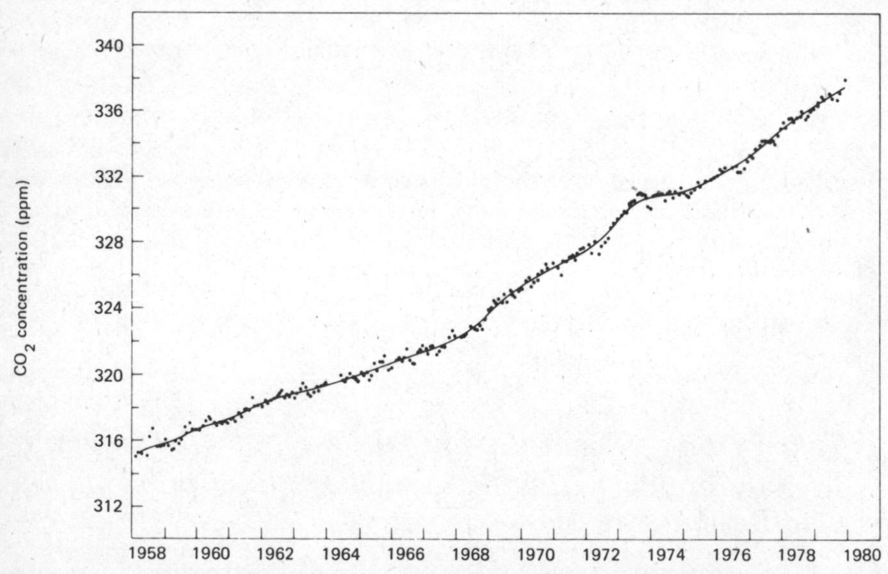

Source: C.D. Keeling and Co-workers, Scripps Institution of Oceanography.

global use of fossil fuels has grown markedly, and the burning of these fuels is believed to have been the principal cause of the increase in atmospheric CO_2. Simply stated, carbon dioxide is produced from the combustion of fossil fuels by the chemical combination of carbon in the fuel with oxygen in the atmosphere to release thermal energy and CO_2.

CO_2 in the atmosphere creates a so-called greenhouse effect. As the concentration of CO_2 increases, more heat, on balance, is trapped in the lower atmosphere, thus increasing its temperature. However, unlike a real greenhouse which warms primarily by reducing convection losses of heat, this CO_2 "greenhouse" warms by reducing infrared radiation losses. Theoretical calculations indicate that, other things being equal, a doubling of atmospheric CO_2 will lead to significant warming of the earth's atmosphere. The earth's climate will continue to change in a natural but presently unpredictable manner, even if CO_2 concentrations were to remain constant. In view of this uncertainty, most simulations of future global climate changes associated with increased CO_2 levels assume that the total climatic change caused by these other factors will be small (hence, the use of the term "other things being equal" in this report).

Because global fossil fuel use is a major contributor to the increase of atmospheric CO_2 levels, many estimates of global energy use suggest that atmospheric CO_2 levels could reach twice the preindustrial level about the middle of the next century. The resulting climatic changes could markedly affect agricultural productivity over large areas and could eventually lead to a rise in sea levels on the order of 5 meters, which would cause significant coastal flooding. Increases in atmospheric CO_2 and the associated climatic effects could also markedly affect the less managed biosphere, including fisheries and forests. Such a course of events could be severely disruptive both within and among nations. . . .

It is estimated that a doubling of CO_2 in the atmosphere could eventually increase average annual global surface temperatures by about 3° C and by as much as 7°C–10°C in the north polar region during the winter. The possible climatic and socioeconomic effects of such a global warming . . . include alterations in wind, ocean currents, and precipitation patterns. If large-scale climatic changes occurred, they could lead to major social, economic, and political impacts. These changes would affect both the managed and the less managed biosphere.

If the warming were great enough, and persisted long enough to lead to the disintegration of the West Antarctic ice sheet, ocean levels could rise 5–8 meters in several decades, though the time scale is uncertain. This rise would force a gradual evacuation of cities, towns, and the countryside located along coastlines. A 5-meter rise in sea level would flood a coastal area of the United States occupied by about 11 million people (5 percent of the population).

Shifts in rainfall could lead to major and disruptive changes in global agricultural patterns. In some regions, agricultural infrastructure could be rendered obsolete, while in other areas increased atmospheric CO_2 and rainfall could benefit agriculture and reduce heating requirements. If agriculture were seriously disrupted in regions that are now productive, major refugee and hunger problems could result unless production increased elsewhere and food could be imported.

The impacts of increased atmospheric CO_2 on the less managed biosphere, although unpredictable in detail, might include shifts in the location and productivity of fisheries, changes in species composition, and the possible extinction of some species with currently unpredictable consequences on ecosystem productivity or resource values for man.

In sum, increased atmospheric CO_2 concentrations could cause widespread and pervasive changes in global climatic, economic, social, and agricultural patterns. The need to adapt to these changes would be placed on a world which is expected to be already heavily burdened with increased political, economic, and environmental troubles in the decades ahead. . . .

OIL

OUR collective image of the history of oil in the United States is that of the wildcatter, a John Wayne figure, a loner whose shrewd gamble brings in a gusher of oil and makes him a millionaire. The oil industry often fosters such imagery in its own advertising, and behind the image lies a certain truth about the early discovery and development of oil fields in America. However, looked at historically, such images represent little more than a minor subtext to the real story of American oil, which is a story of concentration and monopoly.

Before 1850 in the United States oil was skimmed from the surface of creeks and wells and sold as medicine. It was often found by prospectors drilling for salt in western Pennsylvania. Kier's Petroleum became a well-known medicine: three teaspoonsful three times a day as a liniment or for bronchitis, cholera, and liver complaints. At the same time there was a much smaller market for oil as an illuminant, and a trade in oil for that purpose sprang up between Pittsburgh and New York.

Then a professor and journalist, George H. Bissell, came upon so-called rock oil and decided its potential for lighting lamps had been underestimated. Bissell formed the Pennsylvania Rock Oil Company and obtained an expert analysis from Yale University that confirmed his hunch. The analysis found that oil not only could be made into a luminant but yielded gas, paraffin, and lubricating oil. Subsequently the company dispatched a minor shareholder, one Edwin L. "Colonel" Drake to Titusville, a hamlet along a stream called Oil Creek in western Pennsylvania, and told him to dig an artesian well and find oil. Drake, a former railway express clerk, was ill equipped for the job, but amid catcalls about "Drake's folly" he began and to everyone's surprise hit oil. In no time at all Oil Creek was crawling with prospectors, teamsters, and roustabouts. Thus was the modern oil industry launched.

Soon refineries were developed by chemists who had experience in making illuminating oil from coal. Realizing that oil could replace coal, they immediately threw themselves into the task at hand and soon found ways of making different kinds of oils for lighting, lubricating, and paraffin. By 1872, scarcely a decade after Drake had hit oil in Pennsylvania, oil had become the fourth most important export of the United States.

Over the next thirty years the search for petroleum expanded westward from Pennsylvania until by the end of the century crude oil was being produced in fifteen states. Large discoveries were made in California and Oklahoma in the early 1900s, and the two states became the nation's leading producers. In 1928 Texas became the largest producer, and ever since the Southwest has remained the undisputed leading oil territory. It is well to remember, however, that in recent years the finds at Prudhoe Bay in Alaska, offshore along the California coast, and in the western mountains are altering the landscape of production.

Within ten years of the discovery on Oil Creek, Cleveland had become the refining center of the nation. It commanded all markets to the West and was the terminus for trunk lines heading east. It was there that a young merchant named John D. Rockefeller established himself in the produce business on the docks. His business flourished during the Civil War, and then, together with a partner, Rockefeller invested in a refinery. It was a success, and as Cleveland grew as a refining center, he launched a larger venture. Within five years Rockefeller had combined his different ventures into one company, the Standard Oil Company. It was soon the largest firm in the nation, accounted for 85 percent of all the oil refined, and became the first major industrial monopoly in the United States. Ida Tarbell, the great muckraker, describes the origins of the famous business in a selection that follows.

From the standpoint of the structure of the industry, the success of the Standard Oil Company was all-important. Many of the most significant oil companies of the present time are offshoots of Standard, and three of the biggest came from the breakup of the Standard monopoly.

However, from an international point of view an equally important date in the origins of the modern oil industry is 1911, the year in which Winston Churchill, as you will recall from our earlier selection, "The Romance of Design" (see p. 20), took the decision to switch the fueling of the British fleet from coal to oil. Churchill's decision set in motion a train of actions that led to Britain's intervention in Persia and Mesopotamia in the years immediately preceding the First World War and the development of a worldwide oil industry controlled by the West.

After World War I, Standard, by then broken up by the Justice Department, took the lead in pushing the U.S. government into demanding access to Middle Eastern oil. The United States, at the time, claimed it was facing a domestic oil shortage and felt threatened by the possible incursion of foreign oil companies into hitherto-sacrosanct U.S. markets. In the mid-1920s the various Western oil companies worked out a system for splitting up Middle Eastern oil through an international petroleum cartel.

Seven large international companies, the Seven Sisters (Exxon, Mobil, Standard Oil of California, Gulf, Texaco, BP, and Shell), prospered as a result of the cartel system. These companies controlled the worldwide production and distribution of oil well past the end of the Second World War. Their presence fostered (and was eventually circumscribed by) the rise of Middle Eastern nationalist political forces, from Nasser and Mossadegh to the Iranian revolution, which eventually led to the formation of the Organization of Petroleum Exporting Countries (OPEC). To mount their challenge to the Seven Sisters, the OPEC countries first had to pierce the aura of mystery which has always surrounded oil technology, the prevalent idea being that nobody knows anything about petroleum except the oil companies themselves. As Anthony Sampson points out, OPEC's first breakthrough was in the arena of technology, where Middle Eastern engineers, trained in America for the big oil companies, gained sufficient expertise to challenge their former employers.

Today about a quarter of all crude oil consumed in the United States comes from abroad. Its single biggest use is gasoline, with fuel oil, employed for heating and transportation, the second largest category. During the 1960s oil became a major fuel burned by utilities, which found it as cheap as and less polluting than coal. Today the utility market is still the third largest.

The future of domestic oil in the short term may depend on increased exploration in areas previously too expensive to be profitable—such places as the deep basins beneath mountain chains in the West and East; the outer continental shelf in the Atlantic, off Alaska, and off California; throughout the Arctic Circle; and in the Caribbean. Advanced technology may permit recovery of oil remaining in existing wells. And over the long term the future of oil may well come to be tied to synthetic fuels made from coal or oil shale.

Yet, while the industry is normally portrayed in terms of shortage, history tells us something different—namely that the central problem to the current time has been surplus, too much oil, not too little. The immediate problem along Oil Creek was how to keep up prices in the face of a seemingly endless and uncontrollable flood of oil. The same problem in the Middle East more than half a century later led to the formation of an international oil cartel. It was this problem in the southwestern part of the United States which eventually led producers to seek government help in controlling the production of oil. It was surplus that led to the formation of OPEC, and as we shall see in the entries ahead, it was the threat of surplus which prevented OPEC from achieving its ultimate potential of creating a new political fabric in the Middle East. Big Oil's answer to surplus has been concentration, a device repeatedly employed to control oil gluts.

A central question for the industry has always been whether or not and to what extent within the United States the government should be permitted to allocate production to enhance the industry's goals of controlling the surplus and keeping oil prices high. Should production be controlled through the federal government, through state governments, or by a cartel system? As we shall see in John Blair's account, the industry and government coalesced in different ways. The oil industry has used the government's system of leasing out oil on public lands to restrict entry into the business. None but the largest firms can afford to bid on public leases. At the same time the major firms control the flow of oil from wellhead to market through their joint partnerships in pipelines. Because the companies could not bring themselves entirely to trust the federal government, control over actual production was placed in the hands of state governments through the Connally "hot oil" act of the 1930s. In practice, two states, Texas and Louisiana, acting on the advice of the industry, set production levels for the companies and used their governmental powers to enforce them.

A final point: While U.S. claims to Middle Eastern oil historically have been set within the rubric of containment policy toward the Soviet Union, the oil companies themselves plainly have another reason to fear the Russians: the prospect of the Soviet Union, the world's largest single producer of petroleum, unloosing surplus petroleum into their neatly organized marketplace. In 1981, with the signing of a gas pipeline agreement between Germany and the Soviet Union whereby Russian gas will be piped into Europe, it seems that may be precisely what is beginning to happen.

SCARE TACTICS

While there is ample evidence to suggest that the world will exhaust its supplies of fossil fuels, including oil and natural gas, over a relatively short period of time in the next century, it should be remembered that the single most potent weapon in the public relations arsenal of the oil industry has always been the fear of shortage. The following chart illustrates just how often since the discovery of oil in western Pennsylvania in 1859 the United States has supposedly come close to running out of oil.

The most recent scare, of course, was in the 1970s, when the oil industry was hard at work attempting to exempt the price of both natural gas and oil from federal control. Then, as in previous instances, the charge was that the government, by strangling the domestic oil industry through controls, had doomed the nation to become dependent on foreign oil, indeed to be at the mercy of the Arabs. If only the nation would permit oil and gas prices to rise, said the industry, then the scarcity would disappear. Congress duly removed controls from domestically produced oil and natural gas. Soon there was a glut of both fuels.

Taken from A National Fuels and Policy Study, *Hearings on Senate Resolution 45, U.S. Congress, Senate Committee on Interior and Insular Affairs, Washington, D.C., 1972.*

1866—Synthetics available if oil production should end—U.S. Revenue Commission.
1883—Little or no chance for oil in California—U.S. Geological Survey.
1891—Little or no chance for oil in Kansas or Texas—U.S. Geological Survey.
1908—Maximum future supply of oil 23 billion barrels—officials of U.S. Geological Survey.
1914—Total future production only 6 billion barrels—officials of U.S. Bureau of Mines.
1920—United States needs foreign oil and synthetics; peak domestic production almost reached—director, U.S. Geological Survey.
1931—Must import as much foreign oil as possible to save domestic supply—Secretary, U.S. Department of the Interior. (East Texas field discovered in 1930 but full potential not immediately recognized.)
1939—U.S. oil supplies will last only thirteen years—U.S. Department of the Interior.
1947—Sufficient oil cannot be found in the United States—chief of Petroleum Division, U.S. Department of State.
1949—End of U.S. oil supply almost in sight—Secretary, U.S. Department of the Interior.

STANDARD OIL

John D. Rockefeller built the first great industrial monopoly in the United States in the form of the Standard Oil Company. Within ten short years of the first oil well in western Pennsylvania, Rockefeller had gained control of most of the oil in the nation. Today Standard (Exxon) and its successor companies continue to dominate the industry.

Rockefeller's most dogged critic was a journalist, Ida Minerva Tarbell, a feminist and one of the nation's great muckrakers. She grew up in Titusville, Pennsylvania, in the heart of the oil regions, but in her early years she had little interest either in oil or in Rockefeller. Instead, she lived in Paris and wrote biographies. Back in the United States as editor of *McClure's* magazine she tried to find someone to write about Rockefeller and, failing, plunged into the task herself. Her history of the Standard Oil Company began to appear in 1902 and was issued as a book in 1904.

Tarbell succeeded in tarnishing Rockefeller's image, and despite the immense amounts of money the family has since poured into philanthropic enterprises, it never has escaped the image she painted, of a man who had become the "victim of a money-passion which blinds him to every other consideration in life" and whose example had steeped American life in "commercial Machiavellism." The selections from her famous history which follow describe the origins of the Standard Oil Company and show how it dealt with its competition.

From The History of the Standard Oil Company, *by Ida Tarbell, New York, Macmillan, 1904.*

. . . By rail and water Cleveland commanded the entire Western market. It had two trunk lines running to New York, both eager for oil traffic, and by Lake Erie and the canal it had for a large part of the year a splendid cheap waterway. Thus, at the opening of the oil business, Cleveland was destined by geographical position to be a refining center.

Men saw it, and hastened to take advantage of the opportunity. There was grave risk. The oil supply might not hold out. As yet there was no certain market for refined oil. But a sure result was not what drew people into the oil business in the early sixties. Fortune was running fleet footed across the country, and at her garment men clutched. They loved the chase almost as they did success, and so many a man in Cleveland tried his luck in an oil refinery, as hundreds on Oil Creek were trying it in an oil lease. By 1865 there were thirty refineries in the town, with a capital of about a million and a half dollars and a daily capacity of some 2,000 barrels. The works multiplied rapidly. . . .

Among the many young men of Cleveland who, from the start, had an eye on the oil-refining business and had begun to take an active part in its development as soon as it was demonstrated that there was a reasonable hope of its being permanent, was a young firm of produce commission merchants. Both members of this firm were keen business men, and one of them had remarkable commercial vision—a genius for seeing the possibilities in material things. This man's name was Rockefeller—John D. Rockefeller. He was but twenty-three years old when he first went into the oil business, but he had already got his feet firmly on the business ladder, and had got them there by his own efforts. The habit of driving good bargains and of saving money had started him. He himself once told how he learned these lessons so useful in money-making, in one of his frequent Sunday-school talks to young men on success in business. The value of a good bargain he learned in buying cord-wood for his father: "I knew what a cord of good solid beech and maple wood was. My father told me to select only the solid wood and the straight wood and not to put any limbs in it or any punky wood. That was a good training for me. I did not need any father to tell me or anybody else how many feet it took to make a cord of wood."

And here is how he learned the value of investing money:

"Among the early experiences that were helpful to me that I recollect with pleasure was one in working a few days for a neighbour in digging potatoes—a very enterprising, thrifty farmer, who could dig a great many potatoes. I was a boy of perhaps thirteen or fourteen years of age, and it kept me very busy from morning until night. It was a ten-hour day. And as I was saving these little sums I soon learned that I could get as much interest for fifty dollars loaned at seven per cent —the legal rate in the state of New York at that time for a year—as I could earn by digging potatoes for 100 days. The impression was gaining ground with me that it was a good thing to let the money be my slave and not make myself a slave to money." Here we have the foundation principles of a great financial career.

When young Rockefeller was thirteen years old, his father moved from the farm in Central New York, where the boy had been born (July 8, 1839), to a farm near Cleveland, Ohio. He went to school in Cleveland for three years. In 1855 it became necessary for him to earn his own living. It was a hard year in the West and the boy walked the streets for days looking for work. He was about to give it up and go to the country when, to quote the story as Mr. Rockefeller once told it to his Cleveland Sunday-school, "As good fortune would have it I went down to the dock and made one more application, and I was told that if I would come in after dinner —our noon-day meal was dinner in those days—they would see if I could come to work for them. I went down after dinner and I got the position, and I was permitted to remain in the city." The position, that of a clerk and bookkeeper, was not lucrative. According to a small ledger which has figured frequently in Mr. Rockefeller's religious instructions, he earned from September 26, 1855, to January, 1856, fifty dollars. "Out of that," Mr. Rockefeller told the young men of his Sunday-school class, "I paid my washerwoman and the lady I boarded with, and I saved a little money to put away."

He proved an admirable accountant—one of the early-and-late sort, who saw everything, forgot nothing and never talked. In 1856 his salary was raised to twenty-five dollars a month, and he went on always "saving a little money to put away." In 1858 came a chance to invest his savings. Among his acquaintances was a young Englishman, M. B. Clark. Older by twelve years than Rockefeller he had left a hard life in England when he was twenty to seek fortune in America. He had landed in Boston in 1847, without a penny or a friend, and it had taken three months for him to earn money to get to Ohio. Here he had taken the first job at hand, as man-of-all-work, wood-chopper, teamster. He had found his way to Cleveland, had become a valuable man in the houses where he was employed, had gone to school at nights, had saved money. They were two of a kind, Clark and Rockefeller, and in 1858 they pooled their earnings and started a produce commission business on the Cleveland docks. The venture succeeded. Local historians credit Clark and Rockefeller with doing a business of $450,000 the first year. The war came on, and as neither partner went to the front, they had full chance to take advantage of the opportunity for produce business a great army gives. A greater chance than furnishing army supplies, lucrative as most people found that, was in the oil business (so Clark and Rockefeller began to think), and in 1862, when an

Englishman of ability and energy, one Samuel Andrews, asked them to back him in starting a refinery, they put in $4,000 and promised to give more if necessary. Now Andrews was a mechanical genius. He devised new processes, made a better and better quality of oil, got larger and larger percentages of refined from his crude. The little refinery grew big, and Clark and Rockefeller soon had $100,000 or more in it. In the meantime Cleveland was growing as a refining centre. The business which in 1860 had been a gamble was by 1865 one of the most promising industries of the town. It was but the beginning—so Mr. Rockefeller thought—and in that year he sold out his share of the commission business and put his money into the oil firm of Rockefeller and Andrews.

In the new firm Andrews attended to the manufacturing. The pushing of the business, the buying and the selling, fell to Rockefeller. From the start his effect was tremendous. He had the frugal man's hatred of waste and disorder, of middlemen and unnecessary manipulation, and he began a vigorous elimination of these from his business. The residuum that other refineries let run into the ground, he sold. Old iron found its way to the junk shop. He bought his oil directly from the wells. He made his own barrels. He watched and saved and contrived. . . .

These qualities told. The firm grew as rapidly as the oil business of the town, and started a second refinery—William A. Rockefeller and Company. They took in a partner, H. M. Flagler, and opened a house in New York for selling oil. Of all these concerns John D. Rockefeller was the head. Finally, in June, 1870, five years after he became an active partner in the refining business, Mr. Rockefeller combined all his companies into one—the Standard Oil Company. The capital of the new concern was $1,000,000. The parties interested in it were John D. Rockefeller, Henry M. Flagler, Samuel Andrews, Stephen V. Harkness, and William Rockefeller.

The strides the firm of Rockefeller and Andrews made after the former went into it were attributed for three or four years mainly to his extraordinary capacity for bargaining and borrowing. Then its chief competitors began to suspect something. John Rockefeller might get his oil cheaper now and then, they said, but he could not do it often. He might make close contracts for which they had neither the patience nor the stomach. He might have an unusual mechanical and practical genius in his partner. But these things could not explain all. They believed they bought, on the whole, almost as cheaply as he, and they knew they made as good oil and with as great, or nearly as great, economy. He could sell at no better price than they. Where was his advantage? There was but one place where it could be, and that was in transportation. He must be getting better rates from the railroads than they were. In 1868 or 1869 a member of a rival firm long in the business, which had been prosperous from the start, and which prided itself on its methods, its economy and its energy, Alexander, Scofield and Company, went to the Atlantic and Great Western road, then under the Erie management, and complained. "You are giving others better rates than you are us," said Mr. Alexander, the representative of the firm. "We cannot compete if you do that." The railroad agent did not attempt to deny it—he simply agreed to give Mr. Alexander a rebate also. The arrangement was interesting. Mr. Alexander was to pay the open, or regular, rate on oil from the Oil Regions to Cleveland, which was then forty cents a barrel. At the end of each month he was to send to the railroad vouchers for the amount of oil shipped and paid for at forty cents, and was to get back from the railroad, in money, fifteen cents on each barrel. This concession applied only to oil brought from the wells. He was never able to get a rebate on oil shipped eastward. . . .

. . . The rebate had come, and, as we have seen, it soon was suspected and others went after it, and in some cases got it. But the rebate seems to have been granted generally only on oil brought from the Oil Regions. Mr. Alexander claims he was never able to get his rate lowered on his Eastern shipments. The railroad took the position with him that if he could ship as much oil as the Standard he could have as low a rate, but not otherwise. Now in 1870 the Standard Oil Company had a daily capacity of about 1,500 barrels of crude. The refinery was the largest in the town, though it had some close competitors. Nevertheless on the strength of its large capacity it received the special favour. It was a plausible way to get around the theory generally held then, as now, though not so definitely crystallised into law, that the railroad being a common carrier had no right to discriminate between its patrons. It remained to be seen whether the practice would be accepted by Mr. Rockefeller's competitors without a contest, or, if contested, would be supported by the law. . . .

It would seem from the above as if the one man in the Cleveland oil trade in 1870 who ought to have been satisfied was Mr. Rockefeller. . . . [The railroad rebate was the mechanism that Rockefeller employed to build his business. However, the idea of a pipeline for carrying oil caused an immense change in the young industry, immediately reopening the possibility of competition because of the new, efficient, and much cheaper means of transport. Here is how Rockefeller dealt with this threat.]

The project for a seaboard pipe-line to be built by the producers and to be kept independent of Standard capital and direction had been pushed with amazing energy. Early in the fall of 1878 General Haupt reported that his right of way was complete from the Allegheny River to Baltimore; contracts were let for the telegraph line and preparation begun to lay the pipe. Before much actual work had been done it became clear to the company that it was not from the Butler oil field but from that of Bradford that a seaboard pipe-line should run; that the former field was showing signs of exhaustion, while the latter was evidently going to yield abundantly. With a promptness which would have done credit to Mr. Rockefeller himself, Messrs. Benson, Hopkins and McKelvy changed their plan. The new idea was to lay a six-inch line from Rixford, in the Bradford field, to Williamsport, on the Reading Railroad, a distance of 109 miles. The Reading, not having had so far any oil freight, was happy to enter into a contract with them to run oil to both Philadelphia and New York until they could get through to the seaboard themselves. In November, 1878, a limited partnership, called the Tidewater Pipe Company, was organised with a capital of $625,000 to carry out the scheme. Many of the best known producers of the Oil Regions took stock in the company, the largest stockholders being A. A. Sumner and B. D. Benson.

The first work was to get a right of way. The company went at the work with secrecy and despatch. Its first move was to buy from the Equitable Pipe Line, the second independent effort to which, as we have seen, the Producers' Union lent its support in 1878, a short line it had built, and a portion of a right of way eastward which Colonel Potts had been quietly trying to secure. This was a good start, and the chief engineer, B. F. Warren, pushed his way forward to Williamsport near the line which Colonel Potts had projected. The Standard, intent on stopping them, and indeed on putting an end to all future ventures of this sort, set out at once to get what was called a "dead line" across the state. This was an exclusive right for pipe-line purposes from the northern to the southern boundary of Pennsylvania. As there was no free pipe-line bill in those days, this "dead line," if it had been complete, would have been an effectual barrier to the Tidewater. Much money was spent in this sordid business, but they never succeeded in completing a line. The Tidewater, after a little delay, found a gap not far from where it wanted to cross, and soon had pushed itself through to Williamsport. With the actual laying of the pipe there was no interference which proved serious, though the railroads frequently held back shipments of supplies. At Williamsport, where the pipe crossed under the railroad, it was torn out once. The Tidewater had no trouble in this case in getting an injunction which prevented further lawlessness.

By the end of May the company was ready for operation. The plant which they had constructed proposed to transport 10,000 barrels of oil a day over a distance of 109 miles. The apparatus for doing this consisted simply of tanks, pumps and pipes. At Coryville, on the edge of the Bradford field, two iron tanks, each holding 25,000 barrels of oil, were connected with an enormous pump of a new pattern devised by the Holly Company especially for this work. This pump, which was driven by an engine of seventy horse-power, was expected to force the oil through a six-inch pipe to a second station twenty-eight miles away and about 700 feet higher. Here a second pump took up the oil again, driving it to the summit of the Alleghanies, a few miles east. From this point the oil ran by gravitation to Williamsport.

It was announced that the pumps would be started on the morning of May 28. The experiment was watched with keenest interest. Up to that time oil had never been pumped over thirty miles, and no great elevation had been overcome. Here was a line 109 miles long, running over a mountain nearly 2,600 feet high. It was freely bet in the Oil Regions that the Tidewater would get nothing but a drizzle for its pains. However, oil men, Standard men, representatives of the Pennsylvania Railroad, newspaper men and natives gathered in numbers at the stations, and indeed all along the route, to watch the result.

The pump at station one was started by B. D. Benson, the president of the company. . . . Without a hitch the oil flowed in a full stream into the pipe and began its long journey over the mountains. It travelled about as fast as a man could walk and, as the pipe lay on the ground, the head of the stream could be located by the sound. Patrolmen followed the pipe the entire length watching for leaks. There was now and then a delay from the stopping of the pumps; but the cause was trivial enough, never anything worse than chips under the valves or clogging in the pipe by stones and bits of wood which the workmen had carelessly left in when joining the pipe. When the oil reached the second station there was general rejoicing; nevertheless, the steepest incline, the summit of the Alleghanies, had yet to be overcome. The oil went up to the top of the mountain without difficulty, and on June 4, the seventh day after Mr. Benson opened the valve at Station One, oil flowed into the big receiving tank beyond Williamsport. A new era had come in the oil business. Oil could be pumped over the mountains. It was only a matter of time when the Tidewater would pump to New York.

Once at the seaboard, the Tidewater had a large and sure outlet for its oil in the group of independent refiners left at the mercy of the Standard in the fall of 1877 by the downfall of the Empire Line. These refiners had most of them run the entire gamut of experiences forced on the trade by the railroads and the Standard. . . .

The success of the Tidewater experiment brought Mr. Rockefeller face to face with a new situation. Just how serious this situation was is shown by the difference in the cost of transporting a barrel of oil to the seaboard by rail and transporting it by pipe. According to the calculation of Mr. Gowen, the president of the Reading Railroad, the cost by rail was at that time from thirty-five to forty-five cents. The open rate was from $1.25 to $1.40, and the Standard Oil Company probably paid about eighty-five cents, when the roads were not protecting it from "injury by competition." Now, according to General Haupt's calculation in 1876, oil could be carried in pipes from the Oil Regions to the seaboard for 16⅔ cents a barrel. General Haupt calculated the average difference in cost of the two systems to be twenty-three cents, enough to pay twenty-eight per cent. dividends on the cost of a line even if the railway put their freights down to cost. This little calculation is enough to show that the day of the railroads as long-distance transporters of crude oil was over; that the pipe-lines were bound to replace them. Now, Mr. Rockefeller had by ten years of effort made the roads his servant; would he be able to control the new carrier? A man of lesser intellect might not have foreseen the inevitableness of the new situation; a man of lesser courage would not have sprung to meet it. Mr. Rockefeller, however, is like all great generals: he never fails to foresee where the battle is to be fought; he never fails to get the choice of positions. He wasted no time now in deciding what should be done. He proposed not merely to control future long-distance oil transportation; he proposed to own it outright.

Hardly had the news of the success of the Tidewater's experiment reached the Standard before this truly Napoleonic decision was being carried out. Mr. Rockefeller had secured a right of way from the Bradford field to Bayonne, New Jersey, and was laying a seaboard pipe-line of his own. At the same time he set out to acquire a right of way to Philadelphia, and soon a line to that point was under construction. Even before these seaboard lines were ready, pipes had been laid from the Oil Regions to the Standard's inland refining points—Cleveland, Buffalo and Pittsburgh. With the completion of this system Mr. Rockefeller would be independent of the railroads as far as the transportation of crude oil was concerned. It was, of course, a new department in his business, and, to manage it, a new company was organised in April, 1881—the National Transit Company—with a capital of five million dollars, and a charter of historical interest, for it was a mate of the charter of the ill-fated South Improvement Company, granted by the same Legislature and giving the same omnibus privileges—the right in fact to do any kind of business, except banking, in any part of the world. The South Improvement Company charter . . . was repealed. The charter which the National Transit Company now bought seems to have gone into hiding when the character of its mate was disclosed and so had been forgotten. How it came to be unearthed by the Standard or what they paid for it, the writer does not know. However, as H. H. Rogers aptly told the Industrial Commission in 1899, when he was asked if a considerable sum was not given for it: "I should suppose every good thing had to be paid for; I should say a man owning a charter of that kind would sell it at the best price he could get."

And while Mr. Rockefeller was making this lavish expenditure of money and energy to meet the situation created by the bold development of the Tidewater, what was his attitude toward that company? One would suppose that Mr. Rockefeller, of all men, would be the first to acknowledge the service the Tidewater had rendered the oil business; that in this case he would have felt an obligation to make an exception to his claim that the oil business was his; that he would have allowed the new company to live. But Mr. Rockefeller's commercial vision is too keen for that; that would *not* be business. The Tidewater had been built to feed a few independent refineries in New York. If these refineries operated outside of him, they might disturb his system; that is, they might increase the output of refined and so lower its price. The Tidewater must not be allowed to live, then. But how could it be put out of commission? It had money to operate. There were plenty of oil producers glad to give it their product, because it was independent. The Reading Railroad had gone heart and soul into its fight—it had refiners pledged to take its oil, and these refiners had markets of their own at home and abroad. What was he going to do about it? There were several ways to accomplish his end; in two of them, at least, Mr. Rockefeller excelled from long practice. The first was to get out of the way the refineries which the Tidewater expected to feed, and this was undertaken at once. The refiners were approached usually by members of the Standard Oil Company as private individuals, and terms of purchase or lease so generous made to them that they could not afford to decline. At the same time they were assured confidentially that the Tidewater scheme was a pure chimera, that they understood the pipe-line business better than anybody else and they knew oil could not be pumped over the mountains. All but one firm yielded to the pressure. Ayres and Lombard stood by the Tidewater, but soon after their refusal to sell they were condemned as a public nuisance and obliged to move their works! The Tidewater met the situation by beginning to build refineries of its own—one at Bayonne, New Jersey, and another near Philadelphia—in the meantime storing the oil it had expected to sell.

Having done his best to cut off his rival's outlet, Mr. Rockefeller called upon the railroads to carry out that article of their contract with him which bound them to protect him from "injury by competition." What was done was told a few months later to the Committee on Commerce in the House of Representatives by Franklin B. Gowen, the president of the Reading Railroad. According to Mr. Gowen the Tidewater and Reading were no sooner ready to run oil than a meeting of the trunk lines was held at Saratoga, at which the representatives of the Standard Oil Company were present, and on that day the through rate on oil was reduced to twenty cents per barrel to the Standard Oil Company. "It was subsequently reduced to fifteen cents," Mr. Gowen told the Committee, "and I believe, though I do not certainly know, to ten cents per barrel in cars of the Standard Oil Company; . . . and I am told that at the meeting at Saratoga a time was fixed by the Standard Oil Company within which they promised to secure the control of the pipe-line—provided the trunk lines would make the rate for carrying oil so low that all concerned in transportation would lose money.

"I know this, that only three or four months ago we were told—I do not mean myself, but the gentlemen who directly represented the pipe-line which leads to our road—that if they would agree to give all their oil to the Standard Oil Company to be refined, we could carry 10,000 barrels a day, and the rates would be advanced by the trunk lines. But, to use the language of those making the offer, 'we' (meaning the Standard Oil Company) 'will never permit the trunk lines to advance the rate on oil until your pipe-line gives us all its product to refine,' and the prophesy of four months ago has become the history of to-day." . . .

This was the Tidewater's first year's experience. The second and third were not unlike it. But the company lived and expanded. It bought and built refineries, it sent its president to Europe to open markets, it extended its pipe-line still nearer to the seaboard, and it did this by a series of amazingly plucky and adroit financial moves—borrowing money, speculating in oil, exchanging credit, chasing checks from bank to bank, "hustling," in short, as few men ever did to keep a business alive. And every move had to be made with caution, for the Standard's eye was always on them, its hand always outstretched. Samuel Q. Brown, the present president of the organisation, when on the witness stand in December, 1882, said that so much did the Tidewater fear espionage that they were accustomed to keep their oil transactions as a private and not a general account, in order that they might not be reported to the Standard; that even matters which they believed they were keeping in an absolutely private way frequently leaked out, to the injury of the business.

By January, 1882, the Tidewater was in such a satisfactory condition that it decided to negotiate a loan of $2,000,000 to carry out plans for enlargement. The First National Bank of New York, after a thorough examination of the business, agreed to take the bonds at ninety cents on the dollar, but trouble began as soon as the probable success of the bond issue was known. The officials of the First National Bank were called upon by stockholders of the Tidewater, men holding nearly a third of the company's stock, and assured that the company was insolvent, and that it would be unsafe for the bank to take the loan. The First National declined to be influenced by the information, on the ground that the disgruntled stockholders had sold themselves to the Standard Oil Company, and were trying to discredit the Tidewater, so that the Standard might buy it in. . . .

These manoeuvres failing to ruin the Tidewater's credit, a more serious attack was made in the fall of 1882, by the filing of a long bill of complaint against the management of the company, followed by an appeal that a receiver be appointed and the business wound up. The appeal came from E. G. Patterson, a stockholder of the Tidewater, and a man who, up to this time, had been one of the most intelligent opponents of the Standard in the Oil Regions. Mr. Patterson was one of the few who had realised, from the first development of Mr. Rockefeller's pretensions, that it was a question of transportation, and that, if the railroads could be forced by courts and legislatures to do their duty, the coal-oil business would not belong to Mr. Rockefeller. He had been one of the strongest factors in the great suits compromised in 1880, and his disgust at the outcome had been so great that he had washed his hands of the Producers' Union. Later he had been engaged by the state of Pennsylvania to collect evidence on which to support a claim against the Standard Oil Company for some $3,000,000 of back taxes. The Standard had made Mr. Patterson's services unnecessary by coming forward and giving the attorney-general all the information as to its financial condition which he desired. Exasperated as the result of all his efforts, and feeling that he had been deserted by the public he had tried to serve, Mr. Patterson sent word to the Standard that he proposed still further to attack them (just how he never explained) unless they would give him, not to attack, as much as there was in the contract from the state. They seem to have thought it worth while to buy peace, and agreed to give Mr. Patterson some $20,000 in all, and secure him a position for a term of years. The first payment was made at the end of April, 1882, and $5,000 of the money received Mr. Patterson paid to the Tidewater for stock he had taken at its organisation. No sooner was the stock in his hands than he began the preparation of the bill of complaint above referred to, and in December the case was heard.

The Oil Regions watched it with keenest interest. That Mr. Patterson had made some settlement with the Standard was generally known, and the charge was freely circulated that they had bribed him to bring this suit in hopes of blasting the credit of the Tidewater and getting its stock for a song. The testimony brought out in the trial did not bear out this popular notion. The case was rather more complicated. That the suit was backed by the Standard, one would have to be very naïve to doubt, but they were using other and stronger parties than Mr. Patterson, and that was a faction of the company known as the "Taylor-Satterfield crowd." These men, controlling some $200,000 worth of Tidewater stock, had been professing themselves dissatisfied with the management of the business for some months, though always refusing to sell their holdings at an advanced price. It was generally believed in the Oil Regions that their "dissatisfaction" was fictitious, that they were in reality in league with the Standard in an attempt to create a panic in Tidewater stock, a belief which was strengthened when it was learned that a big oil company, which the gentlemen controlled, the Union, had been sold about that time to the Standard Oil Trust for something like $500,000 in its stock. The first manoeuvre of the Taylor-Satterfield faction had been the attempt to dissuade the First National Bank from taking the Tidewater loan referred to above. Failing in this, they seem to have imbued Mr. Patterson thoroughly with their pretended dissatisfaction and to have persuaded him to bring the suit. For some reason which is not clear they failed properly to support him in the suit, and when it came off they practically deserted him. The Tidewater had no trouble in proving that the complaints of insolvency and mismanagement were without foundation, and Judge Pierson Church, of Meadville, before whom the case was argued, refused to appoint the receiver, intimating strongly that, in his judgment, the case was an attempt to levy a species of blackmail, in which it must not be expected that his court would co-operate. Judge Church's decision was given on January 15. Two days later a sensation came in Tidewater affairs, which quite knocked the Patterson suit out of the public mind; it was nothing less than a bold attempt by the Taylor party, or, as it was now known, "the Standard party," to seize the reins of government. It was a very cleverly planned coup.

The yearly meeting for the election of officers in the company was fixed for a certain Wednesday in January. By verbal agreement it had been postponed, in 1882, to some time in February, the controller, D. B. Stewart, a member of the Taylor faction, representing that he could not have his statement ready earlier. No notices were sent out to this effect, although this should have been done. Taylor and his party, taking advantage of this fact perfectly well known to them, appeared at the Tidewater offices on January 17, and although one of the Benson faction, as the majority was known from the name of the company's president, was present with sufficient proxies to vote nearly two-thirds of the stock, they overruled him and elected themselves to the control. They also elected to the Board of Managers,

Franklin B. Gowen, the president of the Reading, and James R. Keene, the famous speculator, both large holders of Tidewater bonds. They followed their election immediately by sending out notices to the banks with which the company did business not to honour checks drawn by the Benson party, and to the post-office to deliver mail to no one but themselves. . . .

The Benson party took immediate action, applying for an injunction restraining the new board from taking possession of the books and offices. This was granted and a date for a hearing appointed. Up to the hearing the old board did business behind barricaded doors! The case was heard in Meadville before Judge Pierson Church—the same who had heard the Patterson case. As it was a case to be decided on purely technical matters—the rules governing elections—no sensation was looked for, but one came immediately. It was a long affidavit from James R. Keene, even more notorious then than now—there were fewer of his kind—for deals and corners and devious stock tricks, declaring that both the Patterson case and this attempt to obtain control were dictated by the "malicious ingenuity" of the Standard for the purpose of destroying the Tidewater and getting hold of its property. . . .

Such was the character of the charges and countercharges in this purely technical case. The judge took little notice of them in his decision, but, after an exhaustive discussion of the points involved in the election, decided it was illegal and continued the injunction he had granted against the new board. Judge Church's decision aroused general exultation in the Oil Regions—as any failure of the Standard to get what it wanted was bound to do, and with good reason. The Tidewater's growth in the face of the Standard's constant interference with its business was proof that independent pipelines and independent refineries could be built up if men had sufficient brains and courage and patience. What one set of men had done, another could do. Their hope of restoring freedom of competition to the oil business was still further brightened in June by the news that the Legislature of Pennsylvania had passed a free pipe-line bill—the measure that they had been urging for twelve years without avail. With a sturdy example of independence, like the Tidewater, before them, and the right of eminent domain for pipes, the future of competition in oil seemed to be up to the oil men themselves.

But the Oil Regions have always been prone to jump at conclusions. They were forgetting Mr. Rockefeller's record when they concluded that he was through with the Tidewater. Because he had failed in his old South Improvement Company trick, that is, failed to create a panic among Tidewater stockholders, and so get their property at panic prices, was no reason at all to suppose he had abandoned the chase. There still remained a legitimate method of getting into the company, and, as a last resort, Mr. Rockefeller accepted it. He bought the minority stock of the concern, held by the Taylor party. Up to this time Mr. Rockefeller had appeared in Tidewater affairs as a destroyer. He now appeared in a role in which he is quite as able—as a pacifier, and his extraordinary persuasiveness was never exercised to better effect. "We own $200,000 worth of your stock," he could tell the people he had been fighting. "If you will consent to confine yourselves to a fixed percentage of our joint business, and will sustain pipage rates and the price of refined oil, we will let you alone. Let us dwell together in peace."

The Tidewater, tired of the fight, accepted. And so these men—to whom the oil business owes one of its most remarkable developments, who, in face of the most powerful and unscrupulous opposition, had in four years built up a business worth five and one-half millions of dollars—signed contracts in October, 1883, fixing the relative amount of business they were henceforth to do as 11½ per cent. of the aggregate, the Standard having 88½ per cent. The two simply became allies. The agreement between them was the same in effect as all Mr. Rockefeller's running agreements—it limited and kept up prices. Any benefit the oil business might have reaped from natural and decent competition between the two was of course ended by the alliance. For all practical purposes the two were one. In the phrase of the region, the Tidewater had "gone over to the Standard," and there it has always remained. The contract was made for fifteen years, but since its expiration it has been lived up to honourably by both parties without other than a verbal understanding. For, note this: Mr. Rockefeller always keeps his word. Indeed, in studying his career, one is frequently reminded of Tom Sawyer's great resolution—never to sully piracy by dishonesty!

The Tidewater has prospered within the boundary Mr. Rockefeller drew for it, as those who have accepted submissively his boundaries have never failed to do. Mr. Rockefeller is right when he says, as he does so often, that all who come with him prosper. That the company would have succeeded in becoming eventually a formidable rival of the Standard, and in controlling much more than eleven per cent. of the business, no one can doubt who knew Mr. Benson, Major Hopkins, Mr. McKelvy, and their colleagues. They were business men of the first order, as their tremendous work from 1878 to 1883 shows.

Once more the good of the oil business was secure, and Mr. Rockefeller at once proceeded to arrange his great house in the new order made necessary by the introduction of the seaboard pipe-line. The entire transportation department of the business had to be reorganised. When the seaboard pipe-line became a factor in the oil business, in 1879, the Standard Oil Company owned practically the entire system of oil-gathering pipe-lines—that is, the lines carrying oil from the wells to the storing or shipping points. These lines were organised under the name of the United Pipe Lines, and the organisation was magnificent in both extent and in character of service rendered. Never, indeed, has the ability of the men Mr. Rockefeller gathered into his machine shone to better advantage than in the building up and management of the pipe-line business. At the end of 1883, when the alliance was made with the Tidewater, the United Pipe Lines were taking from the wells of Pennsylvania fully a million and a half barrels of oil a month. Their pipes, of an aggregate length of 3,000 miles, connected with thousands of wells scattered all over the wide Oil Regions. . . .

THE INTERNATIONAL PETROLEUM CARTEL

The dream of empire and desire for military supremacy over the German fleet led Winston Churchill to decide to fuel the British navy on oil, not coal (see p. 3.) That decision, in turn, led the British to develop an inexpensive, secure source of oil first in Persia (Iran) and later in Mesopotamia (Iraq). In 1911, the year of Churchill's decision, the U.S. Supreme Court issued an equally important ruling and in a major antitrust case broke up Rockefeller's Standard Oil Trust. The decision ordered Standard Oil to divest itself of thirty-eight different subsidiaries. Three of Standard's offspring are today members of the Seven Sisters (Exxon, Mobil, and the Standard Oil Company of California). Half of the sixteen major oil companies are descendants of companies divested by Standard Oil. They are Exxon, Mobil, Standard Oil of California, Standard Oil of Indiana, Standard Oil of Ohio (now owned by BP), Continental (now owned by DuPont), Marathon (owned by U.S. Steel) and Arco. Each of these splintered sections subsequently sought markets and sources of supply across the world.

By the mid-1920s the British and Dutch who controlled most of the oil outside the United States, were exploiting and expanding their holdings with such efficiency that cheap Middle Eastern oil was beginning to flood onto world oil markets. The threat of major competition worldwide, of foreign penetration into U.S. domestic markets, and the specter of worldwide glut which might send prices tumbling out of control led Jersey Standard and other major American companies to launch an uphill struggle to gain a foothold in the Middle Eastern fields, which the British were anxious to sequester for themselves. The result of this initially intense struggle, involving, before it was over, the governments of both the United States and Britain, was a general agreement among the largest oil companies to create an organization for the purpose of ordering and controlling the production of oil in the Middle East. This was the great international oil cartel, and its vehicle was a company called the Iraq Petroleum Company. The IPC, in essence, was a cooperative with each of the major companies of the era—Anglo-Persian (now BP), Royal Dutch Shell, Compagnie Française des Pétroles, and a consortium of U.S. firms led by Standard Oil of New Jersey—holding a quarter share. Its formation signaled the true beginning of large-scale international control and manipulation of the oil business from well to marketplace which has affected the history and development of our world to this day.

A detailed report and analysis of the workings of this cartel were published by the Federal Trade Commission in 1951. The full report is far too lengthy to present in this book, but what follows are its major summary points on the immensely intricate organization and activities of IPC. Over the years the form of the cartel changed as different agreements among the main companies came and went, but the principle on which it was founded can be seen in similar organizations, most recently in the Iranian consortium that allocated oil during the period of the shah's rule in Iran.

Taken from The International Petroleum Cartel, a Staff Report to the Federal Trade Commission, *Select Committee on Small Business, U.S. Senate, 82nd Congress, August 22, 1952*

... *Control by Seven International Petroleum Companies.*—The outstanding characteristic of the world's petroleum industry is the dominant position of seven international companies. These seven companies are:

Standard Oil Company (N.J.): American.
Standard Oil Company of California: American.
Socony-Vacuum Oil Company, Inc.: American.
Gulf Oil Corporation: American.
The Texas Company: American.
Anglo-Iranian Oil Company: British.*
Royal Dutch-Shell Group: British and Dutch.

Control of the industry by these seven companies extends from reserves through production, transportation, refining, and marketing. All seven engage in every stage of operations, from exploration to marketing. The typical movement of petroleum from producer until acquired by the final consumer is through inter-company transfer within a corporate family. Outright sales, arms-length bargaining, and other practices characteristic of independent buyers and sellers are conspicuous by their absence. Control is held not only through direct corporate holdings, by parents, subsidiaries and affiliates of the seven, but also through such indirect means as interlocking directorates, joint ownership of affiliates, inter-company crude purchase contracts, and marketing agreements.

Control of World Crude Reserves.—In 1949, the seven companies owned 65 percent of the world's estimated crude oil reserves; 82 percent of all foreign (outside United States) reserves, 34 percent of the United States (domestic) reserves, and 92 percent of estimated crude reserves outside United States, Mexico and Russia.

Control over World Crude Oil Production.—In 1949, the seven companies accounted for more than one-half of the world's crude production (excluding Russia and satellite countries), about 99 percent of output in the Middle East, over 96 percent of the production in the Eastern Hemisphere, and almost 45 percent in the Western Hemisphere. If U.S. production is excluded, their share of the output of the rest of the Western Hemisphere is 80.5 percent. If U.S. production plus that controlled by U.S.S.R. and her satellite countries is excluded, these seven companies accounted for 88 percent of the remaining world's production. This figure understates the degree of control of the private petroleum industry because some of the output outside of the United States and Russia is produced by countries with state monopolies. Since the production of these countries must first satisfy internal demands, it is evident that only a relatively small quantity of crude is available from any source other than one of the seven large companies.

Control over World's Crude Oil Refining Capacity.—In 1950, the seven companies controlled almost 57 percent of the world's crude oil refining capacity. In the Western Hemisphere, excluding the United States, they held more than 75 percent; and in the Eastern Hemisphere, 79 percent. Excluding the United States and Russian controlled capacity, the seven companies owned more than 77 percent of the rest of the world's refining capacity.

Control of World's Cracking [*refining*] *Capacity.*—Control over cracking capacity is potentially of greater economic significance than control over crude refining capacity. The cracking process enables a refiner to obtain a greater quan-

*Fifty-six percent of the stock ownership of this company is held by the British Government.

tity of higher-valued products (for example, gasoline as compared to residual fuel oil) from a given quantity of crude than can be obtained by the straight-run distillation method of refining. The cracking process also enables the refiner to vary the proportions of products produced, thus giving greater flexibility to the refining operation. Moreover, it is only by using cracking processes that the petroleum industry is able to produce high octane gasoline and many of the chemicals which are the basic raw materials for synthetic rubber and many plastics. Thus the cracking process has made the petroleum industry an important supplier of products to other industries, and the concentration of control over the world's cracking capacity thereby affects a broader segment of the world economy than control over crude refining capacity.

In 1950, the seven companies owned 47 percent of the cracking capacity of the United States, 53 percent of that of the Western Hemisphere, 84 percent of that of the Eastern Hemisphere, and 55 percent of that of the world. If the cracking capacity of the United States and Russia (including her satellites) is excluded, the seven companies held 85 percent of all cracking capacity in the rest of the world as compared with 77 percent of the crude refining capacity of the same area.

Control of World's Petroleum Transportation Facilities.—In international trade petroleum and petroleum products are usually transported by tanker. Pipe lines are important in areas where extended movements overland are necessary and feasible; but, outside the United States, this use is limited to moving crude petroleum from producing areas to refineries or water terminals.

As with reserves, production and refining capacity, petroleum transportation facilities outside the United States are also largely controlled by the seven companies.

Tankers.—At the end of 1949, Anglo-Iranian Oil Company and Royal Dutch-Shell, two of the seven companies, controlled approximately 30 percent of the world's tanker tonnage. The other five of the seven, the American companies, controlled more than 20 percent. Thus, the seven companies control at least 50 percent of the world's tanker fleet, and perhaps more, since most of the large oil companies have added substantial tonnage to their tanker fleets in 1950.

If tanker tonnages owned or controlled by governmental agencies are excluded, the percentage of control of the seven companies is about two-thirds of the total privately-owned tanker fleet as compared to one-half of the world's total tanker tonnage.

Pipe Lines.—Outside the United States, every important pipeline in existence or even proposed is controlled by the seven companies, individually or jointly.

Control over Marketing.—While a detailed analysis cannot be given due to the scarcity of statistical information, it would appear that the seven companies are dominant forces in nearly all foreign markets. It does not appear necessary to develop any elaborate statistical argument to support this conclusion. Highly concentrated control over marketing would seem to be inevitable for the simple reason that there are no other companies operating in international markets capable of supplying petroleum products in substantial quantities. Upon the secure basis of their control over production, refining and transportation, the seven companies have built extensive marketing organizations reaching into consuming areas in all parts of the world. The power of these major companies is so substantial as to be virtually unchallengeable, except perhaps, in particular local marketing areas.

Importance of Inter-Corporate Relationships in the International Oil Industry. —The influence of the seven companies on the world's oil business is increased by close corporate relations existing between them.

Joint Ownership of Subsidiary and Affiliated Companies.—Outside the United States, Mexico and Russia, the operations of the seven companies are combined through various inter-company holdings in subsidiary and affiliated companies. These holdings constitute partnerships in various areas of the world. Each of the companies has pyramids of subsidiary and affiliated companies in which ownership is shared with one or more of the other large companies. Such a maze of joint ownership obviously provides opportunity, and even necessity, for joint action. With decision-making thus concentrated in the hands of a small number of persons, a common policy may be easily enforced.

Interlocking Directorates Among the International Petroleum Companies.— . . . A considerable number of the directors of the seven companies hold multiple directorships in subsidiary companies. For example, it is stated, the directors of the Standard of N.J. and Socony-Vacuum, who determine the policies of Arabian-American Oil Co. (Saudi Arabia) are the same men who help to shape the behavior of the Iraq Petroleum Company. The directors of Anglo-Iranian Company who assist in making high oil policy for Iraq and Iran, participate, along with the directors of Gulf, in planning the price and production policies in Kuwait. . . .

The significance of this high degree of concentration for the cartel problem lies in the fact that concentration facilitates the development and observance of international agreements regarding price and production policies. Indeed, the concentration of an industry into a few hands may be regarded as the *sine qua non* of effective cartel operations.

. . . Development of Joint Control Over the International Petroleum Industry

. . . *Background.*—American oil companies went into the foreign field after World War I for four reasons:

1. Fear of an Oil Shortage in America.
2. High cost of purchasing Private Mineral Rights in America.
3. Discovery of Foreign Reserves.
4. Fear of Foreign Monopoly.

Prior to 1920 American companies either had been indifferent to foreign reserves or they had been largely frustrated in their efforts to acquire reserves in the Eastern Hemisphere, owing to restrictive national and colonial policies of foreign governments and of private oil interests. After 1920, however, they became actively interested in foreign reserves, spurred by the dual fears of a prospective shortage of American oil and of a British-Dutch monopoly of foreign reserves. This increasing interest was also stimulated by the rising costs of American oil and the current and prospective discoveries of large foreign reserves which would afford to their owners a ready supply of cheap oil, advantageously located to important consuming markets. . . .

. . . THE IRAQ PETROLEUM COMPANY, LTD. (IPC)

The Iraq Petroleum Company, Ltd., was the first joint venture in which important American and foreign oil companies were united in one operation. In the words of one of its founders, IPC is a "unique company born of prolonged and arduous diplomatic and economic negotiations. IPC was not organised and operated as an independent corporate entity: rather, its policies and management were determined by and made to serve the mutual interests of the major international oil companies which jointly owned the majority of its shares." . . .

The history and development of the Iraq Petroleum Co., Ltd., is a striking illustration of the evolution of joint control through common ownership. By operating through the common ownership [mechanism], the major international companies were able not only to achieve a near-monopoly of oil concessions in a large area of the Middle East, but also to limit production, control prices, and generally restrain competition. As one authority has put it:

"Only groups with world-wide interests and command of proportionate resources could, for instance, afford to bottle up the Iraq production for so many years . . . The largest operator is, more than anyone else, interested in comparative stability, and he will always be prepared to pay for what he thrives on. It is not difficult to appreciate what would have happened to oil markets in general, if the potential production of the Middle East had been unloaded on world markets in the early 'thirties. This is probably the greatest service the major groups—who were all shareholders of the 'Iraq Petroleum'—have rendered to the industry at large."

IPC was not operated as an independent profit-making company. It was essentially a partnership for producing and sharing crude oil among its owners. Its profits were kept at a nominal level as a result of the practice of charging the member groups an arbitrarily low price for crude—a practice which reduced IPC's tax liability to the British Government and permitted the refining and marketing subsidiaries of the groups to capture the major share of the profits resulting from IPC's operations.

Although the origin of IPC dates back to the early 1900's, it did nto become important in world oil circles until after World War I. Restrictive arrangements came early in the life of the company, e.g., the Foreign Office Agreement of 1914. For the most part, however, the significant restrictions were not developed until the mid-twenties.

In the early twenties, when the American oil companies first became interested in oil concessions in the Middle East, they placed great emphasis on what was termed the "open-door" policy, and, in fact, made the acceptance of this policy a [*sine*] *qua non* of their participation in IPC. In this, they were actively supported by the American Government. In its initial stages the "open-door" policy was broadly interpreted to mean freedom for any company to obtain without discrimination, oil concessions in mandated areas, particularly in [Mesopotamia]. It was designed to promote active competition among the various companies for oil concessions and to prevent the establishment of a monopoly of oil rights. However, the "open-door" was gradually closed and then "bolted, barred, and hermetically sealed" by a series of deliberate and systematic acts on the part of the owners of

IPC. The first of these acts was the concession agreement between TPC (later IPC) and the Iraq Government of March 14, 1925, which made it practically impossible for a nonmember of IPC to obtain a lease or concession in the areas that were to be opened for competitive bidding. Competition for these areas was changed from public or auction bidding to sealed bidding, with IPC given the authority to open the sealed bids and make the awards. In the original "open-door" plan, IPC had been prohibited from bidding on plots to be offered at public auction. This prohibition, however, was omitted from the 1925 concession agreement. Thus, IPC was enabled to outbid any outsider, since (a) under the concession agreement all proceeds from bidding were to go to IPC, and (b) IPC had the right, upon meeting any submitted bid, to award the concession to itself. Secondly, when the groups signed the Red Line Agreement in 1928 and agreed not to be interested in the production or purchase of oil in the defined area (the old Ottoman Empire which included Turkey, Iraq, Saudi Arabia and adjoining sheikdoms, except Kuwait, Israel and Trans-Jordan) other than through the IPC, they "bolted and barred" the "open-door" insofar as their own activities were concerned. Finally, the concession agreement of 1931 closed the door not only on the groups themselves, but on all others as well by eliminating all references to a selection of plots to be offered outsiders, thus giving IPC a monopoly over a large area of Iraq. The "open-door" policy which had been so strongly advanced was discarded in subsequent years without a single test of its adequacy as a practical operating principle.

During the period between 1922, when the "open-door" policy was first advanced, and 1927, when it was in the process of being discarded, radical changes took place in the world oil situation. The fears of an oil shortage which were [so] widespread in 1922 were drowned in a surplus of oil. Instead of competing for the development of oil resources, the international companies turned their attention to limiting output and allocating world oil markets.

With the admission in 1928 of the American group to a share interest in IPC, four of the large international oil companies (Anglo-Iranian, Royal Dutch-Shell, Standard Oil Company (N.J.), and Socony-Vacuum) were united for the first time in a joint venture. The American group, acting as a unit through the Near East Development Corporation (NEDC), along with Anglo-Iranian and Royal Dutch-Shell, comprised the three major groups necessary to control and shape the operating policies of IPC. Following the discovery of oil in Iraq in October 1927, these three groups employed a variety of methods to retard developments in Iraq and prolong the period before the entry of Iraq oil into world markets. Among the tactics used to retard the development of Iraq oil were the requests for an extension of time in which to make the selection plots for IPC's exclusive exploitation, the delays in constructing a pipeline, the practice of preempting concessions for the sole purpose of preventing them from falling into other hands, the deliberate reductions in drilling and development work, and the drilling of shallow holes without any intention of finding oil.

Restrictive policies were continued even after a pipeline was completed, for in 1935, IPC's production was shut back several hundred thousand tons. Moreover, for a time, a sales coordinating committee was established to work out a "common policy regarding the sale of Iraq oil." Again in 1938 and 1939, the Big Three opposed any "enlargement of the pipe line and the corresponding increase in production" on the ground that additional production would upset the world oil market. Although the Big Three eventually conceded to the demands of the French (CFP) for some expansion, no action was taken until after World War II.

An important restrictive feature of the IPC was the Red Line Agreement of 1928, which prevented the member groups of IPC from competing with themselves and with IPC for concessions in an area which included most of the old Ottoman Empire. One writer in commenting upon the Red Line Agreement stated:

"This agreement is an outstanding example of a restrictive combination for the control of a large portion of the world's oil supply by a group of companies which together dominate the world market for this commodity."

Although the strongest proponents of the Red Line Agreement were the French and Gulbenkian, the Big Three were not unalterably opposed to its adoption. The American group, although opposed to the Red Line when first advanced, later agreed to its adoption.

The Red Line gave adequate protection against independent action by the groups within IPC, as was evidenced by IPC's refusal to permit Gulf Oil Corporation from exercising its option to purchase a concession in Bahrein. However, there was a loophole in the agreement in that it did not prevent non-members from seeking concessions within the Red Line area. When an independent organization, the British Oil Development Co. (BOD), obtained a concession in the Mosul area of Iraq, and when another outsider, Standard of California, obtained concessions in Bahrein and Saudi Arabia, IPC began to secure as many concessions as possible within the Red Line area, principally for the purpose of keeping them out of the hands of competitors. To effect the BOD and Standard of California's encroachments in the Red Line area, IPC subsequently obtained control of the BOD concession by secretly purchasing its shares, while the Big Three attempted to come to an understanding with Standard of California regarding the Bahrein and Saudi Arabian concessions.

But the Red Line Agreement proved to be a serious handicap to the Big Three in their efforts to make a deal with Standard of California. It was a handicap to the Big Three because the French and Gulbenkian were unwilling to waive their rights under the Red Line Agreement which entitled them to their pro rata share of any concessions, of any crude produced, or of any products derived from crude produced within the Red Line area. The Big Three tried, either individually or collectively, for almost seven years, to alter the Red Line Agreement in such a way that they would be able to neutralize the competitive effects of Standard of California's operations[,] with[,] however, only partial success. When World War II interrupted negotiations, the IPC groups had reached a temporary understanding among themselves in the form of an Agency Agreement for purchasing Bahrein's production. This agreement, however, fell far short of their real objective, which was a partnership agreement with Standard of California and Texas Co. covering the Arabian concession.

During the war, the Red Line Agreement was more or less put aside. Some of the groups, like, CFP [Compagnie Française des Pétroles] and Gulbenkian, were considered enemies and could not share in IPC's production nor actively participate in the management of the company. Others, like Standard Oil Company (N.J.), could not lift their share of crude because of shipping restrictions. Despite the disruptions of the war, IPC followed its established price policy which assured a low price to the groups able to take IPC crude, although such a policy was of course unfavorable to the interests of the inactive parties.

At the end of the war, CFP and Gulbenkian were reinstated and the question of reaffirming the Red Line Agreement became a pressing issue. The American group, instead of reaffirming the Agreement, declared it dissolved because (a) some of the owners had been enemies during the war, and (b) its restrictive provisions violated the American antitrust laws. It must also be remembered that at this time, Jersey Standard and Socony-Vacuum (the American group in IPC) were extremely anxious to purchase an interest in the Arabian American Oil Co. (Aramco), the company which held the Standard of California and Texas Co.'s concession in Saudi Arabia. It was the Red Line Agreement which before the war had blocked their efforts to secure a participation in these same concessions, the value of which had increased immensely during the war. It not only had been proved, but had developed into one of the world's most important oil concessions. As long as the Red Line Agreement hung around their necks like a millstone, the Big Three were placed in the role of unwilling outsiders, watching Standard of California develop this great new area, with possible disastrous effects on world price markets.

Following declaration by the American group that the Red Line Agreement was dissolved, the French (CFP) filed a suit in the British courts to enforce the Agreement and to obtain their proportionate share of any interest which the American group might secure in Aramco. But in November 1948, before the court case came to trial, a new agreement was negotiated freeing the IPC groups from many of the restrictive provisions of the Red Line Agreement and permitting the American group to purchase an interest in Aramco. The new agreement made it somewhat easier for a member of IPC to obtain oil in excess of its pro rata share. This was of considerable benefit to CFP, which for years had desired more oil from IPC, but under the Red Line Agreement was permitted to take only its pro rata share of IPC's production, as determined by the majority of the groups.

Under the new agreement, the groups were free to engage not only individually but also in common ownership arrangements with other sections of the Red Line area. The groups continued to obtain crude at an arbitrarily low price, and the Big Three retained their position of control over IPC's policies and management. That its long-established policy of restrictionism still continues is suggested by a proposal to restrict IPC's 1950 drilling budget to actual requirements; this proposal was advanced because of a fear that the development of any additional producing capacity would enable CFP to bargain for higher production rates.

The major groups in IPC not only restricted IPC's output, but after World War II, when the exigencies of the moment made it necessary for IPC to operate a refinery at Tripoli, they concertedly acted together to control the prices and the distribution of the refinery's products in such a manner as to discriminate against outsiders and further the interests of the major groups' marketing organizations. Also, the prices established by IPC for products at the Tripoli refinery, as well as the prices charged consumers in Iraq, ignored their natural economic advantage of location near a low cost source of supply.

In summary, the fundamental purposes and objectives of IPC were described by the French in a confidential document:

"The incorporation of IPC and the execution of the Red Line Agreement marked the beginning of a long term plan for the world control and distribution of oil in the Near East."

IPC was so operated as: ". . . to avoid any publicity which might jeopardize the long term plan or the private interests of the group . . ." It would appear there is no evidence that this "long term plan" is still not in effect. . . .

CONCENTRATION OF CONTROL IN DOMESTIC OIL

Although the Supreme Court had broken up the Standard Oil Trust, this hardly spelled the end of Big Oil in the United States. Quite the opposite was actually the case, as John Blair makes clear in the next selection. While the international companies—the Seven Sisters—controlled the oil industry abroad through a cartel, at home a relatively small number of firms employed a variety of means to maintain and exercise control, including joint ownership of federal offshore leases and ownership of refineries and pipelines. The U.S. government played a crucial role in assisting these major companies in their organization of the industry.

John Blair, who for years examined the workings of the oil industry as chief economist of the Senate Antitrust Subcommittee, provides a detailed analysis of how the industry actually functioned at home. Here again, as we have already seen in both Tarbell and the Federal Trade Commission report, concentration—not competition—is the rule of the game.

Taken from The Control of Oil, *by John Blair, New York, Pantheon, 1976.*

From its earliest days the production of crude oil in the United States has been widely dispersed among numerous producers. Although the concentration of domestic crude production has been rising as the result of mergers and other causes, it still remains well below the levels of oil-producing countries elsewhere. Among the factors that have combined to bring this about is a legal principle not present in most other oil-producing lands; the private ownership of subsoil mineral rights. A philosophic principle that has emerged in the development of Western civilization is the right of the individual to own property, including the ownership not only of the surface land but of what lies below. Where the subsoil mineral rights are the property of the state or the ruler, as in the Middle East, the obtaining of concessions has involved negotiations only with the governing body. But in the United States, the right to withdraw oil must be negotiated with individual private property owners whose number is legion.

Moreover, unlike the Middle East, where most of the output comes from a few large fields, production in the United States is scattered among a large number of small and medium-size fields, each of which has its own independent producers and royalty owners usually tracing back to discovery by independent wildcatters. Although over the years the major oil companies have been able to acquire control over most of their output, the circumstances of their discovery left behind a legacy of individual ownership. In a statement to the Temporary National Economic Committee in 1939, Karl A. Crowley, an attorney of Fort Worth, Texas, testified: "The independent wildcatter must be given credit for practically every major discovery of oil in the United States. It was due to the faith of independents that the great Ranger field was discovered when the world was faced with a shortage of oil during the World War. Independents opened the gigantic Burkburnett pool, Cushing, Seminole, Spindletop, and countless others. The hardy independent has discovered and used new methods for locating oil pools, and time after time he has gone into territory condemned by the majors and unearthed a new store of nature's riches." Of fifteen large oil pools discovered in Oklahoma and West Texas between 1912 and 1926, the majors found only one—Oklahoma's Hewitt field, discovered by the Texas Co.

Crowley went on to describe the discovery of the Great Permian Basin in Winkler County: "There the majors had condemned that entire area as being worthless for oil—said that it was impossible to produce oil from the formations that were to be found there. It was condemned as being so utterly worthless that the fool-hardy wildcatter there was unable to sell any of his leases to the major companies and had to depend upon individual speculators to obtain a few dollars from time to time until he literally worried his well down to production. He and his associates found themselves the possessors of a great well located in a block of nearly 30,000 acres of land that has proved to be immensely rich and productive."

The great East Texas field owned its discovery to the persistence of an impoverished wildcatter, the legendary "Dad" Joiner. Volume from this field quickly rose to about 1 billion barrels a day, or about one-third of the national requirements. In Crowley's words:

> It remained for a true independent, C. M. "Dad" Joiner, to discover the world's largest oil pool and to add billions of new wealth to the State of Texas and an unheard-of supply of cheap oil for the people of the nation. Joiner spent more than a year drilling his well. He often was compelled to shut down operations for lack of money and was only able to finish his well by borrowing money from his friends and selling a few leases to individuals. Not a dollar did he ever get from any major company. Joiner's well came in October 3, 1930; it produced 300 barrels of oil a day and it encouraged others to drill in the area and three months later on December 28, 1930, another independent drilled 15 miles farther north and completed a well with an initial production of 10,000 barrels daily. Approximately one month later, about January 26, 1931, another independent brought in still another well, 15 miles farther and this one came in for 12,000 barrels of oil daily.
>
> With the discovery of the latter two great wells by independents, the majors found themselves with very few leases in the field. They sent their buyers, land men and lawyers to the field by the hundreds, all armed with plenty of money, and entered into an unprecedented buying campaign to acquire the choicest leases, covering land that they had before condemned

as being utterly worthless. The independents, however, had secured a toehold and even at this time owned half of the leases in that great field.

And so it was that the East Texas field, the greatest oil field in all history, came into existence through the adventuresome spirit, faith, confidence and capability of independent wildcatters.

Although decentralization was thus inherent in the circumstances of crude production, the subsequent stages of refining and transportation offered the potential for centralized control. And John D. Rockefeller was quick to seize the opportunity, gathering into the hands of the old Standard Oil "Trust" control over the great bulk of the nation's refining capacity. When in 1911 the Supreme Court dissolved the trust, the way was opened for the subsequent growth of other major companies. Had it not been for its dissolution the "Trust," through its control of transportation and refining, could have brought concentration in crude production to even further heights by continuing to determine which producers could get their oil transported and refined. Nonetheless, the Court's order was badly flawed in one respect: the assets of the holding company were distributed back to its own stockholders—assets consisting of the stock of the operating companies, which were spread over production, transportation, refining, and marketing. The result of leaving the ownership of the operating companies in the hands of those who had owned the old parent corporation was of course to leave the dominant ownership with the Rockefeller interests. After an investigation eleven years later, the Federal Trade Commission noted: "There is, as is generally known, an interlocking stock ownership in the different organizations [of the Standard Oil group] which has perpetuated the very monopolistic control which the courts sought to terminate."

Not long after the old Standard Oil "Trust" had been broken up in 1911, the newly divided operating companies resumed their growth by merger. As early as 1921, Standard (Ind.) acquired a sizable rival, Midwest Refining, with assets of $85.9 million. Four years later, it absorbed an even larger company, Pan American Petroleum and Transportation, with assets of $179.5 million. In the same year, Standard of N.Y. (Mobil) acquired one of the nation's largest independents, Magnolia Petroleum, with assets of $212.8 million, and in 1926 it purchased General Petroleum ($102 million). Also in 1926, Standard (Calif.) made two important acquisitions, Pacific Oil and Pacific Petroleum ($181 million and $95 million, respectively). These acquisitions formed an important part of the foundation on which the subsequent growth of the Standard companies was based.

While the descendants of the old trust have continued to grow by merger and otherwise, so also have other integrated majors—companies with their own reserves, refining facilities, and retail outlets. Together with the nonintegrated independents, they make up a threeway division of the domestic industry. In years past it was customary to speak of the "20 majors," but a recent Staff Report of the Federal Trade Commission identifies "17 majors." The reduction is the result of mergers: e.g., Richfield with Atlantic, Pure with Union, Sinclair with ARCO and BP. Within this group of seventeen, the ubiquity of their leadership positions at each of the industry's stages suggests that the eight largest companies represent a group clearly separate from and above the other majors, who are usually an important factor only at one stage. For example, the ninth-ranking firm in ownership of reserves and crude production (Getty) ranks sixteenth in refining capacity and was not even among the twenty largest in retail gasoline sales. The ninth largest in retail sales and refining (Sun) ranked eleventh in crude production and fourteenth in ownership of reserves. Unlike the international industry, the domestic industry has evolved, not into a dichotomy ("majors" and "independents"), but into a trichotomy ("the top eight," "lesser majors," and nonintegrated "independents").

Measured by the customary "four-company" concentration ratio, domestic oil is certainly not one of the nation's most concentrated industries, a fact frequently cited by its defenders. Commenting on this line of argument, John W. Wilson has observed:

> Despite its size, conventional concentration ratio measurements indicate that oil is not particularly concentrated in comparison with other major industries . . . while the concentration ratios for the top four or top eight crude oil producers have increased substantially in the last twenty years, the industry still seems to compare favorably with other leading manufacturing industries, such as automobiles, copper, computers, and aluminum. Thus, argue the industry's defenders, right-thinking rational men should direct their antitrust interests toward more critical targets like breakfast cereals and beer, and leave oil alone.

But this reasoning overlooks the joint ventures and communities of interest among the largest companies and, above all, the use of government to supplement and strengthen private methods of control.

THE CONCENTRATION OF DOMESTIC SUPPLY

On July 12, 1973, Senator Henry M. Jackson, chairman of the Permanent Senate Subcommittee on Investigations, made public as a committee print a sixty-two-page document entitled "Preliminary Federal Trade Commission Staff Report on Its Investigation of the Petroleum Industry." This report presents concentration figures in terms of individual companies for each of the four sectors of the industry —reserves, production, refining, and retail marketing.

Nearly all (93.6%) of the nation's proved reserves of crude oil are held by twenty major oil companies. The United States can thus secure domestic oil that "with reasonable certainty" is "recoverable from known reservoirs under existing economic and operating conditions" only to the extent that this small group of companies agrees to its extraction. Any policies on price, taxes, etc., with which these companies disagree can result in their oil simply being left in the ground, where its value will appreciate as demand and price levels continue to rise.

Nearly two-thirds of the reserves are held by the eight largest firms, and over one-third (37.2%) by the four largest, each of which holds about 9 percent of the total. The top eight in the control of reserves were also the top eight in each of the industry's successive stages. As Table 6-1 reveals, their rankings may differ somewhat from stage to stage; but in ownership of reserves, crude production, refining capacity, and retail sales, the top eight invariably consist of Exxon, Texaco, Gulf, SoCal, Standard (Ind.), Atlantic-Richfield (ARCO), Shell, and Mobil. For the top eight as a group, their aggregate share of retail sales (55.0%) is firmly based

TABLE 6-1 Eight Top Companies: Shares and Ranking at Successive Stages of the Petroleum Industry, 1970

	Domestic Reserves		Crude Production*		Refining Capacity		Retail Gasoline Sales	
	Share	Rank	Share	Rank	Share	Rank	Share	Rank
Exxon	9.9%	1	9.8%	1	8.6%	1	7.4%	3
Texaco	9.3	2	8.5	2	8.1	3	8.1	1
Gulf	9.0	3	6.8	3	5.8	7	7.1	5
SoCal	9.0	4	5.3	5	7.7	5	5.0	8
Standard (Ind.)	8.5	5	5.1	7	8.2	2	7.3	4
ARCO	7.5	6	5.1	6	5.4	8	5.6	7
Shell	5.9	7	6.1	4	8.0	4	7.9	2
Mobil	4.9	8	3.9	8	6.3	6	6.6	6
Top eight	64.0		50.5		58.1		55.0	

*1969.
Source: 1973 FTC Staff Report, pp. 13–22.

on a slightly higher percentage of refining capacity (58.1%), and their share of refining capacity on an even higher proportion of domestic reserves (64.0%). In a period of diminishing supplies, the last will, of course, be the critical determinant.

While it is the *level* of concentration that is associated with differences in an industry's behavior, the direction and rate of change is also of great importance from the point of view of public policy. For economic as well as legal reasons, it is far harder to restore competition than to preserve it. It is by preventing increases in concentration that antitrust has its best opportunity to preserve competitive behavior. Although petroleum has presented an almost ideal opportunity for the preservation of competition through the application of the existing law against mergers, the opportunity has not been seized. Partly as a result, concentration has increased markedly in both the ownership of domestic reserves and the production of crude oil, as can be seen in Table 6-2. From just over a third, the six companies which with BP make up the "seven sisters" increased their share of domestic reserves during 1949–70 to slightly less than a half. Three of the six—Gulf, SoCal, and Shell—nearly doubled their ownership proportions. In terms of crude production, the share held by the six during the more limited period 1960–69 rose from a third to over two-fifths, with by far the largest gain (from 6.5% to 9.8%) being recorded by the industry's largest firm. These increases, it should be noted, took place despite a vast proliferation in the number of producers.

THE CONCENTRATION OF REFINING CAPACITY

In contrast to production, the capital entrance requirements in refining are high and rising, and the number of refiners is low and falling. Although many older refineries are smaller, the minimum optimal size of a new refinery has been placed at about 150,000 barrels a day, costing $250–$400 million. As would be expected

TABLE 6-2 Six Major Oil Companies: Change in Concentration of Domestic Proved Reserves and Crude Production

	Reserves		Production	
	1949	1970	1960	1969
Exxon	11.1%	9.9%	6.5%	9.8%
Texaco	5.4	9.3	8.9	8.5
Gulf	4.6	9.0	5.1	6.8
SoCal	4.6	9.0	4.8	5.3
Shell	2.9	5.9	4.8	6.1
Mobil	5.0	4.9	3.4	3.9
Total	33.6	48.0	33.5	40.4
Top four	25.7	37.2	25.3	30.4

Sources: International Petroleum Cartel, p. 23; 1973 FTC Staff Report, pp. 13, 14.

from the higher capital entrance requirements, the level of concentration is higher in refining capacity than in production. Between 1961 and 1972, the number of domestic petroleum refineries fell from 311 to 282, while the number of refining companies dropped from 175 to 129. Accompanying this decline in the number of refineries, concentration moved steadily upward. As can be seen from Table 6-3, the top four increased their share of domestic refining capacity from 28.5 percent in 1960 to 32.9 percent in 1970, while the top eight enlarged their proportion from 46.0 to 58.1 percent. The effective control over refining capacity is undoubtedly even higher. Concerning the concentration ratio for refining, the FTC report noted that: "due to the existence of processing arrangements between major oil companies and independent refiners through which major oil companies supply crude oil in return for refined product, this figure may substantially understate effective refinery concentration."

In any event, the majors' position at the refining stage has enabled them to

TABLE 6-3 Changes in Concentration of Domestic Refining Capacity, 1960–70

	1960	1970
Exxon	—	8.6%
Texaco	—	8.1
Shell	—	8.0
SoCal	—	7.7
Mobil	—	6.3
Gulf	—	5.8
Total	—	44.5
Standard (Ind.)	—	8.2
ARCO	—	5.4
Top four	28.5	32.9
Top eight	46.0	58.1

Source: 1973 FTC Staff Report, p. 18, n. 18.

eliminate excess capacity by the simple expedient of not building new refineries. Because of the large number of crude producers, the limitation of production required government intercession. But in refining, the number of companies is sufficiently limited and the concentration sufficiently high to make possible an effective tailoring of capacity to demand without such intercession. As Chart 6-1 shows, the growth of refining capacity in relation to demand has undergone three distinct stages during the past quarter century. In the first period, 1952–59, capacity and demand rose closely in tandem with each other, with capacity showing a

CHART 6-1 Domestic Demand* and Refining Capacity, 1950–72

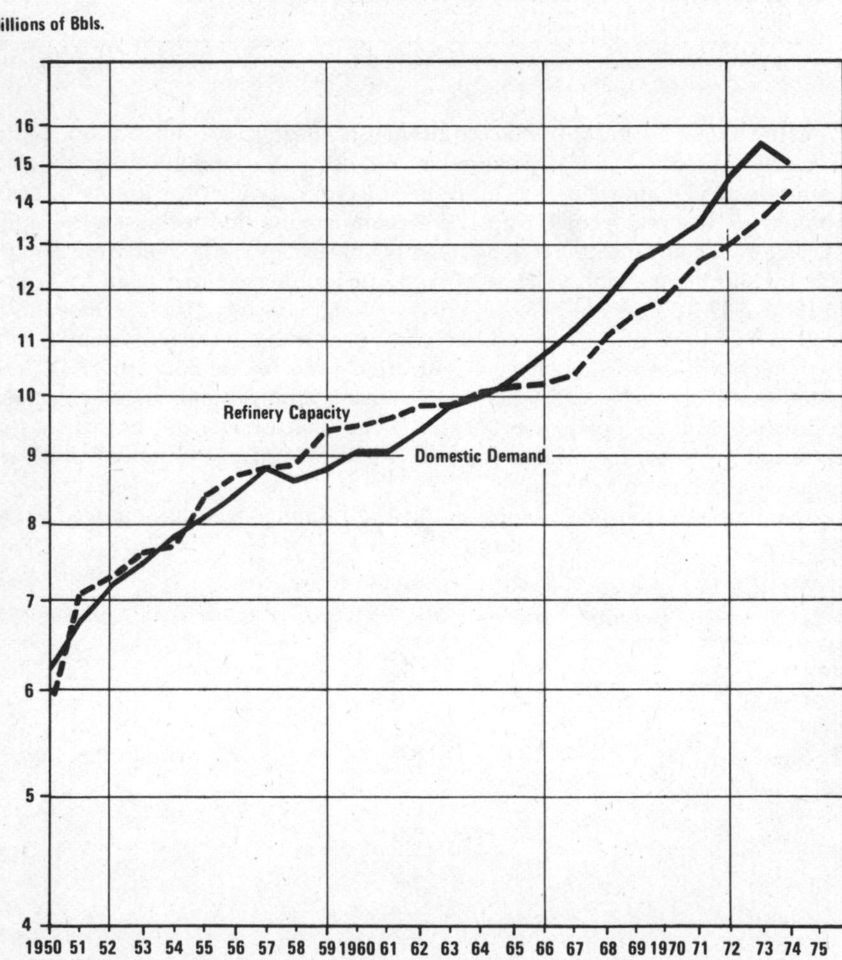

*Primary supply minus production of natural gas liquid plants minus exports and crude losses.

Sources: Bureau of Mines and American Petroleum Institute.

higher average growth rate (3.71%) than demand (2.85%). As a result, refining capacity by 1959 was some 600,000 b/d [barrels per day] in excess of demand. Although in the second period, 1959–66, demand continued to rise at nearly the same rate (2.68%), the annual growth rate of capacity was cut back to only 1.28 percent.

TABLE 6-4 Average Annual Growth Rate for Domestic Refining Capacity and Demand, Selected Periods

	To		
From	1959	1966	1972
1952 Capacity	3.71%	2.51%	2.59%
Demand	2.85	2.39	3.04
1959 Capacity		1.28	2.45
Demand		2.68	3.76
1966 Capacity			4.22
Demand			4.68

Sources: Bureau of Mines and American Petroleum Institute. To secure comparability with the series for refining capacity, the measure used for domestic demand is the production of domestic refineries plus that of natural gas liquid plants (whose output is largely for sale) minus imports.

During 1959–66, average net additions to distillation capacity fell from an annual level of 330,000 to 170,000 barrels a day. Thus, by 1966 the former relationship had been reversed, with capacity falling some 500,000 b/d below demand. During the third period, the expansion of capacity went forward at a more rapid rate (4.22%), but this was not sufficient to enable supply to catch up with demand, since the latter was rising at the still more rapid rate of 4.68 percent. Capital expenditures on petroleum refineries were reduced from $825 million in 1957 to $350 million in 1959, near which level they remained for the next five years. Some of the largest companies reduced not only their financial outlays for expansion but their actual capacity as well. Exxon's refining capacity in Texas, Louisiana, and the Gulf Coast was lowered from 919,040 b/d in 1956 to 879,000 b/d in 1964; Gulf's from 477,490 to 457,000 b/d; and Sun's from 160,000 to 155,000. Others in the face of rising demand kept their capacity unchanged, e.g., Atlantic-Richfield at 210,000 b/d and Cities Service at 199,300 b/d.

The retrenchment in refinery construction can hardly be attributed to an inability to obtain the necessary capital since at the very time the oil companies were reducing their investments in refineries at home, they were greatly expanding their refining capacity abroad. According to the Office of Oil and Gas of the Interior Department, some 1,720,000 b/d of refining capacity was "exported" by American oil firms to foreign locations. Moreover, the majors were also embarked on a vigorous invasion into the U.S. chemical industry. Chart 6-2 indicates that the halving of their capital outlays on petroleum refineries was accompanied by a tripling of their investments in chemical plants, with the result that in the first half

CHART 6-2 Capital Expenditures by Petroleum Companies in the United States for Oil Refineries and for Chemical Plants, 1957–67

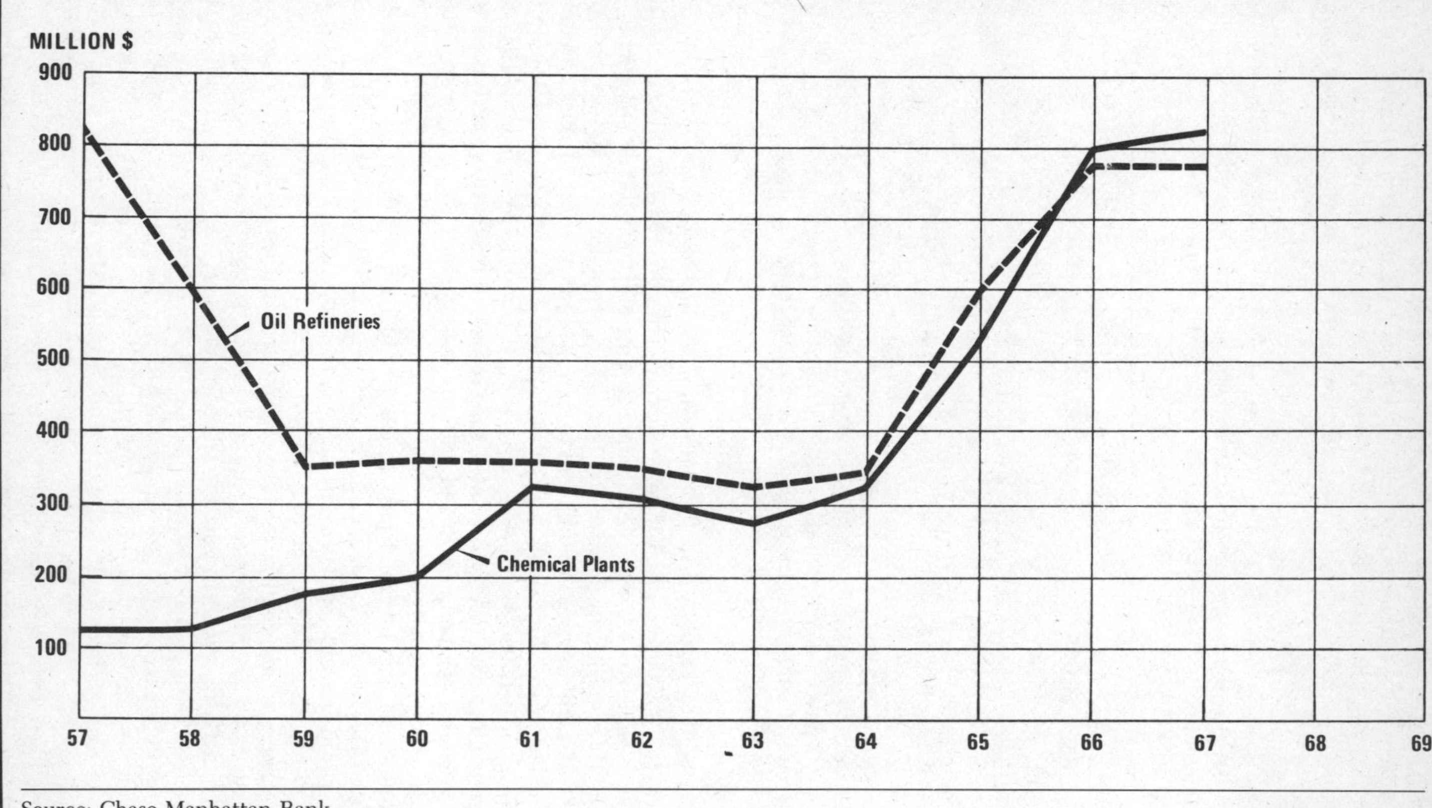

Source: Chase Manhattan Bank.

of the 1960's their expenditures in new chemicals closely approximated outlays in their primary field. By 1967, their investments in chemicals had exceeded their outlays in petroleum by some $50 million. As a consequence, no fewer than eleven of the thirty top sellers of chemicals had by 1968 become petroleum companies; the leaders were Standard (N.J.) which ranked sixth in chemical sales, Occidental (eleventh), Shell (thirteenth), Phillips (seventeenth), and Mobil (nineteenth).

Nor can the industry's failure to expand capacity during the 1960's be traced to environmental objections. The widespread concern with protecting the environment from oil dates from the Santa Barbara oil spill, which did not occur until 1969. In a survey conducted in 1973 by the Senate Commerce Committee, each major oil company was asked how many refineries it had specifically proposed in the continental United States since 1958 that were *not* built because of citizens' law suits based upon environmental issues. Of the ten majors responding, not one stated that it had failed to build a refinery because of environmentally based civil law suits. The most logical explanation, occasionally alluded to in the trade press, is of course the most obvious one. In the words of the *Oil and Gas Journal,* "the conviction of many refiners—who point to widespread price-warring and distressed gasoline—is that a lull in construction is needed to let demand catch up a bit." By 1972 that objective had been largely achieved.

INTERCORPORATE RELATIONSHIPS

The analysis of market concentration presented above has presumed the leading companies to be separate and independent, free from any influence through intercorporate relationships that would affect their competitive behavior. In the case of the petroleum industry, such an assumption is a fiction. Through interlocking corporate relationships and joint ventures of every conceivable form, the opportunities for substituting collective for independent judgment are legion. Indeed, it is the view of John W. Wilson (former chief of the Division of Economic Studies, Federal Power Commission) that the effect of bringing "horizontally and vertically juxtaposed firms into close working relationships with each other" is to make cooperation a necessity:

> They *must* work together to further their joint interests. Consequently, each becomes familiar with the others and with each other's operations. Men in such close working relationships learn to consider one another's interests. This process of learning to live together is, of course, quite laudable in certain social and political contexts. The success of our Nation's international relations, for example, depends greatly upon this process. But it is, most assuredly, not the kind of institutional setting within which a free market economy can be expected to function efficiently. Real economic competition is made of tougher stuff. . . . In order to function both efficiently and in the public interest, free markets *must be competitive.* This means that the participants must be structurally and behaviorally independent of each other. That precondition quite apparently does not apply to the petroleum industry.

Among the many ways in which rival companies are brought together is the joint venture, which for its specific purpose necessarily subordinates individual interests to a concern for the common good. No other industry begins to approach petroleum in the number and importance of jointly owned enterprises. While found in practically every stage of the industry, they have been particularly important with respect to foreign oil reserves, pipelines, and offshore oil leases. Among vertically integrated companies, the conduct of such a series of successive activities through joint ventures has a cumulative effect, progressively narrowing the area in which independent rivalrous conduct is even possible. The joint venture's inhibiting effect on competition is obvious where a company is confronted with the alternative either of embarking on a potentially rewarding (and potentially dangerous) course of independent competitive behavior or of avoiding the competitive struggle by forming a common enterprise with its rivals.

JOINT OWNERSHIP OF PIPELINES. By its very nature the pipeline is a bottleneck, invariably owned and controlled by the majors but of critical importance to the independents. Without the services of a gathering line, the independent producer cannot get his product to a refinery. And without the continuous, assured supply provided by a pipeline, a refinery, because of its high fixed costs, cannot operate efficiently. Even where his supply is provided by independent producers, the independent refiner using a major-owned pipeline is still not free from the influence of his larger competitors.

The opportunities presented by the pipeline for securing monopoly control have long been recognized. When first incorporated in 1870, the Standard Oil Co. controlled only about 10 percent of the nation's petroleum refining capacity. Three years later, it began to gather and transport crude bought from others through pipelines. By 1879, less than a decade after the original incorporation, it had increased its control over refining capacity to 90 percent. This astonishing increase was achieved in large part through control over transportation—both pipelines and railroads.

Today, approximately 75 percent of the crude produced in the United States flows to the refinery by pipeline, 17 percent by tanker and 8 percent by truck. Pipelines transporting crude oil across state lines are common carriers, subject to regulation by the Interstate Commerce Commission, and the egregious tactics employed by the old Standard Oil "Trust" are unlawful. In its recent investigation, however, the FTC Staff found that much the same objectives can be accomplished by more subtle means. The flow of crude to independent refiners can be stopped or limited by: "(1) requiring shipments of minimum size, (2) granting independents irregular shipping dates, (3) limiting available storage at the pipeline terminals, (4) imposing unreasonable product standards upon independent customers of pipe-lines, and (5) employing other harassing or delaying tactics." Although pipeline owners must obtain ICC approval for rates providing a fair return on their pipeline investment, the rates approved may be well above the competitive cost of transporting oil. For the vertically integrated firm, this merely increases the profitability of its pipeline operation and decreases that of its refinery. For the nonintegrated refiner, an excessive pipeline charge is a real cost not transferrable to any other department.

Whether because of their potential for monopoly control or their formidable capital costs, or both, nearly all petroleum pipelines throughout the world have long been owned and controlled by the major oil companies, usually as joint ventures. In 1952 it was found that outside the United States, "... every important pipeline in existence or even proposed is controlled by the seven principal international oil companies, individually or jointly." These included such important arteries as the Trans Arabian Pipeline (Tapline), from Qaisuma, Saudi Arabia, to the Mediterranean, a distance of 753 miles, owned by Exxon, SoCal, Texaco, and Mobil; the Interprovincial Pipeline from Edmonton, Canada, to Superior, Wisconsin, a distance of 1,100 miles, owned by Exxon; a 143-mile line running from Lake Maracaibo in Venezuela to Amsay Bay on the Caribbean, owned by Exxon and other international majors; as well as the complex system of pipelines serving Iran, Iraq, and Bahrein.

That the largest oil companies continue as the principal owners is apparent from data relating to U.S. pipelines presented by Wilson to the Senate Antitrust Subcommittee. Table 6-5 presents the ownership share held by the top eight domestic producers for seven domestic lines (with assets of more than $20 million). In each case companies among the top eight held a majority position. The line with the largest number of companies required to achieve majority control is Dixie, where majority control takes five firms. For the group as a whole, it takes an average of only 3 companies among the country's top eight to hold majority stock ownership.

JOINT OWNERSHIP OF OFFSHORE LEASES. The major oil companies have also joined together in the ownership of, and bidding for, producing leases on offshore lands. Embracing some 16 million acres, of which 80 percent consists of undisputed federal area, the outer continental shelf area off Louisiana (though not off Texas) has proved to contain a large reservoir of oil. The granting of leases to these federal lands is under the jurisdiction of the Department of Interior, whose policies have been criticized as unduly favoring the major oil companies on two grounds.

In the first place, permitting competing companies to join together and submit one bid on their collective behalf contravenes the spirit and objective of the antitrust laws. If in the normal course of business the same group of companies were to meet together privately and agree on the price, who was to get the business, and how the costs and benefits were to be divided, they would be in obvious violation of Section 1 of the Sherman Act. As Walter J. Mead has put it:

> In any given sale, it is obvious that when four firms, each able to bid independently, combine to submit a single bid, three interested, potential bidders have been eliminated; i.e., the combination has restrained trade. This situation does not differ materially from one of explicit collusion in which four firms meet in advance of a given sale and decide who among them should bid (which three should refrain from bidding) for specific leases and, instead of competing among themselves, attempt to rotate the winning bids. The principal difference is that explicit collusion is illegal.

The second criticism goes to the method of bidding; i.e., the practice of "bonus bidding" under which the Department, after requiring a flat one-sixth royalty from all bidders, makes its award on the basis of the cash bonus bid (above a minimal per-acre figure). With individual bids exceeding $100 million per lease, it is difficult to conceive of a bidding procedure more favorable to the largest firms and more disadvantageous to the independents. Even if any independent, or

TABLE 6-5 Company Shares of Top Eight in Selected Pipelines

	Colonial	Plantation	Dixie	Laurel	Texas-N. Mex.	Wolverine	Four Corners
Exxon		48.8%	11.1%				
Mobil	11.5%		5.0			26.0%	
Texaco	14.3		5.0	33.9%	45.0%	17.0	
SoCal							25.0%
Shell		24.0	5.5				25.0
Gulf	16.8		18.2	49.1		7.0	20.0
Standard (Ind.)	14.3		12.1				
ARCO	1.6		7.4		35.0	25.0	10.0
Total	58.5	72.8	64.3	83.0	80.0	75.0	80.0
Assets ($ million)	$480.2	$176.2	$46.4	$35.9	$30.5	$21.8	$20.9

Source: Compiled from Testimony by John W. Wilson before the Senate Subcommittee on Antitrust and Monopoly, Hearings on the Natural Gas Industry, Pt. 1, pp. 456 ff.

group of them, were able to outbid the majors, the cost of the bid itself would absorb cash capital better devoted to undertaking an adequate drilling program. In place of bonus bidding the present procedure could, without change in the law, be simply reversed. Under a proposal originally advanced by E. Wayles Browne, a flat dollar amount per acre would be fixed; the variable would be the royalty percentage, with the award going to the bidder who offered the government the greatest share. Under such a "royalty" bidding procedure, any independent company that is able to contract for an offshore well could enter the bidding, with some possibility of success. Without having to tie up its funds for a lease bonus, substantially all of its working capital would be available for use in geological and geophysical work and in drilling. Moreover, during the foreseeable years of apparently continuing inflation, such a procedure would have the very real advantage of yielding payments to the government in dollars of constant purchasing power. Until such an alternative is adopted, the present "bonus" system will bar even sizable independents from access to these government-owned resources. Testimony to this effect was cited by Wilson:

> As the president of an established oil company with annual revenues of over $100 billion recently testified in an FPC hearing, it would now take a consortium of 15 or more firms like his to surmount the offshore entry barriers which have been erected under Interior's watchful eye. Consequently, his company and others like it have been effectively precluded from entering these producing areas except by obtaining limited farmouts of unwanted acreage from the dominant majors or perhaps by joining one of the established combines as a junior partner.

As an experiment, the Interior Department in October 1974 put up several plots for royalty bidding. The refusal by several of the largest companies even to offer bids was taken by the Department as evidence of the procedure's unworkability. To the majors royalty bidding meant not only greater competition but a lessening of immediate tax benefits. If, under bonus bidding, the lease turns out to yield dry holes or is abandoned for other reasons, half of the bonus can be deducted immediately as a business expense. If the property is income-producing, the company can reclaim half the bonus in equal installments over five years.

As might be surmised from this governmentally imposed barrier to entry, concentration in production from offshore areas is even higher than in the industry's other stages. To measure the concentration of ownership, Walter S. Measday of the Senate Antitrust Subcommittee examined sixty-four fields accounting for 94 percent of all production on federal lands in the Louisiana Outer Continental Shelf (OCS), the results of which are shown in Table 6-6. In comparison with their share of 50.5 percent for total domestic crude production, the top eight accounted for 64.5 percent of the output from the offshore area. Nearly half came from just three of the top eight—Shell, Exxon, and SoCal.

Much of the offshore output is produced by joint ventures, thus affording the majors still another opportunity for the development of commonalities of interest. Exxon shares ownership of federal offshore leases with Gulf and Mobil; Shell shares ownership with SoCal; Gulf with Mobil, SoCal with Mobil and ARCO; and Standard (Ind.) with Texaco and Mobil. But an analysis of the data reveals something else. By and large, the companies with the greatest financial resources, (e.g.,

TABLE 6-6 Company Shares of Sales of Crude and Condensate, Federal Gulf of Mexico, Louisiana Outer Continental Shelf, 1974

Top Eight	Thousands of Barrels	Percent
Shell	60,807	18.8%
Exxon	44,828	13.9
SoCal	36,467	11.3
Gulf	21,610	6.7
ARCO	16,380	5.1
Texaco	11,701	3.6
Mobil	9,026	2.8
Standard (Indiana)	7,801	2.4
Top 8	208,620	64.5
Lesser Majors	65,190	20.3
Others	49,217	15.2
Total	323,027	100.0

Source: 94th Cong., 1st Sess., Senate Subcommittee on Antitrust and Monopoly, Hearings on S. 2387 and Related Bills, Pt. 1, pp. 51–70 (Statement of Walter S. Measday), September 23, 1975.

Exxon, Gulf, Shell, and SoCal) have little need to spread the costs or share the risks. Hence, it is not surprising to find that most of the leases held by these companies are individually owned, without participation by other firms. Forty-three out of 52 leases held by Exxon are individually owned; 64 of 68 held by Shell Oil, 34 of 51 held by Gulf, and 86 of 105 held by SoCal are individually owned. In contrast, the lesser majors rely heavily on participations with other companies. All but 1 of Continental's 119 and of Cities Service's 101 leases are joint ventures; the same is true of all but 2 of Getty's 100 leases. All of the leases of Amerada Hess (15), Marathon (18), and Sun (19) are joint ventures. For companies of this intermediate size, offerings under the bonus bidding procedure appear to be possible only if the cost is shared. But while the joint venture makes participation possible, it also lessens the value to the lessee of any possible discovery.

The present bidding procedure thus has several strategic advantages for the largest companies: it virtually excludes the independents; it dilutes the value of a discovery to any potential maverick by forcing the "lesser majors" into joint offerings; and it gives to the largest firms the option of either spreading the cost through a joint offering or reaping the full benefit through an independent offering. With good reason Wilson has criticized the offshore leasing program as "one of the most onerous anticompetitive cartelization devices at work . . ."

INTERLOCKING DIRECTORATES. In 1914, Congress addressed itself for the first and last time to the problem of interlocking directorates. The occasion was the consideration of what became known as the Clayton Act, a keystone of President Wilson's New Freedoms. In a message to Congress on January 20, 1914, the

President called for the enactment of "laws which will effectively prohibit and prevent such interlockings of the personnel of the directorates of great corporations—banks and railroads, industrial, commercial, and public service bodies—and in effect result in making those who borrow and those who lend practically one and the same, those who sell and those who buy but the same persons trading with another under different names and in different combinations, and those who affect to compete in fact partners and masters of some whole field of business." In their reports accompanying the measure, the House and Senate Committees likewise showed their concern with the general problem of concentrated economic power: "The concentration of wealth, money and property in the United States under the control and in the hands of a few individuals or great corporations has grown to such an enormous extent that unless checked it will ultimately threaten the perpetuity of our institutions. The idea that there are only a few men in any of our great corporations and industries who are capable of handling the affairs of the same is contrary to the spirit of our institutions."

As finally enacted, however, the provision dealing with interlocking directorates (Section 8) was based not on any broad standard directed to the concentration of economic power but on a much narrower test. Specifically, it provided that no person could be a director of two or more industrial or commercial enterprises (with capital, surplus, and undivided profits of more than $1 million), if the concerns were, or are, competitors, "so that the elimination of competition by agreement between them would constitute a violation of any of the provisions of any of the antitrust laws." The principal weakness of the law, although not its only deficiency, is its failure to reach indirect interlocks—the coming together of directors of two or more competing companies as directors of another concern, particularly a financial institution. This loophole has certainly not been overlooked by the major oil companies. In a study of interlocking directorates as of 1946, the Federal Trade Commission found that:

> The third, fourth, fifth, sixth, and eighth and ninth largest of the oil companies were linked with one another through three banks. Standard of Indiana, Standard of California, Gulf Oil and Continental Oil all had directors who were on the board of the Chase National Bank. Standard of Indiana and Texas Co. were linked through Continental Illinois National Bank and Trust Co., while Texas Co., Shell Union Oil and Tidewater Oil were linked through Central Hanover Bank and Trust Company.

Somewhat to its surprise, the Commission also found a number of direct interlocks which would appear to have represented outright violations of the law: "While there were no direct interlocks among the top six oil companies, several of the medium-sized companies did have such ties. Thus, Sinclair had three directors in common with Richfield, which in turn had three directors in common with Empire." "Conspicuous by their absence" among companies with interlocks—direct or indirect—were Standard of New Jersey and Socony-Vacuum. The Commission noted, however, that ". . . these two companies had a series of ties with each other and with other petroleum companies through joint stock ownership in third companies." In fact, the Commission emphasized the importance in the petroleum industry of "other types of close relationships":

> Opportunities for joint action occur, for example, when two or more petroleum companies own affiliated domestic petroleum companies, foreign or domestic companies which produce or market petroleum in foreign countries, domestic natural gas pipeline companies, domestic crude oil pipeline companies, foreign crude oil pipeline companies, domestic gasoline pipeline companies, and various other interests. If the directors or operating executives of major oil companies jointly work out problems in connection with affiliated companies, the consequence may be much the same as if they are linked by interlocking directorates.

Since the time of the FTC study, the frequency with which directors of the major oil companies come together on the boards of the largest banks seems, if anything, to have increased. Chart 6-3 shows the indirect interlocks among thirteen major oil companies whose directors met together in 1972 on the boards of eight of the

CHART 6-3 Indirect Interlocking Directorates Among Major Oil Companies Through Commercial Banks, 1972

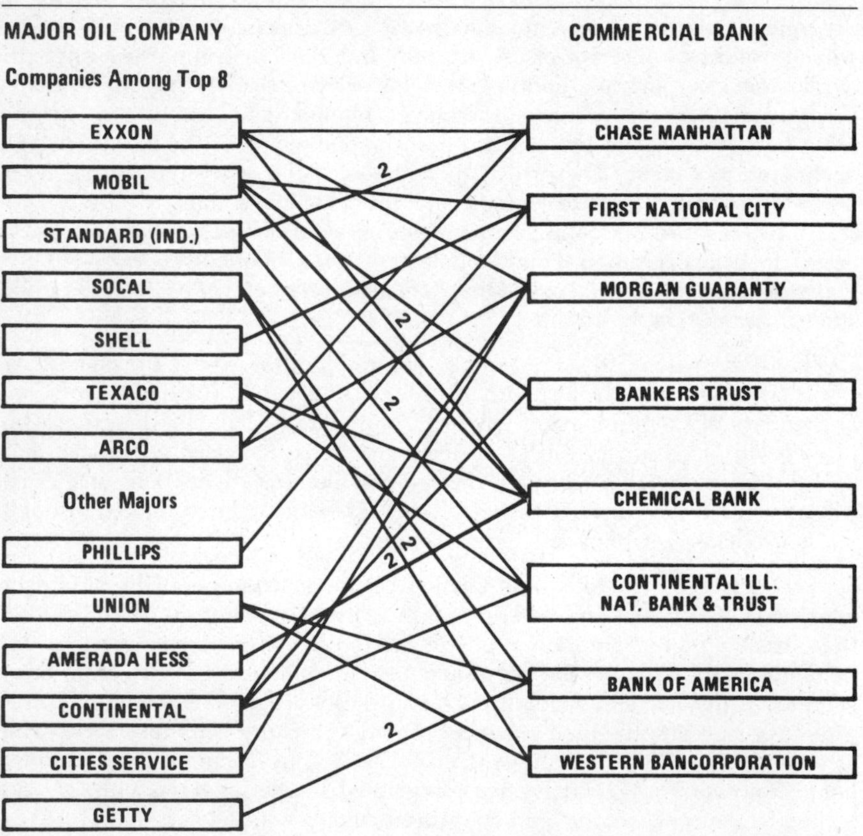

Source: Compiled from Stanley H. Ruttenberg and Associates, *The American Oil Industry —A Failure of Antitrust Policy,* Washington, D.C., 1974, pp. 83, 147–60.

nation's largest commercial banks. At the top left are seven of the top eight companies; below are six other majors who are linked with each other or with the top eight through indirect interlocks with the eight commercial banks.

With the exception of Gulf and SoCal, all of the eight largest oil companies were interlocked in 1972 through large commercial banks with at least one other member of the top group. Exxon had four such interlocks—with Mobil, Standard (Ind.), Texaco, and ARCO. Mobil had three (with Exxon, Shell, and Texaco), as did Standard of Indiana (with Exxon, Texaco, and ARCO), as well as Texaco (with Exxon, Mobil, and Standard of Ind.). ARCO was interlocked with Exxon, and Standard (Ind.), and Shell with Mobil. Whenever all of the six commercial banks shown in the chart (exclusive of Bank of America and Western Bancorporation) hold their board meetings, directors of the top eight (excluding Gulf and SoCal) meet with directors of, on the average, 3.2 of their largest competitors.

Since the 1946 FTC study, the most notable change has been the abandonment by Exxon and Mobil (formerly Socony-Vacuum) of their earlier reticence. By 1972, Exxon had become indirectly interlocked with Standard (Ind.) and ARCO (through Chase Manhattan), with ARCO, Continental, and Cities Service (through Morgan Guaranty), and with Mobil, Texaco, and Amerada Hess (through Chemical Bank). In addition to its ties with Exxon, Mobil had forged links with Shell and Phillips (through First National City Bank), with Continental (through Bankers Trust), and with Texaco and Amerada Hess (through Chemical Bank). These two companies, which had no indirect interlocks in 1946, had by 1972 established such interlocks through five large commercial banks with each other and with eight other major oil companies. The interesting question is why the increase, particularly if the interlocks are without competitive significance? One possible explanation is that in 1946 the oil companies must have had fresh in their minds the investigations of the Temporary National Economic Committee, in which they had been a prime target, whereas by 1972 antitrust activity against the oil industry had been quiescent for over a decade and a half.

The information on interlocking directorates also bears a number of interesting regional implications. When the Bank of America holds its board meetings, for example, directors of the three leading oil producers in the Far West (SoCal, Union, and Getty) sit down together. Further cohesiveness is provided by Western Bancorporation, whose board meetings provide a handy occasion for directors of SoCal and Union to meet together. In the Midwest, the leader (Standard of Ind.) and the sixth largest refiner (Texaco) sit on the board of Continental Illinois Bank and Trust. The area's fifth and eighth largest refiners (Shell and Mobil) meet on the board of First National City Bank. And the third and seventh largest refiners (Standard of Ohio and Marathon) are indirectly interlocked.

Because the necessary information is available, establishing the fact of interlocking directorates is a feasible, though tedious, undertaking. Because the information is conspicuously not available, determining their real significance is quite another matter. At the very least, meeting together presents directors of competing companies with potential conflicts of interest:

> A director, whether direct or indirect, of two competing corporations cannot in good conscience recommend that either shall undertake a type of competition which is likely to injure the other. . . .

> A director on the board of an oil company and a financial institution would find it hard in good conscience to encourage his bank to finance expansion by competitors of his oil company thereby jeopardizing its prosperity. Nor can he in good conscience encourage the oil company to obtain its credit through other channels.
>
> If a person is a director of an oil company and a bank in which the latter is the caretaker and advisor of a pension trust fund of the former, he would feel it incumbent upon himself as a director of the bank to influence the trust department to vote those common stock holdings in favor of management of the oil company of which he is a part. Other directors on the bank board would feel it incumbent upon themselves, in order to retain the business of the oil company, to be mindful of the pressures which are brought by the director serving both companies to keep an eye out for the interest of those two companies.

A potentially adverse effect on competition can arise when a medium-size company and a large firm are represented on the board of a bank which supplies funds to both. If the lesser firm wishes to obtain additional credit to finance a course of competitive conduct that will adversely affect the larger firm, the probable reaction of the bank is not hard to envision. Yet in the oil industry indirect interlocks between the largest firms and other majors are a commonplace. Thus, through First National City Bank, Phillips is interlocked with Shell and Mobil; through the Chemical Bank, Amerada Hess is interlocked with Exxon, Mobil, and Texaco; through Morgan Guaranty, Cities Service is connected with Exxon and ARCO. But by far the most widely represented among the second tier of companies is Continental Oil, which through Bankers Trust is related to Mobil, through Continental Illinois National Bank and Trust to Standard (Ind.) and Texaco, and through Morgan Guaranty to Exxon and ARCO. Such relationships pose an inherent conflict of interest to the banks on whose board the oil companies meet.

THE "ROCKEFELLER" COMPANIES: AN INNER COMMUNITY? Do the "Rockefeller" companies constitute a tight, cohesive grouping within the larger community of the major oil companies? This is a question that has long intrigued students of the petroleum industry. The successors to the old Standard Oil Trust, broken up in 1911—Exxon, Mobil, Standard (Ind.), and SoCal—own 32.2 percent of domestic reserves, hold 30.8 percent of domestic refining capacity, and make 26.3 percent of all retail gasoline sales.

Although the managers of the operating companies and the Rockefeller interests have undoubtedly seen eye to eye on most issues, at least one open conflict over the locus of power did take place. The controversy involved control over Standard of Indiana:

> . . . the most striking illustration of this fight for control was presented by the open warfare between Mr. John D. Rockefeller, Jr., and the management of the Standard Oil Company of Indiana. Mr. Rockefeller actually held 14.9 percent of the voting stock. He had been in substantial control of the company for years. Colonel Stewart, the chairman of the board of directors and undeniably the driving force behind much of that company's activity, displeased Mr. Rockefeller in connection with certain transactions which were the subject of

discussion during the administration of President Harding. He asked Colonel Stewart to resign; Stewart refused and did not grant to Mr. Rockefeller the use of the proxy machinery at the following annual election of directors. Thereupon Mr. Rockefeller waged a most dramatic proxy battle against him. He circularized the stockholders at considerable expense, asking for proxies. He engaged the most eminent legal talent to guard against any "technical mistakes." He brought to bear the tremendous influence of his standing in the community. The *Wall Street Journal* pointed out at the time that the fight marked the first time the Rockefeller domination in a large Standard Oil unit "had been really in question." In opposition, Colonel Stewart obtained the full support of the existing board of directors and sought the support of the 16,000 employees who were stockholders. At this most opportune moment the company declared a 50 percent stock dividend. The issue was for long in grave doubt. Four days previous to the election both sides are reported to have claimed the support of a majority, the one of votes and the other of stockholders. In the final election of directors, Mr. Rockefeller won 50 percent of the votes outstanding or 65 percent of the votes cast being in favor of his candidates. Control may be said to have remained in his hands. Colonel Stewart's connection with the company was brought to a close.

Since managers can readily comprehend the probable personal repercussions of losing in a fight with an important stock-owning group, such episodes are a rarity. And this understandable reticence also extends to the making of competitive moves against a rival corporation whose stock is significantly held by the same owning group. In this way competition can be lessened without either directions to management or meetings, and certainly without publicly aired controversies.

The one and only occasion when ownership of the largest corporation has been traced back through the "owners of record" to the real or "beneficial" owners was a study by the Securities and Exchange Commission for the Temporary National Economic Committee, entitled *The Distribution of Ownership in the 200 Largest Nonfinancial Corporations.* For the four "Standard" companies, the holdings in 1938 of the Rockefeller family as individuals, through trusts and estates, foundations and other "Rockefeller-dominated corporations," were as follows:

TABLE 6-7 Holdings of the Rockefeller Family in Equity Securities of Four "Standard" Oil Companies, 1938 (percent of total stock outstanding)

Company	Individuals	Trusts & Estates	Foundations	Rockfeller-Dominated Corps.	Total
Exxon	6.45%	2.24%	4.82%	6.69%*	20.20%
Mobil	8.64	7.70			16.34
Standard Oil (Ind.)	2.44	4.39	4.53		11.36
SoCal	7.37	4.49	.46		12.32

*Through Standard Oil Co. (Ind.).

Source: 76th Cong., 3rd Sess., Temporary National Economic Committee, Monograph 29, The Distribution of Ownership in the 200 Largest Nonfinancial Corporations, 1940, p. 127.

Since in each case the remainder of the stock was widely dispersed, these holdings were considered sufficient by the Securities and Exchange Commission to give the Rockefeller family control over the corporations. Of Exxon, the Commission stated: "The combined block aggregating 13.5% of the common stock represented by far the largest holding and in view of the wide distribution of the majority of the stock should carry with it an amount of influence equivalent to working control. Furthermore, Standard Oil Co. (Indiana) owned 6.7 percent of the Standard Oil Co. (New Jersey), bringing direct and indirect holdings of the Rockefeller family to 20.2 percent." For Mobil (Socony-Vacuum): "Members of the family owned 16.3 percent of the common stock. . . . As this was by far the largest single block and most of the stock was widely distributed the Rockefeller interests seemed to have safe working control. . . ." Of Standard (Ind.), it was stated, "Members of the family owned 6.8 percent and family foundations 4.5 percent of the common stock. . . . The combined holdings of 11.4 percent appear to carry working control. . . ." And for SoCal (Standard of Calif.), "The Rockefeller family owned 11.9 percent of the common stock . . . and family foundations held another 0.5 percent. The block appeared to carry working control. . . ."

As a result of the vast growth of these companies, the "dilution" of existing holdings resulting from the flotation of new issues, and the emergence of important new stock-owning institutions (mutual funds, pension funds), the relative importance of the Rockefeller holdings since the T.N.E.C. investigation has probably diminished. But has it fallen below the level required for working control? R. H. Larner has used as his standard of the proportion of stock required for control the ownership by a stockholder group of 10 percent. Jean-Marie Chevalier, however, maintains that this is too high, contending that large corporations can be subject to effective minority control if a group owns 5 percent of the stock and is represented on the board of directors. In addition to stock ownership, there is the linkage through interlocking directorates. Directors of Exxon and Standard (Ind.) come together as directors of Chase Manhattan, long identified as the "Rockefeller" bank. Directors of Exxon and Mobil meet together on the Chemical Bank. And, of course, there are the additional linkages among the companies through numerous joint ventures, some of which have been noted above.

Finally, there is the matter of the geographic division of markets. Years ago it was contended that each of the Standard companies tended to confine its operations to one or two contiguous regions, that in these areas it was usually the leading seller, and that as a result the individual Standard companies were able to dominate particular markets without encountering substantial competition from other Standard companies. Considering their resources and marketing abilities, such an orderly division of markets would be unlikely to take place without some coordinating influence. Some credence to this line of argument is lent by current data on retail gasoline market shares. In 1972, Standard (Ind.) was the leading seller in thirteen states—all in the Midwest and Great Plains areas; in only one was Exxon among the four largest sellers. Conversely, Exxon was the leader in twelve other states—all along the Eastern seaboard or in the South; in nine, Standard (Ind.) was not among the four largest. Mobil was the leading seller in four states—New York and three New England states; in none was Standard (Ind.) among the four largest. Moreover, SoCal was the leader in eleven states—six in its historical region of the Far West and five in the South, the latter acquired in its absorption of Standard of Kentucky. In none of these eleven was Exxon among the four largest sellers, and in only two was Standard (Ind.) among the four largest.

On their face the concentration ratios would place the industry in what has been referred to as the "moderately-concentrated" category, whose behavior has usually been found to lie between that of the "concentrated" sector (industries with concentration ratios of 50% or more) and the "unconcentrated" category (those with ratios of less than 25%). If concentration ratios were all that mattered, the behavior of the petroleum industry would presumably be more competitive than that usually associated with oligopolistic industries. But there are other factors to be considered. Concentration in this industry is supplemented by a complex of intercorporate relationships imparting to separate companies a cohesiveness and commonality not approached in any other industry. As Wilson has put it, "The key structural feature of the petroleum industry is that virtually all of its corporate entities are extensively tied together through a very large number of joint venture arrangements and other types of intercorporate interlocks. Consequently, these firms cannot be viewed in parallel with independent unrelated market rivals in other industries." Moreover, competition has been further lessened by the control of the market achieved through the artful use of government. . . . Petroleum thus represents the case, *par exemple,* where concentration is simply one of a series of interlocking building blocks on which an effective control of the market has been erected.

THE TURNING POINT

It is now possible to see the year 1953 as a turning point in the history of oil. In that year the Central Intelligence Agency, with British help, engineered a coup against Mohammed Mossadegh, the premier of Iran, and installed the young shah of the Pahlevi dynasty on the Peacock Throne. Mossadegh had nationalized the oil industry, and although the Western companies could undoubtedly have learned to live with him, in the context of the Cold War and American policies of containment, the Eisenhower administration believed Iranian oil to be in imminent danger of falling under Communist control.

The well-planned coup in Iran had a number of momentous short-term and long-term consequences. On the domestic side, as the following selection indicates, the Justice Department had been on the verge of moving against the international oil cartel. However, the invocation of the Soviet threat in the Middle East caused this cartel case, which might have rivaled the breakup of the Standard Oil Trust, to be dropped. Instead, the Eisenhower administration drew the ostensibly reluctant oil companies more closely into a joint partnership aimed at increasing American hegemony over the world's main oil supply areas. All this was laid out in papers and documents published in 1974 by the subcommittee on multinational corporations under the leadership of Senator Frank Church. Excerpts from his introduction are included here.

As the Church papers indicate, a vital element of U.S. policy was not only to quash the cartel-breaking move by the Justice Department, or even to assure a friendly government which would stand up to the Russians in Iran, but also to reorganize the world's oil industry on far more favorable terms to the United States. Internationally, then, the Iranian coup marked the end of the turning point period of British hegemony in the Middle East, which had started with the Churchill naval decision of 1911 (see p. 3). In this sense the Iranian events described in Fred Halliday's selection ushered in a quarter-century of American control, which ensured a steady flow of cheap oil to the West. This oil, in effect, was subsidized by the Iranians and the Arabs, who received little for the non-renewable resource being taken out of their ground, while they financed the prosperity of the industrial West.

From an even longer range point of view, the overthrow of Mossadegh and the grabbing of the Iranian oil, while suppressing early stirrings of Middle Eastern nationalism, planted the seeds for a future explosion of nationalist feelings far more powerful than any that could have been imagined in 1953. As Anthony Sampson indicates in the selection from his book on the Seven Sisters, the formation of OPEC more than fulfilled Mossadegh's dreams, and as we all know now, the costs incurred by twenty-five years of cheap oil from Iran were paid off in full with the fall of the shah in 1979.

Taken from The International Petroleum Cartel, the Iranian Consortium and U.S. National Security, *Subcommittee on Multinational Corporations, Committee on Foreign Relations, U.S. Senate, 93rd Congress, February 21, 1974.*

The Senate Foreign Relations Committee Subcommittee on Multinational Corporations has decided, with the consent of the Departments concerned, to make public certain hitherto secret documents from the files of the National Security Council, the Department of State and the Department of Justice. These documents explain and relate two conflicting policies of the United States Government in the field of international oil. These policies were 1) prosecution of the International Petroleum Cartel Case, and 2) creation of the Iranian Consortium. The first of these actions accused the five major American oil companies of illegally combining and contracting in the production, refining, transportation, and marketing of oil; the second encouraged the same companies to combine and contract in the first three of these areas. The decisions taken to resolve this conflict have shaped our national energy policy for the past twenty years.

On July 17, 1952, after several months of debate within the administration, the Attorney General announced that a grand jury investigation of the international oil industry would be undertaken. The investigation was based on a staff report of the Federal Trade Commission which had been completed that spring. From the outset the State Department opposed the initiation of this investigation. . . . Nevertheless, subpoenas were issued in August against 21 large oil companies, and a request for the empanelling of a grand jury quickly followed.

Meanwhile, on the other side of the world, the Anglo-Iranian Oil Company (AIOC) was engaged in a bitter dispute with the Government of Iran. Since AIOC (now British Petroleum) was a British corporation the majority of whose stock was owned by the British Government, that government was naturally deeply involved in the dispute. In March 1951, Iran had nationalized all local assets of the company, which until that time had held exclusive concessionary rights over virtually all of Iran's oil producing areas as well as the Abadan refinery, the world's largest. American efforts to mediate the dispute had foundered on an irreconcilable difference between the parties as to whether a valid nationalization had taken place. There was growing concern in the State Department that Iran was going to slip within the Soviet orbit. Because of British and Iranian intransigence. Secretary of State Dean Acheson began considering the advisability of developing an American capability to deal with the Iranian problem. The most convenient method of accomplishing this objective would be to find some way of restoring Iranian oil production, even in the absence of AIOC. But, as Secretary of State Acheson later wrote, "an independent American solution over British opposition was also more easily said than done. Aside from the damaging ill will it would create between our two countries, it would require the cooperation of the major American oil companies, who alone, aside from Anglo-Iranian, had the tankers to move the oil in the volume necessary." . . .

Whether an American solution indeed required the cooperation of the established major oil companies is an important historical question. The Justice Department believed that it did not. Because of the strong objections of the Antitrust Division to the plan proposed by State, an alternative plan was developed for consideration by the Attorney General. That proposal involved the participation of independent American oil companies which did not already have substantial interests in the Near East.

Although these conflicting policies were debated at the highest levels of government throughout the remainder of 1952, no decision was reached until January 1953, in the last days of the Truman Administration. By that time contact had been made with the American majors and they had expressed their reluctant willingness to take over some part of the old AIOC concession. In return for this cooperation, President Truman took the first step in limiting the Cartel Case. On January 12, 1953, he wrote a letter to Attorney General McGrannery ordering him to proceed against the oil companies by way of civil suit rather than grand jury investigations. This order was conditional, however, on the voluntary production by the companies of the documents sought by the Government through grand jury subpoenas.

Pursuant to the direction of the President, the Department of Justice terminated its grand jury investigation and filed a civil complaint on April 14, 1953, in the United States District Court for the District of Columbia. The complaint named five companies as co-defendants; Standard Oil of New Jersey (now Exxon), Socony-Vacuum Oil Company (now Mobil), Standard Oil Company of California (Socal), The Texas Company (now Texaco), and Gulf Oil Corporation (Gulf). It alleged violations of sections 1 and 2 of the Sherman Act during the period from 1928 to the date of filing. Some of the more specific allegations were monopolization of foreign production, division of foreign markets, fixing of prices worldwide, exclusion of competition, and monopolization of refinery patents. . . .

In the meantime, however, the Eisenhower Administration had taken office. One of the new President's first actions was to appoint Herbert Hoover, Jr. as special representative to deal with the Iranian problem. Against the wishes of the Antitrust Division, Hoover proceeded on the assumption that the only solution to the Iranian problem lay in the utilization of the major oil companies as a vehicle for restoring Iranian petroleum production. On August 6, 1953, in National Security Council Action Memorandum No. 875b, the President designated the Attorney General to "develop a solution which would protect the interests of the free world in the Near East as a vital source of petroleum supplies," including development of "new or alternative legal relationship(s) between the oil companies of the Western nations and the nations of the Near East." The terms of reference under which the Attorney General was to solve this problem provided that, "It will be assumed that the enforcement of the Antitrust laws of the United States against the Western oil companies operating in the Near East may be deemed secondary to the national security interest. . . ."

Then, in October 1953, overall authority to direct a solution was transferred from the Attorney General to the Secretary of State. Although the American majors still expressed little enthusiasm for entering Iran, they were encouraged by the downgrading of the Cartel Case to a civil action and stated that they would be willing to participate in achieving a solution because of the "large national security interests involved." . . . Negotiations were begun in London at the instigation of the Chairman of AIOC between that company and the American majors. The Justice Department was not encouraged to play an active role in these negotiations, and the role of the Government itself was rather limited. . . .

On January 13, 1954, the broad outlines of the proposed Iranian Consortium agreement were discussed in the Justice Department. The objections of the Antitrust Division were noted, but the decision was out of their hands. The very next day the National Security Council decided that "the security interests of the United States require the United States petroleum companies to participate in an international consortium to contract with the Government of Iran, within the area of the former AIOC concession, for the production and refining of petroleum. . . ." Pursuant to this decision, on January 20, 1954, the Attorney General rendered an opinion to the President that the proposed consortium plan, when viewed in connection with the security requirements of the United States as determined by the National Security Council, would not in itself constitute an unreasonable restraint of trade. These decisions were communicated to the companies and serious negotiations among them began over the structure and operation of the proposed Consortium. . . .

The National Security Council's decision to place the major American oil companies in the Iranian Consortium effectively killed any chance of the Cartel Case being successfully prosecuted. But the Council in making this decision did so without statutory authority. The only way in which the executive branch may give antitrust immunity to private corporations is under the provisions of the Defense Production Act. . . . Two years later, on September 15, 1954, Leonard Emmerglick wrote: "It seems to me that the Attorney General would have to stultify himself to give an opinion that these agreements would be lawful." By requiring this stultification the National Security Council not only perverted the law, but precluded the creation of a competitive international oil industry.

As one peruses these documents, the reader will note a glaring omission: nowhere is there any reference to consultation with the United States Congress. The decisions reflected in this record were taken in secrecy, debated in secrecy, and never exposed to public debate and inquiry. Yet, these decisions helped seal the basic structure of international oil for 25 years. Today we are living with the consequences of the breakdown of this structure. As we struggle to evolve a new structure, we must ensure that spurious claims of national security are not again used to shut off public inquiry and debate on this vital subject.

FRANK CHURCH,
U.S. Senator.

Taken from Iran: Dictatorship and Development, *by Fred Halliday, New York, Penguin, 1979.*

. . . Since the end of the second world war, nationalist feeling in Iran had been directed against the continued ownership of the country's oil by the British-owned Anglo-Iranian Oil Company; when in 1944 the Soviet Union had also tried to acquire an oil concession in the north, it too had become the object of similar antagonism. The leader of the oil protest movement, Mohammad Mossadeq, became prime minister in 1951: he led a coalition of Majlis [parliamentary] deputies who formed a group called the National Front, and although this Front was never a coherent political organization it enjoyed a wide following in Tehran and other towns. The oil industry was nationalized soon after Mossadeq became premier and within a few months his government was in direct conflict with the Shah and through the Shah with the U S A, despite Mossadeq's initial attempts to win the latter over. In the end Mossadeq was ousted in August 1953 by a coalition of forces within and outside Iran. . . .

While Mossadeq had tried to gain U S support, he had met with little success, in particular because the 1952 U S Presidential elections had brought to power the more aggressively anticommunist administration of Eisenhower and Dulles. Although Mossadeq himself was not a communist, he was seen as opening the door to communist influence, and given Iran's geographic position on the borders of the Soviet Union, and the strained international climate at that time, the U S A was unwilling to take risks in that country. Had Mossadeq been able to consolidate his position, the U S A might have accepted him—especially since it was only in the last year of his government that the Tudeh [Communist] Party supported Mossadeq openly. But Mossadeq was not able to stabilize the situation, and in the end he was overthrown by a coalition of internal and external foes.

There is now no doubt that the U S government, and specifically the C I A, played an active part in organizing the coup of 19 August 1953 that ousted Mossadeq, and that this intervention was the fruit of a build-up of the U S presence in Iran that had been under way since the war. But it is misleading to attribute everything to this factor alone: Iranian nationalists tend to do so—and so, on occasion, does the C I A, keen to claim credit for a successful operation. The reality is not so simple since the C I A intervention was only possible because of the internal balance of forces in Iran, the existence of elements within the dominant class that were interested in acting against the Mossadeq régime and the weaknesses of Mossadeq's own position. Without the latter it would have been impossible for the U S A to act as it did; had Mossadeq had a following that was organized, and based on the oppressed in town and country, the resistance to the coup would have been much more substantial than it was. Moreover, there is no doubt that as the oil conflict continued and as the economic situation deteriorated following the end of oil revenues, so Mossadeq's popular support also declined. His attempt to challenge the monarch and the army was not based on any comparable alternative social base and the attempt which he led to alter the pattern of Iran's internal and international political alignments therefore failed. As a consequence the Pahlavi state emerged stronger than it had been prior to the oil crisis. . . .

THE RISE OF OPEC

Between the end of the Second World War and 1960 the major international oil companies and the Middle Eastern oil-producing nations adjusted but did not fundamentally change the structure of their relationship created by the cartel during the 1920s. The companies paid the producing nations a small royalty for each barrel of oil. In 1950 they adopted a profit-sharing arrangement under which the corporations supposedly split their profits with the countries on a fifty-fifty basis. But this was not real profit sharing since the corporations loaded all their expenses onto the deal, thereby reducing total profit. The arrangement was, in addition, a bonanza for the major corporations since the U.S. government allowed them to treat the "profit" paid out abroad as a tax, which could be written off against profits recorded in the United States.

The profit-sharing setup did, however, importantly affect the oil-producing nations, vastly increasing the amounts of money they received from the sale of oil. As a result, oil began to play an ever more important role in their overall revenues, paying a substantial portion of the cost of their militaries, civil services, and, of course, the lavish royal households of the reactionary regimes. Profit sharing gave the Middle Eastern nations a real stake in what oil was sold for. Thus, it came as a serious blow when the international corporations determined unilaterally to cut prices in February 1959 and again in August 1960. The price cuts caused the producing nations to gather in the first important meeting of the Organization of Petroleum Exporting Countries (OPEC), described in the following selection by Anthony Sampson.

OPEC went on to become a crucial force in international politics during the next twenty years. The oil embargo of 1973 forced the United States for the first time to come to grips with the unpleasant facts of the "energy crisis." The embargo brought home to the Western public what insiders had long known: that sooner or later the cheap oil of the 1950s and 1960s would have to be paid for, that sooner or later the Arabs and Iranians, with a growing sense of their "modern" nationalism, would demand a hefty share of their major nonrenewable resource. But whether or not the "energy crisis" was to become a causative factor in creating an altered political framework over the long term is unclear and is the subject Joe Stork contemplates in his analysis of OPEC after twenty years.

Taken from The Seven Sisters: The Great Oil Companies and the World They Shaped, *by Anthony Sampson, New York, Viking, 1975.*

. . . There had been earlier attempts to bring together the oil-exporting countries. The Venezuelans, . . . influenced by the shrewd Pérez Alfonso, had for long been determined to safeguard their own conservation policy by spreading it abroad. With their very limited reserves, their long history of independence, and their bitter resentment of the United States, they were much more militant than the Arabs, and their proselytizing had helped to establish the principle of "fifty-fifty" in the Middle East. The Arabs had a growing, if vague, realization of the importance of collaborating over oil, ever since the Arab League was formed in 1945 with oil in its terms of reference.

President Nasser of Egypt, in his own book *The Philosophy of a Revolution,* first published in 1954, described petroleum as one of the three chief components of Arab power. Like so many Arab radicals, he had got his ammunition from America. He had then just been reading a treatise on petroleum published by the University of Chicago, which revealed to him that it cost only ten cents to extract a barrel of oil from Arab countries; and that the average output of a single Arab oil well was 4,000 barrels a day, compared to eleven barrels in America. "Petroleum," Nasser told his Arab brothers, "is the vital nerve of civilization, without which all its means cannot possibly exist." But the Arabs with the most oil, led by the Saudis, were not keen on sharing their revenues with Egypt, who had almost none, and it was not until 1958 that there were the beginnings of some unity. The Iraqis, who were soon negotiating with the IPC, felt the need for support from other Arab countries. The new oil adviser in Saudi Arabia, Abdullah Tariki, was a radical who was determined to unite the producers. Tariki was one of a new generation of Arabs who had seen the oil industry from the inside; he had been educated at the University of Texas, had been a trainee in Texaco—a bitter ordeal—and was married for a time to an American girl. He was left with a detailed knowledge of oil and of the antitrust arguments inside America; once again, America was educating its adversaries.

The first price reduction in 1959 had provided the first spur to unity. Two months later the first Arab Petroleum Congress was convened in Cairo, including observers from Iran and Venezuela, and recommended that there should be no reduction in the posted price without consultation with the governments. And there were private talks between Tariki and Pérez Alfonso, which led to a secret gentleman's agreement which, according to Alfonso, "constituted the first seed of the creation of OPEC." But the oil-company men at the congress were not too worried, and Iraq, the most militant producer, was too angry with Egypt to attend.

But the second reduction, led by Exxon, transformed the whole atmosphere in the Middle East. In Iraq, it came just when the oil companies were deadlocked in their negotiations, and the Iraqis suspected it was aimed at bringing pressure upon them. They were determined to fight back, and on September 9, a month after the announcement, they convened a meeting at Baghdad of five countries who were responsible for eighty percent of the world's exports of oil: Saudi Arabia, Iran, Iraq, Kuwait and Venezuela. The key alliance was between Saudi Arabia and

Venezuela, and the meeting was dominated by Tariki and Pérez Alfonso. The two men already trusted each other: Tariki had been much influenced by [Pérez Alfonso's] arguments about conservation, and the fact that Venezuela had been excluded from the posted price cuts enabled [Pérez] Alfonso to show the advantages of being tough, and made him more determined to show unity with the Arabs.

The Shah, too, was furious about the price cuts of which he was given no warning: "[E]ven if the action was basically sound," he said afterward, "it could not be acceptable to us as long as it was taken without our consent." In his indignation he was now prepared to join up with the revolutionaries of Iraq, and the Shah's support was very important to the new movement. But he still kept aloof from the Arab members, continuing to supply oil to Israel, and he was not at all confident of the power of the producers: "I must admit we were just walking in the mist," he explained to me fifteen years later: "not in the dark, but it was a little misty. There was still that complex of the big powers, and the mystical power and all the magic behind the name of all these big countries."

The new price cut was most serious for Iran, which had far the biggest population, but it also came at a bad time for Saudi Arabia, which was just embarking on a massive expenditure on social services. Some other Arabs did not mind the thought of the Saudis having to cut down: thus the *Egyptian Economic and Political Review,* which was close to the Arab League, commented with some gratification that the loss of revenue "should mean fewer Cadillacs in Arabia." But among the oil producers the price cut generated a surge of unity, between the conservative kingdoms of Saudi Arabia and the antimonarchists of Iraq; and between the Arabs and two states, Iran and Venezuela, right outside the Arab world.

THE BIRTH OF OPEC

The five nations met in Baghdad in a mood of excited confidence: "It was quite clear from the start," wrote the ebullient owner-editor of the *Middle East Economic Survey,* Fuad Itayim, "that the price cuts might precipitate the establishment of what some delegate chose to call 'a cartel to confront the cartel,' It had precisely that effect!" They decided on the foundation of the Organization of Petroleum Exporting Countries, or OPEC. The first resolution made clear that their chief enemy was the oil companies, and they stated:

> that members can no longer remain indifferent to the attitude heretofore adopted by the oil companies in affecting price modifications; that members shall demand that oil companies maintain their prices steady and free from all unnecessary fluctuation; that members shall endeavor, by all means available to them, to restore present prices to the levels prevailing before the reductions . . .

The preamble expounded the common predicament of all the oil exporters, with unexceptionable logic; that they all depended on oil income to finance their development and balance their budgets; that oil was a wasting asset, which must be replaced by other assets; and that fluctuations in the price of oil dislocated not only their own economies, but those of all consuming nations.

Would OPEC, or some such body, have formed itself at about this time, without the urgent prodding from the oil companies? Certainly the tide was already flowing toward militancy. The tide which moved the Mexicans to nationalization, which gave the Venezuelans their toughness, and which swept Mossadeq into power in Iran was now carrying the Arabs to the awareness of their potential, and these countries would have found common cause before long. But the critical point about Exxon's decision was that it was unilateral, with no attempt at consultation; and it compelled the countries to respond in the same fashion. Confronted by the unity of the seven, they had to oppose with the same kind of unity. As one Kuwaiti insisted to me, "OPEC couldn't have happened without the oil cartel. We just took a leaf from the oil companies' book. The victim had learned the lesson."

The founders of OPEC owed much to the oil companies, and to their critics in the West. The new generation of young Arab technocrats like Tariki knew the history of conservation in Texas, and they had followed carefully each attack on the "oil cartel." The facts from the Federal Trade Commission's report[*] in 1952 were repeated through OPEC speeches. Like the anticolonialists in the British Empire, they took their weapons from their masters, and the awakening could be interpreted as a reflection of American democracy as much as of Arab nationalism. The concept of the cartel provided an ideal common enemy; and the oil companies were very conscious of being isolated and unloved. As one director of Shell recalled: "OPEC could count on some support from the consuming countries in putting forward their notion of a cartel. When the industry was attacked, it was without friends."

OPEC began with a flourish. A month after its foundation, the Arab Petroleum Congress held another meeting in Beirut, attended by oil-company men. Tariki took the opportunity to lash out at them, accusing them of rigging their profits to deprive the producing countries of more than two billion dollars over the previous seven years. He accused Aramco of having concealed from the Saudi Arabians that they received a discount on their oil; so that the fifty-fifty agreement was really 32–68. The oil companies protested, but would not reveal the true figures: the extent of their Middle East profits, buried in their complex accounting, remains hidden to this day. Tariki had made his point to the other delegates, that the companies were concealing the facts, and the common indignation gave a new fillip to OPEC.

The new organization was duly set up in Geneva, with an Iranian secretary general, Fuad Rouhani. He was an urbane and very moderate man, an international lawyer and a talented musician, and he was determined (as he recalled to me) to keep OPEC out of both politics and religion: he would tour the offices to make sure that officials stuck to oil and economics. But he soon realized that the oil companies were determined to pretend that OPEC simply did not exist; and insisted on negotiating separately with each country. So he turned up at each negotiation, "wearing a different hat." While the companies insisted that OPEC was a would-be cartel, Rouhani observed that the companies were clearly in cahoots, coordinating their terms with each country.

From the beginning, OPEC achieved one important aim: it prevented further reductions in the posted price, even though competition was becoming still more

[*See report on p. 102.]

intense. As Nadim Pachachi, a later secretary general, described it, OPEC froze the "managerial prerogative" of unilateral fixing of prices. The companies tried to get individual countries to give tax rebates in return for extra production: but they stood firm and resisted the temptation. But it did not restore the posted prices to the previous levels, which was another of its aims. And, more serious, its members could not agree about how to fix prices, or to restrict production. At the second conference, in Caracas in January 1961, OPEC resolved to make a detailed study to arrive at a "just pricing formula." But each of the members desperately wanted a bigger share of the market, and the notion of conservation, however much preached by the Venezuelans, had little appeal in the free-for-all. The countries were back in the predicament of the oil drillers in Pennsylvania a century before: divided and ruled by the men who controlled the market.

And the Russians, who could have helped the Arabs to cut back the glut, were still spoiling the market. At one point they actually showed interest, through Rouhani, in becoming members of OPEC, but they took it no further. Instead they explained to successive meetings of the Arab Petroleum Congress that they wanted to get back their position as major oil exporters, and they would not support artificially high prices. For the time the Russians were the chief bogey, both for the Arabs and the companies, and the Americans became increasingly worried that the Russian "dumping" of oil was an attempt to sabotage the West. In November 1962 the National Petroleum Council in Washington produced a long report analyzing the dangers, which reckoned that Soviet exports had cut the income of producing countries by $490 million in five years. However, the Russian threat soon afterward faded away, as the Russians needed more oil for themselves and their satellites; by the late sixties they were actually importing oil from the Middle East.

The first surge of OPEC unity did not last long. The Iraqis, preoccupied with their own problems, did not turn up at the meetings. The radical Arabs resented the moderate Rouhani: he was eventually succeeded by an Iraqi, Abdul Rahman Bazzaz, who encouraged talk of both religion *and* politics. Tariki fell into disfavor and was replaced as oil minister in March 1962 by a young lawyer who seemed a much more pro-Western influence. Sheikh Zaki Yamani, then only thirty-two, was the son of a judge in Mecca, who had studied law first at Cairo, then at New York University, then at Harvard. He had come back to Saudi Arabia, sophisticated and westernized, to start a private law practice.

His appointment as oil minister and as director of Aramco was very welcome to the four companies in Aramco: he became friendly with the directors, and loved visiting New York. And the State Department, as well as Aramco, had taken pains to cultivate the Saudi royal family. King Saud, who had succeeded his father Ibn Saud in 1953, had been an increasing embarrassment to the diplomats; but by 1962 he had been ousted by his brother King Faisal, whose hooked nose and sinister expression had so struck Dean Acheson sixteen years earlier. King Faisal was still implacable on the question of Israel; but he was also deeply conservative and very wary of the Arab radicals, particularly after Nasser was threatening the Saudis through the war in Yemen. The King looked to Washington as an anti-Communist ally, to maintain the most special of special relationships. Moreover, King Faisal, though his revenues were increasing, could always spend more, and had no wish to hold back production to help his Arab rivals.

OPEC was still totally failing to achieve any kind of effective prorationing of oil production between its members, of the kind that had maintained prices in Texas for the past thirty years. Saudi Arabia was becoming the Texas of the Middle East: if they would not restrict production, no one else would. But they showed no interest in restriction, and the problem was now harder than in 1960, for new oil producers were starting up all the time, including Nigeria, which was right outside OPEC. Iran and Iraq were proposing "programming" production according to population—both having large populations—but others wanted programming according to need. At the ninth OPEC conference, in Tripoli in July 1965, members set limits for each country's increase on an experimental basis: Saudi Arabia and Iraq would go up 9 percent in the next year, Iran 14 percent, Kuwait 5 percent, Libya 33 percent. But Saudi Arabia was not at the meeting, having had a row with Iraq about an apology, and the Saudis vetoed the decision: their increase for the year was in fact 18 percent. "The argument was really nothing to do with programming as such," said Yamani afterward, "it was about resources and economic factors." By 1967 OPEC had given up the attempt.

The companies were not now seriously worried by the threat of OPEC. They continued to deal separately with each government, and to play them against each other, while the governments remained in some awe of the power of the companies. But OPEC did have one significant achievement. In June 1962 they resolved to establish a uniform rate for royalties in each country, which would not be deductible from the income tax paid to them. The companies resisted stubbornly, claiming at one point that it would reduce their profits by a quarter, and the argument dragged on for over two years. Eventually in Geneva in December 1964 they reluctantly agreed, thus enabling the producers to increase their revenue at a time when the price was going down. To the oil companies it seemed a generous concession, involving an extra four cents a barrel, and to OPEC it seemed a great victory. But they had not touched the central question of the price of oil, for they were quite unable to control the flow of it. . . .

Taken from "Opec at 20 (1980)," by Joe Stork, in America's Energy, *edited by Robert Engler, New York, Pantheon, 1980.*

The creation of OPEC, however significant it appears in retrospect, was incidental to the main forces at work in this transition period. The continuing trend toward greater production weakened prices where the market was competitive (chiefly Europe), resulting in a fall in the price per barrel of crude from around $1.85 in early 1960 to as low as $1.20 in 1969. The collision of this tendency, rooted in the specifics of the industry, with the economic nationalism of the producing states, led to OPEC, and was resolved in a way that exacerbated the problem. The demands of the producers for higher revenues could not be met by higher prices in this circumstance, but only by still higher rates of production, especially for the compliant regimes of Iran and Saudi Arabia.

OPEC's main achievement in this first decade of falling prices was to bar further reductions in their own revenue per barrel, and to reduce the inventive discounts and accounting rubrics used by the companies to secure profits by calling them something else. In 1963 the regimes received an average of 67 cents per barrel, compared with the companies' 82 cents; by 1969 this had shifted in favor of the regimes, 85 cents to 40 cents. The countries did pay a significant price for this financial accomplishment, though. First, they never secured the companies' recognition of OPEC as a collective bargaining agent, and acceded to company insistence on bilateral country-company negotiations. Second, the oil producers allowed the companies to determine the pace of negotiations, focusing interminable discussion on minor issues and ignoring larger ones altogether. Production scheduling was sabotaged within OPEC itself. Demands like participation in company management were not seriously pursued. And the major purpose of OPEC, to restore crude prices to the level of early 1959, was not accomplished at all in this decade.

One immediate reason for this rather lackluster performance in OPEC's first decade was the elimination of Tariki following the U.S.-supported palace coup in Saudi Arabia in October 1962 that brought Crown Prince Faisal to power. Tariki was removed from his influential position and permanently banished from the country. His replacement, Ahmad Zaki Yamani, came to play as important a role in OPEC as Tariki, but inflected it in a much different direction.

Yamani is far more typical than Tariki had been of the technocrats representing their respective countries in OPEC. Tariki was an articulate exponent of the economic nationalism then surging in the area. Yamani and his fellows saw their mission in terms of insulating oil matters from "the realm of ordinary politics." This approach was inculcated in the Western training the technocrats typically received. True, these technocrats had a much higher level of understanding of the industry they were dealing with than did the princes and courtiers who had "negotiated" the original concessions, and were thus able to strike more beneficial arrangements for the regimes in the financial domain. In the final analysis, though, they represented a modification in the evolution of the prevailing pattern, and not a radical challenge to it.

The class predilections of the technocrats who staff OPEC are subsidiary to the fact that OPEC is, after all, an association of regimes of varied political hues, and can be no more radical than the common political denomination of its components. The dominant states, Saudi Arabia and Iran, were both closely tied to the capitalist consuming countries and the oil companies, and to the United States in particular. Iraq was under severe pressure from the companies in the struggle over the nationalization of Iraqi reserves after 1960; the Shah and the Saudis were only too happy to expand their own production at Iraqi expense. Algeria's significance was limited due to its low production capacity and its exclusive ties to the French market.

The character of OPEC was thus effectively determined by those regimes that most owed their place to the companies and Western governments. Any threat to the companies was seen as a threat to themselves. Their strategic aim was to modulate the popular nationalist pressures underlying OPEC in order to establish a more equal "partnership" with the companies and make themselves more indispensable to the continued functioning of the system. For the dominant regimes, one important OPEC task was to pre-empt more radical associations. In the words of one source close to both the companies and the Saudi regime, "Oil has aroused certain emotions in the Middle East which must be satisfied, and this is OPEC's task."

The June War of 1967 marked a watershed in the intersection of the politics of oil and Palestine, a combination that grew more potent by the time of the next war in 1973. The decisive defeat in 1967 of the radical nationalist regimes in Egypt and Syria initiated a period of political ascendancy for Saudi Arabia and the oil-producing sheikdoms of the Gulf, enhancing the efficacy of the "protection money" with which they bankrolled the front-line states but entangling them in the conflicts and pressures surrounding the Arab nationalist struggles. At the same time a new polarization developed with the rise of the Palestinian resistance and revolutionary movements in Yemen and Oman. Most importantly, through its impact on Libya as a major oil producer, the 1967 war laid the groundwork for OPEC's transition in 1969–71.

Libya, an Italian colony through World War II, was then ruled by a weak monarch, Idris, beholden to Britain and the United States. It was, in the words of one high State Department official, "one of the most corrupt regimes in the world." Libya was to play the same kind of catalyzing role in the evolution of OPEC and the oil industry as Iran would play a decade later. Both Libya in 1969 and Iran in 1979 illustrate several features central to an analysis of OPEC. First, the achievements of OPEC as a group in both periods were precipitated by the respective political upheavals in Libya and Iran rather than through any concerted determination of OPEC. Second, these upheavals were closely related to the social and political impact of the oil industry in these two countries, and in particular to the avaricious character of the companies involved and the local ruling classes. Third, in each case the expansion of the oil industry and the growth of oil revenues was a response by international capital and its local adherents to the contradictions and tensions of the previous phase.

A sketch of the Libyan case will suffice. Exploration and development in Libya took on significant dimensions after the 1956 Suez crisis. The companies desired to diversify their Middle East operations into areas not susceptible to blockages of the Canal or the pipelines serving the eastern Mediterranean. Exports commenced in 1961, but production escalated sharply after the 1967 war closed the Canal and Palestinian forces had taken to sabotaging the Trans-Arabian Pipeline. On top of this, the British announced plans in 1968 to withdraw militarily from the Gulf. Libyan production zoomed by 49 percent in 1968, against 12 percent for the Middle East as a whole, and by another 23 percent in 1969. By early 1970 production reached 3.5 million barrels a day, just under the rate of long-established producer Saudi Arabia.

The political incentives to increased Libyan production were reinforced by its concession and pricing system. In contrast to the traditional concession patterns, where a closely held consortium of major companies controlled a country's reserves and production, Libya let out separate acreage blocks to various companies and consortia, including virtually all the majors but a number of smaller, independent American and European companies as well. For most of these, Libya represented their only stake in low-cost Middle East production. Moreover, the monarchy accepted its profit share based on the market price rather than the official posted price. A major like Exxon was impelled by its more substantial interests to the east to refrain from undercutting Saudi or Iranian production and paid Libya too according to the official price. The independents, though, with no such stake in the status quo, paid as little as 30 cents a barrel in taxes and contributed mightily to the continued price cutting in Europe.

By September 1, 1969, when the code "Palestine is ours" flashed among the lieutenants and captains taking part in the coup led by Colonel Muammar Qaddafi, Libyan production represented a substantial portion of crude supplies for several European countries, notably West Germany and Italy, and the only low-cost crude for a number of the smaller companies. For the industry as a whole, the pell-mell exploitation of the "Libyan Klondike" led to a far more serious vulnerability to interruption than the situation they sought to diversify from in the Gulf.

The new regime moved smartly to redress its paltry share of crude profits by tackling first the highly vulnerable independents with supply contracts to meet and no alternative sources. Any inclination of the majors to stand with the independents by making supplies available was offset by their satisfaction at seeing these corporate upstarts forced to pay at their level. The "conservation" cutbacks used by the Libyans to force agreement from the independents, combined with interruptions in pipeline deliveries to the eastern Mediterranean and galloping demand in the industrial countries, created temporary and localized shortages in the European markets. The price trend of a decade was reversed.

The resulting price increases buttressed Libyan demands for still higher revenues per barrel, and Libya's success was not lost on the rest of OPEC. The companies' long-standing argument that the market would not tolerate an increase was proven, at the least, outmoded. Quaddafi's militance proved infectious, and the regimes in Iran and Saudi Arabia could not demand less without undermining their admittedly thin nationalist credentials. OPEC's twenty-first regular meeting in December 1970 laid out demands for an increase in the tax rate from 50 to 55 percent, a hike in the posted price, an end to all remaining company discounts, new and more lucrative adjustments for quality and transportation differentials, and, taking the lesson of the last decade to heart, set a firm timetable for negotiations.

The majors did finally accede to these demands, but in a highly abrasive manner calculated to generate an atmosphere of crisis and confrontation totally unwarranted by their mutual interest in a higher price plateau. These negotiations of early 1971, OPEC's *first* successful effort at collective bargaining, demonstrated the value of suppressing political differences in pursuit of common financial goals, and ratified the new, upward trajectory for oil prices. Pressures built up quickly for further increases, and the inertia of the 1960s was reversed with a vengeance in the 1970s.

OPEC in and of itself was little more than a medium in this process, coordinating and tempering often radical popular demands in the turbulent transitionary societies that the oil-producing countries had become. In this time, as later, it could have done no less than it did. First, the slight shift in power represented by the outcome of these negotiations was cumulative and developed out of the contradictions in the world oil industry and the erosion of the monopoly power of the largest companies. Praise or blame for this rests not with OPEC but with the readiness of the more radical regimes to seize advantage of the unique and to some extent temporary conjuncture.

Second, the achievements in these negotiations were *strictly* financial in character and arbitrary in amount. The regimes raised their take of the market value of a barrel of oil, which sold then at a composite product price of $14 in Europe, from about $1 to $1.30. For the majors, the price structure was raised and strengthened, and the leverage of the independents in securing lower-cost crude and underselling in the market was sharply reduced. In short, their monopoly position was, if not restored, measurably strengthened. And this was accomplished in a manner where the blame could be laid at the feet of OPEC. The link between OPEC and the "energy crisis" in the United States, which was fomented by the oil companies in their concerted effort after 1968 to remove price controls on natural gas and raise prices for coal and uranium, was successfully forged in the media and the public consciousness.

Subsequent price hikes, though much more substantial, share these same features: they were largely precipitated by developments outside of OPEC's control —the 1973 war, convulsions in the world economy—and they were perfectly compatible with the interests of the major companies.

Given the symbolic importance of the October War and the embargo by the Arab oil-producing states (not OPEC) that accompanied it, several observations are in order. First, the increasing participation of the oil producers in the world market and its attendant regional political complexities has permanently altered their previous insulation from transcendent political crises such as the struggle for Palestine. The trajectory of Saudi ascendancy, so conducive to Western interests after 1967, could only intensify nationalist pressures in 1973 to implement an embargo. Second, the successful implementation of production cuts in the 1971 negotiations for financial ends reduced the plausibility of the argument that such tactics would not be useful for political purposes. Third, the essential function of the "oil weapon," once it was unsheathed in the waning days of the war, was as a class weapon, a device to reassert the hegemony of forces represented by Faisal and Sadat. As such, it is primarily a defensive weapon, to be brandished in the face of pressures from more militant regimes and political forces, such as the Palestinian movement.

OPEC's agenda in the '70s was not limited to the price question. From its very first meeting in Baghdad in September 1960, the matter of national control of resources, and the local oil industry was enshrined in the demand for "participation." This was a term well suited to the political ambiguity that was OPEC: it could mean as much as nationalization, or as little as a pro-forma share in the management of the Western consortia. For Saudi Arabia's Yamani, it was a device for "appeasing patriotic sentiments."

On this question, even more than on prices, OPEC under Saudi and Iranian domination was primarily a force for undercutting rather than advancing the cause of national control. This was especially evident in Yamani's subversion of Iraq's struggle against the Western companies in the mid-1960s. Here, too, satisfaction of this demand was the cumulative result of the struggles of individual countries whose eventual success left OPEC's hierarchs little choice but to follow suit. The companies have been reduced in most instances to the status of "offtakers," or crude purchasers, but still have considerable operating responsibility as contractors in Saudi Arabia and the small Arab Gulf states as well as dominant positions in other stages of the industry.

One component essential to both administering prices and exercising national sovereignty is the control of production and its collective coordination in OPEC. This too was confirmed in OPEC's very first resolutions and was a key objective for Tariki and Perez. In this regard as in no other, Saudi resistance has been decisive until recently. For the whole argument for the indispensability of the giant companies was postulated in the end on their unfettered determination of how much crude would be produced and exported from each country. Their ability to play off one producer against another—against Iran under Mossadeq, against Iraq after Qassem—rested on this capacity to sow divisions among the producers by raising or lowering production and thus revenues. Nowhere was the substitution of Yamani for Tariki more profound in its impact on OPEC's evolution than on this question. The unwavering refusal of Yamani and the regime behind him to consider "production scheduling" under OPEC's aegis has been key to the preservation of Western oil interests in the Middle East. To this very day Yamani refuses to entertain the concept. After an OPEC meeting in March 1979, he testily responded to a reporter: "Sir, we refuse to talk about the level of production in Saudi Arabia with the OPEC member countries. It is not their affair. It is our own affair. And it has been our policy since the early 1960s to avoid any production program. Nothing has changed. We impose our ceiling. We raise or lower it—it is our affair."

This precious prerogative, Saudi ability to maneuver in this realm, is now confined within progressively narrowing parameters in which they must strive to balance off the collective weight of OPEC, the gluttonous needs of the West and the United States, and their own grossly exaggerated physical production capacity. The overthrow of the Pahlavi regime and the consequent sharp reduction in Iranian production over the period ahead has nearly eliminated the Saudi capacity to stabilize or lower prices. Moreover, a struggle has . . . ensued within the Saudi regime over appropriate production levels as dictated by revenue needs, global economic disquietude, and political responsibilities vis-à-vis the Palestinians and the separate Egyptian-Israeli peace.

This is the most important consequence of the Iranian revolution for OPEC's course in the years just ahead, and the salient feature of the current period of transition, which promises to be far more wrenching than those we have experienced to date. For the pace of local political disorders, the intractability of the global economic crisis, the intensity and velocity of the social contradictions in the oil-producing countries and in the industrial and poor countries as well presage a decade where OPEC may be no more than a relic of squandered opportunity.

A main structural feature of the period ahead is OPEC's more limited capacity to serve as "residual producer"—providing on call the oil the consuming world needs but cannot produce or secure from non-OPEC sources. At today's prices, and in light of the last decade's experience, the trend in OPEC is to limit production to meet proximate revenue needs and maximize long-term production capacity. According to OPEC, its ratio of proven reserves to production has fallen from 68.6 in 1960 to 41.2 in 1978. In the 1950s the OPEC countries added 100 billion barrels to their reserves, while cumulative production amounted to 12 billion barrels. In the 1960s, new reserves totaled 180 billion barrels; cumulative production was 33 billion barrels. Between 1971 and 1978 this relationship was drastically reversed: reserves added were only 28 billion barrels, while cumulative production reached 60 billion barrels.

One consequence of the transfer of majority ownership to the producing regimes has been more careful scrutiny of the producing companies' recovery techniques and other factors which affect the maximum productivity of a field. In many instances this has led to production restrictions and downward revision of capacity. The most startling instance of this has been Saudi Arabia: in 1972 Yamani was proposing, based on Aramco figures, production rates of over 20 million barrels a day by the mid-1980s. Today it is thought that Saudi capacity does not exceed 12 million barrels a day. Yamani himself alluded to this last year in commenting on the current Saudi production ceiling of 9.5 million barrels a day: "On paper we have a much greater capacity and a greater sustained capacity. But in reality we do not know exactly how much we are able to produce until we reach a certain level and then we start to face certain problems in the reservoir behavior."

These geological and technical constraints are more than matched by the political constraints deriving from the tremendous social tensions in the producing countries directly attributable to the influx of oil revenues, the heightened penetration of capitalist relations of exchange and production, and the consequent disruption of traditional patterns and identities. The prevailing social fabrics—which had accommodated until now the archaic and outmoded political forms congenial to Western control—are disintegrating under the impact of forces internal to but largely beyond the control of the separate OPEC states or of OPEC as a whole. The upheaval in Iran, the disquieting incidents in Mecca, the manifestations of great power interventions in the region all point to the perilously fragile character of the oil-producing regimes. . . .

OIL AND THE DECLINE OF THE WEST

What does the future hold for oil? In the selections that follow we have two sides of the oil argument: the cheating of the Third World and how it can fight back, presented by Michael Tanzer, versus the decline of the West and the need for collective defense, by Walter Levy.

Tanzer, a former Exxon employee who has advised Third World nations on how best to organize their petroleum resources, knifes through much of the public relations rhetoric that surrounds the industry. He says, for instance, that it is not prohibitively expensive to drill for oil. And while the industry confronts the Third World as an impenetrable monopoly, there exists within this business a competitive group of companies that hire out for drilling. Overall capital requirements are not so large as Third World nations are led to believe. Tanzer lays out a new course for oil exploration in the underdeveloped world.

Levy, the noted petroleum economist whose views are carefully considered within the councils of Western governments and corporations, argues that from the point of view of the consuming nations the only way forward is to forge a unified front against OPEC. But as he notes, this has not yet happened. There is a note of despair to his essay.

But the decline of the West in Levy's sense by no means ineluctably leads to the decline of Big Oil or the Seven Sisters. It should be kept in mind that they have so far weathered the storm caused by the rise of Middle Eastern nationalism and OPEC by jumping into other fuels (coal and uranium, for instance) in other, safer parts of the world (Australia, Canada, and the United States) and hence, if anything, have widened and strengthened their base of operations (see monopoly section, p. 315).

When you read these two selections, it is well to keep in mind that the authors use different sets of facts and figures. Levy, for example, accepts at face value the picture of the world resources future presented by Exxon.

Taken from "Oil and the Decline of the West," by Walter Levy, Foreign Affairs, *Summer 1980.*

. . . The producing countries, having taken full control over their national oil operations, in fact do not recognize as binding supply or price arrangements even if freely concluded by them. Recently they have gone so far as to change agreed-upon prices retroactively. This, they argue, they are entitled to do under the doctrine of sovereign control by producing countries over their natural resources. Because the contracting party in the producing country is also a government-owned oil company, they contend that any change the government requests in the terms and conditions affecting crude oil production and sales would in fact constitute a sovereign act, so that the government oil company that had entered into a contract would be entitled to claim *force majeure* vis-à-vis its customers.

But, undoubtedly, the increasing unilateral application of this doctrine is also related to the ease with which the host countries have been able to apply it, and to the lack of opposition by the affected private or public interested parties against unilateral expropriation or the cancellation of legal and contractual rights. Because of the fear of being arbitrarily cut off from supplies, Western nations and their companies now accept within a wide range practically any economic or political terms that a producing country may impose on them. This subservience, however, rather than safeguarding the remaining rights and position of the companies, in fact encourages the host countries to continue to proceed as they see fit. We have thus entered a period in international oil of near "lawlessness" in the relationship between producing countries, the oil companies and the importing countries.

The issues are not only supply and price stability. They also include exploration and development efforts that are now exclusively dependent on policies of producing countries, which obviously are not interested in creating any surplus of supplies that might endanger OPEC prices.

Moreover, especially since 1979, producing countries have cut back the oil they supply to the major international oil companies, frequently below the level of their direct requirements. The "Internationals," therefore, can no longer provide oil supplies to third parties as in the past. More and more of the oil is sold directly (or sometimes through trading companies) by producing to importing countries. As a matter of fact, the share of the Internationals in world oil trade has declined from 78 percent in 1974 to about 44 percent in 1979, and is declining even further.

At the same time, the terms imposed by producing countries for oil supplies include more and more political and other extraneous conditions, related, for instance, to the interest of the producing countries in the Palestinian problem, or in their nuclear capabilities or in the political postures of their government customers.

Thus, oil companies no longer perform an effective independent role as a buffer in the relationship between oil-producing and oil-importing countries. They have practically no bargaining leverage with regard to any decisions affecting their operations in producing countries. Moreover, any action by OPEC on supplies or prices that would lead to a higher cost of its oil would, as OPEC is fully aware, also tend to benefit the oil companies, as their own non-OPEC production would also become more valuable.

This is at best a messy situation all around, where the producing countries can have it nearly all their way, because there are no countervailing powers they have to consider. The only question they face is whether, because of their own interest in the economic and political well-being of their customers, it would be prudent for them to exercise self-restraint.

This interdependence is indeed a very weak reed to lean on. It is unlikely to become a controlling factor in the decision-making process of OPEC countries as long as the various importing countries and their oil companies, in the spirit of *sauve qui peut,* are willing to go to practically any length in order to secure their individual oil supplies.

Ideally, one might perhaps have hoped that the major importing countries would have formulated an effective energy policy, and also established a coordinated approach to OPEC with regard to supply and financial problems caused by its actions. Instead, what has dominated international oil relations has been the fear of importing countries and their companies that OPEC may cut off their supplies, or impose even stiffer conditions at the slightest sign of resistance or of a common policy approach by the importing countries. The latter have acted as if they were in such a weak position that in order to obtain continued supplies they must act separately and try to gain favors by ingratiating themselves with OPEC countries by any means feasible.

This policy has been a failure. And the experience of 1979 . . . has demonstrated how ineffectiveness resulting from fear and lack of common purpose has badly hurt the West, and in fact accelerated the disintegration and Balkanization of the world oil economy. Now again individual importing countries move in various directions, each one suspicious of the other, while pretending on the surface some desire for a unified approach.

The International Energy Agency (IEA), which was specifically established to deal with emergency supply situations, operates under terms of reference which do not allow it to deal with the actual situations as posed now or for that matter in 1979. And when its terms of reference did in fact permit it to intervene, the Agency apparently tried its utmost to avoid any actions, perhaps out of fear that OPEC might not like it.

Without going into details, it would appear that in order to cope with current problems where oil importers might be confronted by OPEC countries with extraneous or detrimental terms on supply or on pricing, the importing countries should agree among themselves on a common policy, backed up by an allocation scheme. . . . Interestingly enough, Saudi Oil Minister Zaki Yamani recently suggested that the developed and developing countries should jointly adopt a scheme for the equitable distribution of world energy consumption.

Under such a scheme, all the quantities available on regular terms should be shared equitably among the various countries. It would at least reduce the fears of some countries or companies of being left out of the supply stream unless they were prepared to make special deals on basically unreasonable terms—which, when once accepted, might set the pattern for all later OPEC transactions.

However, it is clear that as a result of recent developments affecting the international oil trade, it has now become much more difficult for importing countries and their oil companies to participate in an international oil allocation program. Any allocation scheme would require some redistribution of the flow of world oil; it is predicated on a substantial degree of flexibility in the world oil supply system that had previously been assured by the dominant role of the international oil companies in controlling and directing most of the movements of oil in world trade. As mentioned earlier, this role has now been greatly reduced.

Instead, restrictions on destinations in many recent OPEC export contracts and the proliferation of direct oil supply deals between the governments of importing countries and OPEC national oil companies might deprive the importers of the necessary flexibility for the diversions of oil shipments. Moreover, the importers might well fear that if they arrange any such diversion, the producing country might cancel their oil supply arrangements. And in those cases where the consuming country has obtained oil supplies only by granting the OPEC country special political or economic advantages, it would, in any case, most likely be reluctant to make such oil available for reallocation to other countries.

There is thus a clear and present danger that recent developments in the structure of world oil trade may have undermined the basis for the emergency reallocation system of the IEA and for a self-defense program of the importing countries as suggested here.

This is a matter for urgent consideration by the governments of the importing countries. They are now confronted with a challenge to their ability to try to cope as a group with major oil supply shortages or with a continued deterioration of the terms under which OPEC oil is made available to them.

The importing countries might well be unable to agree on a joint policy. But if they should fail to take a common stand on protecting their freedom to reallocate purchased oil among themselves, they would in fact endanger their capacity for an effective self-defense against a loss of vital oil supplies and hence seriously jeopardize their future economic, political and strategic viability. . . .

. . . Not only are all the economic and political problems . . . likely to remain with us; but in addition, even by the year 2000, the massive challenge of moving from a mostly oil-based energy economy worldwide to one that can largely draw on other more amply available energy resources will probably still remain largely unresolved.

A comprehensive and authoritative projection of the overall energy picture up to the year 2000 that is currently available is the Exxon publication, *World Energy Outlook,* released in early 1980. This study postulates a very high rate of expansion of energy production from non-oil sources during this period. Specifically, it forecasts a nearly 120 percent increase over 1980 in the non-communist world's use of coal; a more than quintupling of nuclear power; a more than doubling of hydro-power including solar, geothermal, etc.; and a buildup of synthetic fuel production from coal, tar sands, and oil shale, from virtually zero to seven million barrels per day.

In addition, the Exxon projections reflect a highly successful effort in improving the efficiency of energy use. . . .

. . . However, the Exxon study concludes that there would remain in the year 2000 a demand for oil of 60 million barrels daily, which would be 15 percent above the 1978 demand level. Oil and gas combined would by the year 2000 contribute 86 million barrels daily oil equivalent, or 52 percent of total non-communist world energy demand as compared with 72 percent in 1978. . . .

With a continued decline in the reserve-to-production ratio during the 20-year period, it is almost inevitable that real prices for oil would take off. The ensuing financial and economic problems could far exceed those which would be incurred between 1980 and 1985 and would—within the framework of our society and institutions—appear to be beyond our current capacity to cope. Moreover, many of the producing countries would certainly, for reasons of economic or political policy or because of physical limits set by productive capacity, reduce their production when their reserve-to-production ratio declines below a certain minimum. There is thus a "self-destruct" element in the relationship between the projected size of oil production and the economic and political consequences that it could entail. . . .

. . . We will probably be confronted by a series of major oil crises which might take any or all of several forms: fighting for control over oil resources among importing countries or between the superpowers; an economic-financial crisis in importing countries; regional conflicts affecting the oil-producing area; or internal revolutions or other upheavals in the Middle East. At best, it would appear that a series of future emergencies centering around oil will set back world progress for many, many years. And the world, as we know it now, will probably not be able to maintain its cohesion, nor be able to provide for the continued economic progress of its people against the onslaught of future oil shocks—with all that this might imply for the political stability of the West, its free institutions, and its internal and external security.

Taken from "Oil Exploration Strategies: Alternatives for the Third World," by Michael Tanzer, Monthly Review, *March 1978.*

. . . Turning to the general question of the present practices of underdeveloped countries in the oil exploration area, we find a wide range of approaches. At one extreme there are countries where the state is essentially a passive tax collector, turning over the risk of oil exploration and full control of such exploration and development to private foreign companies, in exchange for a share of the profits from the sale of the oil, which remains in the control of the foreign companies (the "state tax-collector role"). In the middle are the countries where the state essentially becomes a partner with private foreign companies on the basis of the companies putting up the funds for exploration, and if oil is found the production is shared on some basis between the company and the government. . . . Finally, at the other extreme there are the cases where the state itself bears the risk of exploration, retains full control over exploration and development, and gets 100 per cent of any oil found (the "100 per cent state-control role").

If we were to characterize today's underdeveloped countries by these roles, we would probably find that the passive tax-collector states are the smallest number, the production-sharing states the largest number, and the 100 per cent state-control cases an intermediate number. However, this static head-count would be misleading in an important sense because, looked at dynamically in terms of historical development, we would see that the passive state role is more or less rapidly dying out, having been largely replaced by the production-sharing role, and that in crucial countries the 100 per cent state role is itself replacing the production-sharing approach.

At the risk of some oversimplification, I would argue that the tax-collector role was a product of colonialism, the production-sharing role a product of neocolonialism, and the 100 per cent state-control role is a product of a drive for economic independence in the underdeveloped countries. Thus, while until the 1960s the passive tax-collector role was the dominant form, the countries which still accept this role tend to be extremely weak countries which are virtually colonies. The production-sharing approach, which was popularized by Indonesia in the 1960s, while progressive in form, was in substance often similar to the passive tax-collector role. This is because while the state got some of the oil itself rather than just the money profits, often the state simply sold back its share of the oil to the companies and ended up in the same position. The 100 per cent state-control approach, of which there are examples going back many years, has begun to gain greater influence in the underdeveloped countries, particularly since the jump in oil prices following the 1973 OPEC price revolution, and the consequent huge effect that oil, or the lack of it, has had on underdeveloped countries.

Why are more countries now turning to a 100 per cent state oil-exploration effort? There are a number of reasons, but among them I would like particularly to discuss the increasing spread of knowledge concerning the workings of the international oil industry, and in particular the beginning of the erosion of myths about the oil industry—myths which, being highly profitable to the companies, are perpetuated by them and by some international agencies in order to deter governments of underdeveloped countries from entering the oil industry, and exploration in particular. In sum, these myths are that only the big international oil companies possess the technology and capital necessary to carry out oil exploration and development and can afford to risk failure. . . .

As to myth number one, that *only* the big oil companies control vital exploration *technology*, the facts are that in today's world, most oil-exploration efforts, both onshore and offshore, are *not* carried out by the big international oil companies, like Mobil or Exxon, but by smaller specialized drilling firms which sell their services to anyone, usually for a flat fee and not for a share of the profits. While it is true that in the underdeveloped countries these drilling firms work to a large extent for the big oil companies, this is so because the governments of these underdeveloped countries usually leave the control of exploration to the oil companies under the production-sharing arrangements. What is more relevant, however, is that any government which is willing to pay the going market rate for these drilling operations can obtain them without recourse to the big oil companies, and without giving up a share of production or profits. (And, I might note, this is also true of pre-drilling exploration, such as geological and seismological surveys. . . .

As to myth number two, that *only* the big oil companies have the *capital* necessary for exploration and development, this falsehood exists because of a failure to recognize that while very large amounts of capital are required for finding *and developing* an oil field, only a small part of these funds (perhaps 5 per cent or less) is needed for the truly risky function of exploration. The great bulk of the capital required is for development of an oil field once found, and this is not a risky job. Moreover, given the great value of oil in the world today, oil in the ground is an extremely bankable asset, and the necessary development capital can easily be raised by loans, on quite favourable terms. Such loans, as we shall see, can be obtained from international agencies, commercial banks, equipment suppliers, or countries and oil companies that are anxious to secure future supplies of crude oil.

As for myth number three, that *only* the international oil companies can *afford the risk* of oil exploration, this falsehood exists because of excessive concentration on the cost of exploration, with little attention being paid to the benefits. Whether or not a risk is worthwhile, or affordable, as the oil companies know so well, depends not only on the costs but also on the possible benefits, and what resources can be diverted from other uses to take the gamble. If, by way of a not-so-hypothetical example, $10 million has to be spent on exploration, and the chance of finding a one-billion-barrel field worth 1,000 times the oil exploration investment is one out of two, surely no rational person would say the country cannot afford the risk. After all, any country—no matter how small—has some resources available which it could shift to such an exploration "gamble."

Further, it should also be pointed out that exploration is not an all-or-nothing thing, but a series of steps seeking information, which can be cut short if the initial information indicates that prospects are dim. Thus, if four wells cost $10 million, but the first two give very bad results, then you can cut your losses by ending exploration, and hence your actual risk capital will turn out to be much less than the maximum.

Finally, . . . one must also ask whether the country can afford to give up control of a large share of its oil resources to a giant multinational company which has many interests all over the world. This is particularly important because in today's world oil is a scarce resource whose value is often far greater than its market price. This may be particularly true for a country which might hope to use oil as a basis for further industrialization—a point I will return to below.

By way of footnote to this topic of the possible state role in oil in underdeveloped countries, I should also point out a very fundamental reason why many of them have not moved beyond production-sharing agreements, even where they have penetrated these myths. And that reason is the historically very strong opposition of the international oil companies backed by their powerful home governments, and international lending agencies like the International Monetary Fund and the World Bank, to state companies entering into the oil companies' highly profitable business.

Now, having examined some of the reasons why it is possible for governments of underdeveloped countries to move into 100 per cent state roles in oil exploration, I would like to give some specific examples. There are a number of countries in which the government has set up a state oil corporation which carries out oil exploration, either with its own personnel, or through contracting for such services on a fee basis. I will discuss briefly three illustrative examples: Mexico, India, and Vietnam. Mexico is of interest because it has a long history of 100 per cent state control of oil; India is a case study of a government shift from production-sharing to 100 per cent state control in the offshore area, and the benefits it has reaped; Vietnam is an example of a war-torn country new to the oil industry which in only two years has leaped ahead to develop a pioneering approach to 100 per cent state control.

Petróleos Mexicanos, or Pemex, the country's state oil company, was born in 1938 when the Mexican government nationalized the oil industry because of its arrogant refusal to accept the sovereignty of the government. Pemex, which started as a struggling operation, inherited some oil refineries and a declining oil-production sector; it faced almost universal hostility from the powerful oil companies and their home governments, which attempted to boycott and strangle it from the beginning. Nevertheless, despite continuing hostility from these sources, Pemex built in its first three decades an enviable record in the oil-exploration area.

According to some calculations I made about ten years ago, at a time when crude oil was selling at around $2 per barrel, Pemex had invested, between 1938 and 1966, an estimated $600 million in exploration efforts, finding seven billion barrels of oil reserves worth approximately $14 billion, or $24 in oil found for every $1 invested, with all of the oil and its profits going to the country. In more recent years Pemex has far outstripped even this performance, finding huge new reserves onshore and offshore, which are officially put at 14 billion barrels but unofficially estimated as high as 60 billion barrels. Where once the big foreign lenders boycotted Pemex, now they fall all over each other to make loans for oil development, on very favourable terms. Indeed, one of the ironies of the present situation is that those forces in the United States which continually scoffed at Pemex's efforts and called it a "failure," now look to Pemex as a possible saviour from OPEC, hoping that it will provide the United States with a major supply source which might undermine OPEC's power.

The enormous monetary value of the oil which Pemex has found, through its own drilling operations carried out by Mexican personnel, has clearly been far greater than Pemex's exploration expenditures. All profits were kept within the country. Equally important, however, Pemex as a state oil company played a major role in helping to promote the growth of Mexico's economy, through such means as selling oil at low prices, encouraging indigenous production of oil-field supplies like steel pipe (which in turn helped develop a steel industry in Mexico), producing petrochemicals which aided agriculture, and even providing social services such as roads, schools, and water systems for some of the poorer rural regions.

The second country to be discussed here is India, which is one of the poorest countries in the world, with a per capita income of about $100 per year. Surely India would seem to fit the myth of a country whose government cannot afford the risk of exploring for oil on its own, yet it has very successfully carried out such exploration at great benefit to the country.

The background to this story is that there has been a long struggle in India during the post-Second World War period over the extent to which the government could carry out oil exploration on its own, as opposed to granting concessions to foreign companies. In particular, India was strongly pressured by the foreign oil companies (including Exxon and Mobil), their home governments (particularly the United States), the World Bank, and the International Monetary Fund to leave oil exploration to the private companies. As a result, even though hardly any exploration was carried out by the companies, which at that time had huge reserves in the Middle East, the government did relatively little in the oil-exploration area, although it had some success with onshore drilling directly carried out by government personnel. However, in the more technologically difficult offshore area, the conflicting pressures resulted in delay and indecision, until the 1973 oil price jump forced the country to take action. In 1974 the government compromised by awarding two production-sharing concessions to foreign oil companies, and reserving one area for the state oil entity, the Oil and Natural Gas Commission (O.N.G.C.).

The result of that decision is that the O.N.G.C. found a major offshore oil field (the "Bombay High"), while the two private company groups, after some unsuccessful drilling, have now ceased operations. As for the Indian government's efforts, the sequence of events was as follows. The government bought what is called a "jack-up rig," which is the simplest and cheapest kind of drilling platform suited for shallow waters up to 250 feet. . . . The rig was built in Japan, and the Indian government hired a U.S. offshore drilling company to operate it and also to train Indian nationals to carry out this work in the future, on a fee basis. The cost of buying the rig was probably about $25 million, while the management and training fee was in the neighborhood of $1 million per year.

Five exploration wells were then drilled between mid-1974 and mid-1975, and these wells "proved out" a field estimated to contain in the neighborhood of one billion barrels of oil, worth at today's prices about $14 billion. The total exploration costs (allowing for the fact that the Indian government did not have to buy the rig but could have rented it, and hence only a part of the investment should be charged to the one year's effort) was probably in the order of $20 million. Thus, by "risking" $20 million in exploration expenditures, the government found oil worth more than 500 times as much, all of which now belongs to the country. Surely no other area of economic endeavor offers such tremendous potential return for such relatively small outlay!

The development expenditures to bring the Bombay High field into full production—about 200,000 barrels per day by the early 1980s (an amount which will be worth about $1 billion per year at today's oil prices)—are estimated at about $600 million in total. While this is a great deal of money for India, . . . the country has had no trouble obtaining loans on very favorable terms for such oil development purposes. Even the World Bank, which has historically resisted making loans to state oil companies because it favored private capital in the oil area, has made its first such loan to the Indian government, of $150 million, at 8.2 per cent per year. One can rest assured that, had World Bank money not been available, other private capital would have been eager to fill the gap—as evidenced by the fact that the Indian government recently got its first commercial bank loan (at "a mere 1 per cent above the London Interbank Offered Rate"), based partly on its new-found oil reserves.

The Indian government also has been able to help "self-finance" the oil-field development, and thus to reduce the need for loans. . . . This is to bring the field quickly into production by loading the oil onto tankers at sea and carrying it to shore. This serves the dual purpose of not having to hold up production until an expensive pipeline from the offshore field to the land can be completed, and also providing a cash flow to help pay for the pipeline. Thus, while the pipeline being built is to be finished by mid-1978, the Indian government, by starting production in mid-1976, will have achieved production of 50,000 barrels a day by that time. It will have produced several hundred million dollars' worth of oil before the pipeline is completed, which is more than enough to pay for the entire cost of the pipeline! By way of footnote, this initial success has stimulated the Indian government to additional exploration, and thus far it has found at least one more promising offshore oil field.

Finally, the experience of the Socialist Republic of Vietnam since the end of the war in 1975 illustrates how quickly an underdeveloped country can develop a highly advantageous and sophisticated approach to offshore oil exploration. Essentially the Vietnamese undertook an intensive investigation of the realities of today's international oil industry. As a result, the government has established a two-pronged approach to offshore oil exploration. This has dramatically reversed the previous situation under the Saigon regime which had awarded concessions offshore South Vietnam to foreign companies on terms highly disadvantageous to the country.

. . . The government appears to have reserved some of the most promising offshore areas for its own exploration efforts, to be undertaken at its own risk, with technical services and financing from Norway. . . . Norway is also building an offshore exploration training center in Vietnam.

. . . [The] Vietnamese government also is negotiating arrangements for exploration in other offshore areas in the form of service contracts with state oil companies of Western European countries which are particularly anxious to obtain assured longterm supplies of crude oil. . . . These service contracts reportedly provide that the companies will take the risk of exploration and get the right to buy up to 45 per cent of any oil found at 7 to 10 per cent below world market prices. On that basis, after deduction of costs, Vietnam would end up with 95 to 97 per cent of the oil profits, and the foreign state oil companies 3 to 5 per cent. . . .

In the final analysis, in the world of today, just as war is too important to leave to the military, so oil is too important to leave to the private oil companies. This fact is being recognized in strongholds of private enterprise like Western Europe and Japan, as well as in Canada where the government has set up an integrated state oil company to do everything from exploration and producing oil to operating refineries. Even in the United States itself, where the power of the big oil companies is greater than anywhere else, the federal government is now proposing to get into the business of oil exploration by contracting for drilling on the outer continental shelf. . . .

A NOTE ON NATURAL GAS

Thus far we have traced the growth in the use of both coal and oil from the latter part of the Industrial Revolution to the present. We have seen how these industries grew into large entities. In the case of coal, the myriad small firms congealed into large corporations only after the Second World War. In oil, the pattern was established within a decade of the drilling of the first well. In retrospect, we can observe the signposts along the way toward this concentration: the creation of Standard Oil and its children with the antitrust decision in 1911; the formation of the international cartel in the 1920s; the mechanization and rationalization of the coal-mining industries eagerly pursued by John L. Lewis; and the concentration of the industry as practiced by George Love.

As we shall see in the sections just ahead, the coal and oil industries generally merged in the 1960s, bringing together different fuels under the umbrellas of a few very large "energy" corporations. However, there is another strand in this historical development which we have not yet mentioned: natural gas. (We have not previously discussed it because its fortunes are so intertwined and synonymous with those of oil.) Gas is often discovered with oil, and for many years it was flared (burned) at the wellhead. Trillions of cubic feet of gas, for example, were wasted in this way throughout the Middle East. Whereas coal is dirty, bulky, and cumbersome to handle as a cargo, gas is elusive, evaporating into thin air unless contained under pressure. Its wide use awaited the development of a continental pipeline system, which could transport the gas under pressure from the oil fields of the Southwest to markets in the East and West. The first such pipelines were built during the Second World War, initially used for oil, and after the war turned over to gas. Subsequently processes were developed whereby gas could be frozen, turned into a liquid, and shipped in special tankers.

Although gas is generally produced by the major oil companies, unlike the other fuels, it has been under direct federal regulation, and as indicated in the next entry, it was the oil industry's effort to free gas from federal control that led to the energy crisis of the late 1960s. Under the administration of Jimmy Carter regulations were removed from the production of natural gas, and Carter's successor, Ronald Reagan, argued against government regulation of gas and other fuels. As a result of these policies, initiated by Carter and encouraged by Reagan, the price of gas rose steadily, along with the supply. As we shall see in the next section, the politics of natural gas was inextricably interwoven with the development of synthetic fuels.

Taken from "Out of Gas: Notes on the Energy Crisis," by James Ridgeway, Ramparts, *October 1973.*

THE "REAL" ENERGY CRISIS

. . . If the public thinks of the energy crisis as essentially a gasoline crisis, the major oil companies see it much more as a natural gas crisis. In fact, official talk of an "energy crisis" began with reports from the majors that natural gas reserves were running low. Gas supplies about one third of all energy in the country. In the late 1960s there was a particularly keen demand for the clean burning natural gas because of air pollution in big metropolitan areas.

Oil companies produce most of the natural gas, which is then fed through interstate pipeline companies to markets on the east and west coast. The companies claimed that unless the price of gas was raised at the well-head, there would not be sufficient incentive for them to discover more, and hence there would be a shortage.

The alleged natural gas shortage is at the crux of the energy crisis, for it is the hinge on which the oil companies base future fuels policy. That policy is fairly simple: the gas shortage can be used to force the Federal Power Commission to increase the price of natural gas, then as a lever in the Congress to deregulate its price altogether. As the price is forced upward, it becomes economically feasible in the industry's terms to introduce synthetic gas made from coal. The oil companies have been buying up coal companies and amassing reserves for the last 10 years.

Again, to understand developments in the natural gas business, it is useful to place them in a historical setting:

In the Phillips decision of 1954 the Supreme Court ruled that the government, through the Federal Power Commission, must regulate the price paid for gas by the big interstate pipeline companies to the major oil companies which produce the bulk of the gas. That decision represents a substantial effort to regulate the oil industry. Much gas is discovered in the search for oil, and in order to properly regulate gas prices, the commission would need to inquire into the costs of the oil exploration. That in turn conceivably might lead to regulation of the entire oil industry.

Shortly after the Phillips decision was announced the gas men warned of a short supply of natural gas because, they said, there would no longer be any economic incentive to drill. There was a move in Congress to deregulate the price of gas. In 1955, A. P. King, Jr., representing the Texas Independent Producers Royalty Owners Association, said, "The supply of natural gas available in years past—at least in large part—was priced artificially low at the well and will rapidly fall short of growing demand unless allowed to reach normal competitive levels." The Independent Petroleum Association of America declared, "Federal regulation of natural gas will inevitably result in diminishing supplies and higher cost of this essential and desirable fuel."

Between 1954 and 1961, the FPC did not attempt in any serious way to regulate the price of gas. Then, during the Kennedy administration, Joseph Swidler, chairman of the FPC, worked out a system of price control based on average existing rates for the different gas producing areas. The oil industry fought area pricing through the courts and finally lost in the Supreme Court in 1968. Again gas producers warned of an "energy crisis," and sure enough, by 1969 gas reserve figures published by the industry began to decline.

Since the federal government relies exclusively on the industry reports for estimates of gas reserves, it has little way of checking whether the reserve estimates are correct or not. In 1971 FPC economists noted what they thought to be discrepancies in the figures of the American Gas Association, the trade organization which draws up gas reserve statistics. The staff economists asked the commission for permission to make an independent inquiry into gas reserves. The industry vigorously opposed such a study, and the full commission eventually denied the staff permission to make one. Instead, for cosmetic purposes the commission ordered a gas survey where FPC staff members checked the industry reserve accounts, but did not inquire into the background data on which the reserve estimates were based.

In 1971 the FPC accepted the industry figures, agreed there was indeed a gas shortage and an "energy crisis," and said the price of gas should be made higher to offer additional incentives to companies that searched for new gas. Thus, the price at the well-head for gas offshore Louisiana was raised from 18½ cents per thousand cubic feet (mcf) to 26 cents per mcf. Recent statistics for the year 1972 suggest the price increase had a distinct effect: the opposite of the intended one. More successful gas wells were drilled in 1972, but strangely, gas reserves continued to decline.

FORCING PRICES UP

In June 1973 James T. Halverson, director of the Federal Trade Commission's Bureau of Competition, testified before Senator Hart's antitrust subcommittee that there was "serious under-reporting" of reserves by natural gas producers to the Federal Power Commission. He went on to say that the procedures for reporting reserves by the American Gas Association "could provide the vehicle for a conspiracy among the companies involved to under-report gas reserves."

While the Federal Trade Commission experts were reporting their findings to Senator Hart, the Federal Power Commission was busily granting yet another price rise to the oil producers, an increase that would lift the price from 26 to 45 cents per mcf. Both the Federal Power Commission and the White House additionally sought to pressure Congress and the courts to deregulate the price of gas. If successful, the price of natural gas probably would go a lot higher than 45 cents.

It is important to understand that so far, the Federal Power Commission's incentive program has raised the price more than double without any indication that the industry has discovered new supplies of gas.

As the price of natural gas has climbed, the oil companies have begun to take a more active interest in synthetic gas, made from naphtha, or from coal. Once the price of natural gas reaches a high enough level, then synthetic gas can become profitable, and it will be introduced to ease the "energy crisis" by supplementing the supposedly dwindling natural gas supplies. This is slowly beginning to happen.

Development of synthetics was hastened by the El Paso Natural Gas Co.'s much publicized scheme to import large quantities of Algerian liquefied natural gas (LNG) for use along the East Coast. This project has been approved by the Federal Power Commission, and while it represents a large and important deal in its own right, it was crucial to the oil industry for little noticed reasons.

Liquefied natural gas costs much more than natural gas. The gas must first be piped from wells in Algeria, run through a processing plant where the gas is frozen, then loaded into tankers for the trip across the Atlantic. The frozen gas is finally unloaded at East Coast ports, and turned back into a gas so it can be intermingled with natural gas flowing through the pipelines.

Among the major questions to be decided in the El Paso case was whether gas companies which purchased the Algerian LNG could "roll in" its high price. The commission eventually gave its approval. That decision is viewed as a precedent for the proposed synthetic projects, laying the way for the industry to "roll in" or pass along the extremely high prices of these schemes to the consuming public.

The major synthetic projects involve changing coal into a gas that can be intermingled in the pipeline system with natural gas. The technology is complex with certain problems unresolved, but the profitability from the companies' point of view seems to be clearly established. That is likely to mean that these coal gasification projects—some 200 of them have been planned in the mountain states—will go forward. Coal gasification requires large amounts of strip mine coal, large quantities of water and construction of expensive plants. If it goes ahead, it means large scale development of coal resources in the mountain states, attendant decline in the existing agricultural economy, and most important, a tremendous strain on the already scarce water resources of the region.

And so it is possible to discern certain ongoing trends amidst all the confusion generated by the "energy crisis": After the oil companies recognized the seriousness of Arab nationalism, they moved to diversify their oil holdings through stepped up exploration programs in other parts of the world, primarily in Southeast Asia and in the Arctic. At the same time, they bought into other fields, particularly coal, which could be used as the base for synthetic fuel in the future.

The short-term fuel oil and gasoline shortages were convenient vehicles for the major oil companies to tighten their grip on independents, and drive them out of business. Then again, the energy crisis was a lever to force up the price of natural gas, and for a campaign to deregulate the price of gas. If successful, that would formally remove the federal government from regulation of fuel prices. More importantly, it would permit raising fuel prices to the point where oil companies could begin to seriously exploit synthetic gas made from coal, with enormous consequences for the nation's economy and ecology.

Whether or not they succeed now in this scheme, we can be certain that the majors will keep up the pressure. Moreover, the nation does have serious energy problems which it will have to cope with in the years ahead. Its ability to handle them well, and with foresight, will likely hinge on its ability to handle the major oil companies, to distinguish what is in their interest and what in fact serves the needs of the population at large.

NUCLEAR POWER AND SYNTHETIC FUELS

OIL, natural gas, and coal are valuable energy resources which one day will be exhausted. There is little doubt about that. The debatable question is when. As we have seen, since the 1920s, there have been dire predictions that oil will soon run out, and in the midst of our most recent energy crisis in the 1970s scientists argued that both oil and natural gas supplies would begin to decline during the latter part of this century. As the decade of the eighties began, however, the main problem was a market once again glutted by oil and gas at a time of what seemed to be persistent world economic decline.

Nonetheless, for decades there has been an ongoing debate about how best to switch the industrial world to a more renewable source of energy. Nuclear power and synthetic fuels were two responses to this problem. Both are the dream children of military-industrial technicians and bureaucrats. Each involves startingly similar histories: extravagant, indeed almost mystical early claims to success and the need for an industrial apparatus of extraordinary scale requiring enormous government subsidies and costly technical support systems. Both nuclear power and synthetics represent big government, big industry, big military solutions to relatively intractable human energy problems. In the next section we will see how different were the assumptions behind the small-scale alternative energy movements that took root in the 1970s.

Both the nuclear power and synthetic fuels industries were the direct outgrowths of national military and foreign policies and must be examined in that light.

Einstein had explained that there were vast stores of energy in the atomic nucleus, but scientists did not know how to release that energy. In 1933, Leo Szilard, a Hungarian physicist setting out to warn the nonfascist nations of the dangers of Hitler, tried to convince the British and Americans that they could make an atomic bomb. He advanced a theory of how to unlock atomic energy.

An atom is the smallest unit of an element, which itself is the basic substance of nature. Each atom is made up of electrically charged particles. These particles can be positive, negative, or neutral (neutrons). In most elements these are stuck fast to one another and never move. But when a neutron hits the nucleus, or center, of an atom of uranium 235 either spontaneously in nature or because of human intervention, the atom splits, releasing more neutrons along with a great deal of energy.

Once begun, the splitting process can be made self-propagating, setting off a chain reaction. Thus, in the proper circumstances, one neutron splits one atom which produces two neutrons which split two atoms which produce four neutrons which split four atoms, and so on. If this chain reaction is made to happen rapidly, a huge release of energy takes place.

The theories for splitting the atom provided the basis for the creation of the Manhattan Project to build an atomic bomb.

The Manhattan Project touched off a one-nation race for the bomb—actually the two bombs which obliterated the Japanese cities of Hiroshima and Nagasaki. Thus, at the very inception of nuclear power lies not a vision of the hopeful release of energy for human use, but an appalling vision of nuclear annihilation. However, in the early 1950s, as if by some miracle a wonderful new idea suddenly sprang from this truly horrible specter: What if in the deadly bomb there were indeed an elixir of life and peace? "What better place to find the elixir than in the very source of evil itself?" write Peter Pringle and James Spigelman in *The Nuclear Barons.* "Atoms for Peace, the propaganda buzz phrase of Eisenhower's 1953 speech became a term of magic, of witchcraft; it seemed capable of driving off the evil spirit of atomic warfare. . . . An infectious wave of nuclear enthusiasm spread from the United States throughout the world."

From the most serious new proponents of nuclear power came sky's-the-limit claims of infinitely abundant electrical energy resources for all time: electricity "too cheap to meter," nuclear cargo ships, nuclear airplanes, nuclear-propelled rockets, cures for cancer, sterilized sewage, irradiated food that was safe from disease and spoilage, even the "irradiated food luncheon." Project Plowshare in the late 1950s promised to redirect rivers, move mountains, dig harbors and canals with peaceful nuclear explosions. Such explosions would release natural gas trapped deep within the earth's surface. The hazards of radiation and problems of disposing of nuclear wastes were swept aside in celebration of imagined productive uses of the bomb. As late as the energy crisis of the 1970s nuclear power was celebrated as a cure-all for Arab oil.

It was in this spirit of hope and hokum that the nuclear industry began, and thirty years later this gusto lives on in statements such as the one by Edward Teller which follows. The reality of nuclear power, however, has been rather different, as this section indicates, and today few believe that nuclear energy is destined to be the "oil" of the future.

As a framework for the selections that follow, it is worth keeping in mind a few salient points. First, nuclear power is a child of the military, and the industry it spawned was created initially for military reasons. In part, the nuclear power industry was viewed by men such as Admiral Hyman G. Rickover as a way to enhance one branch of the military over another—in this instance, the Navy with its nuclear-powered submarines and aircraft carriers over the Army and Air Force. More important, military planners viewed the creation of a nuclear power industry as a way to develop and encourage the use of a basically military technology.

Secondly, in government circles, nuclear power was viewed as a handy form of American aid to the rest of the world. We would offer nuclear technology with its promises of untold cheap energy to energy-poor nations, and once they were hooked into such a large-scale system of technology—one which we would have to service perhaps indefinitely with our own technical know-how—then they would also be further ensnared in America's sphere of influence.

Thirdly, like the other energy systems we've examined, nuclear energy has proved hazardous to its workers. Moreover, in the case of nuclear power its hazard to the general public goes beyond any other energy technology ever developed because of the particular and intractable properties of radiation.

Finally, looked at realistically, nuclear energy's main problem has been purely economic. Despite the billions of dollars of government subsidies poured into it, it has proved so far unable to compete with oil, natural gas, and coal, all of which have been on the market in the early 1980s in abundant quantities.

ADMIRAL RICKOVER AND THE CREATION OF THE NUCLEAR INDUSTRY

Historically, it is clear that no military was ever involved in an energy development to the extent that the U.S. military was in inspiring and creating the U.S. nuclear power industry, and more than anyone else Admiral Hyman G. Rickover was the man who helped in the birth of that industry. When Rickover's guiding vision of an atomic navy, preeminent among the armed forces of the future, came into being, the Army's Manhattan Project scientists had already created the bomb.

However, between December, 1942, when Enrico Fermi, the Italian refugee scientist, demonstrated the principle of nuclear power on a squash court at the University of Chicago (or even the creation of the first atomic bomb), and the actual production of electricity by a commercial nuclear reactor lay an immense engineering feat. The nuclear chain reaction had to be changed into steam, and the steam used to drive turbines. Whole new systems of coolants, valves, pumps, and control systems had to be designed and built. It was Rickover who almost single-handedly organized this feat.

Taken from "The Nuclear Power Structure, Where It Came from, What It Is," by Alexander Cockburn and James Ridgeway, Village Voice, *May 7, 1979.*

The story of America's civil nuclear program really begins beneath the waters of the North Atlantic during World War II. Although the German U-boats had ultimately failed in their objective of blocking American supplies of men and materiel to Europe, they had taken a terrible toll. Naval planners and strategists were keenly aware that if a true submarine were ever developed, it could change the shape of war forever. And by 1945, the Germans seemed on the verge of bringing just such advanced submarines into production. Although the submarine already had a 40-year life behind it, it did not begin to approach the vessel envisaged by Jules Verne, in which Captain Nemo literally lived beneath the sea. The bastard contraption in use in the '40s generally lived on the surface while stalking its prey, submerging only at the last moment to launch its torpedoes before attempting a dash to safety. Its electrical and diesel engines were short-lived and unreliable.

Immediately after the war the U.S. Navy, under the guidance of Admiral Chester Nimitz, began to survey its needs for the future. Nimitz had taken charge of the Navy in the Pacific in the month after Pearl Harbor and had built it into the most powerful battle fleet in history. He was a submariner and shared with Eisenhower himself the status of preeminent war hero. Nimitz and his planners soon saw one irresistible avenue of development.

Already, by the late '30s, the Navy had become aware of the potential of atomic power. In November, 1939 the government, in response to scientific pressure (including that of Einstein), was grappling seriously with the same issue. Even at that time there was talk—in a memorandum by Dr. Ross Gunn, for example—of nuclear-powered vessels as well as bombs.

But during the war the Navy played only a small part in the Manhattan Project, which was controlled by the Army. In March 1946 the Navy's research laboratory issued a report arguing for construction of a nuclear submarine to be built in two years, based on advanced German hull designs. In that same month Monsanto Chemical Company proposed that the Navy, along with the other services, cooperate with private industry in building an experimental power reactor at Oak Ridge, in Tennessee.

Six Navy men traveled to Oak Ridge. At their head was the person who turned out to be the most influential figure in the development of U.S. nuclear power, both military and civilian, between that year and today.

Captain Hyman G. Rickover, at the time age 46, had graduated from Annapolis in 1922 and had taken a master's degree in electrical engineering in 1929. He was qualified to command submarines, had worked as chief engineer on a battleship, and as commanding officer on a minesweeper. In 1939, he was assigned to the rapidly growing electrical section of the Navy's Bureau of Ships in Washington.

Rickover's genius showed in his mastery of naval bureaucracy, of wartime engineering requirements, and in knowing how to get what he wanted from the industrial sector. Whereas previously, for example, electrical equipment was based on designs dating to the 1920s, Rickover produced his own specifications—often based on British battle-damage reports and his own personal inspections—and forced the private contractors to build along those lines. He would personally select the contractor staffs. In doing so, Rickover built up close working relationships with the major electrical contractors—most notably, General Electric and Westinghouse.

He was and is also one of the most single-minded, persistent, intelligent, and intractable personalities ever produced by the U.S. Navy.

Rickover and his team at Oak Ridge soon came to the conclusion that it was imperative for the Navy to build a nuclear-powered submarine. . . .

As the Rickover team pushed forward, it suddenly found itself caught up in naval bureaucratic politics. Rickover himself was, of course, a relative nonentity in the Naval hierarchy. The prevailing sentiment among the brass was that the Navy should not get involved in a wild-goose chase toward a nuclear submarine, but should take what seemed to be a more secure road, and bank on the bomb. . . .

It had always been Rickover's hope that the development of a nuclear submarine would be taken up by G.E., which was not only a large corporation, but one equipped with a first-class laboratory. G.E. was interested, but there were problems. The company had agreed to run a plutonium-production plant for the government at Hanford in the state of Washington. The government had in turn agreed to provide G.E. with a nuclear-development laboratory in Schenectady. Soon enough, government bureaus and the Navy began to eye the giant electrical manufacturer nervously, fearing—in the case of the latter—that its new lab in Schenectady would prove a distraction from participation on a nuclear-vessel project. G.E. had decided to place the bulk of its effort in the development of a breeder reactor—a project many years from completion and which Rickover saw as being essentially off-target, as indeed it was.

But Rickover continued to lobby for his point of view in Washington. He induced Nimitz to sign a letter to the Secretary of the Navy, endorsing the nuclear sub as a top priority. The secretary agreed. He fought hard to get the Atomic Energy Commission to cooperate in a reactor-research program, beyond its previous enthusiasms for the mere manufacture of bombs. His efforts paid off. The AEC, with Rickover ensconced in its command structure, opened a new section on reactor research and development. In the same year, Rickover induced Westinghouse to take seriously the possibilities of nuclear power.

He held classes for Westinghouse executives, set up a special division of the company, and plunged into the job of designing a nuclear submarine. He also persuaded MIT to set up a new department for training nuclear engineers, and his overall efforts in this direction provided much of the manpower for the nuclear industry over the next generation.

In 1953, the land-based reactor for the nuclear submarine Nautilus reached "criticality"—the first time in history that man had obtained practical power from the atom. A year earlier President Truman had officiated over the laying of the Nautilus's keel at Groton, Connecticut. In the course of his remarks, Truman said, "The peaceful significance of the Nautilus is even more breathtaking. When this ship has been built and operated, controllable atomic power will have been demonstrated on a substantial scale."

Thus it was Rickover, in the postwar years, with the help of cold war sentiment, who shaped the organization of the nuclear industry and established its imperatives. Not that many other crucial figures weren't involved. But it was Rickover above all who understood the relationship of the state to corporations. And in the end, it was Rickover who forged the essentials: a cadre of nuclear engineers, a system of contracting, and a sense of direction amid bureaucratic anarchy.

The next turning point in the history of nuclear power in the U.S. came in April 1953, with Eisenhower's decision to terminate a Rickover project for a nuclear-powered aircraft carrier. At this point Rickover took the remnants of the carrier project and, with the blessing of the AEC, reshaped it into a program that culminated in the construction of the world's first full-scale nuclear electric generating plant. Under Rickover's overall control this reactor, designed by Westinghouse and built in conjunction with the Duquesne Light Company of Pittsburgh, was established at Shippingport, Pennsylvania. Ground was broken in 1954 and the reactor went on line in late 1957.

The Eisenhower administration was anxious to yield to private industry far greater latitude in the construction of the postwar U.S. economy. In 1951 the AEC had encouraged private utilities to take an interest in the long-term prospects of nuclear power by making classified atomic data available to a group of companies. Industry responded favorably. Walker L. Cisler of the Detroit Edison Company, preeminent in the utility industry, stated that a group of companies under his leadership was prepared to undertake the construction of a power reactor.

Responding to this threat by private industry, the public-power advocates in the Interior Department and Tennessee Valley Authority hastened to form an alliance with the military adherents of a nuclear carrier. Their plan was to build a prototype multi-purpose reactor, which could run a carrier, produce plutonium for bombs, and generate electricity. Adroitly taking advantage of these conflicts Rickover won support for the government-owned Shippingport reactor.

A major impetus for nuclear power came from the advocates of public power, especially the TVA. The TVA had been headed by David Lilienthal, who later became the first chairman of the AEC. Indeed, the role of the TVA had immense repercussions for the energy industry overall. In its early years, TVA had concerned itself largely with the construction of a web of hydroelectric projects, with the aim of modernizing the Tennessee Valley. As the cold war developed, TVA found itself having to rapidly expand its operations for very specific military reasons.

As a consequence of the arms race, larger and larger amounts of enriched uranium were needed for atomic bombs. The process by which uranium is enriched requires vast amounts of electricity. Much of that initial electricity was provided by TVA, which sent the power to the AEC enrichment plants in Kentucky. The hydroelectric facilities of TVA were not able to meet the demand of the enrichment plants during the 1950s and in order to step up generating capacity the Authority turned to coal. To this end TVA sponsored, through a series of unusual (at that time) long-term contracts with coal companies in Appalachia, the reorganization of the coal industry. The industry was mechanized, small operators were driven out, and the way was paved for the subsequent concentration of the coal industry, which finally fell under the control of the oil industry in the late 1960s.

The process then became circular. TVA created the electricity which enriched the uranium. These supplies of uranium, at first used to make bombs, later became the fuel for the nuclear power plants. Among the most important customers was TVA itself which needed nuclear fuel to generate electricity in its reactors, which was used in part to create yet more fuel. The U.S. is now left to deal with the consequences of that dire bargain.

Thus the development of the civil nuclear industry in the U.S. stemmed not so much from rational assessment of the country's energy requirements—later touted as the lodestar of the nuclear option—as from military incentives and the desires of corporations to profit from same.

While the nuclear industry itself—as we have indicated above—was first developed as a government-sponsored enterprise urging major corporations forward, it has come to depend in the most important respects on a network of petroleum and mining conglomerates.

Since the nuclear power plants operating in the U.S. today do not produce their own fuel (the aim of the "breeder" dreamed of by General Electric after the war), they must be supplied with constantly increasing amounts of uranium. Such a requirement has engendered a large industry, dominated by a handful of corporations.

The two biggest suppliers of uranium in the country are Gulf Oil and Kerr-

McGee. Kerr-McGee alone is said to control 35.4 percent of all U.S. uranium reserves. Gulf follows with 19 per cent. The control of these reserves again results from public policy decisions. Much of the uranium in the U.S. is found in public-domain territories, especially in the West. Government-leasing policies, culminating in the 1960s, promoted this private domination of public assets. A 1974 Federal Trade Commission study showed that seven companies controlled 70 per cent of the uranium business in the U.S. in 1971. At hearings held before Senator Edward Kennedy, Exxon officials said that oil company reserves of uranium amounted to 60 per cent of total reserves. And with the expansion of the nuclear industry, the search for uranium has gone well beyond the U.S. itself. Canada, South Africa, and Australia have become major suppliers. Here again, the resources are controlled by a small number of large companies.

Two firms in particular have played an important role in organizing the international uranium market. They are Rio Tinto Zinc, the British mining conglomerate much influenced by the Rothschild banking family, with extensive holdings in Australia, Canada, and Southern Africa; and Anglo-American Corporation of South Africa, the huge mining concern run by the Oppenheimer family. Anglo-American produces uranium in South Africa as a by-product of gold mining. It also has a controlling interest in Engelhard Minerals, the U.S. company which is the largest producer of precious metals in the world. Both RTZ and Anglo-American are interlinked through their directors, and Anglo-American has maintained a financial interest in RTZ as well.

Once again, we find a circular process at work. One of the chief arguments of the nuclear industry has been that while the prices of fossil fuels will increase, the price of nuclear power should hold steady or decline—in part because of the stable price of uranium. Such proclamations are confounded by the spiraling price of uranium. Accounting for this mortifying rise is the natural desire of producers to make more money. This ambition was achieved by the most traditional of methods: the creation of a cartel in 1972. RTZ joined with the governments of Canada, France, and South Africa in its formulation. The intention was to maintain the price of uranium, and projected demand caught up with supply.

What, then, are the forces with a long-range vested interest in the well-being and continued expansion of nuclear power in the U.S.?

An important segment of the state (the U.S. government) remains entrenched in its commitment to nuclear power. As we have shown, the long-term impulse has come from the military, and remains a potent factor. Of almost equal importance in the state sector are the large public-power groupings: most importantly, TVA, and Bonneville Power in the Northwest. . . .

On the private side, favoring nuclear power, we find the uranium suppliers, which now include in this country the major oil companies—Kerr-McGee, Gulf, Conoco, Getty, and Exxon, along with the international mining companies (RTZ and Anglo-American). Most obviously dedicated to nuclear power are the manufacturers of the plants: General Electric (which now owns Utah International, which also mines uranium), Westinghouse, Babcock & Wilcox, and Combustion Engineering. G.E. and Westinghouse are prime military contractors and participated in the earliest formation of the nuclear industry.

It is common for antinuclear advocates to rail most urgently against the utilities, who most visibly are the perpetrators of the nuclear menace. This belief is somewhat illusory and leads to certain miscalculations about who the enemy actually is.

It is true that the private electric utility companies—200 of them—provide about 78 per cent of all electricity in the country. They operate as virtual monopolies within their own territories, and have considerable capacity, through fuel escalation clauses and the like, to force their will on the populace—in the form of higher prices and misconceived priorities. But at the same time it is an incontestable fact that the private utilities, especially along the populous Eastern Seaboard, are senescent mechanisms, with second-rate personnel and little ability to adapt to modern circumstances.

Seen from a neutral perspective, it is possible to conclude that the utilities are not so much enthusiastic advocates of nuclear power as they are hesitant fellow-travelers. They were nudged into the nuclear option in the 1950s, encouraged along the road by subsidies and inducements such as the Price-Anderson Act, which limits accident liability, and general ignorance.

With nuclear power, as with all other issues involving energy, the question relevant to utilities is who owns and controls them. Behind the utilities—as has been amply documented by the late Senator Lee Metcalf and others—stand banks, insurance companies, mutual funds, and other financial institutions.

These businesses have no structural commitment to nuclear power beyond the well-being of their investments. Affection for the status quo will retain their loyalty to nuclear power only so long as it seems prudent and safe to do so. This is not to say that the major institutions can so easily abandon the ramshackle, costly, and foundering nuclear industry after a generation of sponsorship. Continued adherence to the nuclear industry in its present state, however, raises the spectre of rippling bankruptcies and allied inconveniences.

As in its beginning, so in its end. The nuclear industry in the U.S. survives because of government policy—policy most recently restated by President Carter, who made the continuance and expansion of nuclear power a major part of his energy program. . . . [President Reagan also has continued government support for the nuclear industry.]

ALVIN WEINBERG AND THE NUCLEAR ELITE

The dream of the nuclear industry has long been the breeder reactor. Although all nuclear reactors produce plutonium, only breeder reactors are designed to run on it. Because they would actually generate more fissionable material than they consume, they would "breed" their own fuel and theoretically free themselves from the need for further infusions of uranium, thus turning the nuclear industry from a nonrenewable to a renewable energy system. The process of producing enough plutonium in one breeder reactor to feed a second breeder reactor will, however, take not just a few years but many decades. Nonetheless, the first breeder reactor in the United States is scheduled to be built at the Clinch River in Oak Ridge, Tennessee.

Even as the members of the nuclear community persisted in their dream of a functional nuclear energy system based on breeder reactors, the industry as a whole was coming under increasingly harsh attack. By the mid-1970s all around the world antinuclear groups were organizing to ban nuclear power because of the hazards of radiation. Even within the industry economic criticism mounted, while the plants themselves revealed serious flaws in construction and the costs of running them were becoming prohibitive. Because of unexpected excess electric capacity, utilities actually stopped ordering new plants.

It was at this point that the nuclear community seriously needed to take stock of the situation and that Alvin Weinberg, director of the Oak Ridge National Laboratory in Tennessee, began to offer a series of cool assessments of what the future held in store. Weinberg, who was at the University of Chicago during the wartime Manhattan Project, subsequently originated pressurized-water reactors and later became director at Oak Ridge.

Science magazine has referred to Weinberg as the "iconoclast" of the nuclear community. By any measure he is a sober scientist. As will be clear from the following selection, in attempting to broaden the concerns of nuclear power insiders so that they confront in a serious way the issues brought up by antinuclear groups, he has provided the industry with its most complex and sophisticated defense to date. At Oak Ridge itself he sought to widen the scope of the laboratory's research to take into account the social implications of atomic power. Under his directorship scientists conducted genetics research, explored sources of nonnuclear energy, and looked at the environmental effects of all energy sources.

Weinberg always has been a strong believer in the ability of science to solve technical problems. He has felt that risks, such as meltdowns or the theft of bomb materiel, could be controlled by an elite nuclear priesthood. He has soberly predicted that in a nuclear energy future a meltdown might occur as often as once every four years and has argued that with all the plutonium being reprocessed for breeders, the public will just have to begin to accept the dangers. The arguments he offers in the following article are fundamental to the expansion of nuclear power.

Taken from "Is Nuclear Energy Necessary?" by Alvin W. Weinberg, Bulletin of the Atomic Scientists, *March 1980.*

Two questions dominate the nuclear issue: Is nuclear energy necessary? Can nuclear energy be made acceptable? Unless the answer to the first is affirmative, there is little incentive to devise the improvements in nuclear energy necessary to rescue it from its present malaise. In my view, nuclear energy is highly desirable, if not absolutely necessary. It can be made acceptable. And rather than continue the bitter confrontations between proponents of renewable sources and proponents of nuclear sources, the energy community ought to put its efforts into achieving an acceptable nuclear system. We shall need all sources of energy; we cannot afford to reject nuclear energy because its current embodiments are faulted.

The fission chain reaction is a bit of a scientific fluke: for example, there is no theoretical reason why the number of neutrons emitted per fission must be sufficient to maintain a chain reaction. One cannot therefore argue that mankind would perish had fission not been discovered. Indeed, before 1939 energy futurologists, recognizing that fossil fuels were finite, speculated on the possibilities of drawing energy in the long run from the various solar sources—including wind, waves, ocean thermal gradients, and biomass—as well as geothermal sources. Nevertheless, the outlook at the time was rather pessimistic. Most pessimistic was the assessment of Charles G. Darwin, descendant of the biologist. In his book *The Next Million Years,* published in 1953, he predicted a brutish, Malthusian future for man unless he developed an inexhaustible energy source other than the sun. Darwin's candidate for such a source was controlled fusion.

Many of us in the fission community have recognized that in the fission breeder man had another path to salvation from Darwin's ultimate Malthusian disequilibrium. It is therefore understandable that we addressed the development of the breeder with such enthusiasm: here was an embodiment of Darwin's inexhaustible energy source that would, to use H. G. Wells' words of 1914, "Set Man Free."

Given this noble, perhaps noblest, of all technological dreams, it is almost incomprehensible to us why the world is now asking: Is fission necessary? Is not the relevant question: What can be done to eliminate the deficiencies of fission, rather than eliminating fission itself?

The short range: to 2000. What can we say about the necessity of fission in the near term, roughly to the year 2000? Obviously the need for fission depends upon the availability of alternative fuels or sources of energy, and upon the future demand for energy. These are not matters that can readily be settled for the whole world. In the United States, with its abundant coal, for example, a moratorium on fission would be less serious than it would be in Japan or France. The Institute for Energy Analysis (IEA), in its study "Economic and Environmental Implications of a U.S. Nuclear Moratorium, 1985–2010," concluded that the United States could weather a limited moratorium with a loss of 0.5 percent in GNP. The moratorium would allow completion of all reactors under construction by 1985; no new reactors would be built after 1985.

The moratorium would place great pressure on coal or imported oil or both. It was estimated that between 18 and 27 billion tons of additional coal would be needed by 2010 to fuel those stations that would serve in place of nuclear plants not built; alternatively, the additional imported oil would amount to from 6 to 9 billion tons. Re-examining these estimates three years after they were first made, I would say the impact might be overstated, particularly because we expected electricity to capture 46 percent of the energy market by 2000, compared to its present market share of 30 percent. While electricity's market share will probably increase, it seems unlikely that it will increase this much. Nevertheless, in view of the great environmental problems associated with coal mining, let alone the political tensions created by expanded import of oil, I conclude that even this limited nuclear moratorium is very undesirable.

Most other countries do not have coal. For them, rejection of nuclear energy would certainly entail costly importation of coal and oil. A one-gigawatt[*] (elec-

[*One billion watts.]

tric) oil-fired power plant uses 1.4 million tons of oil per year. Throughout the world 800 million tons of oil are burned annually in central electric power stations; this represents 25 percent of the world's consumption of oil in the year 1978. Should all the oil-fired plants be replaced over the next decade with nuclear plants, the pressure on oil would be reduced significantly.

In recent years it has become fashionable to fault this line of argument as simplistic. Rather than replace oil in electric power stations with coal or uranium, we are asked to believe we can so reduce our energy demand as to make many existing, let alone future, electric power plants superfluous. In any case, the use of electricity for such purposes as heating of houses or water is deemed inelegant and wasteful and ought to be discouraged.

It goes without saying that conservation must be central to any energy policy; indeed, much has already been accomplished. For example, D. Reister of the Institute for Energy Analysis points out that in the United States, the ratio of energy to gross national product has decreased by 10 percent between 1970 and 1978. But as Stobaugh and Yergin point out in the Harvard Energy Futures study, conservation requires decisions by innumerable consumers; by contrast, increased supply requires far fewer decisions. Thus the prediction of how much conservation is actually achieved—as contrasted with how much is theoretically achievable—is intrinsically less certain than is the prediction of how much supply can be increased. (To be more accurate, since energy supply and demand must balance, at issue is the relative freedom of choice afforded by policies that depend on conservation rather than on increased supply.) The difficulty has recently been analyzed by P. C. Roberts of the United Kingdom. Roberts gave evidence that, in the United Kingdom, the amount a family is likely to spend to retrofit its house with energy-conserving devices goes as the square of the family income. Roberts thus estimates that, even if fuel costs double, the amount of conservation induced by market forces in the next 25 years is about 35 percent of the theoretical. Conservation in houses, at least in the United Kingdom, does not happen automatically; subsidies of various sorts seem to be necessary. This is not to say that conservation is unimportant; it is simply that conservation in the residential sector is probably more difficult to achieve than in the industrial sector.

The current mood of rejection of electricity seems irrational. If oil is scarce and coal and uranium are abundant, it makes sense to replace oil with coal and uranium, even if in so doing one must resort to inefficient resistive heating or other devices that use electricity. After all, we are not driven by thermodynamic imperatives: economic or political considerations, such as reducing our dependence on foreign oil, certainly take precedence over the much discussed, but often irrelevant, stricture to improve the second law efficiency.

Two technical developments, the electric car and the heat pump, could swing the balance toward an electrical future dominated by large central stations. The recent announcement by General Motors of a car powered by a zinc battery whose lifetime is 50,000 kilometers, with a cruising speed of 80 kilometers per hour and a range between recharges of 165 kilometers, could, if realized, alter our attitude toward the electric future. In addition, the electrically-driven heat pump is a proven device. In the United States 560,000 heat pumps were installed last year, and this number has been increasing by 40 percent each year.

If one concedes that:

- a predominantly electric future is at least as plausible as a nonelectric one,
- oil will continue to be scarce,
- the solar technologies will not penetrate on a large scale (cost, intermittency, storage?),
- coal is not generally available except in countries that possess indigenous deposits (would the United States be prepared, in 50 years, to mine an additional billion tons of coal, to be shipped overseas?)

then it seems inescapable that fission is necessary, at least in some parts of the world. Beyond this, if the cost per joule of coal reaches that of oil—that is $80 per ton of coal at present, possibly $140 per ton with oil at $40 per barrel—then even though the cost of nuclear reactors is high (say, $1,500 per kilowatt), electricity from current reactors probably will still be cheaper than electricity from coal-fired stations.

There are uncertainties in these assumptions. But it is because we cannot know with certainty even the next 20 years that we ought to preserve all our energy options, including nuclear. In this sense, I would judge nuclear energy in the short term to be a necessity.

The long term—beyond 2030. We must look at the time, perhaps 50 to 100 years from now, when oil and gas have become scarce. Fission, if it survives, eventually would be based on breeders, though not necessarily fast breeders. Three issues dominate the long-term outlook for fission: the availability and acceptability of alternatives, the long-term energy demand, and carbon dioxide.

On the scale under discussion, only fusion or the various solar sources are large enough to compete with fission. Here I must admit to being agnostic. Fusion *may* turn out to be technically and economically feasible, but there is no way of knowing. And in good measure this is true of solar energy. Despite the many claims of technological and economic breakthroughs, the uncertainties remain. Such figures as 50 cents per peak watt, the aim of the Department of Energy for solar cells, are still no more than a hope. Given these uncertainties about alternatives to the fission breeder, prudence requires us to develop the breeder, and to deploy it if the alternatives prove too costly or turn out to be unfeasible. In short, it is far too early to reject any of the long-term energy options, particularly the breeder.

Long-term scenarios. Here I can do no better than to borrow extensively from recent studies completed at the International Institute for Applied Systems Analysis (IIASA). These scenarios, which are close to those developed by R. Rotty, at the IEA, contemplate a world population of 8 billion in 2030. Because China, Latin America and possibly India are likely to increase both their per-capita energy expenditure and their populations faster than the developed world, it is plausible to expect these countries to use a much larger fraction of the world's energy than they do now. This, of course, could change somewhat if China's announced program of one child per family succeeds.

At present, the primary per-capita energy demand averaged over the entire world comes to about 2.1 kilowatts per year. The total primary energy demand comes to 8.2 terrawatts (1 terrawatt = 1 trillion watts). If the average per capita demand grows to about 4.3 kilowatts per capita, the total primary energy demand might reach around 35 terrawatts; should it grow to only about 2.8 kilowatts per capita, then the total might be 22 terrawatts. These projections are designated by IIASA as "high" and "low"; the IEA scenario falls between these IIASA projections. (Table 1 summarizes the IIASA estimates of how the high and low energy demands might be met.)

Nuclear energy provides about one-fourth the world's energy in each of the scenarios, whereas hydro, solar, and others provide about 8 percent in the high scenario, 10 percent in the low. Can the renewables replace the 25 percent provided by nuclear energy? Here there is a sharp divergence, with nuclear opponents, such as A. Lovins, insisting that nuclear is unnecessary, that the various solar sources will suffice. To be sure, the total primary energy demand contemplated by these authors is around 17 terrawatts—an amount available from fossil sources according to IIASA, and a little more than twice the world's present energy budget. Whether a 17-terrawatt world, especially one that is increasingly urbanized, can be socially stable, no one can say. My own view is that in planning the future we do best to prepare for a higher rather than a lower energy demand. It almost goes without saying that the less energy shortages become the focus for social tensions, the better for all.

One must recognize that even the 5.2 terrawatts supplied by fission in the IIASA low scenario is formidable: some 1,500 reactors, each producing about 1,000 megawatts (electric) or 3,300 megawatts of heat. And if, in the very long run, fission takes over the role now played by oil and natural gas, the number of required reactors, even in IIASA's low scenario, would rise to over 4,000! In the high scenario these numbers would be roughtly doubled.

Carbon dioxide—a sword of Damocles? The possible constraint on fossil fuel, imposed by accumulation of carbon dioxide in the atmosphere, may be demonstrated by a few numbers. The world's total fossil fuel reserve is estimated to contain about 10 trillion tons of carbon. Should all of this be burned, and if 50 percent of the resulting carbon dioxide remains airborne, the total carbon dioxide in the atmosphere might increase some sevenfold. The temperature of the lower atmosphere is estimated by Manabe and Weatherald to increase by from 2.5 to 3

TABLE 1 Projected Supply Patterns in 2030 (in terrawatts)

	1975	2030 high	2030 low
Oil	3.6	6.8	5.0
Natural gas	1.5	6.0	3.5
Coal	2.2	11.4	6.5
Light water reactor	0.12	3.2	1.9
Fast breeder reactor	—	4.9	3.3
Hydro	0.5	1.5	1.5
Solar	—	0.5	0.3
Other	0.2	0.8	0.5
Total	8.2	35.1	22.5

Source: International Institute for Applied Systems Analysis.

degrees centigrade for every doubling of carbon dioxide in the atmosphere. Thus a sevenfold increase could raise the temperature of the lower atmosphere by as much as 8 degrees centigrade.

H. Flohn has estimated the climatic regimes that might prevail if various amounts of carbon dioxide were added to the atmosphere. He characterizes each regime by comparing it with similar regimes in the geologic past (Table 2). Flohn's estimates of the temperature rise caused by a given addition of carbon dioxide are somewhat higher than those of other authors, largely because he includes the effects of other "greenhouse" gases.

Perhaps the most alarming aspect of Flohn's estimates is that the burning of only 20 percent of the world's fossil fuel would lead to an ice-free Arctic; and he argues that an ice-free Arctic would profoundly change the entire world's climate —to a regime that last occurred two million years ago. Flohn also offers evidence, from the very rapid disappearance of forests at the end of previous interglacials, that once a climate change begins, its ecological consequences could be manifested over a few decades.

Whether the climatic changes induced by carbon dioxide accumulation produced by fossil fuel would constitute the enormous catastrophe envisaged by Flohn is controversial. Nevertheless, we must ask: What is a prudent course in the face of such predictions, even granting their inherent uncertainty? The answer seems obvious. Reduce consumption—a feat far easier to achieve in the energy-rich parts of the world than in the energy-poor parts; and be prepared to shift to energy sources that produce no carbon dioxide. In the latter category are the solar sources, the nuclear sources (fission and fusion), and geothermal.

If the geothermal source is as small as it now appears, and if fusion remains far from technical realization, the sun and uranium are the only remaining alternatives. And if one further concedes that the solar sources may remain expensive, especially if one tries to provide reliable power from inherently stochastic sources

TABLE 2 Climatic Regimes[a]

Period	Degrees centi-grade	Carbon dioxide[b] (parts per million)	Total carbon injected (billions of tons)	Fossil fuel reserve burned (present)	Time[c] (years, high)	Time[c] (years, low)
Present	0	330	180	1.8	1980	1980
1000 A.D.	1	405±25	530	5.3	2015	2034
6,000 before the present	1.5	455±25	760	7.6	2037	2053
Interglacial, 120,000 before the present	2	510±50	1,000	10.0	2050	2073
Ice-free Arctic	4	755±125	2,100	21.0	2110	2165

[a]After H. Flohn, "Possible Climatic Consequences of a Man-Made Global Warming." [b]Hypothetical carbon dioxide concentration necessary to cause the temperature rise given in preceding column. [c]Time to reach carbon dioxide concentrations given in Column 3, according to IIASA high and low scenarios.

like the wind and the sun, then caution dictates that we be prepared to use the only other technically feasible, very large energy source that does not add carbon dioxide to the atmosphere—nuclear fission. To be sure, in making this judgment I am implicitly calculating the risk of nuclear energy to be less than the risk of a carbon dioxide catastrophe. Moreover, I am assuming that if and when (perhaps in a decade or two) the reality of carbon dioxide emerges as a clearly defined political issue, then the move to nuclear and solar, coupled with conservation, can be made fast enough to forestall the catastrophe envisaged by Flohn.

We cannot as yet invoke the carbon dioxide catastrophe as justification for a nuclear future because there is still so much scientific controversy surrounding it. But if we are, as Palmer Putnam put it in 1953, "prudent custodians of man's future," then we would be acting irresponsibly if we reject any energy source, including fission, that produces no carbon dioxide.

There is a likelihood that the world may see many thousands of nuclear reactors within, say, the next 100 years. Is such a world feasible? In short, can man live with fission?

I set aside the issues of proliferation, of waste disposal, and of low-level radiation: the first because it is a political, not a technical question; the second because, as the Interagency Review Group established by President Carter asserted, satisfactory confinement of wastes for periods of several thousand years is technically feasible (after about 1,000 years the ingestion toxicity is comparable to that of the original uranium from which the wastes were derived); the third, because the hazard of low-level radiation has been grossly overplayed. But the matter of reactor accidents is not so easily disposed of. As the incident at Three Mile Island demonstrated, an accident in a nuclear plant is a real possibility; nuclear energy may not survive many incidents like Three Mile Island, even though no one was harmed there.

The *a priori* probability of an accident that releases sizable amounts of radioactivity was estimated by Rasmussen to be 50 millionths per reactor year. This number has since been criticized as being too low. In any event, the Three Mile Island accident—which released about a dozen curies of iodine-131 and, according to the Kemeny commission, probably caused no bodily harm—occurred after a few hundred reactor-years of operation. Its *a priori* probability has been estimated at around one in 400 reactor-years.

For any given reactor, a satisfactory accident probability would appear to be 50 millionths per reactor-year. A particular reactor, during its 40 years of operation, would have a likelihood of one in 500 of suffering an accident. But if the world energy system involved as many as 5,000 reactors—that is, 10 times as many as are now either in operation or under construction—one might expect an accident that released sizable amounts of radioactivity every four years. Considering that a nuclear accident anywhere is a nuclear accident everywhere, I believe this accident probability is unacceptable. If man is to live with fission over the long term, he must reduce the *a priori* probability of accident by a large factor—say, 100.

A relevant comparison is today's volume of air travel, which would have been impossible had not the accident probability per passenger mile been reduced drastically as the number of passenger miles increased. This was accomplished in air transport by a combination of technical and organizational improvements, and the same kinds of improvements will be needed in nuclear energy. Can we visualize the needed changes?

Perhaps the easiest are the technical improvements. Certainly the deficiencies that led to Three Mile Island will be corrected: German light water reactors, for example, have two relief valves in series so that if one fails to close, the other is available. Control panels will be provided with positive indication of valve position, something that was lacking at Three Mile Island. And other technical improvements will be forthcoming.

But beyond the technical fixes, various institutional changes are needed. Among these I mention first the establishment by the utilities of the Institute for Nuclear Power Operations and the Nuclear Safety Analysis Center. These are very significant developments. But I believe, in the long run, even more important is adherence to the principle of confined, permanent siting in relatively remote areas, which is already characteristic of most of the sites in the United States. We have estimated that a nuclear system of 615 gigawatts (electric) could be accommodated in the United States on 80 of the present 100 sites, augmented by 20 new sites to replace those not suited for expansion. My proposal, at least for countries well embarked on nuclear energy, is essentially a moratorium on new sites, not on new reactors. The ultimate nuclear system would consist of large centers, located at those existing sites that are adequately remote, plus a few new sites that are also remote.

The advantages of clustered, permanent locations seem compelling to me. They include a larger cadre of experts available on site; better organizational memory, and therefore better operation; more effective security and easier control of fissile material; handling of low-level wastes and spent fuel elements on site; easier surveillance of decommissioned reactors; and, as at existing nuclear sites like Oak Ridge, a surrounding population that understands radiation and is prepared to respond in case of accident. Beyond this, the entities operating large clustered sites are likely to be stronger than are entities operating, say, a single reactor. This certainly appears to be the case in Canada, where Ontario Hydro operates Pickering, Bruce and Darlington, each with four or more reactors; and the Tennessee Valley Authority in the United States, which intends to confine all its reactors to the seven sites now under construction. Soviet nuclear specialists N. Dollezhal and Y. I. Koryakin (*Bulletin,* Jan. 1980) have proposed a similar confined siting policy for the Soviet Union.

The measures I suggest may not be sufficient to rescue nuclear energy from its present disaffection. But in view of the strong incentive to maintain the nuclear option, it seems important to devise the fixes that will make nuclear energy acceptable. To do less might impose on those who follow us a future much bleaker than one that uses all energy sources—including an acceptable nuclear energy.

TELLER SPEAKS

In March 1979, the near meltdown at Three Mile Island in Pennsylvania occurred. Popular fervor against nuclear power grew dramatically. It was met by the impassioned argument of Dr. Edward Teller, father of the

H-bomb, speaking through a newspaper advertisement, placed by Dresser Industries, a leading nuclear technology company.

Taken from Dresser Industries, Inc., Dresser Building, Dallas, Texas

"On May 7, a few weeks after the accident at Three-Mile Island, I was in Washington. I was there to refute some of the propaganda that Ralph Nader, Jane Fonda and their kind are spewing to the news media in their attempt to frighten people away from nuclear power. I am 71 years old, and I was working 20 hours a day. The strain was too much. The next day, I suffered a heart attack. You might say that I was the only one whose health was affected by that reactor near Harrisburg. No, that would be wrong. It was not the reactor. It was Jane Fonda. Reactors are not dangerous.

"Now that I am recovering, I feel compelled to use whatever time and strength are left to me to speak out on the energy problem. Nuclear power is part of the answer to that problem, only a part, but a very important part.

"I have worked on the hydrogen bomb and on the safety of nuclear reactors. I did both for the same reasons. Both are needed for the survival of a free society. If we are to avoid war, we must be strong and we must help to generate the progress that makes it possible for all nations to grow and prosper.

"And what is the greatest present-day threat to the prosperity and even the survival of nations? A lack of energy. Both developed and developing nations are threatened.

"The citizens of the United States have just begun to recognize the impact of the world's growing energy shortage. Gasoline lines, electrical brownouts and higher prices are minor irritants. They are nothing compared to what may lie ahead. In a struggle for survival, politics, law, religion and even humanity may be forgotten. When the objective is to stay alive, the end may seem to justify the means. In that event, the world may indeed return to the 'simpler' life of the past, but millions of us will not be alive to discover its disadvantages.

"When our existence is at stake, we cannot afford to turn our backs on any source of energy. We need them all. When it comes to generating electricity, we especially need nuclear power. Contrary to what Nader and Fonda, and their friends such as Steinglass, Wald and Kendall, would have you believe, nuclear power is the safest, cleanest way to generate large amounts of electrical power. This is not merely my opinion—it is a fact. Due to [sic] the lessons learned at Three-Mile Island, the nuclear way of generating electricity will be made even safer.

"I have attempted to respond briefly to some of the questions which people ask about nuclear power. The problems that these questions raise are problems because of political indecision or public fear. Technically, they are nonproblems, because the dangers they imply either do not exist or else we have the know-how to solve them. I am absolutely convinced of this, after a lifetime of work as a nuclear scientist.

"I was once asked how I would like for my grandson, Eric, to think of me and my life's work after I am gone. Eric is nine years old. He is a terrible guy—he beats me at the game of 'GO.' I am enormously fond of him, but I have not given much thought to what he will someday think of my life's work. I have given a great deal of thought to whether he will be alive in the next century, and whether he will be living in freedom or in slavery. If he is living under communism, he will know I was a failure.

"I believe that we have reached a turning point in history. The anti-nuclear propaganda we are hearing puts democracy to a severe test. Unless the political trend toward energy development in this country changes rapidly, there may not be a United States in the twenty-first century.

"The President has recognized the danger of the energy shortage. As yet, he has given only some of the answers. I think—I hope—that democracy has enough vitality to evaluate the risks and to recognize the great benefits of nuclear power to human health and well-being, and to the survival of our free society."

QUESTION. Can a nuclear reactor explode like an atomic bomb?

ANSWER. No. Energy cannot increase fast enough in the reactor. Therefore, it is absolutely impossible for a nuclear power plant to explode like a bomb. For this to happen, the laws of nature would have to be repealed.

QUESTION. What is the risk of nuclear power compared to other forms of producing electricity?

ANSWER. It is far safer than coal or hydroelectric power, but all three are necessary to meet our need for energy. It may sound strange to say it, because coal has been around so long, but we know more about controlling radiation than we do about controlling the pollutive effects of burning coal. And, of course, a dam has no backup system to protect those who live below it. Indeed many of these people have lost their lives and more their homes.

QUESTION. I live within 50 miles of a nuclear power plant. What are my chances of being injured by a nuclear accident?

ANSWER. About the same as being hit by a falling meteor.

QUESTION. What about the effect of an earthquake on a nuclear plant?

ANSWER. At the first sign of a tremor, the reactor would shut down automatically. Also, reactors are built to withstand enormous structural damage. The only man-made structures I can think of that are more stable are the pyramids of Egypt.

QUESTION. Is it true that we still have no satisfactory way to dispose of nuclear wastes?

ANSWER. No. Ways do exist. What we have *not* had is a decision by our government on which way to go. Waste disposal is a political problem, not a technical problem.

QUESTION. How much radioactive waste materials are produced by nuclear plants?

ANSWER. At the moment, about 12½% of our electricity is generated by nuclear power. If *all* of it were produced this way, the wastes from these plants over the next 20 years would cover a football field to a depth of about 30 feet.

To dispose of this waste a mile underground would add less than one percent to the cost of electricity.

QUESTION. How dangerous is the release of low-level radiation from a nuclear power plant?

ANSWER. If you sat next to a nuclear power plant for a whole year, you would be exposed to less radiation than you would receive during a round-trip flight in a 747 from New York to Los Angeles.

Let me put it another way: The allowable radiation from a nuclear plant is five mrems* per year. In Dallas, people get about 80 mrems per year from the natural background of buildings, rocks, etc. In Colorado, people get as much as 130 mrems per year from the natural background. Therefore, just by moving from Dallas to Boulder you would receive ten times more radiation per year than the person gets who lives next to a nuclear power plant.

QUESTION. How much radiation were the people around Three-Mile Island exposed to during the accident?

ANSWER. Let me put it this way. Your blood contains potassium 40, from which you get an internal dose of some 25 mrems of radiation in one year. Among the people not working on the reactor, a handful may have gotten as much radiation as 25 mrems.

QUESTION. Should "spent" nuclear wastes be reprocessed to save the plutonium and other by-products?

ANSWER. Yes. Plutonium, for example, is as valuable as the original uranium fuel, because of its potential use to produce still more energy. In the end, reprocessing is needed to make nuclear energy abundant and lasting.

QUESTION. Is there a danger that the plutonium produced by nuclear reactors might be stolen by terrorists and used to construct homemade nuclear explosives?

ANSWER. I believe that reactor products can be properly safeguarded from terrorists. This can be much more easily done than the guarding of airplanes. Also, any terrorist who puts his mind to it can come up with ways to terrorize a population that are less dangerous to himself than handling plutonium. The answer is not to get rid of the reactors—let's get rid of the terrorists.

QUESTION. Will the expansion of nuclear power by other countries enable them to produce nuclear weapons?

ANSWER. Unfortunately, yes. This is already happening. Two-thirds of the reactors in operation in the free world today are outside the United States. Since we can't stop other nations from building nuclear plants or weapons, what we must do is find better solutions to international problems. An energy-starved nation is much more likely to make and use nuclear weapons as a last resort to survival. The only way to prevent that is to see to it that there is enough energy to go around, and to strengthen cooperation and confidence among the nations.

QUESTION. What have we learned from the accident at Three-Mile Island?

*A mrem is an appropriate unit used to make comparisons.

ANSWER. Two things. First, that nuclear reactors are even safer than we thought. Despite many human errors and a few mechanical failures at Three-Mile Island, the damage was contained. No one was killed, or even injured. We have also learned that a lot can be done by better educated, better paid and more responsible reactor operators, and by a more efficient display of the state of the reactor by modern instrument panels.

Three-Mile Island has cost $500-million, but not a single life. We must pay for safety and, even after we have paid for it, nuclear energy is the cheapest source of electrical power. It is most remarkable that in the case of nuclear energy we are paying for our lessons in dollars, not in lives.

NUCLEAR FUTURES

Despite the numerous setbacks the nuclear industry continues to suffer, scientific research (with government and industry backing) is proceeding with the aim of creating an ever more nuclear future. Perhaps the most startling and long term of the options being investigated is the fusion frontier, as reporter Amanda Spake found out when she visited the Princeton Plasma Physics Laboratory, which is the largest fusion energy research center in the world.

Taken from "The Nuclear Frontier," by Amanda Spake, Mother Jones, *September/October 1979.*

. . . Fusion is the source of energy for the stars; fusion is also the technological basis for the hydrogen and neutron bombs. It is a process whereby two atoms of hydrogen are fused together to make one atom of helium and one free neutron, releasing energy as the atoms are joined. Dwight Eisenhower, when he was president, suggested to the old Atomic Energy Commission that the public be kept "confused about fission and fusion," since even then fusion was regarded as the clean relative to the radioactive technology of fission. In fact, fusion and fission are opposites. Unlike in fusion, during which atoms are joined together; in fission, the center of a heavy atom such as uranium is split apart. . . .

You have probably heard about fusion. Fusion power has been consistently promoted to the public as a clean, safe, non-radioactive—if distant-future—source of power, an alternative to nuclear fission. Glowing reports on fusion have been commonplace, like this one from a March 1978, Department of Energy publication: "Fusion releases no chemical pollutants to the atmosphere since there are no combustion products. There are also no 'ashes,' except helium, a harmless and useful gas. There is no inventory of weapons-related uranium or plutonium materials associated with fusion; hence, there is no risk of diversion."

If fusion sounds like the source of power we've all been waiting for, hold on. A *Mother Jones* investigation has turned up evidence that fusion will first be used *not* as an alternative to nuclear fission power, but as a way of *extending its use.*

This is the fusion "application" Daniel Jassby and a number of other scientists, including Nobel laureate Hans Bethe, are promoting to their colleagues. . . . Little has been written about it outside of scientific journals.

Our investigation shows that industry and government scientists are designing power plants that would marry fusion and radioactive fission into a new type of reactor called "the fusion-fission hybrid." The hybrid reactor would be primarily a breeder of nuclear fuel.

This is not the type breeder proposed for the Clinch River reactor in Tennessee . . . This is a breeder that has not yet been discussed publicly. It is technologically different and many times more efficient. Estimates indicate that one hybrid reactor alone could produce enough plutonium or uranium to run 3–10 (and some "optimists" say as many as 20) traditional nuclear power plants.

From the utility and reactor industries' point of view, hybrids could save the current generation of "light water" reactors from certain death when the usable uranium supply runs out. Hybrids would allow the existing style of Three Mile Island-type nuclear power plants to operate well beyond the 25–75 years our uranium supply is expected to last. Hybrids used as nuclear "fuel factories," as Westinghouse has proposed, would allow the fission economy to go on forever.

The Department of Energy is spending about $2 million yearly for conceptual design studies of hybrids, and industry is spending at least $1 million more. These are on-paper studies, since fusion is not yet a working technology. The DOE spends about $500 million a year on the entire fusion energy program. And while some energy officials think it's too early to tell yet if hybrids will be used, Dr. C. Martin Stickley, at one time a top DOE fusion official, acknowledged that hybrid reactors would probably represent fusion's first application.

"We're not highlighting that use of fusion," Stickley cautioned, implying that the DOE was not publicly advertising the fact that fusion might be used for breeding plutonium. Breeding nuclear fuel was "colored by political problems," he added. "But you're right. Breeding fissile fuel [the fuel used in conventional nuclear reactors] is a nearer term thing than pure fusion-generated electricity."

Scientists who are working on plans for hybrids would agree. Despite the fact that Princeton's new Tokamak Fusion Test Reactor is designed to bring the U.S. closer to a working, pure fusion plant, Jassby and other scientists hope to breed small amounts of nuclear fuel in the TFTR. They also hope the electric utility industry will fund future experiments on the TFTR, which would aid in the design of a real hybrid to be built elsewhere later.

There is now a scientific bandwagon in favor of hybrids, and the effect of having a Nobel laureate on board should not be underestimated. Hans Bethe is a one-time Nobel prize winner, Professor Emeritus in physics at Cornell University, decidedly pro-nuclear and considered by government and industry to be the heavyweight champ when it comes to choosing which of the new, complicated technologies may have a chance of success. Three different scientists I spoke with stressed the overwhelming effect Bethe's endorsement of hybrids would have on the fusion program. "When a guy like Bethe starts writing articles supporting these machines," one said, "the chances are very good at least one will be built."

If hybrids really are closer to operation than pure fusion reactors, then that entire $500 million we're spending every year on developing fusion power has to be looked at a little differently. In the end, no matter how many bureaucrats try to deny it, that $500 million is going to benefit radioactive fission. It constitutes a quiet subsidy toward extending the life span of conventional nuclear plants.

The drawbacks of nuclear fission power plants are all too familiar now: no safe solution for the disposal of radioactive waste, toxic for 250,000 years; small and not-so-small releases of radioactivity; long-term, low-level radiation exposure for plant workers and the nearby population; and the probability that a big, China Syndrome-type accident is not nearly so remote as the nuclear industry would have us believe.

Pure fusion, while ostensibly cleaner, is likely to be an extremely complicated and even more cumbersome technology than fission:

- Fusion requires the heating of hydrogen gas to temperatures of 100 million degrees Celsius, more than *six times* the estimated temperature of the sun's interior.
- The tokamak, a large, doughnut-shaped magnetic chamber that holds the hot gas, was invented by the Soviets in 1965 and is still the most advanced machine for fusion energy production. Commercial reactors based on tokamaks would cost several times more than today's $1 billion-apiece conventional nuclear plants.
- Fusion requires enormous amounts of electricity to heat and confine the gas. Running Princeton's small, "experimental" TFTR will require enough electricity to power a city of half a million.
- Breaking even—matching the amount of electricity used to produce fusion with the amount of energy gained from the resulting fusion reaction—is what scientists are aiming for now. In hopes of accomplishing this, they have settled on a fusion fuel made up of two different kinds of hydrogen. The first is deuterium, extracted from sea water. Deuterium—safe, clean and plentiful—is an inexhaustible source of energy and has always represented fusion's most attractive asset. But the other compoenent of this fuel is tritium, a different sort of hydrogen. Tritium is man-made and is radioactive. Princeton's TFTR will be the first fusion reactor in the world to use this mix of deuterium and tritium.

As if these problems weren't enough, there is still another, potentially more damaging: no one yet knows of a safe, workable way to capture the energy generated in the fusion reaction. A reaction using a combination deuterium and tritium fuel releases a high-speed neutron (an uncharged particle); such neutrons will make the inside of a fusion power plant so incredibly radioactive that steel and other materials will not stand up long to the intensity.

All of this brings us full circle, back to fusion-fission hybrids. Because they promise the additional benefit of fission fuel in recompense for all these expensive problems, hybrids might rescue the jobs of scientists who had built their careers on the hope of an early use for fusion power. Hybrid reactors would not, however, correct the engineering or environmental drawbacks of pure fusion. In fact, the engineering difficulties associated with hybrids may be worse than those with either fission or fusion individually. The Clinch River-type fast breeder reactor is undoubtedly the most complex engineering feat the nuclear industry has yet tackled. Yet one DOE breeder official told a meeting of his colleagues that he was "overwhelmed" by the design problems he saw on the horizon with hybrids. "We have all of the problems of breeder reactor development," he said, "squared."

So why build them? Because, if you capture the high-speed neutrons released when deuterium and tritium atoms are fused, you have a key ingredient of nuclear fuel. These neutrons transform useless, depleted uranium ore—the estimated national stockpile is over 250,000 tons—into plutonium. They make thorium, abundant in the earth's crust, into uranium 233. Both of these materials can be used to fuel either traditional nuclear plants or fast breeders if they are ever built.

But hybrids do more than put those neutrons to use. They also multiply the energy output of an otherwise-inefficient pure fusion reactor. The materials used to breed nuclear fuel are wrapped snugly around the hot hydrogen gas in a tokamak. This nuclear fuel "blanket" actually increases the total power output by 5–40 times over that of a pure fusion reactor. As a result, a fusion reactor that only comes close to breaking even on the amount of energy produced versus the electricity necessary to power it would probably function more than adequately as a hybrid. As *Science* magazine puts it, "A fusion concept which would be only marginally successful by itself might be salvaged by making it the fusion core of a hybrid."

Shazam! Suddenly, fusion power doesn't look like such an economic liability anymore. Fusion-fission hybrids are a classic example of the way American industry adds technological fix onto technological drawback until it comes up with something that, if you step back and squint and don't examine too closely, looks as if it might work.

The term "fusion-fission hybrid" is creeping into the lexicon of scientists who used to think of fusion as a clean way to generate electricity in some distant century. Fusion power, no longer a non-radioactive alternative and with enough problems of its own, is being retooled to fit the future needs of an expanding collection of nuclear power plants.

THE ANTINUCLEAR POSITION

Antinuclear activists are deeply concerned, as we shall soon see, with America's nuclear landscape. In responding to this nuclear world, the assault on the nuclear industry has taken place on four major fronts. The first of these is an attack on the claims of proponents of nuclear power that it will provide us with a particularly cheap form of energy for the foreseeable future. While Charles Komanoff shows how disastrously the economics of nuclear power have worked out in practice, Joseph Bowring indicates the way in which massive federal subsidies which helped the industry and continue to keep it afloat were never calculated into its "costs."

The second area of attack is on the dangers of radiation and the seemingly intractable problem of what to do with the spiraling amounts of nuclear waste now being created. The radioactive elements given off in the various processes involved in the nuclear energy cycle have active lifetimes, ranging from less than a second for plutonium 214 to 4.5 million years in the case of uranium 238. All of them are potentially dangerous to human health, and many of them may be around in the form of radioactive waste for as long as any of us can imagine (as the Union of Concerned Scientists' study excerpted here indicates). This does not take into consideration the nuclear power plants themselves, which have a functional energy-producing life span of a quarter of a century. Decommissioned, they will then assumedly sit in our landscape as "hot" sealed-off mausoleums to nuclear power for untold generations to come.

This brings us to our third area of criticism: the plants themselves. As examples from Robert Pollard's *The Nugget File* show, the inherent risks of technical breakdown as well as of human error are constant. At its extreme we see in the meltdown scenario by the Nuclear Information and Resource Service what such technical or human failures could lead to should another Three Mile Island incident occur.

The fourth area of attack is on the issue of nuclear proliferation, which Amory Lovins, L. Hunter Lovins, and Leonard Ross argue is integrally connected with the failures of the nuclear industry as a whole.

THE NUCLEAR LANDSCAPE

Antinuclear activists consider the simple profusion of nuclear plants across the United States, the transport network which hauls nuclear products around the nation, the accidents and near accidents involving nuclear weapons over the years, and even the nuclear energy cycle itself to be symptoms of the danger we all are in from this form of power—as the following three maps, the cartoon excerpt from *The Anti-Nuclear Handbook,* and the list of accidents indicate.

The maps of the routes by which radioactive materials are transported back and forth across the country offer a particularly graphic portrait of the potential dangers of nuclear power. The first, taken from *Southern Exposure* magazine, lays out the routes used for different kinds of radioactive materials in the southeastern part of the country. The second, from Oak Ridge National Laboratory, shows a projected southern Nevada waste storage and disposal site, which would naturally create a nuclear waste funnel whose massive corridors from eastern and midwestern reactors, would run along highway I-40 from Tennesee to Nevada and along I-80, I-80/90, I-80 again, I-76, and I-70 from Pennsylvania to Nevada.

NUCLEAR SHIPMENT ROUTES

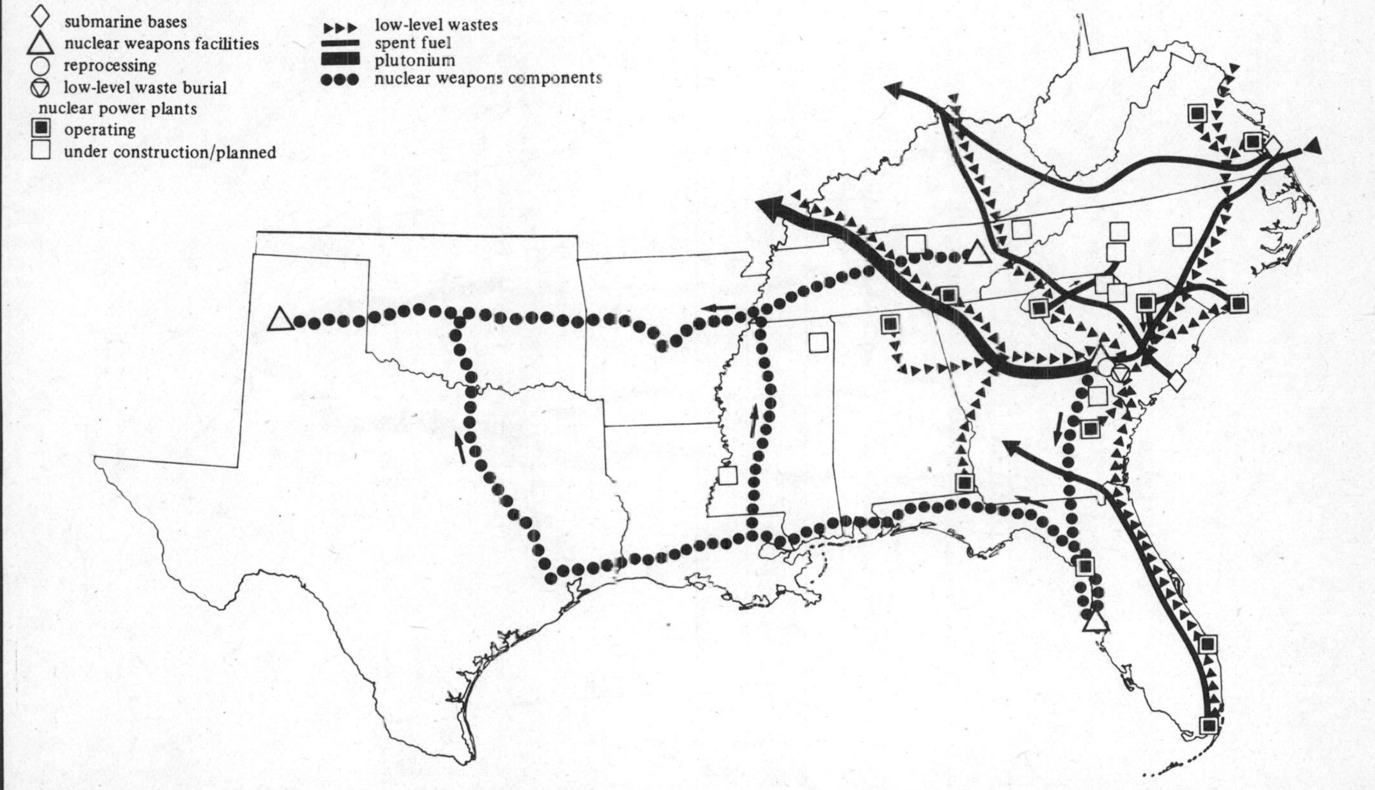

Source: *Southern Exposure,* Winter 1979.

NUCLEAR WASTE STORAGE ROUTE

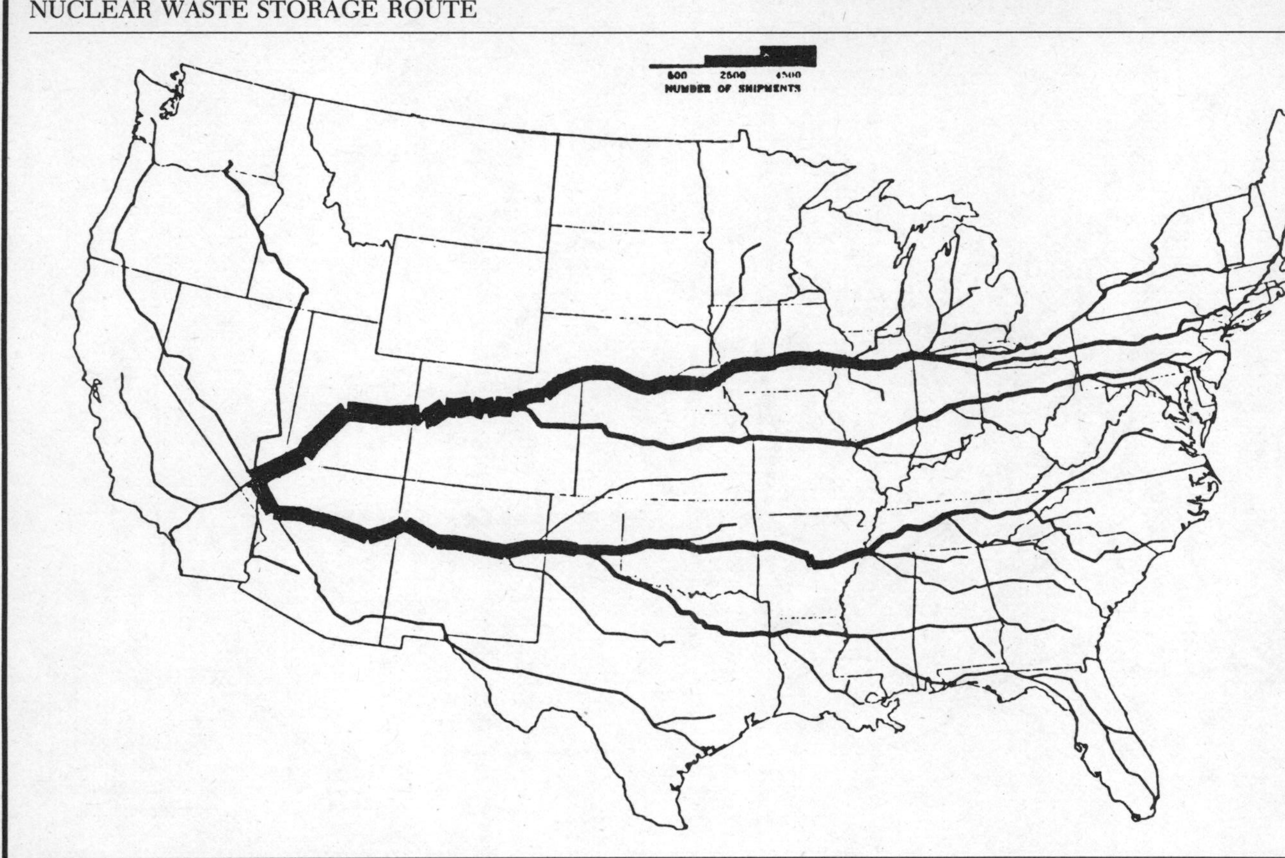

Source: Oak Ridge National Laboratory, 1982.

NUCLEAR POWER REACTORS IN THE UNITED STATES

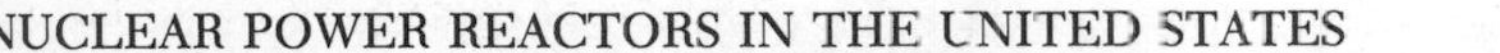

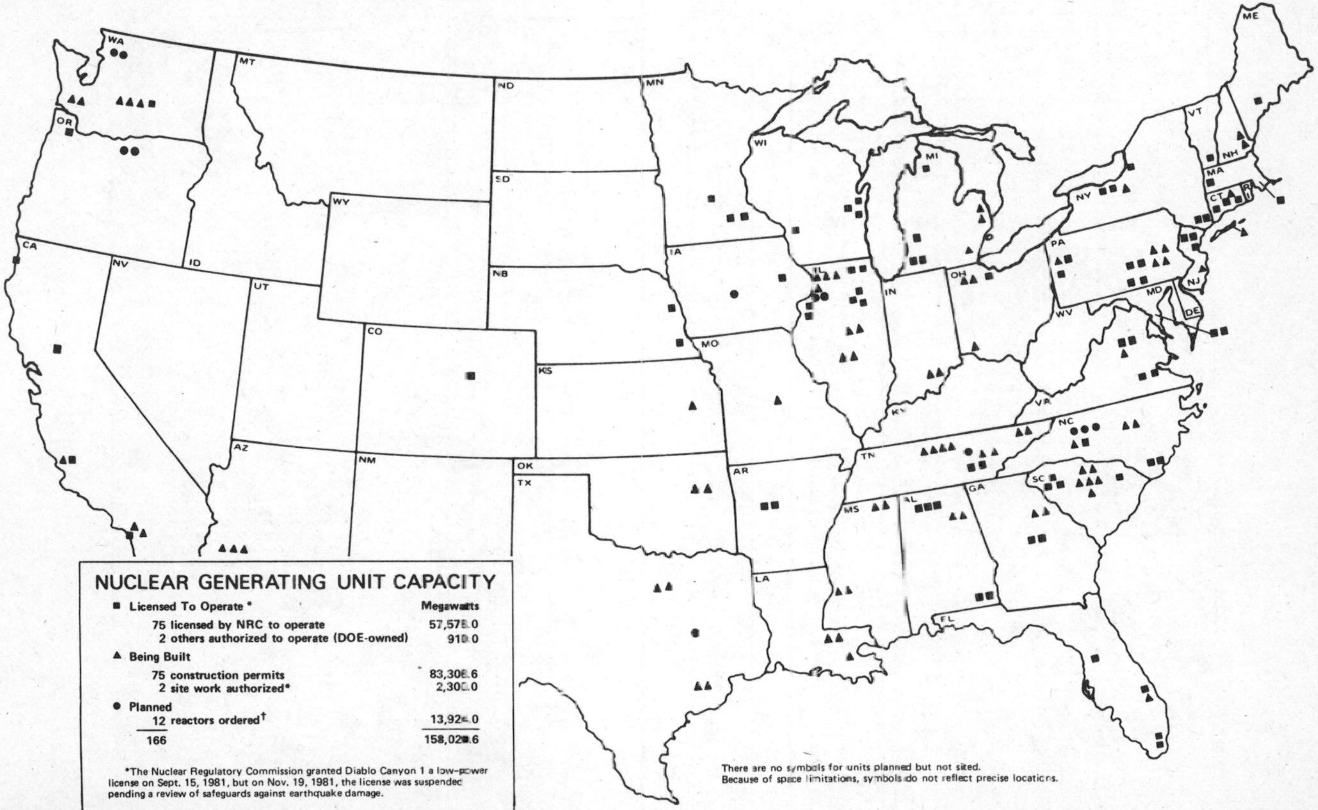

NUCLEAR GENERATING UNIT CAPACITY

	Megawatts
■ Licensed To Operate*	
75 licensed by NRC to operate	57,57[illegible].0
2 others authorized to operate (DOE-owned)	910.0
▲ Being Built	
75 construction permits	83,30[illegible].6
2 site work authorized*	2,30[illegible].0
● Planned	
12 reactors ordered†	13,92[illegible].0
166	158,02[illegible].6

*The Nuclear Regulatory Commission granted Diablo Canyon 1 a low-power license on Sept. 15, 1981, but on Nov. 19, 1981, the license was suspended pending a review of safeguards against earthquake damage.

†There are no symbols for units planned but not sited.
Because of space limitations, symbols do not reflect precise locations.

Department of Energy Revised Mar 1, 1980

THE NUCLEAR FUEL CYCLE

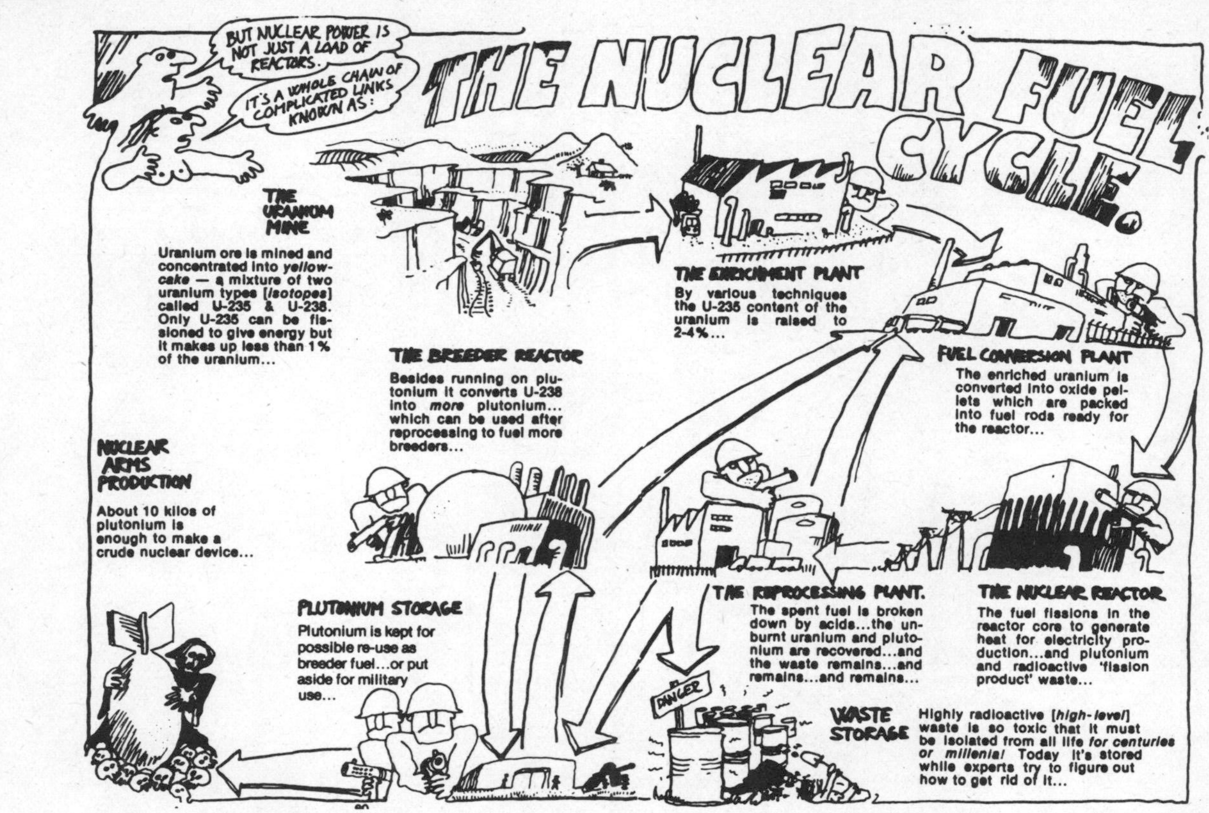

Taken from *The Anti-Nuclear Handbook,* by Stephen Croall and Kaianders, New York, Pantheon Books, 1978.

U.S. Nuclear Weapons Accidents (1950–80) Acknowledged by the Pentagon

Date	Weapon System	Location	Description*
1. February 13, 1950	B-36	Pacific Ocean, off Puget Sound, Washington	B-36 on simulated combat mission dropped nuclear weapon from 8,000 feet over Pacific Ocean before crashing. "Only the weapon's high explosive material detonated. . . . A bright flash occurred on impact, followed by a sound and shock wave."
2. April 11, 1950	B-29	Manzano Base, New Mexico	B-29 crashed into a mountain, killing the crew, three minutes after takeoff from Kirtland Air Force Base. Bomb case demolished, high explosive burned, nuclear components recovered.
3. July 13, 1950	B 50	Lebanon, Ohio	B-50 on training mission from Biggs A.F.B., Texas, crashed, killing sixteen crewmen. "The high explosive portion of the nuclear weapon aboard detonated on impact."
4. August 5, 1950	B-29	Fairfield-Suisun A.F.B., California (now Travis A.F.B.)	B-29 carrying a nuclear weapon crashed on takeoff and the high explosive material detonated. Nineteen crewmen and rescuers killed, including General Travis.
5. March 10, 1956	B-47	Mediterranean Sea	B-47 carrying "two capsules of nuclear weapons material" from MacDill A.F.B. to an overseas base disappeared in clouds while preparing for midair refueling. "An extensive search failed to locate any traces of the missing aircraft or crew."
6. July 26, 1956	B-47	Overseas Base	B-47 with no weapons on board crashed into "a storage igloo containing several nuclear weapons. The bombs did not burn or detonate."

Source: "Nuclear Weapons Accidents: The H-Bombs Next Door," by Stephen Talbot, *The Nation*, February 7, 1981.

U.S. Nuclear Weapons Accidents (1950–80) (Continued)

Date	Weapon System	Location	Description*
7. May 22, 1957	B-36	Kirtland A.F.B., New Mexico	B-36 ferrying a nuclear weapon from Biggs A.F.B., Texas, to Kirtland dropped the bomb in the New Mexico desert. "The high explosive material detonated, completely destroying the weapon and making a crater approx. 25 feet in diameter and 12 feet deep . . . no radioactivity beyond the lip of the crater."
8. July 28, 1957	C-124	Atlantic Ocean	C-124 aircraft en route from Dover A.F.B., Delaware, lost power in two engines and jettisoned two nuclear weapons over the ocean. "No detonation occurred from either weapon." The nuclear weapons were never found. The plane landed near Atlantic City, N.J.
9. October 11, 1957	B-47	Homestead A.F.B., Florida	B-47 crashed shortly after takeoff with a nuclear weapon and a nuclear capsule on board. "Two low order detonations occurred during the burning."
10. January 31, 1958	B-47	Overseas Base	B-47 crashed and burned during takeoff with one nuclear weapon "in strike configuration. . . . There was some contamination in the immediate area of the crash."
11. February 5, 1958	B-47	Savannah, Georgia (Hunter A.F.B.)	B-47 on simulated combat mission out of Homestead A.F.B., Florida, had a midair collision with an F-86 aircraft. The B-47 jettisoned the nuclear weapon "five miles southeast of the mouth of the Savannah River (Georgia) in Wassaw Sound off Tyber Beach." The weapon was never found.

U.S. Nuclear Weapons Accidents (1950–80) (Continued)

Date	Weapon System	Location	Description*
12. March 11, 1958	B-47	Florence, South Carolina	B-47 left Hunter A.F.B., Georgia, with three other B-47s en route to an overseas base. "The aircraft accidentally jettisoned an unarmed nuclear weapon, which impacted in a sparsely populated area 6½ miles east of Florence, South Carolina. The bomb's high explosive material exploded on impact. The detonation caused property damage but no injuries on the ground."
13. November 4, 1958	B-47	Dyess A.F.B., Texas	B-47 caught fire on takeoff and crashed, killing one crew member. The high explosive in the nuclear weapon on board exploded, leaving "a crater 35 feet in diameter and six feet deep."
14. November 26, 1958	B-47	Chennault A.F.B., Louisiana	B-47 caught fire on the ground. Single nuclear weapon on board was destroyed by fire. "Contamination was limited to the immediate vicinity."
15. January 18, 1959	F-100	Pacific Base	F-100 caught fire on the ground while loaded with unarmed nuclear weapon.
16. July 6, 1959	C-124	Barksdale A.F.B., Louisiana	"A C-124 on a nuclear logistics movement mission crashed on takeoff. The aircraft was destroyed by fire, which also destroyed one weapon. . . . Limited contamination. . . ."
17. October 15, 1959	B-52 & KC-135	Hardinsberg, Kentucky (Glen Bean, Kentucky)	B-52 and KC-135 operating out of Columbus A.F.B., Mississippi, collided during refueling over Kentucky. D.O.D. summary provides no information about nuclear weapons, but previous reports said two unarmed nuclear weapons were recovered undamaged.

U.S. Nuclear Weapons Accidents (1950–80) (Continued)

Date	Weapon System	Location	Description*
18. June 7, 1960	Bomarc missile	McGuire A.F.B., New Jersey	"A Bomarc air defense missile in ready storage condition (permitting launch in two minutes) was destroyed by explosion and fire after a high pressure helium tank exploded and ruptured the missile's fuel tanks. The warhead was also destroyed by the fire although the high explosive did not detonate. Contamination was restricted to an area . . . approx. 100 ft. long."
19. January 24, 1961	B-52	Goldsboro, North Carolina	B-52 crashed during airborne alert mission and dropped two nuclear weapons near Goldsboro, North Carolina. "A portion of one weapon, containing uranium, could not be recovered despite excavation in the waterlogged farmland to a depth of 50 feet. The Air Force subsequently purchased an easement requiring permission for anyone to dig there. There is no detectable radiation and no hazard in the area." The D.O.D. summary does not mention the fact that five of six interlocking safety triggers on the bomb failed. "Only a single switch," reported Dr. Ralph Lapp, head of the nuclear physics branch of the Office of Naval Research, "prevented the 24-megaton bomb from detonating and spreading fire and destruction over a wide area."
20. March 14, 1961	B-52	Yuba City, California (Beale A.F.B.)	B-52 with two nuclear weapons on board crashed after pilot succeeded in "steering the plane away from a populated area." No high explosive detonation and no

U.S. Nuclear Weapons Accidents (1950–80) (Continued)

Date	Weapon System	Location	Description*
			contamination. Safety devices worked.
21. January 13, 1964	B-52D	Cumberland, Maryland	B-52D en route from Westover A.F.B., Massachusetts, to its home base at Turner A.F.B., Georgia, crashed with two unarmed nuclear weapons on board, which were recovered "relatively intact."
22. December 5, 1964	LGM 30B (Minuteman ICBM)	Ellsworth A.F.B., South Dakota	LGM 30B Minuteman I missile was on strategic alert at Launch Facility L-02, Ellsworth A.F.B., South Dakota, when a "retrorocket" accidentally fired during repairs. There was considerable damage but "no detonation or radioactive contamination."
23. December 8, 1964	B-58	Bunker Hill A.F.B. (now Grissom A.F.B.), Indiana	B-58 crashed while preparing for takeoff on icy runway at Bunker Hill A.F.B., Indiana. "Portions of the nuclear weapon burned, contamination was limited to the immediate area of the crash and was subsequently removed."
24. October 12, 1965	C-124	Wright-Patterson A.F.B., Ohio	Fire during refueling on ground burned "components of nuclear weapons and a dummy training unit. . . . The resultant radiation hazard was minimal."
25. January 17, 1966	B-52 & KC-135	Palomares, Spain	B-52 and KC-135 collided during midair refueling and both aircraft crashed near Palomares, Spain. The B-52 carried four nuclear weapons. One was recovered on the ground and one was finally found in the sea after an intensive, four-month search. "Two of the weapons' high explosive materials exploded on impact with the ground, releasing some radioactive

U.S. Nuclear Weapons Accidents (1950–80) (Continued)

Date	Weapon System	Location	Description*
			materials. Approximately 1,400 tons of slightly contaminated soil and vegetation were removed to the United States for storage at an approved site." The D.O.E. has reported that the cleanup operation has cost $50 million and that the Palomares area is still being monitored for radiation today.
26. January 21, 1968	B-52	Thule, Greenland	B-52 from Plattsburgh A.F.B., New York, crashed and burned some seven miles southwest of the runway at Thule A.F.B., Greenland. "The bomber carried four nuclear weapons, all of which were destroyed by fire. . . . Some 237,000 cubic feet of contaminated ice, snow and water, with crash debris, were removed to an approved storage site in the United States over the course of a four-month operation."
27. September 19, 1980	Titan II ICBM	Damascus, Arkansas	During routine maintenance in a Titan II missile silo, an Air Force repairman dropped a socket wrench, which punctured a fuel tank and caused an explosion. One Air Force man was killed, 21 injured. The nuclear warhead, which was hurled from the silo by the explosion, was recovered intact. Local residents were evacuated. "There was no radioactive contamination."

*The descriptions of each accident are based on and include quotations from the D.O.D. *Summary.* Additional comments are those of the author, Stephen Talbot.

SOURCE: Department of Defense document, *Summary of Accidents Involving Nuclear Weapons, 1950–1980 (Interim),* released to Stephen Talbot, KQED-TV, San Francisco, December 1980. An accompanying D.O.D. memo states: "Due to differences in record-keeping among the Services, it is difficult to say that this list is complete, particularly with respect to the earlier period covered by the summaries. The Navy and Air Force may have experienced a few more accidents and we are researching this possibility. The

Marines have no nuclear weapons. The Army reports that it has never had an accident with nuclear weapons comparable in seriousness with those on this list. We feel confident that there are fewer than 10 accidents for which we do not yet have summaries, but we cannot give an exact number at this time pending further research. . . . This list does not contain *every* event reportable under safety regulations as an 'accident/incident involving nuclear weapons.' . . . Criteria for inclusion in this summary included the severity of the event, e.g., an airplane crash, radioactive contamination, weapon actually involved in the event, etc."

MELTDOWN

What nuclear activists fear most in a reactor accident is meltdown. What follows is a basic description of what could happen, culled from various studies by the Nuclear Information and Resource Service, a public interest organization, in Washington, D.C.

Taken from "Nuclear Dangers," Energy Fact Sheet Number 2, Nuclear Information and Resource Service, Washington, D.C.

A nuclear reactor is an elaborate machine for boiling water to make steam. Heat for boiling the water comes from the splitting—or fissioning—of uranium atoms.

In the process, tremendous temperatures are reached, requiring constant cooling to prevent a "meltdown" of the fuel. This cooling is crucial, for the fission process produces vast amounts of deadly, long-lasting radioactive waste products. (Today's typical large reactor, after six months of operation, contains about 1,000 times the radioactive materials released by our Hiroshima A-bomb.) If the reactor core is not kept properly cooled at all times—even when the fission process is stopped—a meltdown could occur, leading to the release of the radiation.

There is such potential for harm to all living things in a large area surrounding the reactor that considerable expense and care are taken to ensure that the power plants operate properly. But what would be a minor problem at a gas, oil or coal power plant—such as a stuck valve—could be the start of a disaster in a nuclear facility.

The people who build, own and regulate nuclear power reactors have known for years that accidents can happen. They've known that a major accident involving a core meltdown or other malfunctions could cause thousands of deaths, and contaminate large areas of the country.

A study done for the old Atomic Energy Commission (AEC) in 1965 found that a meltdown could kill 45,000 people, injure another 100,000, and cause $17 billion (in 1965 dollars) worth of property damage. In 1975, the AEC's successor (the Nuclear Regulatory Commission, or NRC) commissioned a new analysis hoping to show that the risks weren't all that bad. The new report—the Rasmussen "Reactor Safety Study"—concluded that a "worst case" accident would mean:

3,300 immediate human deaths
45,000 human deaths from cancer
45,000 radiation sickness victims requiring hospitalization
240,000 people suffering from thyroid tumors
5,000 children born with genetic defects in the first generation following the accident
350,000 males suffering temporary sterility
40,000–100,000 females suffering prolonged or permanent sterility
10,000–100,000 people experiencing severe vomiting.

The analysts made the doubtful assumption when computing those figures that everyone within 25 miles downwind of the nuclear facility would be evacuated. Thus, shifting winds and evacuation difficulties could produce a worst case worse than Rasmussen's worst case.

In addition to human casualties, hundreds of square miles of land would be made uninhabitable, and unfit for agricultural use. Thousands of square miles would be severly contaminated with radiation. Property damage would reach $14 billion (in 1975 dollars). Decontamination would be difficult, dangerous and costly —because all contaminated items (carcasses, air, soil, machines, cars, houses, schools, hospitals, etc.) would have to be thoroughly cleaned or placed in long-term, secure isolation.

Nuclear industry leaders and government regulators do not deny that a serious accident could happen. They assure us, however, that the probability of such an accident is low. As the Rasmussen Report put it, large accidents happen less often than small accidents.

For all the computer models and scientific analysis in the Rasmussen Report—heavily used by industry to sell nuclear power to the people—the NRC in 1979 withdrew endorsement of its accident risks. The NRC acknowledged with this unprecedented action the impossibility of predicting accident probabilities and consequences.

Accidents—or "abnormal occurrences" as the industry sometimes prefers to label them—have taken place at many nuclear facilities:

- The most famous is the near meltdown at the Three Mile Island unit 2 plant near Harrisburg, Pennsylvania, which began on March 28, 1979. Today, controversy rages over the cause, the effects of the accident on neighboring communities and citizens, and who should pay the costs of "clean up," replacement power and rebuilding (if it is possible to rebuild). The reactor's owner, Metropolitan Edison, tried to blame first its employees and second the reactor builders. It then sought to get its customers to cover the costs of the accident.
- In 1966, a near-meltdown occurred at Detroit Edison's fast breeder reactor near Detroit and Toledo. Today, that reactor is shut down and emtombed.
- In 1975, a massive fire crippled what was the world's largest reactor at Brown's Ferry, Alabama. Officials believe that the reactor was only hours from a meltdown when cooling was restored with rubber bands.
- An accident at the SL-1 military reactor in Idaho, in 1966, left three workers dead when steam explosions rocked the reactor vessel. Hundreds of other

"abnormalities" have occurred, resulting in radioactive leaks, worker exposures, lengthy shutdowns and costly repairs. In a 1980 report, researchers at the government's Oak Ridge National Laboratory concluded that at least 20 such incidents could have led to core meltdowns in 1979.

Since the Three Mile Island accident, the nuclear industry has mounted an advertising campaign to persuade the public that nuclear power is necessary and safe and that they have learned the "lessons" of TMI. The industry claims that new safety requirements and improved operator training make the chances of another serious accident negligible. But major gaps still exist in nuclear power safety systems.

- Some systems in nuclear reactors are classified as "non-safety related"—even though "safety related" systems often depend on them—and are not required to meet high reliability standards. These systems include equipment that failed at TMI.
- The TMI accident also involved "common cause" failures, in which two or more safety systems failed due [*sic*] to a single cause. Such failures do not have to be considered in nuclear plant licensing procedures.
- Plants are designed with the assumption that core melt accidents will not happen. Containment buildings are not designed to withstand the hydrogen and steam explosions that could occur in such an accident (and nearly did occur at TMI).

In 1977, the NRC presented Congress with a list of 177 serious, unresolved problems in American nuclear reactors. In 1979, the Kemeny Commission investigating the TMI accident found that only 2 of those 177 problems had been resolved, and that neither solution had been implemented at the affected power plant. Said the Kemeny Report: "The NRC has a history of leaving generic safety problems unresolved for many years."

Despite the continuing problems and the dangers which reactors pose, the NRC is again issuing operating licenses for new reactors. Meanwhile, nuclear companies have moved to protect themselves financially by creating an industry-wide insurance pool for nuclear accidents. In addition, the industry has kept the pressure on Congress for continuation of the Price-Anderson Act, which limits its liability for a nuclear accident to only $560 million.

Across the land, people worry about the reactors in their backyards. But the nuclear industry is rushing to put its "don't blame us" house in order.

WHY NUCLEAR POWER CAN'T COMPETE

In the following selection Charles Komanoff, a New York-based energy consultant to numerous state and local government agencies, including those in New York, New Jersey, and California, explains why the costs of nuclear power make it an unlikely competitor with oil. Komanoff is the author of three major books on the U.S. electric utility industry, including *Power Plant Cost Escalation: Nuclear and Coal Capital Costs, Regulation and Economics* (1981).

Taken from "Doing Without Nuclear Power," by Charles Komanoff, New York Review of Books, *May 17, 1979.*

What are the relative costs of energy from nuclear power? They are rarely compared to the costs of burning oil in engines or furnaces, yet such a comparison is central if we are to weigh the prospects of substituting nuclear power for oil. If we carefully estimate the different kinds of costs involved in producing kilowatts at nuclear plants and in obtaining barrels of oil, we find that the cost of energy from a nuclear plant built today can be calculated at $100 for the "heat equivalent of a barrel of oil." This figure reflects fuel, maintenance, and—most important—the cost of constructing the nuclear plant itself. It is over four times the cost of heat from oil at OPEC prices. [Since this article was written in 1979 nuclear power costs have risen even faster than the price of oil.]

The heat in electricity, of course, can be made use of with more efficiency than can heat from oil and gas—as much as twice as efficiently. For example, electric furnaces produce about 50 per cent more glass, per unit of applied heat, than gas-burning furnaces. When we allow for this, nuclear electricity still remains two to three times as expensive as oil. As a result, the market for nuclear electricity has slowly but inexorably been drying up. Notwithstanding plans to build hundreds of reactors, the projected demand for nuclear power—and with it the financial backing for its expansion—has not materialized.

It wasn't always this way. At the start of 1972, the first plants purchased by the electric utilities on a commercial basis were entering service at a cost of $225 million for a standard thousand-megawatt generator. This cost converts to the equivalent of about $25 per barrel of oil. Costs were expected to fall as more plants were built. The tripling of prices for crude oil and coal in the wake of the 1973 Arab oil embargo was expected to put nuclear power in a commanding market position. Not only was it apparently cheaper than coal as a source of electricity, but nuclear electricity seemed competitive with oil both for heating and for industrial purposes. Nuclear electricity cost only twice as much per British thermal unit —i.e., per unit of delivered heat; and since this heat was available in more efficient form, it was therefore close to oil in energy value. Moreover, nuclear electricity was expected to decline in cost while oil rose. Few doubted the Atomic Energy Commission's projection in 1974 that 1,000 thousand-megawatt reactors would be built by the end of the century—capable of producing roughly the equivalent of the entire US energy supply in 1972.

Instead, nuclear costs have soared as the industry expanded, and primarily for two reasons: safety systems had to be added to meet rising public concerns; and improvements in design were needed to correct defects that emerged as operating experience increased. By the end of 1977, a thousand-megawatt reactor cost $900 million, four times the cost of a 1972 plant. The rate of increase was an astounding 26 percent per year. This was triple the rate of general US inflation and half again as great as the increase in construction costs of power generators using coal, notwithstanding new emission controls. It was about the same rate of increase as that for the price of oil, despite the actions of the OPEC cartel. Nuclear power had thus lost its edge over coal in the electric power market, and had lost the opportunity to make inroads on the larger market occupied by oil and gas. . . .

NUCLEAR SUBSIDIES

Joseph Bowring, an economist, was an employee of the U.S. Department of Energy during the Carter administration when he made a detailed study entitled "Federal Subsidies to Nuclear Power Reactors." The subsidies, as you will see from the following excerpts, are extensive and ongoing. The DOE suppressed the study, and after Bowring left the agency, the government took his work and redid it before making the study public.

Taken from "Federal Subsidies to Nuclear Power: Reactor Design and Fuel Cycle," by Joseph Bowring, March 1980, prepublication draft.

The Federal Government has provided substantial research, development, and demonstration (RD&D) funds to develop nuclear power since 1948. These expenditures were critical to the development of the private nuclear power industry and critical to its continuation.

The Federal Government has provided a variety of subsidies to uranium producers. The subsidies include production incentives, exploration assistance, and an embargo on foreign uranium. These subsidies were initially designed to encourage the development of a uranium industry and, later, to ensure a smooth transition from AEC fuel ownership to commercial ownership. The waste disposal program of the Federal Government has also provided a subsidy to the nuclear power industry. Direct expenditures on RD&D were and are essential to finding a solution to the problem of waste disposal upon which the viability of the nuclear industry depends.

The enrichment stage of the nuclear fuel cycle is owned by the Federal Government. The government provides a subsidy to the nuclear industry through the mechanism of enrichment pricing policy. The government pricing formula does not include provision for a rate of return, for State and local taxes, for insurance, for Federal income taxes, for interest on the uranium inventory required for enriching, or for eventual decommissioning of the enrichment plants.

Each of the subsidy types has reduced the cost and/or the uncertainty to private firms of investing in nuclear power. The result has been that current production of electricity from nuclear power stations is substantially larger than it would have been in the absence of such subsidies. . . .

The total constant dollar value of these subsidies from 1950 to 1979 is just over thirty-seven billion dollars.

Several additional calculations may help to put this overall subsidy figure in perspective. Subsidies contributed to the growth of the nuclear power industry which, in turn, has supplied nuclear electricity since 1957. It is possible to estimate what the cost of nuclear power would be in the absence of the government subsidies considered here, that is, if all these expenditures had been incurred directly by private firms. In order to do this, the subsidy costs must be distributed across the total output to date of nuclear electricity.

An immediate problem is that there is no currently accepted method for treating expenditures on research and development within a business accounting framework. However, by using two extreme possibilities for treating such expenditures, the range of per kilowatt hour subsidy can be established. If RD&D costs are charged against the total electrical output to date from nuclear power plants, the result is a subsidy of 2.50 cents per kilowatt hour. The other extreme alternative is to spread all the RD&D costs over the depreciation life of a nuclear power plant. In this case the subsidy per kilowatt hour is 1.66 cents.

The cost of nuclear generated electricity in 1979 was 2.22 cents per kilowatt hour. Thus, in the absence of subsidies nuclear electricity would probably range in cost from about *one and one-half* to twice its current cost.

An equally important result of the subsidies to nuclear power is non-quantifiable. The subsidies in particular, and the government commitment that they represent in general, have reduced the uncertainty surrounding the development and ultimate commercial applications of nuclear power. Early research and development subsidies demonstrated the technical viability of nuclear reactors at a time when private firms were reluctant to pursue the technology. Subsidies to uranium production virtually created the industry and sustained it until the commercial demand was adequate. Continued and growing subsidies for waste disposal contribute perhaps the greatest reduction in current uncertainty about the viability of commercial nuclear power. They promise a solution to what is one of the larger barriers to the expansion of nuclear power. . . .

RADIOACTIVE WASTES

Radioactivity poses a special hazard to living things because of its peculiar nature. Radiation can penetrate matter and affect its chemistry. It can kill cells and disrupt molecular bonds, causing damage or decomposition of molecules. These interactions can cause various effects: damage or death to exposed cells; cell mutation; cancer; injury or even death to exposed organisms. The problem of radioactive waste has yet to be solved and, as the following selection suggests, poses a nightmare.

Taken From Radioactive Waste: Politics, Technology and Risk, *a Report of the Union of Concerned Scientists, by Ronnie D. Lipschultz, Cambridge, Massachusetts Ballinger Publishing Co., 1980.*

. . . A great deal of radioactive waste is presently buried or stored at numerous locations around the United States. Some 17,000 spent fuel assemblies—the product of only about 450 reactor years[1] of plant operation—are stored temporarily in spent fuel pools. This number is currently increasing by about 4,000 each year. About ten million cubic feet of high level liquid and solid waste produced by the reprocessing of plutonium for defense purposes resides in aging steel storage tanks at Hanford, Savannah River, and Idaho Falls, and some 600,000 gallons of high level waste are stored at the now abandoned West Valley plant [in New York State]. There are sixty-five million cubic feet of low level wastes—of which fifteen million contain transuranic nuclides[2]—in shallow burial or storage at various government sites, and another sixteen million cubic feet of commercially generated low level radioactive materials are buried in six licensed waste facilities (of which three are permanently closed). Approximately 140 million tons of radioactive uranium mill tailings have been left in unstabilized or partially stabilized piles. Some of these tailings, used in construction, contaminate thousands of public and private buildings. Finally, many hundreds of obsolete, radioactively contaminated buildings at government defense facilities await decommissioning, dismantling, and disposal.

Even though these quantities are already quite impressive, they will inevitably increase. This nation's nuclear power program is still slated to expand, and as reactors now planned or under construction are completed . . . , they will begin to produce not only electricity but also ever-increasing quantities of radioactive waste. By 1995, the annual production of commercial spent fuel could equal today's total inventory. By the century's end, the United States may have as many as 300,000 spent fuel assemblies in temporary storage—some 100,000 metric tons . . . —or seventeen times the number in storage today. The uranium requirements of a growing nuclear program could result in the production of up to one billion tons of uranium mill tailings. Low level waste inventories will run into the hundreds of millions of cubic feet. Quantities of this magnitude will greatly strain the storage capacities of temporary facilities and underline the pressing need for development of a permanent means of disposal.

The radiological hazard posed by these wastes is of potentially great significance. For example, the plutonium-239 contained in the radioactive spent fuel discharged by one reactor after one year of operation would be sufficient to cause fatal lung cancers in the entire population of the United States if dispersed as fine particulates and inhaled. While we do not suggest that such material would be released to induce such damage, even the escape of small amounts of radioactive waste into the environment may result in a perceptible increase in the number of cancer deaths in a population. Or radionuclides, free in the environment, may be concentrated in marine organisms and terrestrial animals and plants and so enter food chains, thereby risking exposure of populations to potentially hazardous levels of radioactivity. Inevitably, in the absence of a working disposal technology, an increase in the quantity of radioactive waste in storage will mean an undesirable increase in the risk of radioactivity escaping into the biosphere. Should the levels

1. One reactor year is the equivalent of one reactor operating for one year.
[2. A nuclide having an atomic number greater than that of uranium.]

of escaping material reach significant proportions, an increase in the overall cancer death rate could well result.

. . . The customary approach to waste management and disposal involves solidification of liquid waste into glass blocks followed by encapsulation in metal canisters and emplacement of the canisters in geologic formations or, perhaps, seabed sediments. Ultimately, transmutation of some actinides[3] or possibly disposal into solar orbit might become practical. Other disposal options are too costly, too risky, or too impractical. But even the most advanced technology—geologic isolation—is still no more than a promising concept. Large-scale vitrification of liquid waste is still years from implementation in the United States, and serious questions being raised about the suitability of the glass matrix suggest that it could turn out to be a poor choice. No one has actually constructed and tested a waste canister that will last for more than a few decades, even though many proposals are predicated on canister survival for centuries. Aside from some brief and generally inconclusive experiments in the 1960s, no one has actually placed a canister of radioactive waste in salt or granite or seabed sediment. Undoubtedly, the engineering capability to place a canister of waste in a geologic formation does now exist; the trick, in the words of Senator John Glenn, is whether we can ensure that the wastes won't "come bubbling up 100 miles away 50 years later.". . .

. . . Carroll Wilson, the first general manager of the Atomic Energy Commission, writing about the early days of radioactive waste management, stated:

> Chemists and chemical engineers were not interested in dealing with waste. It was not glamorous; there were no careers; it was messy; nobody got brownie points for caring about nuclear waste. The Atomic Energy Commission neglected the problem. . . . The central point is that there was no real interest or profit in dealing with the back end of the fuel cycle. . . .

As a result of this quasi-official disinterest, the waste management program was severely compromised, with leaks of waste and instances of incompetence becoming the rule rather than the exception. Even where storage measures seemed to be clearly inadequate from an early date, as in the case of the Hanford tanks, the AEC chose to disregard or downplay the scope and significance of the problem. As with many other nuclear-related matters under its jurisdiction—the hazards of weapons-testing fallout and reactor safety are two such examples—the AEC chose to ignore, mislead, or deceive the public about radioactive wastes.

We still face the consequences of this official mismanagement today. Leaks of radioactive wastes have become commonplace, and uncontrolled old radiation dumps, their locations lost, are being rediscovered with alarming regularity. A more serious casualty of the AEC's failures has been government credibility on the waste issue. The perhaps naive faith in the infallibility of the federal government's actions that existed in the 1950s has been replaced by a public cynicism and

[3. Series of elements beginning with actinium 89 and continuing through lawrencium 103. Includes uranium and all man-made transuranic elements.]

distrust that will constitute a continuing burden on future efforts to safely dispose of radioactive wastes. This is the legacy of the Atomic Energy Commission.

As we have made clear, the management and disposal of radioactive wastes has come to be recognized from both a health and economic viewpoint as a problem most critical to the future of the nuclear power program. This concern appears to be evenly spread over many sectors of our society. Nonetheless, the common concern has not produced a convergence of action. Various interest groups see the waste problem as a means to an end: the government, to make its energy policy more attractive; the nuclear industry, to achieve economic viability; and the environmental movement, to halt nuclear power. The desire to eliminate this environmental pollutant is frequently secondary. One result of these conflicting interests has been development of a program of "technical fixes" geared to getting the wastes out of sight and out of the mind of the public as soon as possible. . . . Continuation of the domestic nuclear power program in the face of a prolonged failure to resolve the waste issue will surely be seen as irresponsible. The option of a limitation on the further generation of radioactive wastes, once viewed as the cry of an extremist minority, must now be considered a serious possibility. . . . [The] radioactive waste problem is not one simply amenable to technical fixes. A solution will require careful consideration of not only technical, but also societal and political requirements. . . .

NUCLEAR BREAKDOWN

From among the hundreds of technical and human malfunctions at nuclear power plants cited by Robert Pollard, here are seven chosen because they are so ordinary. It was a series of such mishaps, one triggering or coming right after another, which set the stage for Three Mile Island as well as the other near disasters which have occurred at plants in the United States and elsewhere.

Taken from The Nugget File, *edited by Robert D. Pollard, Union of Concerned Scientists, Cambridge, Massachusetts, January 1979.*

NORTH ANNA UNITS 1 AND 2 MINERAL, VIRGINIA
MAY 1976
VITAL TIMING RELAYS IN EMERGENCY POWER SYSTEM FAILED—DEFECTIVE MANUFACTURE

During an operational test on the emergency diesel generators, it was found that some of the timing relays were not operating at the correct time. The diaphragms of these timers were not manufactured properly and would not hold the air pressure necessary to permit correct timing operation. The replacement timers underwent shop testing prior to installation. No information was offered that would explain why the original timers had not been tested prior to installation.

Dr. Hanauer labeled the report "Nugget-CMF." A CMF (common mode failure) is a failure which affects all identical equipment such as, in this case, all emergency electric power supplied. Nonrandom multiple failure, which is another name for common mode failure, is one of the multitude of generic safety problems relevant to both pressurized water and boiling water reactors which the NRC characterizes as unresolved.

OCONEE UNIT 2 SENECA, SOUTH CAROLINA SEPTEMBER 1975 FAUCET REPAIRS AFFECT REACTOR WATER LEVEL—WRONG VALVES WERE CLOSED/PERSONNEL ERROR

With Oconee Unit 2 operating at full power, chemistry personnel were attempting to isolate the filtered water supply to the chemistry lab to make faucet repairs. Isolation valves for an air system were inadvertently closed instead. This isolated the control air supply to two other valves. These valves control the rate of water drainage and addition to the reactor cooling water system. Prior to the error, the two flows balanced each other. After the air supply was isolated, one valve failed closed, preventing reactor coolant letdown flow, and the other valve failed open, allowing excess reactor coolant makeup. This sequence of events allowed the reactor cooling system pressurizer level to increase the letdown storage tank level to decrease.

This event was apparently caused by personnel error in tracing the filtered water system to find an isolation valve. The close proximity and similarity of the valves in the chemistry lab water system and the control air system contributed to this error.

SEVERAL UNIDENTIFIED REACTORS APRIL 1970 SAFETY SYSTEM COMPONENTS FAILED—PAINT CAUSED STICKING OF MOVABLE PARTS

The AEC requested General Electric to provide information on relays that had failed at several nuclear plants. In accordance with "fail-safe" design principles, many relays used in safety systems are energized when plant conditions are normal and perform their safety function when they are deenergized following an accident. However, several relays had failed to open when deenergized.

The cause of the sticking was the paint on the pole pieces which adhered to the steel armature plate of the energized relay. The heat from the continuously energized relay affected the paint and caused otherwise movable parts of the relay to stick together.

The relay in question has been manufactured and used for thirty years without problems and with a record of high reliability. Discussions indicated that prior to purchase of the relays which failed, the vendor moved his manufacturing plant and was in the process of training new personnel. This change in personnel and lack of control of paint thickness resulted in the failures.

MAINE YANKEE WISCASSET, MAINE JUNE 1975 EMERGENCY CORE COOLING SYSTEM INOPERATIVE—VALVES IN WRONG POSITION

Part of the emergency core cooling system in pressurized water reactors consists of tanks of water pressurized with nitrogen. These tanks, sometimes called accumulators, have been referred to as "fail-safe" by nuclear proponents. The proponents assume, among other things, that the reactor operators will remember to open the tank discharge valves during each startup of the plant.

At the Maine Yankee plant, the discharge valves for all the tanks were found closed. The operator who completed the emergency core cooling valve checklist noted the locked handwheels and mistakenly assumed the valves to be locked open when, in fact, the valves were locked closed.

INDIAN POINT UNIT 2 BUCHANAN, NEW YORK APRIL 1976 RADIATION OVEREXPOSURE—INADEQUATE RADIATION CONTROL PROCEDURES

The Nuclear Regulatory Commission's regulations state that "a licensee may permit" its employees to receive up to 3 rems[*] of radiation dose per calendar quarter. This "permissible" dose is often inadvertently exceeded.

At Indian Point Unit 2, an individual had been assigned to determine the lighting requirements in the area beneath the reactor vessel in preparation for installation of a pump. A radiation survey performed five days earlier had shown the radiation level in the area to be substantially below the "permissible" level. However, highly radioactive components had since been withdrawn from the reactor vessel into the area beneath the reactor vessel. Consequently, the maximum radiation field to which this individual was exposed was approximately 600 R/hr.[†] It was estimated that the individual spent approximately 100 seconds in the area and his film badge indicated he received a whole body radiation dose of 10.06 rem. This dose was more than the total lifetime occupational dose he had accumulated up to that time.

MILLSTONE POINT UNIT 2 WATERFORD, CONNECTICUT JULY 1976 TOTAL INABILITY TO SUPPLY ELECTRIC POWER TO SAFETY SYSTEMS—FIRST EVENT: INHERENT DESIGN DEFICIENCY; SECOND EVENT: "INAPPROPRIATE" CORRECTIVE ACTION FOLLOWING FIRST EVENT

In the event of an accident, the following sequence of events is supposed to take place and result in supplying electric power to the plant's safety systems. The reactor automatically is shut down, resulting in loss of the electric power output from the plant. Automatic switching aligns circuits to deliver electric power from the utility's transmission network (i.e., from other generating plants) to the safety

[*rem: a measure of biological damage done by ionizing radiation.]
[†R/hr: rems per hour.]

systems. If this "off-site power" is unavailable (abrupt loss of power output from a nuclear plant can, and frequently does, result in a blackout) or if the voltage is too low to operate the safety equipment, automatic switching equipment disconnects the off-site power source and aligns circuits so that power from the on-site emergency diesel generators can be supplied to the safety systems. As in so many aspects of nuclear power, what is supposed to happen and what actually happens are two different subjects.

Following an automatic shutdown of Millstone Unit 2, several motors powered from 480-volt power control centers failed to start as required. The failure of the 480-volt motors to start was traced to blown control power fuses on the individual motor controllers.

Northeast Nuclear Energy Company's investigation disclosed that, as a result of the plant trip, the off-site power voltage dropped. This voltage drop, in conjunction with additional voltage drops associated with the transformers involved, reduced the control power to a voltage which was insufficient to close the motor controller contacts. As a result, when the motors were signaled to start, the control power fuses blew. The licensee concluded that under similar low voltage conditions, *THE OPERABILITY OF 480 V ENGINEERED SAFETY FEATURE EQUIPMENT COULD NOT BE ASSURED.* In other words, if the control power fuses blow, it is not possible automatically or manually to start any of the safety equipment from either off-site power or the emergency diesel generators.

The immediate corrective action was to raise the setpoint of the safety systems' "loss of power" undervoltage relays to assure that the plant would be separated from off-site power and emergency power system operation would be initiated before the control voltage fell below that required for contactor operation. A trip of the undervoltage relays causes the emergency buses to be deenergized, the loads to be disconnected from the emergency buses, and the diesel generators to start. The required safety related loads are then sequentially connected to the emergency buses.

Three weeks later the licensee reported that the earlier corrective action was no longer considered appropriate. During the starting of a large motor, the voltage dropped below the new higher setting of the undervoltage relays. This resulted in disconnecting the emergency buses from off-site power. This deenergized the emergency buses, caused load shedding to occur, started the diesel generators and began sequencing loads onto the emergency buses in accordance with the design. However, during sequencing loads onto the buses, the voltage again dropped below the new, higher undervoltage relay setting which caused each load to be disconnected. *THE RESULT WAS ENERGIZED EMERGENCY BUSES WITH NO LOADS CONNECTED.*

Reference: 1975–76 #5 [However, the above is not from the Nugget but from the NRC "Description of Events–Millstone Unit 2."]

NUCLEAR PROLIFERATION

Today six countries belong to the "nuclear club" (the United States, Britain, France, Soviet Union, China, and India), possessing their own nuclear weapons and the means to distribute them over the face of the earth. Two other nations—Israel and South Africa—are thought to have secretly produced such bombs. Pakistan and South Korea should soon have the capacity to do so, and forty other nations have the knowledge and expertise to acquire nuclear arms over the next decade.

As Amory Lovins, L. Hunter Lovins, and Leonard Ross make clear in this summary article, the very nature of the nuclear industry (from its economics to its technical weaknesses) makes nuclear proliferation in one form or another a certainty—with all its dangers to life on earth—as long as the nuclear industry itself exists.

Taken from "Nuclear Power and Nuclear Bombs," by Amory B. Lovins, L. Hunter Lovins, and Leonard Ross, Foreign Affairs, *Summer 1980.*

. . . All concentrated fissionable materials are potentially explosive. All nuclear fission technologies both use and produce fissionable materials that are or can be concentrated. Unavoidably latent in those technologies, therefore, is a potential for nuclear violence and coercion. Most of the knowledge, much of the equipment, and the general nature of the organizations relevant to making bombs are inherent in civilian nuclear activities, and are "in much of their course interchangeable and interdependent" for peaceful or violent uses.

All commercial nuclear fuel cycles are fueled with uranium. Natural uranium as mined contains only 0.71 percent of the fissionable isotope uranium-235. Both this concentration and the few percent of uranium-235 present in "low-enriched uranium" (LEU) are too dilute to be explosive. Practicable bombs require concentrations of tens of percent; highly efficient bombs, about ninety percent ("highly enriched uranium" or HEU). A few minor types of commercial reactors, notably the Canadian CANDU, are fueled with natural uranium. The dominant world type, the U.S.-designed light-water reactor (LWR), is fueled with LEU. One prospective commercial type (the high-temperature gas-cooled reactor) and many research reactors are fueled with directly bomb-usable HEU.

The irradiation of uranium fuel in any reactor produces plutonium, which is a bomb material regardless of its composition or chemical form. The plutonium is contained in the discharged spent fuel, highly diluted and intimately mixed with fission products whose intense radioactivity makes the spent fuel essentially inaccessible for at least a century. The plutonium is thus a proliferation risk only if it is extracted by "reprocessing" the spent fuel behind heavy radiation shielding—chopping up and dissolving the fuel bundles and chemically separating the purified plutonium. It is then in a concentrated, homogeneous and divisible form that can be safely handled, is hard to measure precisely, and is therefore much easier to steal undetected. Extracted plutonium can be made into bombs so quickly (in days or hours) that even instant detection cannot provide "timely warning," the cardinal principle of safeguards since the start of the nuclear age.

U.S. nonproliferation policy since 1976 has rested on distinctions between proliferation-prone fuel cycles and fuel cycles thought to be proliferation-resistant.

LWRs were considered highly proliferation-resistant so long as technologies or services which could further enrich the LEU fresh fuel or extract plutonium from the spent fuel were not available to non-weapons states. It was considered possible for such states to obtain these technologies on their own, but only at high cost, with great technical difficulty, and with a large risk of timely detection. Reprocessing spent LWR fuel in conventional large plants, for example, is so difficult that no country has yet succeeded in doing it on a reliable commercial basis.

In return for an open-ended fee with no guarantee of performance (estimated costs rose thirteenfold in 1974–78 and are still rising), Britain and France are nonetheless proposing to expand their existing, rather unsuccessful, reprocessing plants to provide export services, thus relieving others of the technical difficulties. However, proposed technical measures to inhibit the use of the extracted and re-exported plutonium in bombs—chiefly by diluting or radioactively contaminating it so that further treatment would be needed—have been shown to be impracticable or ineffectual (especially against governments). International management or weapons-state siting of the reprocessing plant cannot affect how the re-exported plutonium is used.

Because commerce in plutonium therefore poses grave risks to peace, and because neither it nor the reprocessing plants supplying it can be safeguarded even in principle, the United States sought by its own example, and for a time by mild persuasion (but not by exercising its legal veto over reprocessing U.S.-enriched fuel), to discourage Britain and France from breaching the formidable barrier offered by the difficulties of reprocessing. As further recommended by the Ford-MITRE report,[*] the United States also sought to defer as long as possible domestic and foreign commitments to widespread use of fuel cycles requiring reprocessing—recycling plutonium in LWRs and breeding it in fast reactors. "Once-through" (no-reprocessing) LWRs, on the other hand, were encouraged for domestic use and for export because of their alleged proliferation resistance.

Advocates of reprocessing and plutonium commerce assaulted the U.S. policy on two contradictory grounds: that power reactors did not make plutonium that would be attractive to bomb-makers, and that if they did, commercial reprocessing was not the only way to extract it. The first limb of this argument claimed that the "reactor-grade" plutonium made by normal operation of power reactors—currently some 30 tons (about 10,000 bombs' worth) per year, a third of it in non-weapons states—could produce only weak and unreliable explosions, and posed exceptional hazards to persons working with it. Countries seeking bombs would therefore pass up this inferior material in favor of "weapons-grade" plutonium whose greater isotopic purity offered optimal performance. Weapons-grade plutonium could be made in existing research reactors (now operating in about 30 countries) or in "production reactors" specially built for the purpose from published designs. This route was claimed to be easier, cheaper, more effective, hence more plausible than using power reactors. Concern over power reactors was thus deemed to be far-fetched.

The technical premise behind this reasoning, however, is false. A detailed

[*]*Nuclear Power Issues and Choices: Report of the Nuclear Energy Policy Study Group.* Sponsored by the Ford Foundation. Administered by The MITRE Corporation, Cambridge, Mass.: Ballinger Publishing Co., 1977.

analysis of weapons physics has now shown that any practical composition of plutonium—including both "reactor-grade" plutonium and plutonium to which inseparable interfering ("denaturing") isotopes have been deliberately added—can be made by governments or by some subnational groups into bombs equivalent in power and predictability to those made from "weapons-grade" plutonium. Alternatively, power reactors can be so operated as to produce modest amounts of the latter without significantly increasing costs, decreasing efficiency, or being detected.

More sophisticated bomb design is needed to achieve the same performance from reactor-grade as from weapons-grade plutonium, but this may be a small price to pay for the greater ease of obtaining the former in bulk. The power reactor has an innocent civilian "cover" rather than being obviously military like a special production reactor. It is available to developing countries at zero or negative real cost with many supporting services. It bears no *extra* cost in money or time if one were going to build a power reactor anyhow. And it produces extremely large amounts of plutonium: so large that theft of a few bombs' worth per year is within the statistical "noise" and can be made undetectable in principle, while nearly a hundred bombs' worth per reactor per year—more than from any other option—is available if overtly diverted. Power reactors, then, can be considered large-scale military production reactors with an electricity by-product rather than benign electricity producers with a militarily unattractive plutonium by-product. They are not, as INFCE held, an implausible but rather potentially a peculiarly convenient type of large-scale factory for bomb material.

Of course plutonium in spent fuel from any kind of reactor is unusable in bombs until extracted by reprocessing, and it is here that plutonium advocates mounted their second line of attack. The official U.S. view was that reprocessing is very hard, whereas making bombs is relatively easy, so reprocessing should be inhibited. Plutonium advocates retorted that, on the contrary, making bombs is very hard but reprocessing relatively easy. To support this claim, Oak Ridge scientists developed a conceptual design for a "quick-and-dirty" reprocessing plant which could allegedly separate a bomb's worth of plutonium per week, with only a modest risk of detection during the relatively short construction time (of the order of a year). Restraints on commercial reprocessing (its advocates then argued), and indeed the timely warning concept itself, were futile because any country seeking bombs could build its own crude reprocessing plant and get plutonium from its domestic spent fuel anyhow.

This double-edghed argument was inconsistent, however, with the same advocates' reassurances that providing commercial reprocessing services would dissuade recipient countries from building their own plants: that international safeguards could be relied upon; and that bomb-making could be prevented by returning the plutonium "spiked" with unapproachably radioactive contaminants. (The recipient country could use its crude reprocessing plant to winnow out the plutonium from the spikants even more easily than from the original spent fuel.)

Thus the measures supposed to make reprocessing "safe" do not work. An argument meant to show there was no point [in] discriminating against plutonium technologies showed only the wider dangers of all fission technologies. Far from showing plutonium cycles were safe, it showed only that the rival once-through cycles were nearly as dangerous. For the real implication of the Oak Ridge design was that the reprocessing barrier is not so substantial after all: that both bomb-making *and* reprocessing are relatively easy (if normal requirements of profitability, environmental control, and worker safety are greatly relaxed).

This conclusion has been reinforced by the recent invention in several countries of unconventional medium- and small-scale methods of plutonium recovery, as yet untested, that are alleged to be substantially cheaper, simpler and less conspicuous than normal reprocessing plants. If, as appears likely, at least one of these new methods or the Oak Ridge concept proves valid, then it does not mean merely the end of the old timely warning concept; it means rather that timely warning can be provided neither for separated plutonium *nor* for spent fuel, so that *all* nuclear fission will be unsafeguardable in principle.

The Ford-Carter policy that reprocessing is very dangerous, therefore, was correct but did not go nearly far enough. By emphasizing that plutonium fuel cycles are *more* dangerous than once-through cycles, it glossed over the risks of the latter. The INFCE findings that there is no technical solution to the plutonium problem, and that once-through fuel cycles are not necessarily far less proliferative than plutonium cycles, are also broadly correct; for they imply, however unintentionally, that reactors of *any* kind are significantly proliferative, and that matters are much worse than the Ford-MITRE analysis and the Ford-Carter policy supposed.

To make matters worse still, more careful scrutiny of the supposedly innocuous front end of the fuel cycle—the use of natural uranium or LEU as fresh reactor fuel—has lately suggested a similar conclusion on independent grounds. Natural uranium can be gradually enriched to bomb-usable concentrations using low-technology centrifuges. LEU can be enriched more than twice as easily. An effective centrifuge design was published 20 years ago. Better versions—much less efficient than high-technology commercial versions, but still adequate—can be, and have been, made by a good machinist in a few weeks. Non-nuclear commercial centrifuges may also be adaptable to uranium enrichment. Though tens or hundreds of centrifuges and tons of uranium would be needed for patient accumulation—perhaps requiring years—of even one bomb's worth of HEU, the centrifuges are simple, modular, concealable, relatively cheap, and highly accessible. The uranium, mined in tens of thousands of tons per year worldwide, would be even easier to get. Thus even without assuming any breakthroughs in fast-moving new enrichment technologies—simplified laser methods, or perhaps the newly discovered magnetochemical methods—old, straightforward centrifuge designs suffice to make even natural uranium, as Bernard Baruch noted in 1946, a "dangerous" material.

There are also disquieting indications that without using any conventional facilities such as LWRs or reprocessing plants, and without serious risk of detection, one unirradiated LWR fuel bundle (about a hundredth of a reactor's annual fuel requirement) could be made into one bomb's worth of separated plutonium in one year by one technician with about one or two million dollars worth of other materials that are available over the counter and apparently subject to no controls. So far as is publicly known, this novel basement-scale method has not yet been used, but the calculations suggesting its feasibility—unpublished for discretion—appear valid. U.S. authorities were apprised of this method during 1978–79, but no published assessment mentions it. A vivid if indirect confirmation that no fuel-cycle material is officially considered "safe," however, comes from the new U.S.-sponsored Convention on the Physical Protection of Nuclear Material. This makes it an extraditable international crime (like genocide or piracy) for unauthorized persons to meddle with any fissionable material other than uranium ore or tailings, and explicitly *including* both LEU (such as LWR fuel) and purified natural uranium.

The proliferative routes just mentioned are only the latest additions to an already long list; conventional enrichment technologies, research and production reactors, direct use of bomb materials of which many tons have been exported (mainly by the United States) for worldwide research, theft of nuclear submarine fuel, theft and dismantlement of military bombs, theft of military bomb components. Collectively, both familiar and newly emerging routes to bombs imply that *every* form of *every* fissionable material in *every* nuclear fuel cycle can be used to make military bombs, either on its own or in combination with other ingredients made widely available by nuclear power. Not all the ancillary operations needed are of equal difficulty, but none is beyond the reach of any government or of some technically informed amateurs. The propagation of nuclear power thus turns out to have embodied the illusion that we can split the atom into two roles and easily and irrevocably as into two parts—forgetting that atomic energy is a-tomic, indivisible.

Can conceivable "safeguards" weaken this stark conclusion? Political arrangements for safeguards must rest on technical measures for materials accounting and for physical security. The former measures are so imprecise and *post hoc* that they cannot, even in principle, provide reasonable assurance that many bombs' worth of plutonium per year are not being removed from a good-sized reprocessing plant. Primary reliance must therefore be placed on physical security measures to limit access to materials and to deter or prevent their removal (or, if they are removed, to recover them). These measures must forestall well-equipped groups, perhaps including senior insiders acting in concert with the host government or a faction of it. Even modestly effective measures would be costly, fallible and intrusive. In the Federal Republic of Germany, for example, they would exceed the authority of the Atomic Energy Act; amending it to permit them would be unconstitutional; and amending the Constitution to permit them would conflict with human rights instruments to which the Federal Republic is a party.

The institutional arrangements which rely on these inherently inadequate accounting and security measures are woven around the International Atomic Energy Agency (IAEA), the Non-Proliferation, EURATOM, and Tlatelolco Treaties, and bilateral agreements. Though these are a considerable achievement, they have well-known and collectively fatal flaws, including: non-adherence of half the world's population, including two of the five acknowledged weapons states (France, China), all three suspected ones (India, Israel, South Africa), and all major developing countries except Iran and Mexico; freedom to renounce; no prohibition on designing bombs or building and testing their non-nuclear components; unsafeguarded duplicate facilities; inadequate inspection staff, facilities and morale; virtual absence of developing-country nationals in key IAEA safeguards posts; high detection threshold; freedom of host governments to deceive, reject, hinder or intimidate inspectors or to restrict their access (especially their unannounced access); unknown effectiveness owing to confidentiality; ambiguous agreements; and unsupported presumption of innocent explanations. The IAEA has already detected diversions of quantities too small for bombs and decided they did not justify even notifying the supplier states concerned. IAEA inspectors "have found many [suspicious] indications and acts . . . , but the IAEA has never taken action on any of them. This will probably continue to be true." It is no wonder. All the resources of the U.S. government, in more than a decade of repeated investigations, were unable to determine whether suspected plutonium thefts at the Numec plant in Apollo, Pennsylvania had occurred. Large HEU losses over many years at an Erwin, Tennessee plant crucial to U.S. naval reactor fuel supply led in 1979 to relaxed accounting standards that would make the losses look "acceptable." How, then, could suspected thefts in and perhaps by a recalcitrant foreign country be investigated?

Finally, the momentum and bureaucratic entrenchment of nuclear programs generally prevent effective sanctions against even an obvious sharp violation, let alone a dimly suspected, creeping one. The breach of EURATOM safeguards by the theft of a 200-ton shipload of natural uranium in 1968 was kept secret for nearly ten years. A decade's advance knowledge of the Indian bomb program by the U.S. and Canadian governments produced only diplomatic murmurs, and the actual test, as Albert Wohlstetter remarks, "inspired only ingenious apologies" from the U.S. State Department—anxious to conceal the U.S. contribution of heavy water—and a congratulatory telegram from the chairman of the French Atomic Energy Commission. As front pages heralded the Pakistani bomb program, Pakistan was being unanimously elected to the IAEA's Board of Governors.

In short, we can have proliferation with nuclear power, via either end of any fuel cycle. We cannot have nuclear power without proliferation, because safeguards cannot succeed either in principle or in practice. But can we have proliferation without nuclear power?

It is true that naval reactor fuel and military bombs provide non-civilian routes to more bombs; but that means only that nuclear armaments encourage their own refinement, multiplication and spread, not that there are significant civilian bomb routes unrelated to nuclear power. With trivial exceptions unimportant to this argument—radioisotope production reactors, large particle accelerators, proposed fusion reactors—*every* known civilian route to bombs involves *either* nuclear power *or* materials and technologies whose possession, indeed whose existence in commerce, is a direct and essential consequence of nuclear fission power. Apologists, apparently intending to be reassuring, often state nonetheless that since power reactors themselves are only one of (say) eight ways to make bombs, restraining power reactors is like sticking a thumb in one of eight holes in a dike. But the other holes were made by the same drill. Arguing that reactors have little to do with bombs is like arguing that fishhooks do not cause the catching of fish, since this can also involve rods, reels and anglers.

The foregoing reasoning implies that eliminating nuclear power is a necessary condition for nonproliferation. But how far is it a sufficient condition? Suppose that nuclear power no longer existed. Again, with trivial exceptions, there would no longer be any innocent justification for uranium mining (its minor non-nuclear uses are all substitutable), nor for possession of ancillary equipment such as research reactors and critical assemblies, nor for commerce in nuclear-grade graphite and beryllium, hafnium-free zirconium, tritium, lithium-6, more than gram quantities of deuterium, most nuclear instrumentation—the whole panoply of goods and services that provides such diverse routes to bombs. If these exotic items were no longer commercially available, they would be much harder to obtain; efforts to obtain them would be far more conspicuous; and such efforts, if detected, would carry a high political cost because for the first time they would be *unambiguously military* in intent.

This ambiguity—the ability of countries, willfully or by mere drift, to conduct operations (in Fred Iklé's phrase) "indistinguishable from preparations for a nuclear arsenal"—has gone very far. An NPT signatory subject to the strictest safeguards can quite legally be closer to having working bombs than the United States was in 1947. For example, precisely machined HEU spheres have recently been seen in Japan, doubtless for purely peaceful criticality experiments. But they could also be hours away from bombs.

Bernard Baruch warned in 1946 that the line dividing "safe" from "dangerous" (proliferative) nuclear activities would change and need constant reexamination. No mechanism to do this was ever set up. The variety and ease of proliferative paths expanded unnoticed to embrace virtually all activities once presumed "safe," while most of those activities were enthusiastically broadcast worldwide. Yet their direct facilitation of bomb-making was probably a less grave threat than the innocent disguise which their pursuit lent, and lends, to bomb-making. Baruch, noting the importance of adequate "advance warning . . . between violation and preventive action or punishment," had sought a technological monopoly so that visible operation or possession of "dangerous" steps other than by a special international authority, regardless of purpose, "will constitute an unambiguous danger signal." Today, with dozens of countries on the brink of a bomb capacity, such a neat solution is temporarily forestalled. But the principle remains sound: detection and deterrence of bomb-making require that it be unambiguously identifiable; and for that, phasing out nuclear power and the supporting services it justifies would be both a necessary and a sufficient condition.

Removing the present ambiguity will not make proliferation impossible. Pakistan, both operating and planning power reactors, sought a French reprocessing plant rationalized as an aid to energy independence, then, when thwarted, decided to pursue bombs more directly with clandestine centrifuges whose advanced design was stolen (as predicted) from the Netherlands. Pakistan probably did not expect that effort to be accidentally unmasked at an early stage, but was presumably willing to bear the political cost of eventual detection (if there was one: India has not yet been made to bear such a cost). Yet the key point is that the reactors, the uranium supply allegedly needed for them, the hoped-for reprocessing plant, the participation of the Pakistani spy in the Dutch project, the existence of that project and of the uranium-mining industry itself—all were justified and cloaked in benignity by nuclear power.

For bomb-making by any route, denuclearization would greatly increase the technical difficulty of obtaining the ingredients, and would automatically stigmatize suppliers as knowing accessories before the fact, hence clear violators of NPT Article I in letter or spirit. By providing unambiguous danger signals, denuclearization would make the political costs and risks to all concerned very high—perhaps prohibitively high. This does not mean that a determined and resourceful nation bent on bombs can by non-military means be absolutely prevented from getting them: much is already out of the barn. But denuclearization would brand as military the use of those escaped resources and inhibit their augmentation and spread. It would narrow the proliferative field to exclude the vast majority of states —the latent proliferators who sidle up to the nuclear threshold by degrees, and those easily tempted.

Yet is not the complete civil (and, in due course, military) denuclearization required to remove every last shred of ambiguity, a fantastic, unrealistic, unachievable goal? On the contrary, as the following sections show, that goal—and more straightforward interim steps on the way to it—would follow logically and practically from obeying the economic principles to which most governments pay allegiance.

Nuclear power has been promoted worldwide as both economically advantageous and necessary to replace oil. Potential proliferation, in this view, is either a small price to pay for vast economic advantages or an unavoidable side effect which we must learn to tolerate out of brutal necessity. But rational analysis of energy needs and economics strongly favors stopping and even reversing nuclear power programs. Their risks, including proliferation, are therefore not a minor counterweight to enormous advantages but rather a gratuitous supplement to enormous disadvantages.

Replacing oil is undeniably urgent. But nuclear power cannot provide timely and significant substitution for oil. Only about a tenth of the world's oil is used for making electricity, which is the only form of energy that nuclear power can yield on a significant scale in the foreseeable future. The other nine-tenths of the oil runs vehicles makes direct heat in buildings and industry, and provides petrochemical feedstocks. If, in 1975, *every* oil-fired power station in the industrialized countries represented in the Organization for Economic Cooperation and Development (OECD) had been replaced *overnight* by nuclear reactors, OECD oil consumption would have fallen by only 12 percent. The fraction of that oil consumption that was imported would have fallen from about 65 to 60 percent (compensated by greatly increased dependence on imported capital and uranium), and would have fallen by much more for the United States than for Japan, France, West Germany or the U.K. In practice, U.S. nuclear expansion has served mainly to displace coal, not oil, by running coal-fired plants less of the time: the utilization of their full theoretical capacity dropped from 62 to 55 percent during 1973–78. In overall quantitative terms the whole 1978 U.S. nuclear output could have been replaced simply by raising the output of partly idle coal plants most of the way to the level of which they are practically capable. And, contrary to the widespread assumption that a nuclear shutdown would cause serious regional shortages, an analysis of the balance within each regional power pool found that in 1978 all but 13 U.S. reactors, or all but two if surplus power were interchanged between regions, could have been shut down forthwith without reducing any region's "reserve margin" (spare capacity) below a prudent 15 percent of the peak demand. Further confirming the loose coupling between nuclear output and oil saving, between 1978 and 1979 the United States reduced by 16 percent the amount of oil used to make electricity, while U.S. nuclear outputs simultaneously *fell* by 8 percent: the oil saving came instead from conservation and coal and gas substitution. Between the first quarters of 1979 and of 1980, total U.S. oil-fired generation fell 32 percent while nuclear output simultaneously fell 25 percent—hardly a substitution.

The OECD calculation above for 1975 exaggerates potential oil displacement by nuclear power, partly because reactors take not one night but about ten years to build. Reactors ordered today can replace no oil in the 1980s—and surprisingly little thereafter. The example of Japan, widely considered the prime case of need for nuclear power, illustrates reactors' relatively small eventual contribution to total energy supply. Quadrupling Japan's nuclear capacity by 1990 would reduce officially projected oil import dependence by only about ten percent. An 18-fold increase by the year 2000—costing about a hundred trillion of today's yen and requiring a large reactor to be ordered every 20 days—could theoretically meet half of all Japan's delivered energy needs then, but fossil-fuel imports would still *increase* by more than two-thirds. "Rate and magnitude" calculations for other countries are equally discouraging.

It may be said that without nuclear power, these examples would look even worse. But even prohibitively large nuclear programs cannot go far to meet officially projected energy needs. The official projections reflect an inability to face the fact that nuclear power cannot physically play a dominant role in any country's energy supply. Solving the oil problem will clearly require, not a nuclear panacea, but a wide array of complementary measures, most importantly [*sic*] major improvements in energy efficiency.

It is therefore necessary to *compare* the elements of this array in costs, rates, difficulties and risks, to ensure that one is displacing oil with the cheapest, fastest, surest package of measures. Just as a person shopping for the most food on a limited budget does not buy caviar simply for the sake of having something from each shelf, but seeks the best bargain in a balanced diet, so every dollar devoted to relatively slow and costly energy supplies actually *retards* oil displacement by not being spent on more effective measures. Nuclear power programs have been justified not by this rational test but by intoning the conventional wisdom stated in 1978 by Brian Flowers of the U.K. Atomic Energy Authority:

> Alternative sources will take a long time to develop on any substantial scale. . . . Energy conservation requires massive investment . . . , and can at best reduce somewhat the estimated growth rate. Nuclear power is the only energy source we can rely upon at present with any certainty for massive contributions to our energy needs up to the end of the century, and if necessary, beyond.

Failure to assess *comparative* rates of oil displacement . . . runs the risk that, having like Lord Flowers dismissed alternatives as slow, conservation as costly, and both as inadequate, one may choose a predominantly nuclear future that is simultaneously slow, costly *and* inadequate.

Nuclear power is not only too slow; it is the wrong kind of energy source to replace oil. Most governments have viewed the energy problem as simply how to supply more energy of any type, from any source, at any rice, to replace oil—as if demand were homogeneous. In fact, there are many different types of energy whose different prices and qualities suit them to different uses. It is the uses that matter: people want comfort and light, not raw kilowatt-hours. Assuming (as we do) equal convenience and reliability to the user, the objective should be to supply the amount and type of energy that will do *each task most cheaply.*

This common-sense redefinition of the problem—meeting needs for energy services with an economy of means, using the right tool for the job—profoundly alters conclusions about new energy supply. Electricity is a special, high-quality, extremely expensive form of energy. This costly energy may be economically worthwhile in such premium uses as motors, lights, smelters, railways and electronics, but no matter how efficiently it is used, it cannot come close to competing with present direct fuels or with present commercial renewable sources for supplying heat or for operating road vehicles. These uses plus feedstocks account for about 90 percent of world oil use and for a similar or larger fraction of delivered energy needs. The special, "electricity-specific" applications represent typically only seven or eight percent of all delivered energy needs—much less than is now supplied in the form of electricity.

In most industrial countries, therefore, a third to a half of all electricity generated is already being used, uneconomically, for low-temperature heating and cooling. Additional electricity could *only* be so used. Arguing about what kind of new power station to build is thus like shopping for brandy to burn in the car or Chippendales to burn in the stove.

The economic absurdity of new power stations is illustrated by an authoritative calculation of how much energy Americans would have bought in 1978 if for the preceding decade or so they had simply met their end-use needs by making the cheapest incremental investments, whether in new energy supply or in efficiency improvements. Had they done so, they would have reduced their 1978 purchases of oil by about 28 percent (making the stripping of the American West unnecessary), and of electricity by 43 percent (so that over a third of today's power stations, including the whole nuclear program, would never have been built). The total net cost of such a program: about 17 percent less than Americans *did* pay in 1978 for the same energy services. Detailed studies of the scope for similar measures throughout the industrial world (and, where data are available in developing countries) have given qualitatively similar results.

If we did want "more electricity," we should get it from the cheapest sources first. In virtually all countries, those are, in approximate order of increasing price:

1. Eliminating waste of electricity (such as lighting empty offices at headache level).
2. Replacing with efficiency improvements and cost-effective solar systems the electricity now used for low-temperature heating and cooling.
3. Making motors, lights, appliances, smelters, etc., cost-effectively efficient.
4. Industrial cogeneration, combined-heat-and-power stations, solar ponds and heat engines, modern wind machines, filling empty turbine bays in existing dams, and small-scale hydroelectricity.
5. Central power stations—the slowest and costliest known source.

The notion that despite all constraints—time, money, politics, technical uncertainties—nuclear power stations are at least a source of energy, and as such can be substituted for significant amounts of the dwindling oil supply, has long exerted a powerful influence on otherwise balanced imaginations. But it does not withstand critical scrutiny. It is both logistically and economically fallacious. The high cost of nuclear power *today* limits its conceivably economic role to the baseload fraction of electricity-specific end-uses: typically about four percent of all delivered energy needs. In purely pragmatic and economic terms, therefore, nuclear power falls on its own demerits. . . .

As costs rise and credibility falls, the market for more electricity is quietly evaporating. With the inevitable response to higher prices beginning, forecasts of electricity demand growth in most countries have been falling steadily. Some are nearing zero or negative values. U.S. electricity demand has consistently been growing more slowly than real GNP of late, and all the trends are downward. Forecasters unfortunately responded more slowly than consumers: over the past six years, U.S. private utilities forecast that peak demand for the following year would grow by an average of 7.8 percent, but the actual growth averaged only 2.9 percent. Overcapacity in the United States will probably hit 43 percent in 1980 and continue to rise (perhaps past the British level of about 50 percent). U.S. overcapacity in excess of a prudent 15 percent reserve margin is already well over twice the present nuclear contribution. It is indeed so large that if *all* U.S. power-plant construction were stopped immediately, growth in peak demand at an annual rate of 1.2 percent—twice that experienced in 1979—would still leave a national reserve margin of 15 percent in the year 2000. Growth by at least 2.2 percent per year could be accommodated if the economically advantageous industrial cogeneration potential were tapped. The market for power stations of any kind is simply imaginary.

Finally, nuclear (or fossil-fueled) power stations and their grids incur such extraordinary capital costs and take so long to build that utility cash flow is inherently unstable. Any utility, whether public or private, regulated or not, which persists in building such plants will sooner or later go broke, and many are already doing so. Funding for new plants is scarce and costly; and even if it is available, building new plants is simply no longer in utilities' financial interest.

These problems, singly and interactively, have taken their toll on industry morale, investor confidence, and resulting expectations. In only six years from 1973, nuclear forecasts for 2000 fell by a factor of five for the world, nearly four for West Germany (no new orders since 1975), and eight for the United States (*minus* 27 net orders during 1974–79). Nuclear forecasts worldwide are still plummeting—more for economic than political reasons. The U.S.S.R., for example, achieved only a third of its nuclear goal for the 1970s, half for the past five years. And although there have been essentially no procedural barriers to building reactors in Canada, the pattern of decline in nuclear capacity forecast for the year 2000 has been all but identical in Canada and the United States.

Despite intensive sales efforts and universal subsidies (often up to or exceeding total costs), the drop in expectations for nuclear power has been even faster in developing countries, paced by Iran, which projected 23,000 megawatts for 1994 and will probably get zero, and by Brazil, which projected 75,000 megawatts for the year 2000 and is unlikely to want more than the 2,000 megawatts that are now in serious difficulties. Total nuclear capacity in all developing countries in 1985 is now unlikely to be as much as 13,000 megawatts, or about the present West

German level. Even if giveaway offers tempt new customers (perhaps Mexico, Kenya, Turkey, Zaïre) to undertake the well-known problems of integrating gigantic, very costly, complex units into rather small grids in countries poor in infrastructure, that extra "business" would be a tiny fraction of the loss elsewhere. It would not even be profitable business—only a way to inject export-bank funds into the vendors' ailing cash flows.

The collapse of nuclear markets has already sealed the fate of an industry tooled up to meet the inflated expectations of the early 1970s. Even with continued domestic and export subsidies, withdrawals by major firms seem inevitable. While rhetorically the world nuclear enterprise is pressing forward, in reality it is grinding to a halt and even slipping backward. The greatest collapse of any enterprise in industrial history is now underway. Thus, as Harry Rowen and Albert Wohlstetter remark,

> . . . the argument sometimes shifts subtly from the needs of a robust and inexorably expanding industry to the sympathetic care required to keep alive a fragile industry that is on the verge of expiring altogether.

The industry's long-term hope has been "advanced" plutonium technologies. But their first stage, recycling plutonium in conventional power reactors, was officially acknowledged in the U.K. and West Germany in 1977–78 to save too little uranium to pay for the reprocessing and other costs. Even the INFCE study, generally enthusiastic about plutonium, failed to find recycling inviting. Contrary to one of the earlier arguments advanced for reprocessing, INFCE has now concurred in the official positions of Canada, the United States and Sweden that reprocessing is not necessary for waste management. (Some experts believe reprocessing may even make it more difficult.) Similarly, one of the strongest arguments earlier advanced for reprocessing and plutonium-related technologies—that fission reactors would need so much uranium as to create shortages—is rapidly receding.

In short, the economics of fast breeder reactors look ghastly until far into the next century. There are indications that prospects for funding and finding acceptable sites for the extremely costly next-stage breeder projects range from only fair (in France and the U.S.S.R.) to poor (in West Germany, Japan, the United States and the U.K.). Even sympathetic officials are realizing that the 50-fold potential improvement in uranium utilization that successful breeders might produce cannot in fact be achieved for well over a century because of the time it takes the breeder's fuel cycle to come to equilibrium; for the next 50 to 80 years, the modest uranium savings that could be realized through breeders could be achieved much more cheaply and surely through uranium-efficient thermal reactors instead. Costly, difficult breeder programs are thus looking increasingly like a commercial blunder, akin to pushing the Concorde while others developed jumbo jets. Further attempts to deploy breeder reactors in an already hostile political climate could indeed jeopardize the limited acceptance now enjoyed by thermal reactors.

The loss of momentum for the breeder, and for the nuclear program which it was to culminate, is reflected at the highest political levels in all the main nuclear countries of OECD and beneath the surface throughout the Soviet scientific community. . . .

How has U.S. policy affected the foreign nuclear debate at all political levels?

U.S. technological dominance of the nuclear arena, though still preeminent, is no longer hegemonic; but U.S. political dominance of world energy policy effectively is. So far it has been exercised in exactly the wrong direction.

U.S. policy pretends that the nuclear collapse is not happening, or that if it is, it shouldn't be and deserves no encouragement.[*] The Energy Secretary has just committed two-fifths of his budget for the next five years to nuclear power. The State Department says that *not* using nuclear power would make proliferation worse. Presidential confirmations of the necessity and the large energy potential of nuclear power have bolstered sagging programs in countries poorer in fuels. Promotional rhetoric has given the nuclear industry a license to present in Europe a false but largely uncontested image of a flourishing American nuclear program (and vice versa). The State Department does not know, and seemingly does not want to know, that however monolithic the policy front presented by other countries (an appearance carefully orchestrated by the U.S. nuclear industry), every national nuclear policy is riven from top to bottom by doubt and dissent. Whatever the United States has done, in policy or in rhetoric, has helped one side of those internal debates and hurt the other. Yet the State Department, maintaining a meticulously lopsided neutrality, has never appreciated that the most powerful U.S. lever for affecting foreign nuclear policies in either direction was not blunt instruments like fuel supply, but rather the *political example* of stated and applied U.S. energy policy in its broadest terms.

Ignoring this influence on domestic energy politics abroad, advocates of continuing subsidized nuclear exports have argued that if the United States does not supply sensitive nuclear technologies, others will, so the United States might as well—and that since others can, the United States has no "leverage" to justify abstention. As Harry Rowen and Albert Wohlstetter put it, "We can retain our leverage only if we never use it. A lever is a form of abstract art rather than a tool giving us a mechanical advantage." Today the United States proclaims itself anxious to be seen as a "reliable supplier," spends five billion dollars on a gratuitous expansion of a centrifugal enrichment capacity to take on new fuel export commitments, and seeks to make those commitments irrevocable; yet at the same time it asks itself, half aloud, how much "leverage" it can obtain by exporting more U.S.-fueled reactors as hostages to later sanctions. Both kinds of exports leave the United States in the unpalatable position of vigorously proliferating in the name of nonproliferation, sacrificing for a weak and counterproductive physical leverage a strong and positive political leverage. . . . In sum, the forces of the market—in combination with new and more searching analysis of other factors—have made the future of nuclear power so precarious that a change in policy by the United States, or by several other countries, would greatly hasten the dawning realization that nuclear power has no valid future either in industrialized or developing countries. The issue is not whether to maintain a thriving enterprise, but rather whether to accept the verdict of the very calculations on which free market economies rely. . . . [See Denis Hayes, p. 291, for the sorts of solutions that Lovins et al. advocate for a nuclear-free world.]

[*Although this article was published during the Carter administration, it applies equally, if not more so, to the Reagan era.]

SYNTHETIC FUELS

Various attempts have been made to find a substitute for natural oil. Among the most promising have been the different efforts to produce both an imitation, or synthetic, gasoline and a gas from coal. Like oil, coal is a hydrocarbon. The trick was to find a way to turn coal into a liquid or a gas at a profit and without losing much of its energy potential. The modern efforts to create a synthetic fuels industry have partially resembled that in the nuclear field because both were spin-offs of military endeavors. While nuclear power arose from military research and the military applications envisioned by Admiral Rickover, synthetic fuels were first brought to fruition in Hitler's Germany during the Second World War. Just as the production of electricity in the United States was a new outlet for atomic power, a way to employ the technology created in the manufacture of the bomb, so the Germans built synthetic fuels plants to make oil from coal because they had no indigenous supply of petroleum to power their war machine.

As will be clear from the selections that follow, hopes for a synthetic fuels industry have soared in periods when fears that world oil supplies would be used up have been high. (You will remember the scare chart in the section on oil.) It is then also that the public is reminded, in a media blitz of hopeful articles and reports, of the vast reserves of oil shale, tar sands, and coal available to be turned into petroleum products. A typical such report from the New York *Times,* November 6, 1981, headlined SHALE OIL IS COMING OF AGE, says, "The two trillion barrels of shale oil in the vast Piceance Basin and others in the [American] west represent three times the world's proved reserves of conventional oil. . . ." Similar articles have been written in virtually the same language since at least the 1920s. However ballyhooed, the synfuels industry has never actually taken off, its hopes always torpedoed by technical failures and by the oil industry's continual gluts.

As you read this section, it is worth asking why this has been so. As a start, it is well to keep in mind the immense scale of synthetics. The mining requirements, support systems, and actual plants are so vast that massive infusions of government aid, whether as subtle subsidies or, in the case of the Carter administration, as outright grants of money and federal guarantees, are necessary simply to set up noncommercial pilot operations.

Just as important, nothing of this scale could succeed without the wholehearted backing of the large oil corporations—the only ones, with their big coal subsidiaries, that could afford the commercial development of a synthetic fuels industry. Several articles in this section explore the unsettling question of whether these oil companies are actually as interested in setting up such an industry as they claim to be, or in reality, have they worked to assure that such an industry will never be built (as they surely did in the 1920s, when a cartel was formed to block the development of synthetics)—at least not built until there are no longer oil profits for synthetics to compete with?

Whether or not, from a human point of view, such an industry would be a boon or an environmental disaster remains an open question, as the articles at the end of this section indicate. Right now this question cannot be settled since a synfuels industry does not yet exist.

It is, of course, inconceivable that either nuclear power or synthetics could survive in the atmosphere of a free market economy, but such an economy does not, in any case, exist in the world of large-scale energy systems. That point was made clear in the previous section on oil. So the real questions become, At what point do industry and government agree that synthetics should be brought into the energy arena? and What will be the effects of this decision on our lives? Despite the actions of the Carter administration, and the slightly more cautious stance of Reagan in the synfuels area, and despite recent moves by the oil corporations to set up commercial synfuels plants with government help, as long as oil remains plentiful and profitable, development of synthetics probably will be postponed.

SYNTHETIC FUELS AND HITLER'S GERMANY

The idea of synthetic fuels is not new. Gas made from coal in the nineteenth century was used to light streetlamps in many cities. But the first real breakthrough in the production of synthetic fuels came in 1909, when Friedrich Bergius, a German scientist, invented a way to produce a synthetic gasoline from coal and hydrogen under high pressure by a process called hydrogenation. During the First World War Bergius sought without initial success to adapt his hydrogenation process to large-scale production.

At this period the companies which were soon to make up the empire of I.G. Farben were in their formative stage. The dynamic chairman of this new industrial giant, Carl Bosch, saw hope for oil-scarce Germany in the Bergius process, and so, as the next selection shows, the modern history of synthetic fuels began.

Taken from The Crime and Punishment of I. G. Farben, *by Joseph Borkin, New York, Macmillan, 1978.*

. . . By far the most ambitious undertaking of the new I.G. [Farben] was a project which had become [company chairman Carl Bosch's] dominant interest and, in fact, had been the real impetus for his insistence on the merger of the I.G. companies into a single financially powerful giant. It was Bosch's dream to liberate Germany from dependence on foreign oil wells. Without a single domestic oil well worthy of the name, Germany had been strangled by the British fleet during [World War I]. Bosch would do for oil what he had done for nitrates. Through the magic of high pressure chemistry and his own genius he would convert Germany's plentiful coal into a torrent of gasoline. He would recreate a past triumph in a new setting.

Events were already taking shape in Germany that provided a pressing demand for oil. Clandestine rearmament through systematic violations of the Versailles treaty was under way. In 1924 mobilization plans projected a sixty-three-division army. The Black Reichswehr required a "safe" source of gasoline. In the mechanized war of the future the need for liquid fuel would be astronomical.

The lure of great profits in peacetime also entered into Bosch's calculations. The automobile boom was on its way, consuming great portions of the available gasoline, and promising to consume continually greater amounts. The immediate energy question confronting the industrial countries of the world was whether oil discoveries could keep up with the accelerating demand. The reply of oil authorities was generally negative, some even predicting the imminent exhaustion of the world's oil reserves. In the United States President Calvin Coolidge gave official recognition to this dismal prophecy by creating the Federal Oil Conservation Board, composed of the secretaries of war, navy, interior, and commerce. The board's mission was to investigate and report on the state of the world's reserves of petroleum. The fact that it was considered necessary to involve such a commission was itself regarded as a grim portent. To the prescient the signs were already discernible that oil would be the vortex of international diplomacy and power politics. Such developments foreshadowed the time when the wealth of nations would be measured by the dipsticks of oil.

Finally, there was a more immediate concern nudging Bosch. His company's domination of the world's synthetic nitrate industry was coming to an end. He had given France a plant as well as the secret of the Haber-Bosch process, and the other major industrial countries were developing their own nitrate capabilities. The time was fast approaching when these foreign plants would lead to a glut of the world's supply. Soon, Bosch recognized, he would have to shut down a large part of the costly, high pressure installations at Leuna and Oppau. Finding a new and profitable use for their expensive equipment became a pressing matter.

To push the project forward, Bosch decided to acquire the Bergius process for converting coal into oil under high pressure. Bosch was aware that Bergius, like Haber, could carry out his process successfully only in the laboratory. All attempts during the war at large-scale industrial production had failed. It was a problem made to order for Bosch. He had the supreme confidence that what he had done for Haber he could do for Bergius. Only one impediment confronted him, but that was monumental: cost. Acquisition of the Bergius patents would be expensive enough; however, the outlays required to adapt the process to large-scale industrial production were beyond even the resources of Badische Anilin Und Soda-Fabrik of Ludwigshafen, already hobbled by the loss of the war.

Although Bosch's plan was to rely on the financial resources of I.G. to develop domestic production, he planned to bring in an American company like Standard Oil (New Jersey) as a partner in the worldwide exploitation of the process. Moreover, Standard had more than enormous financial resources: it had a huge and well-staffed research and development organization that had achieved important breakthroughs in petroleum technology.

Standard, the dominant force in the American oil industry, was also one of its more imaginative members. Since the early 1920s, when depletion of the world's natural oil reserves first became a matter of concern, Standard had searched for alternatives to crude oil. It pioneered in testing shale as a commercial source, and in 1921 it even purchased 22,000 acres in Colorado in the hope that a commercially adaptable method of extracting oil from shale could be found. Standard was also exploring the feasibility of the Bergius process since the United States, like Germany, had tremendous coal deposits. In 1922, Frank A. Howard, head of the Standard Oil Development Company, had sent a young assistant to Germany to study the Bergius process but had been advised that it was still far from ready for commercial exploitation. . . .

In March 1926 Howard arrived at Ludwigshafen . . . and was given a tour of the BASF laboratories, by now officially a part of I.G. Farbenindustrie. He was stunned. Although Howard was the head of research and development of one of the world's largest and most scientifically advanced corporations, he reported that he was "plunged into a world of research and development on a gigantic scale such as I had never seen." He was especially overwhelmed by BASF's experiments in synthetic oil. Howard fired off a message immediately to Walter C. Teagle, president of Standard Oil, then on a visit to Paris, to come to Ludwigshafen without delay:

> Based upon my observations and discussions today, I think that this matter is the most important which has ever faced the company since the dissolution [the breakup of the Standard Oil Trust by a Supreme Court decision in 1911]. The Badische [BASF] can make high grade motor fuel from lignite and other low quality coals in amounts up to half the weight of the coal. This means absolutely the independence of Europe in the matter of gasoline supply. Straight price competition is all that is left.

The urgency of Howard's message brought Teagle to Ludwigshafen within a few days. An examination of BASF's high pressure installation left him just as impressed as Howard: "I had not known what research meant until I saw it. We were babies compared to what they were doing." When Teagle and Howard retired to their quarters, they talked over "the effect the startling scientific developments . . . would have on the world's oil industry." For Standard's own protection, it was obviously imperative to find a way for closer cooperation with I.G. The vision of thousands of obsolete oil wells was enough of a spur.

At first Howard and Teagle considered the possibility of purchasing the world rights to the Bergius synthetic oil patents from I. G. However, millions had already been spent on the process, and it was obvious that only a tremendous price would be acceptable to I.G. At the moment Standard was not prepared to make a large expenditure on a process that was still in the early stages of development and not yet ready for commercial exploitation. Teagle and Howard decided to proceed cautiously. They concluded that at least for the present the most sensible arrangement was a simple partnership to develop and perfect the process without any large financial commitment. Bosch agreed in principle to the proposal. Although he would have preferred a broader agreement, it nevertheless was a concrete demonstration of Standard's interest.

Until this meeting Bosch had limited the hydrogenation project to a few experimental high pressure furnaces. After the reaction of the Standard executives, he threw caution to the winds. On June 18, he ordered a huge Bergius plant to be built next to the Haber-Bosch plant at Leuna. He had decided that the process was sufficiently advanced for I.G. to start mass-producing synthetic oil—100,000 tons a year. It was a step that many I.G. officials considered financially imprudent in view of the fact that the process still had some way to go before it was perfected. But Bosch was too powerful to be thwarted.

On September 1, 1926, at the first stockholders meeting of the incorporated

I.G., plans were announced for construction of the big new synthetic oil plant at Leuna. The wisdom of pushing the project seemed to be corroborated a few days later when President Coolidge's Federal Oil Conservation Board submitted its preliminary report on the question of "national petroleum conditions" in the United States. The board found that "the total present reserves in pumping and flowing wells . . . has been estimated at about 4½ billion barrels, which is theoretically but six years' supply . . . future maintenance of even current supplies implies the constant discovery of new fields and the drilling of new wells." Even the worst pessimists were taken by surprise by the six-year estimate.

Shortly after the announcement of I.G.'s new synthetic oil plant, Bosch himself arrived in the United States to begin negotiations with Standard. He was interested mainly in financial support. By now Teagle and Howard realized that their enthusiasm and stunned appreciation of the hydrogeneration process had reduced their bargaining power with Bosch. They decided to put on a counterdemonstration. Teagle invited Bosch to accompany him on his annual tour of Standard's vast properties. For three weeks they drove across the United States inspecting Standard facilities. On the trip it became clear to Bosch that the Standard Oil officials were not ready to make the large payment to I.G. he had expected. In mid-December he returned to Germany without a definite agreement or financial commitment. Again he slipped into the depression that periodically afflicted him.

It took until August of the next year for Teagle and Bosch to reach a relatively limited understanding. Standard agreed to embark on a cooperative program of research and development of the hydrogenation process to refine crude oil. It also agreed to build a new plant for this purpose as soon as possible in Louisiana. In return Standard was given the right to exploit the process in the United States and to share half of the royalties with I.G. on licenses to other parties. However, Standard was not entitled to exploit the process in any of its far-flung plants outside the United States.

Modest as the arrangement was, the *New York Times,* in its news story of the agreement dispatched by its German correspondent, was almost euphoric about the possibilities of I.G.'s synthetic oil process.

> What experts in chemical fields admit is that the world is on the threshold of a new fuel era, and that he often predicted failure of the gasoline supply is now shoved centuries in the future. . . . The discoveries in these fields are more marvelous than inventions which enable rapid strides in the development of radio, other uses of electricity and in airplanes, a prominent industrialist told the correspondent of the *New York Times.*

It was estimated by "conservative authorities" that twenty percent of the gasoline used in 1928 would be synthetic and that within a very few years Germany would be completely self-sufficient. So great was the confidence in making synthetic oil, concluded the *New York Times* article, that the price for the synthetic fuel was expected to be less than that of natural oil imported from the United States and the Soviet Union.

The story was a public relation man's dream. The true situation was quite different. The Bergius plant at Leuna, which had begun production in June, was beset by operational failures and extremely serious technological problems. Expenditures had soared so far beyond the original estimates that if continued they would threaten the very financial structure of I.G. Farben itself.

In the following months, pressure developed within the I.G. managing board to scrap the synthetic oil project entirely. Bosch paid no attention to the carping of his colleagues: "Nitrogen production took fifteen years to reach today's levels," he told them. "Obviously gasoline production has to be given more time before it becomes profitable." As usual Bosch's power in I.G. was decisive. The managing board agreed to continue the costly synthetic oil project, at least for the time being. However, it was obvious that Bosch would have to find a way to relieve the severe financial strain on I.G. or face more trouble from the board.

In the meantime, Standard Oil officials, probably unaware of I.G.'s problems, had become increasingly bullish about the prospects for the Bergius-Bosch process. A research staff under the direction of Robert T. Haslam, a professor of chemical engineering on leave from M.I.T., had gone to work at the new experimental plant in Louisiana on the hydrogenation of crude oil, and Standard had already concluded that the process was the most important scientific development that had ever occurred in the oil industry. The application of the hydrogenation process to crude oil was nothing less than amazing. In the past, two barrels of crude oil had been required to produce a barrel of gasoline; with hydrogenation, only one barrel of crude would be required. However, under the terms of the 1927 agreement with I.G., Standard's affiliates all over the world were still not permitted to use the process. It could be exploited by Standard only in the United States and then only in conjunction with crude oil, not coal.

In August 1928, Teagle and other top Standard officials went to Germany hoping to convince Bosch and his I.G. advisers to expand the I.G.-Standard partnership to allow joint exploitation of the Bergius-Bosch process all over the world and to give Standard the right to apply the process to coal as well as crude oil. Bosch brushed the Standard request aside. Although he did not say so, he was having enough troubles with his I.G. colleagues about the cost of the hydrogenation project in Germany. This was obviously not the time for I.G. to embark on an expensive program of world exploitation even in partnership with Standard.

What Bosch really wanted was a large lump payment from Standard to extricate I.G. from its present financial difficulties and still enable him to continue the hydrogenation project in Germany. With the help of Hermann Schmitz[,] Bosch devised a counterproposal that he did not believe Standard could afford to refuse. He offered to sell the world rights to the Bergius-Bosch hydrogenation process for the production of gasoline. The only territorial exception was that the rights in Germany were reserved to I.G. Obviously, the German authorities would never permit I.G. to surrender to a foreign company the German rights to a process so crucial to military and economic self-sufficiency. Even so, I.G. did not reveal to its government that it was selling the hydrogenation rights to Standard. As Bosch anticipated. Standard jumped at the offer.

The parties negotiated their agreement in the manner of two great powers forging a treaty to divide the world into separate spheres of influence. They agreed to observe the sovereignty of each in their respective fields. In the words of a Standard official, "The I.G. are going to stay out of the oil business—and we are going to stay out of the chemical business." To set up a mechanism to carry out the terms of the agreement the parties agreed to create the Standard-I.G. Company, incorporated in the United States, owned eighty percent by Standard Oil and twenty percent by I.G. This retained for I.G. a minority interest in any future success. I.G. then transferred the world patent rights (except for Germany) on the hydrogenation process to the new enterprise. In return, Bosch finally secured what he so desperately wanted. Standard turned over to I.G. two percent of its entire common stock: 546,000 shares valued on Standard's books at $35 million! As a slight bonus for I.G., Teagle agreed to serve on the board of I.G.'s newly formed holding company in the United States, the American I.G. Chemical Company. . . .

Hardly had the I.G.-Standard marriage been completed than it received a series of staggering blows. The Great Depression, combined with the discovery of enormous oil reserves in Texas, dropped the price of oil so drastically that Standard abandoned any immediate hope for worldwide development of the conversion of coal into oil. . . . [It] took the Arab oil boycott in 1974 to rekindle Standard's interest in making gasoline from coal.

[The first really large-scale development of synthetics took place during World War II, when the Germans, who had little oil of their own, used their large coal reserves as a feedstock for the manufacture of synthetic petroleum. Hitler was a keen advocate of synthetics. Indeed, he overrode scientific opposition to the idea of setting up synthetic plants. Through his coalition with I.G. Farben, Hitler sought to supply his military machine with large amounts of synthetic fuel. Production grew from 10 million barrels in 1938 to 36 million barrels in 1943. By 1943 synthetics accounted for 50 percent of all German fuel. Chief among the recipients was the German air force, which dominated the air war over Europe in the early stages of combat. In May 1944 the U.S. Air Force bombed I.G.'s synthetic plants to smithereens.

One of these synthetics complexes was built in Silesia, where there were ample supplies of water, coal, and, as it turned out, slave labor. It was called I.G. Auschwitz.

After the war I.G. Farben directors were tried at Nuremberg and either acquitted or given light sentences. The company survived. Indeed, the synthetic fuels processes pursued today have their origins in the work of Bergius and other I.G. scientists.]

THE OIL SHALE ALTERNATIVE

In recent years, as earlier in this century, most of the interest in synthetics has focused on coal as a feedstock for the production of synthetic fuels. However, there are other possible bases on which a synthetics industry might arise. Oil shale and tar sands (or bituminous sands) are the two most prominent of them. The stories of the attempts to use each of them as the basis for a synthetic fuels industry are so similar that we concentrate only on oil shale here. Despite much speculation and professed government interest, neither industry has ever gotten off the ground because of the continuing abundant surplus of other, cheaper fuels, notably oil.

Taken from The Elusive Bonanza, *by Chris Welles, New York, E. P. Dutton, 1970.*

[Oil] shale is . . . neither oil nor shale. According to one geological definition, it is a "fine-textured sedimentary rock containing organic matter that yields substantial amounts of oil and hydrocarbon gas by destructive distillation." The source of the energy in oil shale is very similar to that in such other "fossil fuels" as petroleum and coal: the remains of plants and animals which after dying were buried beneath the ground. A dead plant or animal exposed to the air will rot or oxidize, a burning process that consumes the organism's carbon and hydrogen, thus using up its potential energy. But trapped underground, organic material cannot fully oxidize, and the carbon and hydrogen are preserved, so they may be oxidized and converted into energy by man.

The form these underground remains take is dependent on geological and climatic conditions.

In the opinion of many geologists, oil shale, though bearing some resemblances to coal, is really incompletely developed petroleum. Formation of oil shale deposits began, like petroleum, with the accumulation of dying plant and animal matter in bodies of water, usually inland seas and lakes. The organic material mixed with sediments and settled to the water's bottom, but due to insufficient heat and pressure, actual distillation did not occur. Created instead was "kerogen," a rubbery solid about 80 percent carbon and 10 percent hydrogen which mixed chemically with the sediments to form a tough, dense, inelastic, insoluble rock, whose color ranges from light tan to black depending on the percentage of kerogen. The delineation of the layers is often clearly visible.

The chief chemical difference between kerogen and petroleum is geometric: unlike petroleum the kerogen molecules are connected with elaborate chains. To convert kerogen to a close equivalent of petroleum, one need only apply the heat it did not receive from the earth. At a temperature between 850 and 900 degrees F. "retorting" occurs. The molecular chains break, and the kerogen is distilled into, by weight, about 66 percent shale oil (which is usually released as a vapor), 25 percent coke-like solid matter, and 9 percent combustible gas. Thin layers of shale with a high kerogen content can be retorted with a match, which creates a sooty flame and an acrid odor. The amount of shale oil produced varies, of course, with the percentage of kerogen, ranging from less than five gallons per ton of shale rock to nearly 100 gallons per ton. One cubic foot of reasonably rich shale will yield about three gallons of shale oil. The biggest residue from retorting is "spent shale" which weighs only slightly less than the original shale rock and expands during retorting to a volume between 20 and 40 percent greater, meaning that more space is required to dispose of these tailings than the whole from which the shale rock was dug.

Shale oil has important physical differences from petroleum. Depending on the retorting method, it usually has a high viscosity due to a large wax content, and at room temperature it is so thick and tar-like it will not flow. To be moved through a pipeline it must be either heated to over 90 degrees F. or further "cracked" or distilled. Shale oil also contains excessive impurities including sulphur, tars, and such gases as nitrogen and ammonia. But once they are removed, shale oil can be refined easily into a full range of petroleum products from fuel oil and asphalt to gasoline and petrochemicals.

Deposits of shale occur throughout the world on every continent, constituting, in fact, a greater potential energy resource than any other natural material except coal—far greater than petroleum, natural gas, uranium, and hydro power. Significant amounts are known to exist in Brazil, Scotland, Sweden, China, Russia, Australia, Germany, France, Canada, and Thailand. At least 30 states contain shale deposits, and in wide areas just west of the Appalachian Mountains, much oil shale is mixed with coal.

By far the richest and most extensive oil shale deposit in the world is located in what is called the Green River Formation. This is contained in a roughly circular area of about 17,000 square miles extending out about 150 miles from where Colorado, Utah, and Wyoming intersect and through which the Green River, one of the principal tributaries of the Colorado River, flows. About 72 percent of this land, containing between 80 and 85 percent of the shale, is owned by the federal government. . . .

Production of oil from shale occurred in other areas long before interest developed in the Green River Formation. The earliest oil shale operation may have been in England, where a patent was granted in 1694 for a process to distill "oyle from a kind of stone." In the United States, shale oil production predated the inception of the petroleum industry by several decades. During the early 1800s, and possibly as early as Revolutionary times, lamp oil, lubricants, and medicinal substances were produced from the rather lean shales around the Appalachians. Around 1850 there was talk of a shale oil boom, a new answer to the country's fuel needs which at the time were being met mostly by wood. One plant on the Ohio River actually produced 30 gallons of shale oil a day over a short period.

In 1859, however, Colonel E. L. Drake drilled his famous crude oil well near Titusville, Pennsylvania, and as was to occur many times in the future, the fresh new supplies of petroleum collapsed the hopes of shale oil entrepreneurs. Compared to the relative ease in drilling into underground pools and pumping the oil to the surface, production of shale oil was an expensive operation involving difficult technological problems beyond the grasp of early oil shalers.

. . . The first modern mechanism, [for getting oil from shale] developed around 1894 in Scotland, was the Pumpherston Retort. Thirty feet tall, two to three feet in diameter, it contained two significant advances over the batch variety: shale oil production was continuous and the source of heat was, at least in part, the gas and coke by-products. Crushed shale was loaded in the cast-iron top and moved downward by gravity. Heat from burning gas in a brick-lined furnace section moved upward. In the middle, shale oil vapor was formed and was drawn off along with the shale gas. The vapor was condensed and the gas fed back to the furnace. Later modifications employed steam to help sweep the hot gas through the shale and air vents to help burn the residual coke, thus increasing the heat level and the contact of the hot gas with the shale.

The Pumpherston Retort was to serve as the model for most future oil shale industries, but some countries experimented with wholly different retorting ideas. . . . In Sweden, first tests were made in *in situ,* literally "in place" retorting. The hope was that if ways could be found to retort the shale while still in the ground, the costly problems of mining and disposal of voluminous quantities of spent shale could be eliminated. Holes were drilled into deposits which were about 50 feet deep and quite near the surface of the ground. High voltage electricity was introduced, which heated the surrounding shale and caused shale oil to drip to the bottom of the holes from which it could be pumped to the surface.

As ingenious as many of these methods were, shale oil operations in most countries have been sporadic—between 1875 and 1961 about 275 million barrels of oil were produced, or less than a month's supply for the United States. Most arose because of severe shortages of conventional oil and expired as methods of transporting crude oil worldwide cheaply and efficiently were developed. Too, most foreign shale deposits were too lean and production costs were too high. The only shale oil being commercially produced today is from operations in Estonia and in Manchuria. From the latter the Chinese are said to obtain around 30,000–40,000 barrels/day. A number of American engineering firms and others have held periodic talks with the Brazilian government—that country's shales are second only to those in the United States in richness and Brazil possesses rather scanty crude supplies.

For many years, people thought the oil shale in the Green River Formation was only slightly more extensive than the Appalachian shale. The only commercial activity was quarrying slabs of shale which, when polished to a lustrous, dark-wood finish, made handsome table tops. This attitude began to change during the early 1900s when, due to the growing numbers of internal combustion engines and the developing European war, concern grew about possible domestic crude oil shortages. In 1913, the Geological Survey decided to conduct an extensive investigation of the Green River shales which, having been part of a huge 334-million-acre plot obtained from Mexico at the end of the Mexican-American War in 1848 for $15 million, were almost totally government-owned. During the summer of 1915, a USGS geologist named Dean L. Winchester led a party to survey and sample the lands, and after he returned to Washington in the fall he began computations to determine the total amount of the potentially recoverable shale oil. To his surprise, the figure came to 20 billion barrels, more than three times the estimated national petroleum reserves. Skeptical superiors ordered him to recheck his calculations. The following summer, he returned to the shale lands and after an even more detailed analysis, he reported he had indeed been in error. The figure should have been 40 billion barrels. That year, USGS published Winchester's first comprehensive report *Oil Shale in Northwestern Colorado and Adjacent Areas,* which concluded that the Green River Formation constituted "a latent petroleum reserve whose possible yield is several times the estimated total remaining supply of petroleum in the United States." In his annual report the following year, Secretary of the Interior Franklin K. Lane stated that "as a result of the investigation of the western oil shales it is believed that it is now commercially feasible to work selected deposits of shale in competition with oil from oil wells, and that these oil-shale reserves can be considered of immediate importance to the oil industry and to the defense of the nation." Newspapers and magazines leaped eagerly upon these ideas. Perhaps the apogee of euphoria was a 1918 story in *The National Geographic Magazine* titled "Billions of Barrels Locked up in Rocks." It gushed:

> As the great Creator, through his servants of old, caused water to flow from the rock in the wilderness, so, through twentieth century science, He is

causing oil, for ages locked up in the shales of America, to be released for the relief of human necessity. . . .

No man who owns a motor-car will fail to rejoice that the United States Geological Survey is pointing the way to supplies of gasoline which can meet any demand that even his children's children for generations to come may make of them. The horseless vehicle's threatened dethronement [due to oil shortages] has been definitely averted and the uninviting prospect of a motorless age has ceased to be a ghost stalking the vista of the future. . . .

The United States is indeed a country blessed by a generous Providence. . . . No sooner does one of our resources show limitations in production and the pessimists begin to cry, "What shall we do when our reserve is gone?" than immense additional deposits or satisfactory substitutes are discovered. . . . No one may be bold enough to foretell what tremendous figure of production may be reached within the next ten years.

All of this precipitated a wild land rush. Hundreds of prospectors swarmed over the shale lands and under the authority of the 1872 Mining Law staked over 30,000 claims covering some four million acres in Colorado, and perhaps another 120,000 claims in Utah and Wyoming. . . .

The 1920 Mineral Leasing Act prevented further filing of mining claims for oil shale and said publicly owned shale lands could only be leased by the Secretary of the Interior. But the boom did not abate. More than two hundred oil shale corporations were founded. Many were simply stock promotion outfits which bilked unsuspecting investors on the basis of a few acres of shale holdings and grandiose promises of future bonanzas. A concern called the American Oil Shale and Refining Company set up a small model retort in a booth on State Street in Chicago and sold stock certificates to passersby impressed by the billowing clouds of black smoke which, they were assured, represented pure 100 percentage oil, and there was a lot more where that came from.

A large number of the new organizations were legitimate, but their operators found that getting oil from shale was considerably more difficult than panning gold nuggets from a stream or drilling an oil well. Typically, these firms consisted of four or five men who would build a wooden tramway from a cliff-face mine to a crude oven-like retort jerry-built with a variety of belts, pipes, scoops, and the like. A very few, modeled after the Pumpherston Retort, were capable of continuous operation, but most were batch-type contraptions. The presence of scientific controls of any kind was rare. The oil shalers usually found themselves fortunate in the course of a year of sweat, experiment, and expenditure of the group's collective savings to produce a few dozen barrels of oil. The Monarch Shale Oil Company proudly brandished to potential stockholders a certificate signed by the mayor, the head of the Chamber of Commerce, and the chief cashier of the bank in the town of DeBeque, one of several boom towns to spring up on the banks of the Colorado, which read: "To whom it may concern: we personally measured the oil as it came out of the spout [of Monarch's retort] and the flow was continuous and at the rate of 2 gallons each minute." How long this relatively cornucopia-like flow was maintained was not stated, but Monarch's only recorded commercial success was the sale of 25 barrels of shale oil to Glenwood Springs, a town near Rifle, to oil the streets. The output of most retorts ended up as such somewhat ignominious products as sheep dip, soap, dandruff treatments, tars, and various medicinal remedies.

The most ambitious shale undertaking of this era by far was Catlin Shale Products Company, organized by Robert M. Catlin, a native of Burlington, Vermont. In 1875, while working as a mining engineer, he became intrigued by smouldering fires in dumps of waste material near Elko, Nevada, that had been left by the Central Pacific Railroad Company while making tests in coal beds along its right-of-way. He discovered the source of the fires to be beds of paraffin shales, which are similar to oil shales except the organic content of the latter is higher. He resolved to discover whether a commercial operation was feasible. A member of the American Institute of Mining and Metallurgical Engineers and former chief mining officer with the New Jersey Zinc Company, Catlin had no illusions about what he was attempting. "One of the unfortunate features of the matter," he wrote to a friend, "seems to me is that anybody can produce oil from the shale so easily. People take a crooked pipe and in an ordinary fire get some oily results and the imagination does the rest."

Catlin purchased and leased some land from Central Pacific, in the late 1890s and over the next thirty years invested perhaps as much as a half million dollars of his own money—he never sold stock—in a series of three retorts. The last, built in 1921, was quite sophisticated: continuously operating, internally heated, thermally self-sufficient, it was 40 feet high, and assisted by a 16-man crew, it could process 250 tons of rock daily and produce nearly 50 barrels of shale oil. Uniquely, the company was fully integrated: it mined rock, crushed it, retorted it, refined the oil, and even retailed it through a rudimentary marketing organization. Though Catlin Shale Products did not earn a profit as such, it did find a market for many of its products. Fuel oil was sold locally to the power company and to individuals for heating and powering small tractors and motors. Lubricating oil was sold through garages in Nevada and California. Several hundred tons of paraffin wax were shipped overseas—indeed paraffin wax was used by New Jersey Zinc in zinc production, which was probably a principal reason Catlin persisted with the more paraffinic Nevada shales. Union Oil Company of California, the most active of the major oil companies in shale during this period, made a thorough study of his process, though it eventually took no action.

For reasons that are not entirely clear, Catlin closed his retort down in 1924. He apparently had regarded his operations until then as mainly an experiment and had felt that to run his company on a profitable basis he would have to raise a large amount of capital to improve substantially the capacity of his equipment. Especially he needed money for an improved refinery, since many of his products were inadequately distilled and purged of impurities and had difficulty competing against the products of crude oil refineries. The problems he encountered raising funds are unknown. One was probably a decline in crude oil prices due to new oil field discoveries in California, Texas, and Oklahoma. By 1924 the price of crude had dropped to less than half its 1920 level, and prices were to decline much more before the end of the decade. Further, the lean, thin (less than five feet), often tilted and folded shale beds near Elko probably seemed to potential investors a far less likely location for a shale oil industry than the Piceance Creek Basin. Catlin himself was by now well into his 70s, and his zeal may have been waning. In any event, on December 23, 1930, Catlin Shale Products Company, the United States' first and only continuously operating commercial shale corporation, was formally dissolved. Catlin assigned remaining assets, less than $3,800, to his son.

By that year, most of the other oil shale corporations had long since either gone bankrupt or had been otherwise dissolved. Those that had not were soon vanquished by "generous Providence" which in 1930 blessed the nation with the gigantic six-billion-barrel East Texas oil field—until the discovery of the Prudhoe Bay fields on the North Slope of Alaska, the largest ever found in North America. This caused such a glut that crude prices dropped as low as 10¢ a barrel. (Crude prices today average around $3.10 a barrel at the well.)

To this day, the oil shale industry has never revived. There have been periods of heightened interest, caused by fears of crude oil shortages, and at one point students at Cornell University spent six years drawing up plans for a city of 300,000 they felt certain would soon rise up near Rifle. But the only commercially operating shale industry today consists of a man named Mike Cross, a local Rifle jeweler who sells polished oil shale pins and tie clasps to tourists.

The occasional articles on oil shale that have appeared in magazines and newspapers over the past few decades—typical titles are "Colorado's Fabulous Mountains of Oil," "Is Shale-Oil Boom on the Way at Last?" and "Giant Oil Shale Industry is Waking"—have had a common theme; there is certainly a great deal of oil shale out there in the Colorado mountains, but unfortunately it just costs too much money to get the oil out of the shale. . . .

Belief has been solidified, therefore, in the minds of the public, most government officials, and even some people with broad acquaintance with oil shale, in two apparent truisms:

1. *The reason there has been no development of the oil shale is because development is not yet economically feasible.*

2. *As soon as it becomes economically feasible, oil shale development will occur.*

It does not require much investigation to discover serious flaws in these "truisms." One reads for instance numerous statements that shale oil production is "nearly competitive" with crude oil production. Why then, especially if the oil shale deposits are so rich, is hardly any research being directed toward developing shale oil production techniques?

Attempting to get beyond the truisms is like wandering through a massive, high-walled labyrinth enveloped in smoke, with many false exits and dead ends. Finally, two large controlling entities are revealed: the federal government and the oil industry. The federal government, specifically the Department of the Interior, as the guardian of the 85 percent share of the shale contained in public land, has always been considered the logical party to encourage development of the shale land. The oil industry, as the possessor of petroleum technology and the refining and marketing organization through which shale oil must eventually flow, has always been considered the logical party to develop the shale. Both, though, have acted not unlike a reluctant bride and bridegroom at a shotgun wedding. In the face of demands for action, they have inched forward slowly, ever so slowly, toward the altar, but their hearts have not been in it. At the rate they have been progressing, they will not get there for a long, long time. Meanwhile, the old oil shalers in the dusty towns on the banks of the Colorado continue to gaze longingly at the white cliffs and wait and hope.

THE U.S. SYNTHETICS INDUSTRY

Just after World War II the United States entered another of its periodic oil shortages. OIL SHORTAGES HERE TO STAY, proclaimed the headlines, and the U.S. government embarked on a program to build synthetic oil plants. Julius Krug, Harry Truman's secretary of the interior, presided over the opening of two of these new plants. They were to be operated in the town of Louisiana, Missouri, by the Bureau of Mines. "Truly these plants that surround us here today," said Krug at the opening ceremony, "are the forerunners of a vast new oil and chemical industry. . . . We have shown that liquid fuels can be made out of coal at a price not too greatly above oil prices."

These pilot plants were built to test out the commercial feasibility of the very Bergius process for changing coal into liquid petroleum which I.G. Farben had pioneered in Germany in the 1920s and Hitler's synthetics plants had brought to fruition during the war (see p. 221). They were also to test a second German method, the Fischer-Tropsch synthesis gas process, which converts coal first to gas and then to liquid petroleum. Much as the American military with little experience in rocketry called on the assistance of Hitler's V-1 and V-2 missile experts, so American oilmen turned to the German synthetics scientists and technicians who had set up and run synfuels plants during the war. For four years, with the help of German techniques and technicians, the Missouri plants did turn coal into a variety of oil products, including gasoline used by cars near the site, and one million gallons of gasoline used by vehicles at defense installations.

By 1953, however, the oil shortage was over. In fact, the country was drowning in oil, and the new administration of Dwight D. Eisenhower promptly closed the synthetics plants both for economic reasons and because the plants were run by the government, not private industry.

The oilmen who initially had bridled at government intervention in their business when the synthetics plants were built, now wanted the government to stem the tide of cheap Middle Eastern oil that was flowing into the country, endangering their business. Thus ended the first "successful" U.S. experiment in synthetics.

Since then there have been several different efforts to establish a synthetic fuels industry, most notably Jimmy Carter's proposals for creating a large-scale government-subsidized industry. (Despite his stated opposition to government involvement in a business that should be left to private industry, Ronald Reagan went forward with plans for this subsidized industry.) The following article by Donald L. Bartlett and James B. Steele of the Philadelphia *Inquirer* meticulously reports on what happened to some of these experiments.

The general background needs to be kept constantly in mind: By the mid-1960s the major oil companies had bought themselves imposing positions in the coal industry (see p. 54 and p. 315). In part, this diversification was a hedge against ripening nationalist tendencies in the Middle East (see p. 136.). Once more, fearing a loss of Middle Eastern oil profits, they became interested in the feasibility of a synthetics industry. But as Barlett and Steele suggest, while the oil companies prudently kept a hand in synthetics, their real concern was the persistent worldwide surplus of oil which ensured that synthetics would remain on the back burner.

Taken from "Energy Anarchy," by Donald L. Barlett and James B. Steele, Philadelphia Inquirer, *December 7–13, 1980.*

In Rapid City, S.D., the federal government opened a pilot synthetic fuel plant in 1972. For the next several years, the plant converted low-grade coal to synthetic natural gas. An Interior Department report to Congress predicted that "a commercial plant . . . could be in operation early in the 1980s."

Today, the Rapid City plant is shuttered, its equipment in mothballs.

In Princeton, N.J., another federally financed synthetic fuel plant—this one to turn coal into high-grade oil—also was operating in 1972. It was a big success, according to Interior Department reports to Congress in 1972 and 1973, and was certain to "get into the marketplace quite fast."

Today, the Princeton plant has vanished, its equipment dismantled and carted away.

In Bruceton, Pa., the federal government dedicated a pilot coal gasification plant in 1975. Three years later, the Department of Energy told Congress that the plant proved it was possible to make synthetic natural gas from coal and to price it competitively with conventional natural gas.

Today, the Bruceton plant sits empty, the engineers and technicians who ran it long gone.

Those abandoned synthetic fuel plants and more than a half-dozen others like them litter the nation's landscape, monuments to a national energy policy gone wrong. . . .

Thirty-three years ago, in December 1947, an internal memorandum circulated in the Interior Department projected that within "a period of four to five years" a federally subsidized synthetic fuels industry could result in "the production of 2 million barrels" of petroleum products daily. (A barrel contains 42 gallons.)

But in June 1979, after President Carter's call for just such an undertaking, a Library of Congress study concluded that "even if substantial federal incentives" were offered," synthetic fuel production would total no more than "160,000 to 200,000 barrels" daily by 1998.

Incredibly, after four decades of research, funded with hundreds of millions of taxpayers' dollars, the federal government has concluded that this country is capable of producing only one-tenth of the goal set in 1947—and taking twice as long to accomplish even that.

Why is this?

The technology for converting coal to synthetic oil and gas has existed in the United States for a half-century or more, and through most of those years various federal agencies have engaged in synthetic fuel research.

In 1949, for example, the Bureau of Mines opened twin synthetic fuel plants at Louisiana, Mo., that turned coal into a variety of petroleum products, including gasoline used in plant vehicles and diesel fuel used experimentally to power Burlington Railroad engines.

The tests established, according to government reports, that gasoline made from coal would cost about "3 to 4 cents" a gallon more than gasoline made from crude, or about 30 to 31 cents per gallon. It was expected that cost could be reduced through experience and the sale of by-products.

Ever since, the federal government has been opening and closing similar experimental plants. But all have failed in their avowed purpose of setting the stage for timely production of synthetic fuels for sale to the general public.

They have failed because Congress has refused to set specific, mandatory long-range synthetic fuel objectives—and then stick by them.

They have failed because the oil industry for many years actively discouraged serious synthetic fuel research, especially during the years when the oil companies had no coal holdings.

They have failed because the same oil industry, which now possesses substantial coal holdings, still prefers to buy oil from foreign suppliers rather than produce synthetic fuels from domestic resources.

And they have failed because there are enormous reserves of conventional crude oil worldwide, and it is more profitable to produce and sell that oil than invest in costly coal conversion plants.

None of this, though, has stopped the federal government from squandering hundreds of millions of dollars on devising a growing number of different ways of turning coal into liquid petroleum products and gas—without ever actually following through with commercial production.

With all this emphasis on research, one might assume that the process of converting coal into synthetic fuels is awaiting some major technological breakthrough.

Such is not the case. In truth, the technology for turning coal into synthetic gas has been around for almost two centuries. The technology for turning coal into synthetic crude oil has been around for more than a century. . . .

The new industry that turned coal into oil and gas flourished for about 75 years. But with the introduction of the electric light, and the growing use of conventional oil and natural gas for heating, demand for oil and gas made from coal gradually eroded, disappearing in the 1930s.

Still, as late as 1920, there were nearly 1,000 gas plants in this country that produced gas made from coal to either light or heat 9 million homes and businesses.

Throughout World War II, German industry kept the Luftwaffe flying largely on aviation gasoline made from coal in plants that produced nearly 100,000 barrels of petroleum products daily.

And the government of South Africa, which has operated a coal-fed synthetic fuel plant since the mid-1950s, currently is expanding the facility into the world's largest commercial coal-to-oil-and-gas complex, reducing that country's dependence on foreign oil.

The world's nearly 200 years of synthetic fuel experience notwithstanding, the United States has yet to build its first modern commercial coal conversion plant.

What it has managed to do is build one pilot plant or demonstration plant after another—all financed by the American taxpayer—to conduct an endless series of tests.

Each of those plants was a scaled-down version, from a tenth to a hundredth the size of a commercial facility. Each was built and operated at a cost of about $100 million or less.

Now the government is gearing up to spend not hundreds of millions, but billions and billions of taxpayers' dollars on yet a new generation of synthetic fuel testing facilities.

With passage in June of the Energy Security Act—an energy Christmas tree that provides something for everyone—Congress created the Synthetic Fuels Corporation, which has the power to dole out $88 billion over the next 10 years.

The billions will finance still more pilot and demonstration plants and an assortment of lesser energy experiments—from schemes for the production of soybean oil to replace diesel fuel to the production of synthetic natural gas from rice hulls.

The government's grand multibillion-dollar energy giveaway plan will do nothing to end American dependence on hostile foreign oil producers in the 1980s—the period when the nation will be most vulnerable to supply disruptions because of a large imbalance between U.S. oil production and consumption—but it will please some powerful constituencies.

For the nation's largest oil companies, the marketing of commercial synthetic fuels will be delayed until the companies are ready to profit handsomely from their introduction.

For the federal energy bureaucracy, it means more dollars than ever to spend, more work to oversee, more studies to complete, more positions to fill—with salaries that now range up to $175,000 a year.

For politicians in Congress, Democrats and Republicans both, it means concrete examples—albeit meaningless ones—of their efforts to solve the nation's energy problems.

And for the cottage industry supported by the federal research dollars—universities, think tanks and research firms across the country—it means more contracts, more jobs. . . .

While President-elect Ronald Reagan expressed some skepticism over the projects in the early days of the campaign, he has since tempered his views.

More importantly, some of Reagan's key advisers are as deeply committed to the new synthetic fuel ventures as are the departing Carter administrators.

William J. Casey, the head of Reagan's transition team [now director of the CIA] is a founder and director of Energy Transition Corporation, a Washington consulting firm that specializes in helping companies to win lucrative government energy contracts.

The company—whose president is Robert W. Fri, former acting administrator of the Energy Research and Development Administration—describes its services, in part, this way:

"To minimize the risk and enhance the profitability of [energy] projects, Energy Transition Corp. serves its clients by . . . assisting in the conception, planning, and management of major projects, new ventures, and technology introduction . . . [and] interpreting the policies of, and assisting in relations with, U.S. and foreign governments."

So it is, then, that enthusiasm for synthetic fuels crosses administrations and party lines. It has been ever so. . . .

Back in the spring of 1951, James Boyd, director of the Bureau of Mines in the Interior Department, advised a House Appropriations subcommittee that his department's research would "provide the basis for a new industry in this country . . .

"As we improve [the technology]," Boyd said, "we improve the economics. It has reached the stage of an economic question as affected by new techniques in the process. We have produced oil from coal, but we are trying to reduce the cost of it."

More than a quarter-century later, during the spring of 1978, Robert D. Thorne, assistant secretary for energy technology in the Energy Department, assured a Senate Appropriations subcommittee that work on coal gasification and liquefaction processes was proceeding nicely.

In response to a question as to whether the government was moving "as rapidly as (it) could," Thorne declared:

"I believe we're moving ahead at a satisfactory, even somewhat accelerated, pace."

An "accelerated pace"?

In August 1963, Interior Secretary Stewart L. Udall signed a $10 million contract with Consolidation Coal Co. to build a pilot synthetic fuel plant at Cresap, W. Va., to test a Consolidation process to turn coal into gasoline.

Nearly three years later, the Cresap plant, designed to convert 24 tons of coal a day into 72 barrels of gasoline, was still under construction.

Nonetheless, Office of Coal Research officials confirmed for members of Congress projections that the Consolidation process, designated "Project Gasoline," would produce gasoline that would sell for less than 14 cents a gallon.

Sidney D. Larson, an Office of Coal Research budget director, told a House Appropriations subcommittee in February 1966 that the pilot plant, which was to begin shakedown operations in the fall of that year, "was intended to prove out the process which will produce gasoline for this range of 10½ to 13 cents in a commercial plant."

In March 1969, Neal P. Cochran, chief of the division of utilization in the Office of Coal Research, reassured members of the same House Appropriations subcommittee that—even after three years of rising costs and inflation—Project Gasoline still would produce gasoline at under 14 cents a gallon. "We believe we are, even with the increased costs, under the proper assumptions of success with what we are currently doing at Cresap and in other parts of the program, that we would not change those numbers today. They would still be in the range of 11½ to 13½ cents per gallon," Cochran testified.

A year later, in February 1970, an official of Consolidation Coal Co., by then a subsidiary of Continental Oil Co., reasserted the favorable economics of making gasoline from coal during a synthetic fuel symposium at the Colorado School of Mines.

"The pilot plant program to date has yielded very encouraging results," the Consolidation executive said, adding that "an economic evaluation of the process, based on these results, reaffirms the conclusion that gasoline can be produced to sell at the refinery in the range of 11 to 13 cents per gallon."

At the time, dealers paid 17 to 18 cents a gallon and the retail price of gasoline at service stations, including taxes, averaged 34 to 35 cents a gallon.

The glowing predictions of federal and coal company officials notwithstanding, the Cresap plant—whose technology was hailed by Consolidation as the "farthest advanced" of synthetic fuel processes—shut down in April 1970.

The Cresap facility, which employed about 150 persons, never did produce gasoline from coal that could be sold for 11 to 13 cents a gallon, as everyone had confidently promised. In fact, it produced very little gasoline at all.

As federal officials later explained in a report to Congress:

"Mechanical problems causing interruption to process runs and data collection precluded proof of the process. . . . The Consolidation Coal Co. endeavored to obtain good experimental operation of the plant. This was never achieved." . . .

The Cresap synthetic fuel plant remained idle until 1974, when the Office of Coal Research awarded a contract to the Fluor Corp. to start up the plant and conduct experiments with another process, this one to convert coal into fuel oil.

The federal agency explained its newest venture this way to the House Appropriations subcommittee in March 1974:

"The program for reactivation of facilities at Cresap, W. Va., will modify the existing pilot plant to produce clean low-sulfur fuel oil from coal for power generation and industrial use."

That synthetic fuel venture fared no better than Project Gasoline, and by 1975 the Energy Research and Development Administration (ERDA) was using the elaborate Cresap facility, according to a report submitted to Congress, "to determine the reliability of conventional equipment such as valves, pumps, etc., all of which are equipment common to most liquefaction processes."

A year later, in the spring of 1976, ERDA's assistant administrator for fossil energy, Philip C. White, told a House Appropriations subcommittee that his office was continuing to test equipment at Cresap—where the federal government's total investment had passed the $62 million mark.

White explained his office's thinking on Cresap thusly:

"One of the things we are trying to do in this program is to do enough auxiliary work so that the reliability of these plants when we build them will be significantly high . . . This is sufficiently important, we feel, to be worth a pretty good part of our budget, and Cresap is aimed in that direction." . . .

Today, the Cresap plant, located along the Ohio River about 19 miles south of Wheeling, is abandoned. The costly equipment for converting coal into synthetic fuels, spread over acres of land, sits idle. The buildings and laboratories are boarded up.

The plant that failed to develop the promised commercial process for turning coal into 13-cent-a-gallon gasoline also failed to develop the promised commercial process for converting coal to low-sulfur fuel oil, and gave up on conducting equipment tests once-deemed essential to the successful operation of other synthetic fuel facilities.

In 1973, while the Cresap plant was resting between experiments, engineering design work was started for the construction of a process development unit—a miniature pilot plant—at the Battelle Memorial Institute's engineering station at West Jefferson, Ohio, just outside Columbus.

The pilot plant was designed to test the agglomerating burner gasification process, converting 25 tons of coal a day into 1 million cubic feet of synthetic natural gas.

In the spring of 1973, the Office of Coal Research told a House Appropriations subcommittee that the Battelle research work was "important to all other gasification projects."

A year later, in another report on coal conversion research, the Interior Department described the Battelle project as "vital to coal gasification efforts," saying its "potential contribution to technological and economic feasibility is critical."

The plant started up in 1976, and in the spring of 1978 the Energy Department expressed satisfaction with experimental runs in a report to a Senate Appropriations subcommittee.

Shortly thereafter, the "vital" pilot plant was shut down. A spokeswoman for Battelle now says only that the Energy Department "decided to discontinue the plant." The results of the tests, she said, are unknown.

An Energy Department official was more forthright. Asked why the plant, once described as "critical" to the federal government's coal gasification efforts, had closed, he replied:

"It [the agglomerating burner process] just didn't look commercially attractive. . . ." . . .

At the same time the Office of Coal Research was financing construction of the Chicago pilot plants operated by the Institute of Gas Technology, it also was underwriting work on a synthetic fuel plant in Rapid City, S.D.

This project dated to June 1964, when the Office of Coal Research awarded another contract to Consolidation Coal Co., which was already building its government-funded coal-to-gasoline pilot plant at Cresap, W. Va., to develop another coal conversion technology.

The second Consolidation process, the "CO_2 Acceptor Process," was designed to turn lignite—a brown, wood-like sub-bituminous coal—into synthetic natural gas.

Consolidation subcontracted the building and operation of the Rapid City plant to Stearns-Roger Corp., a Denver-based engineering and construction company.

In the spring of 1972, eight years after the first contract had been awarded to Consolidation, the Office of Coal Research advised a House Appropriations subcommittee that "the CO_2 Acceptor Process bench-scale research has been successfully completed and a pilot plant has been constructed. . . ." The report continued:

"The pilot plant, completed in February 1972, is undergoing 'shakedown' operations. Technical information and data based on operations will begin to accumulate during 1972. Assuming successful operations, a commercial plant producing pipeline gas from lignite could be in operation early in the 1980s."

Two years later, in March 1974, S. William Gouse, Jr., acting director of the Office of Coal Research, told a House Appropriations subcommittee that the Rapid City pilot plant was "showing substantial progress towards operation, according to design . . . The whole plant is onstream." He added:

"What these pilot plants are showing us now is that the chemical process is functioning as we thought it would, producing gas as we thought it would and producing the right amounts from the coal."

Today, the multimillion-dollar gasification plant is closed, the equipment to convert lignite into synthetic natural gas in mothballs. A spokesman for the Department of Energy now says, "The test program was successfully completed."

But the tests indicated, he said, that "it was not economically feasible to use that process to make gas." There will be no commercial plant using the CO_2 Acceptor Process in the early 1980s—as federal officials had once predicted—or even the late 1980s.

The record of the federal government and the Consolidation Coal Co., which became a subsidiary of Continental Oil Co. in 1965, stands at 0-3 in the testing of synthetic fuel technologies at two different pilot plants built at a cost to taxpayers of about $100 million.

While the three processes worked technically, in that the plants turned lignite or coal into synthetic natural gas, gasoline or fuel oil, the development of the technologies has failed to lead to the construction of a full-scale commercial plant. . . .

Not all the federal government pilot synthetic fuel plants have been abandoned. Some are still operating like the coal gasification facility in Homer City, Pa., that is testing the Bi-Gas process.

Nearly a decade ago, in the spring of 1971, the Office of Coal Research, seeking funds to build the Homer City plant, submitted a report to a House Appropriations subcommittee offering this assessment of the Bi-Gas project:

"Conclusion of the pilot plant program can be expected to provide data and process variables to design complete commercial plants."

During an appearance before a House Appropriations subcommittee the following year, [Robert] Dole, the assistant interior secretary, gave a progress report on construction and reaffirmed his department's belief that the Homer City plant would lead to the building of commercial synthetic fuel facilities:

"We have let the contracts out, and are receiving them at the present time. We expect to have these bids accepted sometime later on, and hopefully, groundbreaking will come sometime this spring . . .

"The purpose of the whole program is to arrive at high-BTU [British thermal unit] gas through the pilot plant stage, so that we can get into the demonstration scale plant sometime around 1975–76, in order that a commercial plant will be available for construction sometime around the end of the decade [1970s], the early part of the next decade [1980s]."

The formal groundbreaking followed in July 1972. Six years later, in May 1978, the Energy Department forwarded this report on work at the Homer City plant to a Senate Appropriations subcommittee:

"Construction of a fully integrated pilot plant was completed in fiscal year 1976, but due to the complexity of the process considerable delay was encountered and a long period of shakedown and start-up activities were required, and it was not until fiscal 1978 that short, continuous operations could be achieved."

Today, when the Bi-Gas process, by the prediction of federal energy officials, was to be ready for use in commercial synthetic fuel plants, the Homer City facility is still running tests.

When an Inquirer reporter visited the plant in October 1979, a spokesman for Stearns-Roger Corp., which is operating the facility under contract to the Energy Department, said, "We still have another year or two to define the economics of the process."

At the time, the plant—scaled to a hundredth the size of a commercial plant —had failed to process the five tons an hour, or 120 tons a day, that it had been designed to handle.

Instead, the plant was run for two to four days at a stretch, at below the five-ton-per-hour design, and then shut down.

The coal then being gasified at the Homer City site, which is surrounded by some of the richest coal fields in western Pennsylvania, was shipped in from Montana because it was easier to process.

As for the synthetic natural gas made from the coal, it was flared—burned off —because it was too impure to use as fuel even in the plant's specially designed boilers.

Commenting on the work in progress, a plant spokesman said in October 1979: "We feel we should have another two years to either complete the project or define what must still be done."

In September 1980, one year after the visit to the Homer City facility, an Inquirer reporter asked the same Stearns-Roger official how work was progressing at the plant, where the government's investment will soon pass $100 million. Said he:

"Still basically the same. We are making more progress in our operation. We are still operating up and down, you know, and that kind of thing, but making more progress all the time.

"The Department of Energy has decided they want to continue at least one more year, through fiscal 1981, so we're still right on target, right on course, moving right along."

Has the plant operated for any longer periods than the two-to-four-day runs of last year?

"We've had a good five-day run."

And how much synthetic natural gas was produced during those five days?

"Oh, we don't measure it. We really don't look at it, you know. It's just no advantage to us. We're more interested in looking at the performance of the gasifier . . . So we just haven't really pinned it down."

Has any of the synthetic natural gas been burned to generate heat or power?

"No, we strictly run it through a thermal oxidizer, burn it in a thermal oxidizer. That's an environmental word for flare."

And the coal is still being shipped in from Montana?

"Oh, yes, Rosebud coal. Yeah, we're still on that. We'll probably be on that for a while longer."

Obviously, no commercial Bi-Gas plant was built in the late 1970s, as had been envisioned by the Interior Department at the beginning of the decade. Nor, does it seem likely, will there be any commercial Bi-Gas plants in the late 1980s.

This, then, is the federal government's record in synthetic fuel development:

More than a dozen pilot coal conversion plants and experimental facilities erected since the 1940s, some abandoned, some still sputtering along.

All proved what has been known for at least 100 years: that it is chemically possible to turn coal into synthetic fuels—with some processes potentially competitive, in price, with conventional oil and gas, some not.

All failed to come close to meeting their advance promises. All failed to result in the production of synthetic fuels for sale to the general public.

All these plants were built to test a different coal conversion technology. In simplest terms, coal is turned into synthetic oil or gas simply by adding hydrogen.

But there are scores of different processes. The coal may be heated in the absence of air. It may be reacted with steam and air or oxygen. It may be reacted with hydrogen.

A variety of different catalysts may be introduced to improve the conversion.

Temperature and pressure may be adjusted up or down. The coal may be ground into a granular form, mixed in a slurry or processed in lumps. The equipment may be adjusted to turn out all liquid fuel, solid fuel, gas or some combination of the three.

All these variations may be likened to recipes. Assume for the moment that Nabisco intends to market a new chocolate cookie.

The company's bakers experiment with any number of recipes, adding or subtracting ingredients until they come up with the desired formula. Eventually they agree on a single recipe and begin mass production of chocolate cookies.

But the government and the oil industry, after a half-century of experiments, are still testing recipes, substituting ingredients, unable to settle on one, two or even three, and to then actually begin mass production of synthetic fuels.

Energy Secretary James R. Schlesinger himself acknowledged the problem in April 1979, when he testified about federal energy research projects before a House Appropriations subcommittee.

"In the gasification area," Schlesinger said, "we have got half a dozen processes. We have got the Hygas, Synthane, Bi-Gas, slagging Lurgi, normal Lurgi and so forth, and each of these things has cost differentials of 5 cents per thousand cubic feet, or maybe it's 9-cents per thousand cubic feet.

"The real question is whether you are going to have a process that looks reasonably good commercially. In my judgment, we should pick one and get on with it, or pick two or three and get on with them, instead of going on and inventing more and more new processes.

"We could go on. The number of processes is virtually infinite. We could have 50 to 75 processes that we could continue to put a little bit of money into each year.

"It is not going to solve the national problem, but it is going to keep a lot of research and development types happy."

And indeed it will. For the federal government has already started to spend not hundreds of millions, but billions of taxpayers' dollars to build and operate more pilot and demonstration synthetic fuel plants.

One of these test facilities, operated under a government contract by Ashland Oil Inc., started up in June at Catlettsburg, Ky. Designed to test a technology known as H-Coal, the plant is supposed to process 600 tons of coal a day into about 1,800 barrels of synthetic oil.

More than 120 years ago another synthetic fuel plant started up in Kentucky. By the close of the 1850s, the facility was turning Kentucky coal into 2,000 barrels of synthetic oil every week, and selling its products as far west as Chicago.

A century later, progress is not so swift.

HEALTH HAZARDS

Were a large-scale synthetics fuel industry to be set up, it would necessarily be linked to the extensive coal strip mining planned along the eastern slope of the Rockies and out onto the Great Plains where ecosystems are fragile. The result would undoubtedly be to increase the sorts of environmental damage to which strip mining is already prone. Many of the same phenomena we have already seen associated with strip mining (see p. 72) would occur with a synthetics industry consuming enormous amounts of coal or oil shale. Huge towns or even small cities, with populations of tens of thousands, would spring up in remote rural areas to support such an industry (these, in turn, putting undue pressure on the resources of fragile ecosystems). For the synthetics plants themselves, in addition to the coal, enormous amounts of potentially scarce water supplies would have to be drawn from depleting water tables mainly to moisten the hot spent shale before disposal, and as the following article indicates, the actual health hazards to industry workers and to those who might live in the vicinity of a synthetics operation would potentially be high.

Taken from "Synthetic Fuels and Cancer," by Diane Yale Sauter, Scientists' Institute for Public Information, November 1975.

. . . The carcinogenicity of synthetic fuels results from the chemical composition of the raw materials from which they are derived—the kerogens in oil shale and bitumens in coal—and also from the temperatures at which they are processed, which form and release a wide range of polycyclic aromatic hydrocarbons (PAH). PAH as a family are the earliest known carcinogens. Those established in their carcinogenicity to humans are benzopyrenes and benzanthracenes.

Polycyclic aromatic hydrocarbon compounds are lipid soluble, and enter cells easily. Because of their circular molecular shape, they fit into the structure of DNA —hence their designation as "intercalating agents"—and begin to react with it. Enzymes in the cell are mobilized to repair damage thus caused to the DNA, but the repair process itself initiates mutation in the genetic material where the PAH occurred. The mutation is duplicated in daughter cells when the parent cell divides, and can be the beginning of cancer.

Healthy mouse embryo cells have been morphologically transformed by the addition of pure benzo(a)pyrene (formerly called 3, 4 benzpyrene) under laboratory conditions. When these cells were inoculated back into mice, subcutaneous sarcomas [cancers] developed. . . .

Workers with occupational exposure to synthetic fuels will be in particularly serious jeopardy, although even with controlled plant emissions, the general public will also be at risk. This was acknowledged in the Synfuels Interagency Task Force report submitted to the President's Energy Resources Council: "Some damage to . . . humans from air pollutants may be unavoidable. Adverse human health effects, including cancer, might result from long-term exposure to polycyclic aromatic hydrocarbons and trace elements emitted from synthetic fuel plants in the form of or adsorbed on fine particulates. Some increase in sulfur dioxide, nitrogen oxides, trace elements, hydrocarbons and respirable particulates will occur even though emission controls are employed and air quality standards are enforced." . . .

A synergistic as well as additive hazard is indicated by some researchers. The air-borne presence of nitrogen- and sulphur-containing molecules (present in relatively low concentrations in the petroleum industry) could agument the development of skin and lung cancer, . . . a co-carcinogenic effect which has been confirmed in animal experiments. . . .

The Task Force report continues: "Construction and use of synthetic fuels processing plants can . . . cause release of toxic waste into streams, and return of production water to stream channels. Even with controls, some release would occur . . ."

SHALE OIL

The human carcinogens benzo(a)pyrene, benzo(e)pyrene, and benzo(a) anthracene and other PAH are present in shale oil. Benzo(a) pyrene would be contained in the waste processing waters, and in compounds used to remove the benzo(a) pyrene from waste water. . . . Shale oil fractions without benzopyrene have as well been shown to be carcinogenic when applied to mice. . . .

The carcinogenic potential of shale oil has been known since 1876, when cancer of the scrotum was first described in a Scottish shale oil worker. Between 1920 and 1943, there were over 1,000 verified cases of skin cancer in the British mule spinning industry, which then used shale oil to lubricate spindles. . . . Skin cancer has also been reported in workers in contact with the retort (combustion) tars . . . light oils, waxes and cutting oils derived from shale. . . .

Shale oils are generally more carcinogenic than any of the petroleum oils. A worker exposed to shale oil is at worst fifty times more liable to get skin cancer than a worker in contact with oil from a Pennsylvania well. . . .

Each shale oil plant of the size currently being proposed—50,000 barrels per day—would process up to 30 million tons of oil shale per year. . . . Spent (waste) shale from surface retorting would amount to as much as 26 million tons per year, containing over 300 tons of carcinogenic materials, and covering 50 surface acres of waste for each year of operation. . . .

Disposal would include the filling of canyons in the West, and the building of soil banks in the East. Leachate into the groundwater and surface run-off containing polycyclic aromatic hydrocarbons, as well as lead, mercury and other toxic trace metals, would enter the food chain. In addition, 300 million gallons of PAH-laden waste water would be produced during the retorting process alone.

One such facility would employ 1,100 to 1,500 operating personnel. The total incremental population of a surrounding new town to support the plant is estimated to be about 11,000 to 14,000 people. . . . The Federal Energy Administration's Project Independence Blueprint projects five of these plants in operation by 1985, in towns housing up to 70,000 people, including up to 7,500 shale oil workers.

LIQUEFIED COAL

At least 200 individual chemicals have been isolated and identified which are liberated when coal is liquefied, including benzo(a)pyrene.

Between 1952 and 1959, the Union Carbide Corporation operated a coal liquefaction plant in Institute, West Virginia, employing a total of 359 workers in the hydrogenation process. . . . From evidence with experimental animals and from experience in related industries handling coal tar products and shale oil, it was suspected in advance that skin cancer might be induced. Protective garments standard to "dirtier" chemical operations were therefore used from the beginning.

By 1954, it was determined that extensive contamination was nevertheless occurring. A Health Hazards Committee was formed. Workers were cautioned to avoid unnecessary contact with oils, were given instruction in regard to decontamination practices, and were provided with changes of clothing. Sampling studies were initiated. Efforts were made to identify and correct hazardous equipment and techniques. . . .

Despite these precautions and repeated, careful examinations of the workers, the incidence of skin cancer in the seven years of operation of this coal liquefaction plant was between 16 and 37 times that previously reported in the literature. Skin cancer developed after as little as nine months' exposure. . . . This is in contrast to experience reported in the petroleum industry, where no cancer was observed in workers after 15 years' exposure to petroleum oils which had been highly carcinogenic to the skin of mice. . . .

While the early, unavoidable debugging period was held responsible for some excessive exposure, as late as 1956 air samples showed as much as 1,870 micrograms of benzo(a)pyrene per 100 cubic meters of air on the plant premises. This compares with air samples taken in 1953 in a high traffic area of Los Angeles, showing 2.9 micrograms of benzo(a)pyrene per 100 cubic meters of air. . . .

In retrospect, it was suggested that skin contamination resulting from airborne dusts, vapors, fumes and mists derived from the coal tars may have been more detrimental than direct contact with liquids in the manufacturing process, which forbodes danger to the public from plant emissions.

Prior to 1952 there had been 17 years of exposure of a great many men to the coal liquefaction process in laboratory-sized and small-pilot plants. No cancer had been observed until this large-pilot, but still not commercial-sized plant, began operation. . . .

GASIFIED COAL

Coal tars appear in the gas produced from bituminous or sub-bituminous coal at commonly used gasification temperatures. . . . Benzo(a)pyrene has been isolated from coal tar.

The history of coal tar cancers began in 1775 with the observation of scrotal cancers in chimney sweeps, and ranges through contemporary observations on cigarette smoking and cancer. Skin cancers in coal gas workers were reported in 1892. . . . In comparison with a general population rate of scrotal cancer mortality of 4.2 per million, producer gas men (those who generate coal gas to meet the demands of the plant where it is produced) have been reported to have rates of 10.9 per million, and coal gas and coke makers who work on top of the ovens, where the effluents are greatest, have an incidence of 1,239 per million. . . . A much higher skin cancer rate has been reported for tar distillery workers handling gas works tar than for those handling coke over tar. . . .

A 26-fold excess of lung cancer mortality over the general population and 33 times the rate in other steelworkers was observed in Japanese bituminous producer gas workers in 1936. . . . An excess has also been noted in British coal gas producermen . . . , and coal gas retort workers. . . . Bladder cancer, possibly caused by B-naphthylamine found in gas retort effluents, has been reported in Swedish coal gas workers. Excesses of cancers of the larynx, stomach, and pancreas, as well as leukemia, have also been reported. . . .

The literature does not support ERDA's optimism in concluding that the synthetic fuels program is a "viable environmental protection strategy". . . . In fact, questions raised by research and experience make clear that caution is warranted, and that measures to prevent the induction of cancer must be given serious attention.

ALTERNATIVES

THE alternative energy movement, as it came to be known in the 1970s, took its name from the desire to develop a renewable, relatively small-scale, safe, and healthful energy path for the world—everything, that is, that the current nonrenewable oil-coal-nuclear-based system is not. In this sense, "alternative" energy has come to include a range of energy possibilities including energy from the sun (whether in the form of direct light and heat or indirectly through the use of plants), from wind, from waves and tides, and from small-scale hydroelectric projects. However, as we shall see, it also has incorporated many energy-conserving concepts which are now integral to the very idea of an alternative energy path. In embracing all these areas, the alternative movement is the very antithesis of the world of the mine and the modern energy industry with which this book began. In the most fundamental sense it is in opposition to the present world of military-industrial-rooted energy complexes. For that reason alone its acceptance comes slow and hard.

It is important to keep in mind while reading this chapter that there is nothing new about alternative energy. When, long before Christ, the Greeks denuded their hillsides of trees to build ships with which to trade, they turned to the sun to heat their houses, building courtyards with living rooms facing south for warmth. The courtyard form of housing, subsequently carried into northern Europe by the Romans, remains a usable, attractive method for conserving energy and making use of the sun. The adobe dwelling of the American Southwest follows a similar principle in that it stores up a summer night's cool in its thick walls for natural air conditioning during the next day's scorching heat and holds heat during the winter. Architecture which takes advantage of local environment is a particularly sound, inexpensive, energy-efficient method of both conserving and creating energy.

As for the actual technology and apparatus of alternative energy, that too has a lenthy history. For example, many of the houses in California during the 1880s were equipped with solar hot-water heaters because wood and gas were scarce. At the turn of the century there actually was a thriving industry in solar hot-water heaters in both California and Florida.

In recent years there has been much talk about alternative energy in America, both governmental and industrial bodies having jumped on the verbal bandwagon, yet the "official" approach has been extremely limited and limiting in practice. Although, as Denis Hayes and others show in this section, large-scale, society-wide planning would be necessary to give alternative energy systems a reasonable chance, all governmental and industrial emphasis has been placed on the responsibility of the individual citizen. That citizen, not the government, must spend the money to conserve energy or introduce solar technology in the home. After doing so, the person may attempt to recover some of the cost through credits or deductions on his or her tax return. For those who rent houses, for the huge numbers of people who will never have the funds to own their own houses in today's high-priced real estate market, almost all forms of alternative energy are out of reach.

By contrast, when government formally endorsed nuclear power after the Second World War or in the late 1970s took steps to encourage a synthetic fuels industry, it poured enormous sums of money into creating those industries. Companies were provided money outright or through guarantees simply in order to build those enterprises. That is the main difference between what has happened to alternative energy systems and other sectors of the energy industry. It helps explain why alternatives are and will undoubtedly remain a tiny part of the overall energy picture.

Equally important, alternative energy is not now in the interest of the major energy corporations. Oil companies, electrical equipment manufacturers, mining conglomerates, and others stand to lose from any of its immediate successes. While major oil companies have indeed committed substantial funds toward research on and development of solar energy, their short-term emphasis will be on the profitability of oil, gas, and coal—and alternative energy will be kept in the wings (see p. 343).

Finally, a hopeful note. Despite the ominous tendency within the federal government to develop nuclear power and exploit remaining oil and gas reserves, there are signs that various towns and cities around the nation have, on their own, undertaken ambitious, imaginative ventures, reorganizing their energy infrastructures to make themselves less dependent on major petroleum corporations. Without doubt, the political momentum for useful and progressive change in energy policies will come from such localities and regions, not from the central government.

This section is broken down into three general categories. First there is a look at conservation, then an examination of what can and should be done on the local level, and finally a practical vision of what a renewable energy future might be like.

CONSERVATION

Alternative energy is often seen as a dream of the future, but some of the most effective alternative techniques for energy conservation not only are practical now but have been successfully tried out in other countries, as the following article makes clear. Many such techniques are neither expensive nor complicated, including such simple but energy-efficient acts as turning out office building lights at night. As Marc H. Ross and Robert H. Williams indicate in the following article, the level of energy wastage in the United States is awesome, and the amounts of energy to be gained by proved conservation techniques are impressive. G. N. Hatsopoulos and his colleagues provide a specific illustration of conservation in their short piece.

Taken from "Achieving the Goals of the Employment Act of 1946—Thirtieth Anniversary Review," Paper #2, "Energy and Economic Growth," Joint Economic Committee, August 31, 1977.

. . . Future growth in energy consumption will likely be considerably slower than in the "business as usual" energy projection . . . because of sharply increased energy prices and new policies to encourage fuel conservation. Foreign experience is suggestive of the opportunities for fuel savings. Here we summarize results of studies of energy use in Sweden by Schipper and Lichtenberg and in Germany by Goen and White. The fact [that] the per capita gross national product is similar in these countries and the United States, and that the proportion of heavy industry is similar suggests that comparisons may be useful. Nevertheless conditions differ in these countries, and energy accounts and gross product levels are hard to calibrate accurately, so that comparisons must be made with some care.

In figure 15, per capita energy use is plotted with respect to per capita GDP

FIGURE 15 Per capita energy consumption and gross domestic product of the United States and West Germany for 1967, 1969, 1971, and 1973. Careful examination of the figure shows that both the E/GDP ratio and its rate of change are substantially smaller for Germany than for the United States. Thus, substantially less energy—about two-thirds as much—is associated with each dollar of product in Germany compared with the United States, and there was no tendency for the energy per dollar of product in Germany to change over the period 1969–73. It is especially noteworthy that the high level of affluence achieved by Germany during that period was not associated with an increase in energy consumption per dollar of product. The GDP numbers are expressed in 1970 dollars. . . .

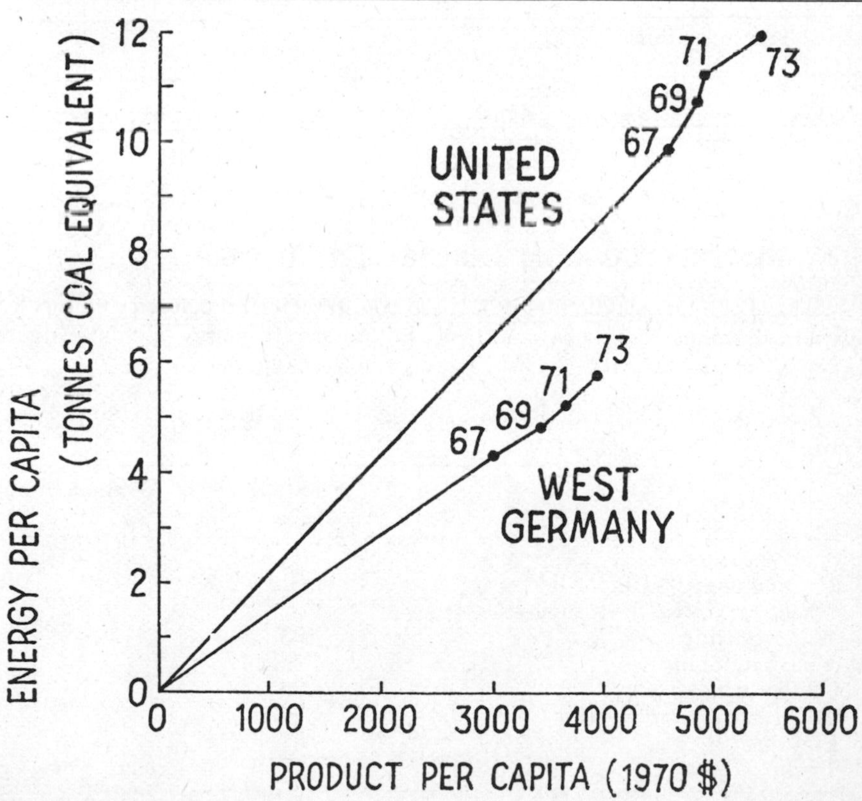

[gross domestic product] for West Germany and the United States. Also the change in recent years prior to the 1973 oil embargo is shown. It is seen that not only is the E[nergy]/GDP ratio smaller in West Germany, but also the increase in energy consumption associated with an increase in GDP has been smaller on the average in recent years.

Summary information on per capita gross national product and energy use by economic sector for these countries is presented in table 3. For each sector, we shall discuss the international differences in per capita energy use, showing by examples how energy consumption varies with the type of equipment used in the different nations, and how it depends on the detailed nature and mix of the products consumed.

TABLE 3 Swedish and German per Capita Indicators Relative to the United States [In percent of U.S. levels]

	Sweden, 1971	West Germany, 1972
Gross national product per capita	88	70
Energy use per capita:		
Residential/commercial	76	52
Industrial	75	61
Transportation	32	26
Total energy	65	49
Net energy	59	46
Energy per gross national product	67	66

. . . RESIDENTIAL-COMMERCIAL ENERGY USE

The use of energy in buildings in these countries is summarized in table 4. In Sweden, the climate is much more severe but per capita energy use for residential

TABLE 4 Per Capita Residential Energy Use Relative to the United States [In percent of U.S. levels]

	Sweden, 1972	West Germany, 1972
Space heating	74	67
Heating energy without taking into account district heat savings	(87)	
Water heating	105	37
Air-conditioning	Nil	Nil
Clothes drying	Nil	Nil
Refrigeration and cooking	70	
Lighting	31	28
Total	76	48

heating is somewhat less than in the United States. In Germany, the climate is somewhat more severe and per capita energy use for residential heating is two-thirds that of the United States. In order to interpret this information it is important, to consider the role of climate and floor space.

In Sweden the floor area per capita is similar to that in the United States but the energy use for heating, corrected for both climate and floor space differences, is roughly half that of the United States, reflecting better construction. The better construction reflects, in turn, tough regulations coupled with a centralized building industry. This Swedish achievement is illustrated in figure 16 where building performance is shown for different climatic conditions. The figures show that the quality of construction improves with severity of climate in the United States, but that Swedish results are substantially better than would be expected from U.S.

FIGURE 16 The heating performance of typical fossil-fuel heated housing in the United States and Sweden versus severity of climate in degree days. Performance is measured in thermal kilowatt hours per square meter of floor space area per degree day.

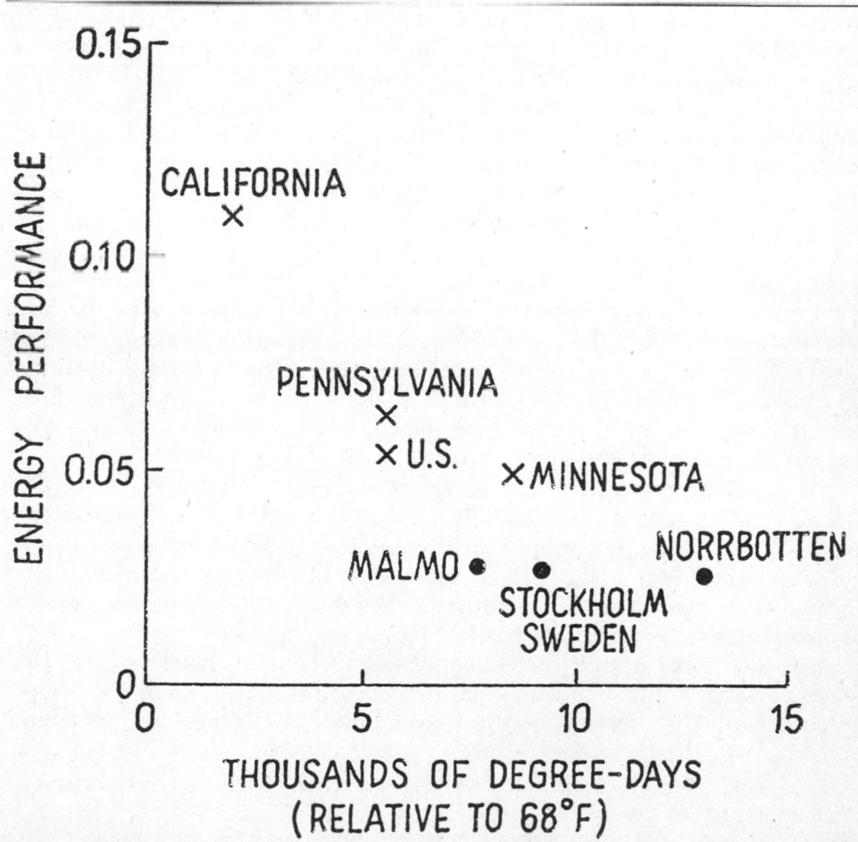

experience. It is noteworthy that Sweden has recently revised its building codes with the objective of reducing heating fuel requirements in new buildings by another 40 percent.

A further, though less important, reason for the lower overall fuel consumption for residential, and commercial, space heating in Sweden is the use of "district heating," where a centralized boiler generating steam provides heat for several buildings or for a whole area of a city. About one-third of these centralized heating systems involve the cogeneration of electricity and hot water or steam near the point of heat use. As much as one-third of the fuel can be saved in such cogeneration systems compared to separate generation of heat and electricity. In Sweden the overall net savings associated with district heating systems is 14 percent of the heating energy, equivalent to 2 percent of total national energy consumption.

In Germany, lower per capita floor area, the custom of allowing some rooms to drift to low temperature,[*] and lower interior temperatures generally appear to be the major factors in the reduced use of fuel for heating compared with the United States. Differences in construction standards are less important. In both Sweden and Germany multiple family dwellings are more prevalent than in the United States. One would expect that multiple family dwellings would require less heating fuel per unit of floor space than single family dwellings,[†] but, because of poor control equipment and perhaps because energy use for heating is not metered and charged separately in multiple family dwellings, no significant fuel saving advantage accrues to those countries on this account. Support for the importance of the mode of metering is provided in a study of master metered versus individually metered apartments in the United States, where it was found that the master metered apartment dwellers consumed about 35 percent more electricity than those who paid for their own electricity use. Separate metering of heating energy in multiple family dwellings is now being introduced in Europe; initial results are promising.

Per capita energy use for water heating is about the same in Sweden and the United States but is much lower in West Germany. In Germany spot water heaters —which are located at the point of use and heat water on demand—are widely used, while many apartments in Sweden have centralized hot water systems with no separate metering. The performance of the German system is suggestive. In principle, spot heating can be far more efficient because heat losses from hot water storage and transport are eliminated.

Air-conditioners and clothes dryers are essentially not used in Sweden and West Germany. Refrigerators are typically smaller and not frost free. Little data is available on lighting. Other appliances are not important energy users.

Data available on energy use in commercial buildings in Germany is sparse. Overall energy use in Swedish commercial buildings is 30 percent lower per unit of area than in the United States. Heating energy, corrected for floor space and climate differences, is, as in the residential sector, about one-half that of the United States. Tighter lighting standards in Swedish commercial buildings mean that air-conditioning for central cores of large buildings is not necessary in winter as

[*]Maintaining different temperatures in different areas of a building, or zonal heating, is a common practice in Europe.

[†]Because the ratio of exterior surface area to floor area is less for multiple family dwellings.

it is in the United States [Since heat from lighting accounts for up to 60 percent of the air conditioning load].

. . . MANUFACTURING ENERGY USE

Because the mix of industrial product differs among Sweden, West Germany, and the United States, and because energy consumption is much greater for basic materials production than for fabrication or other light manufacturing, care must be taken in making comparisons among these countries, even though all are heavily industrialized. For broad industrial categories, energy use per dollar of product is typically somewhat greater in Sweden and substantially less in Germany than in the United States. Swedish industry, however, is concentrated more in the production of basic materials—steel, cement, bulk chemicals, pulp, et cetera—than is American industry. When particular processes are compared, then German and Swedish practices are more efficient than in the United States. Compared with the United States, for example, steelmaking requires 85 percent as much fuel input per physical unit in Sweden and 68 percent in Germany. Paper manufacture requires 77 percent as much fuel in Sweden and 57 percent in Germany. Swedish performance in these areas is actually better than these figures suggest. In fact it is roughly comparable to the German performance, because the primary fuel inputs are exaggerated in the Swedish case—where there is much use of hydropower—by nominally associating three units of fuel with each unit of electricity, and also because the Swedish paper industry makes extensive use of wastes for fuel. (Energy conversion efficiencies are often lower with wastes than with fossil fuels.)

Factors that contribute to the better energy performance of some basic Swedish and German industrial processes include more modern equipment, a tradition of minimizing obvious energy waste because of higher fuel costs, and more cogeneration of electricity and heat. Schipper and Lichtenberg assert that because of energy efficiency differences for specific manufacturing processes Swedish technology is 10 to 15 years ahead of corresponding U.S. technology.

Aggregate consumption of energy by industry per dollar of output depends on the mix and design of consumer products as well as the performance of basic industrial processes. We have seen no systematic comparison of the mix and design of products in Europe and the United States. The fragmentary evidence we have seen suggests that this is not the major factor in the lower industrial energy use per dollar characterizing Sweden and Germany.

. . . ENERGY USE IN TRANSPORTATION

The most striking statistic in this international comparison is found in the transportation sector: per capita energy use for passenger travel in the European countries is roughly one-fourth that of the U.S. (See table 5.) Auto travel—in passenger miles—is the dominant travel mode in all three countries, but the average distance each person travels annually in the European countries is roughly one-half that for the United States, and the energy use per passenger mile in the European countries is again about one-half that of the United States.

The reduced level of travel in Germany and Sweden can be accounted for by

TABLE 5 Relative Use of Energy for Transportation in Sweden, West Germany, and the United States [In percent of U.S. level]

	Sweden (1970–72)	West Germany (1972)
Passenger travel:		
Passenger-miles per capita	54	48
Fuel per passenger-mile*	52	52
Fuel per capita	28	25
Freight:		
Ton-miles per capita	†45	21
Fuel per ton-mile	†115	189
Fuel per capita	73	39

*For automobiles only.
†Road and rail only.

the facts that the metropolitan areas are more compact (so that commuting distances are shorter) and that bicycling and walking instead of driving are relied on for short distances. The primary reasons for lower energy per passenger mile in Sweden are: Higher vehicle occupancy and better gas mileage. Better gas mileage, attributable mainly to lower auto weight, is the most important single explanation of this superior performance. While public transportation is much more important in Sweden and Germany than it is in the United States, it has been too small a factor to affect overall transportation energy use greatly.

The greater use of energy per ton-mile for transporting freight in Germany (see table 5) probably reflects the fact that more freight is moved short distances by truck, while in the United States, coastal and inland water transport and pipelines are relatively more important.

. . . THE RELEVANCE OF EUROPEAN EXPERIENCE FOR THE UNITED STATES

Comparison of specific uses of energy in Sweden and West Germany to those in the United States shows that both the use of better equipment and the prevalence of tasks demanding less energy account for the lower energy use in Europe. Better equipment seems evident in better housing insulation in Sweden; systems for cogenerating electricity and heat in municipalities (in some district heating systems) and in industry; and the general use of modern process equipment throughout industry. Examples of less energy demanding tasks include lower indoor temperatures in winter and, in Germany, zonal heating; clothes drying; and air conditioning other than by machine; lower lighting levels in commercial buildings; smaller cars; and reduced daily transportation needs arising because population is concentrated in small centers near work and shopping.

The existence of these differences in nations of comparable affluence and level of industrialization suggests some possibilities for reducing the energy/GNP ratio that are practical and could be adapted for the United States. Also some of the European policies that shaped energy saving practices may be relevant for the United States. The more important policy measures limiting energy demand in these countries include: Much higher prices for road fuel because of high taxes; excise taxes on large cars; enhancement of urban communities by zoning against sprawl-type expansion, and by maintenance of good public transport, and other public services; and assistance for industrial capital formation. The price mechanism has been used only for some energy forms. In Sweden prices much higher than those in the United States have tended to limit both road fuel and natural gas use, while the prices of heavy oils, heating oils, coal, and electricity have been comparable to those in the United States.

While much of the European experience provides valuable insights about possible future directions for the United States, the best prescription for change in the United States is not necessarily to adopt all Swedish and German experience. In some cases (e.g., clothes drying) many Europeans have clearly accepted a lower material standard than many Americans enjoy, suggesting that tradeoffs are associated with different levels of energy use for some activities. However, as we shall show below, it is in the areas where the differences between United States and European habits are most apparent that there are also the greatest opportunities for improved energy performance. As we shall show, existing and new technology could be used to provide the material amenities to which many Americans have become accustomed with much less energy use. . . .

. . . ILLUSTRATIVE EXAMPLES OF CONSERVATION OPPORTUNITIES THROUGH TECHNICAL CHANGE

We have described elsewhere fuel conservation opportunities in four illustrative areas which together account for 40 percent of total U.S. energy use: The automobile, residential space heating, commercial air-conditioning, and industrial process steam. In each case the potential savings that could be achieved over the next 10 to 15 years are estimated. Here we only briefly highlight the principal results.

In the case of the automobile, presently available technology could be introduced in the next couple years to boost average fuel economy in new cars to over 20 miles per gallon with only a modest reduction in auto weight, say 20 percent. Going further, technological innovations like new engine designs—lightweight diesel, Rankine, or Stirling—and improved transmissions, could lead to an average fuel economy of 30 to 35 miles per gallon for new cars after a decade or so. Of course, these goals have already been achieved with small cars.

In the area of space heating, modest innovations in design and development of new devices and materials, such as better windows and improved insulation to reduce both heat conduction and air infiltration, could cut heat losses in homes by nearly 75 percent. Such a reduction has far-reaching implications for the heating system, because, except for very cold days, no supplemental heating beyond what is provided by sunlight through the windows, the electric load, and body heat would be needed. But even further savings possibilities exist for days when modest supplemental heating is needed. A small electric heat pump that uses well water or lake water as a heat source would be twice as efficient in providing heat as a gas furnace.

It may come as a surprise that, in the case of commercial air-conditioning, heat from lighting is often the largest component of the air-conditioning load, accounting for up to 60 percent of the total. Here, substantial savings can be achieved by adopting task-specific instead of uniform lighting strategies now often employed and by turning off lights when they are not in use. In new buildings, greater use of natural lighting could be achieved. After lighting, the next largest component of the air-conditioning load is typically the cooling requirement for the ventilation system. While a certain amount of outside air is needed to control odors, to keep carbon dioxide levels down, and to provide adequate oxygen, typical ventilation rates are far in excess of what is required. Moreover, the use of heat exchangers in the ventilation system could substantially reduce the air-conditioning requirements for the fresh air that is needed. With reduced use of lighting, an improved ventilation system, and more insulation, air-conditioning demand could often be reduced to less than one-third of its present level. With this greatly reduced air-conditioning demand, it becomes feasible to think of meeting a substantial fraction of the energy requirements for air-conditioning in a commercial office building with solar energy. Heat-driven refrigeration devices are presently widely used to provide air-conditioning for large buildings. Solar-assisted, heat-driven air-conditioners may well be commercially available within a decade. Implementing all these innovations could cut fuel requirements for air-conditioning in a typical New York City office building to one-sixth of what they are now.

In producing steam today for industrial process heat uses, fuel is burned to boil water much as one boils water in a kettle. While the first law of efficiency for this process is an impressive 85 percent (that is, 85 percent of the fuel energy ends up in the steam), the second law efficiency is typically a much more modest 32 percent. The usual process of steam generation wastes the high quality energy in fuel. If, instead, the combustion energy of the fuel is used first to produce electricity, with the "waste heat" from power generation utilized as process steam, the second law efficiency of combined electricity and steam production could be increased to 40 or 45 percent, compared to an efficiency of about 33 percent for the separate production of steam and electricity. The resulting fuel savings are actually much more impressive expressed another way: If only the excess fuel beyond what is required for steam production is attributed to electricity generation, the fuel required to produce 1 kilowatt hour of electricity is reduced to about half of that required in conventional powerplants. At the national level, the potential fuel savings from the cogeneration of electricity and process steam is truly great, because process steam is a major energy-consuming activity in the economy, accounting for about 14 percent of total U.S. fuel consumption.

The most promising application of steam-electricity cogeneration[*] appears to be in industrial plants, where electricity could be produced as a byproduct whenever steam is needed. Various cogeneration technologies could be employed. In a steam-turbine system, steam used to drive the power-generating turbine would be exhausted from the turbine at the desired pressure and (instead of being condensed with cooling water, as at a conventional powerplant) delivered to the appropriate industrial process. With a gas-turbine system, the hot gases exhausted from the power-generating turbine would be used to raise steam in a waste heat boiler. The gas-turbine system is the more efficient of the two, typically with a second law efficiency of 45 percent, compared to 40 percent for a steam-turbine

[*See p. 265 (Barry Commoner) for an explanation of one cogeneration process.]

system; in addition, because it produces several times as much electricity for a given steam load, the gas-turbine cogeneration system could yield several fold greater total fuel savings than the steam-turbine system.

Recent studies on the overall potential for cogeneration have been carried out by Dow Chemical Co. and by Thermo Electron Corp. The latter's study shows that by 1985, electricity amounting to more than 40 percent of today's U.S. consumption (generated with about 135,000 megawatts electrical of equivalent baseload central station generating capacity) could be produced economically with gas turbines as a byproduct of processs steam generation at industrial sites. Through displacement of conventional central station generating capacity that would otherwise be built, the fuel savings would amount to about 5 percent of the present level of U.S. energy consumption. (While the gas turbines in use today must be fueled with gaseous or liquid fuels, it is likely that over the next decade high-pressure fluidized-bed combustors will be available as an economic method of firing gas turbines directly with coal.

To produce power most economically, an industrial installation that generates electricity as a byproduct of process steam production would often produce more electricity than could be consumed onsite. Thus the cogeneration unit should be interconnected with a utility and could substitute for some central-station baseload generating capacity. But such an arrangement is often difficult under existing utility policies. Considerable modification of utilities' transmission, control, and perhaps storage systems may be necessary if interconnected cogeneration capacity is developed on a large scale.

The production of process steam as a byproduct of power generation at large central station powerplants is an alternative to cogeneration at industrial sites. However, such steam production does not lead to a significant increase in second law efficiency, since there is very little useful work left in the powerplant cooling water, which has an average temperature of about 100°F. If the waste heat is to be useful for industrial processes, powerplant operations would have to be modified to produce heat at more useful temperatures (200° to 400°F.). But this would reduce the electrical output, and this change could lead to a net loss of overall efficiency unless essentially all the heat were put to effective use. Not only are the potential gains of byproduct steam generation small, but there are serious implementation difficulties as well. Because it is uneconomic to transport steam long distances, steam-using industries would have to be near the powerplants from which their heat is supplied, and this is a condition often difficult to fulfill. There is also a serious mismatch in time: Large central-station powerplants require 6 to 10 years for construction and are designed for a quarter century or more of service. For these reasons, cogeneration at industrial sites is favored.

. . . THE FUEL CONSERVATION POTENTIAL FOR THE ECONOMY TODAY

We turn now to estimating the potential fuel savings from pursuing fuel conservation measures throughout the economy. Because we wish to focus on what can be implemented on a wide scale within roughly the next two decades, the proposals taken into account are somewhat less ambitious than some of those discussed in the previous subsection. Tables 7a, 7b, 7c, and 7d show the potential savings

TABLE 7A. Potential Annual Fuel Savings in the Residential Sector [In 10^{15} Btu]

Conservation measures	Potential savings
Replace resistive heating with heat pumps having a coefficient of performance† (COP) of 2.5	0.60
Increase air-conditioning COP to 3.6	.40
Increase refrigerator efficiency 30 percent	.27
Cut water heating fuel requirements in half	1.07
Reduce heat losses 50 percent with better insulation, improved windows, reduced infiltration	3.30
Reduce air-conditioning load by reducing infiltration to 0.2 air exchanges per hour	.42
Introduce total energy systems into ½ multifamily units (15 percent of all housing units) with a net 30 percent fuel savings	.31
Use microwave ovens for ½ of cooking, with 80 percent savings	.25
Total savings	6.62
Actual fuel use in 1973	14.07
Hypothetical fuel use with conservation	7.45

[†Ratio of the amount of heat removed from the room to the amount of energy used to remove it.]

TABLE 7B. Potential Annual Fuel Savings in the Commercial Sector [In 10^{15} Btu]

Conservation measures	Potential savings
Increase air-conditioning COP 30 percent	0.37
Increase refrigeration efficiency 30 percent	.20
Cut water heating fuel requirements in half	.31
Reduce building lighting energy by 50 percent:	
Direct savings	.82
Increased heating requirements	−.21
Reduced air-conditioning requirements	.34
Net savings	.95
Reduce heating requirements 50 percent	2.25
Reduce air-conditioning demand 10 percent with better insulation	.08
Reduce air-conditioning demand 15 percent by reducing ventilation rate 50 percent (to 0.5 air exchanges per hour) and by using heat recovery apparatus	.10
Use total energy systems in ⅓ of all units—save 30 percent	.64
Use microwave ovens for ½ of cooking	.06
Total savings	4.96
Actual fuel use in 1973	12.06
Hypothetical fuel use with conservation	7.10

TABLE 7C. Potential Annual Fuel Savings in the Industrial Sector [In 10^{15} Btu]

Conservation measures	Potential savings
Good housekeeping measures throughout industry (except for feedstocks), save 15 percent	3.85
Fuel instead of electric heat in direct heat applications	.17
Steam/electric cogeneration for 50 percent of process steam	2.59
Heat recuperators or regenerators in 50 percent of direct heat applications—save 25 percent (references 31 and 5)	.74
Electricity from bottoming cycles in 50 percent of direct heat applications	.49
Recycling of aluminum in urban refuse	.10
Recycling of iron and steel in urban refuse	.11
Fuel from organic wastes in urban refuse	.70
Reduced throughput at oil refineries	.87
Reduced field and transport losses associated with reduced use of natural gas	.80
Total savings	10.43
Actual fuel use in 1973	29.65
Hypothetical fuel use with conservation	19.22

TABLE 7d Potential Annual Fuel Savings in Transportation [In 10^{15} Btu]

Conservation measures	Potential savings
Improve auto fuel economy 150 percent	5.89
35 percent savings in other transportation areas	3.20
Total savings	9.09
Actual fuel use in 1973	18.96
Hypothetical fuel use with conservation	9.87

which would have been achieved in 1973 had the set of indicated conservation technologies been implemented. The potential savings for the economy as a whole are summarized in figure 18, where actual and "hypothetical" energy budgets for 1973 are compared. It is seen that the hypothesized technical change, providing the same products as in 1973, would have reduced energy consumption from 75 quads[*] to 44 quads. In other words if the fuel conservation measures considered here had been in effect in 1973, fuel consumption would have been less than 60 percent of its actual level. These savings are in addition to what could also be achieved through measures involving changes in lifestyle—a heavy shift to small cars, enforced 55 miles-per-hour speed limits, lowered thermostats in the winter, and the like.

[*In describing large amounts of energy the term "quad" is often used. A quad is equivalent to a quadrillion (1 million times 1 million times 1,000) British thermal units (BTUs). One quad equals 172 million barrels of oil. The United States uses 75 quads of energy a year. We burn up a quad in four days. The current world population uses about 300 quads of energy a year.]

FIGURE 18 Summary of the fuel saving potential in the various energy consuming sectors detailed in Tables 7a–d. The savings are associated with technical change alone. The goods and services provided by energy in the hypothetical economy would be the same as in the actual economy for 1973.

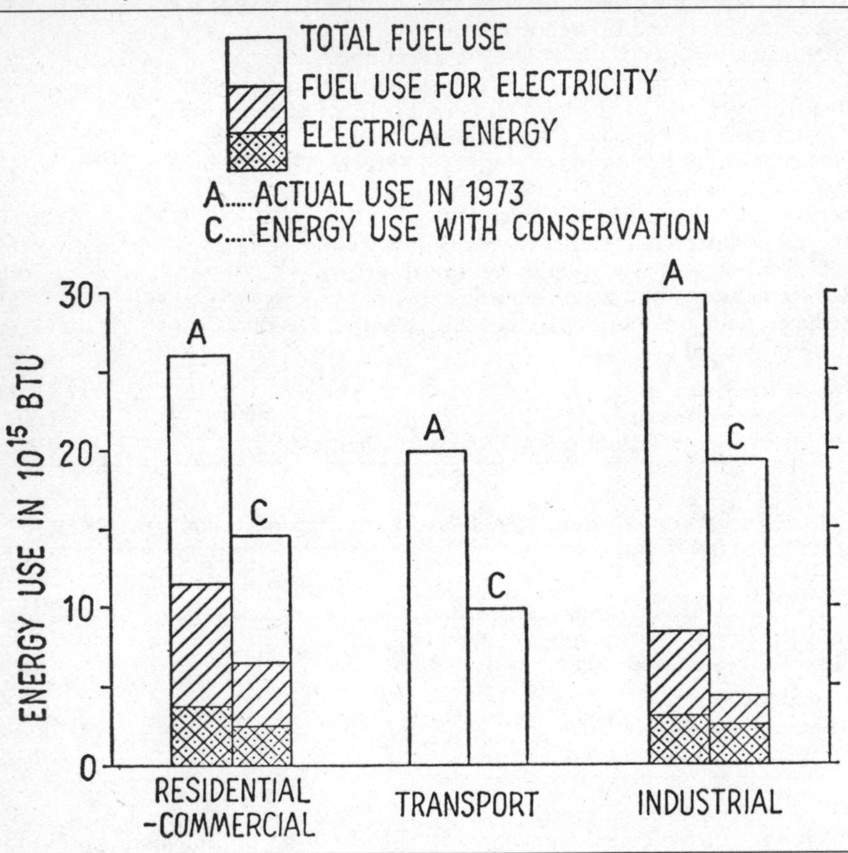

Looking beyond the program implied by tables 7a to 7d we can get a rough idea of further opportunities for conservation from the second law efficiencies associated with these improvements. In the residential, commercial, and transportation sectors, the efficiencies still would be relatively low (typically in the range 8 to 15 percent, compared to 2 to 10 percent today). This suggests that opportunities still will exist for substantial further improvements through technological change. However, for energy intensive activities in the industrial sector, operations may well be approaching the practical limits to efficiency improvement. This suggests that further industrial fuel savings would depend mainly on shifting the industrial product mix toward less energy intensive products.

If the degree of technical improvement represented by the fuel savings shown in figure 18 were accomplished over the remainder of this century, the rate of decline in the E/GNP ratio would be about 2.3 percent per year faster than the long-term historical rate. Since . . . , energy consumption following "historical trends" would grow no faster than 2.3 percent per year in the period 1985 to 2000, the result of pursuing these fuel conservation measures would be zero energy growth beyond 1985. Since the "historical trends" projection is based on the optimistic assumptions of sustained full employment and a return to a high rate of growth in labor productivity, the efficiency improvement rate assumed here is roughly the maximum rate needed to achieve zero energy growth in a vigorously expanding economy. Opportunities for substantial technological innovation are not reflected in this estimate; pursuing these opportunities would enable a continuation of zero energy growth, or even negative energy growth, for the period near the turn of the century and beyond.

This result that in the future zero growth in energy use could be compatible with maintaining a strong economy will not be readily accepted by those who believe firmly in the persistence of historical trends. However, it is worth noting that the historical growth in energy use has not been so persistent as most people think. Figure 19 shows the long-term record of per capita energy use in the United States. What we find remarkable about these data is that, while certain periods have been characterized by rapid growth in per capita energy use, there also have been long periods where per capita energy use has grown hardly at all. Thus the historical record itself provides evidence that "trend is not destiny.". . .

FIGURE 19 Per capita energy use in the United States (million Btu per year).

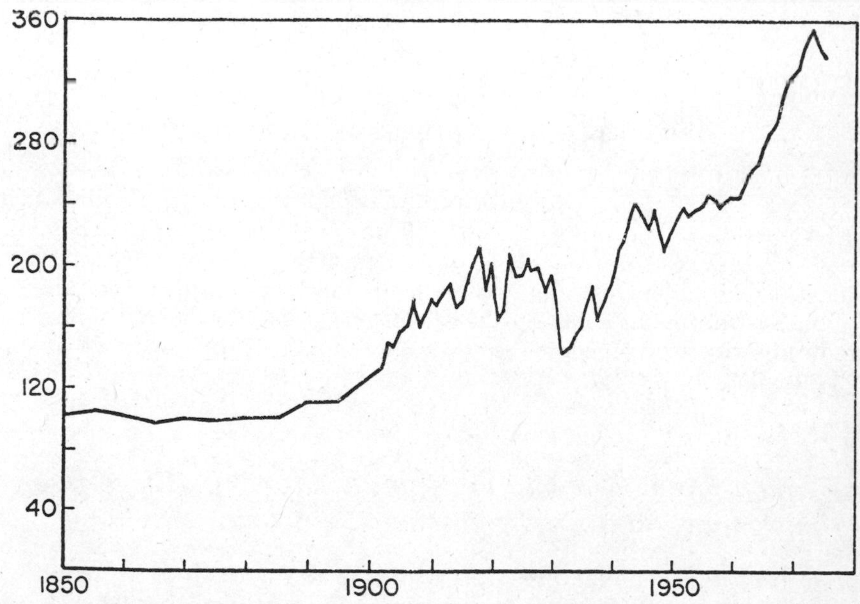

Source: "Historical Statistics of the United States," and U.S. Bureau of Mines news releases.

Taken from "Capital Investment to Save Energy," by G. N. Hatsopoulos, E. P. Gyftopoulos, R. W. Sant, and T. F. Widmer, Harvard Business Review, *March–April, 1978.*

ELECTRIC MOTORS

Now consuming about two-thirds of the electricity used in manufacturing, electric motors afford one of the simplest opportunities to improve efficiency. By 1985, they are expected to account for about 710 billon kwh [kilowatt hours] of electricity consumption, or about 17% of the total energy consumed in manufacturing.

Such motors now cost about $40 per horsepower. Increasing the amount of copper and magnetic materials used and making certain design improvements could raise efficiency by about 10% at a cost of about $10 per horsepower.

If all new motors purchased by industry incorporated this better design, the annual energy saving by 1985 would amount to about 2% of industrial electricity consumption. The capital cost penalty for motors used in new installations, $10 per horsepower, represents an incremental investment of $300 million over the next seven years.

The cost of using high-efficiency motors in all new and existing industrial installations (at $50 per horsepower) amounts to $6.3 billion and translates into an electricity cost of 1.2 cents per kwh. In the absence of such an investment, the operation of less efficient motors through 1985 will require the generation of new electricity at a capital cost of about $13.8 billion and a total cost of 4.4 cents per kilowatt hour.

THE CLOTHESLINE PARADOX

For most people the possibility of the "soft path"—that is, solar energy—seems so hopelessly far off in the future that despite higher and higher energy costs, it is easier to ignore it. One of the reasons for that is the figures published by both industry and government, which apparently demonstrate how minute a contribution is made to the whole "energy pie" by the sun. As Steve Baer indicates with some humor in the next excerpt, these figures are deceptive, to say the least.

Taken from "The Clothesline Paradox," by Steve Baer, Sunpaper, *Summer 1975.*

A few years ago Peter Van Dresser mentioned the Clothesline Paradox.

Solar energy advocates are continuously humiliated by being shown "energy pies." Slices are assigned to coal, gas, oil, hydroelectric and even nuclear energy, but solar energy is evidently too small to appear. I have a typical energy pie from the Ford Foundation whose source is the U.S. Bureau of Mines. The large pie is split into five pieces: petroleum 46 percent, coal 18 percent, natural gas 31 percent, hydropower 4 percent, and nuclear 15 percent. (An asterisk notes that wood has been omitted. Why?) We are frequently reminded that the energy we advocate—solar energy—must, after the proper technical efforts, appear alongside coal, oil, natural gas and nuclear before it will make an "impact." ERDA [Energy Research and Development Administration] in its different energy consumption predictions assigns only a thin wedge of the pie to solar energy and then only as a faint hope 15 to 25 years from now. The demoralized reader is then ripe to be persuaded of the necessity of nuclear power plants or offshore drilling. The accounting system shows that he has done absolutely nothing with solar energy. He lacks even a trace of a useful habit or activity that he could build on. As Peter and I discussed—if you examine these figures you find the cards are stacked against solar energy.

If you take down your clothesline and buy an electric clothes dryer the electric consumption of the nation rises slightly. If you go in the other direction and remove the electric clothes dryer and install a clothesline the consumption of electricity drops slightly, but there is no credit given anywhere on the charts and graphs to solar energy, which is now drying the clothes.

The poor old sun is badly mistreated by such graphs. In the first place the obvious should be pointed out; that coal, oil, and natural gas are all solar energy products stored ages ago by photosynthesis, and hydroelectric power is solar energy no older than the weather patterns which dropped the precipitation flowing through the turbines.

The graphs which demonstrate a huge dependence on fossil fuels are fine in one respect. They are alarming. But they are very bad in another respect. They are misleading. Misleading to such an extent that they blind people to obvious answers and prime them to a frenzy of effort in poor directions. Attention given to such graphs and charts trains people to attempt to deliver what is shown in these accounting systems rather than what is needed.

If you drive a motorcycle, the gasoline you consume appears in the nation's energy budget. If you get a horse to ride and graze the horse on range nearby, the horse's energy which you use does not appear in anyone's energy accounting.

If you install interior greenhouse lights the electricity you use is faithfully recorded. If you grow the plants outside no attempt is made at an accounting.

If you drive your car to the corner to buy a newspaper the gasoline consumption appears. If you walk—using food energy—the event has disappeared from sight, for the budget of solar energy consumed by people in food is seldom mentioned.

The Ford Foundation's energy study shows the U.S.'s energy consumption in 1968 at about 62 quadrillion Btu or 310,000,000 Btu/person/year or 310/365 = 850,000 Btu/day. If the average daily calorie intake is 2,500 Kcal., this is approximately 10,000 Btu/day/person—about 1.2 percent of the total consumption listed by the Bureau of Mines. But this 1.2 percent doesn't appear anywhere on the graphs. Nuclear energy with 1 percent does appear. The food is obviously solar energy. Why is it not included?

What about the question of the energy used in growing the food? Can't we treat this in the same way as the coal burned to generate electricity? If we use the figure of .5 percent efficiency . . . , this means we have consumed approximately

2,000,000 Btu/person/day of sunlight in producing the 10,000 Btu/person consumed. Solar energy then immediately fills over two-thirds of the new energy pie. If we aren't allowed to show the actual sunlight required for our 10,000 Btu/person, then what about power plants? Why is it that when they burn 4 Btu of fuel for every Btu delivered as electricity, all the consumption appears in the energy accounts rather than the 1 Btu?

Why wouldn't it be fair to expand the slice—4 percent (Bureau of Mines, 1973) given to hydroelectric power by a similar factory of efficiency—for the solar energy consumed in raising the water to its working head? After all, in most cases, the rain or snow fell through long unexploited distances before it went to work in a power plant.

Then there is the question of heating houses. Every time the sun shines on the surface of a house and especially when it shines through a window there is "solar heating" to some extent. How do we measure this? How do we account for this in our discussions of energy use? According to the NSF/NASA Energy Panel of 1972, the percentage of thermal energy for buildings supplied by the sun was too small to be measureable. But is that accurate? Shouldn't we recalculate the energy consumption of every building assuming it were kept in the shade all day and then attribute the difference between this amount and its actual consumption to solar energy? I most cases this would result in an enormous difference. Almost every building is solar heated to some extent. I would guess the average shaded fuel consumption to be at least 15 percent higher, and then of course our next concern in heating the building is what keeps the earth as warm as it is? What supplies the United States with the necessary energy to maintain an average temperature of 60 degrees Fahrenheit as it spins in empty space at absolute zero? This is a heating contract no oil company would be quick to try and fill.

Clearly it would be a very difficult thing to account for every calorie or Btu that passed through us or by us every day in the various forms. It doesn't seem to be a particularly urgent job, but it is very important to examine what the limits of an accounting system are to know what the numbers and quantities displayed really mean.

If you go to a drive-in movie to watch the flickering lights on a screen, the energy consumption of the automobile and the drive-in is dutifully recorded and appears in the statistics. If you walk out on a hillside, lie on your back and look at the stars, no attempt is made to measure the power output of the distant stars.

I don't advocate an enormous effort to measure all these things. It would just be more helpful if the graphs stated more clearly what they are about.

The design of houses can be stilted by such graphs. Now that the experts have started this infantile accounting system, which evidently finds us completely independent of the sun, solar energy will be admitted only so long as it has been properly collected, stored and transferred. Legislation aimed at encouraging the use of solar energy equipment by subsidizing the price of certain hardware must end by being pathetic and blundering. It would take an enormous crew of experts to determine the efficiency of different orientations of windows, different arrangements of shade trees, etc., etc. To ignore these efforts and only to reward the purchase of "off the shelf hardware" is to further the disease of narrow-minded quantification.

It should be pointed out to the people promoting the use of solar energy in the place of fossil fuels that the accounting systems used by the experts are rigged against them. As I understand it, we are being prepared to accept that there are legitimate and illegitimate ways of using the sun. If you purchase certain kinds of hardware to exploit solar energy it will be accounted for and a credit will be given to the sun. If you depend on more customary, old fashioned uses of solar energy —growing food, drying clothes, sunbathing, warming a house with south windows —the sun credit is totally ignored.

Our present accounting system with its promise of a credit to the sun after the right hardware has been installed can only discourage good house design. If the natural solar contribution to house heating from windows is ignored, then the designer knows that expanding this share done by the sun will also be ignored. No tax incentives—no credit given to the sun in ERDA's graphs.

I think we would be much better informed if alongside every graph showing our use of oil, coal and uranium there were also an indication of the total energy received from the sun. Since we can't do without it, let's not omit it from our accounts. In the case of the United States, a conservative estimate of the solar energy received in one year might be:

> (3,000,000) square miles (5280^2) $ft.^2/mile^2 \times 350 \times 10^3$Btu received/$ft^2$/year $= 3 \times 10^6 \times (5.28)^2 \times 10^6 \times 3.5 \times 10^5 = 293 \times 10^{17}$Btu/year. [That is] 29,300 quadrillion Btu as opposed to the 62 quadrillion shown as used during 1968 by the U.S. Bureau of Mines.

When small children first start paying close attention to money and to their allowances they briefly commit their whole minds to their few coins and what chores they did to earn them—without even considering the budget of the family's household. We can't allow our entire civilization to be similarly ignorant for long. We must ask who's keeping score and why they have such peculiar methods.

URBAN CONSERVATION

The preceding entries point up general conservation principles and estimates of savings achieved through conservation. When these principles are applied in a realistic way even to urban settings, where energy conservation might at first seem impossible, major benefits can be achieved. Leonard Rodberg and Geoffrey Stokes set forth their plan for New York City. Part of my own report from Davis, California, is also included to show what a small city can do.

But first Barry Commoner, a longtime critic of nuclear power and one of the nation's leading proponents of alternative energy, describes how cogeneration, one of the main energy-saving processes in the New York plan, might really work.

Taken from The Politics of Energy, *by Barry Commoner, New York, Knopf, 1979.*

. . .Where the local sources of solar energy are not sufficient to meet the local needs, as in a densely urbanized area, . . . solar energy must be brought in from elsewhere.

And to conform with the imperatives of the solar transition, the energy must be transmitted in a form, and used in a way, that maximizes efficiency. This brings us to a major segment of the solar picture: cogeneration, the local production of both useful heat and electricity from a combustible fuel. A cogenerator is an electric power plant that is so designed as to make use of the "waste" heat that a conventional plant ejects into the environment. For example, one recently designed cogenerator is simply a four-cylinder gasoline engine, ordinarily used to drive a Fiat automobile. The engine's drive shaft turns a generator that produces electricity; the engine's cooling system, which in the automobile gives off its heat into the environment by way of the radiator, is connected instead to a heat exchanger. This is a nest of interwoven pipes that transfers the heat produced by the engine to, let us say, a building's heating system. Thus the cogenerator produces energy in two useful forms—heat and electricity—which together can usually account for up to 90 percent of the energy originally contained in the fuel. In contrast, if the same engine were used to produce only electricity, with the heat wastefully ejected into the environment, its power output would represent, at most, 30 percent to 40 percent of the fuel's energy. Any engine that produces motion from a burning fuel can be used as a cogenerator: a gasoline or diesel engine, a gas turbine, or for that matter an old-fashioned steam engine. Installed in a residence, commercial building, or factory, a cogenerator can very efficiently heat it in winter, cool it in summer, and throughout the year drive its electrically operated appliances. And since the cogenerator is sized to match the local need, capacity and demand are automatically tied together, so as to avoid the inefficiencies that occur whenever a large power plant is built to meet demand which increases in small, gradual steps. Because they can make very efficient use of liquid and gaseous fuels—which will be in relatively short supply in a solar system—cogenerators are a crucial part of such a system.

Here we come to the next part of the puzzle, for to take advantage of cogenerators we need to find a supply of solar fuel that is nonpolluting (so that it can be used in densely settled urban areas) and that can be transmitted efficiently (so that cogenerators can be used when the local supply of solar fuel is inadequate). . . . [Solar] methane is by far the best choice: It takes relatively little energy or capital to transmit it; it could be fed into the transmission line at numerous points, wherever the varied solar sources that can be converted to methane—sewage, garbage, manure, seaweed, crops—are available; it can readily be used to fuel a cogenerator driven by an internal combustion engine or a turbine; it can be burned anywhere without polluting the environment. Using methane in this way also fits nicely into those situations in which some local biomass is available, but in amounts that are too little or untimely to match the local demand. For example, at the height of the canning season, a cannery might produce more methane (from its waste) than is needed, and feed the surplus into the pipeline. At other times, when the local supply is short, the cannery might draw methane from the pipeline.

Now, with a pipeline for widespread collection and distribution of solar methane in place, we can see how to fit another major feature into the solar picture. This concerns the possibility of collecting electric power from photovoltaic cells and windmills, produced in places where it is readily available in excess of local needs, in order to bolster the total national energy supply. The energy will have to be transmitted over considerable distances, but. . . that can be done more efficently if the electricity is first converted to gas. This can be accomplished by using the electricity to produce hydrogen gas (from water), which can then be readily converted to methane, chemically or through the action of certain microorganisms. Alternatively, the hydrogen can simply be added to the methane pipeline. (Mixtures containing 10 percent to 20 percent hydrogen can be piped and used in equipment designed for pure methane.) In this way, wherever electricity can be produced in excess of local needs, it can be shipped to more needy places in the form of a gaseous fuel, and there converted into electricity and heat by a cogenerator, or into electricity alone by a fuel cell. (A fuel cell is a device that, supplied with oxygen and a gaseous fuel such as hydrogen or methane, very efficiently produces electricity.)

The environment also forms a vital part of this solar picture. Fortunately, the solar devices that make economic sense are also quite compatible with the environment. Solar collectors, photovoltaic cells, and windmills simply transfer solar heat from one place to another. Their effects would be unnoticeable in the heat-transfer processes which occur naturally in the changes of the weather. The production of fuels from biomass fits nicely into the natural ecological cycles that support agriculture, and when burned, these fuels (or hydrogen produced from solar electricity) produce only water and carbon dioxide. And since the carbon dioxide produced when a solar fuel burns is exactly equal to the amount absorbed photosynthetically, when the fuel is produced, this process does not contribute to the untoward environmental effects of rising levels of carbon dioxide in the atmosphere. Unlike the present high-tension power lines which disrupt the landscape, methane pipelines would be underground—where, unfortunately, they would be subject, as are the present natural gas pipelines, to fires and explosions.

A final piece of the solar picture puzzle concerns storage. Since the availability of solar energy depends on the natural cycles that govern the planet's behavior —the alternation of day and night, the seasonal changes in solar intensity, changes in cloud cover—there are times when energy is needed but is not immediately available. Storage is therefore essential. There are wel-known devices capable of storing the different forms of solar energy in the amounts required to meet local short-term needs: tanks of hot water, bins of grain and other forms of biomass, rechargeable batteries, tanks of liquid fuels or of pressurized hydrogen or methane. However, a national solar system also requires storage on a national scale —a fact that is usually overlooked by both the proponents and the opponents of solar energy. The annual output of a wholly solar national energy system would depend on the weather, and if the system was just large enough to meet the national demand in a relatively sunny year, it might fail disastrously in a particularly cold or cloudy year. One can, of course, deal with this problem by building a solar system large enough to operate effectively in the worst conceivable annual weather. But this would incur a large added cost that would be unnecessary in most years. The more efficient way to deal with the problem is the ancient one that has been traditional in our oldest solar enterprise, farming: grain overproduced in good years is stored in preparation for bad years. The same thing could be done by storing energy on a national scale. But again, methane is the only form of energy that could be handled in this way. (Constructing tanks and bins large enough for a national store of liquid fuel, or biomass, would be prohibitively expensive.) With a national methane pipeline system in place, in good years excess methane could be produced and then pumped for storage (perhaps mixed with some hydrogen) into the underground formations that once held natural gas, many of which will then, of course, be empty. The same strategy could be used to compensate for the seasonal imbalance between energy production (which is likely to be highest in the summer) and energy demand (which is likely to be highest in the winter). . . .

Taken from "The Big Switch, a Plan to Save New York," by Leonard Rodberg and Geoffrey Stokes, Village Voice, *February 18, 1980.*

By the casually profligate standards of energy consumption this country has grown used to, New Yorkers are heroes. On a per capita basis, we use only half as much energy as the average American. We live close to each other, in row houses and apartments that expose only two walls; we use the bejeezus out of our mass transit systems; our economy is based on commerce and service industries, not energy-hungry manufacturing. But this is less heroism than happenstance; the days of Manhattan mansions are long past, and driving—or parking—a car is often more trouble than it's worth. With relatively modest effort, we could score even higher on the energy conservation scale.

And we have to, for the pat on the back we get from raw consumption figures is dangerously misleading. Like the rest of the country, we are in trouble—not just because we are yoked to Kansas highways and Los Angeles freeways (even if we wanted to, we couldn't pretend it was their end of the boat sinking), but because of the sources of the energy we do use.

Much more than the rest of the country, we are oil-dependent. Nationwide, less than half the energy Americans use is drawn from oil, but New York City derives 80 per cent of its energy from that increasingly scarce and costly fuel. Even more important, the oil used in the rest of the country is concentrated in transportation. Half of what they use goes into their gas tanks, and though there would of course be political resistance to policies that forced less automobile use, such policies do exist—at least on the drawing boards—and if put into play, would be inconvenient at worst. The inconvenience might be considerable—for many rural people, their car is the only physical link to jobs or neighbors—but a reasonable limit on driving wouldn't be a matter of life or death.

In New York City, the picture is radically different. Less than a quarter of the oil we use goes to cars, trucks, or buses; the rest goes for heat and electricity. Other areas use 15 per cent of their oil to heat their homes and workplaces; we use three times as much. They use only 12 per cent of their oil to generate electricity; we use 28 per cent—more than twice as much. And if the national supply of heating oil ran out on a mythical day when the temperature was an even zero all over the country, two out of every three New Yorkers would freeze; outside the city, almost four out of five households would stay warm.

Though such a magic cutoff is, one hopes, unlikely, the real-world consequences of our dependence on oil remain dramatic. When prices—over which we have no control—go up all across the country, New Yorkers (except perhaps those who own large chunks of Mobil and Exxon) suffer disproportionately. Businesses flee to the

Sunbelt, unemployment increases, and taxes rise in a desperate attempt to keep pace with the increased costs of human government. Homeowners—hit with high real estate taxes and a doubled fuel bill—put their houses on the market for whatever they can salvage, and stable neighborhoods deteriorate. Marginal landlords abandon their buildings, and the so-called "best" ones demand ever higher rents. With each turn of the screw by OPEC or the oil companies, the cycle of disaster grows worse; in a painfully unexaggerated sense, our survival as a city depends on our ability to overcome our addiction to oil.

Fortunately, there are some ways we can help ourselves. We can conserve energy. Not just by turning out the lights when we leave the room (though that's by no means a bad way to begin), but by a major, *governmental* program designed to break the oil suppliers' stranglehold on New York. And once overall use is down, we can move toward full independence by building renewable energy sources to supply the power we really do need. Finally, by financing such a two-step program in the tax-free money market, we can not only salvage the city's longterm economic future, but put thousands of New Yorkers to work in meaningful jobs as we do it.

You would think that the crisis facing us is so obvious that even a municipal government as hard-pressed as New York's would be hastening to formulate a coherent response. That's what you'd think but you've got to remember that the city seems incapable even of picking up the garbage on time, much less indulging in rational planning. To say that the current administration's attitude mirrors Louis XIV's—*"Apres moi, le déluge"*—is not to exaggerate by much. Amazingly, the city is now putting *less* effort into energy planning than it did a decade ago. . . .

. . . To cope with the day-to-day problems of gasoline allocation and heating oil prices, mayoral assistant Robert Herzog has only a staff of six people and a position of virtually no clout. And even if the staff somehow managed to shake free from its daily workload to address the long-range crisis, the odds on its achieving the radical reforms that the situation demands are astronomical. Its work, you see, is overseen by the Mayor's Energy Advisory Committee. Among its members is one Charles Luce—who also, not so incidentally, is the chairman of Con Ed. His business is to sell energy, not save it. . . .

Curiously, the same budgetary limitations that work against us in trying to keep the streets clean or the subways running on time work for us in the energy crisis. We are forced to look where we should be looking—at smaller, decentralized, renewable energy sources. And, of course, at conservation.

We can do what we need to do—and strengthen New York in the process by making it more attractive to businesses and residents—without putting even the slightest dent in our precarious municipal finances. The first step is to reduce our need for fuels of any sort.

CONSERVATION

Conservation is not sexy. Worse, it is the tiniest bit scary, carrying with it those misleading images of shivering in the darkness. It makes good economic sense—as homeowners and large real estate operators have come to understand—but it lacks the glamour of the synfuel program. That's all right, though; New York can't *afford* glamour.

We can afford—and desperately need—a real conservation program along the following lines.

Let's take heating as an example. Over half the energy used by New Yorkers goes to heat our homes and commercial buildings. This year, that heat is going to cost about $2.8 billion. A large chunk of that money is wasted. Burning fuel that we don't need to burn is a free gift to the oil companies and to OPEC. This is silly; they already have more money than we do. And there are opportunities for very great improvements in the efficiency of energy use in our homes, stores, and offices. With reasonable care and with a sufficient initial investment of funds, at current fuel prices, we can save $1.4 billion—half of what we're spending—each year.

Studies of even the relatively well insulated homes of the early '70s have shown that controlling the heat flows in these buildings can reduce fuel usage by as much as two-thirds; because a large part of the city's housing stock isn't even adequately insulated, our savings can be greater. And in offices, for example, a few relatively inexpensive changes in lighting and temperature control let the new Citicorp headquarters reduce its projected energy costs by 45 per cent.

There are two general ways to reduce energy consumption: performing the same activities in a more efficient way; and changing some of our work patterns and domestic behavior to reduce the need for energy.

The first is obviously easier. It involves some one-time change in the way we equip our buildings—through investment in either materials or services. These have the distinct practical advantage of requiring no further attention from the residents of the building once they are in place—and if you've ever despaired of teaching your kids to turn out the bathroom light, you understand the difficulty of getting people to change their behavior. Finally, such structural and operating changes carry an economic bonus; they create jobs in New York rather than surplus profits in Texas.

A compact—and by no means complete—list of conservation measures that are already available to reduce heating costs in buildings includes:

- adding insulation to walls, ceilings, attics, and basements;
- weatherstripping doors and windows;
- installing clock-controlled thermostats and thermostatically controlled radiator valves;
- tuning furnaces for greater efficiency;
- insulating heating pipes and ducts;
- sealing any cracks in the foundation or walls.

In addition, the hot water system can use at least 50 per cent less energy if flow restrictors are installed, temperatures are lowered below scalding, waste hot water is rechanneled to preheat incoming water, and the person doing the laundry uses the cold-water cycle.

Lighting energy can be reduced by substituting fluorescent bulbs where appropriate, and by using incandescent bulbs of the proper wattage in other rooms. Finally, appliance energy drain can be reduced by installing high-efficiency appliances as old ones wear out, improving ventilation and installing sunscreens or awnings to cut air conditioning loads, and, obviously, by using air conditioning only when it is absolutely needed.

This list seems reasonable, for the only significant change it proposes in conventional behavior is a modest reduction in air conditioning. But it will cost money —between $1,500 and $2,000 per household (or its equivalent commercial space). How can the city possibly afford such expenditures?

It can't. On the other hand, it doesn't have to. All the government needs to do is leverage the banks into making loans at reasonable rates to cover the initial investment. The people who save on their energy bills can then use this surplus to pay off both the principal and the interest.

That surplus will mount very quickly. According to Operation Open City's experience with a federally funded weatherization program, the one-time expenditure of as little as $150 for weather-stripping, caulking, and new window panes per household can save 25 per cent on a typical New York City heating bill. With larger investments for all and ceiling insulation, storm windows, and furnace improvements like those we've suggested for an energy-efficient loft (see box, page 272.), much greater savings are possible. At a rough approximation, a $1,500 per-household investment will reduce the heating bill by 50 per cent. (To determine the cost and measures needed in *your* home, you should arrange an energy audit.) With an additional $500 (perhaps spread over a number of years, as new, more energy-efficient appliances are purchased), costs for hot water, lighting, and other household uses should also fall by half. Since the average energy bill for a New York City household this year will be more than $1,000, this $2,000 investment will literally pay for itself in less than four years.

If *every* household and commercial building in New York were to make this investment, we would save 52 million barrels of oil every year—40 per cent of what we now use. This is about five times as much as Con Ed hopes to save by spewing coal smoke into the environment. Even more important, such a program would reduce our *future* energy costs. A conservation program of this size could actually *cut* the use of electricity by more than 30 per cent from current usage. This means Con Ed could phase out its obsolete plants, scheduled for shutdown in the next 15 years, without having to replace their 1,700 megawatts with power purchased from PASNY [Power Authority, State of New York].

This last would not make Con Ed happy, and many people are quite reasonably afraid that the company will force conservation to backfire by raising its rates to make up for lost revenue. This would almost certainly happen if conservation were limited to uncoordinated action by individuals and firms. But if government guides an integrated plan, then the shutdowns can be designed to reduce Con Ed's costs and thus lower its rates (or, depending on the mayor's courage, to get rid of Con Ed altogether). . . .

A final note on costs: though it's obviously *possible,* using only existing equipment and technology, to cut our usage of heating fuel in half, it won't be cheap. Using constant dollars, a program of the size we've outlined will cost the residents and businesses of the city about $8 billion dollars over a 15-year period. But over that same 15-year period, energy *savings* will total more than $17 billion.

The $9 billion dillar difference between what we would have been paying for energy and what we *could* pay if we adopted a conservation strategy is enough

An Energy Audit of a Loft

The typical loft building uses energy very inefficiently. The huge interior spaces and the rising cost of energy make conservation a necessity. We have conducted an energy audit of a typical loft building in Soho. The building has five stories measuring 50′ × 20′, divided into 10 apartment units. The building is oil-heated and has front and back facades of granite and side walls of brick (partially adjoining adjacent buildings). This year the residents of the building will spend $18,000 on fuel oil. Our audit showed the following results:

	Cost	Savings (%)	Payback Period
Insulate roof	$6,000	30	11 months
Insulate walls	$7,500	19	1.8 years
Install storm windows	$4,000	5	3.4 years
Insulate ceiling of sub-basement	$2,800	5	2.4 years
Clean and adjust boiler	$60	5	1 month
Install thermostatic/control valves on radiators	$980	10	6 months
Weatherstrip doors and elevator shaft	$100	2	4 months
Insulate heating pipes in unheated areas	$110	1	7 months
Total	$21,550	77	1.6 years

More than three-quarters of the heating load can be eliminated, and the investment will pay for itself in less than two years. Solar hot water on the roof would cost $20,000 to $25,000, cut the (electric) hot water bill by 60 per cent, and pay for itself in 10 years. One of the masonry facades faces south; a solar wall built there would cost $5,000 and save 20 per cent of the remaining heating bill, with a payback period of 6 years. All of these costs could be greatly reduced if some of the work were done by the residents

—Lisa Alexandra Reindorf

to pay the bankers interest on the bonds to finance the initial investment (bankers always get their share, even in Utopia), and leave a substantial bonus left over. And that's just the beginning.

ALTERNATE SOURCES: THE SUN

Conservation is the most essential component of any rational energy plan for the city, but it's only a part of the picture. Once our overall consumption of energy is reduced, we can then further our independence from OPEC's oil by substituting available, renewable energy sources. The first of these is sunlight.

Sunlight is valuable. Because other energy sources cost so much, the sunlight we now waste can be assigned a very significant price. In New York, the solar energy that falls on a single square foot in an average year is "worth" $8 if it's used to replace electric heat, $2.70 if it replaces oil heat. Even though the available technology won't let us capture and convert all of the sun's energy, the aggregate value of *usable* solar energy is staggering. In it, we have the local equivalent of inexhaustible oil wells pumping tens of billions of dollars every year.

But, as the oil companies remind us with every price hike, collecting the moving energy isn't cheap. At the moment, commercial rooftop solar collection systems cost between $40 and $70 per square foot, though prices should drop as sales increase. Though the time such systems take to pay for themselves is shortened with every jump in the price of oil, their cost has made them attractive primarily to those with readily available cash. There are, however, simpler, less expensive techniques for using the sun's energy that can make solar power an important natural resource for New York.

The sun's energy is present in abundance; the technical problem is to move it from "out there" to "in here"—where it can provide us heat and hot water. The usual way of doing this involves "collectors"—glass-covered boxes containing a maze of black-painted pipes. The collector is set on a roof, and water is pumped through it. In its trip through the labyrinth of pipe, the water absorbs sufficient heat either to be used immediately or stored for later (night-time) use.

But water is neither the only, nor the best, medium to carry the sun's energy. Air, for instance, has a number of advantages: if the system leaks, it won't cause structural or cosmetic damage; there are no freeze-ups; and the system is cheaper to install. Finally, it's a more efficient collector of energy. Best of all, New York's skyscraper canyons are almost perfect for the collection of solar energy striking their towering walls.

New York buildings have millions of square feet of south-facing walls. Because many of them are brick and masonry, they absorb heat so well that they remain warm to the touch for hours after sunset. But as a rule, this heat is wasted. If these walls were, like the pipes in a conventional collector, painted black and covered with glass or clear plastic—and if they were vented into the space behind them —they would provide millions of dollars' worth of solar heat every winter.

One group of teenagers built such a "solar wall" on the Lower East Side, just north of Houston Street. Last heating season, that wall provided heat worth almost $1.50 a square foot to the gymnasium behind it, and as a summer bonus, when the vents were opened, it created a ventilating stream which helped cool the gym. Such walls—commonly called "passive" solar systems—require no external source of energy besides the sun, need little or no maintenance, and cost about $10 per square foot to build; at today's oil prices, a solar wall pays for itself within six years.

The average home or apartment building could—if it had previously adopted the kind of conservation measures we've discussed—meet nearly half of its remaining heating needs by converting 200 square feet per family of its southern facade to a solar wall. If only 20 per cent of the structures in the city carried out such conservation, we would save over three million barrels of oil every year.

We would also change the New York skyline. Instead of the night-time incandescence that once greeted visitors with proof that New York had led the way into the electric age, arriving sailors would see evidence that New York had come into the solar age.

Already, there are more than a dozen solar collectors installed on the New York rooftops; fully 40 per cent of our structures could have such additions to supply their hot water.

It would make a difference of at least a million barrels of oil each year. The average New York household uses about 70 gallons of hot water a day. If the conservation we've talked about cut this consumption in half, 40 square feet of solar collectors would provide the remaining energy requirements on a year-round basis (prudence would demand a backup system, for cloudy mid-winter conditions). Such a solar collector, homemade, costs about $100 to build; a $1,500 estimate for a mass-production commercial model seems generous. At the latter price, a system that replaced electrically provided hot water would pay for itself in 10 years on a private house. But in apartments, where most New Yorkers live, one bank of collectors could serve many households, enabling the system to pay for itself much sooner.

WIND POWER

One doesn't want to come on like Bob Dylan, but vast amounts of energy are present in the winds that sweep across New York. Though wind has obviously been a primary source of energy for centuries—to move ships, pump water, or grind wheat—its most exciting potential for New Yorkers lies in our ability to convert it to heat or electricity.

Though most cities are generally considered to be low-wind areas, New York City is exposed to bodies of water on all sides and has many areas where strong winds are the norm. LaGuardia Airport, probably the most thoroughly measured spot in the city, has an average wind speed of more than 12.5 mph—more than enough to run wind-powered electric generators effectively. Such wind machines could be dotted along the shoreline, on tops of buildings, or even on artificial "islands" off the south shore of Long Island.

In addition, small wind generators—with rated power in the one to 20 kilowatt range—could be set up to serve individual homes or clusters of homes and apartments. According to Con Ed's figures, the typical New York household uses 3,400 kilowatt hours per year; on average, a 2 kw generator would meet this need. Larger generators, in the 100 to 10,000 kw range, might be installed on a commercial basis by Con Ed or—preferably—by a specially created city agency. One such generator, with a power of 2,000 kw, is already operating in Boone, North Carolina.

The logical place for such generators (which are not as aesthetically problematic as conventional power sources) is on the shoreline. The city has 578 miles of coastline, and if, for instance, a 2,000 kw windmill were installed every quarter mile along even half of it, these wind-powered systems would replace the equivalent of 15 million barrels of oil every year—almost half of Con Ed's present consumption.

FREE AS AIR?

With our still comparatively primitive technology, wind systems generate electricity at an average cost of between 9 and 12 cents per kwh; the best available estimates are that this cost will fall to about 5 cents per kwh within a decade. This isn't free, but it already compares favorably with Con Ed's present charge of 9 cents per kwy—a cost that can only rise with the price of oil or synfuel. But even today, a $6,000 2 kw generator would reduce a consumer's Con Ed bill by about $300 per year today, paying for itself in less than 20 years.

Because wind speeds vary widely, such residential generators need to connect with an existing utility system. At certain days and times, they put their surplus power into the existing grid; at others when the home needs more power than the generator is supplying, it draws from the system. When the existing utility system serves as a storage device for wind generators, batteries and other costly storage devices need not be purchased. Indeed, as a result of a lawsuit brought by the group that constructed the city's first wind generator at 519 East 11th Street, Con Ed is now required to accept such interconnections (on the other hand, they now charge exorbitant rates for this service).

Note that a network of wind-powered generators, no matter how extensive, would not lead to a substantial reduction in Con Ed's generating *capacity*. Because of the wind's ebb and flow, the utility system would have to be able to provide virtually as much power as it does now. But it wouldn't have to provide its full capacity on a daily basis and could therefore save vast amounts of oil. Indeed, the utility could contribute to the savings by placing windmills on top of the substations it maintains across the five boroughs, thus capping practicality with appropriate symbolism.

GOLDEN GARBAGE

More than a decade ago, in what then seemed a visionary book, Jane Jacobs proposed "mining" the city's garbage for recyclable materials. A rapidly developing technology has not only made her dream an achievable reality, but has done even more. Because those parts of the garbage that aren't economically recyclable can be burned to generate power, the normal processes of city life are creating a daily gusher.

Municipal waste is already producing electric power in Ames, Iowa, and Hempstead, Long Island; in addition, there are a number of commercial firms eager to convert trash into a powdered or pelletized fuel selling for less than the current price of oil. Westchester County is building a Peekskill plant that will convert 1,500 tons of waste every day. In New York, where we produce 20,000 tons of garbage a day, we could use 10 plants that size.

Some of this is already happening:

The Koch administration has announced plans to build a 3,000-ton-per-day plant in the Brooklyn Navy Yard which will produce steam to be fed into the Con Ed steam distribution system. The state's Urban Development Corporation, in conjunction with a private firm, is planning to construct a plant in the South Bronx that will convert 3,000 tons per day of waste into a powdery fuel that can be burned alone or with oil or coal to make electricity.

Unlike "raw" trash and garbage, this "refuse derived fuel" (RDF) is easily transportable and can be readily stored for use in times of heavy electrical demand. The U.S. Environmental Protection Agency has not yet established standards for the burning of municipal waste, partly because there are few studies so far of its pollution effects. But even if these prove to be serious, New York's RDF could be shipped to a plant that currently burns coal—rather than being burned within the city at Con Ed's oil-burning plants—whose electricity we could buy in return. (It is likely that RDF will give off less pollution than coal, though more than oil. PASNY's proposed Staten Island plant will burn both coal and refuse, giving us the worst of both!)

The burnable portion of each ton of municipal waste has an energy content equivalent to 1.8 barrels of oil. The waste collected in New York City, when burned to produce steam or electricity, will replace 13 million barrels each year. In addition, materials such as steel, aluminum, and glass can be recycled, saving the country (not New York City, which doesn't produce these products) another three million barrels per year and swelling the municipal treasury.

The city can also make use of decaying garbage to produce methane, the primary ingredient of natural gas, and Brooklyn Union Gas is already planning to extract methane from the Fountain Avenue landfill in Brooklyn. However, natural gas is not now in short supply, and space for new landfills is scarce. Toward the end of this century, when the process of producing electricity through wind and photocells should be complete, we might want to shift over to using our waste matter for the production of methane.

The conventional method of producing electricity is inherently inefficient; two-thirds of the heat released in fossil-fuel plants is sent up the stacks or into surrounding bodies of water. In a society where people get cold in winter, this waste is silly. Large buildings and industrial complexes can use oil-or gas-powered generators to produce electricity on-site and put this "waste" heat to productive use. Overall, such processes of "cogeneration" produce electricity with about twice the efficiency—i.e., half the fuel—of conventional power plants. . . .

And if the cogeneration equipment used natural gas instead of oil, it would save an additional four million barrels annually—while using a fuel that is more readily available than oil, yields fewer pollutants, and can be developed from renewable sources. At present, consistent with its hard-nosed opposition to cogeneration, Con Ed is refusing to sell gas to cogenerators. This—along with several other of the company's unsavory policies—will have to be changed.

We've focused only on current available technologies; the idea is that this is a plan the city could begin *now.* But that doesn't mean that other—and better—options might not become available during the years of the plan's implementation.

- Solar Cells: For years, solar cells (also called photovoltaic cells) have been used in the space program. By the 1990s, we are likely to see solar cells installed fairly widely, generating electricity and providing heat—captured by moving water or air behind the cells—as well. This "solar cogeneration" is applicable to any building with access to the sun. And it provides yet another reason we need to break Con Ed's opposition to conventional cogeneration, for that process would pave the way for wide-scale decentralized energy production.
- Fuel Cells: Like solar cells, the hydrogen-based fuel cell received its initial push from the space program. These combine hydrogen with oxygen to produce electricity (and water). Under federal grant, Con Ed is even now testing a fuel cell at its East 15th Street plant.
- Fluidized Bed Furnaces: Before too long it may be possible to use coal as a

fuel for cogeneration in "fluidized bed boilers." These burn crushed coal which has been suspended in air above a bed of limestone. Now being tested here and in Europe, they are twice as clean as new coal-fired plants of the conventional type, and up to 10 times cleaner than coal-burning plants in operation today. Another five years or more are needed, however, before they can be proven reliable and clean enough for widespread use.

Though the measures in this plan will save each New York household about a thousand dollars a year, taxpayers have no doubt noticed they will cost money. Not in the long run—when we use phrases like "pay for itself," we mean it—but immediate money to finance these capital improvements. How and where that money is raised depends on a fundamentally political perception: whose job is this? . . .

. . .[The] decentralized nature of these measures makes it difficiult to finance the necessary steps. Utilities or oil conglomerates can raise billions of dollars in the money market, but the costs of conservation fall on millions of consumers—homeowners, small businessmen, institutions—each of whom must raise several thousand dollars. In the face of double-digit inflation and soaring interest rates, this seems a lot to ask. . . .

So what we need to make this program work is a large pot of money which can be loaned, for long terms, at reasonable rates of interest with sensible repayment plans. Conventional home improvement loans, which are short term and carry relatively high rates of interest, won't work. Energy Saver Loans should have repayment terms equal to the expected life of the purchased equipment, usually 20 years or more. In addition, such loans should be modeled on the so-called "young couples" mortgages—in which payments start low, rising (with inflation) as the years pass. With such graduated payment loans, the consumer will get *immediate* savings, because the savings on energy will be greater than the loan payments.

The problem, alas, is that such funds are generally not available, and a workable alternative energy program must find a way to get local banks and credit unions to provide them. Here, the city or state government could play a key role. It could guarantee them, or it could actually finance them by using its bonding authority to raise money on the tax-exempt (low-interest) market and passing the savings on to consumers. Portland, Oregon, already offers such interest subsidies.

Direct government action of this sort might not be necessary, however, for energy-saving investments don't represent an *additional* cost that the borrower must take on, but an actual reduction in his or her monthly expenditures. By definition, loans of this sort are attractive risks to bankers, and there are many mechanisms which could be used to make them widely available.

Perhaps the most appealing of these is the monthly utility bill. The TVA, along with the municipal power system in Los Angeles and other West Coast cities, already installs insulation, storm windows and solar water heaters without requiring any cash down payment from its customers. Instead, these conservation measures are financed through payments on the customers' regular monthly utility bill —which is often lower than before the loan. . . .

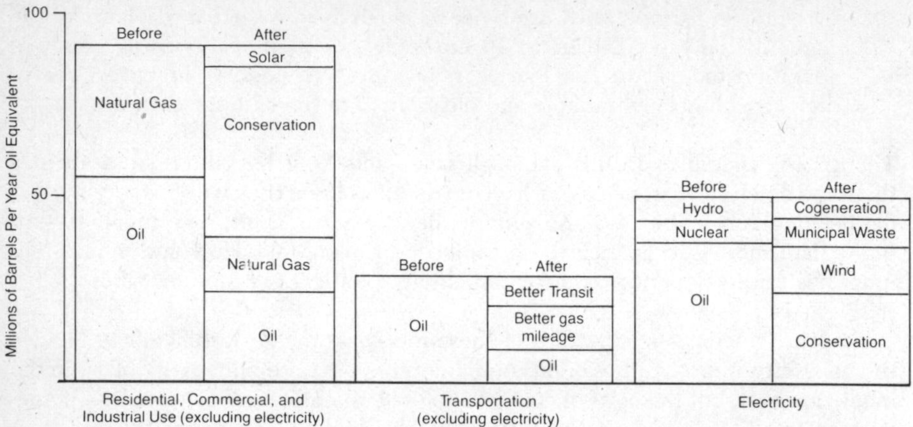

. . . If the energy shortage is really a crisis, then something more than mere persuasion is required. If we want planning for an energy-independent future (so that, for instance, utility construction schedules are consistent with growing conservation), we can't afford to rely on the shifting conditions of the market. After all, why should a landlord weatherize his apartment building when he can simply raise his tenants' rents? Or why should a businessman curb his energy use when he—along with his competitors—can mark up his price tags?

Under our present laws, there's no reason. And so they must be changed. New York, as a number of other cities have already done, should phase in *mandatory* energy conservation requirements. In San Diego County, for instance, all new homes by law must be equipped with solar water heaters. More striking, Portland, Oregon, now requires that by 1984 *no* home may be sold unless it has been retrofited with all energy conservation measures that have payback periods of less than ten years. And no rental unit may be rented unless it has been similarly reconditioned. New York should do the same thing.

There will, obviously, be some opposition to this. Yet we have done it before; the federal government has set mandatory standards for air and water pollution, and regulates automobile fuel efficiency. Locally, New York State has a law requiring that starting in 1981 only high-efficiency air conditioners be sold within the state. The city can certainly move in the same direction. . . .

The city should immediately establish a strong energy agency, with the initial task of developing a comprehensive, detailed plan along the lines of this one. It might follow the lead of Seattle, which took a year-long look at its energy future that involved all segments of the city—consumer, business, labor, environmentalist, utilities, city, state, and federal government—in developing an energy plan for the city.

However, if a plan like ours is adopted, this agency will very soon have operating responsibilities as well as planning ones. It might begin by providing consumer certification for the various kinds of conservation materials and equipment that consumers will be purchasing—insulation, storm windows, replacement oil burners, clock thermostats, etc. Consumers need reliable advice on the effectiveness of such products.

The agency might then move on to the actual installation of energy systems, for instance, solar units or wind generators. (Los Angeles already does this.) As the use of renewable energy development grows, the role of Con Ed will become increasingly questionable. Like all utilities, it is wedded to an old style method of energy production which is nearing the end of the road. Determined in its dying days to "protect" its investment and to extract a maximum profit from us, it is a barrier to effective progress along the path we have outlined. Eventually, Con Ed's oil-fired generating capacity will be replaced by renewable energy sources. This can take place only if these plants are operated by a public agency in the public interest. (An interesting case in point: Seattle's groundbreaking conservation plan was possible because its utility, municipally owned, had to respond to the city government's energy-saving mandate.) . . .

This year New Yorkers will spend over $5 billion on energy, with over half of that flowing out of the New York City economy, to purchase oil and gas and fatten the coffers of sheiks and multi-national oil companies. That money could better have been used by the residents of New York to purchase other goods and services, producing jobs for the hundreds of thousands of unemployed workers in this city.

We know that conservation and renewable energy measures could substantially reduce our consumption of fossil fuels, and would sharply curb this outflow of dollars from our economy. Furthermore, they could create jobs in their own right. Most of the steps we have suggested involve the investment of capital, and when capital is invested, people are put to work.

Finally, a new conservation and renewable energy industry could be created in this city. Construction workers of all kinds would find employment here, and firms producing electrical equipment and components, sheet metal gear, and other light manufacturing would enjoy expanded sales and be able to hire many new workers. In fact, if one billion dollars were to be spent each year of the next fifteen years, we could meet many of the energy goals we have outlined, while more than 15,000 jobs would be created in the direct manufacture and installation of this equipment. An additional 30,000 jobs would be found in supplying this new industry and providing consumer goods and services for the newly employed workers. In addition, New Yorkers would save increasing amounts of money as their energy consumption started to drop; when they spent this money on goods and services within the city, additional tens of thousands of jobs would be created. . . .

Taken from Energy-Efficient Community Planning, *by James Ridgeway, with Carolyn Projansky Emmaus, Pa., JG Press, 1979.*

Davis is close to the Sacramento River, which flows into the San Francisco Bay 50 miles downstream. The terrain is flat. Big farms stretch out in all directions.

The city proper was established in the 1850s as a depot where rail lines from San Francisco met those that connected with the transcontinental railroad. Subsequently Davis became an important junction for the Southern Pacific Railroad, linking the railroad's lines running down the Valley with those going east and west. A few decades after the railroad arrived, the University of California decided to locate the state's agricultural experiment station at Davis, and that gave the community the beginnings of an important second industry.

The basic shape of the city remained much the same until the late 1950s when the agricultural school was expanded to become a full-fledged campus of the University of California. A medical school and liberal arts college were added to the veterinary and agricultural colleges already on the Davis campus.

With rapid growth of the city, citizens became increasingly concerned about planning. In 1968, after lengthy debate, a progressive City Council moved to curb growth.

It turned against the automobile and embraced the bicycle and bus as means of transport. After sponsoring an inquiry into energy use, the Council endorsed a series of measures aimed at reducing energy use by as much as one half. That meant regulating how a new house or apartment building is situated on a lot, what kind and how much insulation builders use, where and how much glass is to be employed, and so on. It encouraged developers and builders to begin adopting solar energy. The city obtained funds and hired consultants to design model solar buildings. It has begun to develop a program for retrofitting existing dwellings.

Davis is experimenting with energy-saving ideas in other areas. It has decided to cut back on the use of pesticides on thousands of trees and shurbs that shade the streets, opting instead for a policy of biological control for insects. The city's fleet of cars and trucks has been transormed into a fleet of compact vehicles. When a Davis employee has to get around town, he borrows a bike from the city rack. Davis even passed a law to formally and solemnly sanction the clothesline.

Two years after the city began to enforce its energy-conscious building code, the results were manifest. Figures for 1977 electricity consumption revealed a 12 percent drop in consumption per customer in the community.

Even more remarkable is that while the number of customers increased by seven percent from 11,600 to 12,500, the total consumption of electricity by all customers declined by six percent. Since 1973, the year of the Arab oil embargo and the beginning of a national energy consciousness, electricity consumption per customer in Davis declined by nearly 18 percent. (Nationwide, in 1974 with the shock of higher utility prices, there was virtually no growth in electricity consumption. Since then, however, consumption has been going up at about three percent per year.)

What follows is a collection of codes, ordinances, drawings, photographs and plans that make up the Davis experiment. It puts special emphasis on conservation of land, water, energy and other natural resources, and moves towards a general limit on growth. While many of the provisions of these papers are designed to meet Davis's unique needs, the ideas and plans will be of use elsewhere.

GENERAL PLAN

Gloria McGregor, the city's community development director, explains basic features of the general plan:

California has, for many years, taken the position that it wishes local government to solve and guide its own destiny, within a very loose framework. Within that context, it has been the evolving position, as evidenced by the recently adopted General Plan, that Davis has some very distinct responsibilities to its citizens, which it accepts, but that it feels considerably less need to take up the burdens of surrounding communities, most importantly Sacramento. From this ethic sprang the policies and ordinances which circumscribe growth management in Davis.

The most important of the enabling documents is termed the Housing Development Priority Program. Its preamble calls for orderly residential development to meet the needs of the community, protection of adjacent prime agricultural land, provision of housing and services for the student body and faculty of the University of California at Davis, in an environmentally and socially responsible manner. A strong expression of the need for adequate housing in Davis for those persons of low, moderate, or fixed incomes whose work, study, or other connections with the city of Davis led them to desire to live here threads throughout the document. This is the single most important part of the Davis General Plan which removes from it the sting and flavor of exclusion which might otherwise be present.

The method to determine the need for housing in Davis is the Annual Needs Survey, which, in as detailed a way as possible, compares the existing housing stock in the planning areas of the city with the need for new housing stock, and sets an annual needs number. This Annual Needs Survey is conducted during the summer and the allocation of approvals to build is granted in the fall for the following three years.

The Needs Survey, first completed in 1974, attempts to identify the number of low, moderate and high income single and multiple family housing units needed in each of the planning areas of Davis. Another important principle of the General Plan, of significant social and economic importance, is the direction to achieve a similar mix in types of housing available across the city, so that property values and social interaction will be maintained wherever one lives in the city. This aspect of the control of housing construction contributes a great deal to the general atmosphere of good will between the University and the city, not often present in other similarly dominated cities.

The second of these important expressions of policy is called the Amplification of Housing Development Priority Criteria. Upon the completion of the Annual Needs Survey, all those builders who wish to receive an allocation must present their plans to the Housing Review Board at the same time, to be examined in the light of the ten criteria set forth in this Resolution. (The property must be already in the right timing phase of the General Plan, and have the proper zoning; the zoning must be planned development to allow for mix of types.) These are, in order of their importance: internal growth needs, economic mix, low and moderate income housing, environmental impact, availability of public services and facilities, compactness, design diversity, economic impact, feasibility and competition. Since each application must be in the form of a planned development, over which the city has complete control, refusal of an allocation can be based on the failure to satisfactorily meet these criteria. This is the strong mechanism, for example, under which the city can assure that an adequate supply of low and moderate income housing is to be built.

The third significant feature of the adopted General Plan is the Phasing Map, which sets forth the order in which the city shall develop, based on 21 criteria developed by the General Plan Committees and the Planning Commission and Council. Roughly speaking, Phase I and Phase II are to be completed by 1990, which would result in a population of approximately 50,000; those areas designated Urban Reserve will then be considered.

This is a capsule view of the growth Management Plan of Davis. It is a sincere and responsible effort to state the acceptance of the city to provide the housing and services which people whose work, study or other connections need to enable them to live in Davis. It is equally plain in its expression of disinclination to allow destruction of its attractive character and ambience by its regional location and magnetic pull for those who work elsewhere. Whether any city, without backing at the regional or state level, is able to maintain its uniqueness may be questioned, but Davis is making a strong effort in that direction.

ENERGY USE

In order to achieve the General Plan objective of energy conservation, a research group at the University of California, Davis, was funded to develop an energy conservation building code. The first task of the group was the collection of data on the energy use of Davis households. The goals of the research were twofold: 1) determine how design features of dwellings affect gas and electric consumption, and 2) to identify household management practices and appliance use which would reduce energy consumption.

Temperature records for apartments and houses were collected over a period of months, in summer and winter, to provide data which would contribute to understanding how design features affect energy use. In addition, utility bills were evaluated to determine actual energy use during a period of several years. The results of this data collection and evaluation formed the basis for the Davis Energy Conservation Building Code.

In the summer, the second floor rooms averaged 12°C(52°F) warmer than those on the ground floor, and north-south exposures were much cooler than east-west. The coolest units were north-south facing on the ground floor, reaching a maximum of 24°C(75°F), perfectly comfortable in hot summer weather. The hottest apartments were those facing east-west on the top floor. The results of the temperature tests were perfectly paralleled by the actual electrical use of the apartments.

In the winter, the south facing apartments performed significantly better than those facing north, east, and west. On several occasions, south facing apartments had high temperatures in the 80s F on sunny winter days, with a maximum of 87 F. During several days the high temperatures were 24°F above ambient, and 17°F above apartments with north, east, or west exposure. These high temperatures occurred in selected vacant apartments built with solar exposures that were far from ideal. By comparison, a specially constructed research room with nearly ideal south window exposure registered an interior maximum temperature 48°F above the maximum ambient.

Tests on single family detached houses provided less clear results than apartments. However, it was evident that the houses in the core area used less electrcity for cooling per square foot than other dwellings. This was attributed to the shade trees in the area which prevented the hot summer sun from reaching the dwellings. West Davis homes had the best insulation and this accounts for their superior performance in both summer and winter.

Research on building in the Central Valley climate has continued for more than thirty years at the University of California, Davis. Most of this work on design with climate has been carried out by L.W. Neubauer, F.A. Brooks, and Richard Cramer. Their achievements provided much of the background for the Davis Energy Conservation Ordinance, and supported the contention that it is possible to achieve good thermal performance by providing proper orientation and shading windows.

Precise answers to the second question of how household management practices and appliance usage affect energy consumption were more difficult to obtain because of the high degree of variability from household to household. Data was collected from household interviews and from gas and electric bills. Analysis of the data show that electric consumption is positively correlated with the number of children in the household, the hours of television watched, and the number of washloads per week. Electric consumption in the households is also highly related to the number of appliances owned.

BUILDING CODE

The basic idea of the Davis Energy Conservation ordinance is that new housing built in Davis shall not experience an excessive heat gain in the summer nor [*sic*] excessive heat loss in the winter. The requirements vary depending on the size of the housing unit and are expressed in BTUs gained or lost per square foot of the house each day. Thus, the thermal efficiency of all housing designs presented to the city's building inspection division must be tested against conditions assumed to exist on typical summer and winter "design" days. The designated design days are August 21 and December 21. The conditions considered include the angle of sunlight at Davis's latitude at different times of the day, the intensity of sunlight, wind speed (assumed to be 15 miles per hour) and outside temperature (45 degrees F as a 24-hour average in the winter, hourly variation in the summer ranging from 59 to 100 degrees).

Maximum permissible amounts of heat gain/loss are shown in the following table, taken from section 10 of the ordinance.

Detached Group 1 Dwelling Unit Thermal Standards

Floor Area (sq.ft.)	Winter Heat Loss (BTUs/sq.ft./day)	Summer Heat Gain (BTUs/sq.ft./day)
500	363	118
1,000	239	103
1,500	208	98
2,000	192	95
2,500	182	93
3,000	176	91

The methods used to meet the requirements set forth above include the following:

Infiltration. All swinging doors and windows opening to the exterior or to unconditioned areas such as garages shall be fully weather-stripped, gasketed or otherwise treated to limit infiltration.

Loose Fill Insulation. When blown or poured type loose fill insulation is used in attic spaces, the slope of the roof shall be not less than 2½ feet in 12 feet and there shall be at least 30 inches of clear headroom at the roof ridge. ("Clear headroom" is defined as the distance from the top of the bottom chord of the truss or ceiling joists to the underside of the roof sheathing.)

Pipe Insulation. All steam and steam condensate return piping and all continuously circulating domestic or heating hot water piping which is located in attics, garages, crawl spaces, underground or unheated spaces other than between floors or in interior walls shall be insulated to provide a maximum heat loss of 50 BTU/hr. per linear foot for piping.

Walls. All exterior walls (excluding windows and doors) shall use R-11 batt insulation between studs. Group H structures must have lightly colored or shaded walls.

Roof/Ceilings; Ceiling/Attics. All roof/ceilings and ceiling/attics must use insulation achieving a minimum resistance of R-19 for the insulation itself. Group H occupancies having roof surfaces unshaded on August 21, at 8:00 A.M., 12:00 noon, or 4:00 P.M., shall be no darker than No. 6 on the Munsell chart.

Floors. Suspended floors over a ventilated crawl space or other unheated space shall have insulation with a minimum resistance of R-11. Concrete slabs on grade require no insulation.

Glazing Area. In Group H occupancies, exterior single-pane glazing (windows, skylights, etc.) may not exceed 12½ percent of the floor area. Exterior double-pane glazing may not exceed 17½ percent of the dwelling unit's floor area.

Glazing Shading. All glazing which is not oriented to the north must be shaded to protect it from direct solar radiation for the hours of 8:00 A.M., 12:00 noon, and 4:00 P.M. (P.S.T.), August 21. In Group H occupancies, the total accumulated amount of unshaded glazing may not exceed 1.5 percent of the dwelling unit's floor area. The use of approved shade screen systems may be employed to demonstrate compliance. Tinted, metalized, or frosted glass shall not be considered self-shading.

The regulations are expressed in two forms, Path I and Path II. Path I is a set of prescriptive standards and Path II is a set of performance standards. The city provided two versions so that a builder with a standardized product might have a routine means of compliance, while those using innovative techniques and materials might have additional scope.

Builders can follow Path I and conform to these provisions:

- A light-colored roof with a Munsell rating of six to ten.
- Six-inch insulation (R-19) as a minimum in the roof.
- Three and a half-inch insulation (R-11) in the walls between the studs.
- Light-colored or shaded exterior walls, with a limit of 15 percent dark allowed for trim.

- Glazing limited to 12.5 percent of the floor area for apartments, with an additional 20 square feet of window area allowed for single family homes, intended to benefit especially small houses.
- Unshaded glazing limited to 1.5 percent of the floor area.

The code includes more detail and some additional provisions, but these have the most significant effect on construction.

Or a builder can follow Path I "with exceptions." Essentially, credit is given when standards are exceeded in one part of the dwelling which can then be applied to another portion. Thus, if the builder improves insulation in the floor or wall, applies heat storage concepts or adds double-paned glass, the area of glass in the house may be increased.

Under Path II the builder presents a design which he certifies meets the standards for winter and summer heat loss.

The three different paths involve different fee structures. For plans conforming to Path II, the building inspection division adds $20 to the permit fee.

Once the builder has selected the path he proposes to follow, he then decides which of several possible plan check methods he will use. The city has produced a workbook which leads the builder through the energy-plan check process. The most important variable to be checked at this point is the amount of glazing permissible in the proposed home, since glass has a very low degree of thermal resistance.

The builders choosing prescriptive standards may elect to have their plans checked in any one of three ways. The simplest approach, the "math method," asks the builder to make a few easy arithmetic calculations to determine how much glass is allowable considering building square footage and other variables. In general, window areas may not exceed 12.5 percent of the building's floor area; but the true amount of glazing permissible may be much greater if the windows are properly shielded from the summer sun.

A second method of checking the glazing requires the builder to make a scale model of the building for examination under a solar simulator which is kept in the building inspection division office. The simulator reproduces the position of the sun at different times on the summer and winter design days.

A third, more complicated approach (profile angle method) requires analysis of windows according to shading angles cast by roof overhangs.

Builders choosing performance standards must also submit their designs for a plan check and may, if they desire, simplify the analysis of glazing by using either the solar simulator or profile angle methods.

The building code does not in any way require the use of solar energy, although it is one way to meet its requirements. Davis, however, is concerned about retrofitting existing and new houses with solar systems. To that end, it now requires that all new houses be equipped with plumbing stubs for solar hot water heating.

The construction ordinance is one formal step in the Davis energy conservation program. Another step involves adoption of design standards for subdivisions and city circulation systems. These standards have not been adopted, but they are used in an informal manner in the design of planned developments. Since Davis has a housing development priority program which allows for residential construction by permit only, the city has condiderable control over the type and design of construction. . . .

ENERGY CONSERVATION RETROFITS

The Davis building code applies to new structures, but there has been a good deal of interest within the city for developing a method of dealing with existing dwellings as well. Davis has taken two different tacks to meet this problem.

First, the city enacted an ordinance that requires inspection of all homes when they are put up for sale to ensure that existing codes are met. If a home fails to meet the dictates of the requisite laws, then the buyer would be required to bring it up to standard. This is an unusual ordinance, for in most cities homes are inspected because of complaints or at the request of the buyer or seller. Inspection usually is not mandatory on sale.

This ordinance was adopted in part with a view towards providing a mechanism for administering a retrofit program. Consultants were then engaged to draw up a scheme by which existing dwellings could be made to meet certain basic energy conservation standards. A point system was developed, a plan outlined. The idea is that in expectation of receiving a sizeable amount of cash, the seller of a house will be in a position to make the required changes at the time of sale. . . .

FENCES & HEDGES

Davis is gradually moving to a new approach in setbacks—the arrangement of houses in relation to sidewalks and fences or hedges. If houses are to have large south-facing windows to take advantage of the winter sun, they must also have adequate space between the window and fence to allow the low angled winter sun to enter the window. That means fences must be set back closer to the street when the house faces south.

If zero lot lines (i.e. attached "townhouses") are encouraged, less energy loss will occur because there will be fewer outside walls to heat or cool. In addition, if front yards are allowed to be fenced close to the street, there will be a great deal more private yard space which can be utilized by the occupants. Here again, we see a return to private inner courtyards.

Set forth below are a variety of measures undertaken in a city ordinance to cut down on the use of energy through standards on the location of fences, walls, and hedges:

Fences, walls and hedges may be located in required yards as follows:

(1) If not exceeding at any point four feet in height above the elevation of the surface of the ground at such point, they may be located in any yard or court, except for a corner lot.

(2) If not exceeding at any point six feet in height above the elevation of the surface of the ground at such point, they may be located in any required rear yard or interior side yard.

(3) On a corner lot, a fence or hedge over three feet in height, measured from

the curb gutter grade, shall not be located in a triangular area measured twenty-five feet along the inside face of the sidewalk in either direction from the sidewalk intersection. Where no sidewalk exists, the measurement shall be made along the right-of-way line.

(4) Fences not exceeding six feet in height may be located at the 10-foot setback in the front yard.

(5) The Community Development Director may issue a permit to allow a fence to:

(i) Be located at the five-foot setback for the street side provided that such fence will not conflict with public utility easements; or

(ii) exceed the six-foot height limitation up to a maximum height of eight feet for side and rear yard fences only if such proposed fence design will not have an adverse effect upon adjoining properties.

In 1977, the City Council added a requirement for landscaping in commercial zones. In such areas landscaping must cover 10 percent of the site. Trees are to be distributed throughout parking areas, and landscaping is to be provided to assure screening of loading, storage, refuse and other unsightly areas. Native drought resistant trees are to be used wherever feasible.

WORK AT HOME

One way to reduce the use of energy is to work in the neighborhood where you live. But in many cities, zoning prohibits development of work places in residential areas. In addition, housing if often owned by individuals and organizations outside the community who are engaged in real estate speculation.

Davis is attempting to encourage people to live and work in their neighborhoods with two different ordinances. One requires the purchaser of a house in certain zones to live there. The ordinance (No. 917) does not cover apartments, duplexes or commercial real estate. But in residential zones, buyers must sign a declation that they will move into the house they are purchasing within six months and live there for one year. The declaration is sworn and must be filed within 10 days of the sale. A false declaration is a misdemeanor. Repeated violations may be subject to injunction.

If the new owner does not take up residency within six months and live in his house for one year, he is considered in violation of the law unless it can be shown "that the purchaser's circumstances changed after execution of the sworn declaration so as to prevent such intended occupancy. Examples of good cause would be a job change, a change of marital status, a change in family situation such as ill health of the purchaser or related persons, or other circumstances which raise practical or economic difficulties relating to occupancy of the unit." The ordinance does not apply to foreclosures due to default, or to acquisitions by inheritance or bequest.

A second ordinance backs cottage industry within the home by allowing home owners to operate small businesses. In effect, this law gives formal sanction to home industry. . . .

STREETS

In Davis there has been a move towards narrower streets. The widths of streets are determined primarily by the width of fire trucks, with a minimum acceptable width of a street being equal to two times the width of a fire truck plus some clear space to allow for passing.

Narrow streets are less energy-consuming in several ways. They cost less and savings in land and site development could be as high as $1,000 per lot. They use less asphalt. They probably contribute to lower speeds by autos, thereby enhancing fuel efficiency. If use of alternative transportation systems such as buses, walking or bicycles become important enough, wider streets would be less and less needed anyway. The reduction of local streets from 34 to 28 feet is contemplated, with a possibility of further reduction in width in conjunction with neighborhood parking bays. . . .

SHADE TREES

As part of its far-ranging energy conservation efforts, the City Council organized a street tree committee, made up of five citizens, to advise them [*sic*] on matters pertaining to maximizing benefits from the trees. The committee meets quarterly and all gatherings are public.

The committee originally prepared an ordinance which was made law in 1963. The committee and the park superintendent put together a master list of every tree in the city, and then laid out a plan for planting of trees. A complete inventory and card system of every tree has been established. The basic idea of the ordinance is to develop and maintain a comprehensive plan for planting and maintaining trees and other plants, and to set up rules for planting, maintenance and care of the trees.

The city's basic tree policies are that all planting is done by city crews. One tree is required per lot (on corner lots one on each street front) and is planted in the 10 foot easement behind the sidewalk. Planting is done only after homes are occupied. The street tree committee designates a tree for each street. When it comes to pruning, this too is done by city crews.

In the older section of the city there are about 3,000 trees of various kinds, in the newer areas there are about 6,000, and the city is planting about 700 additional new trees each year. The total tree population is about 17,800. There are some 80 different kinds of trees, and the tree committee has set limits on the numbers of any one kind of tree by establishing use categories.

The planting program calls for evergreen trees to be planted on major streets and either evergreens or deciduous trees on the embounded streets. Evergreens on the major streets reduce the problems of leaf pickups in the fall, provide good scale and give the appearance of a city of trees year around.

Cooling shade trees can help to reduce energy use during the hot Davis summers, when temperatures of streets and walls go as high as 140 degrees Fahrenheit. The city is taking measures to protect streets, homes and commercial buildings wherever possible from the sun by trees. And since there is little rain from May through October, the trees must be drought resistant.

TRANSPORT

Like many suburban communities in California, Davis has been dominated by the automobile. Over the last decade the city has consistently sought to reduce the importance of the car, and establish other modes of transport. As a result, many citizens use bicycles for getting about town, or take a double-deck bus run by university students. . . .

The city itself has moved towards a more fuel-efficient transportation system. It maintains a fleet of bicycles for employees. In addition, the fleet of cars and trucks maintained by the local government has been changed to meet fuel efficiency standards. Thus, in fiscal 1973–74, the city owned eight full-size sedans, 35 one-half ton pickups, four compact cars. In 1977, it owned seven regular sedans, 22 one-half ton pickups and 19 subcompacts. In effect, the one-half ton trucks were replaced by subcompact cars.

BICYCLES

Davis has 28,000 bicycles. Considering that the city has a population of only 36,000, probably no other city in the United States has as high a proportion of its citizens owning bicycles and using them as a regular means of transportation.

In their paper, "Bikeways in Action," Robert Sommer and Dale Lott describe Davis' unique transportation situation:

A number of factors produced this situation—the presence of many young people attending the Davis Campus of the University of California, the flat terrain, the mild weather, and the many wide streets. When the campus was expanded and the population in the area grew rapidly in the early 1960s, the streets became much busier. About the time the first stop light was installed, people riding bicycles began to feel crowded. At the local bicycle shop, it was common to see bikes appearing with damaged front wheels when riders were forced onto the curb by passing cars. Competition, both for space on the streets and for opportunities to cross at intersections, grew between bicycles and automobiles. It was a lopsided competition at best—bicycles are small and frail, automobiles large and sturdy. It became clear to a number of concerned Davis citizens that, if bicycles were to remain a viable part of the city transportation system, they would have to be given a place of their own in city traffic planning.

What was needed was some way to separate bicycles from automobiles, and the plan adopted was the bicycle lane or bikeway—a strip of pavement or concrete from which automobiles would be excluded. At first this suggestion was rejected by the city council; it was considered to be visionary, impractical, potentially dangerous, and its proponents were regarded as cranks. However, as the debate continued, it became apparent that there was widespread support for bicycle lanes. A citizens group circulated a petition asking the City Council to establish bicycle lanes along principal streets and rights-of-way as an integral part of the city's transportation system. This petition was signed by 90 percent of the several hundred voters approached. Bike lanes became the central issue in a city election of 1966 and the pro-bikeway candidates won. Soon after, that, the first bike lanes were established along the sides of existing wide streets.

Since that time, Davis has been developing a bicycle lane network that is probably unique in the United States. New housing tracts in the city are required to set aside space for bicycle lanes separated from traffic, and a special act was passed by the California Assembly to enable the city to formulate traffic regulations for bicycles. It is important to realize that the bicycles are not merely owned, stored or used for recreational purposes; they are an important part of the transportation system. On one heavily trafficked street, traffic counts during the summer (with few university students in town) show that bicycles represented 40 percent of all traffic. During the rush hour, 90 percent of all riders are adults. The emblem of the city shown on many municipal vehicles is a gay nineties two-wheeler. Many business leaders in the community are strong proponents of bike riding, and admit that this is a matter of self-interest. The bicycle has also helped preserve the central city core as a viable shopping district, since parking is not a serious obstacle to shopping downtown. The university and high schools have been able to set aside less space for parking lots than they would ordinarily. The acceptance of the bicycle as a viable means of transportation by virtually all segments of the community provides the unique opportunity to learn the structural and social requirements of safe, efficient and pleasurable bike riding.

The potential of bicycle transportation cannot be realized without the necessary environmental support system. Just as one cannot have a railroad without tracks, or a bus system without highways, so one needs special facilities and regulations for bicycle traffic. This means planning which must rest on firm knowledge of the special requirements of the bicycle. One simply does not design highways for automobiles and sidewalks for pedestrians, leaving bicyclists squeezed in between moving automobiles, parked cars and pedestrians.

First let us review the history of the Davis bicycle lane network. About eight years ago a group of concerned citizens formed the Bike Safety Committee which investigated bicycle traffic problems in the city and made various suggestions about how to alleviate them. The city public works department became interested and made traffic counts to determine the streets most heavily used. There was very little precedent to follow in developing bike lanes. The city public works department believed that the most feasible plan was to create bike lanes on the outsides of the streets over 50 feet wide. Where this contradicted the California Motor Vehicle Code a special bill relating to bike lanes was passed with the help of the state assemblymen. This bill permitted the Davis City Council in 1967 to pass Ordinance 442 creating bike lanes and regulating bike traffic.

The city now operates programs in bicycle education, safety, and enforcement, through the police department. Under this program an officer visits each grade three or four times a year. A specially prepared curriculum introduces bikes in the kindergarten and continues on up through the ninth grade. The curriculum includes a talking bicycle, films, slides, lectures and hand-out materials.

A bike rodeo held on the schools' grounds during the school day tests the rider's ability to balance, turn, stop and signal for turns. On bike safety check day, each bike at school is inspected for safe use. Bolts, nuts, pedals, etc. are checked and minor repairs done by a police officer.

Bike licenses are sold for a three year period at a cost of $4.50 each. The license information is put on a computer, so that lost or stolen bikes can be identified.

All uniformed patrols of the Davis police department can issue citations to individuals, regardless of age, who are in violation of the bicycle ordinance. The "Bike Enforcement Officer" rides a 10-speed bike in uniform and he checks to make sure riders are obeying the bike traffic laws. In addition, the bike aide is responsible for retrieving stolen or abandoned bicycles. He maintains the bike files, assists with licensing at rush times of the year and conducts bike auctions. Abandoned bicycles must be held 90 days prior to being auctioned off. About four auctions are held each year. . . .

A SOLAR-POWERED WORLD BY 2025

Conservation in and of itself can only be considered an early, tentative step along the way to an alternative energy world. A wide range of alternative energy systems would have to be employed together to make such a world work from an energy point of view. The following piece by Denis Hayes sets forth just what sorts of policies, based purely on what we now know works, might lead us to such a world by the year 2025. The entry which follows it by a group of scientists at Washington University describes in detail the way one aspect of such an alternative energy policy—the use of plant energy—would work. It is important to keep in mind that none of this, however, deals with any of the energy breakthroughs which might come about in the intervening years in now-arcane areas like the use of the process of photosynthesis to create an ever renewable source of energy for human societies. It does not even take into account what might happen if appreciable research funds were suddenly to be put into an area like solar energy.

Taken From "The Solar Energy Timetable," by Denis Hayes, Worldwatch Paper *19, April 1978.*

If the transition to a solar-powered world is to be completed within 50 years, major resource commitments must be made immediately. Such a goal can be achieved only if an ambitious timetable of interim goals is met. Failure to begin building the equipment, establishing the infrastructure, and educating people in the skills needed in a solar era will only increase the cost and disruption of the transition and decrease the likelihood of its completion within five decades.

Meeting five-sixths of the anticipated world energy budget in the year 2025 with solar technologies could involve using more than 70 billion square meters of solar collectors and 7.5 million megawatts of solar cells. World hydroelectric capacity would be quadrupled, five million wind turbines would be constructed, and about 15 percent of the world's forests would be devoted to raising wood as an "energy crop." Commitments of this magnitude are certainly possible over a 50-year period, but they are unquestionably ambitious.

A substantial body of literature has documented the technical feasibility and social desirability of solar energy sources. More jobs—and less environmental deterioration—would be created per unit of energy than with any other source. The security of energy supply would be enhanced. Individuals, neighborhoods, regions, and nations would become increasingly self-reliant. And the new energy system would be sustainable for as long as the earth remains inhabitable.

Despite the attractions of a solar-powered world, surprisingly little thought has been given to the sheer physical requirements of a global solar transition. Considering the increasingly tight constraints under which all conventional energy resources are operating, the time has clearly arrived for serious thought to be given to the implications of converting the world economy to solar energy. This proposed timetable is an attempt to sketch one of several possible paths to that goal. It is not a "forecast," and it is certainly not a "projection." Rather it is an attempt to describe a feasible course for a world that needs to move rapidly toward increased reliance upon renewable energy resources.

Oil and natural gas, which now account for about three-fifths of the world's annual fuel consumption, will almost certainly have been reduced to subordinate roles in the global energy picture by 2025. Indeed, world oil production could begin to decline before 1990. While there remains some controversy over the exact date that world oil production will "peak," the Vice Chairman of Sun Oil Company acknowledged a widely perceived truth when he recently remarked, "We are in a business that is dying." Some new source, or combination of sources, will be required to fill the gap.

For some time, planners believed that the gap would be filled mostly by energy from coal and nuclear fission. While it was recognized that problems would attend the development of both these sources, the difficulties were considered to be more manageable than the crises that could result from having too little energy. An emerging body of evidence suggests this assumption may be wrong. Some of the problems associated with the large-scale worldwide development of coal and nuclear power could dwarf the stresses that such development was intended to avoid.

The relative abundance of coal leads many energy planners to think of it as a long-term energy option—a mistake seldom made for oil and gas. Thus coal is expected to be the centerpiece of the post-petroleum energy budgets in such countries as China, Australia, and the United States. While there are many unfortunate, and often unhealthy, consequences associated with coal extraction and combustion, the most intractable long-term problem arises from the atmospheric accumulation of carbon dioxide.

Carbon dioxide is produced whenever any fossil fuel is burned, but more CO_2 is produced per unit of energy released by coal combustion than by burning either oil or gas. Adding CO_2 to the air raises the earths' temperture by slowing down the escape of heat into space. This CO_2 greenhouse effect[*] was a matter of speculation as recently as five years ago, but most meteorologists now agree that it is a matter of concern. An excellent report on the dangers was issued in 1977

[*See article on the greenhouse effect, page 83.]

by the U.S. National Academy of Sciences. Among the consequences would be a decline in food production in "breadbasket" regions, and a shift in agriculture to less fertile areas.

Although there is disagreement over just how soon major changes in the earth's climate could result from the buildup of CO_2 that has already begun, many knowledgeable observers feel dire consequences are possible before 2025. A January 1978 article in the British science journal *Nature* concluded:

> If the CO_2 greenhouse effect is magnified in high latitudes, as now seems likely, deglaciation of West Antarctica would probably be the first disastrous result of continued fossil fuel consumption. A disquieting thought is that if the present highly simplified climatic models are even approximately correct, this deglaciation [and the consequent five-meter rise in sea level] may be part of the price that must be paid in order to buy enough time for industrial civilization to make the changeover from fossil fuels to other sources of energy. If so, major dislocations in coastal cities, and submergence of low-lying areas such as much of Florida and the Netherlands, lie ahead.

Nuclear power, like coal, is beset by myriad difficulties, including the risk of catastrophic accidents (especially with breeder reactors) and the disposal of long-lived radioactive wastes. These difficulties, and the public conern that they have helped to generate, have caused some former nuclear champions to become pessimistic. John O'Leary, Deputy Secretary of the U.S. Department of Energy, remarked in February 1978 that "nuclear power, which ten years ago was the hope of all energy planners, is now a 'has been.' "

The most awesome problem facing nuclear power is posed by the inextricable link between this energy source and nuclear weapons. Depending upon the level of global energy demand postulated for the year 2025, meeting just half of it with nuclear power would require the recycling of between 7 million and 20 million kilograms of some fissile isotope—probably plutonium-239—every year. About five kilograms of any such isotope is all that is needed to make an atom bomb.

The inevitability of "normal" losses during production would allow a thief who operated within the credible margin of error to divert large amounts of bomb-grade materials without detection. As of August 1977, official U.S. inventories showed 1,534 missing kilograms of plutonium and 2,227 absent kilograms of highly enriched uranium—enough material to make 750 atom bombs. It may well be that none of this material has fallen into the hands of criminals, terrorists, or foreign governments, but the material cannot be accounted for. This uncertainty would swell to much more terrifying proportions with the creation of a huge, worldwide nuclear program.

Nuclear fusion may eventually provide significant amounts of commercial electricty, but its future is uncertain at the moment. Conceptual design studies of the fusion approaches, that now receive the lion's share of international research and development funding suggest that such techniques may have little commercial applicability. However, a recent survey of alternative fusion concepts by the Electric Power Research Institute found several promising avenues for research—some of which could lead to comparatively small-scale, decentralized applications. Nonetheless, even this generally encouraging, review was not sanguine about the rapid development and commercialization of "clean" advanced fusion cycles.

Controlled thermonuclear fusion has yet to produce more energy than it consumes. While some advanced fusion process would provide an attractive supplement to solar resources, their successful development cannot now be counted upon.

Even as the other long-term options have begun encountering unexpected problems, extraordinary strides have been made in technologies to harness the essentially inexhaustible energy of the sun. Existing solar technologies can provide energy as heat; as solid, liquid, or gaseous fuels; or as electricity. The sunlight that strikes the earth daily contains 10,000 times more energy than all the conventional fuels burned that day. Obviously, the solar resource base is more than adequate to meet any likely level of human energy use.

Technologies to harness the energy in sunlight, wind, falling water, and biomass are referred to by several names, including appropriate, light capital, intermediate distributed, soft, and renewable. The different names often carry different nuances. The term "light capital," technologies generally refers to inexpensive devices (biogas plants, for example) that Third World villages can build of indigenous materials; "distributed" technologies generally suggest decentralization as a prime criterion; "soft" technologies generally indicate devices that increase the efficiency with which transitional fuels are used as well as those that harness renewable resources. But all refer to an energy system reliant upon energy "income" from the sun, rather than one dependent upon the energy "capital" in fossil or fissile fuels. Many countries have begun to examine carefully such solar alternatives in light of their particular geographical locations and energy needs.

The quality of energy sought from the sun and the costs of collecting, converting, and storing that energy usually correlate directly: the higher the desired quality, the higher the cost. Sources and uses must therefore be carefully matched, so that expensive, high-quality energy is not wasted on jobs that do not require it. For example, a hot bathtub contains more energy than does a small storage battery, but the electricity in the battery is of a higher quality than is the heat in the tub. It is very difficult to power a transistor radio with a hot bathtub, and it is generally wasteful to heat bathwater with electricity. In the course of considering the use of solar technologies in various countries, it will be important to bear in mind the qualitative dimension of energy demand.

Conventional wisdom holds that while solar energy has many attractive characteristics, it is too expensive today for widespread application. As is so often the case with conventional wisdom, yesterday's truth has become today's misapprehension. Five years ago, solar energy could not compete economically with low-priced fuels. But since 1973 the cost of solar equipment has dropped streadily while the costs of all competing energy sources have skyrocketed. Solar technologies can now provide energy for many purposes at no higher cost than new investments in conventional energy sources.

There remains much room for improvement. Many solar technologies can benefit from research advances, and mass production using new materials will doubtless lead to substantial reductions in cost. Increased attention to the solar prospect may lead to break throughs that are not now apparent. In the meantime, it is possible to begin sketching the broad outlines of a global solar strategy to provide almost all of humanity's commercial energy from renewable sources by 2025.

How much energy will be needed in the year 2025? Estimates range widely. Most countries assume that their fuel requirements will continue to grow for the foreseeable future. If the need for an eventual energy ceiling is admitted, the day of reckoning is always thought to lie beyond the horizon of official projections. Studies of future consumption patterns do not generally include an in-depth examination of a spectrum of alternative policies. Policymakers ask only, "Where do we seem to be heading?" They make no attempt to grapple with the question, "What can be?"

This process of gazing into a rearview mirror and proclaiming it to be a crystal ball necessarily results in certain analytical hazards. During the last 25 years, world fuel consumption tripled, oil and gas consumption quintupled, and electricity use grew almost sevenfold. Clearly, such trends cannot long be sustained. The Arab oil embargo of 1973–74 led to the first major global discontinuity in energy growth; others will certainly follow.

In an era of major discontinuities, 50-year forecasts can have only limited value at best. Yet it is necessary to formulate a vision of where we are going in order to be able to design a strategy for getting there. Our vision of 2025 would see a 75-percent larger world population using twice as much energy annually as we now use—and using it about twice as efficiently. This assumes a 50-percent increase in energy use in the industrial world and a 400-percent increase in the Third World. And the energy efficiency target is a reasonable goal given an aggressive world energy conservation effort.

Dollar for dollar, a trillion-dollar investment in increasing the energy efficiency of the world's buildings, industries, and transportation systems would save more energy than the same expenditure on new energy facilities would produce. In the United States, for example, improving the efficiency of air conditioners would save ten times as much electricity as identical investments in new power plants would produce. In India, $10 spent on improving stove efficiency can cut a typical village family's wood consumption in half—saving $10 to $25 per year. In neither case is a loss of benefit or comfort involved. And in both cases, the energy saved is just as useful as new energy would be.

Comparisons between countries and within the same country over a period of years make it clear that economic well-being is not based on increases in fuel consumption. Over the past 50 years the amount of fuel consumed per dollar's worth of goods and services produced has fallen in most countries—despite declining real energy prices. With rising energy prices a near-certainty for the foreseeable future, this trend can be expected to accelerate dramatically. This will merely require increases in the fuel-efficiency of machinery and the improved operation and maintenance of this equipment. Moreover, an intelligent program of energy conservation can actually bolster employment.

Virtually all oil-importing countries have begun to take significant strides to improve energy efficiency. The nature of the energy conservation methods employed sometimes bears no particular relationship to the ideology of the government involved. In the Soviet Union, for example, the price of gasoline was doubled in March 1978, and the marketplace was relied upon to reduce gasoline consumption. In the United States, on the contrary, all efforts to remove price controls from gasoline have been soundly defeated. Reliance is instead placed upon a federal program to regulate the fuel efficiency of new cars.

Assuming, then, a vigorous effort to increase efficiency, annual world energy use from all sources in 2025, could amount to 60×10^{16} kilojoules. (A kilojoule is slightly less than a British Thermal Unit. The proposed energy budget—600 quadrillion kilojoules—equals about 570 quadrillion BTUs.) This is approximately equal to the energy released by burning 21 billion metric tons of coal. Five-sixths of this 2025 energy budget could be met by renewable energy resources if the proposed timetable is followed. (See Figure 1.) Thirty-six percent of this solar energy would be used directly as heat; 44 percent as solid, liquid and gaseous fuels (mostly of biological origin); and 20 percent as electricity. (See Table 1.) This is a fourfold increase in the use of electricity, representing an annual growth rate of about 3.1 percent.

Existing nuclear power plants, which contributed only 0.66 percent of world energy in 1977, would have long since completed their useful lifetimes, and been replaced by solar-electric facilities. Fossil fuels would contribute about one-sixth of all energy use, mostly as backup for solar sources. At that level of usage, these fuels would last more than 1,000 years, and the CO_2 threat would be postponed for at least two centuries—allowing succeeding generations more flexibility in the rate at which they phase out the combustion of fossil hydrocarbons.

It would be possible to have a 100-percent solar energy budget by 2025. Prelim-

FIGURE 1 Proposed World Energy Production Timetable, 1980–2025*

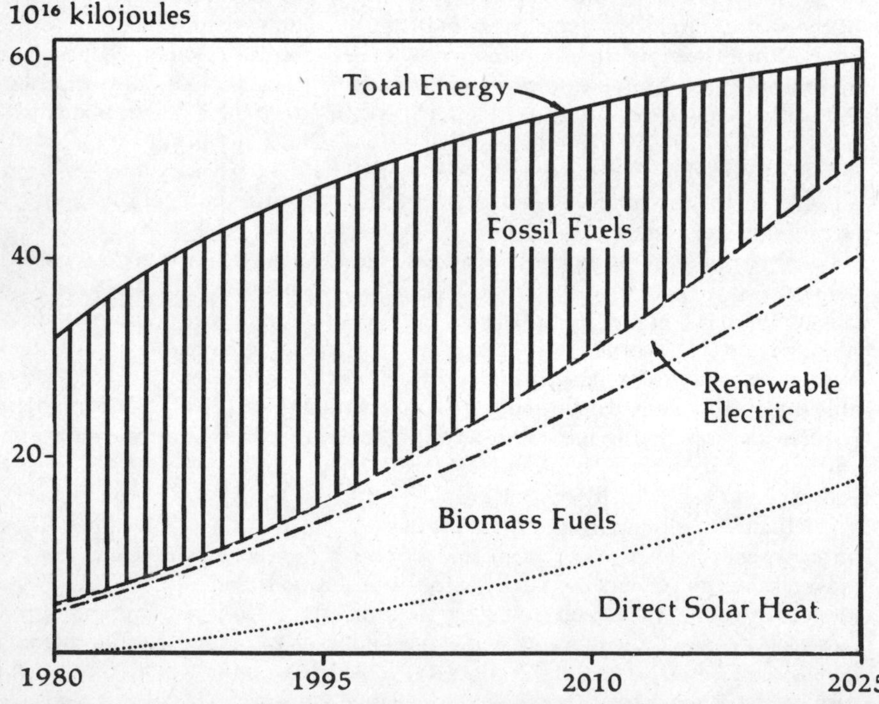

*Energy sources supplying less than 1 percent of total are omitted

TABLE 1 World Solar Energy Timetable, 1980–2025

Energy Source	1980	1995	2010	2025
		(10^{10} kilojoules)		
Active Solar Heating	0	3.0	6.0	11.0
Passive Solar Heating	0	1.0	4.0	7.0
Total Direct Solar Heat	0	4.0	10.0	18.0
Wood	4.0	6.0	7.0	8.0
Liquid Fuels	0	2.0	4.0	8.0
Gaseous Fuels	0	2.0	4.0	6.0
Total Biomass Fuels	4.0	10.0	15.0	22.0
Hydroelectric	0.5	1.0	1.5	2.0
Wind Power	0	0.5	1.0	2.0
Solar-electric	0	1.0	3.0	6.0
Total Renewable Electric	0.5	2.5	5.5	10.0
Total	4.5	16.5	30.5	50.0

Source: Worldwatch Institute

inary studies have suggested how this might be accomplished in Canada, Sweden, and the United States, and it is undoubtedly feasible elsewhere. The State of California, which is equivalent to the sixth largest industrial country in the world, currently has a de facto nuclear moratorium and recently began offering a 55-percent tax credit to encourage solar development. California is now the subject of the most detailed examination of solar energy prospects that has yet been undertaken, and the preliminary results suggest that a complete transition would be possible by 2025.

However, energy transitions have seldom led to 100 percent replacements. Heavy reliance on coal began in the eighteenth century, but wood still contributes about one-sixth of the world's energy today. Heavy reliance on oil began seven decades ago, but coal still contributes more than one-fourth of the world's energy. Fossil fuels, particularly oil and gas, have desirable characteristics. They have high energy densities and they are easily transported and stored. Although they are not sufficiently abundant to long sustain their current role as the world's primary sources of energy, they could and should play some role well into the twenty-first century. The world's principal reliance, however, should shift to solar resources by 2025. In modest ways, this transition has already begun. It needs to be vastly accelerated if this timetable is to be met.

HEATING AND COOLING

Heating water with sunlight is simple. The collector is, in essence, a box with a black bottom and a glass top. Glass is transparent to sunlight but much less so to heat. When the black bottom is struck by sunlight, it warms up, and this heat is trapped inside the collector. When water is pumped through the hot collector, its temperature rises. The hot water is then piped to a very well-insulated storage tank where it is kept until needed.

About 10,000 Cypriot homes, 30,000 American homes, 250,000 Israeli homes, and over two million Japanese homes have solar water heaters. In remote parts of Northern Australia, where fuels are expensive, solar water heaters are required by law on all new buildings. Niger requires them on all new hospitals, hotels, schools, and housing for government employees.

It is also simple to heat buildings with solar energy. "Passive" solar homes have heating systems with just one moving part: the earth, moving around the sun. Passive solar buildings capture sunlight where it strikes the building's walls and floor. Such systems are designed to protect the structure from summer heat while retaining the sun's warmth during the winter. Passive solar architecture is, beyond doubt, the most efficient and cost-effective way to heat and cool new buildings. Modest investments will often provide 80 to 100 percent of a building's heating and cooling requirements. But it demands advance planning; passive features cannot easily be added to existing structures.

"Active" solar heating systems are more expensive, but they can be bolted onto the roof or southern wall of existing buildings as a substitute for—or supplement to—conventional furnaces. In active systems, fans or pumps move solar-heated air or liquid from collectors to storage areas, from which the heat is drawn as needed. Solar self-sufficiency will usually dictate a combination of active and passive features in the temperate regions of the world. In the United States about 4,500 homes and several hundred larger buildings now employ either passive or active solar space heating. The number has been more than doubling each year since 1974.

Buildings can be cooled as well as heated by sunlight. Again, passive solar design is the most important first step, but active solar air conditioners are also now being marketed. Fortuitously, absorption solar air conditioners reach peak cooling capacity when the sun burns brightest, which is when they are most needed. They therefore could reduce peak demands on many electrical power grids. As solar air conditioners penetrate the housing market, the overall economics of active solar heating systems will improve because solar collectors will begin providing a year-round benefit.

Solar-thermal technologies have industrial applications as well. A study of the Australian food-processing industry, for example, found that heat accounted for 90 percent of the industry's energy needs. Almost all this heat was at under 150° C and 80 percent was below 100° C, the boiling point of water. Such low temperature heat can be produced and stored easily using simple solar devices. Solar equipment has been applied on an experimental basis to various agricultural tasks in Australia, including a 56-square-meter solar heating unit for timber drying. In 1977, a commercial soft drink manufacturer near Canberra began using solar collectors. In the United States, solar heating is now being applied to a soup-canning plant in California, a fabric-drying facility in Alabama, and a concrete block factory in Pennsylvania. Solar-powered laundries and car washes are now operating in California, and a St. Louis brewery has turned to solar pasteurization.

Throughout much of the industrial world, solar heating is now more economical than electricity. That is to say, if the energy were to come from a *new* solar unit or a *new* nuclear or coal power plant, the solar investment would be cheapest. The individual homeowner, of course, does not buy electricity just from the expensive new power plant; the utility averages the expensive new eenrgy in with cheap energy from existing sources, so that the true cost of new power is hidden from the individual consumer (though borne, through rising utility bills, by all consumers). In Seattle, Washington, for example, the average price of residential electricity is now less than 1¢ per kilowatt-hour. But electricity from a new nuclear power plant would cost at least 7¢ per kilowatt-hour. At the lower, average prices, only the cheapest solar equipment is economical. But compared to the higher cost for *new* power, virtually all solar heaters look attractive. For society as a whole, the additional energy could be most cheaply harnessed with solar equipment. It is thus in society's interest to encourage—and perhaps subsidize—individual and community solar purchases.

Even where the homeowner must compare the costs of *new* solar equipment with the *average* cost of competing energy sources, solar investments will generally make sense over the lifetime of a building. The most important first step is to incorporate passive solar design into the building's blueprints. Often this costs little or nothing. For example, it costs no more to place most windows in the southern wall than to place them facing north, but southern windows capture the sun's warmth while northern windows merely leak the building's internal heat. Roof overhangs, masonry floors, and working shutters are not expensive. When they are combined with tight construction and good insulation, they can lower the heating load of the building by 75 percent and more. In Arkansas, 200 well-designed houses constructed under a grant from the U.S. Department of Housing and Urban Development cost no more than neighboring houses that were built using conventional construction standards, but their fuel bills are only one-fourth as high.

More elaborate designs can lead to greater savings. In the relatively mild climate of Atascadero, California, Harold Hay's passive solar house was constructed with bags of water incorporated on its roof. These act like a "thermal flywheel," capturing the sun's energy on winter days and storing it to meet nighttime heating requirements. In the summer, the system collects heat from the interior during the day and radiates it outward at night. The cost of these solar features was about $5,000—but the system has provided 100 percent of the home's heating and cooling needs for several years.

In climates where passive solar design will not provide 100 percent of heating requirements, backup fuels or active solar systems are needed. In Princeton, New Jersey, architect Douglas Kelbaugh's passive solar home captures energy through a huge southern window wall during the day and stores it in a concrete interior wall that gives off heat during the night. Like other passive solar homes, the Kelbaugh residence employes no pumps or fans—just careful design. The solar features cost around $9,000, and they provide virtually all the home's requirements. In the unusually cold winter of 1976–77, the heating bill for supplementary conventional fuels in this comfortable northern residence was just $75 for the whole year. Financed with a standard home mortgage, Kelbaugh's solar energy system would require $1,800 cash at the time of construction with monthly payments of $60—far less than his neighbors' fuel bills.

Active solar heating systems can be used to supplement the energy provided by passive solar design. Many different solar collectors, pumps, fans, and storage systems are now on the market, although their prices vary considerably. Solar collectors can be built of durable metals for a materials-cost of about $20 per square meter. Princeton University physicist Ted Taylor believes the use of inexpensive plastic should make it possible to produce fairly durable collectors for a few dollars a square meter. In the United States, professionally installed active solar heating systmes now range from under $100 per square meter to more than $700.

Solar collectors at an installed-cost of $200 per square meter make economic sense when compared with the average costs of electrical resistance heating, except where cheap hydropower is plentiful. At $150 per square meter, they make sense compared with oil heat and electrical heat pumps. At $100 per square meter, they compete effectively with all residential fuels. The use of prefabricated units that are as easily installed as roofing could substantially reduce installation costs.

In order to meet the solar heating goal of 20×10^{16} kilojoules per year by 2025, an ambitious program must soon be undertaken. The "passive" heating contribution assumes a nearly immediate decision to promote intelligent architecture. Schools of architecture and engineering should institute courses teaching the necessary skills, and appropriate training programs could be established in the construction industry. By 1985, all new buildings should employ passive solar design. In March 1978, the U.S. Department of Energy announced that it had under serious consideration a program to require that all new residences incorporate passive solar features. Since building stock turns over at the rate of about 2 percent a year, most of the world's built environment would incorporate at least some passive features by 2025. There remains additional scope for improvement in this area in subsequent years.

As well as supplementing passive designs, "active" systems can meet the special requirements for high-temperature heat in industry and agriculture, and for absorption air-conditioning. To calculate the amount of surface area needed as sites for solar collectors in order to meet the timetable, some assumptions must be made.

The amount of solar energy reaching different inhabited geographical locations varies by about a factor of three. The energy in the sunlight that falls on Stockholm each year contains about 3.5×10^9 joules per square meter. In some arid equatorial regions, however, annual insolation is about 10×10^9 joules per square meter.

In harnessing direct sunlight, the middle latitudes have a marked advantage in consistency over the polar regions. The Kenyan highlands, for example, experience only a 35 percent variation in insolation through the year. In Stockholm, on the other hand, 30 times as much solar energy per square meter is available in June as in December. Thus, far more collector surface will be needed to deliver a given amount of heat in the winter than in the summer. Moreover, the heating required for buildings in Stockholm is obviously greater in the winter than in the summer. In order to capture the solar energy needed in winter, more collector surface must be installed than can be productively employed in the summer. (This disparity can be greatly mitigated by the use of seasonal storage of low-grade heat to warm buildings, but high-temperature industrial heat would be much harder to store for long periods.) So it is necessary to assume that only half the heat harnessed in solar collectors is actually put to productive use. Moreover, the collectors themselves do not capture and retain all the energy in sunlight that strikes them. Some is reflected off the glass or plastic cover; some leaks out of the collector itself. The calculations for this timetable assume that only half the energy that strikes the collector surface is captured, and that only half the energy captured each year is actually used.

Assuming the sunlight striking a typical collector each year contains 6×10^9 joules per square meter, an average square meter of collector surface would "deliver" one-fourth that amount, or 1.5×10^6 useful kilojoules per year. Thus, to meet the goals of the solar timetable, 20.0 billion square meters of collectors must be built by 1995, 40.0 billion by 2010, and 73.3 billion by 2025. If the average collector has a useful life of 25 years, about three billion square meters of new collector would be needed per year to maintain this level of direct solar heating. (It is hoped that collectors with longer life expectancies will have captured the market before 2025.)

These are large figures, but not so imposing that the goal should be dismissed as impractical. They are, however, sufficiently large to lead to the inescapable conclusion that solar features must be incorporated into the basic structural design of new buildings. Because these collectors would be mainly placed on the roofs of buildigns, including factories, the expense involved could be dramatically reduced if all new roofs were constructed at an optimal angle to the sun with a broad southern exposure. This, in turn, may be related to such seemingly trivial considerations as whether communities build roads along due north-south and east-west axes, so that buildings along the road are well oriented to take advantage of the sun. In many such subtle ways, a successful solar transition will involve changing the face of the world.

RENEWABLE FUELS

All fossil fuels were once green plants. Existing technology can harvest "energy crops" directly, without waiting hundreds of millions of years for nature to convert them into oil, gas, and coal. Dry plant material—biomass—contains about as much energy per ton as low-quality coal, and about 60 percent as much as high-quality bituminous coal. The hydrocarbons produced by some plants contain as much energy as oil does.

Because vegetation can be grown almost everywhere, it is relatively immune to international political pressures. Unlike fossil fuels, biological energy resources are renewable; they can be grown as long as the land remains fertile and water is available. Moreover, the use of biomass as commercial fuel involves few of the serious environmental drawbacks associated with the large-scale use of coal and oil. Although not given formal recognition in most official energy statistics, wood and charcoal currently contribute more than 15 percent of humanity's energy budget.

To place the biological resource base in a broader perspective, the energy content of food, fiber, and lumber crops should be considered. In the United States, the potential energy contained in food, paper, and timber each year, when added to the potential energy in the residues of the related industries, equals more than half of all commercial energy use. Yet barely 3 percent of this photosynthetic energy is now harnessed—virtually all by wood and paper companies.

Biological energy sources can be divided into two broad categories: wastes from other biological processes (such as the food and fiber industries), and energy crops grown for use as fuels. Wastes are the easier source to tap for energy, since they must be disposed of in any case. A variety of processes, including biogas production, pyrolysis, fermentation, hydrogasification, and hydrogenation, exist to convert organic wastes into high-quality fuels, and many cities and industries around the world have begun to tap their wastes for usable energy.

In the post-petroleum era, energy crops can be expected to make a far greater contribution to the global energy budget. A variety of trees, grasses, and other types of vegetation have been suggested for intensive cultivation in energy plantations. Different crops will be appropriate for different climates, geographical areas, and energy uses. It also appears increasingly likely that energy crops can be successfully cultivated at sea and in freshwater bodies, thus making available for cultivation some of the 70 percent of the earth's surface covered by water.

Renewable fuels constitute a particularly attractive component of a solar energy budget. They provide a compact way of storing large amounts of energy for very long periods: one gallon of alcohol contains more energy than is easily stored in 100 gallons of hot water in a conventional solar heating system. Moreover, biologically-derived fuel can be directly substituted for the oil and natural gas that are in short supply. For example, existing automobiles can operate smoothly on blends of gasoline with ethanol or methanol, and only minor engine modifications are needed to use pure alcohol fuel. Similarly, methane produced by biogas plants can be fed directly into existing natural gas pipeline systems. And for many purposes, charcoal manufactured from wood can serve as effectively as coke, which is produced from coal. A fair number of countries are already pursuing biological energy sources with vigor. China, for example, has built more than four million biogas plants in the last three years. These are designed to convert animal wastes and human excrement into methane—a clean-burning gas. Less aggressive biogas programs are being pursued by several other countries, including India, Indonesia, Korea, and Taiwan. The residue of the biogas process is an excellent fertilizer—far better than raw manure—and biogas plants also greatly assist the control of such communicable diseases as schistosomiasis.

Brazil is engaged in a determined effort to substitute homegrown ethanol for 20 percent of its imported gasoline before 1985—a goal that will require the production of six billion liters a year. The first distillery built under the program is now producing 60,000 liters a day; 120 additional distilleries, ranging from two to four times as large as the first, are scheduled for construction by 1980. By 1995, Brazil hopes to substitute alcohol produced from sugar cane and cassava for all imported gasoline.

The net efficiency of biomass conversion processes will be of enormous importance to policy, but it will not be the sole criterion. On occasion it is worth paying a premium to convert biomass into a form that is more useful. In the conversion of wood into methanol for example, a large fraction of the original energy is lost, but because it is rather difficult to fuel an automobile with wood, the energy price is worth paying.

Moreover, the nature of any particular nation's biomass strategy will be determined by many factors specific to it: the climate, water, soil, amount of available land, and so on. The different types of fuels that are the logical end products will depend upon what crop is planted. In lieu of a detailed country-by-country inventory of potential energy crops and competing uses for land, and a clear determination as to whether ocean farming will prove feasible and ecologically acceptable, it is not possible to describe all the elements of a biomass strategy.

Nonetheless, we can gain some idea of the magnitude of the effort needed by assuming that all the solid fuel will be wood, that all the liquid fuel will be alcohol, and that all the gaseous fuel will be methane. It must be recognized, however, that by 2025 it is likely there will be a variety of solid, liquid, and gaseous fuels from biomass in the commercial marketplace.

Wood, when dried in the air, has an energy content of about 1.5×10^7 kilojoules per metric ton. Hence, to meet the energy needs postulated for 1980, 2.6 billion metric tons of wood will be needed annually. The 1995 target will demand 4 billion metric tons, the 2010 goal will need 4.6 billion, and the target for the year 2025 assumes the consumption of 5.3 billion metric tons of wood per year. Currently, the net annual increment in forest growth is 36 billion tons, of which about 2.5 billion tons is used as fuel, with about 5.2 billion tons used by society for all purposes. Thus, the amount of wood that would be used for energy in the year 2025 is about as high as is currently used for all purposes.

The productivity of different species under different conditions varies greatly, from a net growth of about two tons per hectare to more than 40 tons for intensively cultivated, short-rotation, fast-growing trees. Some authorities believe that selective breeding, and intensive cultivation could lead to yields on the order of 80 tons per hectare. Assuming net annual growth of 12 tons per hectare on energy farms, the 2025 goal would require the employment of 440 million hectares for forest energy crops. This represents about one-sixth of the land area now heavily forested and about one-eighth of all forest land. It can also be compared with the 1.5 billion hectares currently under agricultural cultivation. This level of production appears sufficiently conservative to avoid the "mining" of forests now practiced in some locations, where forest stocks are depleted at a rate exceeding new biological production, causing diminution of the resource base. The overall efficiency with which this energy is ultimately used will depend upon the conversion process employed. Most wood will probably be burned directly as a backup fuel for intermittent energy sources, though some will doubtless first be converted to charcoal, methanol, or other intermediate fuels possessing specific desired characteristics.

Ethanol has an energy content of 2.2×10^4 kilojoules per liter, and methanol somewhat less. Assuming that an average facility produces 200,000 liters of alcohol per day, or 73 million liters per year, each such distillery will then produce fuel containing 1.6×10^{12} kilojoules per year. Thus, if our goals for liquid fuels were to be met entirely by alcohol from such plants, the 1995 target would require the construction of 12,500 facilities. The 2010 target requires 31,250 alcohol production facilities, and the 2025 goal would require 50,000.

By the year 2025, it should be possible to grow crops yielding more than 3,000 liters of ethanol per hectare. Sugar cane now produces between 3,000 and 3,400 liters per hectare in those regions where it can be successfully cultivated. Increased yields could be achieved with new or improved species, with multiple cropping, or with improved conversion of crops into fuel. However, assuming a yield of 3,000 liters per hectare, meeting the proposed 2025 liquid fuel target entirely from ethanol could require up to 1.2 billion hectares. Again, comparing this with the 1.5 billion hectares now under agricultural cultivation worldwide provides a clearer idea of the enormity of this goal.

Of course, all liquid fuels won't come from "ethanol crops." Methanol can be derived from a variety of sources, and ethanol itself can be manufactured from many organic wastes. Several plant families yield a sap that is rich in complex hydrocarbons, and some of these plants can flourish in dry, inhospitable environments. Yet the central fact remains: the production of liquid fuels as substitutes for oil will be one of the most difficult tasks of the solar transition. If it proves too difficult, liquid fuels will simply cease playing as important a role in human affairs as they now do.

Methane contains about 4×10^4 kilojoules per cubic meter. Hence, 500 billion cubic meters of methane are needed to meet the 1995 goal, 1 trillion cubic meters for the 2010 target, and 1.5 trillion cubic meters by 2025. The biogas[*] produced by anaerobic digestion is only 50 to 60 percent methane, and most of the other gases produced have lower energy values. Hence, more biogas will have to be produced to meet our targets than if it were pure methane. The 2025 goal, for example, might demand over 2 trillion cubic meters of biogas.

About half of this methane can be obtained from the wastes of existing systems built upon biological products. The remaining half could be derived from aquatic plants, such as freshwater hyacinths or giant ocean kelp. If cultivated at sea, approximately one-fifth of 1 percent of the ocean surface would be needed. If successful, such kelp farms could also relieve some of the pressures put on the land by the demand for liquid fuels.

With wise management, the total energy attributed in this timetable to biomass[†] fuels can be harvested on a sustainable basis. It is less clear that there is scope for increasing production much beyond this level. There is a popular tendency to think of renewable resources as infinite resources, but this is a confusion of size with duration. If care is taken, biological crops can be cultivated in perpetuity. But with short-sighted management, energy crops (like all other biological systems) can simply collapse.

Already, vast treeless regions can be found in the Middle East, North Africa, Asia, and South America. Multinational corporations and desperate villagers alike have too often failed to replant seedlings after the harvest of mature trees. If wood is to play a larger role in the coming energy transition, successful reforestation programs must be among the world's highest energy priorities. Moreover, it is essential that reforestation programs be concerned with diversity and stability as well as yield. Extensive monocultures could lead to dependence upon forests that are vulnerable to all sorts of threats. Because several years of growth are required for the maturation of even short-rotation energy crops, the loss of such crops before harvest could be calamitous.

If pursued without foresight, as has too frequently occurred with the development of virgin lands, the biological resource base could be rapidly depleted. Unless nutrients are recycled to the earth, the crops will effectively "mine" the soil. Unless harvested areas are immediately resown with good ground cover, flooding

[*Gas from decaying plant matter.]
[†Waste products from decaying plant matter.]

will strip away irreplaceable topsoil. Unless conversion processes are carefully chosen and matched with crops, more energy will be used to produce a unit of renewable fuel than the fuel itself contains.

Even as they exhibit these various environmental vulnerabilities, biological fuels possess some unique advantages. Notably, unlike the fossil fuels that they could displace, renewable fuels would make no net contribution to atmospheric carbon dioxide. The plants that are the sources of these fuels draw as much carbon dioxide from the air during the process of photosynthesis as is returned to the air when the fuel is burned.

As part of an integrated, sensible strategy of producing energy in perpetuity instead of maximizing short-term production, the use of biological energy sources is one of the most attractive options available. They can provide the ideal buffers in the transition to a post-petroleum era because they are so similar in nature to the fossil fuels on which we currently depend so heavily.

ELECTRICITY

Electricity is, in many respects, a splendid form of energy. It can perform a variety of tasks, from cooking an egg to powering a computer. Large amounts of electrical energy can pass through comparatively tiny wires, permitting the more efficient design of factories and other energy-intensive facilities. Electricity is clean at the point of end-use, and it can be instantly available at the flip of a switch.

On the other hand, electricity tends to be much more expensive than other forms of energy. Electricity is difficult to store for long periods, and transmission grids are vulnerable to natural phenomena, common human error, and conscious malevolence. Major environmental costs are usually associated with the power plant and with the production of its fuel. It would therefore seem sensible to use electricity when it exhibits a marked advantage over competing forms of energy, and to look elsewhere when electricity holds no advantage.

During the next 50 years, the use of electricity will almost certainly grow more rapidly than energy use in general. This assumption is based in part on the belief that electricity will become available to hundreds of millions of people who do not currently have access to it. Partly, also, it is based on the assumption that more of the uses of energy that emerge in the next 50 years will rely on electricity than on other energy sources. On the other hand, these estimates of the growth rate for electricity are far lower than those forecast by most proponents of a nuclear- or coal-dominated future. They include the assumption that a series of foreseeable technical advances will make solar-electric technologies sufficiently inexpensive for the proposed levels of usage to be economically practicable. If this assumption proves in error—if cost reductions do not occur as rapidly as expected—either the total use of electricity will be lower, or some fraction of the chemical fuel supply will have to be allocated to electrical generation, or both.

Currently, the most commonly harnessed solar source of electricity is hydropower (although limited amounts of sugar cane residue, organic municipal wastes, wood, and even coconut husks are also converted into electricity). In 1976, hydropower was the source of 72.6 percent of all Canadian electricity. Most surveys suggest more hydroelectric development globally than would actually be feasible. Conventional surveys too often ignore the flooding of fertile agricultural bottom lands, and plan for the construction of dams in geologically unstable areas (where they may rapidly fill with silt). The more conservative assumption used in this timetable is that global hydroelectric capacity will increase fourfold in the next 50 years. Wind power and solar photovoltaic cells are expected to shoulder the bulk of the remaining electrical generating burden, although ocean thermal-electric stations could provide an attractive supplement if their economic costs and environmental consequences prove acceptable.

Wind turbines once provided significant amounts of electricity. In 1916, Denmark had more than 1,300 operating wind generators. By 1940, the United States had built about six million. Before the American rural electrification program, wind turbines were the only source of electricity available to much of rural America. But cheap fossil fuels and inexpensive hydroelectric facilites, combined with large federal subsidies for integrated electrical grids, priced wind power out of the marketplace in a matter of years. However, now that the cost of fossil fuels is rising dramatically, wind power is once again beginning to receive serious international attention. Many interesting new technologies are being pursued, including vertical axis windmills, that turn in the wind like spinning coins. In many parts of the world, electricity generated from the wind already makes economic sense. With declining costs brought about by mass production and technological innovation, the use of wind power can be expected to increase rapidly, first in rural areas of the developing world and then in the most wind-rich parts of the industrial world.

The most exciting solar-electric prospect is the photovoltaic cell, a simple device that generates electricity directly when sunlight falls on it. Photovoltaic cells have no moving parts, consume no fuel, and produce no bomb-grade materials. Fashioned from relatively abundant elements, they have long lifetimes, and require little maintenance.

Photovoltaic cells are modular by nature, and little is to be gained by grouping large masses of cells, at a single collection site. On the contrary, they are most sensibly used in a decentralized fashion—perhaps incorporated in the roofs of buildings—so that transmission and storage problems can be minimized. With decentralized use, solar cells can be efficiently combined with compatible technologies to use waste heat for space heating and cooling, water heating, and refrigeration. In the summer of 1977, a photovoltaic array in Mead, Nebraska, irrigated 80 acres of corn at 1,000 gallons per minute.

The manufacture of photovoltaic cells is currently a low volume business and the products are consequently rather expensive. But with mechanized mass production, costs should plummet; they are, in fact, already falling rapidly. Solar cells cost about $200,000 a peak kilowatt[*] in the late fifties. By early 1975, the costs had dropped to $31,000; by September 1976, the figure was $15,500. In early 1977, the cost of solar cells fell to $11,750 a peak kilowatt. And in December 1977, an Arkansas Community College contracted for a photovoltaic system for $6,000 per peak kilowatt. Making allowances for the average availability of sunshine versus the average capacity factor of large nuclear power plants, and considering costs and losses during transmission and storage, solar cells are now probably about ten times as expensive as nuclear power in the most favorable regions of the United

[*Measure of maximum output.]

States. Solar cells now cost about one-tenth of what they cost five years ago; nuclear power now costs about twice as much as it cost five years ago.

The earth now has about 100,000 megawatts of nuclear capacity and about one megawatt of photovoltaic capacity. With mass production, solar cell costs are expected to continue falling dramatically. The current goals of the U.S. Department of Energy are to drive prices down to $2,000 per peak kilowatt by 1980, $500 per peak kilowatt by 1985, and $100 to $300 per peak kilowatt by 1990. At present prices, solar cells make economic sense for remote applications of various kinds; at 1985 prices, they will be cost-effective for peak power production in much of the industrial world; and at 1990 prices, they should experience the kind of market penetration needed for a successful solar transition. With a substantial international effort, the pace of these cost reductions might well be accelerated.

One kilowatt-hour of electricity equals 3,600 kilojoules. Hence, to meet the 1995 target for electricity from renewable sources, 5.6 trillion kilowatt-hours would have to be generated by then per year. The 2010 goal would require 12.5 trillion kilowatt-hours, and the 2025 target would need nearly 28 trillion kilowatt-hours. In comparison, current worldwide production of electricity from all sources is about seven trillion kilowatt-hours.

For hydroelectricity, this assumes that additions roughly equal to the current installed capacity will be made every 15 years. Assuming that average wind turbines have a rated capacity of 500 kilowatts allows some estimation of the needed effort in wind power. (These would produce enough electricity to meet the current demand of about 200 average homes in the United States.) These turbines would be located on sites with sufficiently steady wind to produce power at an average of 40 percent of their rated capacity. Under such assumptions, the 1995 wind-power goal would require 800,000 windmills. The target for 2010 will demand some 1.6 million wind turbines, and by 2025 nearly 5 million wind turbines must be operating. Thus by 2025 the world would have about as many large wind turbines as there were small windmills in the United States in 1940.

By 2025, significant amounts of electricity should be available from various solar-thermal devices, including small, low-temperature engines using organic working fluids. It is also possible that large power plants will be using the temperature differences between ocean gradients to produce steady, round-the-clock power. But an assumption that all the solar-electric power will be derived from solar cells allows a rough sense of the magnitude of the required effort.

Averaged worldwide and over an entire year, a kilowatt of photovoltaic capacity should produce some six kilowatt-hours of electricity per day. To achieve the 1995 solar-electric goal will require the production and installation of 1.2 million megawatts of photovoltaic capacity. The 2010 goal will need almost 4 million megawatts of capacity, and the 2025 target anticipates a photovoltaic capacity of about 7.5 million megawatts.

GETTING THERE FROM HERE

Solar energy is now receiving far more international attention than ever before. A recent survey found formal solar research programs in 63 countries. Clearly the leader in research spending is the United States, with a current budget approaching $400 million and reasonable prospects for double that amount in 1979. Yet for all the public interest and enthusiasm, the mainstream energy establishment has remained rather aloof. Even the high U.S. budget represents a mere 4 percent of federal energy research and development spending. Few planners have devoted the sort of time and attention to renewable resources that they have given to nuclear energy or coal—even in countries rich in sunlight but with no domestic reserves of uranium or coal. Only a handful have examined what an aggressive solar path might look like.

Sweden is one that has. The Swedish Secretariat for Future Studies has mapped out in some detail a path that Sweden might follow in order to be entirely dependent upon renewable energy resources by 2015. The report, *Solar Sweden,* assumes that total energy use will increase 37 percent by 2015, and that the existing nuclear facilities will have finished their useful lives by then and been replaced by solar technologies. Of the total energy used, 62 percent would be derived from biological resources, 13 percent from solar heating, 11 percent from hydropower, 9 percent from photovoltaics, and 5 percent from wind power.

Under the Swedish plan, biological sources will require between 6 and 7 percent of the land area of the country. Photovoltaic cells will be placed on the roof areas of densely populated districts. The wind component will require the construction of 250 four-megawatt wind turbines—the energy equivalent of a large nuclear reactor—every year. Two-thirds of the Swedish energy research budget for 1978–81 is concentrated on renewable sources. Nuclear fission and nuclear fusion, by comparison, each receive only 12 percent of the Swedish federal energy research budget. Although the results of this study have not yet been folded into official policy, the prospects for a solar Sweden have at least been officially scrutinized and found plausible.

Japan, on the other hand, is manifestly on an unsustainable energy path but has given little serious attention to a possible change of course. Now utterly dependent upon foreign sources of fuel, Japan hopes to produce domestically 15 percent of its energy needs by 1985, and 22 percent by the turn of the century. These modest projections are misleading, however, because two-thirds of domestic energy would come from nuclear power, which is "domestic" only in a very loose sense since the country must import uranium. Yet, an energy growth rate of 5.2 percent per year is forecast through 1984, and 3.0 percent growth is expected from 1984 through 2000.

The official energy plan in Denmark, unveiled in 1976 showed renewable energy resources constituting just 4 percent of the national energy budget by 1995. Scientists and engineers from leading Danish universities subsequently prepared an alternative energy plan, under which the contribution from renewable sources would be tripled. The alternative plan, produced under very conservative assumptions, effectively undercut the government's rationale for major investments in nuclear power and led to a postponement of the official commitment to nuclear energy.

In Britain, the House of Commons Select Committee on Science and Technology reported in 1977 that the Department of Energy "must accord greater priority to renewable sources in view of their potential importance." It urged the establishment of specified "target dates" for development of working projects "so that those renewable sources which prove to be technically and economically viable are in a position to begin making a worthwhile contribution to the United

Kingdom energy requirements by 1990." This report has not had much policy impact as yet, however. The British Department of Energy is funding the world's most ambitious project for harnessing "wave power," but it remains unexcited about other renewable energy resources.

A report by the Australian Academy of Science recommended that federal research on solar energy and bioconversion be greatly increased. As a target, the report suggested that more than one-fourth of all primary energy be derived from solar resources—chiefly solar heaters and liquid fuel from biomass—by the year 2000. The Commonwealth Scientific and Industrial Research Organization has in fact been sponsoring solar energy research for more than 20 years. In the last few years this research effort has begun to see practical application. Today, about 30,000 Australian homes employ some sort of solar technology—mostly water heaters, the production of which has increased fivefold since mid-1976.

If eucalyptus were used to meet the goal of the Australian Academy for alcohol fuel for automobiles, about 200 million tons of wood would be needed each year. Seventeen factories, each associated with a 740,000-hectare plantation and capable of producing 4,000 tons of alcohol per day, would be constructed. If sugar cane were the energy crop, only one-fourth as much land would be required, but seasonable storage could pose problems. Some combination of crops would doubtless be optimal.

The government of Brazil is actively pursuing a similar course already. It is encouraging the substitution of alcohol, produced from sugar cane and manioc, for 20 percent of the country's gasoline by the early eighties, and for 100 percent of imported petroleum fuels as soon as possible. Sixty billion liters of alcohol would be required to replace current consumption of gasoline, diesel, and fuel oil. Annual production is only 740 million liters of alcohol today, but the program is growing rapidly. To produce 60 billion liters, about 4 percent of the land area of Brazil may have to be dedicated to energy crops.

It is difficult to ascertain China's energy strategy for the future, but it is clear that at least some renewable energy technologies are being pursued vigorously. With 60,000 mini-hydroelectric facilities and 5.4 million biogas plants, China is the obvious world leader in both areas. Passive solar greenhouses are used extensively, and the climate in China is ideal for applying passive solar design to houses as well.

Diverse lands with different geographies, climates, and cultures are turning toward the sun. This is no cause for surprise. The resource base is abundant. Many proven technologies can be employed to harness renewable energy sources. Tapping such resources avoids many of the more disturbing consequences of conventional energy growth. The important question is no longer whether solar energy will be developed. The questions today are, How much and how soon?

No insurmountable technical or material difficulties will hinder the solar transition. The major long-term constraint appears to be competition for land, especially for energy crops versus other crops. Some important questions remain outstanding, such as the net energy delivered by some solar processes, and the possibilities for innovative ways to store sunlight. We have solutions in hand for all these problems, but they are not necessarily the best possible solutions. Nonetheless, we know enough to proceed, realizing that improvements will emerge over time.

Many social questions—some of them trifling, some of them momentous—must also be resolved. What effect will solar energy have on employment? Studies in the

United States found that solar technologies produce more jobs than any other energy sources. Brazilian studies of ethanol production suggest that it will be highly labor-intensive as well. As solar electricity becomes cost competitive, what changes will there be in the regulation of utilities, and in the relation of the utility to its community? Some utilities may try to monopolize the sun; others may decide to oppose it. How is capital to be made available to the family or neighborhood at rates that make purchases attractive? How are warranties to be established for items that may make economic sense only after seven years of use? Whose aesthetic judgment will prevail regarding the attractiveness of various pieces of equipment?

A transition to an efficient, sustainable energy system is both technically possible and socially desirable. But 150 countries of widely different physical and social circumstances are unlikely to make such a transition smoothly and painlessly. Every potential energy source will be championed by vested interests and fought by die-hard opponents. Bureaucratic inertia, political timidity, conflicting corporate designs, and the simple, understandable reluctance of people to face up to far-reaching change will all slow the transition down. Even when clear goals are widely shared, they are not easily pursued. Policies tend to provoke opposition; unanticipated side effects almost always occur.

If the path is not easy, it is nonetheless the only road worth taking. For 20 years, global energy policy has been headed down a blind alley.

ALCOHOL

Among the most popular ideas for creating a substitute fuel for petroleum is alcohol fuel from biomass. A group from the Center for the Biology of Natural Systems, Washington University, in St. Louis, explores these possibilities in the following entry.

Taken from "The Technical Potential for Alcohol Fuels from Biomass," by Richard Carlson, David Freedman, Neil Jacobstein, Jim Kendall, Robert Schneider, and Holly Winger, "Farm and Forest Produced Alcohol: The Key to Liquid Fuel Independence," a Compendium of Papers Submitted to the Subcommittee on Energy of the Joint Economic Committee, U.S. Congress, August 22, 1980.

In 1973, the Center for the Biology of Natural Systems began a five year analysis (supported by the National Science Foundation) of ways to reduce the dependence of U.S. agriculture on petroleum based imports. Our research showed that with appropriate changes in farm production patterns fossil energy consumption in crop production could be cut by 60 percent. This reduction could be accomplished largely by eliminating use of indirect energy inputs (inorganic fertilizers and pesticides), with an 11 percent drop in crop revenue but no reduction in net economic returns per acre, since the decrease in input costs compensates for the loss in revenue. . . .

In 1978, our research efforts turned to ways of reducing U.S. agriculture's dependence on direct petroleum inputs. At the outset, we assumed that with adoption of energy conserving farming practices and on-farm production of energy, farmers could *at best,* totally eliminate their own dependence on fossil energy inputs. We have since discovered that this assumption was too conservative. Indeed, our present research suggests a new concept: U.S. agriculture as a net producer of significant quantities of renewable liquid and gaseous fuels, without reducing the supply of food or livestock feed for domestic consumption or export.

This report makes a preliminary technical assessment of the ultimate potential for alcohol production from agricultural and forestry biomass sources using biological conversion processes. Our basic concept of integrating renewable fuel production with other production activities leads to our estimate that in 2000 some 150 billion gallons of ethanol and butanediol could be produced in the United States. Alcohol could completely replace gasoline as the nation's primary liquid fuel. Some three billion gallons could be produced with surplus grain and food processing wastes; by shifting several million acres from soybean to corn production another seven billion gallons of ethanol could be produced; by planting additional acres in sugar crops, such as sugar beets, another 40 billion gallons of ethanol could be produced; conversion of cellulose in wood, crop residues and municipal wastes could further add 40 billion gallons of ethanol; finally, conversion of the hemicellulose in the same cellulosic material could produce 60 billion gallons (ethanol equivalent) of butanediol, which mixes more easily with gasoline than ethanol does. . . .

CROPPING PATTERNS

The increase in soybean production after World War II is a particularly good example of the rate and extent of change possible in the U.S. crop mix. Between 1949 and 1969, more than 30 million acres of soybeans were brought into production. . . . And in the last decade, another 30 million acres have been added, bringing the total harvested soybean acreage to over 70 million acres for 1979. The shift from corn to soybeans was important for livestock productivity because soybeans contain almost five times as much protein as corn.

A second example of changes in cropping patterns is the recent rapid growth in sunflower production. Stimulated by a demand for polyunsaturated oil, sunflower production grew from less than 200,000 acres in 1969 to more than five million acres in 1979.

Ethanol production from corn could be achieved by replacing soybeans with corn and forage crops. There are virtually no agronomic barriers to substituting corn for soybeans. However, the yield of ethanol per acre from corn is considerably lower than from various sugar crops.

Sugar beets are an attractive alternative because of their relatively high yield of ethanol plus livestock feed coproducts per acre. . . . Unlike sugar cane growing conditions appear to be favorable to sugar beet cultivation on essentially all land presently devoted to corn and soybeans, based on considerations such as precipitation, temperature, and soil slope, composition, and pH. . . . Pest problems, particularly with nematodes, can be avoided by rotating sugar beets (one year in four) with grain and forage crops. . . . Since sugar beets have been grown on as many as 2.5 million acres, there would be very few problems with disseminating crop production knowledge, or providing planting and harvesting equipment to growers.

The capacity of U.S. industry to keep pace with these changes by timely provision of ethanol conversion equipment is also illustrated by the soybean example. Few problems were encountered in supplying soybean processers with equipment for crushing, oil extraction, and protein meal drying. Although concern has recently been expressed about the shortage of fermentation and distillation equipment, this is only a very short-term problem. It is generally recognized that a large-scale (e.g., 20–50 million gallons per year) ethanol production plant can be constructed within two to three years. On-farm units can be custom built in several months. And perhaps most significantly, factory assembled units suitable for on-farm and cooperative-scale application can be constructed by the thousands each year. For example, Solargizer International, Inc., of Bloomington, Minn., is contracting with Winnebago to build prefabricated alcohol plants capable of 500,000 gallons of anhydrous ethanol output per year.

Thus, agriculture is flexible enough to make the necessary changes in the crop production system, and industry is likewise flexible enough to respond to the new demands of agriculture. . . .

COST OF ETHANOL

Critics argue that although limited production of agricultural ethanol may be tolerated because of strong farmer interest in fuel self-sufficiency, total output should be limited to only a few billion gallons per year because other liquid fuels can be produced at a lower cost from abundant fossil resources such as coal, oil shale, and tar sands. As evidence, critics often point to the current wholesale price of ethanol—now about $1.65 per gallon, compared to wholesale gasoline at $.85 per gallon—and the extent to which ethanol is subsidized by the federal government and several states.

To determine whether ethanol from agriculture is cost-effective it is necessary to recognize the following points:

(1) The current wholesale price of ethanol is substantially higher than its profitable manufacturing cost because of subsidies to gasohol retailers and the inability of producers to keep pace with demand. A state-of-the-art analysis by Raphael Katzen Associates (1979) indicates that ethanol can be produced profitably from corn at $2.30 per bushel for $0.89–1.16 per gallon in 1978 dollars. Because the ethanol industry is presently being subsidized—for whatever reason—the existing price of ethanol is greater than its actual cost of production by the federal road tax rebate subsidy of $0.40 per gallon of ethanol, plus various state subsidies.

(2) Without subsidization ethanol would cost slightly more than $1.00 per gallon according to most recent studies. Given that ethanol has only two-thirds the energy content of gasoline, critics charge that even if cost estimates are based on

modern production techniques, ethanol is more expensive than wholesale gasoline since two-thirds of a gallon costs about $0.60 to produce. Here it must be noted that ethanol's market value stems not from its energy content, but from its ability to perform work—to propel vehicles—and its octane-enhancing characteristics when blended with gasoline. The precise data are still lacking to fully qualify these advantages. However, OTA [Office of Technology Assessment] has estimated, these two additional values may amount to $0.35–0.45 per gallon of ethanol, thereby increasing its competitive market value to around $1.00, or roughly equal to its cost of production.

(3) In considering the long-run and dynamic consequences of alternative liquid fuel supply strategies, the cost of renewable alcohol fuel needs to be compared to the cost of synthetic fossil liquid fuels. . . . [Estimates] made during the 1970's on the cost of ethanol produced from corn have been stable, even though more recent estimates account for air pollution control equipment, minimal waste water and energy conservation plant design. In the future, the cost of ethanol can be expected to remain fairly stable because new cost-reducing innovations are continually being developed. Since the construction time for ethanol facilities is four or five times shorter than for synthetic fuel plants, second or third generation ethanol design technology should more accurately be contrasted with the present synthetic fuel technology. Since our estimate of how much alcohol fuel could be produced from biomass (both agriculture and forestry) without reducing food supplies is very large, this means that biomass feedstocks will remain constant in cost no matter how much alcohol is produced. In addition, some of the new technical innovations will allow more abundant and cheaper cellulosic feedstocks to be used.

The cost trend for methanol derived from coal, however, has been escalating exponentially over the same time period. As more environmental and worker health and safety protection measures are incorporated into the conversion plant's capital and operating costs, and as the price of coal rises, the price of methanol must also increase. In all likelihood, based on experience with the chemical industry, nuclear power, and other large complex technologies, capital and operating cost estimates can be expected to continue to rise.

(4) Finally, after accounting for the long-run internalized, private costs of competing liquid fuels, the remaining social damage costs of each alternative must be considered. For ethanol produced from crops or agricultural residues, the OTA and ERAB [Energy Research Advisory Board] reports emphasize that serious environmental damage may result from energy farming. First, they assume that more residue would be removed and row crop acreage expanded to marginal land, exposing the soil to the elements. Soil losses in the United States are large and increasing, according to the Soil and Conservation Service. Second, they assume that energy crop production would result in more intensive use of fertilizer and pesticides. This would consume more scarce petroleum in farming, as well as causing more pollution and health damage. Yet our analysis shows that ethanol production from agricultural crops need not involve expanding row crop land to marginal soils. What is required for ethanol production is a reorganization of tillage practices on *existing* row crop land, replacement of row crops such as soybeans with high-carbon crops such as sugar beets, and the full use of fermentation feed coproducts in livestock rations.

This does not mean, however, that alcohol production cannot be expanded to marginal lands in environmentally benign ways. For example, interplanting of tree crops yielding annual sugar pod crops with forages would allow for alcohol production without exposing the land to erosion. Also, forage crop-to-ethanol and -methanol technologies are currently under development. Cultivation of forage crops from marginal lands does not present a problem of environmental deterioration, reducing soil erosion to virtually zero.

It does not necessarily follow that no more crop residues could be removed from the land because soil erosion is a serious and worsening problem. First, changes in crop mix induced by ethanol production would probably result in somewhat more residue production, allowing more to be harvested with the same amount left on the land. Secondly, if more forage production is forthcoming from an increased carbohydrate price, hilly and marginal land can be better protected from soil erosion. Thirdly, and most importantly, numerous studies have shown that conservation tillage practices (i.e., a primary tillage tool other than the moldboard plow) allow considerable residue removal while greatly *reducing* soil erosion from that of conventional land preparation. Conservation tillage need not also imply liquid fuel-saving *minimum* tillage, although this would be an added benefit. . . .

Finally, energy crops such as sugar beets need not result in any more fertilizer or pesticide application or pollution than corn. Following corn in a rotation[,] sugar beets can utilize nitrogen which has leached below the corn root zone due to sugar beets' deeper roots (which also make it more drought resistant). Pesticide application recommendations for Midwest corn and sugar beets are nearly identical. So increased biomass yields need not result in proportionately higher farming inputs. Careful examination is required on a crop-by-crop basis.

Although environmental damage costs to agriculture from energy farming can be easily alleviated, some of the potential environmental damages created by synthetic fossil fuels will be very expensive or impossible to control. For example, the damage to the world's climate from CO_2 build-up is a serious consequence of fossil fuel burning—especially synthetic fuels—but not of biomass fuels since the carbon released is quickly recycled into growing plants. The destruction of Western lands and the socio-economic consequences of boom towns are difficult to internalize into the private costs of synthetic fuels development. . . .

MONOPOLY

THE vision of the future offered by alternative energy (what Amory Lovins calls the soft path) leads us away from the underground world of the mine to a world embedded in and responsive to nature. In its fundamental contours, it stands dramatically opposed to the big energy world of our military-industrial society with its vast technological apparatus. Despite hopeful snatches of progress here and there, it remains a fragile dream.

If the sort of scenario proposed by Denis Hayes (see p. 291), however logical and compelling it may seem, is unlikely to come about, then what will our real energy future look like? As this book has already indicated, the most basic trend in the energy industries practically from their inception has been toward concentration and monopoly. An energy future based on the present energy industry will undoubtedly be an accentuation of the same. In fact, as this section indicates, such a trend is already well under way with Big Oil moving with rapidity into other energy areas so that in a not-too-distant future it is possible to imagine a single, conglomerated "energy" industry which has absorbed not just oil, coal, natural gas, and nuclear power but even alternative energy (though hardly in the form imagined by people like Denis Hayes).

What consequences would such a future involve for us all? Certainly in contrast with the gentle and humane visions of the environmentalists, the energy industry throws up a harsh world view of its own, grounded in economic and political struggle for the use and control of the world's natural resources. Its view involves the exploitation of these resources in the most profitable manner for itself, without a particular regard for either environment or human health. In the future it will involve even greater flows of governmental funding and ever more massive schemes for the use of large-scale technology. In all these senses, the goals and methods of such a future energy conglomerate would be little different from those of the Standard Oil Trust 100 years ago. Then, as now, the primary problem was to control energy surpluses for the sake of maintenance of a profitable price level.

Even as the environmental movement prospered during the last decade, the petroleum industry was moving rapidly to consolidate and extend its grasp. As we have seen, the overthrow of Mossadegh in 1953 with the active participation of the American CIA set in motion a program of energy diversification on a grand design (see pp. 131ff.). Over the last fifteen years the outlines of a new energy industry have gradually emerged. This industry, centered in the large international petroleum corporations, now increasingly controls other energy areas.

This section includes a variety of reports and statistics that offer a general view of this new energy industry. In this regard, the work of the late Senator Lee Metcalf of Montana, his longtime staff aide, Vic Reinemer, and the researches of the Corporate Data Exchange in New York have proved invaluable.

WHO OWNS THE ENERGY CORPORATIONS?

Other sections of this book have presented facts and arguments to support the contention that the energy industry is highly concentrated, its affairs influenced by a handful of companies. As we have seen, coal reserves, an important base for synthetic fuels, are closely held by a few major energy firms. John Blair has described in detail how the domestic petroleum industry functions through joint ventures, pipeline partnerships, and so forth (see p. 110).

Behind the interlocking companies themselves are the interlocking individuals or organizations that own securities in them. In terms of actually exercising control over the industry, these investors can play an important role. A big bank, for instance, which through its trust department has major holdings in a utility may well be able to persuade the utility to buy fuel from a coal company in which the bank also owns substantial amounts of stock. In addition, by dint of its influence with the utility, the bank can persuade it to provide ample electricity and gas at economic rates to an office building it is helping finance. The following article by Vic Reinemer explains who the major investors in energy are and what their investments can mean.

Taken from "The Dominant Dozen: Who Owns the Energy Corporations?," by Vic Reinemer, Public Power, *November–December 1980.*

Nothing differentiates public and private energy systems more than the matter of where ultimate ownership and control reside.

The 2,200-plus local publicly owned electric utilities which comprise the public power sector are owned by city, town and district governments. Citizen customers have equal votes in deciding who sits on the utility governing boards, or who appoints them.

In contrast, private utilities and other investor-owned energy corporations are responsible to investors. Their interests are quite different from those of the customers who, in public power systems, hold the ultimate control. And the number of investors in a position to influence or control an energy corporation is very, very small.

What constitutes control, or potential control, of the large investor-owned systems? Two eminent authorities often cited are former Federal Reserve Board Chairman Arthur Burns and the late Rep. Wright Patman, who as chairman of the House Banking and Currency Committee was often at loggerheads with Burns. They disagreed on many things but agreed that control of a widely held corporation could often be exercised with less than 5 percent of the voting stock.

How is this so? Five percent of the stock in a corporation with, say, 100 million voting shares, is five million votes. That is frequently several thousand times more than the average stockholding in a large corporation. Large stockholders—usually institutional investors such as banks, insurance companies or investment company (mutual fund) complexes—can arrange representation on the boards of directors. This is especially easy if the corporation permits cumulative voting; all the votes can be cast for one candidate for the board and multiplied by the number of board positions to be filled.

These levers of control—voting power and board representation—can be supplemented by business arrangements, between the investor and the corporation, which provide additional leverage. These arrangements may be loans, with restrictions on the company and favors for the lender written into the agreement; administration of employee stock plans, which provides additional voting authority; or negotiated contracts for services that might be obtained more economically on a competitive bid basis.

Perhaps more significantly, corporate managers are most solicitous of the views and desires of their largest investors. Corporate management dreads the thought that a large investor might abruptly sell its holdings in the corporation, precipitating a run on the stock and a drop in its price.

The control by principal energy corporations of the lions' share of oil, coal, gas and uranium reserves, and the means of producing energy from them, is well-documented. So is their growing share of solar technology. They own almost two-thirds of the domestic copper required by solar collectors. Only two of them —Atlantic Richfield Co. and Exxon Corp.—own half of the photovoltaic cell industry.

But—try to peer up another level, to ascertain control and influence within the major energy corporations, and vision fades. The records on such matters in government regulatory offices are scant—and misleading. Usually articulate officials of large corporations and institutional investors hedge or mumble when specific questions about control and voting are asked. The corporations prefer to deal with the subject through press releases, television commercials, or newspaper and magazine ads which suggest that the companies are owned by millions of hard hats, pensioners and working women.

DIRECTORY LISTS KEY INVESTORS

There now is, however, solid and noteworthy data regarding ownership and control of energy corporations. A stock ownership directory illuminates these pyramids of power as never before. The directory profiles the ownership of 131 of the largest U.S. energy corporations, whose combined revenues total about half a trillion dollars annually; the 10 largest take in about half of that revenue.

The directory was prepared by Corporate Data Exchange (CDE), a nonprofit research organization, five years old, which has identified corporate relationships for congressional committees, labor unions, corporations and the press. CDE's methodology was to collect, evaluate and tabulate literally hundreds of reports filed in 1979 which show who is empowered to vote, buy and sell stock. CDE also identified some of the other business relationships among major investors and the corporations in their investment portfolio.

Here are the principal findings:

- In the 38 major energy corporations, the top 20 stockholders control, on the average, 32 percent of the corporations' stock; the top five stockholders 21 percent. (Table 1)
- These principal investors are usually from among 52 firms. Within the 52 are a dozen dominant investors, including one family group. (Table 2)
- In 53 of the energy firms in the study (the principal petroleum, coal mining, natural gas, electric utility and nuclear-related companies) at least one stockholder controls 5 percent or more of the corporation's stock. (Table 3)

TABLE 1 Stock Ownership Concentration of the 38 Major Energy Corporations

	Company Rank in:					% Stock Managed by Top:		Total Stock Managers Identified:		
Energy Company	Coal Prod.*	Petrol. Refin.	Gas Prod.	Gas Dist.	Uran. Milled	5	20	Number	Stock Held(%)	Number of Stockholders of Record
Amax	3	—	—	—	—	35	48	38	54	26,709
Amerada Hess	—	9	—	—	—	35	51	36	57	30,341
American Natl. Res.	—	—	—	9	—	12	24	61	38	49,576
Ashland Oil	7	15	25	—	—	13	22	23	22	61,278
Atlantic Richfield	—	8	7	—	3	12	26	69	45	196,150
Bethlehem Steel	10	—	—	—	—	12	20	31	22	161,000
Columbia Gas Sys.	—	—	21	6	—	14	21	25	22	157,139
Conoco	2	16	14	—	6	14	27	65	43	70,588
Consol. Natl. Gas	—	—	—	10	—	19	25	21	25	70,204
El Paso	—	—	—	2	—	15	26	28	28	113,872
Exxon	31	1	1	—	5	9	19	61	31	693,176
General Electric	19	—	—	—	4	9	21	67	35	543,000
Getty Oil	—	17	16	—	10	64	71	32	73	19,947
Gulf Oil	16	6	9	—	—	24	31	35	35	357,061
Kerr-McGee	—	19	20	—	1	14	36	56	48	19,100
Mobil	—	7	4	—	—	13	25	51	34	267,995
Northern Natural Gas	—	—	—	8	—	18	33	56	45	31,431
Occidental Petroleum	4	—	—	—	—	8	13	21	14	162,769

Panhandle Eastern	—	—	27	4	—	20	41	56	54	21,274
Penn Virginia	9	—	—	—	—	41	55	20	55	1,675
Peoples Gas	—	—	—	5	—	7	18	36	22	62,424
Phelps Dodge	—	—	—	—	8	13	24	34	29	42,861
Phillips Petroleum	—	12	10	—	—	14	25	67	41	122,624
Pittston	5	—	—	—	—	17	29	38	36	21,884
Shell Oil	32	3	2	—	—	81	85	16	85	34,789
Standard Oil (Cal.)	—	26	—	—	—	16	24	47	32	263,336
Standard Oil (Ind.)	—	4	5	—	—	14	26	59	38	173,211
Standard Oil (Ohio)	13	14	—	—	9	59	67	28	69	41,297
Sun Co.	45	10	12	—	—	51	55	14	55	73,883
Tenneco	—	24	13	1	—	12	22	50	30	231,600
Texaco	—	5	3	—	—	9	16	40	21	431,562
Texas Eastern	—	—	—	3	—	17	32	45	39	52,337
Texas Utilities	8	—	—	—	—	14	28	84	53	59,900
UNC Resources	—	—	—	—	2	25	36	18	36	17,300
Union Carbide	—	—	—	—	7	8	18	51	26	176,079
Union Oil of Cal.	—	13	8	—	—	13	24	50	34	84,996
United Energy Res.	—	—	—	7	—	20	26	21	27	39,498
United States Steel	6	—	—	—	—	20	27	25	28	258,239
Averages for All 38 Companies						21%	32%	41	39%	
							Total Stockholders			5,241,095
Top 10's Market Share	35%	63%	56%	55%	94%					

*The largest coal producer, Peabody Holding Co., is privately held and therefore does not appear in this table.

TABLE 2 The 52 Largest Institutional Investors in the Energy Industry

Investor	Number of Companies in Which Investor Controls 1% or More of the Stock		
	131 Profiled Companies	38 Major Companies	93 Other Companies
TIAA-CREF	31	8	23
Morgan, JP & Co.	30	14	16
Prudential Insurance	26	9	17
Citicorp	23	10	13
Capital Group	23	8	15
Bankers Trust New York	21	10	11
IDS Group	18	7	11
Chase Manhattan	16	9	7
Manufacturers Hanover	15	9	6
Lord Abbett & Co.	15	8	7
Du Pont Family Interests	15	5	10
AmeriTrust	12	4	8
Harris Bankcorp	11	3	8
United States Steel	11	2	9
Marsh & McClennan	10	1	9
State Farm Mutual Auto Ins.	10	1	9
Chemical New York	9	3	6
Dreyfus Corp.	9	3	6
FMR Corp.	9	3	6
First National Boston	9	3	6
Massachusetts Financial Serv.	9	3	6
Mellon National	9	5	4
Pioneer Western	9	3	6
Sarofim (Fayez) & Co.	9	3	6
Bank of New York	8	5	3
First Bank System	8	1	7
First Chicago	8	4	4
Ford Foundation	8	2	6
Lazard Freres	8	2	6
National Detroit	8	3	5
Rowe Price (T.) & Assoc.	8	1	7
Sears Roebuck	8	1	7
Seligman (J & W) & Co.	8	2	6
California, University of	7	—	7
Cal. Pub. Emps. & Teach. Retir.	7	4	3
Equitable Life Assur.	7	2	5
Metropolitan Life Ins.	7	2	5
Stein Roe & Farnham	7	1	6
Batterymarch Financial Mngt.	6	1	5
First Union Bancorp	6	—	6
Robeco (Holland)	6	2	4
Scudder Stevens & Clark	6	3	3
Wellington Management	6	2	4
Continental Corp.	5	2	3
Donaldson Lufkin & Jenrette	5	—	5
Minnesota State Board of Inv.	5	2	3

TABLE 2 (Continued)

Investor	Number of Companies in Which Investor Controls 1% or More of the Stock		
	131 Profiled Companies	38 Major Companies	93 Other Companies
Northern Trust	5	2	3
National City Corp.	5	1	4
Oppenheimer & Co.	5	1	4
Republic of Texas	5	1	4
State Street Research & Mngt.	5	1	4
Wells Fargo	5	3	2

TABLE 3 Managers of 5% of More of Stock in Energy Corporations

Corporation	Manager (%) # indicates interlocking directorate.
Allied Chemical	Textron Inc. (5.08)
Amax	Standard Oil of Cal. (19.32) Selection Trust Ltd. (Eng) (7.51)
Amerada Hess	Hess Family Interests #(20.94) Prudential Insurance (5.06)
American Petrofina	Petrofina S A (Belg.) (72.10)
Armco	Capital Group (7.92)
Ashland Oil	Chemical New York (7.26)
Atlas Corp.	Hughes, Howard & Jr. Estate (7.16) Pioneer Corp. (Texas) (5.82)
Borg-Warner	Bosch (Rob) Gmbh (W. Ger.) (9.98)
CBI Industries	Horton Family Interests # (6.90) Trees, Geo. S. & Family # (5.55)
Cities Service	Bancoklahoma Corp. (8.73)
Coastal States Gas	Wyatt, O. S. Jr. & Family II (9.53) Continental Illinois (7.68)
	Mercantile Texas Corp. (5.44)
Conoco	Bankers Trust New York (5.15)
Duke Power	Duke Family Interests # (20.84)
Du Pont (E.I.) de Nemours	Du Pont Family Interests # (27.31)
Eastern Gas & Fuel Associates	Bankers Trust New York (5.56) Bank of New York (5.08)
Entex	State Farm Mutual Auto Ins. (9.01)
General Dynamics	Crown Family Interests# (20.36) Bankers Trust New York (7.67)
	Morgan, J. P. & Co. (5.32)
Getty Oil	Getty Family Interests# (58.16)
Gulf Oil	Mellon Family Interests# (18.00)
Gulf Resources & Chemical	Hunt Family Group (8.24)
Mobil	Bankers Trust New York (6.39)
Montana-Dakota Utilities	Forester-Orr Family Interests# (5.04)
National Steel	Pittsburgh National Corp (15.52) Hanna Mining Co. (5.73)

TABLE 3 (Continued)

Corporation	Manager (%) # indicates interlocking directorate.
Niagara Mohawk Power	Hong Kong and Shanghai Banking (5.35)
North American Coal	Taplin-Rankim Family Int# (34.64) National City Corp. (12.70)
Northern Natural Gas	Omaha National Corp. (6.91)
Oklahoma Natural Gas	Bancoklahoma Corp. (8.81)
Pacific Gas & Electric	Rothschild Fam. Group (Fr.-Eng.) (6.30)
Panhandle Eastern Pipeline	State Street Research & Mngt. (6.66)
Penn Virginia	Leisenring-Wentz Fam. Int.# (14.09) Fidelcor (12.39)
	Morgan, J.P. & Co. (6.17)
Pennzoil	Sarofim (Fayez) & Co. (6.91)
Phillips Petroleum	First Natl. Bk. in Bartlesville (6.92)
Pioneer Corp (Texas)	Prudential Insurance (5.87)
Pittston	Morgan, J.P. & Co. (7.71)
Pogo Producing	State Farm Mutual Auto Ins. (7.52)
Republic Steel	Capital Group (6.07) Lord Abbett & Co. (5.85)
Rochester & Pittsburgh Coal	Iselin Family Interests# (46.29)
Shell Oil	Royal Dutch/Shell Group (70.16) Shell Oil (7.37)
Southern Union	First International Bancshares (6.42) First Bank System (5.92)
Standard Oil (Ind)	First Chicago (8.71)
Standard Oil (Ohio)	British Petroleum Ltd. (Eng.) (52.16)
Stone & Webster	Kramer, W.J., Whisnand, R. Jr. & Assoc. (6.37)
Struthers Wells	Finkelstein Fam. & Affiliates# (16.14) Wallace, John C. Fam. & Assoc# (6.84)
Sun Co.	Pew Family Interests# (32.44) Thompson, B.R. Fam & Assoc. (8.53)
	Philadelphia National Corp. (5.88)
Superior Oil	Keck Family Interests# (29.88) Union Bancorp (8.91)
Texaco	Manufacturers Hanover (5.21)
Texas Eastern	Sarofim (Fayez) & Co. (6.02)
Texas Gas Transmission	Bankers Trust New York (5.47)
Transco Cos	First City Bancorp of Texas (7.92)
UNC Resources	Hunt Family Group (7.12) Morgan, J.P. & Co. (6.48)
	BEA Associates (5.90)
Union Oil of California	Security Pacific (6.37)
United Energy Resources	Hunt Family Group (6.00)
United States Steel	United States Steel (13.21)

- Pension and employee funds are invested heavily in key energy corporations. However, most of these pension funds are controlled by relatively few large institutional investors, rather than the pensioners or workers, many of whom are employed by local and state governments. Similarly, the large institutions control through trust arrangements much of the stock which individuals have invested.

AD TELLS DIFFERENT STORY

The difference between what some energy corporations say about their ownership, and the facts as assembled by CDE, can easily be shown by the example of Standard Oil of Indiana. It has recently run in dozens of publications the ad "Who really owns Standard Oil (Indiana)?" The ad speaks of the 21,215 institutions, 154,869 individuals and many company employees who "own" the company.

Part of CDE's report on the same corporation is also reprinted there. CDE ranked 59 investors who control 38.24 percent of the corporation's stock. The top 20 control more than a fourth of all the stock. The top five control about 14 percent of it. Thus the ad would be more accurate were the pictures of junior, grandma and the rest replaced by a group shot of the chief executive officers of First Chicago Corp., Citicorp, Harris Bankcorp, Chase Manhattan Corp. and the Prudential Insurance Co.

CDE's findings need to be qualified in three ways:

(1) A corporation's employee savings plan—such as Standard Oil of Indiana's—is often managed by a financial institution, in this illustrative case First Chicago Corp. The employees have the right to instruct the bank how to vote their shares. Many of them do not bother to do this. If the employees do not instruct the bank how to vote at least 10 days before the annual meeting the bank votes the shares, in favor of the candidates and propositions recommended by management.

CDE credits control of stock in such arrangements to the bank. The option of employees described above tends to diminish the reported stock concentration ratio, but probably not by very much. Of those employees who do give voting instructions only a few are likely to record themselves against management, which almost always has enough votes to win overwhelmingly regardless of the issue. First Chicago Corp. refuses to disclose how many Standard Oil of Indiana shares it voted this year without instructions from employee-stockholders.

(2) Stock controlled by an individual generally is not reported publicly unless the person is (a) an officer or director of a publicly held company; (b) a member of an officer's or director's family, or (c) controls more than 5 percent of the corporation's outstanding shares. Some significant stockholdings by individuals, or by institutions which are not subject to or have not complied with government reporting requirements, may not be included in the directory. However, the stock holdings of large institutional investors are so large that they tower over, as far as can be determined, the holdings of all individuals and families except the du Ponts, Rockefellers, Hunts and Rothschilds.

(3) Some of the biggest energy corporations escaped CDE's definition of major energy corporations and are not included in this study. These are the "railroads" —the Burlington Northern (BN) and Union Pacific Corp. These two energy-real

estate conglomerates and Continental Oil Co. (which was profiled by CDE) each control more than 10 billion tons of economically recoverable coal reserves.

THE BN'S SIDELINE

The BN's coal reserves—some 60 billion tons—dwarf those of other energy corporations. The BN also has oil and gas rights to 7.5 million acres in 13 states, 1.5 million acres of timberland, more than a million acres in grazing and farm land, and a railroad network extending from the Pacific to the Gulf of Mexico to the Great Lakes.

The federal government generously granted vast natural resources to the BN as an incentive to build a railroad. The BN sidelined rail passenger service to concentrate on developing those lucrative resources. It is trying to abandon intrastate freight service. Interstate freight service continues, as public power systems in Texas which are fighting the BN's hefty, multiple rate increases are keenly aware.

Increasing oil prices are good news for the BN's principal stockholders—J.P. Morgan & Co., Pacific Power and Light (PP&L) and Peter Kiewit Sons Inc. (PP&L and Peter Kiewit Sons' Inc. jointly own Decker Coal Co., whose subsidiary Westana is the record owner of the BN stock.) As the price of oil increases the proportion of coal reserves which can be mined economically increases. The BN *increased* its estimate of economically recoverable coal from 12 billion tons in 1978 to 14.7 billion tons—up 2.7 *billion* tons—last year. During the same period its proven oil reserves grew 18 percent and natural gas reserves increased 28 percent. Nevertheless for accounting purposes, during the same one-year interval, the BN *decreased* the book value of its identifiable coal and minerals, from $3.1 *million* to $2.7 *million.*

12 KEY ENERGY INVESTORS

Which are the few firms that control sizeable blocks of stock in major energy corporations? Are they subject to any control and guidance from the people who invest in or through them?

The dozen major investors at the top of Table 2 each control one percent or more of the stock in from 12 to 31 major energy corporations; each of the 12 is also among the five largest stockholders in from 10 to 33 major energy corporations. The majority of these 12 major investors are also principal creditors of energy corporations. And there are numerous interlocks among the boards of directors.

These 12 dominant investors include six commercial banks, two insurance companies, three investment company (mutual fund) complexes, and one family group, the du Ponts. The 11 institutional investors are:

INVESTMENT COMPANIES

Capital Group, Inc.
Lord Abbett & Co.
IDS

INSURANCE COMPANIES

TIAA-CREF
Prudential

BANKS

J.P. Morgan & Co.
Citicorp
Bankers Trust Co. New York
Chase Manhattan Corp.
Manufacturers Hanover Corp.
AmeriTrust Corp. (formerly Clevetrust Corp.)

MUTUAL FUNDS

Some of these firms are hardly household words. Capital Group Inc., based in Los Angeles, is one example. Privately held, it does not report to the Securities and Exchange Commission. Neither it nor its subsidiary Capital Research & Management are [*sic*] listed in "Standard & Poor's Register," "Moody's Bank & Finance Manual" or the "Directory of Corporate Affiliations."

The principal affiliates of Capital Group, Inc. are listed on newspaper financial pages under "American Funds" in the mutual fund quotations. Capital Group's principal owner is Jonathan Bell Lovelace, Jr., son of the fund family's founder.

Lord Abbett & Co. is an investment management firm in New York owned by eight partners. On Oct. 1 Alvin H. Berndt replaced Robert S. Driscoll as managing partner.

IDS (Investors Diversified Services), whose tower dominates the Minneapolis skyline, is the largest mutual fund complex in the world. IDS is a subsidiary of the New York-based Alleghany Corp., a conglomerate controlled by the Kirby family. Alleghany Board Chairman F.M. Kirby emphasizes that the mutual funds in the IDS group are—and this is typical—"separate, publicly-owned companies, which elect their own independent boards of directors."

ELECTIONS PREORDAINED

"Elect" is the key word in Kirby's statement. Election results at annual meetings of mutual funds and other major investor-owned corporations are as preordained as in the Soviet Union, inasmuch as the Soviet and corporate ballots are strikingly similar—there is only one candidate for each position.

The key process, of course, is not election, but *nomination.* Service in or aspiration to high political office, and close ties with large energy corporations, are characteristic attributes of persons nominated and elected as outside directors of IDS funds.

Richard Nixon served on four of the fund boards from 1964 to 1968, the year he became president. (He and George E. MacKinnon, then vice president and general counsel of the largest IDS fund, Investors Mutual, had been freshman congressmen together.) Nixon was replaced in 1968 by his friend Donald Kendall, chief executive officer of Pepsico. Kendall also sits on the board of Atlantic Richfield; the IDS group is one of its five major stockholders. Kendall still serves on IDS fund boards of directors with Melvin Laird, former congressman who was Nixon's secretary of defense and is a member of the board of directors of Phillips Petroleum, in which IDS funds are heavily invested.

John Byrnes, who was ranking minority member of the House Ways and Means Committee when he served in Congress, is a member of several of the IDS fund boards. Paul McCracken, chairman of the Council of Economic Advisers in the Nixon administration, sat on the boards' of six of the funds until last year. Board chairman of all the IDS funds is Hamer Budge. Also a former congressman, he went straight to IDS from the job of regulating mutual funds as chairman of the Securities and Exchange Commission, to which Nixon had appointed him.

INSURANCE COMPANIES

The acronym TIAA-CREF stands for Teachers Insurance and Annuity Association—College Retirement Equities Fund. Its assets, including more than $5 billion in stock, constitute the retirement and insurance plans of more than half a million professors and other employees of some 3,300 colleges, universities and nonprofit educational and research organizations.

TIAA-CREF's procedures in deciding how to vote and invest its vast blocks of stock are a far cry from a city council meeting, but more democratic than those of other major managers of other people's money. One-fifth of the trustees are selected by policyholders. While TIAA-CREF occasionally differs with the management of some corporations in which it invests, it does not cast its votes against management on energy policy. The non-elected trustees of TIAA-CREF, who outnumber the elected trustees four to one, include Exxon's chairman, William Garvin. He replaced Atlantic Richfield's chariman, Robert Anderson, on the TIAA-CREF board in 1978.

Newark-based Prudential—whose chairman and chief executive officer is Robert A. Beck—is the largest of the mutual insurance companies, which theoretically are owned by their policyholders. In practice, however, policyholders have fewer rights than stockholders of investor-owned corporations.

Many mutual insurance policyholders are never notified of annual meetings. If a Prudential policyholder wants to nominate someone for the board of directors he has to present a supporting petition with more than 10,000 signatures of other policyholders. However—Catch 22—the list of policyholders is not available until 40 days before an election, and the nomination has to be filed at least five months before the election.

COMMERCIAL BANKS

And who controls the one Cleveland and five New York commercial banks—the dominant group within the 12 principal investors in energy corporations?

Put most simply, the major banks control themselves and each other. A CDE directory of bank and finance corporations also published this year confirmed and expanded upon this finding by two congressional committees. The bank and finance directory, based on 1979 data, shows that:

- AmeriTrust Corp. (formerly Clevetrust Corp.) is an extraordinarily concentrated center of financial power. The bank controls itself by managing more than 26 percent of its own stock. The second largest block of stock is controlled by National City Corp. of Cleveland, also a multibank holding company. Its subsidiaries include National City Bank of Cleveland. National City Corp. is also the top stockholder in Cleveland Electric Illuminating Co. (CEI) and administers CEI's employee savings plan.

  Public Power readers will recall the long efforts of Cleveland banks, led by M. Brock Weir, now chairman and chief executive officer of the new AmeriTrust Corp., to abolish the feisty public power system in Cleveland which competes with the banks' favored CEI. . . .
- Two of the five New York banks, Chase Manhattan Corp. and Citicorp, together control more than five percent of the stock of one of the other five, J.P. Morgan and Co. Along with T. Rowe Price & Associates* and two other banks, First National Boston Corp. and National Detroit Corp., they control more than 13 percent of Morgan's stock. The top 20 investors in Morgan control more than 27 percent of Morgan's stock. Most of the top 20 are banks —including Morgan itself—or insurance companies; IDS and the University of California are exceptions.
- The top five stockholders in Citicorp, with 11.53 percent of the votes, remarkably resemble the five top stockholders of J.P. Morgan & Co. The largest is Morgan, which controls more than 4 percent of the votes in its competitor Citicorp. The other four are First National Boston Corp. (again), T. Rowe Price & Associates Inc. (again), TIAA-CREF and Citicorp itself.
- Bankers Trust New York Corp. controls 7.24 percent of its own stock, which is more than seven times as much as its second largest stockholder, Morgan. More than 5 percent of the stock in Chase Manhattan Corp. is controlled by the bank itself and the Rockefeller family interests. Bankers Trust is the next largest stockholder. Others which control more than 1 percent of the stock are the IDS mutual fund group, California and Ohio public employees' retirement systems and FMR Corp.

  FMR, like Capital Group Inc., is an investment company complex (the "Fidelity Group" in the mutual fund quotations) controlled by the son of another fund pioneer. President of 10 of the funds and board chairman of 11, Edward Crosby Johnson 3rd nevertheless is not listed in "Who's Who in America" or "Who's Who in Finance and Industry." (Both publications, incidentally, are subsidiaries of ITT, in which the Fidelity funds control more than half a million shares.)
- Manufacturers Hanover controls more than 7 percent of its own stock. Morgan and Citicorp together control more than five percent. Another of the top five stockholders in Manufacturers Hanover is Continental Corp., an insurance company in which Manufacturers Hanover is the principal stockholder. (Turnabout is fair play.) The next largest stockholders in Manufacturers Hano-

*T. Rowe Price Associates, based in Baltimore, is an investment counsel firm owned by its 326 employees. Curran W. Harvey is president and E. Kirkbride Miller is board chairman.

ver, with more than 5 percent among them, are the IDS fund group (again), Ameritrust (again), and Bankers Trust New York Corp. (again). And so it goes.

CONCENTRATION BLITHELY UNNOTICED

Ownership means control, according to my dictionary. Control of the energy corporations bears little resemblance to the image the industry expensively projects. Standard Oil of Indiana's ad is of a piece with the press releases—virtually identical—of the American Petroleum Institute and the Chamber of Commerce of the United States, which claim that individuals own 90 percent of the largest oil companies. Put in the same category the message which Bob Hope has dinned into millions of ears via television: "Who owns America's oil companies? Fourteen million Americans, trusting in companies like Texaco!"

On the other hand, the answer to the question of control of the energy industry is not just "Wall Street" or "the banks." To be sure, the inbred New York commercial banks dominate. But there are other pinnacles of power, equally unaccountable to the people whose money they manage, even less known by the public and press.

The Organization of Petroleum Exporting Countries (OPEC) and its control over oil receive a lot of attention. But here at home, relatively and blithely unnoticed, control of energy has concentrated in fewer and fewer hands, farther and farther away from the people who depend on it. . . .

INTERLOCKING CONTROL

The following documents from the Corporate Data Exchange's report on energy show in graphic detail the increasingly intertwined nature of the energy business at all levels. Among them, the first, "Horizontal Integration," is perhaps the most important and ominous, showing as it does the way in which the various energy industries—oil, natural gas, coal, and nuclear—are shading toward a future in which there will simply be a single big energy industry.

Taken from press release accompanying release of CDE Stock Ownership Directory, No. 4, Energy, *published by Corporate Data Exchange, Inc., New York, June 1980.*

HORIZONTAL INTEGRATION

The top twenty petroleum refiners led by Exxon (1), Standard Oil of California (2), and Shell (3) currently control 85 percent of U.S. oil refining and 60% of production. These same oil companies own 92.9 percent of all known U.S. oil reserves. But a look at the last fifteen years of their participation in other energy sectors reveals that these companies have expanded their influence through in-

Horizontal Integration of the Top 20 Petroleum Companies, 1977

	Petroleum			Natural Gas		Coal		Nuclear	
Company	Ref Rank	Prod Rank	Res Rank	Prod[1] Rank	Res[2] Rank	Prod Rank	Res Rank	Mili Rank	Res Rank
Exxon	1	1	1	1	1	31	4	5	4
Standard Oil of Calif	2	5	5	6	6	—	—	—	29
Shell Oil	3	4	7	2	8	32	14	—	—
Standard Oil (Ind)	4	3	6	5	3	—	—	—	—
Texaco	5	2	4	3	—	—	21	—	—
Gulf Oil	6	7	9	9	5	16	13	—	2
Mobil	7	8	10	4	4	—	11	—	8
Atlantic Richfield	8	6	3	7	2	—	15	3	7
Amerada Hess	9	17	19	—	20	—	—	—	—
Sun Co	10	11	13	12	13	—	16	—	—
Marathon Oil	11	15	11	17	18	—	—	—	—
Phillips Petroleum	12	10	15	10	11	—	6	—	14
Union Oil of Calif	13	12	14	8	7	—	—	—	12
Standard Oil (Ohio)	14	16	2	—	9	13	—	9	31
Ashland Oil	15	19	25	25	22	7*	—	—	—
Conoco	16	13	17	14	12	2	1	6	9
Getty Oil	17	9	8	16	17	—	—	10	11
Cities Service	18	14	18	11	16	—	—	—	—
Kerr McGee	19	20	26	20	27	—	23	1	1
American Petrofina	20	22	31	—	**	—	—	—	—
Industry Concentration Ratios									
Top 5 Petroleum Cos	39.2%	28.8%	54.2%	35.3%	24.8%	12.3%	18.1%	38.4%	25.2%
Top 10 Petroleum Cos	63.4	45.8	79.4	56.3	36.7	13.1	23.1	38.4	32.9
Top 20 Petroleum Cos	85.5	60.0	92.9	70.7	44.2	13.1	23.8	38.4	33.3

1. Only includes sales to interstate pipelines.
2. Includes United States and Canada.

*Operators 50% owned by Ashland Oil.
**Ranked below top 30.

creased ownership of America's energy reserves. As windfall profits from decontrol and higher gas pump prices are recorded, the oil companies are investing heavily in coal, nuclear, and natural gas energy companies. Seven companies—Conoco, Exxon, Phillips, Arco, Mobil, Gulf, and Shell—command 18 percent of the nation's coal reserves, up from the 1965 figure of 1 percent. The nuclear industry has its oil base in five companies, led by Kerr McGee, Arco and Exxon, which produce 38.4 percent of U.S. nuclear fuels, up from 21 percent in 1965. A look at oil company participation in the natural gas industry reveals a 70 percent share of present production and a 44.2 percent share of natural gas reserves.

CROSS-OWNERSHIP

CDE's data on intercompany ownership sheds new light on possible antitrust violations. For example, Newmont Mining holds 3 percent of Conoco, the nation's second largest coal company, and 27.5 percent of Peabody Holding Company, the largest coal company in the United States. Newmont's holdings in these two companies give it a key position in 17 percent of the nation's coal production.

Pioneer Corporation owns 5.82 percent of the Howard Hughes estate-controlled Atlas Corporation. Both companies are among the top twenty producers in uranium milling (see table).

Cross-Ownership Among Energy Companies

Company	Holder (Percent)
Amax	Standard Oil of California (19.32)
Atlas Corp	Pioneer Corp (5.82)
Carolina Power & Light	United States Steel (1.12)
Central & South West	United States Steel (1.31)
Conoco	Newmont Mining (3.26)
Florida Power	General Electric (1.87)
	United States Steel (3.83)
Florida Power & Light	United States Steel (2.16)
Middle South Utilities	United States Steel (1.06)
Mobil	Northern Natural Gas (1.42)
Pacific Power & Light	American Electric Power (.92)
Peabody Holding	Newmont Mining (27.50)
Southern	United States Steel (.60)

In addition, J.P. Morgan controls over 5 percent in three competing coal companies—Penn Virginia (6.17 percent), General Dynamics (5.32 percent) and Pittston (7.71 percent)—which together produce almost 5 percent of the nation's coal.

FOREIGN CONTROL

CDE data reveal that 12 percent of petroleum refining and 25 percent of U.S. oil reserves rest with companies the dominant owners of which are foreign interests. With the present concern over dependence on Middle East oil, foreign ownership of American firms is often overlooked. Among the most significant holdings are 52 percent of Standard Oil of Ohio, the nation's fourteenth largest oil company, by British Petroleum; 70 percent of Shell Oil, the third largest oil company, by combined Dutch-British interests; and the Belgian oil company's 72 percent share of American Petrofina, the twentieth largest refiner of U.S. crude oil. Smaller, yet significant holdings appear throughout the corporate profiles. For example, the Saudi Arabian Chaith Rashad Pharaon is the fourth largest holder in Occidental Petroleum, and the British concern, S. Pearson & Son Ltd., ranks number two in Ashland Oil.

LAW FIRMS AND INVESTMENT BANKS REPRESENT COMPETING COMPANIES

CDE data demonstrate that prominent investment banks and law firms are representing companies competing in the same industry, even though they are often privy to strategic information on their clients. Potential conflicts of interest were highlighted by the 1978 lawsuit charging that Morgan Stanley had turned over confidential information to its client Johns-Manville, which was seeking to acquire another Morgan client, Olinkraft. At the same time law firms have been placed on notice for relationships to clients on opposing sides in court cases. In July 1978 Kirkland & Ellis of Chicago was forced to withdraw as legal counsel to Westinghouse in its huge uranium antitrust case because the firm also represented three of the accused firms in other uranium-related proceedings.

CDE found that Baker & Botts of Houston is the nexus of an integrated natural gas complex, serving as the top outside legal counsel to two gas producers including Pennzoil; Tenneco, the largest interstate natural gas pipeline; and two utilities. Its crosstown rival, Vinson & Elkins, services an energy conglomerate of its own with ties to Superior Oil Company; Texas Eastern, the third largest interstate gas pipeline; a coal producer; and a gas utility.

Investment banking relationships are even more concentrated among New York firms. Morgan Stanley is the leading investment banker for six petroleum companies, including Shell and Exxon, and five coal producers. Merrill Lynch services twelve gas and electric utilities, and Dillon Read counts among its clients four interstate gas pipelines.

THE REVOLVING DOOR

Former energy planners such as Federal Energy Administration czar Frank Zarb; his successor, James Schlesinger; Treasury Secretary William Simon; and Alan Greenspan, chairman of the Council of Economic Advisers—all have used their government experience and connections to advise the energy industry. Frank Zarb became a general partner of Lazard Freres, which handles, among others, Allied Chemical, Allis Chalmers, General Dynamics, and the Peabody Holding Company. Schlesinger left his government job to become a senior adviser at Lehman Brothers, working on private financing of the Alaska Natural Gas Pipeline.

The Carter administration had its share of energy industry-related advisers. For instance, Lynn Coleman, from the John Connally law firm Vinson & Elkins, was general counsel to the Department of Energy. Vinson & Elkins has been general counsel to Texas Eastern and Superior Oil, among others.

INTERLOCKING DIRECTORATES

Another clue to the growing relationships among companies are members of boards of directors who serve on several different company boards at the same time. Below are excerpts from the late Senator Lee Metcalf's study.

Taken from "Interlocking Directorates Among the Major U.S. Corporations," a Staff Study, Subcommittee on Reports, Accounting and Management, Committee on Governmental Affairs, U.S. Senate, January 1978.

. . . For a number of years, eight large energy companies[*] had been involved independently and through joint ventures in providing the United States with much of its energy. Formerly, it was just oil and gas, now their product is a total energy package including coal, nuclear, geothermal, and solar. . . .

Hardly a business or population area in this country does not depend in some part on the production and distribution of energy supplies of these corporate giants. A 1976 staff report of the Senate Special Subcommittee on Integrated Oil Operations has suggested that the production of consumer goods such as automobiles, television sets, household appliances, and other energy-consuming products and services are inextricably linked to the growth of energy consumption and the organization of the energy industry. Thus, it follows that where such industry organization affects the pricing and production of energy and energy-using appliances and equipment, the energy industry must necessarily influence the structure and behavior of the U.S. economy itself.

As part of any study of concentration in the structure of the energy industry, a look at the directorate affiliations of its major companies should be one of the first orders of business. From Table 2B . . . it appears that three of the largest energy companies had indirect interlocks with most of their major competitors. . . .

As shown in Table 2B, the Nation's largest energy company, Exxon, indirectly

[*]The eight largest U.S. energy companies in 1976 were: Exxon, Texaco, Mobil, Standard (California), Gulf, Standard (Indiana), Shell, and Atlantic Richfield. Gulf Oil Corp. was not included in the analysis here because it was reported to have no direct or indirect interlocks with the major energy companies, with one exception: Shell (one indirect interlock). Gulf had 2 direct and 11 indirect interlocks with Mellon National; 5 indirects with General Motors; 5 indirects with Metropolitan Life; and 4 indirects with United States Steel. Mellon Bank (100 percent owned by Mellon National) and the Mellon family held a 14.6 percent voting interest in Gulf.

Connections of Former and Present Government Officials to Energy Industry

Individual	Government Position (date)	Former Affiliation to Energy Industry Through Law Firm		
		Law Firm	Legal Serv	Energy Client
Lynn R. Coleman	Gen Counsel to Dept of Energy ('78–)	Vinson & Elkins, TX ('65–'78)	Gen Counsel	Gulf Resources & Chem.
			"	Houston Natural Gas
			Leg Counsel	Halliburton
			"	Superior Oil
			"	Texas Eastern
Robert Carswell	Deputy Sec. of Treasury ('77–)	Shearman & Sterling, NY	Gen Counsel	Combustion Engineering
			Leg Counsel	Con Edison
Warren Christopher	Deputy Sec. of State ('77–)	O'Melveny & Myers, CA	Leg Counsel	Southern California Edison
			Securities Counsel	Standard Oil (Ind)
Lloyd N. Cutler	Counsel to President ('79–)	Wilmer, Cutler & Pickering, DC	Wash Rep	Bethlehem Steel
Robert Strauss	Chmn, Comm to Reelect Pres (79) U.S. Intl Trade Negotiator ('77)	Akin, Gump, Hauer & Feld, TX	Wash Rep	Coastal State Gas
			"	Marathon Oil
			"	Sun Co
Stephen Wakefield	Asst to Gen Counsel, Fed Power Commission ('70–'72); Dep Asst Sec of Interior for Mineral Resources ('72–'73) Asst Sec Interior for Energy & Minerals ('73–'74); Asst Adm Fed Energy Office ('73–'74)	Baker & Botts, TX ('74–)	Gen Counsel	Entax
			"	Pennzoil
			Leg Counsel	Houston Industries
			"	Pogo Producing
			"	Tenneco
			"	United Energy Resources

Connections of Former and Present Government Officials to Energy Industry (Continued)

Individual	Government Position (date)	Current Affiliation to Energy Industry Through Investment Bank	
		Investment Bank (date)	Energy Clients
William E. Simon	Sec. of Treasury ('74–'76); Past Chmn, Oil Policy Com; Member, Pres Energy Resources Council	Salomon Brothers ('64–'72)	15 energy clients including: Atlantic Richfield, Florida Power & Light; Gulf Oil, Sun Co.
		Senior Consultant, Blyth Eastman Dillon ('77–)	12 energy clients including: American Electric Power, Pacific Gas & Elec, Standard Oil of Calif.
Robert H. Baldwin	Under Sec. of the Navy ('65–'67)	Morgan Stanley, Senior Partner ('68–'73), Pres ('73–)	33 energy clients including: Exxon, Shell Oil, Standard Oil (Ind), Conoco, Tenneco, United States Steel
William P. Rogers	Secretary of State ('69–'73)	Board of Directors, Merrill Lynch ('74–)	42 energy clients including: Commonwealth Edison, El Paso, Potomac Elec, Public Service Electric & Gas
James Schlesinger	Secretary of Energy ('77–'79); Chief Energy Adviser to Pres ('77); Sec of Defense ('73–'77); Dir. CIA ('73); Chmn Atomic Energy Commission ('71–'73)	Senior Adviser, Lehman Brothers ('79–)	23 energy clients including: AMAX, Kerr McGee, Long Island Lighting, Westinghouse Electric
Frank Zarb	Adm, Federal Energy Administration ('74–'77); Assoc Dir Office of Mngt & Budget ('73–'74)	Gen Partner, Lazard Preres ('77–)	4 energy clients including: Allied Chemical, Allis-Chalmers, General Dynamics, Peabody Holding

Individual	Government Position	Direct Affiliation to Energy Industry
Alan Greenspan	Chmn, Council of Economic Advisers ('74–'77)	Board of Dir., Mobil Corp ('77–)
Robert S. Ingersoll	Ass. Sec. of State for East Asian & Pacific Affairs ('74); Dep. Sec. of State ('74–'76)	Board of Dir., Atlantic Richfield ('76–)
Adm. Thomas H. Moorer	Chief of Naval Operations ('67–'70); Chmn., Joint Chiefs of Staff ('70–'74)	Board of Dir., Texaco ('74–)

TABLE 2B Energy Industry: Indirect Interlocks Among Major Competitors (1976)

	Atlantic	Exxon	Mobil	Shell	Standard (Cal)	Standard (Ind)	Texaco
Atlantic Richfield		4	3	1	2	5	2
Exxon	4		6	1	6	2	2
Mobil	3	6		3	3	3	4
Shell	1	1	3		1	0	0
Standard (Cal)	2	6	3	1		0	0
Standard (Ind)	5	2	3	0	0		0
Texaco	2	2	4	0	0	0	

interlocked with its leading competitors as follows: Atlantic Richfield (4 times); Mobil (6 times); Shell (once); Standard of California (6 times); Standard of Indiana (twice); and Texaco (twice).

The second largest energy company, Mobil, similarly connected with its sister competitors: Exxon (6 times); Atlantic Richfield (3 times); Shell (3 times); Standard of California (3 times); Standard of Indiana (3 times); and Texaco (4 times).

Texaco, the number 3 company, linked with Exxon twice; Atlantic Richfield twice; and Mobil 4 times.

Atlantic Richfield also interlocked with all 6 competitors: Exxon (4 times); Mobil (3 times); Shell (once); Standard of California (twice); Standard of Indiana (5 times) and Texaco (twice).

The directorate linkages among these giant energy firms appear all the more serious when viewed in the context of where their directors met.

For example, Exxon had two directors—one its chairman—sitting on the board of Citicorp, alongside directors of Mobil and Standard of California. Other energy related companies on the Citicorp board were Halliburton (Brown & Root), Texas Eastern Transmission, General Electric, Stone and Webster and Westinghouse. Major energy users on that board were General Motors, Ford, Monsanto, DuPont, Union Pacific, Southern Pacific and U.S. Steel. Major communications firms represented were A.T. & T., IBM and RCA.

Exxon directors met directors of Mobil, Atlantic Richfield and Standard of Indiana on the board of Chemical New York. Other energy companies on that board were Amerada Hess and Aramco. A member of an advisory committee to the Chemical board was also a director of Texaco. Other energy-related companies on the Chemical board were General Electric, Westinghouse, A.T. & T. and IBM.

Exxon interlocked with Mobil and Texaco on the board of A.T. & T. Also on that board was a director of Continental Oil. Major energy users represented included General Motors, Chrysler, DuPont, Southern California Edison, Southern Railway, Union Carbide and U.S. Steel.

Exxon linked with directors of Standard of Indiana, Utah International, Allied Chemical and Cities Service on the board of Chase Manhattan. Also represented there were Rockefeller Family Associates, General Motors, Chrysler, IBM, Bendix, and U.S. Steel. Exxon also connected with Atlantic Richfield and Phillips Petroleum on the board of Metropolitan Life.

Exxon indirectly interlocked with Mobil on the board of Equitable Life. Represented on the Equitable board were Continental Oil, Chase Manhattan, Ford, and Citicorp.

However, the corporate board that provided the broadest opportunity for a summit discussion on energy was not a financial institution, but a heavy machinery manufacturer. Caterpillar Tractor's board included directors from Exxon, Mobil, Shell, Standard of California and Atlantic Richfield—five of the seven major energy companies in the analysis. Chemical New York—where four majors met—was also directly interlocked with Caterpillar. Similarly, A.T. & T., IBM and United States Steel were on the machinery manufacturer's board. This is perhaps the most extreme example of industry concentration on one company's board of directors found in the study.

Other energy companies also related to each other. Mobil met Shell on the board of General Foods. Mobil connected with Texaco on the board of American Express, and with Atlantic Richfield through Time, Inc. Shell interlocked with Gulf Oil on the board of Ampex Corp., and Standard of California met Atlantic Richfield on the board of Carter Hale Hawley Stores. Standard of Indiana interlocked with Mobil on the boards of Eli Lilly and Bell & Howell.

Mobil's own board of directors is of special interest since it included the former chairman of General Electric who was also a director of Utah International (uranium); a director of Stone & Webster; two directors of American Express Co. (including Mobil's chairman); a director of A.T. & T. (Mobil's chairman again); one director of Citicorp and one of Citibank; the chariman of the Finance Committee of IBM, and the former chairman of Bankers Trust.

Two other possible elements of concentration in the energy field are common use of accounting firms and investment bankers by big energy companies. Exxon's chief auditor is Price, Waterhouse & Co., which also audits Royal Dutch Petroleum, Standard Oil of California, Gulf Oil, Standard of Indiana and Shell, as well as Caterpillar Tractor referred to above. Exxon's lead investment banker is Morgan Stanley, which is also the principal investment banker for Mobil, Standard of Indiana, Texaco, and Shell.

The above described interlocks raise fundamental questions. To what extent do these extraordinary corporate linkages provide a mechanism for stabilizing prices, controlling supply, and restraining competition? What is the effect of major energy company interlocks on industry attempts to influence Government policies? What is the impact of the energy companies' potential boardroom powers to influence decisions on the kinds of energy-consuming products and services marketed by major companies with whom they interlock? . . . They are . . . yet to be answered.

THE CONTINENTAL–CONSOLIDATION DECISION

Probably the most important turning point for the evolving energy industry took place in 1965, when the Antitrust Division of the Justice Department in the Johnson administration declined to block the merger of the Continental Oil Company, then tenth largest in the nation, and Consolidation Coal, the largest coal producer. Following this merger, other oil companies bought coal companies until, as we have seen in the Corporate Data Exchange report, the coal industry is under all but total control of the oil industry. Donald Turner, assistant attorney general for antitrust, later explained the government's reasoning.

Taken from "Concentration by Competing Raw Fuel Industries in the Energy Market and Its Impact on Small Business," hearings, Subcommittee on Special Small Business Problems, Select Committee on Small Business, House of Representatives, July 12, 13, 14, 15, 20, 22, 1971.

We did not attack the acquisition of the Consolidation Coal Co. by the Continental Oil Co. for the following reasons. Only insignificant amounts of Continental's gasoline are sold in Consolidation's market area. Although natural gas and residual fuel oil—which Continental produces—may sometimes compete with coal, Continental sold these products for use only in areas of the country in which Consolidation does not operate and Consolidation did not sell in areas in which Continental's products were sold.

Moreover, Consolidation and Continental are not significant potential competitors. Heavy residual fuel oil requires water transportation if it is to be shipped far from where it is produced. It is thus unlikely that Continental could expand its residual fuel oil sales into Consolidation's markets. Similarly transportation costs made it unlikely that Continental's natural gas would be sold in Consolidation's markets or that Consolidation's coal would be sold in Continental markets.

We were, of course, fully aware that Consolidation was trying to develop a process for making gasoline out of coal. Even if it develops such a process, however, it is unlikely that it would have competed significantly with Continental. Consolidation operates primarily in Pennsylvania, West Virginia and Kentucky and presumably would sell gasoline in that area.

Continental's sales in that area account for only 8/10 of 1% of its total domestic gasoline sales. There is no indication that either company intends to expand its marketing territory significantly. Moreover, if Consolidation succeeds in converting coal to gasoline, it should be anticipated that other companies can do the same and are potential competitors in the gasoline market to the same extent as is Consolidation. In our judgment, therefore, the removal of one of them as a potential competitor was unlikely to affect significantly the behavior of companies that now sell gasoline or have any significant adverse long-run effect on competition.

TVA AND ENERGY MARKETS

As the largest consumer of coal in the nation, the Tennessee Valley Authority has played an important role in organizing the energy industry. As we note in the nuclear power section (see p. 166), it was the TVA which was instrumental in providing the large amounts of electricity required for nuclear power, both bombs and power plants. To do so, it pressured the coal industry into mechanization and, as Tom Bethell has pointed out (see p. 38), in effect joined Lewis and Love in reorganizing that industry.

Since the mid-1960s, however, the TVA has fought the tendency toward horizontal integration within the energy industry, (which the Continental-Consolidation decision helped trigger), seeing itself threatened by a concentrated industry which could set its own terms on energy supply and price. Following are excerpts from a 1979 TVA report on energy markets.

Taken from "The Structure of the Energy Markets: A Report of TVA's Antitrust Investigation of the Coal and Uranium Industries," February 26, 1979.

The big oil companies' attempts to enter and dominate the coal and uranium markets continued during the last 18 months, posing threats to TVA fuel supplies. Thus,

> In the fall of 1978, Standard Oil of California (Socal), the Nation's fourth largest oil company first tried to increase its ownership in AMAX, TVA's fourth largest coal supplier, from its current 20 percent to a majority position. AMAX rejected that offer. Soon after, Socal proposed the takeover of American Nuclear Corporation, a major TVA uranium contractor. TVA strongly opposed this proposed merger and in February 1979 Socal dropped the proposal, giving TVA's resistance as the cause.
>
> Diamond Shamrock, an oil and gas company and, according to the 1978 *Fortune* 500, the 67th largest American corporation in terms of net income, is seeking to acquire Falcon Seaboard, TVA's 3d largest coal supplier and virtually the sole source of supply for TVA's Bull Run Steam Electric Generating Plant, one of our major power plants.
>
> Shortly after TVA's award of a major coal contract to R & F Coal Company in July 1977, Shell Oil Company, the 8th largest oil company and the 14th largest coal reserve owner, acquired Seaway Coal Company and its subsidiary R & F. R & F is an Appalachian coal producer and a large TVA supplier.

> In the fall of 1977, Gulf Oil Corporation, the fifth largest energy company and the owner of Pittsburg & Midway Coal Company, TVA's fifth largest supplier, acquired Kewanee Industries. In addition to its oil and gas interests, Kewanee owned an interest in Westmoreland Resources, Inc. Westmoreland Resources is a major coal producer in the Northern Great Plains.
>
> Standard Oil of Indiana, previously the only major oil company without an interest in either coal or uranium, bought Blue Diamond Coal Company of Knoxville, Tennessee. Blue Diamond produces about 2 million tons of coal a year in east Kentucky and Virginia. Standard of Indiana has also formed a new subsidiary, Amoco Minerals, to engage in uranium exploration and production.
>
> Mapco, Inc., an energy business and TVA's sixth largest coal supplier, acquired Longbranch Coal Co., an east Kentucky coal producer, in February 1978. TVA previously opposed Mapco's proposed 1975 merger with Falcon Seaboard, Inc.
>
> Natomas Company, with interests in oil and geothermal energy, took over Brown Badgett Coal Co., Weebro, Inc., and B&M Terminal in March 1978. Brown Badgett is TVA's ninth largest coal supplier. TVA also has a coal contract with Weebro.

There were at least six other acquisitions or attempted acquisitions by energy companies in the last 18 months, including Mobil Oil Corporation's purchase of Mt. Olive and Staunton Coal Company; Union Oil Company's takeover of Silver Bell Industries (uranium); Cleveland Cliffs Iron Company's (uranium) acquisition of 94 percent of Tiger Oil International, Inc.; Occidental Petroleum Corporation's attempted takeover of Mead Corporation (coal); Panhandle Eastern Pipeline Company's merger with Youghiogheny & Ohio Coal Company; and Tosco Corporation's (oil) purchase of Sanner Brothers Coal Company.

This recent merger activity intensifies our concern for America's energy markets because those markets are already unduly concentrated. It is generally recognized that effective competition may be endangered or even prevented when the four largest firms in a market control over half the industry's production. Three of the Nation's major regional coal markets are that concentrated—including the Midwest market from which TVA buys 70 percent of its coal. The top four firms in the Midwest market now control 56 percent of production, while the four biggest firms in the Northern Great Plains control 53 percent of production there, and the top four firms in the Southwest control 60 percent.

These important regional coal markets—and the other domestic markets to a lesser extent—are not only dangerously concentrated, but are also dominated by companies with other energy interests. Of the 13 companies that hold places at the top of those 3 most concentrated markets, 5 are owned in whole or in part by 5 of the Nation's large energy companies, 1 is owned by a firm principally involved in other energy-related markets (the General Electric Company), 3 produce only captive coal, and 2 of the remaining 4 are owned by conglomerates.

The same is true of the uranium market. It is highly concentrated and is dominated by nine of the Nation's largest oil companies, eight of whom also have major coal interests.

This uncompetitive structure of the coal and uranium markets can adversely affect both fuel prices and supplies. Because the fuel markets are oligopolies, and since oligopolists price their goods above competitive market price, coal and uranium prices are likely to be higher than necessary. Worse, since the same group of energy companies which dominate the coal markets also dominate the uranium market, consumers are even deprived of the potential benefits of price and supply competition between those two competing fuels.

The prices of coal and uranium have increased enormously in recent years. Coal now costs over four times what it cost in 1970. . . . Similarly, although TVA was able to enter into contracts for uranium supplies at base prices of $6 to $9 per pound in 1970, the Department of Energy reports that market price settlements for 1977 uranium deliveries averaged $41.50 per pound and $43.95 for 1978 deliveries. . . .

Portions of the sharp increase in fuel prices have been explained by some as the expected effects of various forces, including: inflation; OPEC oil price and supply decisions; the decreasing supply of gas and oil for boiler uses; the constraints on fuel production and use imposed by environmental laws; increased exploration, development, and mining costs; and short-term supply factors, such as coal miners' strikes. However, there is a basis for believing that a portion of the price increases may be accounted for as the effects of the uncompetitive structure of the coal and uranium markets.

There are vast adverse effects on the Nation, and particularly on power consumers, from the lack of vigorous competition in the fuel markets. Almost 65 percent of the electricity generated in the United States is produced with coal or uranium, and practically all new generating capacity during the foreseeable future will use those fuels. Coal and uranium provide the energy for substantially all of TVA's baseload capacity.

Not only do the Nation's power systems rely heavily on coal and uranium, but the cost of those fuels is one of the major expenses in power generation. TVA's fuel cost—about $909 million in 1977, as compared with $157 million in 1970—accounts for more than half of our total cost of generating power. . . . Most of TVA's fuel expense is for coal. The major increases in the price of coal in the last few years were instrumental in forcing TVA to more than double average residential electric rates and to more than triple industrial rates between 1970 and 1977. . . .

Because of our concern for these sharp price increases, after substantial preparatory work, in September 1977 we published a comprehensive report entitled *The Structure of the Energy Markets: A Report of TVA's Antitrust Investigation of the Coal and Uranium Industries* (June 14, 1977), that considered the structure of the coal and uranium markets in detail. It showed that steam coal is a distinct product which is traded in a distinct national market and in four identifiable regional markets: the Midwest, Appalachia, the Northern Great Plains, and the Southwest.

The report showed that the national and Appalachian coal markets are moderately concentrated and that the national coal market is dominated by energy companies and other conglomerates.

Moreover, we showed that concentration in three regional markets (Midwest,

Northern Great Plains, and Southwest) is even higher and may seriously threaten competition. For instance, we showed that the Midwest market is an oligopoly and that all but one of the principal competitors are energy companies or other conglomerates who have entered the market since the early 1960's. We expressed TVA's particular concern about the high concentration in that regional market since it supplies 70 percent of TVA's coal receipts.

The Northern Great Plains and the Southwest markets are also important sources of low sulphur coal and our 1977 report found each of those fields to be highly concentrated and tending toward increased concentration. In the last decade, the energy companies have become major producers in these markets.

Our report also pointed out that, at the same time the energy companies were acquiring the coal companies and concentration in the coal markets was increasing, the price of coal increased drastically. After TVA's average cost per ton of coal remained relatively constant from 1963 through 1969, it increased steadily from 1970 to 1974, and thereafter rose so sharply that by 1976, coal cost four times more than in 1969.

We concluded that the changes in the competitive structure of the coal industry during the prior 13 years and the major increase in the price of coal were instrumental in forcing TVA to nearly double average residential electric rates between 1970 and 1975.

In our 1977 report, we also considered a distinct national uranium market. We showed that concentration in that market is high and has been high for a long time. In addition, we pointed out that the uranium market is dominated by the same energy companies which dominate the coal markets. Like the price of coal, uranium prices have at least quadrupled since the early 1970's.

Although coal and uranium are traded in distinct markets, those fuels compete for use in new generating capacity. Thus, in 1977 we concluded that together coal and uranium form a third distinct market led by the same energy companies which dominate the separate fuel markets, and all of which entered those markets in the last 10 or 15 years. We concluded that the energy companies exercise sufficient power in the coal and uranium markets to be able to hamper interfuel competition. . . .

In November 1977 TVA filed antitrust suits against 13 foreign and domestic uranium producers or sales agents charging them with conspiring to restrain or eliminate competition in the world uranium market by fixing prices and setting conditions of sale. We alleged that TVA was boycotted and denied the ability to purchase uranium except at prices and under conditions established by the collusion of an international uranium producers cartel.

The suits charge that beginning as early as 1972 and continuing at least through 1974, a number of uranium producers met on numerous occasions in six countries and agreed to fix world uranium prices and allocate world uranium markets. They also agreed not to sell uranium for delivery after 1978 except at a negotiated price prevailing at or near the time of delivery. TVA alleged that the producers had agreed that the "negotiated price" would also be fixed by the defendants. In addition to antitrust violations, the suits charge the uranium firms with violating the TVA Act which prohibits conspiracies to defraud TVA or to defeat the Agency's purposes. . . .

RIPPING OFF THE SUN

Not content with its expansion into the natural gas, coal, and uranium fields, Big Oil is also assuring itself of a potentially outsize position in alternate energy through relatively small initial investments. Whether the purpose of these investments is in fact to promote, to control, or even to suppress alternative energy is a subject the following piece on the budding solar power industry explores. Whatever the answer, it would be a striking irony if the alternative energy movement simply became a part of a future monopolized giant energy industry—a vision which would fulfill the darkest fears of the many present-day alternative energy proponents.

Taken from "Ripping Off the Sun," by Richard Munson, Progressive, *September 1979.*

Not a month goes by without one large corporation or another offering Tony Clifford a lot of money. Corporate executives want to work more closely with Tony. In fact, they want to own his company.

Tony produces solar cells, technically called photovoltaics. In a world of rising energy prices, Tony's ability to convert abundant sunlight into electricity is admired, even relished.

But Tony is rare among his kind. So far, he and his colleagues at Solarex have resisted the large sums the big oil companies tempt them with. They have remained independent. The other firms producing solar cells have not. Of the nine major photovoltaics firms, eight have been purchased by large corporations, five of those by major oil companies. Between them, Exxon and ARCO will soon control more than half the industry.

But the photovoltaic cell is not the only solar technology being absorbed by giant energy firms. Twelve of the top twenty-five solar companies are controlled by firms with annual sales greater than $1 billion, including Exxon, General Electric, General Motors, Alcoa, and Grumman. Such giants as Westinghouse, Bechtel, and Lockheed are not far behind.

Solar technologies are becoming big business. Last year *Business Week* published a special report on "The Coming Boom in Solar Energy." Governor Jerry Brown projects that solar "will be a $4 billion to $7 billion industry by the 1980s" in California alone.

The solar community is divided on the issue of large corporate involvement. On one side are solar advocates who believe that only large companies, especially large oil firms, can offer the investment capital needed to develop solar energy equipment. Some of the oil companies see their roles as more than those of financiers. According to Jo Graves, senior vice president of Exxon's Ventures Corporation, "The management skills, financial resources, and research and development capabilities of companies such as Exxon can be effectively brought to bear on bringing solar energy to fruition."

But others in the solar community believe that the solar transition should amount to more than a simple substitution of windmills for coal-fired plants, of photovoltaic cells for nuclear reactors, and of solar collectors for oil derricks. They also share E. F. Schumacher's contention that solar energy is a "technology with a human face, conducive to decentralization." The Mid-Peninsula Conversion Project goes so far as to assert that "control of solar energy by large corporations would reduce its job-creation potential, keep costs higher than would otherwise be possible, retain low public accountability, provide environmentally destructive energy, tie up massive amounts of capital, and suppress innovative programs capable of responding to community needs."

Many of the Government's antitrust experts are also skeptical of oil company involvement. Alfred Dougherty, director of the Federal Trade Commission's Bureau of Competition, is concerned that the oil firms would suppress the development of solar energy. "If [oil] companies control substantial amounts of substitute fuels, and they act in their rational self-interest, they may slow the pace of production of alternative fuels in order to protect the value of their oil and gas reserves," Dougherty says. "Any decision an oil company makes concerning the production or development of substitute fuels would logically take into account its effect on the value of the company's existing oil and gas reserves and related capital assets."

But Congressional investigators believe that even if the oil firms do not actually suppress development, large firms would retard innovation. A recent report of the House Small Business Antitrust Subcommittee states that "smaller business is not only a prolific producer of innovation, but a more efficient producer than larger business as well."

Government officials also fear that oligopolies or monopolies within the solar industry will raise the costs of solar equipment. According to John Shenefield, Assistant Attorney General in the Antitrust Division, the practice is not unusual. "An industry without competition, or a firm or groups of firms with an ability to force up the price of a product by restricting its supply—an ability we call 'market power'—will usually do so."

But the most significant argument against the oil companies' involvement in solar technology development was presented by the Federal Trade Commission: "The trend toward diversified energy companies, if allowed to continue, threatens to limit decision-making in the crucial energy market to a few powerful firms." The giant oil companies already control a dangerously high percentage of this country's energy resources. According to recent Congressional studies, the eight largest oil companies control 64 per cent of all proven oil reserves, 60 per cent of all natural gas, and 45 per cent of all known uranium reserves.

The intensity of this concern about such concentration of power reflects the oil firms' past practices. That history is most succinctly stated by the FTC's Dougherty: "The oil companies' substantial political and economical power . . . has apparently been abused in a variety of ways, ranging from bribery to political intervention in the internal affairs of foreign nations."

The large oil companies' approach to solar technology development reflects apparent contradictions. On the one hand, these companies play a subtle political game. Since the technology enjoys such widespread popular support, they do not publicly oppose a solar vision. Instead, they usually claim that solar technology should not be supported above conventional energy sources because it cannot make any significant energy contribution in this century. This attempt at a self-fulfilling prophecy has been promoted by several major oil firms. Mobil Oil, for example, launched an expensive media campaign shortly after Sun Day to convince Americans that "a solar powered economy is a lovely idea and a worthy goal, but still a long, long way off."

In 1978, the Shell Oil Company projected that solar sources could contribute only 6 per cent of U.S. energy by the year 2000. (Solar sources already contribute 5 per cent and, according to a Federal interdepartmental task force, the United States could obtain 25 to 30 per cent of its energy from solar sources by the year 2000.) Pacific Gas and Electric, a large California investor-owned utility, recently spent $900,000 to present the same antisolar message.

Despite these public criticisms of solar's potential, the giant energy firms seem to be hedging their bets. The investments Exxon, ARCO, Shell, and Chevron have made in photovoltaic firms are relatively minor items in their portfolios. But the size and nature of the investments indicate that controlling a major portion of the solar industry is the goal.

Besides absorbing other companies, the oil firms have made less conspicuous moves to gain control of the solar industry's growth. Most rankling are the proprietary claims on the resources necessary for the solar transition, especially copper.

According to the Federal Trade Commission, "the availability of copper at stable prices will be essential to the orderly growth of the American solar heating and cooling industry over the next decade." If President Carter's modest goal of 2.5 million solar home collectors is to be met by 1985 (with an average collector size of 250 square feet), between 256,000 and 512,000 short tons of copper will be required. This demand alone equals 33 per cent of all U.S. copper production in 1974, and the oil companies are determined not to let such an opportunity slip through their hands. Through recent acquisitions, the oil industry has increased its control to 63 per cent of all domestic copper production.

The large corporations have also misguided the Government, luring Federal and public financing away from the development of the decentralized applications that Schumacher endorsed. Indeed, when it comes to solar projects, some firms are trying to convince the Government that "large is beautiful."

Perhaps the largest of these yellow elephants is the solar or microwave satellite. "Sunsat," as the seventy-two square-mile (larger than Manhattan) satellite is called, would beam microwave radiation down to huge reception-and-relay stations on Earth. Sunsat's supporters pointedly say that there is no night in space and that a single space station could produce almost twice the output of the Grand Coulee Dam. Many of the largest aerospace firms (including Boeing, Lockheed, McDonnell-Douglas, General Electric, Westinghouse, and Martin Marietta) are actively lobbying for Federal money to cover the initial investments in Sunsat.

Its critics contend that the microwaves are harmful, that the $60 billion price tag is too high, that the satellite would be difficult to protect from sabotage or enemy attack, and that the energy required to build and launch the satellite would exceed the amount it could produce for many years. But more important, the solar/microwave satellite is yet another centralized technology whose power is controlled by a few elite manufacturers and technicians.

Another outsized project is being constructed in California's Mojave Desert. The Barstow "power tower" consists of 2,200 giant mirrors that focus sunlight on a boiler atop a 500-foot concrete tower. The $130 million project is being constructed by McDonnell-Douglas and will produce electricity for Southern California Edison. Despite the White House Office of Science and Technology's comment that the project is "economically unpromising," the Department of Energy continues to spend approximately 15 per cent of its total solar budget for the "power tower."

Regrettably, Federal support of the solar work of large corporations is pervasive. Some solar advocates contend the Department of Energy is, in effect, giving the solar industry to the large energy firms.

Of course, the Department has long been known to prefer large corporations to small. In fact, only 2.6 per cent of the agency's prime contracts in 1977 went to small businesses. On the other hand, the top ten firms accounted for approximately 47 per cent of the contract money.

The trend toward large firms continues in DOE's solar programs, despite the feasibility of turning over much development work to small businesses. According to the Critical Mass Energy Project, 88.7 per cent of DOE's funds for solar research and development during 1978 went to big businesses. A full 70 per cent of the expenditures were received by such well-known firms as Rockwell International, Martin Marietta, General Electric, McDonnell-Douglas, and Westinghouse Electric.

In addition to funding research, DOE has been charged by Congress with purchasing solar equipment for Federal buildings and Government installations. Through these procurements, the Government can help shape the growth of the solar industry. But small businesses are suspicious of the unrealistically low bids some large corporations are making for Government contracts, and fear that the oil companies will take on development work at a loss to gain control of the industry. According to Roger Little of the small Spire Corporation, "It just might be that the DOE procurement program forces us to sell out to some oil company."

Even Government programs for demonstrating solar collectors at homes throughout the country have been steered to the larger firms. Almost 70 per cent of the $6 million available through the Department of Housing and Urban Development's solar demonstration program for 1977 went to seven major corporate solar manufacturers. All but two were solar subsidiaries of large American corporations, including Exxon, Asarco, and Grumman. Some of the long-time solar pioneers were excluded from the program because, ironically, their systems were too cheap.

Harry Thomason is a good example of a pioneer neglected by the Government. In 1958, Thomason built his first solar home, and he now installs the same collector at approximately one-third to one-sixth the cost of other solar heating systems. After years of prodding, the Department of Energy spent $198,000 to test Thomason's system, finding it just as efficient as higher-priced collectors. Despite the revolutionary conclusions, the Federal Government withheld the report for several years and refused to give Thomason any contracts.

The next few years will probably determine the direction of our energy transition from the use of petroleum-based fuels. The arguments favoring a turn toward solar energy are well known. But those advantages are most clear when compared with our other energy choices. Denis Hayes of the Solar Lobby points out:

"Tapping some energy sources demands ever-increasing centralization; solar sources are best used at dispersed locations. Some dangerous sources can be permitted widespread growth only under authoritarian regimes; solar energy can lead to nothing more dangerous than a leaky roof. Some energy sources invite profiteering cartels; solar sources would tend to narrow the gap between rich and poor—both within and among countries. Some energy sources will tend to reduce the size of the workforce; solar sources promise large numbers of new jobs. Some energy sources involve technologies that baffle all but a few specialists; solar energy can be harnessed by individual home owners with simple devices built of local materials."

To make the solar transition, the Federal Government must give renewable energy technologies a fair shake in the energy marketplace. Either the huge subsidies ($14 billion in 1979 alone) the Government now gives to conventional energy sources must be eliminated—unlikely, given the strength of the vested interests promoting coal, oil, and nuclear power—or equivalent incentives must be granted solar energy.

Although solar energy is not a social and environmental panacea, it does provide us with an important opportunity: We can mold the growing solar industry to serve the public interest. That interest is perhaps best expressed by the FTC's Alfred Dougherty: "The goal is to limit or diffuse centralized economic power and to increase the number of decision-making units in the market."

The effort to prevent the formation of centralized power in a new industry has never been made before. Public interest advocates and the Government's antitrust attorneys usually confront entrenched oligopolies or monopolies in lengthy and costly legal battles. The next few years offer our best opportunity to mold the growing solar industry to serve the public interest.

Prevention of centralized power requires promoting small businesses while preventing Government from aiding large corporations to control new industries. Although many opportunities for helping small business will occur on the state and local level, the Federal Government must wield its unique power to direct needed capital to small firms. In 1978, Congress approved $75 million in direct and guaranteed loans for small businesses wishing to enter some aspect of the solar market. Citizen groups are now lobbying Congress to appropriate more money and to have the Small Business Administration aggressively promote the program.

Citizen groups are also working on a variety of other measures to promote small solar firms. Solar Lobby, for example, recently released its *1980 Counter Budget,* calling for a doubling of the Carter Administration's proposed solar effort and directing more of the funding toward commercialization projects managed by small businesses. Solar advocates are lobbying DOE to expand its Massachusetts test program that provides venture capital to small solar firms through a separate financing corporation. And later this year, they will lobby the Congressional Small Business Committees to draft legislation to ensure that small firms receive a larger portion of DOE's research grants and procurement contracts.

At the same time, citizen groups will lobby to kill additional appropriations for such centralized solar applications as the solar/microwave satellite. Last year, the groups successfully blocked a budget increase in the Senate Energy Committee on the very day the large aerospace firms were holding a party across town to celebrate their earlier victory in the House.

One of the strongest protections against big business domination of the solar industry is to have the Government restrict the giant energy firms from participating in the solar markets. The Justice Department already has a program that effectively stops the major oil companies from acquiring more Federal coal lands. Later this year, citizen groups will work with committees headed by Senator Edward Kennedy and Representative Morris Udall to investigate legislation that would divest oil companies of their solar energy holdings.

Some solar advocates believe even more dramatic actions should be taken to prevent big corporations from casting a shadow over the sun. According to William Winpisinger, president of the International Association of Machinists (AFL-CIO), "If we don't get a handle on private industry profiteering we should nationalize all forms of energy."

The transition to an economy based on decentralized solar technologies will not be smooth or painless—for Tony Clifford or for the rest of us. Competing energy sources will be vigorously championed by powerful vested interests. And bureaucratic inertia, political timidity, and conflicting corporate designs will work against a rapid transformation. But the movement for solar energy and for local control of our energy future grows stronger after each OPEC price increase, each nuclear accident, and each shortage of some petroleum-based fuel.

GLOSSARY OF ENERGY PROCESSES

COAL

Most coal mined in the United States is burned to produce heat, which in turn is used to generate steam for industrial processes or employed in the production of electricity. Coal is also employed in chemical reactions, as in the reduction of iron ore, and it can be used as a source of synthetic gas or liquid fuel.

It has been estimated that there is enough coal in the United States to last about 500 years. About 13 percent of the nation's land area has coal beneath it. Some 60 percent of total national production comes from deep mines in Appalachia, which is our traditional supplier of fuel. Another 20 to 25 percent comes from Indiana, western Kentucky, and Illinois. Much of this coal is surface-mined. Within the last decade strip mining has progressed into the virgin coal fields along the eastern slope of the Rocky Mountains and into the Southwest.

Coal is divided into five classes: anthracite, bituminous, subbituminous, lignite, and peat. Peat is the earliest stage of the formation of coal. Heat and pressure underground force the moisture from peat until progressively higher ranks of coal are formed. Thus, anthracite contains the lowest percentage of moisture and the highest percentage of carbon. The chemical and physical properties of the other types lie somewhere between peat and anthracite.

In surface mining, a seam of coal, which lies below the surface, is exposed by gouging the earth (or overburden) away with steam shovels or draglines. With modern equipment it is economical to strip-mine coal that is 150 feet below the surface. Where coal deposits outcrop from hills or mountains, a bend or shelf is cut into the side of the hill.

Underground mining is considerably more complex and more dangerous than strip mining. Where the overburden is too great, the mine operator sinks a passage or shaft into the ground until the coal seam is reached. While there are different ways of mining coal, the most conventional method involves five steps. First a cutting machine carves out a slot at the base of the coal wall, or face. Then a boring machine drills holes halfway up the face, and the holes are stuffed with explosives. The workers retire to safety, set off the charges, and the coal tumbles out of the seam. Then loading machines pick up the coal pieces and put them onto conveyor belts, which carry the coal to shuttle cars. The shuttle cars carry the coal to railway cars, which in turn take the coal out of the mine, where it is washed and broken into manageable sizes.

Beginning in the late 1950s, continuous-miner machines were introduced. These large machines, operated by one or two men, have spinning teeth which gouge the coal out of the seam and deposit it on a conveyor belt, which takes it out of the mine.

As miners work with either cutting machines or explosives against the face of the coal, they must take care to extend roof supports above them or risk the danger of rocks and earth coming down on them. Historically the common practice, one still employed in smaller mines, was to run timber overhead as the mining operation moved forward against the coal seam. In the 1950s mine operators introduced roof bolting, a new technique for securing the roof. After the coal has been taken from the face, a member of the crew goes forward and drills holes up into the stone roof. Then the worker inserts a long bolt with an expanding section at its end. The top expands as it tightens, squeezing the rocks together and, in effect, forming the rocks into a laminated roof.

Longwall mining, employed for many years in Europe, is different from either of the two previous processes. Corridors are first driven into the coal, then interconnected. The long wall of the interconnection is mined in slices. The roof is held up with steel jacks while the cutter makes a pass across the face. The roof jacks are advanced so a new pass can be made. The roof is allowed to collapse in the mined-out area behind the jacks.

OIL AND NATURAL GAS

Prospecting for oil and natural gas, historically often discovered in conjunction with each other, is an expensive and complicated detective game. Before undertaking the actual drilling of a well, whether on land or offshore, the prospectors usually will conduct their own geophysical studies of the terrain or study the geophysical research of the U.S. Geologic Survey. The most common form of geophysical study is the seismic survey. This involves setting off high-explosive charges with electrical detonations in shallow-bore holes located at grid points in promising terrain. The resulting earthquake types of shock waves are recorded from the surface in a moving filmstrip as they come back through the rock. The strip then shows the inclinations, depth, uplifts, faults, and other features of the rock formations far below.

If, on the basis of such geophysical evidence, the terrain still looks promising, an exploratory well may then be drilled. Such wells can be very deep indeed, up to five miles. The act of drilling has been likened to a dentist's drilling a tooth in the mouth of a patient who is several miles away.

A drilling bit, usually with hardened metal teeth—for very hard rocks the teeth are made of industrial diamonds or tungsten—is pushed into the earth. Trailing down behind the bit are a string of pipes, connected one to another as they sink into the earth. This drill "string" can be very heavy, weighing several hundred tons, and it must be hauled back out of the ground when the bit has to be replaced. The string is suspended from a derrick, up to 200 feet high.

As the drill goes down, mud is pumped around the bit, filling the well, both to keep the bit from becoming too hot and to force down any oil and gas. The mud thus helps prevent an uncontrollable gusher—should the bit hit oil—by tamping it down. Usually it's analysis of the mud that first turns up traces of oil or gas in the well. As the well goes down, casings may be inserted near the top. Extending out of the casings are blowout preventers, big rubber-tipped arms that can block off the well if mud doesn't hold back the oil and things get out of control.

Much drilling for oil and gas now is offshore, making it more expensive. In the early days of offshore exploration oil derricks were fitted out on conventional ships. But they tended to drag anchor. Now there are fixed platforms of several different types. A jackup rig, for example, can be towed out to the site. Only then are its legs jacked down to the bottom. A semisubmersible rig is made up of large hulls, which are sunk under the water. Legs extend upward to hold the platform in place.

When oil is discovered, it is pumped up through a pipeline to a tanker or through a pipeline to shore and on to a refinery. At the refinery oil and solids are removed from the crude oil by sedimentation. The oil is then sent through various distilling stages where different products are removed.

NUCLEAR POWER

The turning of uranium from ore into a nuclear fuel involves a fairly intricate process. Most of the uranium ore that is mined contains 0.23 percent of the desired uranium (or U-) 308. Large quantities of ore must be mined, then processed into U-308, or yellow cake as it is known. The yellow cake then is changed into a gaseous state. In this form it can be introduced directly into gaseous diffusion plants, where the uranium is enriched. In this process the fissionable isotope U-235 is concentrated. After enrichment the fuel is fabricated, changed into fuel rods to meet the specific requirements of different power plants.

When these rods are installed in a nuclear reactor, a self-sustaining chain reaction is possible. As fragments of the split uranium atoms fly apart, their kinetic energy is converted to heat. In U.S. reactors, water absorbs the heat generated by the fission process. In one type of reactor the fuel rods are bathed in water which is under pressure so that it becomes hot without boiling. The hot water then is circulated through pipes which go through a secondary boiler where they produce steam that is used to run a turbine electric generator. In another type of reactor, the boiling-water reactor, the water that bathes the fuel rods itself boils and produces steam, which is fed into the turbines. The steam is then condensed to water and returned to the reactor vessel. In both cases the water that bathes the fuel rods becomes highly radioactive.

After the reactor has operated for a time, the fuel is spent and the fuel rods have to be replaced. This is a difficult situation because the rods are highly radioactive. They are stored temporarily in a shielded container, usually under a deep layer of water.

SYNTHETIC FUEL

Synthetic fuels are not new. In 1813 the original London Bridge was lit by a gas made from coal, and lighting on many American and European streets during the nineteenth and early twentieth centuries was provided by town gas, a fuel that was made by reacting steam with coal. The process was expensive, dirty, and inefficient. Even so, town gas played a major role in the United States well into this century, particularly in markets located near coal deposits but far from natural gas fields. When long-distance pipelines connected gas fields in the South and Southwest to markets along the East and West coasts and in the Middle West at the time of the Second World War, town gas disappeared.

Because of the energy crisis, there has been renewed interest in synthetic gas made from coal. The process is basically the same as the one that produced light for London Bridge more than a century ago. Coal is first crushed and dried, then fed into a large vessel, where it reacts with steam and either air or oxygen. The reaction usually occurs at high temperatures (from 1,500 to 3,500 degrees Fahrenheit) and at pressures up to 1,600 pounds per square inch.

Under these conditions the coal begins to break down, and hydrogen atoms from the steam along with oxygen atoms link up with carbon atoms of coal to produce a mixture of gases.

The resulting gas, however, is low in energy because it does not possess nearly as much methane as does natural gas. It is sometimes called low-BTU gas and equals about 100 BTUs (or British thermal units) per cubic foot. When oxygen rather than air is injected into the gasifier, the BTU content can be raised to a medium range of about 300 BTUs per cubic foot. These gases can be used for chemical feedstocks or industrial purposes but still are too low in energy content to be worthwhile transporting long distances through pipelines. To make a high-BTU gas, the percentage of methane must be boosted to 950 to 1,000 BTUs per cubic foot.

To make a high-BTU gas from coal, two steps are necessary. First, some of the carbon monoxide made in the gasifier must be reactivated with steam to form additional hydrogen. This then establishes a proper ratio of gases for the next step, ethanization. In this step the carbon monoxide and hydrogen flow over a nickel-based alloy. The nickel acts as a catalyst, causing gas to recombine to form methane. After purification, this methane can be fed directly into a natural gas pipeline.

But there are problems in making high-BTU gas. To begin with, it is costly. In addition, the type of coal is important. Coals in the United States vary from region to region. Coal, from the East, for instance, is a problem since it tends to swell and stick together in the gasification process. Coals in the West are better suited. However, making gas in the West competes with agricultural pursuits since the manufacture of gas requires large amounts of often scarce water traditionally employed by farmers and ranchers.

Coal also can be turned into a synthetic liquid. Solid coal consists mainly of carbon and ash and contains only small amounts of hydrogen, along with other elements such as sulfur, oxygen, and nitrogen. Oil, on the other hand, is made of molecules with a much higher proportion of hydrogen linked to its carbon atoms.

The basic method of turning coal into oil is to increase the amount of hydrogen. There are three different techniques for accomplishing this. One approach is to break coal into two fractions, one rich in carbon and another that retains most of the hydrogen. The second is to break coal apart with steam and oxygen to form a gas, to rebuild the gaseous molecules into liquids, and finally to add hydrogen to the coal. Most of the recent research and development emphasis has been on these two methods.

Oil shale is another form of synthetic fuel. Actually oil shale is neither oil nor shale. It is a fine-grained rock called marlstone that contains varying amounts of a brown to dark gray organic material called kerogen. When heated to about 900 degrees Fahrenheit, the kerogen reacts to form synthetic oil and gas.

A vast deposit of oil shale exists in the Colorado-Wyoming-Utah area in a region known as the Green River Formation. Here the recoverable shale is estimated at an equivalent of 600 to 700 billion barrels of oil. There is also oil shale, although of much lower grade, in the East—in a triangular region from Michigan to western Pennsylvania to Mississippi. Next to coal, oil shale is the nation's largest fossil fuel resource. Shale can be mined by underground methods similar to those employed in room-and-pillar coal mining or by surface mining. Once mined, the shale is crushed up, then retorted on the surface. Either air or oxygen is introduced into the retorting vessel containing the broken shale. Some of the potential oil and gas and some of the residue on the shale are burned to supply necessary heat. Another indirect method involves a heat-carrying medium such as recycled gas, inert gas or reactant gas being passed through the bed, or hot solids are mixed with the shale.

In another method the shale is broken up *in situ* (i.e., in the ground) by explosives, then slowly burned. As it burns from the top down, the oil seeps out, drops to the bottom of the shale bed, and is recovered. *In situ* processing is thought to have particular effectiveness for relatively low-grade oil shale, which dominates most of the resource base.

SOLAR ENERGY

The most basic form of solar energy is photosynthesis in plants, through which the sun causes carbon dioxide and water to unite with nutrients from the soil, creating oxygen. All our coal, oil, gas, wood, and food are derived over time from photosynthesis.

Solar batteries represent a relatively recent development in the harnessing of the sun's rays to create electricity. Without the solar silicon battery man's exploration of space would not have taken place. In a silicon battery the sun's rays cause an electric current to flow by dislodging electrons from properly treated silicon.

For most people solar energy has come to mean the solar collector, a flat, rectangular device resembling a window frame which is perched on a roof. It absorbs solar radiation on a blackened surface and converts it into heat. The sun's rays pass through a sheet of glass and hit the blackened metal, which is heavily insulated on the side away from the sun. The heat absorbed by the metal may be conducted by water which runs through pipes attached to the metal or by air which is blown past the heated surface. The glass is important as a one-way transmitter of the sun's heat. Rays pass through it and reach the metal, but they don't reflect backward through the glass and out into the atmosphere.

BIBLIOGRAPHY

COAL

Bethell, Thomas N. *Hurricane Creek Massacre.* New York: Harper & Row, 1972.

Caudill, Harry M. *Night Comes to the Cumberlands.* Boston: Atlantic Monthly Press, 1962.

Coleman, McAlister. *Men and Coal.* New York: Farrar & Rinehart, 1943.

Dubofsky, Melvyn, and Van Tine, Warren. *John L. Lewis: A Biography.* New York: Quadrangle/The New York Times Book Co., 1977.

Eavenson, Howard. *The First Century and a Quarter of the American Coal Industry.* Baltimore: Waverly Press, 1942.

Hume, Brit. *Death and the Mines.* New York: Grossman, 1971.

McAteer, J. Davitt. *Coal Mine Health and Safety: The Case of West Virginia.* New York: Praeger, 1970.

McGovern, George S., and Guttridge, Leonard F. *The Great Coalfield War.* Boston: Houghton Mifflin Co., 1972.

Office of Technology Assessment, Congress of the United States. *The Direct Use of Coal.* Washington, D.C.: Government Printing Office, n.d.

Schmidt, Richard A. *Coal in America, an Encyclopedia of Reserves, Production and Use.* New York: McGraw-Hill, 1979.

OIL

Blair, John M. *The Control of Oil.* New York: Pantheon Books, 1976.

Engler, Robert. *The Politics of Oil.* New York: Macmillan, 1961.

Mosley, Leonard. *Power Play: Oil in the Middle East.* New York: Random House, 1973.

Nash, Gerald D. *United States Oil Policy.* Pittsburgh: University of Pittsburgh Press, 1968.

Sampson, Anthony. *The Seven Sisters.* New York: Viking Press, 1975.

Stocking, George W. *Middle East Oil.* Nashville: Vanderbilt University Press, 1970.

Tanzer, Michael. *The Political Economy of International Oil and the Underdeveloped Countries.* Boston: Beacon Press, 1969.

Tarbell, Ida M. *The History of the Standard Oil Company,* briefer version, David M. Chalmers, ed. New York: W. W. Norton, 1969.

NUCLEAR ENERGY

Commoner, Barry. *The Poverty of Power, Energy and the Economic Crisis.* New York: Alfred A. Knopf, 1976.

Gyorgy, Anna, and Friends. *No Nukes: Everyone's Guide to Nuclear Power.* Boston: South End Press, 1978.

Komanoff, Charles. *Power Plant Cost Escalation.* New York: Komanoff Energy Associates, 1981.

Metzger, H. Peter. *The Atomic Establishment.* New York, Simon & Schuster, 1972.

Nader, Ralph, and Abbots, John. *The Menace of Atomic Energy.* New York: W. W. Norton, 1977.

Pringle, Peter, and Spigelman, James. *The Nuclear Barons.* New York: Holt, Rinehart & Winston, 1981.

SYNTHETICS

Borkin, Joseph. *The Crime and Punishment of I.G. Farben.* New York: Free Press, 1978.

Pratt, Larry. *The Tar Sands, Syncrude and the Politics of Oil.* Edmonton: Hurtig Publishers, 1976.

Welles, Chris. *The Elusive Bonanza: The Story of Oil Shale—America's Richest and Most Neglected Natural Resource.* New York: E. P. Dutton, 1970.

ALTERNATIVE ENERGY

Bookchin, Murray. *The Limits of the City.* New York: Harper & Row, 1974.

Butti, Ken, and Perlin, John. *A Golden Thread: 2500 Years of Solar Architecture and Technology.* Palo Alto: Cheshire Books, 1980.

Commoner, Barry. *The Politics of Energy.* New York: Alfred A. Knopf, 1979.

Dickson, David. *The Politics of Alternative Technology.* New York: Universe Books, 1975.

Grossman, Richard, and Daneker, Gail. *Energy, Jobs and the Economy.* Boston: Carrier Pigeon, 1979.

Kendall, Henry W., and Nadis, Steven J. eds. *Energy Strategies: Toward a Solar Future.* Cambridge: Ballinger Publishing Co., 1980.

Lovins, Amory B. *Soft Energy Paths: Toward a Durable Peace.* New York: Harper Colophon Books, 1979.

Ross, Marc H., and Williams, Robert H. *Our Energy: Regaining Control.* New York, McGraw-Hill, 1981.

Schumacher, E. F. *Small Is Beautiful.* New York: Harper & Row, 1973.

Stobaugh, Robert, and Yergin, Daniel, eds. *Energy Future: Report of the Energy Project at the Harvard Business School.* New York: Ballantine Books, 1980.

Talbot, David, and Morgan, Richard E. *Power & Light, Political Strategies for the Solar Transition.* New York: Pilgrim Press, 1981.

MONOPOLY

Blair, John M. *The Control of Oil.* New York: Pantheon Books, 1976.

Corporate Data Exchange. *Stock Ownership Directory* No. 4, *Energy.* New York: Corporate Data Exchange, 1980.

Ridgeway, James. *The Last Play: The Struggle to Monopolize the World's Energy Resources.* New York, E. P. Dutton, 1973.

U.S. Senate, Committee on Governmental Affairs. *Structure of Corporate Concentration, Institutional Shareholders and Interlocking Directorates Among Major U.S. Corporations: A Staff Study.* 2 vols. Washington, D.C.: Government Printing Office, December 1980.

INDEX

ABOUT THE AUTHOR

James Ridgeway is a regular staff writer on the *Village Voice.* He has written numerous books on energy, including *The Politics of Ecology, The Last Play,* and *Energy Efficient Community Planning,* and was the editor of *The Elements,* a newsletter in the field of natural resources. He lives in Washington, D.C.